Scott Foresman

CALIFORNIA
MATHEMATICS

Authors and Advisors

Jennie Bennett   Charles Calhoun   Mary Cavanagh

Lucille Croom   Stephen Krulik   Robert A. Laing

Donna J. Long   Stuart J. Murphy   Jesse A Rudnick

Clementine Sherman   Marian Small   William Tate

Randall I. Charles   Alma B. Ramirez   Jeanne F. Ramos

Editorial Offices: Glenview, Illinois • Parsippany, New Jersey • New York, New York
Sales Offices: Reading, Massachusetts • Duluth, Georgia • Glenview, Illinois
Carrollton, Texas • Ontario, California

ISBN: 0-328-00470-7

Copyright © 2001 Scott Foresman, a division of Addison-Wesley Educational Publishers, Inc.

3 4 5 6 7 8 9 10-DOW-07 06 05 04 03 02 01

Mathematician Content Reviewers

Roger Howe *Grades K–2*
Professor of Mathematics
Yale University
New Haven, Connecticut

Edward Barbeau *Grades 3–4*
Professor of Mathematics
University of Toronto
Toronto, Ontario, Canada

Gary Lippman *Grades 3–6*
Professor of Mathematics and
Computer Science
California State University Hayward
Hayward, California

David M. Bressoud *Grades 5–6*
DeWitt Wallace Professor of
Mathematics
Macalester College
Saint Paul, Minnesota

California Content Standard Reviewers

Damien Jacotin *Kindergarten*
Los Angeles, California

Donna M. Kopenski *Grade 3*
Poway, California

Jennifer Lozo *Kindergarten*
Lodi, California

Armine Aghajani *Grade 4*
Tujunga, California

Sharon Frost *Grade 1*
Burbank, California

Floyd Flack *Grade 4*
Westminster, California

Beth Gould-Golland *Grade 1*
Encinitas, California

Donna Crist *Grade 5*
Turlock, California

Linda Newland *Grade 2*
Santa Clarita, California

Jimmy C. Jordan *Grade 5*
La Crescenta, California

Wendy York *Grade 2*
Merced, California

Felicia Clark *Grade 6*
Compton, California

Shakeh Balmanoukian *Grade 3*
Glendale, California

Vahe Tcharkhoutian *Grade 6*
Pasadena, California

Contents

Whole Numbers and Decimals

2 Multiplying and Dividing Decimals

CHAPTER 3

Using Data and Statistics

4 Number Theory and Fractions

5 Fraction Operations

CHAPTER 6
Positive and Negative Numbers

CHAPTER 8

Ratio and Proportion

Understanding and Using Percent

Equations and Graphs

CHAPTER

12 Perimeter, Area, and Volume

California Mathematics Content Standards
Grade 6

By the end of grade six, students have mastered the four arithmetic operations with whole numbers, positive fractions, positive decimals, and positive and negative integers; they accurately compute and solve problems. They apply their knowledge to statistics and probability. Students understand the concepts of mean, median, and mode of data sets and how to calculate the range. They analyze data and sampling processes for possible bias and misleading conclusions; they use addition and multiplication of fractions routinely to calculate the probabilities for compound events. Students conceptually understand and work with ratios and proportions; they compute percentages (e.g., tax, tips, interest). Students know about π and the formulas for the circumference and area of a circle. They use letters for numbers in formulas involving geometric shapes and in ratios to represent an unknown part of an expression. They solve one-step linear equations.

Number Sense

1.0 (🔑) Students compare and order positive and negative fractions, decimals, and mixed numbers. Students solve problems involving fractions, ratios, proportions, and percentages:

1.1 (🔑) Compare and order positive and negative fractions, decimals, and mixed numbers and place them on a number line.

1.2 (🔑) Interpret and use ratios in different contexts (e.g., batting averages, miles per hour) to show the relative sizes of two quantities, using appropriate notations ($\frac{a}{b}$, a to b, a:b).

1.3 (🔑) Use proportions to solve problems (e.g., determine the value of N if $\frac{4}{7} = \frac{N}{21}$, find the length of a side of a polygon similar to a known polygon). Use cross-multiplication as a method for solving such problems, understanding it as the multiplication of both sides of an equation by a multiplicative inverse.

1.4 (🔑) Calculate given percentages of quantities and solve problems involving discounts at sales, interest earned, and tips.

2.0 (🔑) Students calculate and solve problems involving addition, subtraction, multiplication, and division:

2.1 Solve problems involving addition, subtraction, multiplication, and division of positive fractions and explain why a particular operation was used for a given situation.

2.2 Explain the meaning of multiplication and division of positive fractions and perform the calculations (e.g., $\frac{5}{8} \div \frac{15}{16} = \frac{5}{8} \times \frac{16}{15} = \frac{2}{3}$).

2.3 (🔑) Solve addition, subtraction, multiplication, and division problems, including those arising in concrete situations, that use positive and negative numbers and combinations of these operations.

2.4 (🔑) Determine the least common multiple and the greatest common divisor of whole numbers; use them to solve problems with fractions (e.g., to find a common denominator to add two fractions or to find the reduced form for a fraction).

Algebra and Functions

1.0 Students write verbal expressions and sentences as algebraic expressions and equations; they evaluate algebraic expressions, solve simple linear equations, and graph and interpret their results:

1.1 (🔑) Write and solve one-step linear equations in one variable.

1.2 Write and evaluate an algebraic expression for a given situation, using up to three variables.

1.3 Apply algebraic order of operations and the commutative, associative, and distributive properties to evaluate expressions; and justify each step in the process.

1.4 Solve problems manually by using the correct order of operations or by using a scientific calculator.

2.0 Students analyze and use tables, graphs, and rules to solve problems involving rates and proportions:

2.1 Convert one unit of measurement to another (e.g., from feet to miles, from centimeters to inches).

2.2 (🔑) Demonstrate an understanding that *rate* is a measure of one quantity per unit value of another quantity.

2.3 Solve problems involving rates, average speed, distance, and time.

3.0 Students investigate geometric patterns and describe them algebraically:

3.1 Use variables in expressions describing geometric quantities (e.g., $P = 2w + 2\ell$, $A = \frac{1}{2}bh$, $C = \pi d$—the formulas for the perimeter of a rectangle, the area of a triangle, and the circumference of a circle, respectively).

3.2 Express in symbolic form simple relationships arising from geometry.

Measurement and Geometry

1.0 Students deepen their understanding of the measurement of plane and solid shapes and use this understanding to solve problems:

1.1 (🔑) Understand the concept of a constant such as π; know the formulas for the circumference and area of a circle.

1.2 Know common estimates of π (3.14; $\frac{22}{7}$) and use these values to estimate and calculate the circumference and the area of circles; compare with actual measurements.

1.3 Know and use the formulas for the volume of triangular prisms and cylinders (area of base $\times$ height); compare these formulas and explain the similarity between them and the formula for the volume of a rectangular solid.

2.0 Students identify and describe the properties of two-dimensional figures:

2.1 Identify angles as vertical, adjacent, complementary, or supplementary and provide descriptions of these terms.

2.2 (🔑) Use the properties of complementary and supplementary angles and the sum of

the angles of a triangle to solve problems involving an unknown angle.

2.3 Draw quadrilaterals and triangles from given information about them (e.g., a quadrilateral having equal sides but no right angles, a right isosceles triangle).

Statistics, Data Analysis, and Probability

1.0 Students compute and analyze statistical measurement for data sets:

1.1 Compute the range, mean, median, and mode of data sets.

1.2 Understand how additional data added to data sets may affect these computations of measures of central tendency.

1.3 Understand how the inclusion or exclusion of outliers affects measures of central tendency.

1.4 Know why a specific measure of central tendency (mean, median, mode) provides the most useful information in a given context.

2.0 Students use data samples of a population and describe the characteristics and limitations of the samples:

2.1 Compare different samples of a population with the data from the entire population and identify a situation in which it makes sense to use a sample.

2.2 ( ) Identify different ways of selecting a sample (e.g., convenience sampling, responses to a survey, random sampling) and which method makes a sample more representative for a population.

2.3 ( ) Analyze data displays and explain why the way in which the question was asked might have influenced the results obtained and why the way in which the results were displayed might have influenced the conclusions reached.

2.4 ( ) Identify data that represent sampling errors and explain why the sample (and the display) might be biased.

2.5 ( ) Identify claims based on statistical data and, in simple cases, evaluate the validity of the claims.

3.0 Students determine theoretical and experimental probabilities and use these to make predictions about events:

3.1 ( ) Represent all possible outcomes for compound events in an organized way (e.g., tables, grids, tree diagrams) and express the theoretical probability of each outcome.

3.2 Use data to estimate the probability of future events (e.g., batting averages or number of accidents per mile driven).

3.3 ( ) Represent probabilities as ratios, proportions, decimals between 0 and 1, and percentages between 0 and 100 and verify that the probabilities computed are reasonable; know that if P is the probability of an event, $1-P$ is the probability of an event not occurring.

3.4 Understand that the probability of either of two disjoint events occurring is the sum of the two individual probabilities and that the probability of one event following another, in independent trials, is the product of the two probabilities.

3.5 ( ) Understand the difference between independent and dependent events.

Mathematical Reasoning

1.0 Students make decisions about how to approach problems:

1.1 Analyze problems by identifying relationships, distinguishing relevant from irrelevant information, identifying missing information, sequencing and prioritizing information, and observing patterns.

1.2 Formulate and justify mathematical conjectures based on a general description of the mathematical question or problem posed.

1.3 Determine when and how to break a problem into simpler parts.

2.0 Students use strategies, skills, and concepts in finding solutions:

2.1 Use estimation to verify the reasonableness of calculated results.

2.2 Apply strategies and results from simpler problems to more complex problems.

2.3 Estimate unknown quantities graphically and solve for them by using logical reasoning and arithmetic and algebraic techniques.

2.4 Use a variety of methods, such as words, numbers, symbols, charts, graphs, tables, diagrams, and models, to explain mathematical reasoning.

2.5 Express the solution clearly and logically by using the appropriate mathematical notation and terms and clear language; support solutions with evidence in both verbal and symbolic work.

2.6 Indicate the relative advantages of exact and approximate solutions to problems and give answers to a specified degree of accuracy.

2.7 Make precise calculations and check the validity of the results from the context of the problem.

3.0 Students move beyond a particular problem by generalizing to other situations:

3.1 Evaluate the reasonableness of the solution in the context of the original situation.

3.2 Note the method of deriving the solution and demonstrate a conceptual understanding of the derivation by solving similar problems.

3.3 Develop generalizations of the results obtained and the strategies used and apply them in new problem situations.

Whole Numbers and Decimals

Diagnosing Readiness

In Chapter 1, you will use these skills:

Ⓐ Place Value
(Gr. 5)

Write the value of the 2 in short form.

1. 825,013,000

2. 287

3. 0.21

4. 12

Ⓑ Ordering
(Gr. 5)

Write the numbers in each set from least to greatest.

5. 72, 27, 2.7

6. 2,913; 2,899; 3,684

7. Staci collects thimbles. She has 37 from South America, 49 from Europe, and 111 from the United States. She sells 53 of her U.S. thimbles to another collector for $159.00. From what country does she have the most thimbles?

Ⓒ Estimation
(Gr. 5)

Round each number to the nearest thousand. Then estimate the sum.

8. 12,121 + 13,654

9. 6,570 + 2,119

D Comparing

(Gr. 5)

Write $<$, $>$, or $=$ for each ⬤.

10. $188 - 161$ ⬤ $60 + 60$

11. $320 + 1,400$ ⬤ $145 - 50$

12. $2.3 + 7.8$ ⬤ $4.5 + 5.1$

13. Shay has four horses named Wes, Bess, Mess, and Tess. Wes weighs 1,202 pounds, Bess weighs 1,150 pounds, Mess weighs 1,212 pounds and Tess weighs 927 pounds. If the second-largest horse is Shay's favorite, who is his favorite horse?

E Patterns

(Gr. 5)

Determine the missing number in the pattern.

14. 2, 6, ■, 14

15. ■, 400, 475, 550

16. Maria sells 22 jump ropes in August, 35 in September, and 48 in October. If the pattern continues, predict the number of jump ropes she will sell in December.

F Adding and Subtracting

(Gr. 5)

17. $\begin{array}{r} 2,001,003 \\ -97,111 \\ \hline \end{array}$

18. $\begin{array}{r} 417,387 \\ +623,214 \\ \hline \end{array}$

19. The local library is selling 2,278 books at the book sale. Dana records that 1,156 of these books are fiction and the rest are non-fiction. How many books are nonfiction?

G Variables and Expressions

(Gr. 5)

Find the value of the expression when $x = 212$.

20. $74 + x - 23$

21. $x + x - 400$

22. $1,098 - x$

23. $16 + x + 24$

24. Duane's foot measures 2 inches less than Ty's foot. Jana's foot is 3 inches smaller than Duane's foot. If Ty's foot measures 15 inches, what size is Duane's foot?

To the Family and Student

Looking Back

In Grade 5, students learned place value from the thousandths to the billions.

Chapter 1

Whole Numbers and Decimals

In this chapter, students will learn place value and how to add and subtract whole numbers and decimals from the millionths to the billions.

Looking Ahead

In Chapter 2, students will learn how to multiply and divide whole numbers and decimals.

Math and Everyday Living

Opportunities to apply the concepts of Chapter 1 abound in everyday situations. During the chapter, think about how whole numbers and decimals can be used to solve a variety of real-world problems. The following examples suggest several of the many situations that could launch a discussion about whole numbers and decimals.

Math in Space Saturn is approximately 1,427,000,000 kilometers from the sun. Write this number in word form.

Math and Transportation Order the following gasoline prices from least expensive to most expensive. If the prices represent 89-octane unleaded gasoline, which gas station has the lowest price?

Gas Station	Price
Dairy Mart	$1.49/gallon
Fleet Mart	$1.48/gallon
Service Mart	$1.44/gallon

Math at the Market Last week your family spent $217.02 on groceries. This week your family used coupons to try to save money. With the coupons, the grocery bill was only $175.99. How much less did your family spend this week than last week?

Math at the Ocean

Ocean	Size
Pacific	63,800,000 mi^2
Atlantic	31,800,000 mi^2
Indian	28,900,000 mi^2
Arctic	5,400,000 mi^2

How much larger is the Pacific Ocean than the Atlantic Ocean? Indian Ocean? Arctic Ocean?

Math and Travel At the beginning of a trip the odometer on your family's car read 31,816.3. At the end of the trip it read 35,279.1. To the nearest mile, how many miles did your family travel?

Math and Movies You and a friend see a double feature at the theater. The first movie is 1.5 hours long and the second is 1.75 hours long. There is a quarter hour intermission. How long are you at the theater?

Math and Communication Your family wants to buy a cell phone. Cell phone plans are typically based on the number of minutes per month that the phone is used. Your family estimates that they will use the phone 420 minutes per month. Evaluate each expression for $m = 420$ and determine the cheapest monthly phone plan for your family.

Plan A $9.95 + $0.20m$

Plan B $19.95 + $0.15m$

Plan C $29.95 + $0.10m$

Math and Exercise You decide to train for a 5-mile walk. The first week you walk 0.5 mile. The next week you walk 1 mile, and the third week, you walk 1.5 miles. If this pattern continues, how many miles will you walk the sixth week?

California Content Standards in Chapter 1 Lessons*

Number Sense	Teach and Practice	Practice
1.1 (Grade 5) Estimate, round, and manipulate very large (e.g., millions) and very small (e.g., thousandths) numbers.	1-1, 1-5	
1.1 (🔑) Compare and order . . . decimals	1-2	
2.0 (🔑) Students calculate and solve problems involving addition, subtraction, ...	1-6, 1-7	

Algebra and Functions	Teach and Practice	Practice
1.1 (🔑) Write and solve one-step linear equations in one variable.	1-12	1-6
1.2 Write and evaluate an algebraic expression for a given situation, using up to three variables.	1-10, 1-11	
1.3 Apply algebraic order of operations and the commutative, associative . . . properties to evaluate expressions	1-4	1-9, 1-10, 1-11
1.4 Solve problems manually by using the correct order of operations or by using a scientific calculator.	1-9	

Statistics, Data Analysis, and Probability	Teach and Practice	Practice
2.3 (🔑) Analyze data displays	1-13	

Mathematical Reasoning	Teach and Practice	Practice
1.0 Students make decisions about how to approach problems.		1-1, 1-2, 1-5
1.1 Analyze problems by identifying relationships . . . and observing patterns.	1-8	1-6
1.2 Formulate and justify mathematical conjectures based on a general description of the mathematical question or problem posed.	1-8	1-9
2.0 Students use strategies, skills, and concepts in finding solutions.		1-3, 1-4, 1-7, 1-8
2.4 Use a variety of methods, such as words, numbers, symbols, charts, graphs, tables, diagrams, models, to explain mathematical reasoning.		1-13
2.6 Indicate the relative advantages of exact and approximate solutions to problems	1-3	
3.0 Students move beyond a particular problem by generalizing to other situations.		1-3, 1-8, 1-11

* The symbol (🔑) indicates a key standard as designated in Mathematics Framework for California Public Schools. Full statements of the California Content Standards are found at the beginning of the book following the Table of Contents.

LESSON 1-1 Whole Numbers and Decimals

California Content Standard Number Sense 1.1, Grade 5: *Manipulate very large (e.g., millions) and very small (e.g., thousandths) numbers*

Math Link You know how to use place value with numbers like 257 and 0.3. Now you will learn how place value can help you understand large whole numbers and decimals.

Warm-Up Review

1. 6×100 2. $8 \times 1,000$

3. $9 \times 10,000$

4. $4 \times 1,000,000$

5. Which number has a 3 in the tens place? 3,027; 4,731; 316

6. Jack's dog weighs 78 pounds. Eric's dog weighs 93 pounds. How much more does Eric's dog weigh?

Example 1

The number of people living on the Earth grows daily.

What is the value of the 3 in the number shown on the world population clock at the right?

Use the place-value chart below.

The value of each digit in a number depends on its place. The 3 is in the ten millions place. The value of the 3 is $3 \times 10,000,000 = 30,000,000$.

	BILLIONS			MILLIONS			THOUSANDS			ONES				DECIMALS					
	hundred billions	ten billions	billions	hundred millions	ten millions	millions	hundred thousands	ten thousands	thousands	hundreds	tens	ones		tenths	hundredths	thousandths	ten-thousandths	hundred-thousandths	millionths
			6,	0	3	5,	4	7	9,	5	1	8	.						
											3	6	.	0	0	0	2	5	

Example 2

Write the value of the 2 in 36.00025 in short word form.

Use the place value chart shown above.

The 2 is in the ten-thousandths place. The value written in short word form is 2 ten-thousandths.

Read: 36 and 25 hundred-thousandths

Example 3

Write 6,035,479,518 in expanded form.

Show the value of each nonzero digit.

$6,000,000,000 + 30,000,000 + 5,000,000 + 400,000 + 70,000 + 9,000 + 500 + 10 + 8$

Read: 6 billion, 35 million, 479 thousand, 518

Additional Standards: Mathematical Reasoning 1.0 (See p. 3.)

Guided Practice *For another example, see Set A on p. 38.*

Write the value of the underlined digit in short word form.

1. 3<u>4</u>1,984,654   **2.** 1<u>2</u>,144,754,984   **3.** 144.008<u>6</u>   **4.** 23.00103

5. Ordinary dust is made up of particles less than 625 ten-thousandths mm in diameter. Write this number in standard form.

Independent Practice *For more practice, see Set A on p. 40.*

Write the value of the underlined digit in short word form.

6. <u>5</u>,040,123   **7.** 91,01<u>4</u>,477   **8.** 0.0<u>6</u>2   **9.** 2.000<u>2</u>

10. 10,4<u>5</u>6,789.000 **11.** 17.304<u>8</u>   **12.** <u>4</u>4.444   **13.** 1,506.01<u>0</u>1

Write each number in standard form.

14. 7 ten-thousandths   **15.** 9 billion, 9 million, 9 thousand, 9   **16.** 45 thousandths

17. Write 20,065,289 in expanded form.

18. The population in Asia in 2010 is predicted to reach 3,934,703,000. What is the value of the 9 in this number?

19. Pollen grains range in size from 25 thousandths of a millimeter to 5 hundredths of a millimeter. Write these numbers in standard form.

Mixed Review

20. Find the next three numbers in the pattern.
324, 334, 344 ___, ___, ___

21. Mental Math Find $6 \times 10,000$ **22.** Round 785 to the nearest 100.

23. What is the value of the 5 in 51,644,023?

24. 247 + 738   **25.** 1,091 + 655   **26.** 2,412 − 922   **27.** 7,965 − 87

Test Prep Choose the correct letter for the answer.

28. Algebra If $72 \div n = 8$, then $n =$
(Gr. 5)
  A 576   **C** 9
  B 80   **D** 8

29. Algebra If $n - 16 = 12$, then $n =$
(Gr. 5)
  F 30   **H** 6
  G 28   **J** 4

LESSON 1-2

Comparing and Ordering Decimals

California Content Standard Number Sense 1.1 (🔑): *Compare and order . . . decimals . . . and place them on a number line.*

Warm-Up Review

Compare. Use >, <, or = for each ●.

1. 32 ● 38 **2.** 124 ● 214

3. 1,003 ● 916

4. 847 ● 897

5. 12,867 ● 14,061

6. 291,384 ● 209,782

7. Sue is two years older than Lynn. Lynn is 4 years older than Kevin. Sue is 12 years old. How old are Lynn and Kevin?

Math Link You have learned how to compare and order whole numbers. Now you will learn how to compare and order decimals.

Example 1

Which number is greater, 0.357 or 0.359?

Start at the left and compare digits in the same place.

0.359 > 0.357

```
0 . 3 5 7
0 . 3 5 9    9 > 7
  ‿‿‿
  same
```

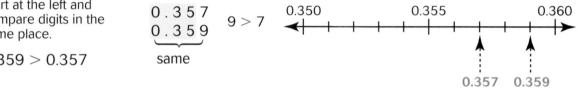

0.357   0.359

Example 2

Which decimal is the greatest, 1.4357, 1.3475, or 1.4375?

Compare two numbers at a time, starting at the left.

```
1 . 4 3 5 7
1 . 3 4 7 5    4 > 3
  ‿
 same
```
1.4357 > 1.3475

```
1 . 4 3 5 7
1 . 4 3 7 5    7 > 5
  ‿‿‿
  same
```
1.4375 > 1.4357   So, 1.4375 is greatest.

More Examples

Once you have compared the numbers in a list, you can arrange them in order, from greatest to least or least to greatest.

A. Order the decimals from greatest to least. Start at the left and compare digits in the same place.

0.347   0.349   0.336

```
0 . 3 4 7
0 . 3 4 9
0 . 3 3 6  ← least
  ‿‿
  same
```

```
0 . 3 4 7  ← less
0 . 3 4 9
  ‿‿‿
  same
```

0.349 > 0.347 > 0.336

B. Order the decimals from least to greatest. You can place zeros so that all of the decimals are to the same place value.

2.71   2.6   2.65

```
2 . 7 1
2 . 6 0  ← less
2 . 6 5
  ‿
 same
```

```
2 . 7 1
2 . 6 5  ← less
  ‿
 same
```

2.6 < 2.65 < 2.71

Additional Standards: Mathematical Reasoning 1.0 (See p. 3.)

Guided Practice *For another example, see Set B on p. 38.*

Compare. Use >, <, or = for each ⬤.

1. 18.499 ⬤ 8.500   **2.** 9.760 ⬤ 9.76   **3.** 6.35 ⬤ 6.357

4. Order 0.04, 0.93, 0.99, and 0.75 from least to greatest and place on a number line.

Independent Practice *For more practice, see Set B on p. 40.*

Compare. Use >, <, or = for each ⬤.

5. 0.34 ⬤ 3.4   **6.** 1.5674 ⬤ 1.59   **7.** 0.7 ⬤ 0.71

8. 1 ⬤ 0.99   **9.** 4.85 ⬤ 4.86   **10.** 36.42 ⬤ 36.52

Write the numbers in each set from least to greatest.

11. 0.56; 0.021; 0.003; 0.9   **12.** 2; 0.15; 1.5; 2.7; 0.05; 17

13. 2.05; 2.106; 4.5; 2.999   **14.** 57; 56.098; 50.897; 50.9; 57.47

15. Write three numbers between 76 and 76.1.

16. Sam bought 1.73 pounds of walnuts, 1.08 pounds of almonds, and 1.7 pounds of pecans. Sam bought the most of which type of nut?

Mixed Review

17. Order the national parks by size from largest to smallest.

National Park	Number of Acres
Yellowstone	2,219,791
Serengeti	3,584,000
King's Canyon	461,901

18. Mental Math Compare 26×60 ⬤ 26×70.

19. Algebra Evaluate the expression $3t + 7$ for $t = 25$.

Write the value of the underlined digit in short word form.

20. 76,0̲32,513.94   **21.** 90.702̲45   **22.** 1,998.39500̲2

⬤ **Test Prep**   Choose the correct letter for each answer.

23. $5,000 \times 60$
(Gr. 5)
    A 3,000   **C** 300,000
    B 30,000   **D** 3,000,000

24. 700×800
(Gr. 5)
    F 5,600   **H** 5,600,000
    G 560,000   **J** 56,000,000

Problem-Solving Skill:

Exact or Estimated Data

Warm-Up Review

1. 200×10 2. 16×100

3. $1,000 \times 40$

4. $25 \times 1,000$

5. Estimate the product of 11 and 28.

6. Ryan's family traveled 1,295 miles by car on their family vacation. They used 4 tanks of gas. About how many miles did they travel on each tank of gas?

🖊 **California Content Standard** Mathematical Reasoning 2.6: *Indicate the relative advantages of exact and approximate solutions to problems . . ..*

Read for Understanding

Students at Edison Middle School took part in a project to reduce home energy usage. About half of the 983 students involved in the project reported some success. Of these successful students, 205 use oil to heat their homes. The rest use electricity, gas, or solar energy.

① How many students were involved in the project?

② How many of the homes where energy usage was reduced use oil?

③ About what fraction of the 983 students reported some success?

Think and Discuss

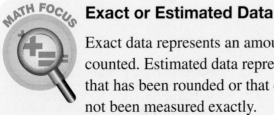

Exact or Estimated Data

Exact data represents an amount that has been counted. Estimated data represents an amount that has been rounded or that cannot be or has not been measured exactly.

Reread the paragraph at the top of the page.

④ Is 983 the exact number of students who participated in the project or is it an estimate? How do you know?

⑤ About half the students involved in the project reported some success. Does this statement give you an exact number or an estimate? Explain your reasoning.

⑥ Suppose 495 students reported some success. About how many students' homes used electricity, gas, or solar energy? Is your answer exact or is it an estimate? Explain.

🖊 *Additional Standards: Mathematical Reasoning 2.0, 3.0 (See p. 3.)*

Guided Practice

Anna used the ad at the right to show how a compact fluorescent bulb can save energy. She explained that a regular 60-watt bulb lasts only about 715 hours and that this 20-watt bulb uses less energy.

Save Energy and Money with
COMPACT FLUORESCENT BULBS

Compared with other electric bulbs, these new bulbs

- use about $\frac{1}{4}$ as much energy!

- last about 10 times longer than a regular 60-watt bulb!

Buy now and get a rebate of
$5 per bulb!
Limit: 4 bulbs

1. Which of these is an estimate?
- **a.** the amount of the rebate
- **b.** the amount of energy saved over the life of the bulb
- **c.** the limit on the number of lightbulbs each person can purchase

2. Based on the information in the paragraph and in the ad, how long should one of the new bulbs last?
- **a.** about 7,000 hours
- **b.** exactly 7,000 hours
- **c.** about 71,000 hours

3. Which number would you estimate?
- **a.** the amount of energy you expect a household to save
- **b.** the rebate given for 3 bulbs
- **c.** both a and b

Independent Practice

Richard's family bought a new car for $17,659.99. The old car got less than 20 miles per gallon. They drove the old car more than 14,000 miles each year. They will drive the new car more than 15,000 miles each year. The new car gets over 30 miles per gallon.

4. Which of these is an exact number?
- **a.** the cost of the new car
- **b.** the gas mileage of the old car
- **c.** the gas mileage of the new car

5. How many miles can the new car travel on 10 gallons of gas?
- **a.** less than 100 miles
- **b.** about 200 miles
- **c.** over 300 miles

6. How many gallons of gas did they buy for the old car each year?
- **a.** less than 700 gallons
- **b.** exactly 700 gallons
- **c.** more than 700 gallons

7. How many more miles per gallon will the new car get than the old car?
- **a.** less than 10 more
- **b.** exactly 10 more
- **c.** more than 10 more

8. Math Reasoning How would you calculate the amount of gas that will be used by the new car in 4 years? Would your answer be an estimate or an exact answer?

Addition Properties

Algebra

California Content Standard Algebra and Functions 1.3: *Apply . . . the commutative, associative . . . properties to evaluate expressions . . ..*

Math Link You have learned how to add and subtract numbers. Now you will learn how properties of addition can help you compute mentally.

Example 1

Use the data at the right. How many species of birds, fish, and reptiles are endangered in the United States?

Addition properties and mental math strategies can help you compute this information in your head.

Animals at Risk	
Animal Group	**Number Endangered**
Mammals	55
Birds	76
Reptiles	14
Amphibians	14
Fish	68
Clams	51

Commutative Property	Associative Property	Identity Property
The order in which numbers are added does not affect the sum.	The way in which addends are grouped does not affect the sum.	The sum of any number and zero is that number.
$8 + 12 = 12 + 8$	$7 + (11 + 5) = (7+11) + 5$	$45 + 0 = 45$

One strategy is to look for *compatible numbers*.
Compatible numbers help you to compute mentally.

$$76 + 68 + 14 = 76 + 14 + 68 \qquad \text{Commutative Property}$$
$$= (76 + 14) + 68 \qquad \text{Associative Property}$$
$$= 90 + 68 \qquad \text{Add } 76 + 14 \text{ mentally.}$$
$$= 158$$

There are 158 endangered species of birds, fish, and reptiles.

Example 2

The *break-apart* strategy and *compensation* strategy are two other strategies that are useful for computing mentally.

A. Break apart numbers to have easier numbers to work with.

$$128 + 64$$
$$= (128 + 60) + 4 \qquad \text{Break apart 64.}$$
$$= 188 + 4 \qquad \text{Associative Property}$$
$$= 192$$

B. Change one number to make it easy to use. Then change the other number to compensate.

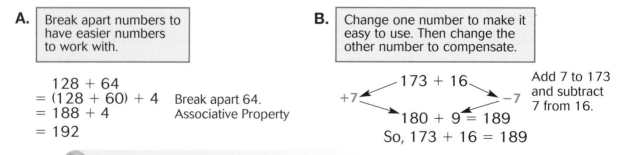

173 + 16
+7   −7
180 + 9 = 189
So, 173 + 16 = 189

Add 7 to 173 and subtract 7 from 16.

Additional Standards: Mathematical Reasoning 2.0 (See p. 3.)

Guided Practice *For another example, see Set C on page 38.*

For each exercise, choose a strategy and compute mentally.

1. $28 + 74 + 32$ **2.** $325 + 225$ **3.** $88 + 64$ **4.** $124 - 79$

5. Use the data on page 10. How many more species of birds are endangered than fish?

Independent Practice *For more practice, see Set C on page 40.*

For each exercise, choose a strategy and compute mentally.

6. $28 + 75$ **7.** $79 + 22$ **8.** $157 + 75$ **9.** $223 + 25$

10. $27 + 81 + 13$ **11.** $683 - 79$ **12.** $324 - 98$ **13.** $113 + 35 + 65$

14. Algebra If $359 + n = 359$, then $n = ?$ **15.** Find the sum of 64 and 36 mentally.

16. In her coin collection, Lauren has 25 pennies dated between 1910 and 1930, 17 pennies dated between 1931 and 1950, and 75 pennies dated between 1951 and 1970. How many pennies does she have in her collection?

17. Use the data on page 10. How many more species of birds and reptiles are endangered than mammals and amphibians?

Mixed Review

18. The height of Mount Rainier in Washington is 14,410 feet. The height of Pikes Peak in Colorado is 14,110 feet. Which mountain is taller?

Write each number in standard form.

19. 73 million, 420 thousand, 29   **20.** 7 and 9 hundred-thousandths

21. Compare. 256.47 ⬤ 253.97

Test Prep   Choose the correct letter for each answer.

22. Find the next number in the pattern.   86, 78, 71, 65, 60, . . .
(Gr. 5)
    A 56   **B** 55   **C** 54   **D** 53   **F** NH

23. A recipe calls for 2 cups of raisins and 1 cup of dried cherries.
(Gr. 5) How many cups of raisins will be needed to make this recipe with 3 cups of cherries?
    F 4 cups   **G** 5 cups   **H** 6 cups   **J** 8 cups

Rounding Whole Numbers and Decimals

California Content Standard Number Sense 1.1, Grade 5: *Estimate, round, . . . very large (e.g., millions) and very small (e.g., thousandths) numbers.*

Math Link You have learned to order and compare numbers. Now you will learn how to round whole numbers and decimals to get an approximate value.

Warm-Up Review

Write the value of the underlined digit in short word form.

1. 1̲7,322,104

2. 75.015̲3

3. 808.941̲3 **4.** 46,0̲76.409

5. Write three numbers that are found between the numbers 12.399 and 12.504.

Example 1

The graph at the right shows the average yearly rainfall for four cities in the United States. How much rainfall, to the nearest tenth of an inch, falls in Los Angeles in one year?

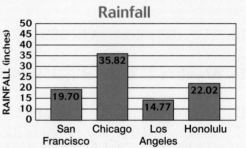

Round 14.77 to the nearest tenth.

Step 1 Find the tenths place.	**Step 2** Look at the digit to the right.	**Step 3** If the digit to the right is less than 5, round down. If the digit is 5 or greater, round up.	Since 7 > 5, the digit in the tenths place increases by 1.
14.7̲7	14.77	14.77 rounds to 14.8.	

About 14.8 inches of rain fall in Los Angeles each year.

Here's WHY It Works

14.77 is between 14.70 and 14.80 on a number line.

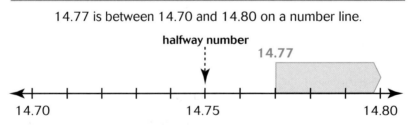

Since, 14.77 is greater than the halfway number, it rounds to 14.8.

Example 2

Round 1,639 to the nearest hundred.

Underline the digit in the hundreds place. Look at the first digit to its right.   1,6̲39

Since 3 < 5, the digit in the hundreds place stays the same.   1,600

To the nearest hundred, 1,639 rounds to 1,600.

Additional Standards: Mathematical Reasoning 1.0 (See p. 3.)

Guided Practice   *For another example, see Set D on page 38.*

Round 2,593.6781 to the place named.

1. nearest hundred   **2.** nearest thousandth   **3.** nearest tenth

4. Use the graph on page 12. What is the average rainfall for Honolulu to the nearest ten inches?

Independent Practice   *For more practice, see Set D on page 40.*

Round 8,930.4692 to the place named.

5. nearest one   **6.** nearest thousand   **7.** nearest hundredth

Round each number to the place underlined.

8. 4̲99.95   **9.** 1̲7.3   **10.** 0.0̲9   **11.** 45̲.59

12. 12̲3.106   **13.** 2̲7.003   **14.** 198̲.789   **15.** 1.146̲

16. Use the graph on page 12. What is the average rainfall for Chicago to the nearest inch?

17. A baseball player's batting average is rounded to the nearest thousandth. Round 0.2545455 to the nearest thousandth.

Mixed Review

18. Math Reasoning Write the following times in order from least to greatest.

5 days, 144 hours, 3,600 minutes

19. Mental Math Find the sum of $99 + 88 + 20$ mentally.

Write the numbers in each set from least to greatest.

20. 3.941; 3.455; 3.099; 3.0992   **21.** 7.4; 3.86; 1.005; 7.392

Test Prep   Choose the correct letter for each answer.

22. Algebra Which value of x will
(Gr. 5) make this statement true?

$x + 60 = 135$

A $x = 185$ **B** $x = 175$

C $x = 85$ **D** $x = 75$

23. Algebra Which value of n will make
(Gr. 5) this statement true?

$210 - (n + 2) = 200$

F $n = 6$ **G** $n = 8$

H $n = 10$ **J** $n = 12$

Adding Whole Numbers and Decimals

California Content Standard Number Sense 2.0: *Students calculate and solve problems involving addition . . ..*

Math Link You have learned about addition properties and mental math strategies. Now you will learn how to use these properties and strategies to add whole numbers and decimals.

Example 1

Glass
2,520 pounds

Paper Goods
12,600 pounds

Other Materials
10,710 pounds

Metals
2,835 pounds

Plastics
2,835 pounds

Use the picture above to find how many pounds of paper goods and metals are discarded by a typical sixth-grade class each year.

Find 12,600 + 2,835.

First estimate the sum by rounding.   13,000 + 3,000 = 16,000

Then find the exact sum.

$$\begin{array}{r} 12,600 \\ +\ \ 2,835 \\ \hline 15,435 \end{array}$$

A typical sixth-grade class discards 15,435 pounds of paper goods and metals each year.

Compare the computed sum to the estimate. The sum 15,435 is close to 16,000. The answer is reasonable.

Additional Standards: Algebra and Functions 1.1 (☞); Mathematical Reasoning 1.1 (See p. 3.)

Example 2

Find 1.8 + 250.03 + 16.196.

When adding whole numbers, arrange addends so that place values are aligned properly. When adding decimals, arrange the addends by aligning the decimal points.

Estimate first by rounding to the nearest whole number.

$$2 + 250 + 16 = 268$$

Then find the exact sum.

Remember to align the decimal points.

$$\begin{array}{r} 1.800 \\ 250.030 \\ + \ 16.196 \\ \hline 268.026 \end{array}$$

Zeros have been written as placeholders in the first two numbers so that all three addends are written in thousandths.

Compare the computed sum to the estimate. The sum 268.026 is close to the estimate, 268.

More Examples

A. $5,250 + $64 + $186

$$\begin{array}{r} \$5,250 \\ 64 \\ + \ 186 \\ \hline \$5,500 \end{array}$$

B. 4.253 + 10.03 + 0.015

$$\begin{array}{r} 4.253 \\ 10.030 \\ + \ 0.015 \\ \hline 14.298 \end{array}$$

C. 684.8 + 2,897

With a calculator:

Press: 6 8 4 . 8 +

2 8 9 7 =

Display: 3581.8

Guided Practice   *For another example, see Set E on page 38.*

Estimate first. Then find the exact sum.

1.
$$\begin{array}{r} 12,375 \\ 450 \\ + \ 1,055 \end{array}$$

2.
$$\begin{array}{r} 15.70 \\ 186.59 \\ + \ 3.00 \end{array}$$

3.
$$\begin{array}{r} \$9,576.00 \\ 3.89 \\ + \ 339.50 \end{array}$$

4.
$$\begin{array}{r} 0.176 \\ 5.000 \\ + \ 445.300 \end{array}$$

5. 1 + 0.678 + 0.55 + 15

6. 43 + 0.15 + 1.2 + 155

7. At the grocery store, Adela spent $4.59 for beef, $0.85 for onions, and $1.87 for carrots. How much did she spend in all?

Independent Practice *For more practice, see Set E on page 40.*

Estimate first. Then find the exact sum.

8. $234.50
    + 187.95

9.   13,005
     + 8,472

10.   0.010
      17.506
    + 12.494

11. $125.08
       0.75
    + 15.17

12. 1,498 + 16 + 1.5 + 0.09

13. 0.999 + 16.7 + 0.98 + 1

Use mental math, paper and pencil, or a calculator to find the sum.

14. $175.75
     325.00
    + 0.55

15.   10.004
       5.808
    + 11.238

16.   0.4002
       19.2004
    + 106.0240

17. 21,425.00
    12,009.95
    + 20.55

18. $705.26 + 12.24 + 0.50 + 32.00

19. 0.418 + 4.018 + 40.18 + 401.8

20. **Mental Math** Find the value of n when
    $(3.7 + 1.8) + n = 3.7 + (1.8 + 1.2)$.

21. **Algebra** Find the value of w when $(15 + w) + 15 = 30 + 9$.

22. Mr. Perry's class recycled 161 pounds of paper, 78.5 pounds
    of metal and plastic, and 57.6 pounds of glass. There are
    24 students in his class. What was the total weight of the
    materials collected by Mr. Perry's class?

Mixed Review

23. Jenny bought jeans for $35. She paid with two $10 bills and one
    $20 bill. How much change did she get back?

Mental Math Find each sum or difference mentally.

24. 14 + 16 + 92

25. 0.9 + 6.2 + 7.1

26. 306 − 98

Round each number to the place underlined.

27. 32.0784

28. 16.9999

29. 27.0836

Test Prep   Choose the correct letter for each answer.

30. Which is not correct?
(Gr. 5)

    A 2.03 < 2.3   B 4.68 = 4.068   C 3.5 = 3.50   D 16.9 < 16.99

31. Round 2.37894 to the nearest thousandth.
(1-5)

    F 2.3789   G 2.3790   H 2.378   J 2.379   K NH

(**Use Homework Workbook 1-6.**)

Subtracting Whole Numbers and Decimals

Warm-Up Review

1. $300 - 100$

2. $275 - 125$

3. $415 - 30$

4. $1,000 - 850$

5. $2,300 - 800$

6. $6,100 - 1,600$

7. Juan has 8 quarters, 6 dimes, and 7 nickels. Ari has 10 quarters, 4 dimes, and 3 nickels. Who has more money? How much more?

California Content Standard Number Sense 2.0: *Students calculate and solve problems involving . . . subtraction . . ..*

Math Link You have used addition properties and mental math strategies to add whole numbers and decimals. Now you will learn how to subtract whole numbers and decimals.

Example 1

Use the data at the right. If each car is driven 100,000 miles, how much more carbon dioxide gas (CO_2) is released by the car that gets 26 miles per gallon of gasoline than the car that gets 45 miles per gallon?

Estimate. Round each number to the nearest thousand.

$79,000 - 52,000 = 27,000$

$$
\begin{array}{r}
{\scriptstyle 7\ 15} \\
78,\!\cancel{5}80 \\
-\ 51,860 \\
\hline
26,720
\end{array}
$$

Regroup to subtract.

The answer is reasonable because 26,720 is close to 27,000.

The car that gets 26 miles per gallon releases 26,720 more pounds of CO_2 into the air.

Example 2

A.
$$
\begin{array}{r}
{\scriptstyle 6\ 18\ \ 7\ 13} \\
78,\!839 \\
-\ 9,256 \\
\hline
69,583
\end{array}
$$

B.
$$
\begin{array}{r}
{\scriptstyle 8\ 12\ 17\ 14} \\
9,\!384 \\
-\ 8,795 \\
\hline
589
\end{array}
$$

With a calculator:

Press: (7) (8) (8) (3) (9) (−)

(9) (2) (5) (6) (=)

Display: 69583

Press: (9) (3) (8) (4) (−)

(8) (7) (9) (5) (=)

Display: 589

Additional Standards: Mathematical Reasoning 2.0 (See p. 3.)

Example 3

You can use the regrouping skills you learned for subtracting whole numbers to subtract decimals. When subtracting decimals, you must remember to align the decimal point.

Subtract: 7.84 − 6.56.

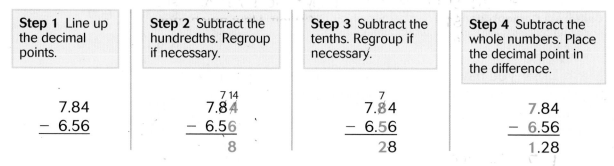

Step 1 Line up the decimal points.	**Step 2** Subtract the hundredths. Regroup if necessary.	**Step 3** Subtract the tenths. Regroup if necessary.	**Step 4** Subtract the whole numbers. Place the decimal point in the difference.
7.84 − 6.56	$\overset{7\ 14}{7.8\cancel{4}}$ − 6.56 8	$\overset{7}{7.\cancel{8}4}$ − 6.56 28	7.84 − 6.56 1.28

More Examples

Sometimes you need to use zeros as placeholders.

A. 76 − 21.5

$$\begin{array}{r} \overset{5\ 10}{7\cancel{6}.\cancel{0}} \\ -\ 21.5 \\ \hline 54.5 \end{array}$$

B. 3.45 − 1.7

$$\begin{array}{r} \overset{2\ 14}{3.\cancel{4}5} \\ -\ 1.70 \\ \hline 1.75 \end{array}$$

C. 8.047 − 1.639

With a calculator:

Press: ⑧ . ⓪ ④ ⑦ ⊖
① . ⑥ ③ ⑨ ═

Display: 6.408

Guided Practice *For another example, see Set F on page 39.*

1.   158,200
   − 119,678

2.   100,000
   − 49,696

3.   24.60
   − 0.45

4. $55.99
   − 9.45

5. 129 − 5.063

6. 1,450 − 1,275

7. 5.3 − 2.27

8. $15 − $5.40

9. Patty spent $26.07 at the farmer's market. Elizabeth spent $19.98. How much more did Patty spend than Elizabeth?

Independent Practice *For more practice, see Set F on page 41.*

10.   12,300
   − 9,438

11.   850.00
   − 225.76

12. $458.19
   − 378.46

13.   87.43
   − 0.76

14.   5.17
   − 2.64

15.   83,429
   − 6,097

16.   107.94
   − 84.68

17.   15.007
   − 9.038

18. 288.55 − 7

19. 8.055 − 6.8

20. $4.78 − 3.25

21. 1,500 − 700

22. $499.75
    − 76.55

23. 7,955.03
    − 7.90

24.   0.9000
    − 0.3333

25. 2,367.0
    − 999.7

26. 7 − 1.55

27. 5,000 − 0.46

28. 8.006 − 6

29. $24.80 − $2.48

30. Lily had $32.50. She gave some money to her sister. After she bought a CD for $12.99, she had $10.39 left. How much money did she give to her sister?

31. Cedric lives 1.87 miles from school, Dana lives 2 miles from school, and Sam lives 2.14 miles from school. How much farther does Sam travel to school than Cedric each day?

32. Algebra Find the value of t when $6,320 − t = 2,400$.

33. Mental Math Is the difference of 77.23 and 34.99 greater than or less than 50?

Mixed Review

Use the table at the right for Exercises 34 and 35.

34. What is the cost of three round-trip tickets with 14-day advance purchase?

35. How much would you save on a ticket if you purchase it 21 days in advance instead of 3 days in advance?

Advance Ticket Purchase	Cost for Round Trip
21 days	$232
14 days	$289
7 days or less	$370

36. Each doll Mrs. Bolt designed was decorated with 215 glass beads. How many packages of beads will she need to decorate five dolls if each package contains 100 beads?

37. Round 50.30521 to the nearest hundredth.

38. 36.134 + 7.9372

39. 45.284 + 90.3721

40. 0.9365 + 83

Test Prep   Choose the correct letter for each answer.

41. What is the decimal form for five and fifty-six thousandths?
(1-1)
   A 5,056   **B** 5,000.56   **C** 5.56   **D** 5.056   **E** NH

42. Which of the following shapes is a quadrilateral?
(Gr. 5)
   F square   **G** triangle   **H** circle   **J** hexagon

Diagnostic Checkpoint

Write the value of the underlined digit in short word form.

1. 9̲83,720
(1-1)

2. 0.002̲
(1-1)

3. 4,715̲,628
(1-1)

4. 25.0036̲8
(1-1)

5. Write the number eighty-seven hundred-thousandths in standard form.
(1-1)

Compare. Use >, <, or = for each ●.

6. 12.44 ● 1.244
(1-2)

7. 3.40 ● 3.4000
(1-2)

8. 117.3 ● 117.7
(1-2)

9. 4.1 ● 4.11
(1-2)

Choose a strategy and compute mentally.

10. 22 + 39 + 18
(1-4)

11. 87 − 9 + 13
(1-4)

12. 189 + 799 + 1 + 11
(1-4)

13. 101 + 105 − 9
(1-4)

14. 421 + 175
(1-4)

15. 999 − 99 + 933 + 67
(1-4)

Round each number to the place underlined.

16. 42̲8,000
(1-5)

17. 39.823̲5
(1-5)

18. 14̲3.914
(1-5)

19. 13.07̲29
(1-5)

20. 0̲.89
(1-5)

21. 61.3̲51
(1-5)

Find the sum or difference.

22. 238,417
(1-6)   725
     + 68,934

23.   4.1006
(1-6)   63.0849
     + 97.3103

24. 42.080
(1-7) − 7.147

25.   39.61
(1-6)   199.07
        + 8,221.77

26. 600,430
(1-7) − 73,789

27. 183.716
(1-7) − 67.829

28. 4.3212
(1-6) 7.0050
     + 0.8716

29. 1.03108
(1-7) − 0.85312

30. In six years, Luanne will be about 60 inches tall. If Luanne
(1-3) stands 47 inches tall now, about how many inches will she grow in six years. Is your answer an exact number, or is it an estimate? Explain your answer.

31. At the school track meet, Cindy beat Casey by 6.28 seconds. If
(1-7) Casey ran the race in 62.10 seconds, how fast did Cindy run the race? Explain your answer.

Multiple-Choice Cumulative Review

Choose the correct letter for each answer.

1. What are the next two numbers in the pattern?

    3, 6, 12, 24, ■, ■

    A 36, 48

    B 48, 64

    C 48, 96

    D 34, 48

2. Which of the following is nine million, nine hundred thousand, twenty-one in standard form?

    F 9,000,210.0

    G 9,900,021.0

    H 0.090021

    J 0.00921

    K NH

3. Chelsea had $21.04. She then purchased two new magazines for $6.49. How much money does Chelsea have left?

    A $27.53   C $15.45

    B $20.39   D $14.55

4. Which of the following has the greatest difference?

    F 299.7 − 92

    G 111.24 − 4.79

    H 426 − 398

    J 80 − 12.44

5. What is the value of the expression when $s = 12$?

    12 + 24 + s + 24

    A 576   D 58

    B 72   E NH

    C 60

6. What is 2,993.0144 rounded to the nearest thousandth?

    F 2,993.014   J 3,000

    G 2,993.1   K NH

    H 2,994

Use the table for Questions 7 and 8.

Softball Throw	
Student	Distance
Bernice	16.60 m
Sean	15.20 m
Sal	16.81 m
Lorena	16.87 m

7. The table lists the distance four students threw a softball. Which student threw the ball the farthest?

    A Sal   C Bernice

    B Lorena   D Sean

8. How much farther did Sal throw the softball than Bernice?

    F 0.20 m   H 0.27 m

    G 0.21 m   J 2.27 m

Problem-Solving Strategy
Find a Pattern

California Content Standard Mathematical
Reasoning 1.1: *Analyze problems by identifying
relationships . . . and observing patterns.*
Also, Mathematical Reasoning 1.2

Warm-Up Review

1. 900 − 325

2. 350 + 80

3. 6,500 + 450

4. 750 + 750

5. How many three-digit
   numbers with a 7 in
   the tens place are less
   than 250?

Example 1

Sam and Rachel want to know how many orders Cardmart
should expect in December. Sam's conjecture is "We
should expect 1,100 orders because the orders increased
by 200 from September to October, so we should expect an
increase of 200 orders each month. Rachel's conjecture is "We
should expect more than 1,100 orders because the increase in
orders from month to month keeps getting larger. Use the table at
the right. How many orders should Cardmart expect in December?

Understand

What do you need to find?

You need to find the number of
orders expected in December.

Greeting Card Orders per Month						
June	July	Aug.	Sept.	Oct.	Nov.	Dec.
200	250	350	500	700	?	?

Plan

How can you solve the problem?

You can find the increase in the number of orders from month
to month. Then find a pattern and predict the number of
orders for December.

Solve

The table shows that the number of orders increases by
50 more than the increase for the previous month. The
increase from October to November should be 250 orders
and the increase from November to December should be
250 + 50, or 300.

November orders: 700 + 250 = 950   December orders: 950 + 300 = 1,250

Cardmart should expect 1,250 orders in December.

Look Back

Was Sam or Rachel's conjecture more accurate?

Additional Standards: Mathematical Reasoning 2.0, 3.0, 3.2 (See p. 3.)

Guided Practice

Greeting cards are arranged in a window display with 1 card in the first row, 3 in the second row, 6 in the third row, and 10 in the fourth row. If the pattern continues, how many cards are in the

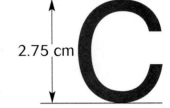

2.75 cm

1. fifth row?   **2.** sixth row?   **3.** tenth row?

Independent Practice

Use the design at the right for Exercises 4 and 5.

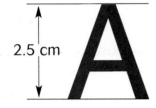

2.5 cm

4. The design for Cardmart's new window sign is being created. How high will the next letter be?

5. Finish Cardmart's window sign by continuing this pattern. How high will the final letter be?

6. Math Reasoning Pat designed the front of a card with the pattern shown below. Make a conjecture about what letter is in the 54th position and explain your thinking. Then solve the problem.

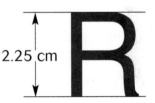

2.25 cm

GOODLUCKGOODLUCKGOODLUCKGOODLUCK

Mixed Review

Try these or other strategies to solve each problem. Tell which strategy you used.

> ### Problem-Solving Strategies
> • *Find a Pattern*   • *Draw a Diagram*   • *Make a Table*
> • *Work Backward*   • *Use Logical Reasoning*   • *Make an Organized List*

7. Erin needs ten 1-meter pieces of ribbon to hang a window display. How many cuts will she need to make in a 10-meter length of ribbon?

8. Sales at Tim's Gift Shop were about $10,000 in 1997, $11,000 in 1998, $13,000 in 1999, and $16,000 in 2000. If this pattern continues, approximately what will sales be in 2005?

9. A customer receives $4.76 in change after buying a box of greeting cards for $15.75, a roll of ribbon for $2.99, and a box of writing paper for $11.50. How much money had the customer given the clerk?

Use Homework Workbook 1-8.

Order of Operations

Warm-Up Review

1. 84 ÷ 12   **2.** 16 × 15

3. 32 + 89   **4.** 140 ÷ 20

5. 11 × 11   **6.** 297 − 165

7. How many ways can you make 50¢ using quarters, dimes, and nickels.

California Content Standard Algebra and Functions 1.4: *Solve problems manually by using the correct order of operations or by using a scientific calculator.*

Math Link You can add, subtract, multiply, and divide whole numbers. Now you will learn how to evaluate expressions using several operations.

Suppose you wanted to evaluate 3 + 4 × 5. You could add first or multiply first.

If you add first, 3 + 4 = 7, and 7 × 5 = 35.

If you multiply first, 4 × 5 = 20, and 3 + 20 = 23.

To make sure everyone gets the same answer for a problem, mathematicians use a set of rules called the **order of operations.** The rules are in the table below

ORDER OF OPERATIONS

1. Compute all values in parentheses first.

2. Simplify exponents.

3. Multiply and divide from left to right.

4. Add and subtract from left to right.

Following the order of operation rules, 3 + 4 × 5 = 23.

Example 1

Evaluate 17 − (3 + 1) ÷ 2.
- Add 3 + 1 inside the parentheses first.
- Next, divide.

- Finally, subtract.

17 − (3 + 1) ÷ 2

17 − 4 ÷ 2

17 − 2

15

With a calculator:

Press: 1 7 − (3 +

1) ÷ 2 =

Display: 15

Scientific calculators follow the rules of order of operations.

Example 2

A. 4 + 6 × 5

4 + 30 = 34

B. 12 − 72 ÷ 8 + 3

12 − 9 + 3

3 + 3 = 6

With a calculator:

Press: 1 2 − 7 2 ÷

8 + 3 =

Display: 6

Additional Standards: Algebra and Functions 1.3 (See p. 3.)

Guided Practice *For another example, see Set G on page 39.*

Use order of operations to evaluate each expression.

1. $3 + 9 \div 3$ **2.** $8 - 5 + 9$ **3.** $7 \times (3 + 1)$ **4.** $14 - 3 \times 2 + 7$

5. On a class trip, Zachary visited 3 museums and 1 monument. Museum tickets were $2.50 each. The monument ticket was $2.00. How much did Zachary spend for tickets?

Independent Practice *For more practice, see Set G on page 41.*

Use order of operations to evaluate each expression.

6. $7 + 3 \times 6$ **7.** $(2 + 3) \times 9$ **8.** $15 - 96 \div 12$ **9.** $12 \times 2 - 12$

10. $16 \div (4 \times 2)$ **11.** $6 - 3 \times 2 + 4$ **12.** $63 \div 7 - 6$ **13.** $3 + (4 \times 6) - 7$

Use parentheses to make each statement true.

14. $7 \times 6 + 2 = 56$ **15.** $2 + 3 \times 4 = 20$ **16.** $9 \times 3 - 1 \div 6 = 3$

17. Mental Math Explain how you can use mental math to evaluate $60 + 60 \div 60$.

Mixed Review

Use the table at the right for Exercises 18 and 19.

18. Find the total number of kilowatts of electricity generated by the plants at the Oroville and Hoover dams.

19. Find the total number of kilowatts generated by the two plants generating the smallest number of kilowatts.

Hydroelectric Plants	
Plant Name	Number of Kilowatts Generated
Oroville	2,500,000,000
Hoover	1,500,000
New Melones	300,000
Hungry Horse	428,000
Grand Coulee	6,500,000

20. $88.146 + 0.95$ **21.** $43 - 0.354$ **22.** $36,084 - 19,375$

Test Prep   Choose the correct letter for the answer.

23. Tamara wants to buy 5 pounds
(1-7) of apples. So far, she has put 1.75 pounds in her bag. How many more pounds does she need?

    A 6.75 pounds   **C** 5.75 pounds

    B 4.25 pounds   **D** 3.25 pounds

24. Billy bought a pack of baseball cards
(1-7) for $4.29. One month later he sold the same pack for $6.75. How much profit did he make?

    F $2.46   **H** $2.56

    G $2.54   **J** $11.04

LESSON 1-10

Variables and Expressions

Algebra

California Content Standard Algebra and Functions 1.2: *[E]valuate an algebraic expression for a given situation, using up to three variables*

Math Link You have learned to evaluate expressions like $3 + (15 - 6)$. Now you will learn to evaluate expressions with up to three variables.

Warm-Up Review

Evaluate each expression for $x = 1$, 2, and 3.

1. $x + 5$ **2.** $11 - x$

3. $4x$ **4.** $12 \div x$

5. Tamara delivers 65 newspapers each morning. The newspapers cost $0.50 each. How many papers does she deliver in one week?

Example 1

You know from evaluating simple expressions such as $3 + n$ for $n = 2$, 4, and 6 that a **variable** is a quantity that can change or vary, and that letters are used to represent variables.

Word Bank

variable

Some expressions have more than one variable.
Evaluate $3x + y$ for $x = 5$ and $y = 6$

$$3x + y$$
$$3 \times 5 + 6 \qquad \text{Substitute 5 for } x \text{ and 6 for } y.$$
$$15 + 6 \qquad \text{Evaluate using the order of operations.}$$
$$21$$

Example 2

Evaluate $2a + (5b - 4c)$ for $a = 15$, $b = 16$, and $c = 0$.

$$2a + (5b - 4c)$$
$$2 \times 15 + (5 \times 16 - 4 \times 0) \qquad \text{Substitute 15 for } a, \text{ 16 for } b, \text{ and 0 for } c.$$
$$30 + (80 - 0) \qquad \text{Evaluate using the order of operations.}$$
$$30 + 80 \qquad \text{Add}$$
$$110$$

Guided Practice
For another example, see Set H on page 39.

Evaluate each expression for $a = 10$ and $b = 5$.

1. $a + b$ **2.** $a \times b$ **3.** $a - b$ **4.** $a \div b$

Evaluate each expression for $x = 10$, $y = 7$ and $z = 2$.

5. $2x + 3y$ **6.** $4x - 5y + 4z$ **7.** $6y \div 3z$ **8.** $(x + y) - 2z$

9. Algebra When Lisa is x years old, her sister is $x + 4$ years old. If Lisa is 11, how old is her sister?

26   *Additional Standards: Algebra and Functions 1.3; Mathematical Reasoning 1.2 (See p. 3.)*

Independent Practice *For more practice, see Set H on page 41.*

Evaluate each expression for $r = 15$ and $t = 2$.

10. $r + 2t$ **11.** $2r - t$ **12.** $r - 5t$ **13.** $4r \div 3t$

Evaluate each expression for $x = 9$, $y = 1$ and $z = 25$.

14. $3x - 2y$ **15.** $2z \div 5y$ **16.** $x - 9y$ **17.** $x + 4z$

18. $5x + 5y + 5z$ **19.** $2 \times (x - y)$ **20.** $4x \times (25y - z)$ **21.** $x + y \times z$

22. Algebra The cost of a movie ticket is $7. The cost of buying x number of tickets is $7x$. The cost of popcorn is $2 a box. The cost of y boxes of popcorn is $2y$. Use the expression $7x + 2y$ to find the cost of 6 movie tickets and 4 boxes of popcorn.

23. Mental Math Explain how you can use mental math to evaluate the expression $10x + y$ if you know that $y = 0$.

Mixed Review

24. Math Reasoning Jacky and Molly used their scientific calculators to evaluate $21 - (12 - 3) \div 3$. Jacky entered

[2] [1] [−] [( ] [1] [2] [−] [3] [ )] [÷] [3] [=]

and the display showed 18. Molly entered [2] [1] [−]

[1] [2] [−] [3] [÷] [3] and the display showed 8. Explain why the parentheses needed to be entered to get the correct answer.

25.   8.906   **26.**   0.987   **27.**   384.12   **28.**   0.541
    $- 1.500$ $- 0.192$ $- 59.60$ $- 0.194$

Use order of operations to evaluate each expression.

29. $(10 - 6) \div 2$ **30.** $8 \times 6 \div 3$ **31.** $6 + 24 \div 3$ **32.** $2 \times 9 \div 2 - 6$

Test Prep   Choose the correct letter for each answer.

33. Convert. 144 inches = __ yards.
(Gr. 5)
   A 432 yards   **B** 12 yards   **C** 4 yards   **D** 3 yards

34. Convert. 6 feet = __ inches.
(Gr. 5)
   F 18 inches   **G** 60 inches   **H** 66 inches   **J** 72 inches

Writing Expressions

Algebra

California Content Standard Algebra and Functions 1.2: *Write and evaluate an algebraic expression for a given situation, using up to three variables.*

Warm-Up Review

Evaluate each expression for $t = 1, 5,$ and 10.

1. $t + 9$ **2.** $38 - t$

3. $8t$ **4.** $30 \div t$

5. California has 840 miles, Oregon has 296 miles, and Washington has 157 miles of coastline. What is the total length of coastline for these states?

Math Link You have learned how to evaluate expressions. Now you will learn how to translate word phrases and situations into mathematical expressions.

Some words in English can be translated into specific mathematical operations.

Word	Definition	Sample Numerical Expression	Sample Variable Expression
Sum	The result of adding numbers	$4 + 7$	$3 + x$
Difference	The result of subtracting numbers	$20 - 5$	$11 - y$
Product	The result of multiplying numbers	2×9	$6t$
Quotient	The result of dividing numbers	$18 \div 2$	$a \div 8$

Example 1

Write an expression for the product of 15 and s.

Product means multiplication.

The phrase *the product of 15 and s* written as a variable expression is $15s$.

To translate situations that don't use words such as sum, product, or difference, you need to choose a mathematical operation that is appropriate for the situation.

Example 2

Sara bought x apples and ate 3 of them. Write an expression that describes how many apples she has left.

The question asks how many apples she has left after starting with x apples. The operation to use is subtraction. Sara ate 3 apples so the expression $x - 3$ describes how many apples she has left.

Guided Practice *For another example, see Set I on p. 39.*

Write each phrase as an expression.

1. 6 less than k **2.** t divided by 8   **3.** m and 3 more

4. Adam raked r bags of leaves. Alex raked 5 bags. How many bags were raked altogether?

Additional Standards: Algebra and Functions 1.3; Mathematical Reasoning 3.0 (See p. 3.)

Independent Practice
For more practice, see Set I on p. 41.

Algebra Write each phrase as an expression.

5. *u* less than 4

6. 6 more than a number *x*

7. 8 more than twice a number *c*

8. 3 times the sum of a number *t* and 15

9. 1 more than the product of *n* and 3

10. 4 times the difference of *y* and 6

11. A 5-foot pine tree was planted and grew 2 feet each year. Write an expression for the height after *y* years.

Math Reasoning Write an expression for the distance around each square.

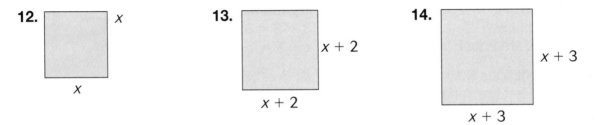

12. *x* / *x*

13. *x* + 2 / *x* + 2

14. *x* + 3 / *x* + 3

Mixed Review

15. Math Reasoning Make a conjecture about the number of 2-digit numbers that can be made by adding two 1-digit numbers. Explain your thinking. Then solve the problem.

16. Use parentheses to make the statement true: $2 \times 10 \div 5 \times 3 = 12$.

Evaluate each expression for $r = 5$, $s = 16$, and $t = 1$.

17. $5r - s$

18. $s \times t + 2r$

19. $5t - r$

Test Prep Choose the correct letter for each answer.

Use the table at the right for Exercises 20 and 21.

20. How many more people attended summer camp during Week 3 than Week 2?
(Gr. 5)

   A 6 people   **C** 37 people

   B 31 people   **D** 42 people

21. What is a reasonable estimate of the number of people attending camp during the four weeks?
(Gr. 5)

   F 300 people   **H** 1,200 people

   G 400 people   **J** 2,400 people

Weekly Attendance at Summer Camp	
Week	Number of People
1	312
2	275
3	306
4	264

Solving Addition and Subtraction Equations

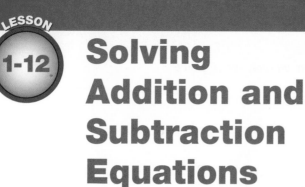

Algebra

California Content Standard Algebra and Functions 1.1: *Write and solve one-step linear equations in one variable.*

Math Link You can use what you know about evaluating expressions to solve equations.

An **equation** is a statement that two expressions are equal.	Expressions		Equations
	$3 + 5$	8	$3 + 5 = 8$
	$x + 3$	7	$x + 3 = 7$

To solve equations like $x - 26 = 85$ or $w + 41.8 = 55.9$ you want to get the variable by itself on one side of the equal sign. Addition and subtraction are **inverse operations.** They "undo" each other. You can solve equations using inverse operations.

Word Bank

equation
inverse operations

Example 1

Solve $x - 26 = 85$. Check your answer.

$x - 26 + 26 = 85 + 26$	To undo subtracting 26, add 26 to **both** sides.
$x + 0 = 111$	Add.
$x = 111$	

Check:

$x - 26 = 85$	Write the original equation.
$111 - 26 \overset{?}{=} 85$	Replace the variable with your answer.
$85 = 85$	Calculate.
When $x = 111, x - 26 = 85$ is true.	

Example 2

Solve $w + 41.8 = 55.9$. Check your answer.

$w + 41.8 - 41.8 = 55.9 - 41.8$	To undo adding 41.8, subtract 41.8 from **both** sides.
$w + 0 = 14.1$	Subtract.
$w = 14.1$	

Check:

$w + 14.8 = 55.9$	
$14.1 + 41.8 \overset{?}{=} 55.9$	Replace the variable with your answer.
$55.9 = 55.9$	When $w = 14.1, w + 41.8 = 55.9$ is true.

Additional Standards: Mathematical Reasoning 3.3 (See p. 3.)

Guided Practice
For another example, see Set J on page 39.

Solve each equation. Check your answer.

1. $a + 17 = 43$ **2.** $x - 22 = 66$ **3.** $138 + g = 150$ **4.** $y + 8.3 = 9.2$

5. The chemical element aluminum was discovered in 1825. This was 18 years after the discovery of element sodium. Use the equation $y + 18 = 1825$ to find the year (*y*) that sodium was discovered.

Independent Practice
For more practice, see Set J on page 41.

Solve each equation. Check your answer.

6. $r - 77 = 99$ **7.** $987 = 16 + m$ **8.** $48 = d + 23$ **9.** $2{,}098 = k - 536$

10. $45 = 36 + f$ **11.** $p + 1.5 = 1.5$ **12.** $f - 63 = 937$ **13.** $651 + c = 800$

14. $1.02 = v - 66$ **15.** $w - 56 = 560$ **16.** $y - 87.4 = 0$ **17.** $7.1 = s - 58.3$

18. Math Reasoning Suppose $a + b = 10$. If the value of *a* increases by 2, how must the value of *b* change so that the equation is still true?

19. Nick has 4 tan shirts, *b* blue shirts, and 5 white shirts. He has a total of 16 shirts. Solve the equation $4 + b + 5 = 16$ to find how many blue shirts Nick has.

Mixed Review

20. Anne has $178 in her savings account. She saved *n* dollars each week. Write an expression for the amount of money in her account in 12 weeks.

21. $8.03 + 10.74   **22.** $28.99 - 12.49   **23.** $10.803 - 6.724$

Evaluate each expression for $a = 2$ and $b = 10.5$.

24. $4b \div a$ **25.** $(6a + 2b) \times a$ **26.** $(5 \times a \times b) - 6.5$

Test Prep Choose the correct letter for each answer.

27. Simplify the expression.
(1-9)

$3 + 6 \times 4 \times 2$

A 48   **C** 72

B 51   **D** 144

28. Simplify the expression.
(1-9)

$(2 + 6) + (3 - 1) \times 4$

F 14   **H** 40

G 16   **J** 44

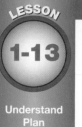

LESSON 1-13

Understand
Plan
Solve
Look Back

Problem-Solving Application:

Using Data From Graphs

Warm-Up Review

1. 5.0 + 2.5 **2.** 7.5 + 14.0

3. 45,000 + 35,000

4. 50,000,000 + 50,000

5. Joe bought 2 CDs that cost $8.99 apiece. He paid with a $50 bill. How much change did he receive?

California Content Standard *Statistics, Data Analysis, and Probability 2.3 (🔑) Analyze data displays . . ..*

Example

The graph shows about how much solid trash is produced in Raetown monthly. Most food waste and yard waste can be composted and used to enrich the soil. About how many pounds of the trash collected in 2 months could be composted?

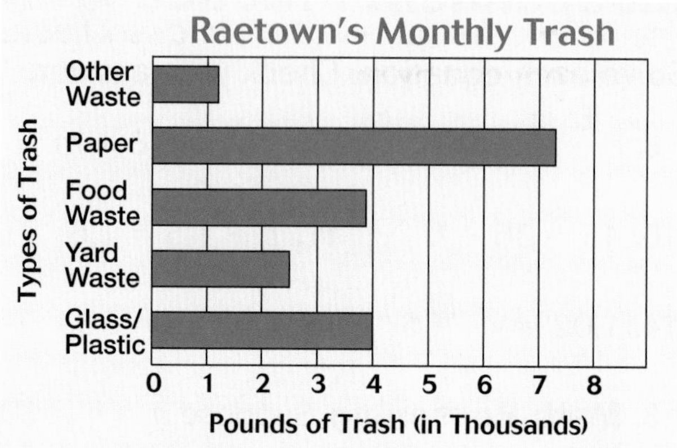

Understand

What do you need to know?

You need to know the approximate number of pounds of food waste and yard waste produced each month.

Plan

How can you solve the problem?

Estimate the amount shown by each bar in the graph. You can add 4 thousand and 2.5 thousand to find about how many pounds of food waste and yard waste are produced in one month. Double this amount to find an estimated number of pounds for 2 months.

Solve

	4.0 thousand		6.5 thousand
+	2.5 thousand	+	6.5 thousand
	6.5 thousand		13.0 thousand or 13,000

About 13,000 pounds of trash could be composted in two months.

Look Back

What number would you choose if you wanted to use a closer estimate for the number of pounds of food waste in one month?

 Additional Standards: Mathematical Reasoning 2.4 *(See p. 3.)*

Guided Practice

Use the bar graph on page 32 to solve Exercises 1–2.

1. Estimate how many pounds of paper are thrown out in 3 months.

2. What material makes up the greatest part of the solid trash in Raetown per month? Does this material make up more than or less than half the town's trash?

Independent Practice

The double bar graph below shows what happens to the solid trash produced by two local towns in one year. Use the graph to solve Exercises 3–5.

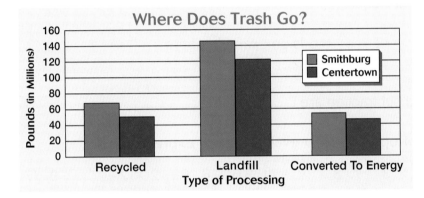

3. In 1 year, about how many more pounds of trash are produced by the people of Smithburg than by the people of Centertown?

4. In 1 year, the town of Greenfield recycles about half as much trash as does Smithburg. Greenfield takes twice as much trash to the landfill as does Centertown, and converts 50 million pounds of trash to energy. About how many pounds of trash do the people of Greenfield produce per year?

5. In 2 years, about how many more pounds of trash is recycled in Smithburg than Centertown?

Mixed Review

6. In a store display, cans are stacked with 20 cans in the first row, 18 cans in the second row, 16 cans in the third row, and so on. If the pattern continues, how many cans are in the tenth row?

7. A machine produces a metal part that is 0.2 inches in length. How much must be trimmed in order to make the part only 0.16 inches in length?

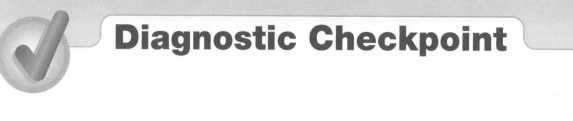

Diagnostic Checkpoint

Complete for Exercises 1–5. Use the words from the Word Bank.

1. _____ represents an amount that has been counted.
(1-3)

2. The _____ states that the sum of any number and zero is that number.
(1-4)

3. An _____ is a statement that two expressions are equal.
(1-12)

4. $2 + (3 + 6) = (2 + 3) + 6$ is an example of the _____.
(1-4)

5. Addition and subtraction are _____.
(1-12)

Use the order of operations to evaluate each expression.

6. $16 - 8 \div 2 \times 3$
(1-9)

7. $3 \times (8 + 4) \div 6$
(1-9)

8. $6 - 2 \times 2$
(1-9)

9. $(7 + 8) + 2 \div 2$
(1-9)

10. $12 + 2 \times 6 \times 5$
(1-9)

11. $(10 - 2) \times 4$
(1-9)

12. $30 \times 0 + 2 \div 2$
(1-9)

13. $16 \div 2 + 4$
(1-9)

Evaluate each expression for $b = 2$, $m = 0$, and $s = 4$.

14. $3b - m$
(1-10)

15. $s + b \times m$
(1-10)

16. $104m + b$
(1-10)

17. $(s - b) \times 6$
(1-10)

18. $s + s - 8 \div 2$
(1-10)

19. $18m + 18b$
(1-10)

20. $12s - 12b$
(1-10)

21. $b \times m + b + m$
(1-10)

Algebra Write each phrase as an expression.

22. 3 more than x
(1-11)

23. the product of 6 and x
(1-11)

24. 6 times the sum of y and 2
(1-11)

25. 18 less than k
(1-11)

Solve the equation. Check your answer.

26. $x + 3 = 20$
(1-12)

27. $y - 10 = 5$
(1-12)

28. $s + 2 = 6$
(1-12)

29. Suppose Natalie saves $0.08 on Sunday, $0.16 on Monday, and $0.32 on Tuesday. If Natalie continues this pattern, how much will she save on Saturday?
(1-8)

Chapter 1 Test

1. Round 160,248.37096 to the nearest ten-thousandth.

2. Write the value of the 8 in 8,374,511.3 in short word form.

3. Compute mentally: $98 + 1,850 + 102$

4. Compare 2.001121 ⬤ 2.00112. Use >, <, or =.

Estimate. Then add or subtract.

5.	6.	7.	8.
95,374 +16,285	18.0573 − 9.3655	$1,487.22 + 288.73	464,600 −28,851

Use order of operations to evaluate each expression.

9. $36 + 6 \div 2$

10. $(14 + 6) \times 2$

11. $9 \times (6 - 3) + 4$

Evaluate each expression for $x = 3$, $b = 2$, and $y = 3$.

12. $4x + 3y$

13. $5b - 2y$

14. $8x - 2b + (8y - 1)$

Write each phrase as an expression.

15. 2 less than a number

16. 6 times the sum of 2 and n

Solve each equation.

17. $x + 5 = 12$

18. $p - 8 = 29$

19. $120 = m + 86$

20. $43 = r - 39$

21. Beginning on Monday, Bobbie will follow this exercise schedule: Swim for 2 days, take a day off, run for 3 days, take a day off, and so on. By following this pattern, Bobbie conjectures that on Monday of the fifth week, she will be swimming. Do you agree? Explain your thinking.

22. An auditorium seats 688 people. About half the seats are full. How many are empty? Is this an exact number or an estimate? Explain.

23. Use the bar graph. What is the difference in jumping distance between the two classes with the farthest average jumping distances?

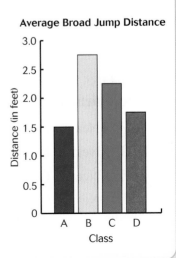

Average Broad Jump Distance

Multiple-Choice Chapter 1 Test

Choose the correct letter for each answer.

1. What is the place value of the 6 in 24.24361?

   A   6 millionths

   B   6 hundred-thousandths

   C   6 ten-thousandths

   D   6 thousands

2. Chance predicts the population of his ant farm to reach 1,117,000 in 20 more years. Which describes the ant population in word form?

   F   One hundred and seventeen

   G   One million and seventeen

   H   One million, one hundred seventeen thousand

   J   One billion, one million seven thousand

3. Select the number set that is ordered least to greatest.

   A   65,0231, 62.2141, 69.1933

   B   617.94, 671, 671.1176

   C   0.4387, 0.43, 0.4289

   D   99.923, 99.928, 0.9999

4. If 4,986.81762 is rounded to 4,986.818, to which place value was it rounded?

   F   Nearest millionths

   G   Nearest hundred-thousandths

   H   Nearest thousandths

   J   Nearest hundredths

5. Sharon planted two types of flowers. She expects the tulips to grow no less than 4 inches high and the sunflowers should grow to about 2 feet. Which describes an exact number?

   A   The height of the sunflowers

   B   The height of the tulips

   C   The number of types of flowers

   D   The number of inches the planted sunflower grows

6. Which indicates how you could find the sum $5 + 118 + 12 + 15$ using compatible numbers?

   F $(15 + 5)(118 + 12)$

   G $(100 + 8 + 15) + 5$

   H $12 + (118) + 5 + 5 + 5$

   J $(118 + 12) + (15 + 5)$

7. $211.9432 + 0.2118 + 72.003$

   A   284.103

   B   284.15

   C   284.1578

   D   284.158

   E   NH

8. Find the difference. Round to the nearest thousand.
   $930,876 - 75,622.61$

   F   860,000

   G   855,253.385

   H   855,253.39

   J   855,000

9. The first month, Jack's dog gained 0.5 kilogram. The second month it gained 0.9 kilogram, and the third month 1.3 kilograms. If this pattern continues for two more months, how much weight will the dog gain in month 5?

   A   0.4 kilogram
   B   1.7 kilograms
   C   2.1 kilograms
   D   2.5 kilograms

10. Which statement is true?

    F $60 \div 5 + 5 = 6$
    G $2 \times 12 \div 6 + 1 = 5$
    H $10 + 12 + 8 \div 2 = 64$
    J $6 - 4 \div 2 \times 2 - 1 = 4$

11. Which expression describes the phrase 16 more than 2 times b?

    A $16 + 2 + b$
    B $2 \times 16 \times b$
    C $(b + 2)16$
    D $2b + 16$

12. Evaluate the expression for $x = 3$, $y = 8$, and $z = 0$.

    $$2x + y - 12z$$

    F   0
    G   2
    H   11
    J   14
    K   NH

13. Solve the equation $22.1 + b = 61.5$.

    A   38.6   C   49.4
    B   39.4   D   83.6

Use the bar graph below for Questions 14 and 15.

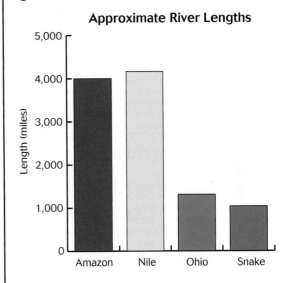

Approximate River Lengths

14. About how much longer is the Nile River than the Snake River?

    F   5,000 miles
    G   4,000 miles
    H   3,000 miles
    J   2,000 miles

15. What would be the approximate combined length of the Amazon River, the Snake River, and the Ohio River if they were laid end to end?

    A   4,000 miles
    B   5,000 miles
    C   6,000 miles
    D   10,000 miles

Reteaching

Set A (pages 4–5)

Write 721 thousand and 721 ten-thousandths in standard form.

						7	2	1	0	0	0	0	7	2	1

hundred billions · ten billions · billions · hundred millions · ten millions · millions · hundred thousands · ten thousands · thousands · hundreds · tens · ones · tenths · hundredths · thousandths · ten-thousandths · hundred-thousandths

721,000.0721

Remember the decimal point is read "and."

Write each number in standard form.

1. 6 thousand and 6 hundredths

2. 23 thousandths

3. 47 and 3 ten-thousandths

4. 80 million

Set B (pages 6–7)

Write the numbers in order from greatest to least.

1**7**.2391   17.**2**391   2 < 3
1**7**.3267   6 < 7   17.**3**267 ← greatest
1**6**.1999 ← least

17.3267, 17.2391, 16.1999.

Remember to compare two digits at a time, starting at the left.
Write the numbers from greatest to least.

1. 0.38765, 0.37721, 0.41171

2. 22.750, 2,300, 2.26

Set C (pages 10–11)

Compute 17 + 6 + 23 mentally.

17 + 6 + 23 = 17 + (23 + 6)   Commutative
              = (17 + 23) + 6   Associative
              = 40 + 6   Add 17 + 23 mentally.
              = 46

Remember the commutative, associative, and identity properties can help you compute mentally.

1. 11 + 3 + 19   **2.** 164 + 14 + 16

Set D (pages 12–13)

Round 16.008216 to the place underlined.

Since 2 < 5, the number rounds to 16.008.

Remember if the digit to the right of the digit to be rounded is 5 or greater, round up. If it is less than 5, round down.

1. 0.6**7**92   **2.** 11**9**.299

Set E (pages 14–16)

Estimate first, then find the exact sum.

2.02 + 16.231 + 9.87

Estimate: 2 + 16 + 10 = 28

Exact: 2.020   Use zeros as placeholders.
         16.231   Align the decimal points.
          9.870
         ─────
         28.121

Remember when adding decimals, align the decimal points.

Estimate first. Then find the sum.

1. 284.236 + 0.8994

2. 16.36 + 19.23 + 29.21

Set F (pages 17–19)

Subtract 12.6 − 3.22.

$$\begin{array}{r} \overset{5\ 10}{12.\cancel{6}\cancel{0}} \\ -\ 3.22 \\ \hline 9.38 \end{array}$$

Regroup to subtract the hundredths.
Subtract the tenths, and whole numbers.
Place the decimal point.

Remember when subtracting decimals, align the decimal points. Insert zeros as placeholders.

1. $87.93 − 64.217$ **2.** $12.342 − 6.76$

Set G (pages 24–25)

Evaluate $11 + (6 − 2) \div 2$.

$11 + (6 − 2) \div 2$ Parentheses first.
$11 + \quad 4 \quad \div 2$ Divide.
$11 + \qquad 2$ Add.
$\qquad 13$

Remember when evaluating an expression, use the order of operations.

1. $(9 \div 3) − 3$ **2.** $16 \times 3 \div 8 − 3$

3. $24 − 10 + 6 \div 2$ **4.** $9 − 3 + 3 \times 9$

Set H (pages 26–27)

Evaluate $2x + 3b \div 12$ for $x = 4$ and $b = 8$.

$2x + \quad 3b \div 12$
$2(4) + 3(8) \div 12$ Substitute 4 for x and 8 for b.
$8 + \quad 24 \div 12$ Evaluate using order of operations.
$8 + \qquad 2$
$\qquad 10$

Remember letters are used to represent variables.

Evaluate each expression for $x = 3$, $b = 7$, and $c = 4$.

1. $b − c − x$ **2.** $6x + 4$

3. $5b + 2c$ **4.** $10c − 16$

Set I (pages 28–29)

Write the phrase, 7 less than the quotient of 2 divided by x, as an expression.

key words: *less than* means subtraction
quotient means division

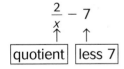

$\dfrac{2}{x} − 7$
quotient   less 7

Remember to look for the words that can be translated into mathematical operations.

Write each phrase as an expression.

1. 3 times k **2.** 8 less than x

3. y divided by 6   **4.** 6 times the sum of b and 3

Set J (pages 30–31)

Solve $p + 1.6 = 1.8$.

$p + 1.6 = 1.8$
$p + 1.6 − 1.6 = 1.8 − 1.6$ Subtract 1.6.
$p + 0 = 0.2$ Add.
$p = 0.2$

Remember to get the variable by itself when solving the equation.

1. $x − 1.4 = 3.2$ **2.** $0 = s − 0.7$

3. $6 + y = 63$ **4.** $52 + m = 74$

More Practice

Set A (pages 4–5)

Write the value of the underlined digit in short word form.

1. 7,2̲05,837   **2.** 48,91̲2,003   **3.** 8.0000̲7

Write each number in standard form.

4. 6 tenths   **5.** 12 and 17 thousandths   **6.** 5 million, 63 thousand, 103

7. Dust particles are no less than 0.0625 millimeters in width. Write this number in short word form.

Set B (pages 6–7)

Compare. Use >, <, or = for each ●.

1. 200,002 ● 88,385   **2.** 6.1137 ● 6.1125   **3.** 0.30058 ● 0.31

Write the numbers in each set from least to greatest.

4. 17,842; 29,987; 77,699   **5.** 5.97; 5.1357; 5.0996

Set C (pages 10–11)

For each exercise choose a strategy and compute mentally.

1. 565 + 35   **2.** 68 − 39   **3.** 22 + 15 + 58

4. A moving truck contains 866 pounds of furniture, 80 pounds of luggage, and 34 pounds of dishware. Determine the total weight of the truck's contents.

Set D (pages 12–13)

Round each number to the place underlined.

1. 5.02̲336   **2.** 9.072̲5   **3.** 12.119̲187   **4.** 89̲0,066,231

5. A baseball pitcher's earned run average is rounded to the nearest thousandth. Round 2.3742 to the nearest thousandth.

Set E (pages 14–16)

Estimate first. Then find the exact sum.

1. 37,543 + 9,824   **2.** $314.09 + $123.55   **3.** 75.31 + 62.575

4. For his art class, Chuck bought 1.58 kilograms of clay and 2.67 kilograms of papier-mâché mix. What was the total weight of Chuck's supplies?

Set F (pages 17–19)

Estimate. Then subtract to find the exact difference.

1. 5,800,000
     $-$ 735,000

2. 320.58
     $-$ 19.88

3. $263.27
     $-$ 108.92

4. 725.8536
     $-$ 6.9922

5. Karen's stone weighs 2.5253 grams. Stella's stone weighs 2.8851 grams. Whose stone is heavier? How much heavier?

Set G (pages 24–25)

Use order of operations to evaluate each expression.

1. $4 \times (10 - 6) + 34$

2. $2 + 6 + 3 \div 1$

3. $18 \times 2 - 2 \div 2$

4. A teacher bought 6 ballpoint pens for $1.79 each and 4 felt-tip pens for $2.12 each. She also purchased a book for $6.49. How much money did she spend?

Set H (pages 26–27)

Evaluate each expression for $s = 10$, $y = 13$, and $b = 3$.

1. $sy - b$

2. $3(b + y) - s$

3. $s \div 2 + b$

4. $y - b - s + b$

5. The expression $3x + 2$ describes the cost (in dollars) of renting a canoe. If $x =$ the number of hours the canoe is rented, what is the cost of renting the canoe for 7 hours?

Set I (pages 28–29)

Write each phrase as an expression.

1. 11 less than b

2. 16 times x

3. 7 more than z

4. The annual rainfall in Miami is about 46 inches more than it is in San Diego. Write an expression that describes the rainfall in Miami if x represents the inches of rainfall in San Diego.

Set J (pages 30–31)

Solve each equation. Check your answer.

1. $10 + s = 73$

2. $s - 120 = 54$

3. $t - 2.2 = 612.7$

4. The local gym has 17 balls. They have 3 footballs, x soccer balls, 6 tennis balls, and 4 racquet balls. Write and solve an equation to find how many soccer balls the gym has.

Problem Solving: Preparing for Tests

Choose the correct letter for each answer.

1. Lonnie made 3 dozen muffins and 12 pancakes. His family ate 7 muffins for breakfast. Which expression can be used to find the number of muffins left?

   A $(3 \times 12) - 7$

   B $3 \times (12 - 7)$

   C $(3 \times 7) - 12$

   D $7 \times (12 - 3)$

   Tip

   Remember that operations inside parentheses are always done first.

2. A scientist is making precise measurements of the diameters of pollen grains and recording those measurements. Her records show measurements of 0.061 mm, 0.037 mm, 0.042 mm, 0.813 mm, and 0.028 mm. Which of these measurements is probably incorrect?

   F 0.813 mm

   G 0.061 mm

   H 0.042 mm

   J 0.028 mm

   Tip

   Look at the four numbers in the answer choices to see which one is significantly different.

3. Eve spends $625 per month on rent and $240 for food. Her gas bill for September was $97.34; her electric bill for the same month was $49.46. Which is the best estimate for Eve's monthly expenses for these items?

   A Less than $650

   B $650

   C About $900

   D More than $900

   Tip

   Start by rounding the rent and the gas and electric bills to the nearest ten dollars.

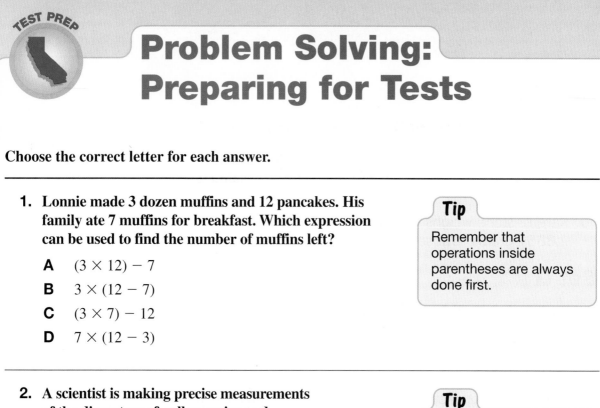

SEPTEMBER EXPENSES
RENT $625.00
GAS $97.34
ELECTRIC $49.46
FOOD $240.00

4. The Maxwell children weigh 128 pounds, 83 pounds, and 72 pounds. Their parents weigh 136 pounds and 212 pounds. Which of these represents the combined weight of the children?

F   631 lb

G   348 lb

H   283 lb

J   200 lb

K   NH

5. The graph below shows the results of a voter survey.

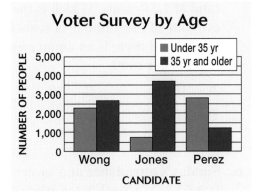

Voter Survey by Age

According to this graph, who is likely to win the election?

A   Wong

B   Jones

C   Perez

D   Jones or Perez

6. George is organizing 147 tapes and 128 CDs. He puts no more than 25 tapes in a box. Which of these is an exact number?

F   There are 25 tapes in every box.

G   George needs about 6 boxes.

H   George will have 3 tapes left over.

J   The total of CDs and tapes is 275.

7. Sid has a garden that is 26 meters wide by 34 meters long. The garden has a fence around it. Between the garden and the fence, there is a path 1.5 meters wide. What is a reasonable length for the fence?

A   It is exactly 63 meters.

B   It is about 100 meters.

C   It is exactly 120 meters.

D   It is more than 120 meters.

8. Hal stacks boxes for a window display. He puts 8 boxes in the bottom row, 7 in the next row, 6 in the third row, and so on. There is 1 box in the top row. How many boxes are in the display?

F   36   H   56

G   46   J   64

9. Paula's car gets about 35 miles to a gallon of gasoline. Which of these is reasonable for the amount of gas Paula needs for a 350-mile car trip?

A   Less than 5 gallons

B   Exactly 10 gallons

C   About 10 gallons

D   Exactly 100 gallons

10. Tom is twice as old as Julie. Julie is x years old. Which expression can be used to find Tom's age?

F $x + 2$

G $2 - x$

H $2x$

J $2x - x$

Multiple-Choice Cumulative Review

Choose the correct letter for each answer.

Number Sense

1. Which numbers are in the correct order from *least* to *greatest*?

   A 68.9, 68.03, 67.91, 67.85

   B 68.03, 67.91, 67.85, 68.9

   C 67.85, 67.91, 68.03, 68.9

   D 67.85, 67.91, 68.9, 68.03

2. In Big Bend National Park, Texas, the Rio Grande Village Nature Trail is $1\frac{1}{4}$ miles long, the Santa Elena Canyon Trail is $1\frac{3}{4}$ miles long, and the Boquillas Canyon Access Trail is $1\frac{1}{2}$ miles long. Which list below shows the trail lengths in correct order from *greatest* to *least*?

   F $1\frac{1}{4}$ mi, $1\frac{3}{4}$ mi, $1\frac{1}{2}$ mi

   G $1\frac{3}{4}$ mi, $1\frac{1}{2}$ mi, $1\frac{1}{4}$ mi

   H $1\frac{1}{4}$ mi, $1\frac{1}{2}$ mi, $1\frac{3}{4}$ mi

   J $1\frac{1}{2}$ mi, $1\frac{1}{4}$ mi, $1\frac{3}{4}$ mi

3. What is 12.46 rounded to the nearest *tenth*?

   A 10

   B 12.4

   C 12.5

   D 12.6

4. Which is the least common multiple of 4 and 10?

   F 2   **H** 20

   G 8   **J** 40

5. There are 3 bleacher sections at the stadium. There are 72 rows with a total of 1,440 seats. Which is the best estimate of the number of seats in each row if there is an equal number of seats per row?

   A 10   **C** 30

   B 20   **D** 33

6. Sunday's attendance at a soccer game was 64,232. A week later, when the team played again, the attendance was only 37,687. Estimate to the nearest thousand how many more people attended the first week than the second week.

   F 20,000   **H** 26,500

   G 26,000   **J** 26,540

7. Which expression describes 14 groups of 3?

   A $14 \div 3$

   B $42 \div 14$

   C 14×3

   D $14 - 1 - 1 - 1$

Algebra and Functions

8. **What expression describes the situation, *d* dollars of savings less $100?**

    F $d + 100$

    G $d - 100$

    H $100d$

    J $100 - d$

9. **Which of the algebraic symbols make the number sentence true?**

    $$1 \blacksquare 2 \blacksquare 8 = 16$$

    A $+$

    B $-$

    C $\times$

    D $\div$

10. **Meg picked 6 apples off a tree. She picked four times that amount the following day. She used 18 apples for baking. How many apples does Meg have left?**

    F 12   **H** 48

    G 6   **J** 42

11. **Solve the equation $d + 8 = 12$.**

    A 1.5   **C** 20

    B 4   **D** 96

12. **An input/output table has the rule multiply by 9. What is the output for an input of 6?**

    F 1.5   **H** 15

    G 3   **J** 54

Measurement and Geometry

13. **Which figure has more than 1 line of symmetry?**

    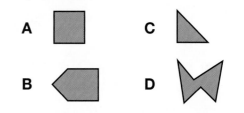

14. **Samantha's baby sister is 54 weeks old, and her younger brother is 3 years old. How many *days* old is Samantha's sister?**

    F 948 days

    G 417 days

    H 378 days

    J 358 days

15. **Which best describes the two pentagons?**

    A The pentagons are not similar.

    B The pentagons are congruent.

    C The pentagons are both symmetrical.

    D The pentagons are reflections of each other.

16. **A three-dimensional figure has 6 faces that are all squares. This figure is a ?.**

    F Cube

    G Cylinder

    H Pyramid

    J Triangular prism

Multiplying and Dividing Decimals

Diagnosing Readiness

In Chapter 2, you will use these skills:

Ⓐ Multiplying and Dividing Whole Numbers

(Grade 5)

1. 9×8

2. $64 \div 8$

3. 6×7

4. $49 \div 7$

5. $2 \times 1 \times 6$

6. $50 \div 5 \div 2$

7. 8×5

8. $4 \times 3 \div 2$

9. Tate plays 8 games of chess in a statewide chess tournament. Each game he plays averages about 3 hours. About how many hours does Tate spend in all playing in the chess tournament?

Ⓑ Comparing Whole Numbers

(pages 6–7)

Fill in the ⬤ with <, >, or = to make each statement true.

10. 43 ⬤ 23

11. $112 ⬤ $126

12. 22 − 9 ⬤ 13

13. 17 ⬤ 64 − 49

C Adding Whole Numbers

(pages 14–16)

14. 23,911 + 17,273

15. 13,806 + 1,264

16. $4,786 + $82,976

17.   94,463
     + 81,002

18.   16,777
     + 23,911

D Multiplying by Powers of 10

(Grade 5)

Complete the table.

	× 100	× 1,000	× 10,000
0.02	2	20	200
19. 0.78			
20. 2.36			
21. 7.003			
22. 21.081			

23. A model airplane is 118 cm long. Greg and 21 other engineers are going to build a real airplane 10 times the size of the model. How long will their plane be?

E Dividing by Powers of 10

(Grade 5)

Complete the table.

	÷ 100	÷ 1,000	÷ 10,000
68,000	680	68	6.8
24. 112,000			
25. 75,000			
26. 189,000			
27. 4,300			

28. A collection has 9,820 clay pots. If there are 10 exhibits, find the average number of pots in each exhibit.

F Solving Equations

(pages 30–31)

Solve for x.

29. $x - 9 = 2$

30. $6 = x + 4$

31. $95 = x - 5$

32. Josie swam 9 laps on Monday, 11 laps on Tuesday and d laps on Wednesday. She swam a total of 31 laps. Use $9 + 11 + d = 31$ to find how many laps she swam on Wednesday.

To the Family and Student

Looking Back

In Grade 5, students performed calculations and solved problems involving simple multiplication and division.

Chapter 2

In this chapter, students will learn how to multiply and divide whole numbers and decimals.

Looking Ahead

In Chapter 5, students will learn how to multiply and divide fractions and mixed numbers.

Math and Everyday Living

Opportunities to apply the concepts of Chapter 2 abound in everyday situations. During the chapter, think about how multiplying and dividing whole numbers and decimals can be used to solve a variety of real-world problems. The following examples suggest just several of the many situations that could launch a discussion about multiplying and dividing whole numbers and decimals.

Math and Landscaping
Your family purchased 11 white pine trees to plant along the border of your sidewalk. The total tree bill, including labor to plant the trees, was $981.23. If labor was $145.23, what was the cost for each tree?

Math and Transportation

The airplane you are traveling on has 45 rows of seats with 6 seats in each row. All the seats on the plane are filled with passengers. The airline allows each passenger two carry-on bags. What is the maximum number of carry-on bags allowed on the airplane? For your return flight, the plane is expected to be only half full. How many carry-on bags should the airline expect on the return flight?

Math at the Zoo You bought three student admission tickets to the zoo. You had $18.36 in your pocket when you arrived. After buying the tickets you only have $13.11. How much did each ticket cost?

Then you bought three bags of popcorn for $1.25 each and two lemonades for $0.85 each. How much money did you have left?

Math at Home Your family installs hardwood floors in the kitchen of your home. The kitchen measures 256.25 square feet. The cost of the material and installation of the new hardwood flooring is $4,668.88. What is the cost per square foot to make this home improvement? Round to the nearest cent.

Math and Health Health experts suggest that people drink 64 ounces of water every day. To obtain this goal, you decide to drink from a 7-ounce sports bottle. How many times a day do you need to fill the container with water so you drink at least the suggested amount?

Math and Publications
The newspaper is delivered to your home every day. The rate is $0.48 per day Monday through Saturday and $1.35 on Sunday. How much money does your family spend for the newspaper in one year? (Use 1 year = 52 weeks.)

Math and Recreation
Horseback-riding rates are $10.25 the first 30 minutes and $8.50 each 30 minutes thereafter. You and two of your family members want to ride from 10:45 A.M. to 1:15 P.M. How much will it cost for all of you to go riding?

California Content Standards in Chapter 2 Lessons*

Number Sense	Teach and Practice	Practice
2.1 (🔑) (Grade 5) Multiply with decimals….	2-2	
2.2 (🔑) (Grade 5) Demonstrate proficiency with division, including division with positive decimals and long division with multidigit numbers.	2-4, 2-5	
Algebra and Functions		
1.1 (🔑) Write and solve one-step linear equations in one variable.	2-7	
1.2 Write and evaluate an algebraic expression for a given situation, using up to three variables.		2-4
1.3 Apply…the commutative, associative, and distributive properties to evaluate expressions and justify each step in the process.	2-1	2-5

Mathematical Reasoning	Teach and Practice	Practice
1.1 Analyze problems by…sequencing and prioritizing information….		2-5
1.2 Formulate and justify mathematical conjectures based on a general description of the mathematical question or problem posed.		2-2
2.1 Use estimations to verify the reasonableness of results.		2-2
2.2 Apply strategies and results from simpler problems to more complex problems.		2-3, 2-8
2.4 Use a variety of methods such as words, numbers, symbols, charts, graphs, tables, diagrams, and models to explain mathematical reasoning.	2-8	
2.5 Express the solution clearly and logically by using the appropriate mathematical notation and terms and clear language; support solutions….	2-3	2-7
2.7 Make precise calculations and check the validity of the results from the context of the problem.		2-4, 2-6
3.2 Note the method of deriving the solution and demonstrate a conceptual understanding of the derivation by solving similar problems.	2-6	
3.3 Develop generalizations of the results obtained and the strategies used and apply them in new problem situations.		2-1

* The symbol (🔑) indicates a key standard as designated in Mathematics Framework for California Public Schools. Full statements of the California Content Standards are found at the beginning of the book following the Table of Contents.

Multiplication Algebra Properties

California Content Standard *Algebra and Functions 1.3: Apply . . . the commutative, associative, and distributive properties to evaluate expressions; and justify each step in the process.*

Math Link You have learned how to use mental math strategies and properties to help you find sums and differences mentally. Now you will learn how multiplication strategies and properties can help you compute mentally.

Warm-Up Review

1. 8 × 7   2. 9 × 6

3. 5 × 4   4. 3 × 30

5. 10 × 40   6. 62 × 10

7. At the sport store, Jeff bought 4 cans of tennis balls and 3 packs of golf balls. There are 3 tennis balls in each can and 6 golf balls in each pack. Did he buy more tennis balls or more golf balls?

Example 1

Find 3 × 17 mentally.

One mental math strategy that can be used is the break-apart strategy.

$3 \times 17 = 3 \times (10 + 7)$ ← "Break apart" a number to give you easier numbers with which to work.

$= (3 \times 10) + (3 \times 7)$ Distributive property

$= \quad 30 \quad + \quad 21$

$= 51$

Example 2

Compatible numbers is another strategy for computing mentally.

Find 2 × (386 × 5)

$2 \times (386 \times 5) = 2 \times (5 \times 386)$ Commutative property

$= (2 \times 5) \times 386$ Associative property

$= \quad 10 \quad \times 386$

$= 3,860$

Example 3

The compensation strategy can also be used to compute mentally.

Find 4 × 598

$4 \times 598 = 4 \times (600 - 2)$ Write 598 as 600 − 2.

$= (4 \times 600) - (4 \times 2)$ Distributive property

$= 2,400 - 8$ Subtract.

$= 2,392$

Multiplication Properties

Commutative Property
The order in which numbers are multiplied does not affect the product.

$5 \times 20 = 20 \times 5$

Associative Property
The way in which factors are grouped does not affect the product.

$3 \times (2 \times 5) = (3 \times 2) \times 5$

Identity Property
The product of one and any number is that number.

$45 \times 1 = 45$

Property of Zero
The product of zero and any number is zero.

$9,999 \times 0 = 0$

Distributive Property
Multiplying a factor by a group of addends yields the same result as multiplying that factor by each addend and then adding the products.

$6 \times (5 + 4) = (6 \times 5) + (6 \times 4)$

Additional Standards: Mathematical Reasoning 3.3 (See p. 49.)

Guided Practice *For another example, see Set A on page 76.*

Use multiplication properties and mental math to simplify each expression.

1. 4×253 **2.** 13×5 **3.** 6×393 **4.** $4 \times (7 \times 25)$ **5.** $(5 \times 188) \times 2$

6. At a museum, Dixie visited 2 exhibit areas on each of 3 floors. Bruce visited 3 exhibit areas on each of 2 floors. Who visited more areas? How do you know?

Independent Practice *For more practice, see Set A on page 78.*

Use multiplication properties and mental math to simplify each expression.

7. $1 \times 9 \times 46$ **8.** 4×72 **9.** $2 \times (5 \times 56)$

10. 6×19 **11.** $5 \times 71 \times 20$ **12.** $1{,}026 \times 84 \times 0$

Find the missing value. Name the property you used.

13. $8 \times (52 + n) = (8 \times 52) + (8 \times 64)$ **14.** $14 \times (76 \times 7) = (14 \times n) \times 7$

15. Tracy collects old sheet music. At a flea market, she found 29 songs at $4 apiece. Find the total cost of the music.

16. What property can you use to find the product of $53 \times 86 \times 892 \times 0 \times 876$ mentally?

17. A collector offered to sell 5 World's Fair posters at $32 apiece. Explain how you can use the distributive property to find the total cost.

Mixed Review

18. Round 2,109.5627 to the nearest one.

Algebra Write each phrase as an expression.

19. 12 more than u **20.** m multiplied by 3   **21.** t decreased by 3

Test Prep   Choose the correct letter for each answer.

22. Algebra Solve for t.
(1–12)

     $404 - t = 176$

     A $t = 124$ **C** $t = 176$
     B $t = 128$ **D** $t = 228$

23. Algebra Solve for y.
(1–12)

     $36.5 + y = 50$

     F $y = 13.5$ **H** $y = 41.5$
     G $y = 14.5$ **J** $y = 86.5$

LESSON
2-2

Multiplying Whole Numbers and Decimals

California Content Standard *Number Sense 2.1(🔑), Grade 5: Multiply with decimals . . ..*

Math Link You can use what you know about multiplication properties to multiply large whole numbers and decimals.

Example 1

The African elephant, the largest land animal, has been known to weigh as much as 26,328 pounds. The blue whale can weigh as much as 15 African elephants. How much can a blue whale weigh?

26,328   ×   15   =   *n*

weight of one   elephants   weight of one
elephant   blue whale

Estimate by finding a range: $20,000 \times 10 = 200,000$
$30,000 \times 20 = 600,000$

Step 1 Multiply by the ones.	**Step 2** Multiply by the tens.	**Step 3** Add the partial products.
26,328 × 15 ——— 131640	26,328 × 15 ——— 131640 263280	26,328 × 15 ——— 131640 263280 ——— 394,920

The answer is reasonable because 394,920 is between 200,000 and 600,000.

A blue whale can weigh as much as 394,920 pounds.

Example 2

The key to multiplying a whole number by a decimal is locating the decimal point in the product.

Find 0.38×86.

Estimate first: Since 0.38 is less than 0.5, the product should be less than half of 86, or 43.

Warm-Up Review

1. $8,354 + 4,350$

2. $9,904 + 213,510$

3. $98 + 680 + 4,500$

4. $605 + 7,234 + 10,659$

5. $462 + 5,100 + 89,700$

6. Alana bought a stamp for $3. She was told that next year it would be worth $6, the year after that $12, and the year after that $24. If the stamp continues to increase in value this way, what will it be worth in 6 years?

52   *Additional Standards: Mathematical Reasoning 1.2 (See p. 49.)*

Step 1 Multiply as with whole numbers.	Step 2 Count the number of decimal places in **both** factors to determine how many decimal places are in the product.

$$
\begin{array}{r}
0.38 \\
\times 86 \\
\hline
228 \\
3040 \\
\hline
3268
\end{array}
$$

$$
\begin{array}{rl}
0.38 & \longleftarrow \quad 2 \text{ decimal places} \\
\times 86 & \longleftarrow \quad + \ 0 \text{ decimal places} \\
\hline
228 & \\
3040 & \\
\hline
32.68 & \longleftarrow \quad 2 \text{ decimal places}
\end{array}
$$

The answer is reasonable because it is less than 43.

Example 3

Multiplying two decimals is almost like multiplying a whole number by a decimal.

Find 94.2×1.08.

Estimate first: Round both factors to the nearest whole number: $94 \times 1 = 94$.

Step 1 Multiply as with whole numbers.	Step 2 Count the number of decimal places in **both** factors to determine how many decimal places are in the product.

$$
\begin{array}{r}
1.08 \\
\times 94.2 \\
\hline
216 \\
4320 \\
97200 \\
\hline
101736
\end{array}
$$

You may wish to write zeros to help you align partial products.

$$
\begin{array}{rl}
1.08 & \longleftarrow \quad 2 \text{ decimal places} \\
\times 94.2 & \longleftarrow \quad + \ 1 \text{ decimal place} \\
\hline
216 & \\
4320 & \\
97200 & \\
\hline
101.736 & \longleftarrow \quad 3 \text{ decimal places}
\end{array}
$$

Check: 94.2 was rounded to 94 and 1.08 was rounded to 1, so the answer should be greater than 94. Since the answer, 101.736, is greater than 94, it is reasonable.

More Examples

A.
$$
\begin{array}{r}
\$3.16 \\
\times 7.5 \\
\hline
1580 \\
22120 \\
\hline
\$23.700 = \$23.70
\end{array}
$$

B.
$$
\begin{array}{r}
0.206 \\
\times \ 0.14 \\
\hline
824 \\
2060 \\
\hline
0.02884
\end{array}
$$

With a calculator:

Press: . 2 0 6 × . 1 4 =

Display: *0.02884*

Guided Practice *For another example, see Set B on page 76.*

1.
$$
\begin{array}{r}
209 \\
\times 36
\end{array}
$$

2.
$$
\begin{array}{r}
1{,}650 \\
\times 412
\end{array}
$$

3. 42.7×2.1

4. 6.21×0.03

5. Mental Math If you paid $5.00 per pound, how much would you pay for 2.5 pounds of cheese?

Independent Practice

For more practice, see Set B on page 78.

6. 399 × 705	**7.** 52.7 × 3.9	**8.** 417 × 26	**9.** 2.637 × 4.36	**10.** 5.03 × 0.07

11. 5.76 × 4.08   **12.** 0.08 × 0.007   **13.** 0.62 × 0.038   **14.** 3.16 × 15.7

To find an object's weight on a different planet, multiply the object's Earth weight by the surface gravity of the other planet. Use the data in the table at the right for Exercises 15 and 16.

Surface Gravity on Each Planet	
Mercury	0.38
Venus	0.90
Earth	1.00
Mars	0.38
Jupiter	2.64
Saturn	1.13
Uranus	1.07
Neptune	1.08
Pluto	0.029

15. How much would Paul weigh on Saturn if he weighs 77.45 pounds on Earth?

16. If your dog, Star, weighs 55.61 pounds on Earth, how much would he weigh on Pluto?

17. Math Reasoning Make a conjecture about whether there are more or fewer than 50 numbers that can be written as the product of three 1-digit numbers, without using the number 1 more than once as a factor. For example, 15 can be written as 1 × 3 × 5 and 24 can be written as 2 × 3 × 4. Explain your thinking. Then solve the problem.

Mixed Review

18. Raul checked his pulse and counted 27 beats in 15 seconds, 54 beats in 30 seconds, and 81 beats in 45 seconds. If this pattern continues, how many beats would he expect to count in 90 seconds?

Algebra Solve each equation. Check your answer.

19. $s - 48 = 79$ **20.** $87 + s = 102$ **21.** $1.67 + p = 2.05$

Algebra Find the missing value. Name the property you used.

22. $93 \times \bullet = 93$ **23.** $40 \times 7 = \bullet \times 40$ **24.** $(6 \times 12) + (6 \times 18) = \bullet(12 + 18)$

Test Prep   Choose the correct letter for each answer.

25. Algebra Evaluate $x + 6y$ for $x = 7.2$ and $y = 9$.
(1–10)

   A 22.2   **B** 44.1   **C** 61.2   **D** 126   **E.** NH

26. Algebra Write an expression for "twice the sum of 6 and n."
(1–11)

   F $2 \times (6 + n)$ **G** $(2 \times 6) + n$ **H** $2 + (6 + n)$ **J** $(2 \times 6) \times n$

   (**Use Homework Workbook 2-2.**)

Multiple-Choice Cumulative Review

Choose the correct letter for each answer.

1. **What is the value of the underlined digit in 260,813.367?**

    A   0

    B   10 thousands

    C   60 thousands

    D   260 thousands

2. **The product of 218 × 1 = 218 is an example of which property?**

    F   Associative

    G   Identity

    H   Commutative

    J   Inverse

3. **Compute mentally.**

    $$2 \times (5 \times 92)$$

    A   900

    B   910

    C   920

    D   930

4. **Complete the pattern.**

    $3 \times 10 \qquad = 30$
    $30 \times 100 \qquad = 3,000$
    $300 \times 1,000 \quad = 300,000$
    $3,000 \times 10,000 = \underline{\qquad}$

    F   300,000

    G   3,000,000

    H   30,000,000

    J   3,000,000,000

5. **Which of the following describes the expression $6x - 6$?**

    A   Six more than six

    B   Six greater than x times six

    C   Six divided by x minus six

    D   Six less than six times x

6. **Evaluate.**

    $$2 + 3 \times 6 - 5 \div 5$$

    F   3

    G   5

    H   19

    J   29

7. **There are 16 tracks in a railroad yard. There are 32 trains with a total of 672 train cars parked on the tracks. Which is the best estimate of the number of cars on each train if there is an equal number of cars per train?**

    A   10 cars   **C**   30 cars

    B   20 cars   **D**   33 cars

8. **A table can support only 80 pounds. Bobi stacks three boxes of fruit, 20.97 pounds each, on the table. How much more weight can the table support?**

    F   60.97 pounds

    G   59.03 pounds

    H   19.09 pounds

    J   17.09 pounds

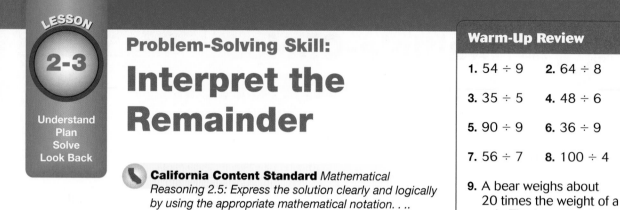

Problem-Solving Skill:

Interpret the Remainder

California Content Standard *Mathematical Reasoning 2.5: Express the solution clearly and logically by using the appropriate mathematical notation. . ..*

Warm-Up Review

1. 54 ÷ 9   2. 64 ÷ 8

3. 35 ÷ 5   4. 48 ÷ 6

5. 90 ÷ 9   6. 36 ÷ 9

7. 56 ÷ 7   8. 100 ÷ 4

9. A bear weighs about 20 times the weight of a cub. The bear weighs 360 kilograms. How much does the cub weigh?

Read for Understanding

A group of eleven sixth-grade students wanted to visit the museum's special exhibit on optical illusions. A sign at the beginning of the exhibit read "Groups of 4 only." After reading the sign, Mary said, "We have to go in groups of 4. I don't think we can all get in."

Sam said, "We can all get into the exhibit if we can get five more people to join us." Ed said, "We don't need as many as five people."

1 How many sixth graders are there?

2 How are people admitted to the exhibit?

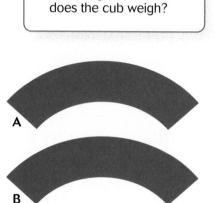

▲ **Optical Illusion:** Is Shape A or Shape B longer? (They are the same length.)

Think and Discuss

MATH FOCUS

Interpreting Remainders

When you use division to solve a problem, a remainder can affect the solution. How you interpret the remainder depends on what is being divided and why.

Reread the paragraph at the top of the page.

3 Is Mary's statement true? Explain.

4 How many students may not be able to visit the exhibit?

5 What was the reasoning behind Sam's statement? Behind Ed's statement?

6 What is the least number of students that must join the group in order for all the students to get into the exhibit? Explain.

7 How was being able to interpret the remainder correctly useful in solving this problem?

Guided Practice

Ms. Hartley's class wants to view the Virtual Reality show. There are 26 students, and Ms. Hartley wants one parent to accompany each group of 4 students. She will go with any remaining students.

1. Which calculation will help you find the number of parents Ms. Hartley needs?

    a. 26 ÷ 5

    b. 26 ÷ 4

    c. 26 ÷ 1

2. Look back at Exercise 1. What does the remainder represent?

    a. The number of groups

    b. The number of parents needed

    c. The number of students in Ms. Hartley's group

3. How many groups will see the Virtual Reality show?

    a. 5 groups

    b. 6 groups

    c. 7 groups

Independent Practice

Boats are lined up at the dock, waiting to take Mr. Ramos, 37 students, and some parents for a ride around the museum's lake. Each boat holds 6 people. There are enough parents for Mr. Ramos to assign one parent and 5 students to each boat. Mr. Ramos joins the remaining students in another boat.

4. Which calculation is most useful for finding the number of boats needed?

    a.
$$\begin{array}{r} 4 \text{ R1} \\ 9\overline{)37} \\ -36 \\ \hline 1 \end{array}$$

    b.
$$\begin{array}{r} 6 \text{ R1} \\ 6\overline{)37} \\ -36 \\ \hline 1 \end{array}$$

    c.
$$\begin{array}{r} 7 \text{ R2} \\ 5\overline{)37} \\ -35 \\ \hline 2 \end{array}$$

5. What part of the calculation in Exercise 4 tells you how many parents are present?

    a. The divisor

    b. The quotient

    c. The remainder

6. Math Reasoning What part of the calculation tells you how many students were in the boat with Mr. Ramos?

LESSON 2-4

Dividing by Whole Numbers

 California Content Standard *Number Sense 2.2* (🔑), *Grade 5: Demonstrate proficiency with division, including division with positive decimals and long division with multidigit divisors.*

Math Link You know how to divide numbers like 72 ÷ 8 and 123 ÷ 3. Now you will learn how to divide by two-digit divisors and how to divide decimals by whole numbers.

Example 1

The gift shop at the science museum donated a carton containing 2,622 wood dinosaur "bones" to a local school. Students assembled the bones in 23 identical model dinosaurs. How many bones does each model contain?

number of bones   models   bones in each model

$$2,622 \div 23 = n$$

Estimate using compatible numbers: 2,400 ÷ 24 = 100.

Step 1 Use your estimate to help you place the first digit in the quotient. Divide the hundreds.	**Step 2** Divide the tens.	**Step 3** Divide the ones.
$$\begin{array}{r} 1 \\ 23\overline{)2,622} \\ -23 \\ \hline 3 \end{array}$$ • Divide. • Multiply. • Subtract. • Compare. 3 < 23	$$\begin{array}{r} 11 \\ 23\overline{)2,622} \\ -23\downarrow \\ \hline 32 \\ -23 \\ \hline 9 \end{array}$$ • Bring down. • Divide. • Multiply. • Subtract. • Compare. 9 < 23	$$\begin{array}{r} 114 \\ 23\overline{)2,622} \\ -23\downarrow \\ \hline 32 \\ -23\downarrow \\ \hline 92 \\ -92 \\ \hline 0 \end{array}$$ • Bring down. • Divide. • Multiply. • Subtract. • Compare. • Write the remainder, if any, in the quotient.

Check by multiplying.
$$\begin{array}{r} 114 \\ \times\ 23 \\ \hline 342 \\ 228 \\ \hline 2,622 \end{array}$$

Each model contains 114 bones.

Warm-Up Review

1. 216 × 12

2. 1,085 × 30

3. 415 × 0.04

4. $86.15 × 6.1

5. 43 × 0.27

6. Jamie wants to buy 5.4 feet of wood for a bookshelf. The wood costs $3 a foot, and Jamie has $17.50. Does he have enough for all the wood he wants? Explain your answer.

    Additional Standards: Algebra and Functions 1.2; Mathematical Reasoning 2.7 (See p. 49.)

Example 2

You can apply what you know about dividing whole numbers to dividing a decimal by a whole number.

Find $26.30 ÷ 5.

Estimate first: $25.00 ÷ 5 = $5.00

Step 1 Place a decimal point in the quotient directly over the decimal point in the dividend.	**Step 2** Divide as with whole numbers. Use your estimate to help you place the first digit.	**Step 3** Check by multiplying.
$$5\overline{)\$26.30}$$	$$\begin{array}{r} \$5.26 \\ 5\overline{)\$26.30} \\ -25 \\ \hline 13 \\ -10 \\ \hline 30 \\ -30 \\ \hline 0 \end{array}$$	$$\begin{array}{r} \$5.26 \\ \times\quad 5 \\ \hline \$26.30 \end{array}$$

Example 3

Sometimes it is necessary to place zeros in the dividend.

Find 37 ÷ 4.

Estimate first: 40 ÷ 4 = 10

Step 1 Place a decimal point in the quotient. Then divide.	**Step 2** Place a zero in the tenths place. Then divide.	**Step 3** Place a zero in hundredths place. Then divide.	**Step 4** Check by multiplying.
$$\begin{array}{r} 9. \\ 4\overline{)37.} \\ -36 \\ \hline 1 \end{array}$$	$$\begin{array}{r} 9.2 \\ 4\overline{)37.0} \\ -36 \\ \hline 10 \\ -8 \\ \hline 2 \end{array}$$	$$\begin{array}{r} 9.25 \\ 4\overline{)37.00} \\ -36 \\ \hline 10 \\ -8 \\ \hline 20 \\ -20 \\ \hline 0 \end{array}$$	$$\begin{array}{r} 9.25 \\ \times\quad 4 \\ \hline 37.00 \end{array}$$

More Examples

A.
$$\begin{array}{r} 0.85 \\ 9\overline{)7.65} \\ -72 \\ \hline 45 \\ -45 \\ \hline 0 \end{array}$$

When the quotient is less than 1, put a zero in the ones place.

B.
$$\begin{array}{r} 0.032 \\ 6\overline{)0.192} \\ -18 \\ \hline 12 \\ -12 \\ \hline 0 \end{array}$$

Since 1 < 6, put a zero in the tenths place of the quotient as a placeholder.

More Examples

C.
$$\begin{array}{r} 0.2075 \\ 24\overline{)4.9800} \\ -\,48\downarrow\downarrow \\ \hline 180 \\ -\,168\downarrow \\ \hline 120 \\ -\,120 \\ \hline 0 \end{array}$$

Since 18 < 24, put a zero in the hundredths place of the quotient and bring down the zero.

D.
$$\begin{array}{r} 5.07 \\ 55\overline{)278.85} \\ -\,275\downarrow\downarrow \\ \hline 3\,85 \\ -\,3\,85 \\ \hline 0 \end{array}$$

With a calculator:

Press: 2 7 8 . 8 5 ÷
5 5 =

Display: 5.07

Guided Practice   *For another example, see Set C on page 77.*

1. $13\overline{)455}$

2. $65\overline{)1,170}$

3. $38\overline{)3,914}$

4. $10\overline{)4,020}$

5. $22.05 \div 70$

6. $18.24 \div 3$

7. $\$32.40 \div 12$

8. $211.4 \div 7$

Check each exercise by multiplying. Indicate whether the quotient is correct or incorrect.

9. $2.7 \div 9 = 0.3$

10. $41.4 \div 6 = 6.8$

11. $6.03 \div 9 = 0.67$

12. Seventeen students each bought two posters in the museum gift shop. All posters cost the same amount. The total cost was $168.30. How much did each student spend?

Independent Practice   *For more practice, see Set C on page 78.*

13. $7\overline{)62.3}$

14. $5\overline{)\$12.20}$

15. $49\overline{)245.098}$

16. $26\overline{)182}$

17. $\$37.50 \div 30$

18. $30.736 \div 8$

19. $234.96 \div 132$

20. $3.654 \div 18$

21. $80\overline{)1,604}$

22. $\$96.81 \div 21$

23. $36\overline{)3.0276}$

24. $7.446 \div 12$

Check each exercise by multiplying. Indicate whether the quotient is correct or incorrect.

25. $62.7 \div 3 = 20.9$

26. $97.5 \div 12 = 8.120$

27. $0.248 \div 2 = 0.124$

28.
$$6\overline{)0.054} = 0.009$$

29.
$$13\overline{)3.003} = 2.31$$

30.
$$9\overline{)100.62} = 1.18$$

31. Mental Math Find $87.42 \div 100$.

32. Algebra Evaluate $(2.5 \div 5) \times 20$.

33. In one room of the library, a wall that is 53.52 feet long is divided into 24 equal sections. How long is each section?

34. On a typical weekend at the video store, sales total $1,367.08. Sales for the rest of the week typically total $2,542.60. How much more money does the video store take in on a Saturday or Sunday than it does on a typical weekday?

35. The distance between San Francisco and Seattle is 820 miles. On a map, the distance was 8 inches. How many miles does an inch on the map represent?

Mixed Review

36. Janine earned $105.40 last week. If she worked 15.5 hours, how much did she earn per hour?

37. Math Reasoning The length of one lap of an auto racetrack is 2.5 miles. One race was 400 miles long. Is this more than, less than, or exactly 200 laps?

38. Coach Green ordered 8 pairs of gym shorts at $16.95 each and 13 shirts at $11.50 each. How much more did the shirts cost than the shorts?

39. $(2 \times 438) \times 50$ **40.** $(83 \times 6) + (83 \times 4)$ **41.** 5×399

42. $\begin{array}{r} 562 \\ \times\ 93 \\ \hline \end{array}$ **43.** $\begin{array}{r} 3.98 \\ \times\ 2.4 \\ \hline \end{array}$ **44.** $\begin{array}{r} 5.06 \\ \times\ 0.38 \\ \hline \end{array}$ **45.** $\begin{array}{r} 0.431 \\ \times\ 0.202 \\ \hline \end{array}$ **46.** $\begin{array}{r} 0.399 \\ \times\ 0.04 \\ \hline \end{array}$

Use the table at the right for Exercises 47 and 48.

47. What distance is needed to stop a car traveling at 30 mph?

Speed of auto (mph)	10	20	30	40	50	60
Stopping distance (ft)	15	40	65	120	175	240

48. How much greater is the stopping distance at 60 mph than at 50 mph?

Test Prep   Choose the correct letter for each answer.

49. One month is $\frac{1}{12}$ of a year. How many months make up $\frac{1}{3}$ of
(Gr. 5)
a year?

   A 4 months   **B** 3 months   **C** 2 months   **D** 1 month

50. If $\frac{1}{4}$ of a pumpkin weighs 8 pounds, how much does the
(Gr. 5)
pumpkin weigh?

   F 2 pounds   **G** 12 pounds   **H** 24 pounds   **J** 32 pounds

2-5 Dividing a Decimal by a Decimal

California Content Standard *Number Sense 2.2 (🔑), Grade 5:* *Demonstrate proficiency with division, including division with positive decimals and long division with multidigit divisors.*

Math Link You can use what you know about dividing decimals by whole numbers to divide decimals by decimals.

Look at the following pattern. Notice that when the dividend and the divisor are multiplied by the same nonzero number, the quotient stays the same.

Dividend		Divisor		Quotient
6	÷	2	=	3

Multiply 6 and 2 by 5: $30 \div 10 = 3$
Multiply 6 and 2 by 10 $60 \div 20 = 3$
Multiply 6 and 2 by 100: $600 \div 200 = 3$

When dividing by a decimal, first multiply the divisor by a power of ten to make the divisor a whole number. Multiply the dividend by the same power of ten. Then divide.

Example 1

Find $13.2 \div 1.65$

Step 1 Think of a power of 10 that will make the divisor a whole number.	**Step 2** Multiply the dividend and the divisor by the same power of 10.	**Step 3** Place the decimal point in the quotient and divide.
$1.65 \times 100 = 165$ $1.65\overline{)13.2}$	$165.\overline{)1320.}$	$\begin{array}{r} 8. \\ 165\overline{)1320.} \\ -\,1320 \\ \hline 0 \end{array}$

Example 2

Find $533 \div 8.2$

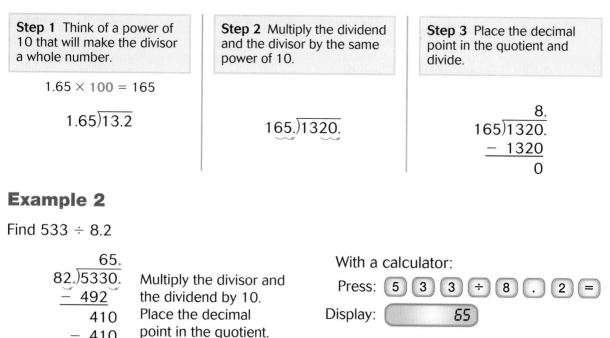

$\begin{array}{r} 65. \\ 82.\overline{)5330.} \\ -\,492 \\ \hline 410 \\ -\,410 \\ \hline 0 \end{array}$
Multiply the divisor and the dividend by 10.
Place the decimal point in the quotient.
Divide.

With a calculator:

Press: ⑤ ③ ③ ÷ ⑧ . ② =

Display: 65

Additional Standards: Algebra and Functions 1.3, Mathematical Reasoning 1.1 (See p. 49.)

Warm-Up Review

Fill in the blank.

1. $3.6 \times$ _____ $= 36$

2. $0.673 \times$ _____ $= 673$

3. $4.31 \times$ _____ $= 431$

4. $0.04054 \times$ _____ $= 4{,}054$

5. $60.9018 \times$ _____ $=$ $609{,}018$

6. The energy output of a normal speaking voice is 0.000024 watt. One million voices produce twice as much energy as a snare drum. What is the energy output of a snare drum?

Guided Practice *For another example, see Set D on page 77.*

1. $0.9)\overline{6.39}$ **2.** $2.5)\overline{12.75}$ **3.** $4.5)\overline{10.755}$ **4.** $0.42)\overline{4.788}$

5. One 8-ounce glass of milk contains 0.4 milligram of riboflavin. An 11-year boy needs 1.6 milligrams of riboflavin each day. How many 8-ounce glasses of milk supply 1.6 milligrams?

Independent Practice *For more practice, see Set D on page 79.*

6. $3.4)\overline{12.92}$ **7.** $0.8)\overline{26.08}$ **8.** $4.5)\overline{22.5}$ **9.** $0.03)\overline{0.228}$

10. $1.08)\overline{3.456}$ **11.** $1.9)\overline{5.738}$ **12.** $0.004)\overline{6.8}$ **13.** $0.013)\overline{0.52}$

14. $1.7)\overline{3.995}$ **15.** $0.81)\overline{3,402}$ **16.** $0.007)\overline{0.868}$ **17.** $0.65)\overline{20.8}$

18. Mental Math Find $96.11 \div 0.01$.

19. Algebra Evaluate $5(0.50 \div 0.025) + 50$.

20. Janna spent half of her money on a poster. Then she spent half of what she had left for a small magnet. She bought lunch for $5.00. When she got home she had $2.50 left. How much money did she have to start with?

Mixed Review

21. Beth bought 25 postcards at $0.33 each and 75 stamps at $0.33 each. How much did she spend?

22. $\begin{array}{r} 235 \\ \times\ \ 84 \\ \hline \end{array}$ **23.** $\begin{array}{r} 9.27 \\ \times\ 0.13 \\ \hline \end{array}$ **24.** $\begin{array}{r} 118 \\ \times\ 0.72 \\ \hline \end{array}$ **25.** $\begin{array}{r} 0.509 \\ \times\ \ \ 208 \\ \hline \end{array}$

26. $2.701 \div 73$ **27.** $32.848 \div 8$ **28.** $0.0195 \div 5$ **29.** $73.594 \div 31$

🖊 Test Prep Choose the correct letter for each answer.

30. Jim saves $4.50 each week. How much will he save in 8 weeks?
(2–2)
  A $4.50   **B** $36.00   **C** $90.00   **D** $360.00

31. Jane practices the clarinet for 45 minutes each day. How many
(2–5) hours will she practice in one week?
  F 4 hours   **G** 4.5 hours   **H** 5 hours   **J** 5.25 hours

Diagnostic Checkpoint

Find the missing value. Name the property used.

1. $82 \times 26 = c \times 82$
(2-1)

2. $4 \times (10 + 9) = (4 \times b) + (4 \times 9)$
(2-1)

3. $64 \times p = 64$
(2-1)

4. $n \times 67 = 0$
(2-1)

5. $s \times 11 = 11 \times 6$
(2-1)

6. $3 \times (12 \times 9) = (3 \times 12) \times y$
(2-1)

Find each product.

7. $\begin{array}{r} 747 \\ \times\ 631 \end{array}$
(2-2)

8. $\begin{array}{r} 252 \\ \times\ 39 \end{array}$
(2-2)

9. $\begin{array}{r} 57 \\ \times\ 29 \end{array}$
(2-2)

10. $\begin{array}{r} 1{,}729 \\ \times\ 67 \end{array}$
(2-2)

11. 2.63×7
(2-2)

12. 12.56×3.4
(2-2)

13. 0.08×72
(2-2)

14. 28.47×13.3
(2-2)

15. $3{,}911 \times 488$
(2-2)

16. 0.007×32
(2-2)

17. 0.009×0.003
(2-2)

18. 3.9×3.6
(2-2)

Find each quotient.

19. $78\overline{)238.68}$
(2-4)

20. $30\overline{)18.9}$
(2-4)

21. $3\overline{)8{,}712}$
(2-4)

22. $41\overline{)492}$
(2-4)

23. $25\overline{)3.75}$
(2-4)

24. $42\overline{)18.9}$
(2-4)

25. $0.8\overline{)19.6}$
(2-5)

26. $7.5\overline{)326.25}$
(2-5)

27. $12\overline{)9.6}$
(2-4)

28. $0.36\overline{)0.7092}$
(2-5)

29. $0.84\overline{)0.4872}$
(2-5)

30. $5.4\overline{)0.945}$
(2-5)

31. If Vinnie were on Mars, he would weigh about 0.38 as much as
(2-5) he weighs on Earth. Vinnie weighs about 92 pounds on Earth. About how much would he weigh on Mars? Round to the nearest whole number.

32. Meg is hired to paint a mural on a wall that is 136 feet long.
(2-4) To prepare the wall, she partitions the wall into 16 sections of equal size. How long is each section?

33. There are 79 garden-club members. Each member needs a new
(2-3) set of garden gloves. The gloves are sold in packs containing 3 pairs each. How many packs of gloves should the garden club buy?

34. Jen went to the farmers' market, where she bought some fresh
(2-2) produce. She bought 5 pounds of apples for $0.79 per pound and 3.5 pounds of oranges for $0.69 per pound. How much did she spend altogether?

Multiple-Choice Cumulative Review

Choose the correct letter for each answer.

1. Pash opens his dog grooming business at 10:00 A.M. and closes at 4:30 P.M. On Tuesday he is scheduled to groom 12 dogs. About how many dogs will he need to groom each hour in order to complete his work for the day?

   A 2 dogs/hour **C** 4 dogs/hour

   B 3 dogs/hour **D** 5 dogs/hour

2. Lou, Max, Kate, Steve, and Riley are standing in line waiting to buy lemonade. Lou is behind Riley and in front of Max. Kate is in front of Lou. Steve is behind Riley and directly in front of Max. Who is at the front of the line?

   F Kate or Lou

   G Riley or Steve

   H Kate or Riley

   J Steve or Max

3. If Tia jogs every week for a year, about how many miles will she jog?

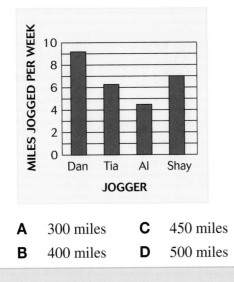

   A 300 miles **C** 450 miles

   B 400 miles **D** 500 miles

4. Evaluate $2x - 3y + 10$ for $x = 8.6$ and $y = 2.1$.

   F 10.0

   G 10.1

   H 20.9

   J 21.0

5. Which makes the statement true?

   $$(6.1 + 2.1) \times 7 \quad \bullet \quad 8.2\overline{)57.4}$$

   A $<$

   B $>$

   C $=$

   D $\leq$

6. Which expression is equivalent to $77 \div 7 - 3$?

   F $2 \times 2 \times 2 \times 2$

   G $66 \div 6 - 2$

   H $\frac{16}{4} + 2$

   J $(311 - 295) \div 2$

7. There are 92 plastic cups in a box. Orange juice will be poured into $\frac{1}{4}$ of the cups. How many cups will contain orange juice?

   A 18 cups **C** 31 cups

   B 23 cups **D** 69 cups

65

Problem-Solving Strategy:
Work Backward

California Content Standard *Mathematical Reasoning 3.2: Note the method of deriving the solution and demonstrate a conceptual understanding of the derivation by solving similar problems.*

Warm-Up Review

1. $23.45 + 61.092$

2. $100.87 - 96.48$

3. 52×23.5

4. 50.5×4.1

5. $\$7.35 \div 5$

6. $3(\$1.75 + \$3.50)$

7. List three numbers between 2.003 and 2.03.

Example

Kim bought 10 ears of corn, one quart of berries and some tomatoes. Use the data given in the table at the right. If Kim gave the cashier $10.00 and received $1.80 in change, how many pounds of tomatoes did Kim buy?

Understand

What do you need to know?

You need to know how much Kim spent on tomatoes.

Plan

Vegetable or Fruit	Price
Berries	$2.00 per quart
Corn	5 for $1.00
Broccoli	$0.80 per lb
Tomatoes	$1.20 per lb

How can you solve the problem?

You can **work backward,** starting with the change Kim received from a $10 bill. Use this information and the information in the table at the right to find how much she spent on tomatoes. Then you can find how many pounds of tomatoes she bought.

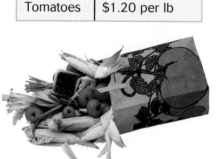

Solve

Money given $10.00	−	Change $1.80	=	Money spent $8.20

Money spent $8.20	−	Cost of 10 ears of corn $2.00	−	Cost of 1 qt of berries $2.00	=	Cost of tomatoes $4.20

Cost of tomatoes $4.20	÷	Cost per pound $1.20	=	Amount of tomatoes 3.5 lb

Kim bought 3.5 pounds of tomatoes.

Look Back

How can you check the answer? Explain.

Additional Standards: Mathematical Reasoning 2.7 (See p. 49.)

Guided Practice

Use the data in the table on page 66 for Exercise 1.

1. Joe bought 4.5 pounds of tomatoes, 10 ears of corn and some broccoli. If he spent $9.60, how many pounds of broccoli did he buy?

Independent Practice

Use the data in the table on page 66 for Exercises 2–4.

2. Jamie bought 5 ears of corn, 2 quarts of berries, and some tomatoes. If she received $2 in change from a $10 bill, how many pounds of tomatoes did she buy?

3. **Math Reasoning** Sue bought 5.5 pounds of tomatoes, a quart of berries, and an 8-pound watermelon. She said the watermelon cost $1.25. If she received $0.65 in change from a $10 bill, was she correct about the price of the watermelon? Explain how you know.

4. Carla spent $8 for tomatoes and broccoli. She bought the same number of pounds of each. How much of each did she buy?

Mixed Review

Try these or other strategies to solve each question. Tell which strategy you used.

> ### Problem-Solving Strategies
>
> - *Find a Pattern*
> - *Draw a Diagram*
> - *Work Backward*
> - *Make a Table*
> - *Write an Equation*
> - *Use Logical Reasoning*

5. Pat bicycled 1.5 miles on Monday. On Tuesday she rode 0.25 mile more than she did on Monday. For the next three days she rode 0.25 mile more than she did each previous day. How many miles did she travel in all over the 5 days?

6. Chad bought 8.5 pounds of apples and some grapes. Apples cost $0.80 a pound and grapes cost $0.75 a pound. He spent $9.05. How many pounds of grapes did he buy?

7. Chris bought 3 pounds of cucumbers for $0.69 a pound, 5.5 pounds of onions for $0.46 a pound, and a head of lettuce for $0.99. How much did he spend in all?

2-7 Solving Multiplication and Division Equations

Algebra

Warm-Up Review

Estimate each product.

1. 31 × 8   **2.** 14 × 58

3. 28 × 52   **4.** 715 × 16

5. 129 × 419

6. 318 × 104

7. A wolf had 10 pups in her third litter. The number of pups was twice as many as in her second litter, and her second litter had 3 more pups than her first. Find the number of pups in her first litter.

California Content Standard *Algebra and Functions 1.1(➤): Write and solve one-step linear equations in one variable.*

Math Link You have learned how to solve addition and subtraction equations. Now you will use these skills to solve multiplication and division equations.

Multiplication undoes division and division undoes multiplication. They are **inverse operations.** To solve multiplication or division equations you need to decide which operation has been applied to the variable. Then you need to "undo" the operation to get the variable by itself on one side of the equal sign.

Example 1

Solve $256x = 1,024$. Check your answer.

$$256x = 1,024$$
$$\frac{256x}{256} = \frac{1,024}{256}$$
$$x = 4$$

To undo multiplying by 256, divide **both** sides by 256. Dividing both sides by the same nonzero number maintains equality.

Check: $256x = 1,024$ Write the original equation.
$256 \times 4 \stackrel{?}{=} 1,024$ Replace the variable with your answer.
$1,024 = 1,024$ Calculate. The answer checks.

Example 2

Solve $\frac{s}{30} = 17$. Check your answer.

$$\frac{s}{30} = 17$$

To undo dividing by 30, multiply **both** sides by 30.

$$\frac{s}{30} \times 30 = 17 \times 30$$

Multiplying both sides by the same nonzero number maintains equality.

$$s = 510$$

Check: $\frac{s}{30} = 17$ Write the original equation.

$\frac{510}{30} \stackrel{?}{=} 17$ Replace the variable with your answer.

$17 = 17$ Calculate. The answer checks.

Additional Standards: Mathematical Reasoning 2.5 (See p. 49.)

Guided Practice   *For another example, see Set E on page 77.*

Solve each equation. Check your answer.

1. $4t = 88$ **2.** $x \div 33 = 66$ **3.** $7.5 = 1.5y$ **4.** $\dfrac{f}{14} = 9.2$

5. Each roll of Mia's film allows her to take 36 photographs. There are 1,224 students at her school. Solve the equation $36n = 1{,}224$ to find how many rolls of film, n, she will need to take a picture of each student.

Independent Practice   *For more practice, see Set E on page 79.*

Solve each equation. Check your answer.

6. $45m = 135$ **7.** $100 = \dfrac{w}{66}$ **8.** $\dfrac{h}{13} = 268$ **9.** $216 = n \div 2$

10. $352 = 8z$ **11.** $7r = 147$ **12.** $m \div 3.4 = 7.25$ **13.** $100 = \dfrac{w}{7.7}$

14. $x \div 3.8 = 60.2$ **15.** $7.4y = 45.88$ **16.** $33j = 19.8$ **17.** $6.5n = 26$

18. Fingernails grow about 1.5 inches per year. The world record for longest fingernails is 56 inches. Solve the equation $1.5y = 56$ to find how many years, y, it might take to grow a fingernail 56 inches. Round your answer to the nearest year.

19. Math Reasoning Look at the two equations $a \times 10 = 40$ and $b \div 10 = 40$. Which variable is greater? Explain your answer.

Mixed Review

20. Algebra Which of these expressions will always have the same solution, no matter what you choose for x: $x + 3$, $5 - x$, or $0x$?

21. $113.16 \div 23$ **22.** $0.176 \div 0.05$ **23.** $0.732 \div 4$ **24.** $27.71 \div 3.4$

Test Prep   Choose the correct letter for each answer.

25. Algebra Write an expression to describe the distance around
(1-11) the square at the right.

m

  A $4 + m$ **B** $\dfrac{m}{4}$ **C** $m - 4$ **D** $4m$

26. Algebra Choose the correct expression for the phrase "three
(1-11) times the sum of a number and 6."

  F $3(n + 6)$ **G** $3 + 6n$ **H** $3n + 6$ **J** $n + 6 + 3$

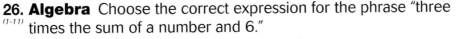

Problem-Solving Application:
Using a Pictograph

California Content Standard *Mathematical Reasoning 2.4: Use a variety of methods, such as . . . graphs . . . to explain mathematical reasoning.*

Warm-Up Review

1. $24{,}000 \div 100$

2. $70{,}000 \div 1{,}000$

3. $8{,}900 \div 1{,}000$

4. $149{,}000 \div 10{,}000$

5. Lauren received $0.55 in change after buying 3 large postcards for $0.75 each and 4 small postcards for $0.55 each. How much money did she give the clerk?

World Population

2000	👤👤👤👤👤👤👤👤👤👤👤👤👤👤👤👤👤👤👤👤👤👤👤
1950	👤👤👤👤👤👤👤👤👤👤
1900	👤👤👤👤👤👤
1850	👤👤👤👤
1750	👤👤👤
1650	👤👤

👤 = 250 Million People

The world population in 1950 was how many times as great as it was in 1650?

Understand

What do you need to know?

You need to know what each symbol in the pictograph represents.

Plan

How can you solve the problem?

Count the symbols used to represent the population in 1650 and 1950. Then divide the number of symbols for 1950 by the number of symbols for 1650.

Solve

For 1650: 2 symbols   For 1950: 10 symbols
Divide: $10 \div 2 = 5$
The population in 1950 was 5 times as great as in 1650.

Look Back

How else could you use the pictograph to solve the problem?

Additional Standards: Mathematical Reasoning 2.2 (See page 49.)

Guided Practice

Use the pictograph on page 70 for Exercises 1–4.

Between which years did the world population

1. double?
2. triple?
3. quadruple?

4. About how many more people were alive in 2000 than in 1900?

Independent Practice

Use the pictograph below for Exercises 5–9.

2015: Projected Populations of 6 Cities

Tokyo, Japan	♀♀♀♀♀♀♀♀♀
São Paolo, Brazil	♀♀♀♀♀♀
Bombay, India	♀♀♀♀♀♀♀♀
Beijing, China	♀♀♀♀♀♀
Jakarta, Indonesia	♀♀♀♀♀♀
Buenos Aires, Argentina	♀♀♀♀

♀ = 3 Million People

5. Which cities are expected to have populations greater than 22,000,000 people by the year 2015?

6. The projected population in Los Angeles in 2015 is approximately 14,300,000 people. How would you show this data in the pictograph?

For Exercises 7–9, answer true or false.

7. By the year 2015, Tokyo is projected to have more than twice the population of Buenos Aires.

8. By the year 2015, the population of Jakarta is projected to be about 9 million people less than that of Bombay

9. The projected populations of Jakarta and São Paolo are about the same.

Mixed Review

10. Laura gave 12 postcards from her collection to Andy. She then received 15 postcards from Kelly and gave 24 to Michael. She now has 62 postcards. How many postcards did she have originally?

Diagnostic Checkpoint

Complete Exercises 1–4. Use the words from the word bank.

1. $(2 \times 12) \times 16 = 16 \times (2 \times 12)$ is an example of
(2-1) the _____.

2. The _____ states that zero is the product of any number
(2-1) times zero.

3. The expression $6 \times 10 + 6 \times 13 = 6(10 + 13)$ is an
(2-1) example of the _____.

4. The _____ states that the product of 1 and any number
(2-1) is that number.

Solve each equation. Check your answer.

5. $8m = 96$ **6.** $p \div 7 = 9$ **7.** $8n = 32$ **8.** $z \div 5 = 7$
(2-7)   (2-7)   (2-7)   (2-7)

9. $j \div 4 = 12$ **10.** $5y = 99.015$ **11.** $d \div 9 = 9$ **12.** $6.8s = 15.64$
(2-7)   (2-7)   (2-7)   (2-7)

13. Paige needs to save $1,850 for a new computer. When she has
(2-6) saved four times as much as she has already saved, she will
need only $116 more to buy the computer. How much has
Paige already saved?

14. Tara spends 45 minutes each morning getting ready for school. She
(2-6) then practices her violin for 15 minutes before she walks 2 minutes
to the bus stop. Her bus ride is about 18 minutes long. At what time
must Tara wake up in order to get to school by 8:15 A.M.?

15. Gary ran a total of 4.5 miles in 18 laps around
(2-7) the track. Use the equation $18d = 4.5$ to find
the distance around the track.

Use the pictograph for Exercises 16–17.

16. The number of adults who like walking is
(2-8) how many times as great as the number
who like rowing?

17. Which exercises are enjoyed by more
(2-8) than 150 adults?

Favorite Type of Exercise Among Adults in Clark County

Walking	🧍 🧍 🧍
Biking	🧍 🧍
Jogging	🧍 🧍
Rowing	🧍

Each 🧍 stands for 100 adults.

Chapter 2 Test

Use multiplication properties and mental math to simplify each expression.

1. 9×28

2. $3 \times 11 \times 2$

3. 99×3

4. $1{,}020 \times 7$

Find the missing value. Name the property you used.

5. $99 \times 8 = n \times 99$

6. $18 \times (8 + 2) = (18 \times n) + (18 \times 2)$

Find each product or quotient.

7. $\begin{array}{r} 328 \\ \times\ 44 \\ \hline \end{array}$

8. $\begin{array}{r} 863 \\ \times\ 3.74 \\ \hline \end{array}$

9. $\begin{array}{r} 8.42 \\ \times\ 0.07 \\ \hline \end{array}$

10. $\begin{array}{r} 0.097 \\ \times\ 0.393 \\ \hline \end{array}$

11. $\begin{array}{r} 13.45 \\ \times\ 5.6 \\ \hline \end{array}$

12. $0.8 \div 1000$

13. $14\overline{)64{,}008}$

14. $0.24\overline{)98.832}$

15. $54.3 \div 1.2$

16. $56\overline{)7{,}322}$

17. $960 \div 0.003$

Solve each equation. Check your answer.

18. $s \div 17 = 13.2$

19. $45 = b \div 15$

20. $11.2x = 89.6$

21. $125y = 1{,}175$

Use the table for Exercise 22.

22. Alyce bought 3 dozen roses, some carnations, 8 bundles of daisies, and 12 sunflowers. She paid $170.00 and received $3.00 in change. How many carnations did Alyce buy?

Flowers	Price
Roses	$24 per dozen
Sunflowers	3 for $8.00
Carnations	$1.50 each
Daisies	$6.75 per bundle

23. Renea plans to make 173 caramel apples. Apples are sold eight to a sack for $3.99 at the farm market. How many sacks of apples does Renea need to purchase?

Use the pictograph for Exercises 24 and 25.

24. The number of students who enjoy fall is how many times as great as the number who enjoy winter?

25. How would you represent 600 students?

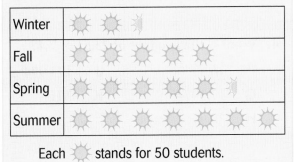

Middle School Students' Favorite Season

Winter	
Fall	
Spring	
Summer	

Each ☀ stands for 50 students.

Multiple-Choice Chapter 2 Test

Choose the correct letter for each answer.

1. Which number sentence is an example of the distributive property?

   A $0 \times 101 = 101 \times 0$

   B $3 \times (8 \times 2) = (8 \times 2) \times 3$

   C $6 \times (6 + 8) = (6 \times 6) + (6 \times 8)$

   D $4 \times (7 \times 10) = (4 \times 7) \times 10$

   E NH

2. Christy, a local gymnast, trains every day for 67 days. She then takes a week's break and resumes her training for another 45 days. Every day she is training, Christy jumps on the trampoline 1,029 times. How many jumps does Christy make on the trampoline during her entire training program?

   F 122,451 jumps

   G 115,248 jumps

   H 68,943 jumps

   J 46,305 jumps

3. $86.233 \div 1.4$

   A 0.162   **D** 86.233

   B 1.4   **E** NH

   C 61.595

4. What is the product of 23.51×7.4?

   F 16.11   **J** 173.974

   G 17.3974   **K** NH

   H 30.91

5. Solve the equation $15x = 12.3$.

   A $x = 0.82$ **D** $x = 184.5$

   B $x = 2.7$ **E** NH

   C $x = 27.3$

6. A school-spirit ribbon costs $1.55. How much would it cost if Tito's father purchased a ribbon for each of the 226 sixth-grade students?

   F $2.50

   G $35.03

   H $350.30

   J $3,503.00

7. Jacki purchased 11 packages of diapers for a daycare company. Each package has three rows of diapers with six diapers in each row. How many diapers did Jacki buy?

   A 198 diapers

   B 84 diapers

   C 51 diapers

   D 50 diapers

8. A dinner reception for 561 people is being planned. Each round table seats 6 people. Determine the number of tables needed to seat all of the guests.

   F 93 tables

   G 94 tables

   H 300 tables

   J 3,366 tables

Use the data from the table for Questions 9–11.

Flood-Relief Volunteer Groups	
Task	Number of Volunteers
Cooking	217
Cleanup	15,580
Construction	1,811

9. The cleanup crew is divided into 76 groups. How many people are in each group?

   A Fewer than 200 people

   B 204 people

   C 205 people

   D More than 250 people

   E NH

10. Each of the cleanup volunteers spent an equal amount of time working. The total amount of hours worked was about 32,000 hours. Which best describes the number of hours one volunteer worked?

   F About 0.5 hour

   G About 2 hours

   H About 5 hours

   J About 50 million hours

11. The cooking volunteers packaged 41,030 pounds of pasta. Each family needing help received two 5-pound containers of pasta. How many families needed help?

   A 8,206 families   **C** 82 families

   B 4,103 families   **D** 41 families

12. Edmund bought a CD player and two CDs. He paid the cashier $200 and received $7.03 in change. The CDs were $17.49 each, including tax. How much was Edmund charged for the CD player?

   F $157.99

   G $165.02

   H $172.05

   J $192.97

13. Which of the following describes how to solve the equation $s \div 18 = 30.5$?

   A Multiply both sides by 30.5.

   B Multiply both sides by 18.

   C Divide both sides by 18.

   D Break apart 30.5.

   E NH

14. A pictograph key shows that * = 150 people. Which would describe 600 people on the pictograph?

   F * * *

   G * * * *

   H * * * * *

   J * * * * * *

15. James and his 7 friends are going to the movies. They can go in cars in groups of 3. Which expression will help you find the number of cars needed?

   A $7 \div 3$

   B $8 \div 3$

   C 7×3

   D 8×3

Reteaching

Set A (pages 50–51)

Find 4 × 27 mentally.

$4 \times 27 = 4 \times (20 + 7)$ Break apart 27

$\qquad = (4 \times 20) + (4 \times 7)$ Distributive
$\qquad\qquad\qquad\qquad\qquad\quad$ property

$\qquad = 80 + 28$

$\qquad = 108$

Remember to use the multiplication properties when computing mentally. They are the commutative, associative, distributive, and identity properties, and the property of zero.

Find each product mentally.

1. 14×6 **2.** 4×29

3. $2 \times 302 \times 5$ **4.** 797×2

5. 5×52 **6.** 8×19

7. 8×150 **8.** $5 \times (23 \times 20)$

9. $25 \times (72 \times 4)$ **10.** 3×48

11. 2×325 **12.** $5 \times 8 \times 21$

Set B (pages 52–54)

Find 44 × 0.68.

Estimate first: Since 0.68 is greater than 0.5, the product should be more than half of 44, or 22.

$0.68 \longleftarrow$ 2 decimal places

$\underline{\times44} \longleftarrow$ + 0 decimal places

272

$\underline{2720}$

$29.92 \longleftarrow$ 2 decimal places

The answer is reasonable because it is greater than 22.

Remember when multiplying decimals to count the number of decimal places in both factors to determine how many decimal places should be in the product.

1. 352×26 **2.** 7.24×0.9

3. 2.2×16 **4.** 421×0.3

5. 6.24×1.2 **6.** 1.62×1.22

7. $\begin{array}{r} 0.043 \\ \underline{\times2.7} \end{array}$ **8.** $\begin{array}{r} 602 \\ \underline{\times38} \end{array}$

9. $\begin{array}{r} 0.013 \\ \underline{\times0.007} \end{array}$ **10.** $\begin{array}{r} 15.3 \\ \underline{\times18} \end{array}$

Set C (pages 58–61)

Find 41.34 ÷ 6. Check by multiplying.

$$\begin{array}{r} 6.89 \\ 6\overline{)41.34} \\ -\ 36\downarrow \\ \hline 53 \\ -\ 48\downarrow \\ \hline 54 \\ -\ 54 \\ \hline 0 \end{array}$$

Check:
$$\begin{array}{r} 6.89 \\ \times\ \ \ 6 \\ \hline 41.34 \end{array}$$

Remember when dividing a decimal by a whole number to place a decimal point in the quotient directly over the decimal point in the dividend.

Check by multiplying.

1. $13\overline{)1{,}326}$ **2.** $512 \div 16$

3. $4\overline{)\$48.64}$ **4.** $28.98 \div 9$

5. $27 \div 4$ **6.** $90 \div 8$

Set D (pages 62–63)

Find $0.7\overline{)4.41}$.

$$0.7\overline{)4.41}$$

$0.7 \times 10 = 7$
$4.41 \times 10 = 44.1$

$$\begin{array}{r} 6.3 \\ 7\overline{)44.1} \\ -\ 42 \\ \hline 21 \\ -\ 21 \\ \hline 0 \end{array}$$

Remember, before you divide by a decimal, multiply the divisor by a power of 10 to make the divisor a whole number. Multiply the dividend by the same power of 10.

1. $2.3\overline{)10.35}$ **2.** $1.2\overline{)2.16}$

3. $0.8\overline{)5.408}$ **4.** $46.8 \div 0.72$

5. $245 \div 3.5$ **6.** $518.4 \div 3.24$

Set E (pages 68–69)

Solve $\frac{b}{3} = 81$. Check your answer.

$$\frac{b}{3} = 81$$

$$\frac{b}{3} \times 3 = 81 \times 3 \quad \text{Multiply both sides by 3.}$$

$$b = 243$$

Check: $\frac{b}{3} = 81$

$$\frac{243}{3} \stackrel{?}{=} 81$$

$$81 = 81$$

When $b = 243$, $\frac{b}{3} = 81$ is true.

Remember that multiplication and division are inverse operations.

Solve each equation. Check your answer.

1. $\frac{w}{12} = 6$ **2.** $16m = 64$

3. $4.4c = 10.56$ **4.** $\frac{x}{5} = 20$

5. $\frac{a}{107} = 3$ **6.** $9b = 32.4$

More Practice

Set A *(pages 50–51)*

Find each product mentally.

1. 8×39 **2.** 7×92 **3.** 4×199 **4.** 9×398

5. $143 \times 50 \times 2$ **6.** $4 \times 83 \times 25$ **7.** $2 \times (5 \times 68)$ **8.** $159 \times 46 \times 0$

Find each missing value. Name the property used.

9. $15 \times 8 = n \times 15$ **10.** $(8 \times n) \times 3 = 8 \times (2 \times 3)$

11. $52 \times n = 0$ **12.** $9 \times n = 5 \times 9$

13. $2 \times (4 + 5) = (2 \times 4) + (2 \times n)$ **14.** $8 \times n = 8$

15. Three students bought 4 gifts each at the museum shop. Four students bought 3 gifts each. Which group bought more gifts? How do you know?

Set B *(pages 52–54)*

1. $\begin{array}{r} 52 \\ \times\ 43 \\ \hline \end{array}$ **2.** $\begin{array}{r} 138 \\ \times\ 28 \\ \hline \end{array}$ **3.** $\begin{array}{r} 419 \\ \times\ 509 \\ \hline \end{array}$ **4.** $\begin{array}{r} 5{,}238 \\ \times\ 447 \\ \hline \end{array}$

5. 9.92×0.53 **6.** 82.7×3.8 **7.** 47.52×18

8. 0.328×0.08 **9.** 3.6×4.8 **10.** 4.23×5.9

11. The diameter of Saturn is about 9.45 times as great as the diameter of Earth. If Earth's diameter is about 7,926 miles, what is Saturn's diameter?

Set C *(pages 58–61)*

1. $5\overline{)3.5}$ **2.** $5\overline{)163.8}$ **3.** $6\overline{)\$5.46}$ **4.** $23\overline{)96.6}$

5. $12\overline{)\$20.40}$ **6.** $40\overline{)25.20}$ **7.** $9\overline{)4.59}$ **8.** $31\overline{)96.1}$

9. $\$24.94 \div 43$ **10.** $283.21 \div 223$ **11.** $117.6 \div 35$ **12.** $264 \div 176$

13. On one weekend, the gift shop in the museum sold 84 model dinosaurs for a total of $662.76. If all the models were the same price, how much did each one cost?

Set D (pages 62–63)

1. $0.5\overline{)2.55}$ **2.** $0.03\overline{)0.711}$ **3.** $0.09\overline{)1.323}$ **4.** $0.56\overline{)53.2}$

5. $0.4\overline{)19.2}$ **6.** $0.25\overline{)52.5}$ **7.** $0.16\overline{)8.32}$ **8.** $4.7\overline{)1.739}$

9. $0.83\overline{)118.69}$ **10.** $2.9\overline{)21.17}$ **11.** $0.007\overline{)3.57}$ **12.** $0.64\overline{)5,508.8}$

13. $42.21 \div 60.3$ **14.** $0.685 \div 2.74$ **15.** $8.7 \div 4.35$ **16.** $34.32 \div 0.165$

17. Anna ran a 6.2-mile race in 47.43 minutes. If she ran the same pace throughout the race, what was her average time per mile?

18. Lance makes $8.75 per hour working at a restaurant. Last week, Lance was paid $210. How many hours did Lance work?

Set E (pages 68–69)

Solve each equation. Then check your solution.

1. $5 \times d = 310$ **2.** $\frac{m}{4} = 24$ **3.** $8 \times u = 72$ **4.** $\frac{a}{7} = 56$

5. $3 \times y = 48$ **6.** $v \div 14 = 7$ **7.** $p \div 15 = 25$ **8.** $7 \times u = 49$

9. $m \div 0.601 = 14$ **10.** $15w = 1,030.5$

11. $33n = 0.66$ **12.** $56.25 = 4.5b$

13. $\frac{m}{3.25} = 14.4$ **14.** $0.465s = 94.86$

15. $1.44b = 72$ **16.** $8.04 = \frac{x}{1.8}$

Write and solve an equation for Exercises 17 and 18.

17. A container of roses was used to make 7 displays, each with 48 roses. How many roses were in the container?

18. Six floral displays used an equal number of carnations. If there were 540 carnations in all, how many were in each display?

Problem Solving: Preparing for Tests

Choose the correct letter for each answer.

1. For a walk-a-thon, Claudia had pledges that totaled $29.28 for every kilometer she walked. If Claudia collected $614.88 and her dad gave her another $10.00, how many kilometers did she walk?

   Tip
   Read the problem and eliminate information you do not need.

   A 15 km

   B 16 km

   C 20 km

   D 21 km

2. For a model-building project, Tricia needs 7 pieces of molding, each 3.4 cm long. How much molding will be left over if she cuts up a piece of molding that is 30 cm long?

   Tip
   Read the problem carefully. Make sure you answer the question asked.

   F 1.8 centimeters

   G 2.38 centimeters

   H 3.8 centimeters

   J 6.2 centimeters

3. Carson divided her age by 3, added 24, divided by 5, multiplied by 2.5, and then added 5. The result was 20. How old is Carson?

   Tip
   Work backward and use inverse operations to solve for her age.

   A 6

   B 11

   C 18

   D 29

4. Use this price table. Which order costs more than $100?

Clothing Prices			
Item	S	M	L
T-shirts	$10	$10	$13
Sweatshirts	$18	$20	$22
Jackets	$38	$42	$42

F 2 small T-shirts, 1 medium sweatshirt, 1 small jacket

G 1 large T-shirt, 2 large sweatshirts, 1 medium jacket

H 2 medium T-shirts, 3 small sweatshirts, 1 medium jacket

J 2 large T-shirts, 1 large sweatshirt, 1 medium jacket

5. Africa has an area of about 11,708,000 square miles. Its area is about four times as great as that of Australia. Which best describes the area of Australia, rounded to the nearest hundred thousand?

A 2,900,000 square miles

B 3,000,000 square miles

C 46,800,000 square miles

D 46,900,000 square miles

6. Roberto buys 36 boxes of greeting cards at $11.87 per box. How much change will he get from $450.00?

F $22.68

G $72.68

H $427.32

J $438.13

7. On a 150-mile car trip, Judy used 6 gallons of gas and traveled at an average speed of 45 mph. She left home at 10:30 A.M. What time is a reasonable arrival time for Judy's trip?

A Exactly 12:30 P.M.

B About 1:20 P.M.

C Exactly 1:30 P.M.

D About 1:50 P.M.

Use the graph for Questions 8–9.

The graph below shows the attendance at a movie theater by type of movie.

Movie Attendance	
Adventure	♀♀♀♀♀♀♀♀♀
Horror	♀♀♀
Science fiction	♀♀♀♀♀
Romance	♀♀♀♀♀♀♀
Other	♀♀♀
♀ = 100 People	

8. How many more people attended romance movies than science fiction movies?

F 700 more people

G 450 more people

H 300 more people

J 250 more people

9. Which two categories represent about half of the people shown on the graph?

A Adventure and romance

B Adventure and science fiction

C Romance and horror

D Science fiction and horror

Multiple-Choice Cumulative Review

Choose the correct letter for each answer.

Number Sense

1. What is the prime factorization of the number 24?

   A $2 \times 2 \times 3$

   B $2 \times 2 \times 4$

   C $2 \times 2 \times 12$

   D $2 \times 2 \times 2 \times 3$

2. Which number sentence is true?

   F $\dfrac{5}{6} > \dfrac{7}{8}$

   G $\dfrac{5}{10} > \dfrac{3}{8}$

   H $\dfrac{2}{5} > \dfrac{2}{3}$

   J $\dfrac{3}{10} = \dfrac{4}{8}$

3. What is the greatest common factor of 15 and 30?

   A 60

   B 30

   C 15

   D 5

4. Jane is making a scrapbook of fall leaves she collected. Her scrapbook has 8 pages. She has 6 orange leaves, 10 red leaves, and 8 yellow leaves. What fraction of her leaves are yellow?

   F $\dfrac{1}{3}$

   G $\dfrac{4}{8}$

   H $\dfrac{3}{4}$

   J $\dfrac{8}{10}$

5. What is the sum of 567.3 and 4.04?

   A 571.34   **C** 575.44

   B 575.04   **D** 607.7

6. What is the missing number in the equation $6 \times 3 \times 7 = b \times 21$?

   F 3

   G 6

   H 7

   J 18

7. What is the greatest number you can divide into 1,000 and get a whole number with no remainder for an answer?

   A 0

   B 250

   C 500

   D 1,000

8. The product of an even number times an odd number is

   F sometimes odd.

   G always even.

   H sometimes even.

   J always odd.

Algebra and Functions

9. A shop has a scale that subtracts 2 ounces from each order of nuts, N, sold by the ounce, to cover bag weight. Which equation shows the total weight of a bag, B, with the nuts in it?

A $N + 2 = B$ **C** $B + N = 2$

B $N - 2 = B$ **D** $N \times 2 = B$

10. Paul walks in a walk-a-thon each year. For every 2 kilometers he walks, Paul raises $14 for charity. What is the ratio of number of kilometers walked to number of dollars raised?

F $\dfrac{7}{1}$ **H** $\dfrac{3}{14}$

G $\dfrac{2}{3}$ **J** $\dfrac{1}{7}$

11. The table shows the relationship between x and y. Which equation can be used to solve for ■?

A $15 \times 8 = $ ■

B $15 + 8 = $ ■

C $11 \times 15 = $ ■

D $15 \div 8 = $ ■

x	y
4	32
7	56
11	88
15	■

12. A pool is 75 meters long. If a swimmer can swim about 10 laps in 7 minutes, how many laps would she be able to swim in 28 minutes?

F 24 laps   **H** 40 laps

G 28 laps   **J** 42 laps

Measurement and Geometry

13. The radius of a circle is shown. Which method would you use to find the diameter of the circle?

A Divide the radius in half.

B Multiply the radius by 2.

C Square the radius.

D Add 2 to the radius.

14. What kind of angle is a 120° angle?

F Right   **H** Straight

G Acute   **J** Obtuse

15. Which of the following sets of angles would form a right triangle?

A 45°, 45°, 90°   **C** 20,°, 40°, 120°

B 40°, 60°, 80°   **D** 30°, 50°, 100°

16. Which of the following illustrates a slide of the letter L?

F   **H**

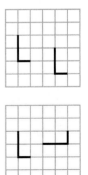

G   **J**

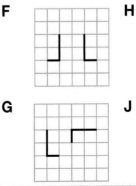

Using Data and Statistics

Diagnosing Readiness

In Chapter 3, you will use these skills:

Ⓐ Ordering Whole Numbers and Decimals

(pages 6–7)

Write the numbers in each set from least to greatest.

1. 46; 58; 47; 49; 51; 52

2. 12; 16; 11.5; 12.4; 11.75

3. 0.26; 0.004; 0.109; 0.205

4. 5.7; 6.3; 5.75; 6; 5.85

Ⓑ Adding Whole Numbers and Decimals

(pages 14–16)

Estimate first. Then find the exact sum.

5. 1,207 + 348 + 2,049

6. 2.6 + 3.7 + 4.1 + 0.64

7. 12.8 + 9.7 + 4.25 + 19.6

8. Shaina measured the rainfall for four days in a row. She found it rained 0.75 inch, 1.4 inches, 0.2 inch, and 1.3 inches. What was the total amount of rain that fell during the four days?

C Subtracting Whole Numbers and Decimals

(pages 17–19)

9. 347 − 92

10. 15.6 − 8.7

11. 2.5 − 0.45

12. 6 − 0.96

13. Maurice had $20 before he spent $14.19. How much money did he have left?

D Order of Operations

(pages 24–25)

Use order of operations to evaluate each expression.

14. (7 + 9 + 12) ÷ 4

15. 7 + 9 + 12 ÷ 4

16. (5 + 8 + 10 + 7) ÷ 5

17. 8 + 7 + (5 + 10) ÷ 5

18. 9 ÷ 3 + 5 × 3

19. 4 × (6 + 5 − 7)

20. 4 × (6 + 5) − 7

E Using Data from Graphs

(pages 32–33)

The double bar graph shows the numbers of males and females in language classes. Use the graph for Exercises 21–23.

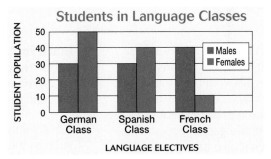

21. In which class do males outnumber females?

22. Which two classes have the same number of male students?

23. How many more females are in German class than are in French class?

F Dividing by Whole Numbers

(pages 58–61)

24. 12.75 ÷ 5

25. 19.48 ÷ 4

26. 21.6 ÷ 6

27. 4.2 ÷ 8

To the Family and Student

Looking Back

In Grade 5, students learned how to read and make graphs and how to find mean, median, mode, and range.

Chapter 3

In this chapter, students will learn how to analyze statistical results.

Looking Ahead

In Grade 7, students will learn how to identify relationships between variables in a data set.

Math and Everyday Living

Opportunities to apply the concepts of Chapter 3 abound in everyday situations. Throughout the chapter, think about how data analysis and statistics can be used to solve a variety of real-world problems. The following examples suggest just several of the many situations that could launch a discussion about data analysis and statistics.

Math in the Newspaper
You often see graphs like the one below in the newspaper. Usually, someone is trying to make a point. What impression does the graph give and how does it give this impression?

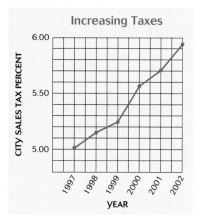

Math in Advertising "Four out of five dentists surveyed recommend our toothpaste for preventing cavities."

Advertisers often use statistics such as those quoted above to convince you to buy their products. But, you would be wise to wonder what methods they used to collect their data. What is the population surveyed? Is the sample representative of the population?

Math at Home Last month your family grocery bills were $157.30, $185.90, $175.12, and $260.08. What is the typical amount your family spent on groceries per week? What effect does the unusually large amount of $260.08 have on this average?

Math in Politics The following question is an example of an unfair question.

"Whom do you plan to vote for in the Congressional race, Tom M., who wants to raise your taxes, or Mary C., who wants to lower them?"

The question is not fair because there are many issues to consider besides taxes. Questions that include viewpoints, supply partial information, or try to influence the answer in any way are unfair. How could the question above be asked so that it would be fair?

California Content Standards in Chapter 3 Lessons*

Statistics, Data Analysis, and Probability	Teach	Practice
1.1 Compute the range, mean, median, and mode of data sets.	3-1	
1.2 Understand how additional data added to data sets may affect these computations of measures of central tendency.	3-2	3-3
1.3 Understand how the inclusion or exclusion of outliers affects measures of central tendency.	3-2	
1.4 Know why a specific measure of central tendency (mean, median, mode) provides the most useful information in a given context.	3-1	3-3
2.0 Students use data samples of a population and describe the characteristics and limitations of the samples.		3-6, 3-9
2.1 Compare different samples from a population with the data from the entire population and identify a situation in which it makes sense to use a sample.	3-5	
2.2 (🔑) Identify different ways of selecting a sample (e.g., convenience sampling, responses to a survey, random sampling) and which method makes a sample more representative for a population.	3-6	
2.3 (🔑) Analyze data displays and explain why the way in which the question was asked might have influenced the results obtained and why the way in which the results were displayed might have influenced the conclusions reached.	3-8, 3-9	
2.4 (🔑) Identify data that represent sampling errors and explain why the sample (and the display) might be biased.		3-5, 3-6
2.5 (🔑) Identify claims based on statistical data and, in simple cases, evaluate the validity of the claims.	3-8	

Mathematical Reasoning	Teach	Practice
1.0 Students use strategies, skills, and concepts in finding solutions.		3-1
2.0 Students use strategies, skills, and concepts in finding solutions.	3-7	3-4, 3-9
2.2 Apply strategies . . . from simpler problems to more complex problems.		3-2
2.3 Estimate unknown quantities graphically and solve for them by using logical reasoning and arithmetic . . . techniques.		3-7
2.4 Use a variety of methods, such as . . . graphs, tables, . . . and models, to explain mathematical reasoning.	3-3, 3-4, 3-7	3-9
3.0 Students move beyond a particular problem by generalizing to other situations.		3-4
3.2 Note the method of deriving the solution and demonstrate a conceptual understanding of the derivation by solving similar problems.		3-7

* The symbol (🔑) indicates a key standard as designated in Mathematics Framework for California Public Schools. Full statements of the California Content Standards are found at the beginning of this book following the Table of Contents.

LESSON 3-1

Mean, Median, Mode, and Range

California Content Standard *Statistics, Data Analysis, and Probability 1.1: Compute the range, mean, median, and mode of data sets. Also, Statistics, Data Analysis, and Probability 1.4.*

Math Link You know how to order, add, subtract, and divide whole numbers and decimals. Now you will learn how to use these skills to find the mean, median, mode, and range of a set of data.

Example

The table at the right shows the number of performances per year given by the City Ballet Company. Find the mean, median, mode, and range of the data.

Performances Each Year								
Year	1992	1993	1994	1995	1996	1997	1998	1999
Performances	90	89	90	100	95	100	104	100

Arrange the numbers in the table in order from least to greatest.

89   90   90   95   100   100   100   104

The **mean** is the sum of all the data divided by the number of data values.

$89 + 90 + 90 + 95 + 100 + 100 + 100 + 104 = 768$

$768 \div 8 = 96$

The mean is 96.

When the data are arranged in order, the **median** is the middle number if the set has an odd number of values or the average of the two middle numbers if the set has an even number of values.

$\frac{95 + 100}{2} = 97.5$

The median is 97.5.

The **mode** is the number or numbers that occur most often in a set of data. Sometimes there is no mode or there is more than one mode.

100 occurs most often.

The mode is 100.

To find the mean using a calculator:

Press:

Display: [96]

Additional Standards: Mathematical Reasoning 1.0 (See p. 87.)

The **range** can tell you if the data are spread far apart or clustered. To find the range, subtract the least number from the greatest number in a set of data.

$104 - 89 = 15.$

The range is 15.

The mean, median, and mode are **measures of central tendency.** They indicate what is typical of a set of data.

Word Bank
range
mean
median
mode
measures of central tendency

Guided Practice *For another example, see Set A on p. 118.*

Find the mean, median, mode, and range for each set of data. Round the mean to the nearest tenth.

1. 12, 14, 22, 16, 18

2. 3, 3, 3, 4, 5, 5, 5, 12

3. 1.2, 3.6, 5.4, 2.4, 3, 4.2

4. 45, 49, 40, 37, 39, 42

5. Katrina practiced dancing 2 hours on Wednesday, 2 hours on Thursday, 1 hour on Friday, 6 hours on Saturday, and 4 hours on Sunday. Find the mean, median, and mode of these data.

Independent Practice *For more practice, see Set A on p. 121.*

Find the mean, median, mode, and range for each set of data. Round the mean to the nearest tenth.

6. 15, 8, 10, 15, 20, 10

7. 60, 80, 50, 30, 70, 10

8. 50, 62, 47, 75

9. 6.9, 7.4, 6.9, 5.2, 8.7, 6.9

10. 300, 500, 200, 400, 200, 200

11. 14, 18, 22, 29, 20, 12, 32

12. Mental Math Use estimation to decide which measure of central tendency is the greatest for the data set: 2, 2, 2, 3, 5, 8, 7.

Use the table at the right for Exercises 13–14.

13. The table shows the number of hours you practiced each week at Dance Camp. Find the mean, median, and mode of these data.

14. If you practiced only 14 hours in week 1, how would the mean, median, and mode change?

Practice	
Week	Hours
1	20
2	18
3	12
4	15
5	19
6	18

15. Math Reasoning After attending camp, Jane planned to practice an average of 3 hours a day for 5 days. She practiced 2 hours one day and 5 hours another day. Decide how many hours she needs to practice the rest of the 5 days to average 3 hours a day.

16. An electrician has 48.5 feet of wire for floor lights. She needs 4.2 feet of wire between each pair of lights and 5 feet of wire from the outlet to the first light. She determines she can install 12 lights. Is this answer reasonable? Explain.

Use the tally chart at the right for Exercises 17–19.

17. How many students have 2 hours or less of homework each night?

18. What is the median number of hours of homework?

19. Math Reasoning Which measure of central tendency is easiest to find from the tally chart? Explain.

Number of Hours of Homework Each Day for Sixth Graders	
Hours of Homework	Tally
1	⫿⫿⫿⫿⫿ I
2	⫿⫿⫿⫿⫿ III
3	⫿⫿⫿⫿⫿
4	I

Mixed Review

20. A dance troupe is putting on a performance with 7 princesses and 7 frogs. The costume designer for the troupe needs 2.5 yards of white lace for each princess's costume. How many yards of lace does she need?

21. $5.3\overline{)21.306}$

22. $0.64\overline{)5.696}$

23. $14.592 \div 0.08$

Algebra Solve each equation.

24. $7k = 42$

25. $\dfrac{x}{4} = 1.2$

26. $0.5n = 7.5$

Test Prep Choose the correct letter for each answer.

27. What property is being used? $(10 + 25) + 75 = 10 + (25 + 75)$
(1-4)

    A Commutative property of addition   **C** Commutative property of multiplication

    B Associative property of addition   **D** Associative property of multiplication

28. Last month, Carrie practiced shooting baskets 4.75 hours
(1-2) per week, Thomas practiced 4.8 hours per week, Maurice practiced 4.7 hours per week, and Marsha practiced 4.5 hours per week. Who practiced the most?

    F Carrie   **G** Thomas   **H** Maurice   **J** Marsha

    (**Use Homework Workbook 3-1.**)

Data with Outliers

California Content Standard *Statistics, Data Analysis, and Probability 1.3: Understand how the inclusion or exclusion of outliers affects measures of central tendency. Also, Statistics, Data Analysis, and Probability 1.2.*

Warm-Up Review

Use the data: 85, 89, 86, 74

1. Find the mean.

2. Find the median.

3. Find the mode.

4. Find the range.

5. Which measure of central tendency is typical of the data?

Math Link You know how to find the mean, median, and mode of a set of data. Now you will learn how one unusual number in a set of data can affect these measures of central tendency.

At the County Fair, a blue ribbon is given each year to the person who enters the largest tomato.

Example 1

Use the table at the right. Find the mean, median, and mode of the data. Round the mean to the nearest tenth.

Mean: $\dfrac{1 + 2 + 1 + 1 + 3 + 1 + 2}{7} = \dfrac{11}{7} \approx 1.6$

The mean is about 1.6 ribbons.

To find the median, list the data in order.

1 1 1 $\boxed{1}$ 2 2 3

The number in the middle is 1. The median is 1 ribbon.

The number 1 appears the most times. The mode is 1 ribbon.

County Fair Blue Ribbon Winners Largest Tomato 1980–1999	
Name	Total Number of Blue Ribbons
Sam	1
Dominik	2
Brianna	1
Paul	1
Mario	3
Erica	1
Maria	2

Example 2

Hannah is not listed in the table. She won the blue ribbon nine times. Add Hannah's data to the data set and recalculate the mean, median, and mode. Round the mean to the nearest tenth.

Mean: $\dfrac{1 + 2 + 1 + 1 + 3 + 1 + 2 + 9}{8} = \dfrac{20}{8} = 2.5$

The mean is 2.5 ribbons.

With a calculator:

Press: (1 + 2 + 1 + 1 + 3 +
1 + 2 + 9) ÷ 8 =

Display: 2.5

Additional Standards: Mathematical Reasoning 2.2 (See p. 87.)

Hannah's data is an outlier. An **outlier** is a number in a data set that is very different from the rest of the numbers. Outliers can have a great effect on the mean. Data sets can have more than one outlier.

The mean is higher with Hannah's total than without it. With Hannah's total it is 2.5; without Hannah's total it is approximately 1.6.

With Hannah's total the two middle numbers are 1 and 2, so the median is 1.5; without Hannah's total it is 1.

The mode, 1, is the same.

Word Bank

outlier

Guided Practice *For another example, see Set B on p. 118.*

Identify the outliers. Then find the mean, median, and mode of the data with and without the outlier. Round the mean to the nearest tenth.

1. 15, 18, 12, 9, 46

2. 48, 52, 50, 8, 52

3. The table at the right lists the number of soccer player of the week certificates earned by four girls. Find the mean, median, and mode of the data with and without the outlier.

Player of the Week	
Name	Certificates
Diane	1
Heather	10
Ann	3
Estella	6

Independent Practice *For more practice, see Set B on p. 121.*

Identify the outliers. Then find the mean, median, and mode of the data with and without the outlier(s). Round the mean to the nearest tenth.

4. 25, 33, 28, 14, 35, 60

5. 24, 24, 18, 56, 25, 12, 15, 22

6. 64, 58, 61, 64, 67, 27, 59, 51

7. 200, 225, 3,000, 500, 325, 311

8. 12.3, 14.8, 9.7, 1.56, 14.8

9. 8.4, 7.5, 8.5, 8.8, 9.9, 7.8, 8.0, 8.4

Use the table at the right for Exercises 10–12.

10. Find the mean, median, and mode of the data in the table. Round the mean to the nearest tenth.

11. Math Reasoning Will the mean of the free-throw data be greater or less without the outlier? Explain.

12. Find the mean, median, and mode of the free-throw data without the outlier.

6th-Grade Free Throws Made			
Name	Free Throws Made	Name	Free Throws Made
Brad	5	Jim	1
Cal	1	Kevin	1
Charlie	3	Matthew	4
Chet	1	Michael	4
Doug	1	Nick	1
Deon	9	Owen	2
Ed	5	Ryan	2
Jason	22	Wayne	11

13. **Math Reasoning** Fill in the blanks. When an outlier that is *greater* than the rest of the data is excluded, the mean _____; when an outlier that is *less* than the rest of the data is excluded, the mean _____.

14. **Math Reasoning** Write an example of a set of data with two outliers.

15. **Math Reasoning** Write a set of data that has 6 numbers, no mode, an outlier; when the outlier is excluded, the mean increases and the median increases.

16. Jason scored 18 points during a basketball game. He did not make any free throws. What possible combinations of 2- and 3-point field goals could he have scored?

Mixed Review

17. A hockey player scored 14 goals in the first 5 games of the season. A newspaper reporter said the player scored nearly 3 goals per game. Is this number reasonable? Explain.

Find the mean, median, mode, and range of each set of data. Round the mean to the nearest tenth.

18. 19, 21, 18, 4, 11, 23, 15, 15   19. 168, 164, 167, 187, 170

Solve each equation.

20. $\frac{x}{5} = 7$ 21. $0.16h = 13.44$ 22. $6.33 + n = 18.9$

Test Prep Choose the correct letter for each answer.

Use the graph at the right for Exercises 23 and 24.

23. Which types of music are liked
(1-13) more by students in Mexico than in the United States?

    A Jazz and Rock

    B Dance and Rock

    C Rap and Country

    D Dance and Rap

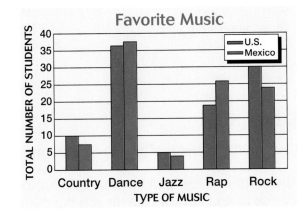

24. How many more students in the
(1-13) United States like Rock than Rap?

    F 9 students   **H** 18 students

    G 11 students   **J** 30 students

LESSON

3-3

Stem-and-Leaf Plots

Warm-Up Review

Find the median and the mode for each set of data.

1. 5, 12, 16, 19, 20, 22

2. 35, 42, 45, 47, 50

3. 15, 18, 24, 24, 24, 30, 31

4. 52, 60, 54, 57, 63, 62

5. 36, 32, 40, 41, 32

California Content Standard *Mathematical Reasoning 2.4: Use a variety of methods, such as . . . graphs [and] tables, . . . and models, to explain mathematical reasoning.*

Math Link You know how to read stem-and-leaf plots. Now you will learn how to make them and how to analyze data in them.

Example 1

The table shows the average number of points scored by the teams in the basketball tournament at the 1996 Summer Olympic Games in Atlanta. Make a stem-and-leaf plot of the data.

Average Olympic Basketball Scores					
Angola	Argentina	Australia	Brazil	China	Croatia
56	70	98	92	72	85
Greece	Lithuania	Puerto Rico	S. Korea	USA	Yugoslavia
80	85	89	81	104	96

Step 1 Title the stem-and-leaf plot.

Step 2 Write the tens digits from the data in order from least to greatest. Write a 10 for numbers from 100 to 109.

Step 3 Next to each tens digit, write the ones digit for each number in the data in order from least to greatest.

Step 4 Write an example that shows what the stem-and-leaf represents. For example, 5 is the tens digit and 6 is the ones digit.

Average Olympic Basketball Scores

Stem	Leaves
5	6
6	
7	0 2
8	0 1 5 5 9
9	2 6 8
10	4

5 | 6 means 56 points

Example 2

Use the stem-and-leaf plot to find the median and the mode.

The stem-and-leaf plot has the data for the 12 teams in order. The sixth and seventh leaves are the middle numbers. They both represent 85 points.

$$\frac{85 + 85}{2} = 85$$

The median is 85 points.

The only leaf that appears more than once with the same stem is 85.

The mode is 85 points.

94   *Additional Standards: Statistics, Data Analysis, and Probability 1.2, 1.4 (See p. 87.)*

Guided Practice *For another example, see Set C on p. 119.*

Use the stem-and-leaf plot for Exercises 1–3.

1. Find the range.   **2.** Find the median.

3. Mental Math Find the mode.

4. Which team in the table on page 94 had the greatest average score?

Number of Students in School Clubs

Stem	Leaves
0	7
1	4 8
2	3 8
3	3 5
4	0 2 5 6

Independent Practice *For more practice, see Set C on p. 122.*

Use the following data for Exercises 5–10.

1998 Winter Olympics Medals Won by Top 12 Countries
29   25   18   17   15   13   12   11   10   10   8   8

5. Make a stem-and-leaf plot.   **6.** Find the median.

7. Mental Math Use the stem-and-leaf plot to find the mode.

8. Make a stem-and-leaf plot of the data for just the top ten countries.

9. Use the stem-and-leaf plot from Exercise 8 to find the median and the mode for the top ten countries.

10. Math Reasoning How do the numbers of medals won by the eleventh- and twelfth-ranked countries affect the median? The mode? Explain.

Mixed Review

For Exercises 11–13, use this information: Abby's test scores in math were 86, 90, 88, 92, 92, and 68.

11. Find Abby's mean and median test scores with the outlier.

12. Find Abby's mean and median test scores without the outlier.

13. Which measure of central tendency is more affected by the outlier?

Test Prep   Choose the correct letter for the answer.

14. Algebra Mike bought several CDs at $7.99 each and the same number of tapes at $4.99 each. Which expression gives the total amount Mike spent on CDs and tapes?
(1-11)

A $7.99 + 4.99$ **B** $7.99x + 4.99$ **C** $7.99 + 4.99x$ **D** $7.99x + 4.99x$

Problem-Solving Skill:

Choosing the Best Graph

Warm-Up Review

Refer to the Olympic basketball scores on page 94.

1. How many teams had an average of 90 points or more?

2. How many more teams had at least 80 points than had fewer than 80 points?

🔔 **California Content Standard** *Mathematical Reasoning 2.4: Use a variety of methods such as graphs, tables, . . . and models to explain mathematical reasoning.*

Read for Understanding

Some of the first dramas were created by the early Greeks. Today, people still study and perform some of these popular plays. The table at the right shows sets of data for a community theater group.

Community Theater Group				
Year	Number of Dramas	Number of Comedies	Attendance	Cost per Ticket
1996	10	8	6,500	$10.50
1997	15	7	4,000	$12.00
1998	12	9	5,500	$12.50
1999	12	10	8,000	$14.00

Look at the data in the table.

1 Which sets of data show totals for each year?

2 Which set of data shows a steady increase over time?

Think and Discuss

MATH FOCUS

Choosing the Best Graph

Line graphs show changes over time. Bar graphs and pictographs show specific numbers, like totals for a year. Circle graphs show parts of a whole.

3 Which type of graph would be best for the data on the number of dramas and number of comedies?

4 Which type of graph would be best for the data on cost per ticket?

🔔 *Additional Standards: Mathematical Reasoning 2.0, 3.0 (See p. 87.)*

Guided Practice

1. The graph shows data on attendance. Which type of graph would *not* be appropriate to use to show attendance?

   a. Circle graph

   b. Line graph

   c. Bar graph

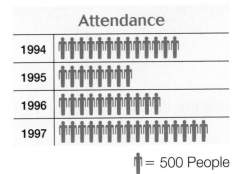

Attendance

1994	♂♂♂♂♂♂♂♂♂♂♂♂♂
1995	♂♂♂♂♂♂♂♂
1996	♂♂♂♂♂♂♂♂♂♂
1997	♂♂♂♂♂♂♂♂♂♂♂♂♂♂♂♂♂♂

♂ = 500 People

Independent Practice

2. Which type of graph would be best to show the data on the number of tickets sold on Saturday?

   a. Circle graph

   b. Line graph

   c. Bar graph

Saturday Ticket Sales

Theater	Number of Tickets Sold
1	292
2	208
3	224
4	195

3. Which type of graph would *not* be appropriate to show the data on Saturday ticket sales?

   a. Circle graph

   b. Line graph

   c. Bar graph

4. Which data from the table would you use to make a double bar graph about the Drama Club?

   a. Adult Actors and Child Actors

   b. Adult Actors and Total Ticket Sales

   c. Child Actors only

The Drama Club

Year	Adult Actors	Child Actors	Total Ticket Sales
1997	30	8	$2,400.00
1998	24	12	$4,000.00
1999	44	14	$6,700.00

5. Which data from the table would be best to make a pictograph about the Drama Club?

   a. Year

   b. Child Actors

   c. Total Ticket Sales

6. **Math Reasoning** Explain why a bar graph would be better than a pictograph for the data on Saturday Ticket Sales.

Diagnostic Checkpoint

Use the data for Exercises 1–6.

The data set below shows the number of minutes that Ms. Lee's students spent at the library in one week.

7, 8, 9, 15, 10, 17, 28, 29, 34, 36, 31, 28, 34

1. Make a stem-and-leaf plot.
(3-3)

2. Use the stem-and-leaf plot to find the median.
(3-3)

3. Use the stem-and-leaf plot to find the mode(s).
(3-3)

4. Find the range.   **5.** Find the mean.
(3-1)   (3-1)

6. Which measure of central tendency best indicates the typical
(3-1)   amount of time spent in the library?

Use the data in the table for Exercises 7–12.

7. Which type of graph would be best to show the
(3-4)   water depths in Lake A and Lake B?

8. What type of graph might you use to show the
(3-4)   number of fish caught each week in each lake?

9. Find the mean water depth in Lake A.
(3-1)

10. Find the mean water depth in Lake B.
(3-1)

11 Does either set of lake data have an outlier? Explain.
(3-2)

12. Find the range of the water depths in Lake B.
(3-1)

Water Depth (ft)		
Week	Lake A	Lake B
1	47	40
2	47	46
3	47	49
4	48	49
5	48	50

For Exercises 13–16, find the mean, median, and mode of the data with and without the outlier. Round the mean to the nearest tenth.

13. 64, 72, 68, 68, 12, 70   **14.** 4.8, 5.3, 5.5, 4.9, 10.4, 4.9, 5.5
(3-2)   (3-2)

15. 18, 16, 14, 15, 20, 31, 19   **16.** 25, 33, 34, 33, 28, 10, 27, 30
(3-2)   (3-2)

17. In Exercises 13–16, which measure of central tendency is most
(3-2)   affected by the outlier?

Multiple-Choice Cumulative Review

Choose the correct letter for each answer.

1. A circle has a circumference of about 113 cm and a diameter of 36 cm. What is its *radius*?

   A   6 cm

   B   9 cm

   C   18 cm

   D   54 cm

2. When Sam kept track of the number of books he read each month, he found a pattern. How many books did he read in June?

Jan.	Feb.	Mar.	Apr.	May	June
5	7	10	14	19	■

   F   23 books   H   25 books

   G   24 books   J   26 books

3. Roy ran for 1 hour at 10 miles per hour and then ran for 2 hours at 3 miles per hour. Which number sentence could be used to find *M*, the total number of miles that Roy ran?

   A $M = (10 + 3) + (1 + 2)$

   B $M = (10 \times 1) + (3 \times 2)$

   C $M = (10 + 1) \times (3 + 2)$

   D $M = (10 + 3) \times 3$

4. $2.85 + 0.432 + 11.9$

   F   14.182   J   836

   G   15.182   K   NH

   H   826

Use the grid for Questions 5–6.

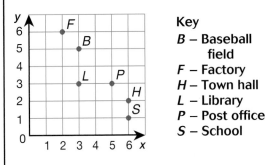

Key
B – Baseball field
F – Factory
H – Town hall
L – Library
P – Post office
S – School

5. Which town landmark is located at (5, 3)?

   A   Post office

   B   Baseball field

   C   School

   D   Town hall

6. Which ordered pair names the location of the factory?

   F   (6, 2)   H   (1, 6)

   G   (3, 5)   J   (2, 6)

7. What is the value of the underlined digit in 19.05<u>4</u>3?

   A   4 thousands

   B   4 hundredths

   C   4 thousandths

   D   4 ten thousandths

   E   NH

LESSON 3-5 Understanding Sampling

California Content Standard *Statistics, Data Analysis, and Probability 2.1: Compare different samples of a population with the data from the entire population and identify a situation in which it makes sense to use a sample.*

Math Link You know how to organize data and find measures of central tendency. Now you will learn how sampling is used to collect data in real-life situations.

Example 1

Jerome sells pets and supplies. He has a large barrel filled with glass marbles that people buy to decorate their aquariums. The marbles are various colors, all mixed together. He wondered what percent of the marbles are green.

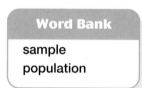

Word Bank

sample

population

It is not practical for Jerome to count all the marbles, so Jerome decided to study two **samples,** or parts, of the population. The **population** in a statistical study is the entire group of people or things being considered. In this case, the population is the entire barrel of marbles.

Sample 1 Jerome scooped out a bucket of marbles. He counted 210 marbles in the bucket and 51 were green.

$$\frac{51}{210} \approx \frac{50}{200}, \text{ or } \frac{1}{4}$$

51 is about $\frac{1}{4}$, or 25%, of 210.

About 25% of the marbles in the bucket were green.

Sample 2 Jerome examined another sample. This time he scooped out 188 marbles and found that 61 were green.

$$61 \div 188 \approx 0.32$$

61 is about $\frac{1}{3}$, or 33%, of 188.

About 33% of the marbles in the second bucket were green.

Since Jerome's two samples gave results of 25% and 33%, he estimated that about 30% of marbles in the barrel are green.

Warm-Up Review

Write each fraction as a decimal.

1. $\frac{1}{10}$ 2. $\frac{2}{5}$

3. $\frac{1}{4}$ 4. $\frac{1}{8}$

5. $\frac{1}{2}$ 6. $\frac{3}{4}$

Find the mean, median, and mode of the data with and without the outlier.

7. 47, 53, 24, 48

8. 3, 9, 5, 3, 4

Additional Standards: Statistics, Data Analysis, and Probability 2.4 (⚷) (See p. 87.)

Samples are often used when it is too difficult or impractical to study the entire population.

Example 2

In each situation, would it make more sense to study the entire population or a sample?

A. David got a new shipment of doggie treats. Each small bag is supposed to contain pieces of real beef jerky. David wants to know the mean number of pieces of beef jerky per bag.

It would take too much time to examine every bag. Also, after David cuts open a bag of treats, he can no longer sell it. It makes more sense to study a sample.

B. Kristen wants to know the mean height of her cat's new kittens.

It is not difficult to measure each kitten. So, it makes more sense to study the entire population.

When you interpret statistical data, it is important to know whether the statistics are based on a sample or on the entire population.

Example 3

The table shows the results of a 1999 poll of 500 dog owners in a large city. Identify the population being studied. Were the statistics drawn from a sample or from the entire population?

The population is all dog owners in the city. The statistics are drawn from a sample, since not all dog owners were polled.

Dog Owners	
Breed	Percent
Beagle	35%
German Shepherd	30%
Retriever	25%
Other	10%

Guided Practice *For another example, see Set D on p. 119.*

For each situation, identify the population studied and tell whether the statistics are drawn from a sample or from the entire population.

1. According to a 1994 survey, 79% of the adults in California have completed high school.

2. The mean elevation of the ten tallest mountains in California is 14,196 feet.

For each situation, tell whether you would study the entire population or a sample. Explain your answer.

3. You want to find what percent of cars on California highways have out-of-state license plates.

Independent Practice *For more practice, see Set D on p. 122*

For each situation, identify the population studied and tell whether the statistics are drawn from a sample or from the entire population.

4. Brett read in an almanac that teens in the United States watch more than 12 hours of television every week.

5. Marisol recorded the scores of her math quizzes. She concluded that the average score was 86.5.

For each situation, tell whether you would study the entire population or a sample. Explain your answer.

6. You want to find the average height of a redwood tree in the 112,000-acre Redwood National Park.

7. You want to find the percent of students in your school who are in the school chorus.

8. You want to know the mean height of middle school students in California.

9. You want to know what percent of the fortunes in a shipment of fortune cookies contain predictions about wealth.

10. You want to find the average height of your school's basketball team.

Mixed Review

Use the stem-and-leaf plot at the right for Exercises 11–13.

11. Find the median number of track medals won.

12. Mental Math Find the mode of track medals won.

13. Mental Math Is there an outlier in the data set? If so, what is it?

Track Medals Won

Stem	Leaves
1	7 7 8 8 9
2	2 6
3	1
4	1 2 3 8 8 9 9
5	0 1 1

Test Prep   Choose the correct letter for each answer.

14. Which number is less than 9 thousandths?
(1-2)

 A 0.08   **B** 0.008   **C** 0.085   **D** 0.0092   **E** NH

15. Which set of data contains an outlier?
(3-2)

 F 2, 1, 3, 15, 3   **G** 4, 7, 5, 6, 8   **H** 5, 0, 1, 4, 4   **J** 9, 9, 9, 8, 7

(**Use Homework Workbook 3-5.**)

Sampling Methods

California Content Standard *Statistics, Data Analysis, and Probability 2.2 (🔑): Identify different ways of selecting a sample (e.g., convenience sampling, responses to a survey, random sampling) and which method makes a sample more representative for a population.*

Math Link You can use what you know about sampling to find how sampling methods can affect the statistical results.

The table below shows the number of school districts in each state.

Warm-Up Review

Use this set of data:

12, 14, 16, 18, 18, 20, 24, 30

1. Find the mean.

2. Find the mean using every other number starting with 12.

3. Find the mean using every other number starting with 14.

4. Find the mean of the four greatest numbers.

Local School Districts

State	Districts	State	Districts	State	Districts	State	Districts	State	Districts
AL	127	HI	1	MA	351	NM	89	SD	176
AK	53	ID	112	MI	674	NY	705	TN	139
AZ	329	IL	929	MN	380	NC	117	TX	1,042
AR	311	IN	295	MS	153	ND	233	UT	40
CA	994	IA	377	MO	525	OH	661	VT	286
CO	176	KS	304	MT	461	OK	547	VA	141
CT	166	KY	176	NE	640	OR	198	WA	296
DE	19	LA	66	NV	17	PA	501	WV	55
FL	67	ME	284	NH	179	RI	36	WI	426
GA	180	MD	24	NJ	608	SC	90	WY	48

Example 1

The ten most populated states are California (CA), Texas (TX), New York (NY), Florida (FL), Illinois (IL), Pennsylvania (PA), Ohio (OH), Michigan (MI), New Jersey (NJ), and Georgia (GA). Find the mean and median number of school districts per state using these ten states as a sample.

FL	GA	PA	NJ	OH	MI	NY	IL	CA	TX
67	180	501	608	661	674	705	929	994	1,042

Mean: $\frac{6,361}{10} = 636.1$ Median: $\frac{661 + 674}{2} = 667.5$

The mean is 636.1 school districts per state.

The median is 667.5 school districts per state.

Word Bank

biased

random sampling

representative

convenience sampling

responses to a survey

A **biased** sample is one which does not mirror the population. The sample in Example 1 is biased because states with large populations are likely to have more than an average number of school districts.

Example 2

The name of each state was written on a piece of paper and placed in a bag. Then ten pieces of paper were selected without looking.

The states selected were Maine (ME), Colorado (CO), Wisconsin (WI), Kansas (KS), Rhode Island (RI), Georgia (GA), Alaska (AK), Arkansas (AR), Alabama (AL), and New Jersey (NJ).

Find the mean and median number of school districts per state using these states as a sample.

Arrange the 10 states in order from the least number of school districts to the greatest number of school districts.

RI	AK	AL	CO	GA	ME	KS	AR	WI	NJ
36	53	127	176	180	284	304	311	426	608

Mean: $\frac{2,505}{10} = 250.5$

Median: $\frac{180 + 284}{2} = 232$

The mean is 250.5 school districts per state.

The median is 232 school districts per state.

Example 2 uses random sampling. In **random sampling,** each person or thing has an equal chance of being chosen.

Since a random sample is usually a good match for the population, it is a **representative** sample.

Example 3

The principal of an elementary school sent a survey letter to each student's parents asking if voters in the school district would support a tax increase to build a new middle school.

Is this sample likely to be representative or biased?

The sample is biased. Parents of elementary students who would be attending the new school are more likely to support a new middle school than would voters in general.

It was convenient for the principal to survey parents of students. In **convenience sampling,** any convenient method is used to choose the sample. Convenience sampling is usually biased.

Asking for **responses to a survey** is another form of sampling that is often biased. People with strong opinions are more likely to take the time to respond to a survey than people in general.

Guided Practice
For another example, see Set E on p. 120.

Tell whether each sample is likely to be representative or biased. Explain your answers. Identify each as random sampling, convenience sampling, or responses to a survey.

1. A state legislator mails questionnaires about literacy to all the eligible voters in her district. Only 12% of the people return the questionnaire.

2. A school principal questions every student whose locker number ends in a 9 to gather student input about plans for the new library.

Independent Practice
For more practice, see Set E on p. 123.

For Exercises 3 and 4, tell whether each sample is likely to be representative or biased. Explain your answers. Identify each as random sampling, convenience sampling, or responses to a survey.

3. The staff of a student newspaper conducts a poll about students' favorite vacations by interviewing every 10th student listed in the student directory.

4. The town council polls the members of the civic orchestra about what type of entertainment the residents want at the Fourth of July Jamboree.

5. The ten least populated states are Wyoming (WY), Vermont (VT), Alaska (AK), North Dakota (ND), South Dakota (SD), Delaware (DE), Montana (MT), Rhode Island (RI), New Hampshire (NH), and Hawaii (HI). Use the table on page 103 to find the mean and median number of school districts per state using these ten states as a sample. Compare your results to those found for the ten most populated states.

Mixed Review

6. Find the range of the data in the stem-and-leaf plot on page 94.

7. You want to find the mean number of students per school district in California. Tell whether you would study the entire population or a sample. Explain your answer.

Test Prep   Choose the correct letter for each answer.

8. **Algebra** Find $6x + 2y$ when
(1-10) $x = 1$ and $y = 2$.

    A 6   **C** 10

    B 8   **D** 14

9. **Algebra** Solve $5n = 156.5$.
(2-7)

    F $n = 31.3$ **H** $n = 332$

    G $n = 33.2$ **J** $n = 782.5$

Use Homework Workbook 3-6.   **105**

Problem-Solving Strategy:
Make a Graph

California Content Standard *Mathematical Reasoning 2.4: Use a variety of methods such as . . . graphs, tables, . . . and models to explain mathematical reasoning.*

Example 1

The Somerset School is having its annual music festival. The table at the right shows the attendance for last year's festival. The planners want to schedule the number of workers needed throughout the day based on last year's attendance. During what part of the day should the planners schedule the greatest number of workers?

Understand

What do you need to find?

You need to find the times of day that attendance is the greatest.

Plan

How can you solve the problem?

To better understand the information in the table, you can **make an appropriate graph**. Since a line graph is used to show change over time, you should make a line graph to analyze how the attendance changed throughout the day.

Solve

You can conclude from the graph that the greatest number of workers will be needed between 4 P.M. and 9 P.M.

Look Back

When would you have most of the workers take lunch? Why?

Attendance Last Year

Time	Total Attendance
9 A.M.	104
10 A.M.	345
11 A.M.	359
12 NOON	339
1 P.M.	137
2 P.M.	373
3 P.M.	405
4 P.M.	488
5 P.M.	534
6 P.M.	545
7 P.M.	568
8 P.M.	561
9 P.M.	555

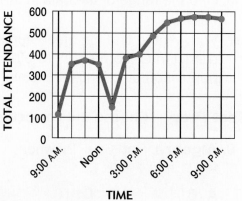

Attendance at Somerset Music Festival

Additional Standards: Mathematical Reasoning 2.0, 2.3, 3.2 (See p. 87.)

Guided Practice

Use the data in the table at the right for Exercises 1–4.

1. Make a graph to show the prices of concert tickets.

2. During which year was there the greatest difference in ticket price between Section A and Section B?

3. Which section had the greater increase in ticket prices from 1995 to 1999?

4. Use a graph to predict the prices for each section in the year 2000.

Concert Ticket Prices (in dollars)		
Year	Section A	Section B
1995	15	24
1996	18	31
1997	22	37
1998	27	46
1999	30	54

Independent Practice

Use the data in the table at the right for Exercises 5–7.

5. Make a graph to show the sales of concert CDs.

6. Based on CD sales, in which year might concert attendance have dropped?

7. Based on your graph, can you predict the number of CDs that might be sold at the next concert? Why or why not?

Concert CD Sales	
Year	Sales
1995	151
1996	178
1997	197
1998	140
1999	210

Mixed Review

Try these or other strategies to solve each problem. Tell which strategy you used.

Problem-Solving Strategies

- *Make a Graph*
- *Find a Pattern*
- *Write an Equation*
- *Make a Table*

8. **Algebra** Ann bought 8 tickets for $210. Adult tickets cost $30 each. Student tickets cost $20 each. How many of each kind of ticket did she buy?

9. During the first hour of the festival, Rick sold 7 posters. He sold 15 during the second hour, 23 during the third hour, and 31 during the fourth hour. At this rate, how many posters will he sell in the seventh hour?

Analyzing Statistical Results

California Content Standard *Statistics, Data Analysis, and Probability 2.3 (🗝): Analyze data displays and explain why the way in which the question was asked might have influenced the results obtained. Also, Statistics, Data Analysis, and Probability 2.5 (🗝).*

Math Link You know how sampling techniques affect statistical results. Now you will learn how wording of questions affects these results.

Example 1

Match each question to the bar graph it is more likely to generate. Explain your answer.

  a. Should bicyclists be forced to wear knee pads?

  b. For safety reasons, should bicyclists be required to wear knee pads?

Question **a** probably generated bar graph **ii.** People are likely to oppose "forcing" individuals to do things.

Question **b** includes the word *safety,* which people are likely to support. So bar graph **i** probably matches Question **b**. Also, *required* is not as strong a word as *forced*.

i

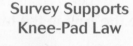
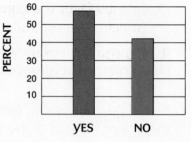

ii

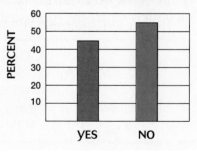

Example 2

Identify the claim made in the following passage. Then tell whether the claim is justified by the statistics.

We found that 88% of those who use Head Set Shampoo have clean and silky hair. So, using Head Set Shampoo will make your hair clean and silky.

The claim is that using Head Set Shampoo will make your hair clean and silky. The claim is not justified, because the sample population is not identified. The people using Head Set might have clean and silky hair with **any** brand of shampoo.

Guided Practice *For another example, see Set F on p 120.*

1. Which question do you think is most fair? Explain your answer.

   a. Are you in favor of restricting excessive gasoline consumption?

   b. Do you favor or oppose gasoline rationing?

   c. Do you want gasoline rationing to limit your driving freedom?

2. Identify the claim made in the following passage. Then tell whether the claim is justified by the statistics. Explain your answer.

   Our survey revealed that 92% of the teachers at East River Middle School favor a longer lunch period. Therefore, Mr. Katz, a math teacher at East River, probably favors a longer lunch period.

For Exercises 3 and 4, tell which question you think is most fair. Explain your answer.

3. a. Do you favor the construction of a new freeway to cut down on traffic jams?

   b. Do you want your tax money spent on the construction of another freeway?

   c. Do you support or oppose the construction of another freeway?

4. a. Should residents of Northfield recycle paper?

   b. Should residents of Northfield be required to recycle paper every week?

   c. Should residents of Northfield pay to recycle paper?

Independent Practice *For more practice, see Set F on p. 123.*

For Exercises 5 and 6, identify the claim made in each passage. Then tell whether the claim is justified by the statistics. Explain your answer.

5. Based on the health club survey at the right, we can assume that Mrs. Buneul, a member of the health club, is more likely to be less than 50 years old than to be 50 years old or older.

6. A serving of Oat Loopies contains 3 grams of fat. A slice of American cheese contains 7 grams of fat. Therefore, Oat Loopies are healthier for you than American cheese.

Health Club Survey	
Characteristic	Percent of Membership
Good Swimmer	64%
Less than 50 years old	81%

7. Match each question to the bar graph it is more likely to generate. Explain your answer.

  a. Do you support increasing the salaries of public servants in the California legislature?

  b. Should the politicians in Sacramento get another raise?

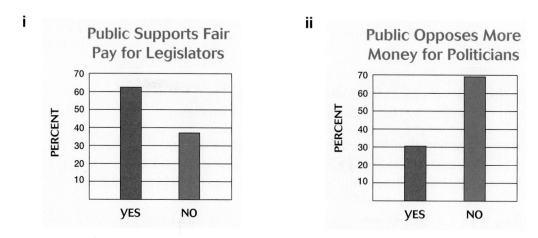

i

Public Supports Fair Pay for Legislators

ii

Public Opposes More Money for Politicians

8. Math Reasoning Explain why the following survey question is not likely to generate fair results.

Should people be allowed to bring portable stereos to public parks even though their loud music ruins the day for other people?

Mixed Review

9. The automotive industry selects driver's license numbers at random. Then it contacts drivers to ask them about their driving habits. Is this sample representative or biased? Explain.

10. A TV news reporter conducted a poll in which she asked viewers to call the station and report their opinions. What kind of sampling did she use? Was the sample representative or biased? Explain.

11. Would you study the entire population or a sample to find what percent of students in your class own dogs?

Round to the nearest one, tenth, hundredth, and thousandth.

12. 26.04923　　　　**13.** 0.00402　　　　**14.** 1.89983

Test Prep　Choose the correct letter for each answer.

15. Algebra Evaluate $k(20 + 1)$ for
(1-10) $k = 12$.

　A 228　　　　**C** 241

　B 239　　　　**D** 252

16. Algebra Solve $25 - x = 16$.
(1-12)
　F $x = 9$　　　　**H** $x = 19$

　G $x = 11$　　　　**J** $x = 41$

Multiple-Choice Cumulative Review

Choose the correct letter for each answer.

1. Round 847.9356 to the nearest hundredth.

  A 800   **C** 847.94

  B 847.9   **D** 847.936

Use the following for Questions 2 and 3.

Joe went to the store. He paid more than a dollar for a dozen eggs, about 2 dollars for a gallon of milk, and about a dollar for a loaf of bread. He gave the cashier $10.

2. Which of these is an exact number?

  F The cost of the eggs

  G The cost of the milk

  H The cost of the bread

  J The money Joe gave the cashier

3. How much change should Joe get?

  A Exactly $5   **C** Exactly $6

  B Exactly $5.50 **D** Cannot tell

4. Which property is shown?

$$(5 + 4) \times 3 = (4 + 5) \times 3$$

  F Associative property of addition

  G Associative property of multiplication

  H Commutative property of addition

  J Commutative property of multiplication

  K NH

5. Find the next number in the pattern.
27, 26, 24, 21, 17, . . .

  A 16   **C** 12

  B 15   **D** 11

Use the graph for Questions 6 and 7.

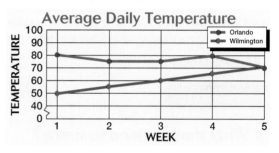

6. Which week had the greatest difference in temperature between the cities?

  F Week 1   **H** Week 3

  G Week 2   **J** Week 4

7. During which two weeks in Orlando was the temperature the same?

  A Weeks 1 and 2

  B Weeks 2 and 3

  C Weeks 3 and 4

  D Weeks 4 and 5

8. Evaluate the expression

$$6 + 9 \div 3 - 2.$$

  F 3   **H** 15

  G 7   **J** 18

Problem-Solving Application:
Representing a Point of View

California Content Standard *Statistics, Data Analysis, and Probability 2.3 (⚷): Analyze data displays and explain why the way in which the results are displayed might have influenced the conclusions reached.*

Warm-Up Review

For each set of data, give an appropriate scale for a graph of the data. Tell if you would include all numbers greater than zero or delete a group of numbers.

1. 100, 125, 250, 175, 150

2. 3, 7, 12, 9, 18, 22, 6

3. 10, 12, 14, 12, 13, 16, 15

Example

Videoland wants to raise video-rental prices to $3.75. Before the owners do this, they want to convince customers that the price increase is small. Which graph might convince you that the price increase is small?

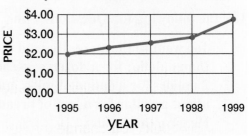

Graph A: Video Rental Prices

Understand

What do you need to know?

You need to know why the graphs look so different even though they show identical data.

Plan

How can you solve the problem?

Compare the data displayed on the graphs. Then interpret the graphs by looking at the scales on both graphs.

Graph B: Video Rental Prices

Solve

The same data is displayed on each graph. The scale on Graph A has $1 intervals, so the price increase appears smaller. The scale on Graph B has $0.50 intervals, so the price increase appears greater. Since the price increase *looks* smaller on Graph A, Videoland would probably use Graph A.

Look Back

How can graphs be used to influence people's thinking?

Guided Practice

Use Graphs C and D for Exercises 1 and 2.

1. About how much did Videoland's profits increase from 1998 to 1999?

2. How does the increase in profit shown in Graph D compare with the increase shown in Graph C?

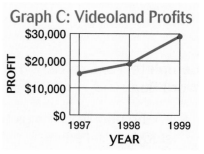

Independent Practice

Use Graphs C and D for Exercises 3–7.

3. Compare the vertical scales on Graphs C and D. How are they alike? How are they different?

4. Which graph might Videoland use to persuade potential shareholders of tremendous profit?

5. How could you change the horizontal scale on Graph D so that Graph D would look more like Graph C?

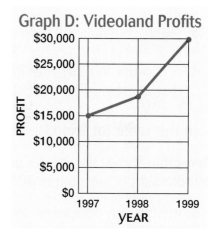

6. **Math Reasoning** How does the scale used for each graph affect the impression given by the graph?

7. **Math Reasoning** Between which two years did profits increase more? How can you tell?

8. Draw graphs to persuade your teacher that you spend a great deal of time doing homework compared to the time you spend watching television.

Mixed Review

9. Cindy spent $6.50 buying souvenirs. She spent $2.50 on a magnet, $3.25 on a mug, and the rest of the money on postcards. How much did she spend on postcards?

10. Bill bought 15 souvenir mugs. He bought 3 more small mugs than large mugs. How many of each size mug did he buy?

11. If the science class is divided into groups of 2, 3, or 5 students, there is 1 extra student each time. What is the least number of students in the science class?

Diagnostic Checkpoint

Complete. For Exercises 1–4, use the words from the Word Bank.

1. All the people or things being considered in a statistical
(3-5) study are called the _____.

2. _____ is usually representative of the population.
(3-6)

3. Mean, median, and mode are _____.
(3-1)

4. A number in a data set that is very different from the
(3-2) rest of the numbers is called _____.

Use the table for Exercises 5–8.

The table shows the results of a survey at Bradford
Middle School, which has 500 students.

Students and Activities				
Grade	5th	6th	7th	8th
Band	5	7	9	13
Choir	7	7	10	12

5. Identify the population studied and tell whether
(3-5) the statistics are drawn from a sample or from
the entire population.

6. Suppose the data are the results of a survey
(3-6) taken in two math classes at each grade. Tell
whether the sample is likely to be representative
or biased. Explain your answer. Identify it as
random sampling, convenience sampling, or
responses to a survey.

7. The students who took the survey claim more
(3-8) students get involved as they get older. Is this
claim justified by the statistics? Explain.

8. Draw a bar graph for just the choir data that
(3-7) gives the impression that more than 3 times
as many 8th graders as 5th graders are in choir.

9. Identify the claim in this passage; then explain whether or not
(3-8) the claim is justified.

Snackies crackers contain 5 g of fat per serving, while Crunchies
contain 7 g of fat per serving. So, Snackies are healthier.

Chapter 3 Test

For Exercises 1–4 use this data set: 1 2 4 5 6 6 25. **Find the**

1. mean. **2.** median. **3.** mode. **4.** range.

Use the stem-and-leaf plot for Exercises 5–11. Find the

5. median. **6.** mode. **7.** range.

8. Identify the outlier.

What effect does excluding the outlier have on

9. the median? **10.** the mode? **11.** the range?

Books Borrowed

Stem	Leaves
0	8 9
1	0 2 4 5 8 9
2	3 3 6 6 6 7 9
3	1 2 3 6
4	8

12. What type of graph would be best to display the data in the table at the right?

13. Make a graph to display the data.

14. Station B claims to play "More music, all the time." Do the statistics justify this claim? Explain.

15. During which hour are the most songs played?

Number of Songs Played

Time	Station A	Station B
1st hour	16	18
2nd hour	14	17
3rd hour	17	13
4th hour	19	24

Use the graph at the right for Exercises 16–20.

16. What is the total number of students surveyed?

17. How would you change the horizontal scale on the graph so that it would appear that almost the same number of girls and boys chose science as their favorite subject?

18. Tell whether the statistics are drawn from a sample or the entire population. Explain.

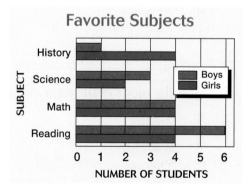

Tell whether each sample is likely to be biased or representative. Identify each as random sampling, convenience sampling, or responses to a survey.

19. Students were surveyed in Literature Club.

20. Students were asked to complete a form and leave it in a box in the hallway.

Multiple-Choice Chapter 3 Test

Choose the correct letter for each answer.

Use the data in the table for Questions 1–7.

Hours Students Spent Playing Basketball One Week					
2	0	8	0	5	2
1	3	0	4	0	1
4	7	16	0	2	3

1. Find the mean of the data in the table. Round to the nearest tenth.

    A 0 hours

    B 2 hours

    C 2.5 hours

    D 3.2 hours

2. Find the median of the data in the table.

    F 0 hours

    G 2 hours

    H 2.5 hours

    J 3.2 hours

3. Find the mode of the data in the table.

    A 0 hours

    B 1 hour

    C 2 hours

    D 3 hours

4. Which measure of central tendency is the most typical of the data in the table?

    F Range

    G Median

    H Mode

    J All of them are typical.

5. Find the range of the data in the table.

    A 12 hours

    B 14 hours

    C 15 hours

    D 16 hours

6. Find the mean of the data in the table without the outlier 16. Round to the nearest tenth.

    F 0 hours

    G 2 hours

    H 2.5 hours

    J 3.2 hours

7. Which measure of central tendency is affected the most by excluding the outlier 16?

    A Mean

    B Median

    C Mode

    D None are affected.

Use the stem-and-leaf plot for Questions 8–9.

Number of Books Read

Stem	Leaves
2	0 3 7
3	0 7
5	2 3
7	8
8	1 5 6

8. **Find the median of the data in the stem-and-leaf plot.**

   F 30 books   **H** 52 books

   G 37 books   **J** 53 books

9. **Find the mode of the data in the stem-and-leaf plot.**

   A 27 books

   B 37 books

   C 27 and 37 books

   D There is no mode.

10. **In which situation would you study the entire population rather than a sample?**

   F You want to know the mean height of all sixth-grade students in California.

   G You want to know the median hand span of students in your Physical Education class.

   H You want to know the mean amount of time it takes students in your school to run the 50-yard dash.

   J You want to know the mean number of hours per week students in California take physical education.

Use the following situation for Questions 11–13.

You want to know whether or not students in your school support a program to plant trees on the school playground.

11. **What is the population you plan to study?**

   A All students in your class

   B All students who like trees

   C All students in your school

   D All middle school students in California

12. **You survey students on your soccer team. What type of sampling is this?**

   F Random sampling

   G Representative sampling

   H Responses to a survey

   J Convenience sampling

13. **Which question do you think is most fair?**

   A Do you support planting trees to take up space on the playground?

   B Do you support planting trees on the playground to help the environment?

   C Do you support or oppose planting trees on the playground?

   D All are fair.

Reteaching

Use this set of data.

19, 25, 22, 22, 26, 18

Find the mean of the data.

The mean is the sum of all the data divided by the number of data items.

$19 + 25 + 22 + 22 + 26 + 18 = 132$

$132 \div 6 = 22$

The mean is 22.

Find the median of the data.

Write the numbers in order. The median is the middle number or the average of the two middle numbers.

18   19 | 22   22 | 25   26

$\frac{22 + 22}{2} = 22$

The median is 22.

Remember that the mode is the number that occurs most often. There may be more than one mode or no mode.

Find the mean, median, mode, and range for each set of data. Round the mean to the nearest tenth.

1. 8, 12, 19, 10, 12, 14, 15, 10

2. 245, 360, 129, 211, 298

3. 20, 40, 50, 30, 60, 30, 50

4. 11, 19, 10, 16, 22, 24, 20, 14

5. 33, 58, 47, 54, 37, 41

6. 9.3, 5.4, 8.2, 8.1, 8.4, 8.2, 9.0, 8.2

Find the median of the data with and without the outlier.

427, 455, 210, 460

Write the data in order:

210 | 427   455 | 460

$\frac{427 + 455}{2} = 441$

With the outlier, the median is 441.

The outlier is 210.

427 | 455 | 460

Without the outlier, the median is 455.

Remember that an outlier is a number in a data set that is very different from the rest of the numbers.

Find the mean, median, and mode of the data with and without the outlier. Round the mean to the nearest tenth.

1. 85, 89, 91, 89, 61, 95, 92

2. 5, 2, 3, 3, 2, 12, 4, 2, 5, 3

3. 23, 96, 14, 19, 25, 27, 11, 9

4. 1,821; 952; 945; 902

5. 283, 282, 288, 282, 283

6. 1.8, 1.6, 1.2, 1.5, 1.6, 0.4, 1.4, 1.9

Set C *(pages 94–95)*

Use the stem-and-leaf plot to find the median.

**Hours Per Week
Students Watch TV**

Stem	Leaves
0	2 5 7 7 9
1	0 1 ①4 8 9
2	1 2 6 8

2|1 means 21 hours

There are 15 leaves.

The middle one is circled.

The median is 11.

Remember that data are the same only when both the stem and the leaf are the same.

Use the data for Exercises 1–3.

Hours Per Week Students Sleep						
56	55	49	60	61	58	53
57	56	60	57	56	52	58

1. Make a stem-and-leaf plot.

2. Use the stem-and-leaf plot to find the median.

3. Mental Math Use the stem-and-leaf plot to find the mode.

Use the data for Exercises 4 and 5.
57, 42, 46, 21, 25, 13, 26, 22, 14, 42, 46, 59

4. Make a stem-and-leaf plot.

5. Use the stem-and-leaf plot to find the median and the mode.

Set D *(pages 100–102)*

Tell whether you would study the entire population or a sample.

You want to find the mean amount of time it takes students to get to your school each morning.

It would be difficult to find out how long it takes every student to get to school, so it makes more sense to study a sample.

Remember that samples are often used when it is too difficult or impractical to study the entire population.

For each situation, tell whether you would study the entire population or a sample.

1. You want to find the number of cars in California that are red.

2. You want to find the number of students in your math class who are left-handed.

Reteaching (continued)

Set E (pages 103–105)

Tell whether the sample is likely to be representative or biased. Identify the type of sampling used.

A polling company questions people leaving a football game to see whether or not voters in the community support plans to build a new stadium.

The sample is probably biased. Most people at the game are more likely to support a stadium than voters in general. Convenience sampling was used.

Remember that random sampling is usually representative of the population.

Tell whether the sample is likely to be representative or biased. Explain your answers. Identify it as random sampling, convenience sampling, or responses to a survey.

1. The manager of a shopping mall uses a suggestion box to determine that most of the shoppers would like more restaurants.

2. A car dealer tallies the colors of cars that pass the showroom in order to determine the most popular color.

Set F (pages 108–110)

Identify the claim and tell whether it is justified by the statistics.

In a survey of the members of the boys' and girls' 6th-grade basketball teams, 22 out of 24 support an extra hour of Physical Education (P.E.) each week. Therefore, all 6th graders support an extra hour of P.E.

The claim that all 6th graders support an extra hour of P.E. each week is not justified. The sample was biased.

Members of basketball teams are more likely to want an extra hour of P.E. than students in general.

Remember that statistical claims are justified only when the sample is representative of the population, questions are worded fairly, and the claim does not go beyond the statistics.

Identify the claim and tell whether it is justified by the statistics. Explain your answer.

1. We found that 65% of the 6th graders surveyed do not want to take swimming lessons as part of P.E. class in the winter. Therefore, 6th graders do not want to swim in P.E.

2. At Lines School, 90% of the kindergarten students know the alphabet. C.J. is in kindergarten at Lines School, so she probably knows the alphabet.

More Practice

Set A *(pages 88–90)*

**Find the mean, median, mode, and range for each set of data.
Round the mean to the nearest tenth.**

1. 14, 7, 5, 3, 7, 6

2. 8, 6, 13, 16, 13, 4

3. 16.3, 7.8, 5.9, 6, 12, 6

4. 3, 5, 7.4, 3.1, 5, 2.7, 11.6

5. 13.6, 22.3, 13.4, 7.2, 3.8, 7.2

6. 1.34, 2.5, 4, 2.52, 0.34, 4

7. Rich and Jerry walked 4 miles on each of 4 days. Then they walked 2 miles on each of 4 days. What was the average number of miles they walked per day in the 8 days?

8. The lengths of the Great Lakes are as follows: Erie—241 miles, Huron—206 miles, Michigan—307 miles, Ontario—193 miles, and Superior—350 miles. Find the average length of the lakes.

Set B *(pages 91–93)*

**Find the mean, median, and mode of the data with and
without the outlier. Round the mean to the nearest tenth.**

1. 25, 28, 27, 42, 25

2. 69, 72, 31, 72, 69, 70, 71, 75

3. 465, 428, 125, 428, 450

4. 19, 15, 12, 11, 12, 15, 12, 15, 25, 18, 17

5. 700, 500, 600, 900, 800, 100

6. 450; 420; 435; 5,500; 440; 425; 460; 450

7. 9.4, 10.2, 3.1, 8.4, 9.4

8. 3.6, 3.55, 3.75, 3.8, 5.2, 3.5, 3.75

Use the table for Exercises 9–10. Round the mean to the nearest tenth.

9. Find the mean, median, and mode of the data in the table.

10. Find the mean, median, and mode of the data in the table without the outlier.

Miles Amy Jogged	
Day	Miles
1	1.6
2	0.9
3	1.5
4	1.6
5	3.5

More Practice

Set C *(pages 94–95)*

Use the stem-and-leaf plot at the right for Exercises 1 and 2.

Stem	Leaves
5	3 6 6 8
6	0 2 5 7 9
7	1 4 6

1. Find the median of the data.

2. **Mental Math** Find the mode of the data.

Use the data in the table for Exercises 3–8.

Sizes of Sixth-Grade Classes in Math, Science, English, and History									
17	18	24	40	25	32	19	25	24	24
26	25	19	28	26	24	25	29	30	16

3. Make a stem-and-leaf plot of the data.

4. Use the stem-and-leaf plot to find the median.

5. **Mental Math** Use the stem-and-leaf plot to find the mode.

6. Find the median without the outlier.

7. **Mental Math** Find the mode without the outlier.

8. What effect does the outlier have on the median? the mode?

Set D *(pages 100–102)*

For each situation, identify the population. Tell whether you would study the entire population or a sample.

1. You want to find the mean size of a math class at your school.

2. You want to find the median cost of renting a videotape in the United States.

3. You want to find the number of raisins in each bag of trail mix.

4. Your principal wants to find the mean score of students in the school on a standardized test.

Set E (pages 103–105)

Tell whether each sample is likely to be representative or biased. Explain your answer. Identify each as random sampling, convenience sampling, or responses to a survey.

1. A company investigating voter opinions about a new tax on gasoline interviews every fifth person getting off a bus.

2. A government committee surveys people whose Social Security number matches randomly chosen numbers.

3. Cathy surveyed the students in all her classes at Murphy Middle School to determine whether they would approve of a dress code requiring students to wear dress slacks to school.

Set F (pages 108–110)

1. Match each question to the bar graph it is more likely to generate. Explain your answer.

  a. Should the cafeteria continue to serve desserts at lunchtime even though the sugar content is unhealthy?

  b. Should the cafeteria continue to serve desserts we love at lunchtime?

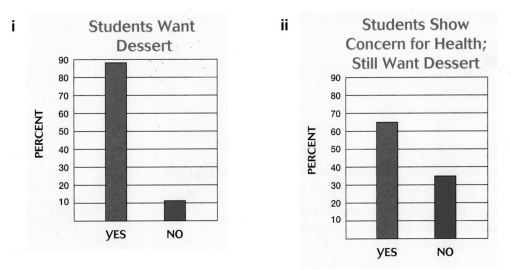

2. Which question do you think is most fair? Explain your answer.

  a. Should cat owners be required to purchase annual licenses for their pets?

  b. Should cats be licensed or not?

  c. Since dog licenses are required, should cat licenses also be required?

Problem Solving: Preparing for Tests

Choose the correct letter for each answer.

1. There is an L-shaped walkway along two sides of Tim's house. The outside length along one side is 10 m. The length along the other side is 18 m. Starting at one end, Tim is putting fence posts 1 m apart along the outside edge of the walk. How many posts does he need?

   Tip

   Draw a Diagram to help you solve this problem. Remember to label your diagram.

   A 31 posts

   B 30 posts

   C 29 posts

   D 28 posts

   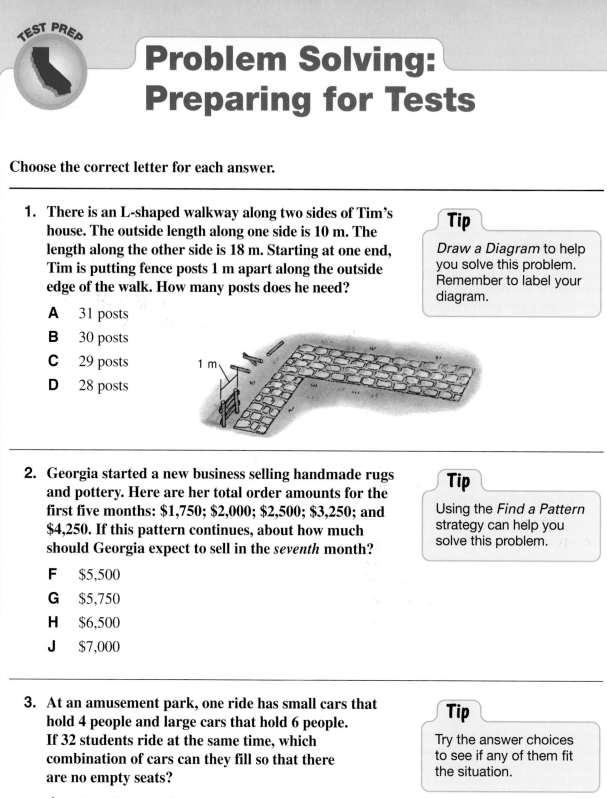

   1 m

2. Georgia started a new business selling handmade rugs and pottery. Here are her total order amounts for the first five months: $1,750; $2,000; $2,500; $3,250; and $4,250. If this pattern continues, about how much should Georgia expect to sell in the *seventh* month?

   Tip

   Using the *Find a Pattern* strategy can help you solve this problem.

   F $5,500

   G $5,750

   H $6,500

   J $7,000

3. At an amusement park, one ride has small cars that hold 4 people and large cars that hold 6 people. If 32 students ride at the same time, which combination of cars can they fill so that there are no empty seats?

   Tip

   Try the answer choices to see if any of them fit the situation.

   A 2 small cars, 5 large cars

   B 3 small cars, 3 large cars

   C 4 small cars, 3 large cars

   D 5 small cars, 2 large cars

4. A box has a volume of about 2,400 cubic inches. It measures 8 inches long by 10 inches wide. Which is a reasonable estimate for the height?

F Less than 36 inches

G About 120 inches

H About 240 inches

J About 360 inches

5. Movie tickets are $5 for children and $7.50 for adults. Which number sentence shows the cost, T, of tickets for 2 adults and 4 children?

A $T = (2 + 4) \times (\$5 + \$7.50)$

B $T = (2 \times \$5) + (4 \times \$7.50)$

C $T = (4 \times \$5) + (2 \times \$7.50)$

D $T = (2 \times 4) + (5 \times \$7.50)$

6. Ike made a line graph showing the change in the height of a plant over 4 weeks. He used the horizontal scale to show time. Which of these is reasonable for the shape of the graph?

F It slopes down from left to right.

G It is a horizontal line.

H It slopes up from left to right.

J It slopes down, then up.

7. Julia and her sister bought 2 tents for $109 each and 2 sleeping bags for $59 each. Which is a reasonable estimate of Julia's share of the purchases?

A Less than $200

B Between $200 and $300

C Between $300 and $400

D More than $400

8. The graph shows the results of a magazine survey.

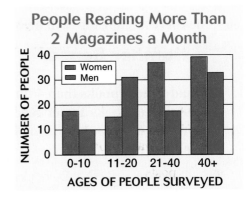

People Reading More Than 2 Magazines a Month

In which age group do about twice as many women as men read more than 2 magazines a month?

F People younger than 21

G Ages 0–10

H Ages 21–40

J People older than 40

9. Mel makes $32,000 a year. He can afford to spend about a fourth of his monthly income for rent. Which of these is a reasonable amount for Mel's monthly rent?

A Between $600 and $700

B Between $750 and $800

C Between $7,000 and $8,000

D About $8,000

10. Jake has scores of 85, 80, 85, and 90 on 4 tests. If Jake takes 1 more test, which of these test scores will give him a mean score of 86 for all 5 tests?

F 75

G 80

H 85

J 90

Multiple-Choice Cumulative Review

Choose the correct letter for each answer.

Number Sense

1. Sal read 2 more books than 4 times the number of books Taylor read. If Taylor read 6 books, how many books did Sal read?

  A   48 books   **C**   24 books

  B   26 books   **D**   12 books

2. What is the sum of 11.99, 112.35, and 0.062?

  F   232.807   **J**   124.402

  G   130.540   **K**   NH

  H   124.960

3. Paul bought 50 sheets of stationery at $0.30 a sheet and 50 matching envelopes at $0.45 per envelope. How much did the stationery and envelopes cost, excluding tax?

  A $15.00   **C** $37.50

  B $22.50   **D** $50.00

4. Kate and Ian hiked $1\frac{1}{3}$ mi before stopping for lunch. After lunch they hiked another $1\frac{1}{6}$ mi before stopping to rest. Then they hiked $1\frac{1}{3}$ mi before setting up camp. How far did they hike?

  F $3\frac{1}{6}$ miles   **H** $3\frac{2}{3}$ miles

  G $3\frac{1}{2}$ miles   **J** $3\frac{5}{6}$ miles

Measurement and Geometry

5. Which quadrilateral always has 4 right angles?

  A   Rectangle   **C**   Trapezoid

  B   Rhombus   **D**   Parallelogram

6. If $\triangle STU$ is congruent to $\triangle JKL$, then which of the following is true?

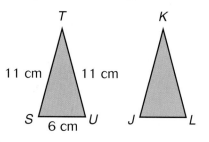

  F   Side JL measures 11 cm.

  G   Side KL measures 11 cm.

  H   Side TU and JL are congruent.

  J   Side JK measures 6 cm.

7. Which of the following illustrates a reflection of the letter E?

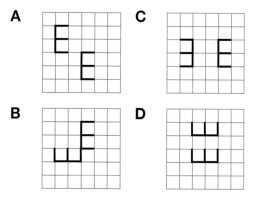

Statistics, Data Analysis, and Probability

Use the following data for Questions 8–10.

Fran's math grades are: 98, 85, 88, 85, and 94.

8. What was Fran's *median* score?

   F 92   H 88

   G 89   J 85

9. What was Fran's *mean* score?

   A 92   C 88

   B 90   D 85

10. What was Fran's *mode* score?

    F 92   H 88

    G 90   J 85

11. What is the range of these data?

    32.6, 34.9, 31.7, 38.8, 40.9, 30.3

    A 10.6   D 2.3

    B 9.2   E NH

    C 7.1

12. What effect does excluding the outlier have on the following data set?

    8, 9, 8.5, 8.75, 4, 8.5

    F The mode is greater.

    G The median is less.

    H The mean is greater.

    J The mean is less.

Use the data below for Questions 13–15.

Student Sport Survey		
Favorite Sport	Number	Percent
1. Baseball	15	30%
2. Basketball	18	36%
3. Football	10	20%
4. Soccer	7	14%

13. The numbers in the circle graphs below refer to the numbers of the sports listed in Column 1. Which graph best represents the data?

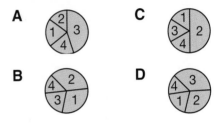

14. How many more students chose football or soccer than chose baseball?

    F 17 students   H 8 students

    G 12 students   J 2 students

15. Based on the survey, what is the probability a student chosen at random would like football best?

    A $\frac{1}{10}$ C $\frac{1}{5}$

    B $\frac{7}{50}$ D $\frac{3}{10}$

Number Theory and Fractions

Diagnosing Readiness

In Chapter 4, you will use these skills:

Ⓐ Multiplying Whole Numbers and Decimals

(pages 52–54)

1. 1.8×3

2. $7 \times 7 \times 7$

3. $3 \times 2 \times 3 \times 4$

4. $13 \times 13 \times 13$

5. $6.2 \times 6.2 \times 10 \times 10$

6. For two days, 4 buses drove 24 students each to summer camp. How many total students attended summer camp?

Ⓑ Writing Expressions

Write each mathematical expression in symbols.

(pages 28–29)

7. eleven less than y

8. twice a number plus 21

9. three times three plus three

10. three multiplied by two

11. two times six divided by four

12. five times five times five

13. Joel walks a mile in 16 minutes. Caleb jogs a mile in x minutes less than Joel. How long does it take for Caleb to jog a mile?

C Evaluating Expressions

(pages 26–27)

Evaluate each expression.

14. $3(y + 6) + 12 \times 2$ when $y = 0$

15. $105 - 5 + 16y - 85 - 3$ when $y = 5$

16. $21x + (18 + 2) \times 10.5$ when $x = 2$

17. $4 \times 8 \times 12 \times b \times 7 + 2$ when $b = 0$

18. The expression $d - (3 \times \$11.98)$ describes the amount of money Mark has left after buying three items for $11.98. If $d = \$50.25$, how much does Mark have left after making his purchases?

D Multiples of Whole Numbers

(Grade 5)

List four multiples of each number.

19. 6

20. 8

21. 10

22. 5

23. 3

24. 11

25. 15

26. 9

27. Bart planted 10 flowers in every row of his garden. How many flowers are there if Bart's garden has 11 rows?

E Solving Multiplication and Division Equations

(pages 68–69)

Solve.

28. $1.5x = 45$

29. $7x = 294$

30. $8x = 8.8$

31. $p \div 13 = 71$

32. $b \div 1.3 = 7$

33. $10 = x \div 0.34$

34. Spencer rides his bike at 8 miles per hour. He gets to the train station in 3 hours. How many miles did Spencer ride?

F Comparing and Ordering Decimals

(pages 6–7)

Write the numbers in each set in order from least to greatest.

35. 1.375, 0.375, 0.75, 1.75, 0.125

36. 1.2, 0.8, 0.09, 2.8, 2.75

37. Elaine's dog weighs 15.4 kilograms. Theo's dog weighs 15.25 kilograms. Which dog weighs more?

To the Family and Student

Looking Back

In Grade 5, students learned how to determine equivalent fractions and how to write fractions in simplest form.

Chapter 4

Number Theory and Fractions

In this chapter, students will find greatest common factors and least common multiples, compare and order fractions, and relate fractions and decimals.

Looking Ahead

In Chapter 5, students will add, subtract, multiply, and divide fractions and write the answer in simplest form.

Math and Everyday Living

Opportunities to apply the concepts of Chapter 4 abound in everyday situations. During the chapter, think about how number theory and fractions can be used to solve a variety of real-world problems. The following examples suggest just a few of the many situations that could launch a discussion about number theory and fractions.

Math in the House On Saturday you spent $2\frac{3}{4}$ hours doing chores. Your sister spent $2\frac{1}{2}$ hours doing chores. Your sister complained that she had to work longer than you. Is she correct?

Math and Transportation You buy a toll pass every 9 days and a subway pass every 7 days. If you buy both passes today, in how many days will you have to buy both a toll pass and a subway pass?

Math and Sewing You cut $2\frac{1}{2}$ inches of ribbon from a spool. Your friend cuts $2\frac{2}{3}$ inches of ribbon from the same spool. The pattern for which you need the ribbon calls for a $2\frac{5}{8}$ inch piece of ribbon. Decide which ribbon you should use. Explain.

Math in Arts and Crafts You are making decorative shelves. You have two wooden planks measuring 63 inches and 84 inches. You want to cut them into the longest possible shelves of equal length. How long will the shelves be?

Math in the Garden You and your family have purchased the following bulbs for your garden. What fraction of the bulbs are tulip bulbs?

Type of Bulb	Number of Bulbs
Iris	24
Hyacinth	12
Tulip	36
Crocus	36

Math and Recreation At a family reunion, you and your relatives went on a white-water rafting trip. The following chart shows the distance each raft traveled.

Raft Number	Distance, in miles
1	26
2	$27\frac{1}{4}$
3	$27\frac{3}{4}$
4	$26\frac{3}{8}$
5	$26\frac{1}{4}$
6	27

Put the rafts in order from greatest distance traveled to least distance traveled.

California Content Standards in Chapter 4 Lessons*

Number Sense	Teach and Practice	Practice
1.0 (Grade 5) Students compute with very large and very small numbers, positive integers, decimals, and fractions, and understand the relationship between decimals, fractions, and percents. They understand relative magnitudes of numbers.	4-7	
1.0 (🔑) Students compare and order positive and negative fractions, decimals, and mixed numbers. Students solve problems involving fractions, ratios, proportions, and percentages.		4-8
1.1 (🔑) Compare and order positive . . . fractions . . . and mixed numbers and place them on a number line.	4-8	
1.2 (🔑) (Grade 5) Find decimal and percent equivalents for common fractions and explain why they represent the same value . . .	4-9	
1.3 (Grade 5) Understand and compute positive integer powers of nonnegative integers; compute examples as repeated multiplication.	4-1	
1.4 (🔑) (Grade 5) Determine the prime factors of all numbers through 50 and write the numbers as the product of their prime factors by using exponents to show multiples of a factor (e.g., $24 = 2 \times 2 \times 2 \times 3 = 2^3 \times 3$).	4-2	
2.4 (🔑) Determine the least common multiple and the greatest common divisor of whole numbers; use them to solve problems with fractions (e.g., to find a common denominator . . . or to find the reduced form for a fraction).	4-4, 4-6	4-7

Algebra and Functions	Teach and Practice	Practice
1.2 Write and evaluate an algebraic expression for a given situation, using up to three variables.		4-1
1.4 Solve problems manually by using the correct order of operations or by using a scientific calculator.		4-1
Mathematical Reasoning		
2.1 Use estimation to verify the reasonableness of calculated results.	4-3	
2.2 Apply strategies and results from simpler problems to more complex problems.		4-5, 4-10
2.4 Use a variety of methods, such as words, numbers, symbols, charts, graphs, tables, diagrams, and models, to explain mathematical reasoning.		4-4
2.7 Make precise calculations and check the validity of the results from the context of the problem.	4-3, 4-10	
3.1 Evaluate the reasonableness of the solution in the context of the original situation.	4-3	
3.2 Note the method of deriving the solution and demonstrate a conceptual understanding of the derivation by solving similar problems.	4-5	
3.3 Develop generalizations of the results obtained and the strategies used and apply them in new problem situations.		4-2, 4-5, 4-6, 4-9

* The symbol (🔑) indicates a key standard as designated in the Mathematics Framework for California Public Schools. Full statements of the California Content Standards are found at the beginning of this book following the Table of Contents.

Exponents *Algebra*

Warm-Up Review

1. $2 \times 2 \times 2 \times 2$

2. $5 \times 5 \times 5$

3. $0.3 \times 0.3 \times 0.3$

4. You earned $2 the first day you baby-sat. The second day you earned $4. The third day you earned $8. If this pattern continues, how much will you earn in all after 5 days?

California Content Standard *Number Sense 1.3 (Grade 5): Understand and compute positive integer powers of nonnegative integers; compute examples as repeated multiplication. (This lesson extends positive integer powers to nonnegative decimals.)*

Math Link You know how to multiply more than two factors. Now you will learn another way to write a product such as $4 \times 4 \times 4$.

Example 1

You call 3 friends to tell them about a carnival. They go to the carnival the first day. Each friend calls 3 other friends to encourage them to go to the carnival the second day. All of these friends go to the carnival, and they call 3 more friends each to tell them to go the third day. If all of these friends go, how many go to the carnival on the third day?

3

3×3

$3 \times 3 \times 3$

The picture shows that $3 \times 3 \times 3$, or 27, friends go to the carnival on the third day.

You can use an **exponent** to tell how many times a number is used as a factor.

$$\underbrace{3 \times 3 \times 3}_{\text{factors}} = 3\overset{\text{exponent}}{\underset{\text{base}}{3}}$$

The number is called the **base.** The exponent is called the **power** of the base. For example, three to the third power is written 3^3.

You can read 3^3 as "three cubed" or "three to the third power." To find 3^3, multiply $3 \times 3 \times 3$.

In general, $n^3 = n \times n \times n$.

Word Bank

exponent
base
power

Additional Standards: Algebra and Functions 1.2, 1.4 (See p. 131.)

Example 2

A. Evaluate 4^3.

$$4^3 = \underbrace{4 \times 4 \times 4}_{\text{3 factors}} = 64$$

With a calculator:

Press: [4] [y^x] [3] [=]

Display: [64]

B. Evaluate 0.5^2.

$$0.5^2 = \underbrace{0.5 \times 0.5}_{\text{2 factors}} = 0.25$$

With a calculator:

Press: [.] [5] [y^x] [2] [=]

Display: [0.25]

Example 3

Evaluate $n^2 - 5$ for $n = 4$.

$n^2 - 5$

$4^2 - 5$ Substitute 4 for n.

$16 - 5$ Using the rules for order of operations, evaluate 4^2 first.

11 Subtract.

$n^2 - 5 = 11$ when $n = 4$.

Guided Practice
For another example, see Set A on p. 162.

Use exponents to write each expression.

1. $2 \times 2 \times 2$

2. $0.8 \times 0.8 \times 0.8 \times 0.8$

3. $b \times b \times b \times b \times b$

Evaluate.

4. 7^2 **5.** 6^3 **6.** 4^5 **7.** 0.5^4 **8.** 4^1

Evaluate each expression when $n = 5$.

9. $n^2 - 2$ **10.** $(n - 3)^4$ **11.** $2n^2$

12. A certain cell doubles every hour. If you begin with one cell, at the end of 1 hour there are 2 cells, at the end of 2 hours there are 2^2, or 4, cells, and so on. After 6 hours how many cells will there be?

Independent Practice
For more practice, see Set A on p. 164.

Use exponents to write each expression.

13. $7 \times 7 \times 7 \times 7 \times 7$ **14.** $0.15 \times 0.15 \times 0.15$ **15.** $k \times k \times k \times k$

Evaluate.

16. 4^4 **17.** 1^{12} **18.** 12^1 **19.** $(0.9)^3$ **20.** $(1.5)^4$

Evaluate each expression when $n = 3$.

21. $n^2 - 5$ **22.** $(n + 4)^2$ **23.** $4n^2$

24. You are going to show pictures of your trip after school. You invite 2 people after first period. They each invite 2 people after second period. This goes on until classes end after eighth period. How many people are invited after eighth period?

25. The area of the rectangle at the right can be found with the expression $2s^2$. Find the area when $s = 8$ feet.

26. Mental Math Compare: 6^1 ⬤ 1^6

In Exercises 27–29, write an expression without exponents. In Exercises 30 and 31, write an expression with exponents.

27. y^2 **28.** t^4 **29.** a^5 **30.** $m \times m \times m$ **31.** $r \times r \times r \times r$

Mixed Review

32. Find the mean number of calendars sold by each student.

Calendars Sold
1, 3, 2, 1, 2, 2, 5, 3, 9, 2

Test Prep   Choose the correct letter for each answer.

33. Which survey question is most fair?
(3-8)

   A Should students be encouraged to sell calendars to raise money for the school?

   B Should students be forced to sell calendars to raise money for the school?

   C What is your opinion about students selling calendars to raise money for the school?

   D Should students put themselves in danger selling calendars door-to-door to buy computers for the teachers?

34. Students question parents leaving a basketball game about the
(3-6) practice of selling calendars to raise money for the school. What type of sampling is this?

   F Random sampling   **H** Responses to a survey

   G Representative sampling   **J** Convenience sampling

LESSON 4-2 Prime Factorization

California Content Standard *Number Sense 1.4 (Gr. 5)(🔑): Determine the prime factors of all numbers through 50 and write the numbers as the product of their prime factors by using exponents to show multiples of a factor (e.g., 24 = 2 × 2 × 2 × 3 = 2³ × 3).*

Math Link You can use what you know about exponents to help you write the prime factorization of a number.

Example 1

If you and two friends collect 144 shells at the beach, can you divide them equally?

To find out, you need to know if 144 is divisible by 3. **Divisible** means "having no remainder after division." You can find out if 144 is divisible by 3 by using the divisibility rule for 3. A number is divisible by 3 if the sum of its digits is divisible by 3.

Step 1 Find the sum of the digits.	**Step 2** Divide the sum by 3.
1 + 4 + 4 = 9	9 ÷ 3 = 3 no remainder

144 is divisible by 3. You and your friends can divide the shells equally.

Divisibility rules help you find out if a number is divisible by 2, 3, 4, 5, 6, 9, or 10.

Divisibility Rules
A number is divisible by
2 if the last digit is 0, 2, 4, 6, or 8.
3 if the sum of its digits is divisible by 3.
4 if the number formed by the last two digits is divisible by 4.
5 if the last digit is 5 or 0.
6 if the number is divisible by both 2 and 3.
9 if the sum of the digits is divisible by 9.
10 if the last digit is 0.

Warm-Up Review

Use exponents to write each expression.

1. 3 × 3 × 3 × 3 × 3

2. 2 × 2 × 2 × 3

3. 2 × 5 × 5

4. A box holds 25 marbles. It is 15 cm long, 8 cm wide, and 6 cm tall. What is the volume of the box?

Word Bank

divisible

prime number

composite number

prime factorization

Remember, an **even** number ends in 0, 2, 4, 6, or 8. An **odd** number ends in 1, 3, 5, 7, or 9.

Additional Standards: Mathematical Reasoning 3.3 (See p. 131.)

Example 2

Is 19 divisible by 2, 3, 4, 5, 6, 9, or 10?

Since the last digit of 19 is 9, 19 is not divisible by 2, 5, or 10. 19 is not divisible by 4 or 6 because it is not divisible by 2.

The sum of the digits is $1 + 9 = 10$. Since 10 is not divisible by 3 or 9, 19 is not divisible by 3 or 9.

It is also not divisible by 7 or 8. Since 19 is only divisible by itself and 1, 19 is a prime number.

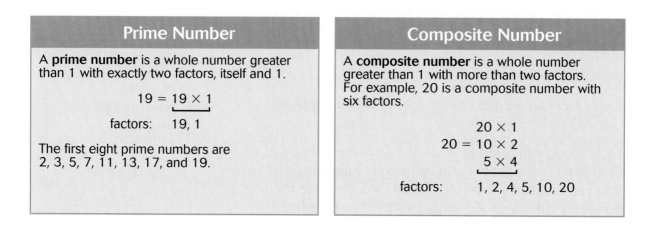

Prime Number	Composite Number
A **prime number** is a whole number greater than 1 with exactly two factors, itself and 1. $19 = 19 \times 1$ factors: 19, 1 The first eight prime numbers are 2, 3, 5, 7, 11, 13, 17, and 19.	A **composite number** is a whole number greater than 1 with more than two factors. For example, 20 is a composite number with six factors. $20 = \begin{matrix} 20 \times 1 \\ 10 \times 2 \\ 5 \times 4 \end{matrix}$ factors: 1, 2, 4, 5, 10, 20

When a number is written as the product of its prime factors, the product is called the **prime factorization** of the number.

When a number is prime, its prime factorization is just that number. For example, the prime factorization of 13 is 13.

Example 3

Write the prime factorization of 40. You can make a factor tree.

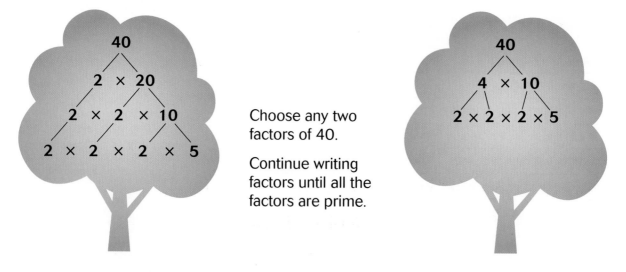

Choose any two factors of 40.

Continue writing factors until all the factors are prime.

The prime factorization for 40 is $2 \times 2 \times 2 \times 5$, or $2^3 \times 5$.

Guided Practice
For another example, see Set B on p. 162.

Tell if each number is divisible by 2, 3, 4, 5, 6, 9, 10, or none of these.

1. 3,742   **2.** 5,310   **3.** 47,388   **4.** 9,999   **5.** 41,112

Use exponents to write the prime factorization of each number.

6. 64   **7.** 48   **8.** 76   **9.** 81   **10.** 90

11. Math Reasoning Is 4,647 a prime number? Explain your answer.

Independent Practice
For more practice, see Set B on p. 164.

Tell if each number is divisible by 2, 3, 4, 5, 6, 9, 10, or none of these.

12. 213   **13.** 550   **14.** 1,032   **15.** 111,000   **16.** 17,985

Use exponents to write the prime factorization of each number.

17. 141   **18.** 56   **19.** 100   **20.** 96   **21.** 2,400

22. Mental Math What is the greatest four-digit number that is divisible by 3?

23. The nature center is creating an exhibit of 356 shells. Decide how many display cases to use if an equal number of shells must be in each case and you want more than 2 but fewer than 10 cases.

Mixed Review

24. Identify the claim in the passage at the right. Then tell whether the claim is justified by the statistics. Explain your answer.

> **Students Will Pay for Bike Rack**
> In a survey of 30 bike riders, 25 said they would donate a quarter to purchase a new bike rack. If all 300 students at Longhorn Middle School donate a quarter, enough money can be raised to buy a bike rack for the school.

Evaluate.

25. 0.3^2 **26.** 15^2 **27.** 20^3

Test Prep   Choose the correct letter for each answer.

28. Algebra Find the value of $a + 2b$ if b is 4 and a is 3.
(1-10)

   A 10   **B** 11   **C** 18   **D** 20

29. Evaluate the expression $72 - 30 \div (3 + 3)$.
(1-9)

   F 7   **G** 42   **H** 65   **J** 67

Problem-Solving Skill:
Reasonable Answers

California Content Standard *Mathematical Reasoning 2.7: Make precise calculations and check the validity of the results from the context of the problem. Also Mathematical Reasoning 2.1, 3.1 (See p. 131.)*

(See p. 131.)

Warm-Up Review

1. $12 \times 8 \times 5$

2. 324×3 **3.** $420 \div 7$

4. 20×60

5. Ten buses are being used to take 435 students on a field trip. The students will tour a museum in groups of 5. About how many students should ride each bus?

Read for Understanding

Some riverboat cruises offer tickets with and without lunch. Today, 60 of the 180 passengers bought tickets that include lunch. Each lunch table can seat up to 6 people. On most cruises, half the passengers eat in groups of 2 and half eat in groups of 4.

① How many passengers are on the cruise?

② How many passengers have lunch tickets?

③ How many passengers can sit at a table?

Riverboat Cruise		
Maximum Capacity	On Board Today	Lunch Tickets Sold
240	180	60

Think and Discuss

MATH FOCUS

Reasonable Answers

When you solve a problem, you should always check to make sure that your answer is reasonable. You can use your estimate or look back at the information in the problem to see if the answer makes sense.

④ Is it reasonable to say that 60 tables are needed? Why or why not?

⑤ The captain has instructed the crew to set up 25 tables for the lunch crowd. Is this a reasonable number of tables? Explain.

Guided Practice

During a 14-day cruise, each of the cruise ship's 275 passengers will sit at the captain's table for at least one meal. The table seats a total of 10 people, including the captain. Three meals are served each day.

1. Which of the following shows how to find the number of passengers who can eat with the captain in one day?

   a. Multiply the number of passengers by 14.

   b. Multiply the number of passengers who can sit at the table at any one meal by 3.

   c. Multiply the number of passengers at the table at any one meal by 14.

2. Is it reasonable to say that the maximum number of people who can dine with the captain during the cruise is 378 people?

   a. No, because $275 \times 3 = 825$.

   b. Yes, because $14 \times 10 \times 3 = 420$.

   c. Yes, because $14 \times 9 \times 3 = 378$.

3. Is it reasonable to say that some passengers will have the chance to eat a meal with the captain more than once?

   a. Yes, because the number of passengers who can eat with the captain is greater than 275.

   b. Yes, because there will be 28 meals in 14 days.

   c. Both **a** and **b**

Independent Practice

The passengers on a whale-watching cruise lined the railings to look for whales. Half of the 90 passengers were on the middle deck. One third of the remaining passengers watched from the upper deck. The rest watched from the lower deck.

4. Which fact in the problem makes it reasonable to say that the middle deck has 45 passengers?

   a. Half the passengers are on the middle deck.

   b. One third of the remaining passengers are on the upper deck.

   c. The rest are on the lower deck.

5. Is it reasonable to say that there were 45 people on the middle deck, 15 on the upper deck, and 30 on the lower deck?

   a. Yes, because $45 + 15 + 30 = 90$.

   b. Yes, because $45 = 15 + 30$.

   c. Both **a** and **b**

6. Math Reasoning A crew member stated that there were 3 times as many passengers on the lower deck as on the upper deck. Was his statement reasonable? Explain.

Greatest Common Factor

Warm-Up Review

Use exponents to write the prime factorization of each number.

1. 12   **2.** 27

3. 36   **4.** 60

5. You have 6 boxes of granola bars with 8 bars in each box. Can you share them equally among 12 people?

California Content Standard *Number Sense 2.4 ( ): Determine the . . . greatest common divisor of whole numbers; use them to solve problems with fractions . . ..*

Math Link You can use what you know about prime numbers to find the greatest common factor.

Example 1

You are putting vacation photos in an album. One section will have 12 photos from Philadelphia, and another will have 30 photos from Boston. You want to have the same number of photos on each page.

To find the greatest number of photos you can have on each page, you need to find factors common to 12 and 30 and then find the **greatest common factor (GCF).** The greatest common factor is also called the greatest common divisor.

Step 1 Find the factors of 12 and 30.	**Step 2** List the factors from least to greatest. Circle the common factors. Find the greatest common factor.

12: 1×12; 2×6; 3×4

30: 1×30; 2×15; 3×10; 5×6

12: ①, ②, ③, 4, ⑥, 12

30: ①, ②, ③, 5, ⑥, 10, 15, 30

The GCF is 6.

You can place 6 photos on each page.

Example 2

Find the greatest common factor of 48 and 60.

With large numbers, it is sometimes easier to write the prime factorization of each number. Then find the common prime factors and multiply.

$48 = ②\times②\times 2 \times 2 \times③$

$60 = ②\times② \qquad \times③\times 5$

Multiply the common prime factors to find the greatest common factor.

$2 \times 2 \times 3 = 12$

The GCF of 48 and 60 is 12.

Word Bank

greatest common factor

Guided Practice *For another example, see Set C on p. 162.*

Find the greatest common factor (GCF).

1. 6, 15   **2.** 21, 49   **3.** 300, 144   **4.** 16, 70, 78

5. You separate some of your pictures into three groups, 16 from Philadelphia, 12 from Boston, and 20 from New York. You want to display them in an album by group with the same number of pictures on each page. What is the greatest number of pictures you can have on a page?

Independent Practice *For more practice, see Set C on p. 164.*

Find the greatest common factor (GCF).

6. 10, 16   **7.** 36, 48   **8.** 18, 42   **9.** 30, 50

10. 84, 120   **11.** 60, 45   **12.** 45, 63   **13.** 90, 105

Use the Venn diagram at the right for Exercises 14 and 15.

14. The Venn diagram shows the prime factors of 24 and 36. What is the prime factorization of each number?

15. What does the shaded area show?

24   36

2   2 2 3   3

16. Math Reasoning Can the greatest common factor of 9 and 27 be greater than 9? Explain your answer.

Mixed Review

17. You want to make some jewelry, using 17 shells. Each piece of jewelry uses either 3 or 4 shells. How can you use all the shells?

Use exponents to write each expression.

18. $9 \times 9 \times 9 \times 9 \times 9$ **19.** 6.4×6.4 **20.** $2.7 \times 2.7 \times 2.7 \times 2.7$

Test Prep   Choose the correct letter for each answer.

21. A plumber has 18 feet of pipe. Use the equation $4.5p = 18$ to
(2-7) find into how many 4.5 feet long pieces, p, the pipe can be cut.

    A 2 pieces   **B** 3 pieces   **C** 4 pieces   **D** 5 pieces

22. Algebra Which expression means 7 less than a number n?
(1-11)

    F $n + 7$ **G** $n - 7$ **H** $7n$ **J** $\dfrac{n}{7}$

Use Homework Workbook 4-4.   **141**

Problem-Solving Strategy:
Using Logical Reasoning

California Content Standard *Mathematical Reasoning 3.2: Note the method of deriving the solution and demonstrate a conceptual understanding of the derivation by solving similar problems.*

Read the newspaper ad. Then use the clues to find the missing phone-number digits.

Understand

What do you need to find?

You need to find values for *a, b, c,* and *d* in the phone number.

Plan

How can you solve the problem?

You can **use logical reasoning** and a table to organize the information.

Solve

Make a table. As you read the clues, cross out incorrect digits and circle the only correct answer.

- **Clue 1:** Doesn't help yet.
- **Clue 2:** Circle 7 and cross off all other digits for *a*. Use Clue 1: Cross off 7 for *b, c,* and *d*.
- **Clue 3:** Cross off numbers that are not prime for *b* and *d*. Cross off numbers that *are* prime for *c*.
- **Clue 4:** Circle 0 and cross off all other digits for *c*.
- **Clue 5:** Circle 5 and cross off all other digits for *d*. Cross off 5 for *b*.
- **Clue 6:** Circle 2 and cross off 3 for *b*. The telephone number is 555-7205.

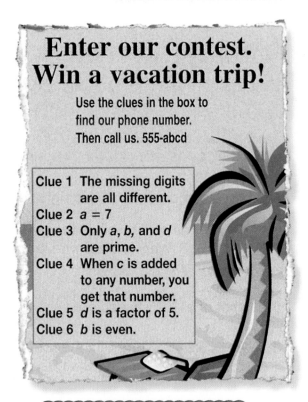

Enter our contest.
Win a vacation trip!

Use the clues in the box to find our phone number. Then call us. 555-abcd

Clue 1	The missing digits are all different.
Clue 2	*a* = 7
Clue 3	Only *a, b,* and *d* are prime.
Clue 4	When *c* is added to any number, you get that number.
Clue 5	*d* is a factor of 5.
Clue 6	*b* is even.

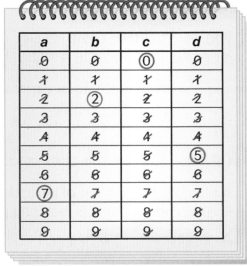

a	b	c	d
0̸	0̸	⓪	0̸
1̸	1̸	1̸	1̸
2̸	②	2̸	2̸
3̸	3̸	3̸	3̸
4̸	4̸	4̸	4̸
5̸	5̸	5̸	⑤
6̸	6̸	6̸	6̸
⑦	7̸	7̸	7̸
8̸	8̸	8̸	8̸
9̸	9̸	9̸	9̸

Look Back

Check that all the digits satisfy each clue.

Additional Standards: Mathematical Reasoning 2.2, 3.3 (See p. 131.)

Guided Practice

1. The table at the right shows students' class trip choices.

   The town has school buses in 3 different sizes. Some can seat 30 students, some can seat 40, and some can seat 48. Which of these buses can be used for all the trips, assuming there will be no empty seats?

Trip	Number of Students
Mountain train ride	150
Harbor cruise	210
Parks and museum	90
Historic tour of the city	240

Independent Practice

Make a table and use logical reasoning to find the missing digits of each telephone number for Exercises 2 and 3.

2. 123-*efgh*
   Clue 1: *e, f, g,* and *h* are different.
   Clue 2: Only f and h are prime.
   Clue 3: Only *e* and *f* are even.
   Clue 4: *e* is a multiple of 3.
   Clue 5: *g* is a factor of every number.
   Clue 6: The sum of *e, f, g,* and *h* is 12.

3. 555-*abcd*
   Clue 1: *a, b, c,* and *d* are different.
   Clue 2: *d* is the only odd number.
   Clue 3: *a* is the only prime number.
   Clue 4: $d = 3^2$
   Clue 5: $c < 8$
   Clue 6: $c - b = a$

Mixed Review

Try these or other strategies to solve each problem. Tell which strategy you used.

Problem-Solving Strategies

- *Use Logical Reasoning*
- *Work Backward*
- *Find a Pattern*
- *Make a Graph*

---

4. The mountain train reaches a speed of 5.4 miles per hour after traveling 2 miles, 6.8 miles per hour after 4 miles, and 8.2 miles per hour after 6 miles. If the speed continues to increase at this rate, how fast will the train be traveling when it has gone 20 miles?

5. Tom, Pat, and Sue decided to share expenses equally for a party. Tom spent $35 for food, Pat spent $26 for a gift, and Sue spent $20 for decorations. What should they do now to make sure each contributes the same amount?

4-6 Least Common Multiple

California Content Standard *Number Sense 2.4 (🔑): Determine the least common multiple . . . of whole numbers; . . ..*

Math Link You can use what you know about prime factorization to find least common multiples.

Example 1

You and some friends set up a two-track model train system—a 10-second track and a 6-second track. If both trains leave the station at the same time, how much time will pass before they are at the station at the same time again?

To find out, you need to find the **least common multiple (LCM)** of 10 and 6. You can find the LCM of two or more numbers by listing their multiples and finding their common multiples. The least of these is the least common multiple.

List some **multiples** of each number.

Multiples of 10: 10, 20, **30**, 40, 50, 60, 70

Multiples of 6: 6, 12, 18, 24, **30**, 36, 42, 48, 54, 60, 66

The least common multiple of 10 and 6 is 30.

After 30 seconds, both trains will be at the station again.

Example 2

Find the least common multiple of 84 and 72. With large numbers, it is sometimes easier to write the prime factorization of each number.

$$84 = 2 \times 2 \quad \times 3 \quad \times 7$$

$$72 = 2 \times 2 \times 2 \times 3 \times 3$$

Write each prime factorization, aligning common factors.

$$LCM = 2 \times 2 \times 2 \times 3 \times 3 \times 7 = 504$$

Write the product as shown, using each common factor once and each other factor once. Multiply.

The least common multiple of 84 and 72 is 504.

🔑 *Additional Standards: Mathematical Reasoning 3.3 (See p. 131.)*

Guided Practice _For another example, see Set D on p. 162._

Find the least common multiple (LCM).

1. 5, 6   **2.** 3, 7   **3.** 3, 9   **4.** 4, 14   **5.** 4, 6, 8

6. Math Reasoning Find the product of the GCF and the LCM of 10 and 6. Find the product of the GCF and the LCM of 4 and 6. What do you notice?

Independent Practice _For more practice, see Set D on p. 164._

Find the least common multiple (LCM).

7. 4, 12   **8.** 3, 14   **9.** 5, 14   **10.** 1, 4, 40   **11.** 9, 12, 18

12. Lenny, Mark, and Liza are going to jog along 3 different trails in the park. To complete one circuit, Lenny takes 6 minutes, Mark takes 12 minutes, and Liza takes 9 minutes. If they start at the same place and the same time, how long will it be before they are together again at the starting point?

13. Mental Math Find the greatest common factor and least common multiple of 12 and 36.

Mixed Review

Use the histogram at the right for Exercises 14 and 15.

14. How many more people saw 2–3 movies than 6–7 moves?

15. Between which two consecutive intervals is there the greatest difference in the number of people?

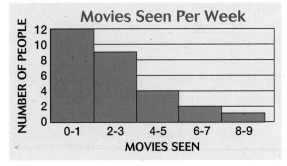

16. Use exponents to write the prime factorization of 140.

17. Find the greatest common factor of 48 and 72.

Test Prep   Choose the correct letter for each answer.

18. Find the next number in the pattern.
(1-8)   1.4, 1.9, 2.9, 4.4, 6.4, _____

    A 6.9   **C** 8.4

    B 7.4   **D** 8.9

19. $(10 + 20) + 30 = 10 + (20 + 30)$ is true
(1-4)   because of which property of addition?

    F Commutative   **H** Identity

    G Associative   **J** Opposite

Diagnostic Checkpoint

For Exercises 1–4, write the product as an exponent and evaluate.

1. $7 \times 7 \times 7 \times 7$
(4-1)

2. $4 \times 4 \times 4 \times 4 \times 4$
(4-1)

3. $11 \times 11 \times 11$
(4-1)

4. $5 \times 5 \times 5 \times 5$
(4-1)

Evaluate.

5. 1^6
(4-1)

6. 3^5
(4-1)

7. 7^2
(4-1)

8. 10^5
(4-1)

9. Evaluate $(n - 8)^4$ when $n = 10$.
(4-1)

10. Evaluate $n^4 - 2$ when $n = 3$.
(4-1)

Tell if each number is divisible by 2, 3, 4, 5, 6, 9, 10, or none.

11. 372
(4-2)

12. 1,488
(4-2)

13. 585
(4-2)

Tell if the number is prime or composite. If the number is composite, write the prime factorization.

14. 14
(4-2)

15. 51
(4-2)

16. 61
(4-2)

17. 720
(4-2)

18. 97
(4-2)

Find the greatest common factor (GCF).

19. 15, 36
(4-4)

20. 32, 48
(4-4)

21. 16, 24, 72
(4-4)

22. 36, 40, 56
(4-4)

23. 9, 6, 24
(4-4)

Find the least common multiple for each set of numbers.

24. 6, 9
(4-6)

25. 1, 6
(4-6)

26. 2, 6, 7
(4-6)

27. 2, 3, 7
(4-6)

28. 4, 5, 8
(4-6)

29. During a 3-day business convention, 118 of the participants
(4-3) will give one lecture. There are 7 rooms that each seat
80 people. Is it reasonable to say that each room will hold about
6 lectures a day during the convention? Explain your answer.

30. Use logical reasoning to find the missing digits of the zip code.
(4-5) $4\ 5\ a\ 3\ b$
Clue 1: a and b are different.
Clue 2: a and b are both even.
Clue 3: b is twice the digit before it.
Clue 4: a is the product of the last two digits divided by the sum
of the first two digits.

31. You want to share your baseball cards with some friends. You
(4-4) have 12 rookie-of-the-year cards, 16 hall-of-fame cards, and
24 world series cards. What is the largest number of friends you
can give equal numbers of each type of card?

Multiple-Choice Cumulative Review

Choose the correct letter for each answer.

1. Each of two different fifth grade classes will be divided into groups of the same size. The classes have 36 and 48 students. Which is the greatest common factor of 36 and 48?

   A   4

   B   8

   C   12

   D   24

2. Which expression shows 60 as a product of prime factors?

   F 6×10

   G $2 \times 6 \times 5$

   H $2 \times 2 \times 3 \times 5$

   J $2 \times 3 \times 10$

3. On a 5-day trip, Katie's family traveled the following distances: 154 miles, 203 miles, 61 miles, 0 miles, and 182 miles. What was the average number of miles traveled each day?

   A   100 mi   C   150 mi

   B   120 mi   D   170 mi

4. Laura's, Gil's, and Matt's towns have these populations: 4,832; 3,397; 9,720. Which is the best estimate for the difference between the greatest and least populations?

   F   13,000   H   7,000

   G   11,000   J   5,000

Use the graph for Question 5 and 6. This graph shows how two groups of people spend their leisure time.

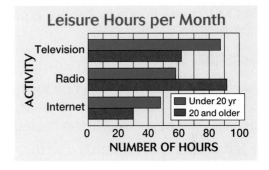

5. About how many more hours per month do people aged 20 and older spend watching television than they spend on the Internet?

   A   25 hours   C   35 hours

   B   30 hours   D   40 hours

6. About how many total hours per month do people under 20 watch television, listen to the radio, and spend on the Internet?

   F   100 hours   H   300 hours

   G   200 hours   J   400 hours

7. Which expression is equal to 14?

   A $2 \times 3 + 4 - 6 + 19$

   B $140 \div 7 - 3 - 3$

   C $64 \div 8 + 6 \times 2 - 5$

   D $196 \div 4 \div 7 + 10$

Equivalent Fractions

California Content Standard *Number Sense 1.0* (🔑): *Students . . . solve problems involving fractions . . ..*

Math Link You know how to find the GCF and LCM of two numbers. Now you will learn how to use the GCF and LCM to write fractions that are equal to each other.

Warm-Up Review

Find the greatest common factor.

1. 18, 12   **2.** 36, 48

Find the least common multiple.

3. 9, 8   **4.** 15, 20

5. You have 12 T-shirts. Five are blue and the rest are other colors. What fraction of your shirts are not blue?

Example 1

Alissha and Jeff went to Texas on their vacation. While they were there, they each bought 12 stamps and 12 picture postcards. The next day, Alissha mailed 4 of her 12 cards, and Jeff mailed $\frac{1}{3}$ of his cards. Did they mail the same number of cards?

You need to decide if $\frac{1}{3}$ equals $\frac{4}{12}$.

Word Bank

equivalent fractions

simplest form

least common denominator (LCD)

12 stamps total

4 stamps

Two fractions with the same value are **equivalent fractions.**

Multiply or divide the numerator and denominator by the same number to decide if $\frac{1}{3}$ and $\frac{4}{12}$ are equivalent fractions.

Multiply $3 \times \blacksquare = 12$ Divide $12 \div \blacksquare = 3$

$$\frac{1}{3} = \frac{1 \times 4}{3 \times 4} = \frac{4}{12}$$ $$\frac{4}{12} = \frac{4 \div 4}{12 \div 4} = \frac{1}{3}$$

Remember $\frac{4}{4} = 1$

Alissha and Jeff mailed the same number of postcards.

Additional Standards: *Number Sense 2.4* (🔑) (See p. 131.)

When you solve problems involving fractions, your answer may be easier to understand if the fraction is written in **simplest form**.

A fraction is in simplest form when the greatest common factor of its numerator and denominator is 1.

Example 2

Write $\frac{12}{42}$ in simplest form.

Step 1 Find the greatest common factor of the numerator and the denominator.	**Step 2** Divide the numerator and denominator by the greatest common factor, 6.
$\frac{12}{42} = \frac{2 \times 2 \times 3}{7 \times 2 \times 3}$ GCF $= 2 \times 3 = 6$	$\frac{12 \div 6}{42 \div 6} = \frac{2}{7}$

$\frac{12}{42} = \frac{2}{7}.$

$\frac{2}{7}$ is in simplest form because the greatest common factor of 2 and 7 is one.

You can use the least common multiple of two numbers to find the **least common denominator** (LCD) of two fractions. The least common denominator is the least common multiple of two or more fractions. Using the LCD will help you compare unlike fractions.

Example 3

Rewrite $\frac{3}{4}$ and $\frac{5}{6}$ as fractions with the same denominator.

Step 1 Find the LCM of the denominators. You can use prime factorization.	**Step 2** Write equivalent fractions, using the LCM, 12, as the least common denominator.
$4 = 2 \times 2$ $6 = 2 \quad \times 3$ $2 \times 2 \times 3 = 12$	The LCM of 4 and 6 is 12. The LCD of $\frac{3}{4}$ and $\frac{5}{6}$ is 12. $\frac{3}{4} = \frac{3 \times 3}{4 \times 3} = \frac{9}{12}$ Think $4 \times \blacksquare = 12$ $\frac{5}{6} = \frac{5 \times 2}{6 \times 2} = \frac{10}{12}$ Think $6 \times \blacksquare = 12$

$\frac{3}{4} = \frac{9}{12}$ and $\frac{5}{6} = \frac{10}{12}.$

Guided Practice   *For another example, see Set E on p. 163.*

Write each fraction in simplest form.

1. $\frac{12}{22}$ **2.** $\frac{14}{28}$ **3.** $\frac{24}{40}$ **4.** $\frac{38}{46}$ **5.** $\frac{24}{54}$

Use the LCD to write each set of fractions as fractions with the same denominator.

6. $\dfrac{5}{6}, \dfrac{5}{20}$

7. $\dfrac{6}{10}, \dfrac{4}{30}$

8. $\dfrac{7}{6}, \dfrac{8}{10}$

9. $\dfrac{8}{9}, \dfrac{4}{12}$

10. $\dfrac{4}{3}, \dfrac{5}{8}, \dfrac{7}{9}$

11. **Math Reasoning** Is there any limit to the number of equivalent fractions one fraction can have? Explain.

Independent Practice *For more practice, see Set E on p. 165.*

Write each fraction in simplest form.

12. $\dfrac{16}{20}$

13. $\dfrac{25}{40}$

14. $\dfrac{70}{100}$

15. $\dfrac{66}{99}$

16. $\dfrac{49}{63}$

17. $\dfrac{33}{99}$

Use the LCD to write each set of fractions as fractions with the same denominator.

18. $\dfrac{2}{24}, \dfrac{36}{48}$

19. $\dfrac{4}{6}, \dfrac{25}{24}$

20. $\dfrac{2}{8}, \dfrac{2}{4}, \dfrac{1}{3}$

21. $\dfrac{7}{8}, \dfrac{1}{6}, \dfrac{2}{8}$

22. $\dfrac{6}{18}, \dfrac{2}{36}, \dfrac{10}{9}$

23. There are 60 pictures in Tom's album, including 12 taken in Boston. Is it true that $\dfrac{1}{6}$ of them are from Boston? Explain your answer.

24. In your friend's album, $\dfrac{1}{5}$ of the 75 pictures were taken in Philadelphia. How many pictures were taken in Philadelphia?

Mixed Review

25. Find the smallest number greater than 1,000 that is divisible by 6.

26. Find the greatest common factor (GCF) of 99 and 27.

27. Find the least common multiple (LCM) of 33 and 15.

Test Prep Choose the correct letter for each answer.

28. A store bought 12 cases of a popular music CD. Each case
(4-3) contains 4 boxes, and each box contains 8 CDs. The store expects to sell about 350 CDs during the first week the CD is advertised. Is it reasonable to say the store will have enough CDs to meet the expected demand the first week?

    A Yes, because $12 \times 4 \times 8 > 350$ **C** No, because $4 \times 12 < 350$

    B No, because $12 \times (4 + 8) < 350$ **D** Both B and C

29. Which of these numbers has the same value as the 5 in 247.358?
(1-1)

    F 50   **G** 5.0   **H** 0.5   **J** 0.05   **K** NH

4-8

Comparing and Ordering Fractions and Mixed Numbers

🪃 **California Content Standard** *Number Sense 1.1(🔑): Compare and order positive . . . fractions . . . and mixed numbers and place them on a number line.*

Warm-Up Review

Compare. Use >, <, or = for ●.

1. 1,254 ● 1,524

2. 0.01 ● 0.001

3. Carla and Carlos each buy 8 pieces of fruit. Carla eats 2 of her pieces. Carlos eats $\frac{1}{4}$ of his. Do they eat the same amount?

Math Link You will use what you know about finding common denominators to compare and order fractions and mixed numbers.

Example 1

Use the map at the right. Rosa and Cari were biking in a state park. Rosa followed the red trail and Cari followed the blue trail. Who rode farther?

To find out, compare $\frac{7}{8}$ and $\frac{4}{5}$.

Rename the fractions so they have the same denominator and compare.

KEY

🚲 Bike Trails

· · · · · · $\frac{7}{8}$ mi

- - - - - $\frac{4}{5}$ mi

Step 1 Find the least common denominator of $\frac{7}{8}$ and $\frac{4}{5}$.	**Step 2** Write equivalent fractions, using the LCD.	**Step 3** Compare the fractions.
The LCM of 8 and 5 is 40. The LCD of $\frac{7}{8}$ and $\frac{4}{5}$ is 40.	$\frac{7}{8} = \frac{7 \times 5}{8 \times 5} = \frac{35}{40}$ $\frac{4}{5} = \frac{4 \times 8}{5 \times 8} = \frac{32}{40}$	$\frac{35}{40} > \frac{32}{40}$ So $\frac{7}{8} > \frac{4}{5}$

The red trail is longer because $\frac{7}{8} > \frac{4}{5}$. Rosa rode farther than Cari.

Example 2

Compare $\frac{1}{4}$ and $\frac{1}{3}$. Then compare $\frac{1}{3}$ and $\frac{1}{2}$. Use the fraction strips at the right.

The fraction strips show $\frac{1}{4} < \frac{1}{3}$ and $\frac{1}{3} < \frac{1}{2}$.

When two fractions have the same numerator, the one with the smaller denominator is the greater number.

$\frac{1}{4}$

$\frac{1}{3}$

$\frac{1}{2}$

A fraction with a numerator larger than the denominator is called an **improper fraction**. Improper fractions can be written as **mixed numbers**.

Word Bank

improper fraction
mixed number

A mixed number is a number written as a whole number and a fraction.

This picture shows two whole oranges and one quarter of an orange, or $2\frac{1}{4}$ oranges.

This picture shows nine quarter oranges, or $\frac{9}{4}$ oranges.

$2\frac{1}{4}$ is a **mixed number**.

$\frac{9}{4}$ is an **improper fraction**.

| To write a mixed number as a fraction, write the whole number as a fraction. Then combine the fractions. | To write an improper fraction as a mixed number, divide the numerator by the denominator. Simplify if possible. |

$2\frac{1}{4} = \frac{8}{4} + \frac{1}{4} = \frac{8+1}{4} = \frac{9}{4}$

$2\frac{1}{4} = \frac{9}{4}$

$\frac{9}{4} = 4\overline{)9}\;\;2\frac{1}{4}$
$\phantom{\frac{9}{4} = 4\overline{)9}}\;\underline{8}$
$\phantom{\frac{9}{4} = 4\overline{)9}}\;1$

Example 3

Write the numbers $1\frac{3}{4}, \frac{17}{8}, \frac{3}{2},$ and $\frac{7}{8}$ from least to greatest and place them on a number line.

Step 1 Write the improper fractions as mixed numbers.

$\frac{17}{8} = 8\overline{)17}\;\;2\frac{1}{8}$
$\phantom{\frac{17}{8} = 8\overline{)17}}\;\underline{16}$
$\phantom{\frac{17}{8} = 8\overline{)17}}\;1$

$\frac{3}{2} = 2\overline{)3}\;\;1\frac{1}{2}$
$\phantom{\frac{3}{2} = 2\overline{)3}}\;\underline{2}$
$\phantom{\frac{3}{2} = 2\overline{)3}}\;1$

Step 2 Write equivalent fractions using the LCD.

The LCM of 4, 8, and 2 is 8.

$1\frac{3}{4} = 1\frac{6}{8}, \quad \frac{17}{8} = 2\frac{1}{8}, \quad \frac{3}{2} = 1\frac{1}{2} = 1\frac{4}{8}$

Step 3 Write the numbers from least to greatest.

$\frac{7}{8} < \frac{3}{2} < 1\frac{3}{4} < \frac{17}{8}$

Step 4 Place the numbers on a number line.

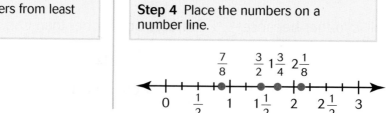

Guided Practice   *For another example, see Set F on p. 163.*

Write each improper fraction as a mixed number and each mixed number as an improper fraction.

1. $\frac{7}{3}$

2. $\frac{22}{3}$

3. $9\frac{4}{7}$

4. $10\frac{3}{5}$

Compare. Write <, >, or = for each ⬤.

5. $\frac{3}{4}$ ⬤ $\frac{1}{4}$ **6.** $\frac{7}{9}$ ⬤ $\frac{2}{3}$ **7.** $3\frac{4}{5}$ ⬤ $3\frac{3}{4}$ **8.** $1\frac{7}{8}$ ⬤ $1\frac{3}{16}$

9. In June, $1\frac{3}{4}$ inches of rain fell. In July, $1\frac{7}{8}$ inches fell, and in August, $1\frac{5}{6}$ inches fell. Which month had the most rain? the least?

Independent Practice   *For more practice, see Set F on p. 165.*

Write each improper fraction as a mixed number and each mixed number as an improper fraction.

10. $\frac{22}{7}$ **11.** $\frac{19}{3}$ **12.** $7\frac{3}{8}$ **13.** $5\frac{2}{3}$

Compare. Write <, >, or = for each ⬤.

14. $\frac{5}{8}$ ⬤ $\frac{5}{12}$ **15.** $1\frac{1}{4}$ ⬤ $1\frac{2}{5}$ **16.** $\frac{17}{10}$ ⬤ $1\frac{4}{9}$ **17.** $\frac{7}{6}$ ⬤ $\frac{9}{6}$

Arrange in order from least to greatest and place the numbers on a number line.

18. $\frac{1}{3}, \frac{5}{9}, \frac{1}{6}$ **19.** $\frac{3}{5}, \frac{1}{2}, \frac{11}{10}, 1\frac{3}{10}$ **20.** $\frac{3}{8}, 3\frac{1}{2}, 2\frac{1}{4}, \frac{3}{4}, 1\frac{1}{8}$

21. Jesse hiked $3\frac{11}{12}$ miles, canoed $3\frac{9}{10}$ miles, and rode his bike $3\frac{5}{6}$ miles. During which activity did he travel the greatest distance? the shortest?

Mixed Review

22. Mental Math You have 2.8 meters of ribbon. You buy 3.2 meters. How much ribbon do you have now?

Find the least common multiple (LCM).

23. 16, 24   **24.** 20, 45   **25.** 15, 24   **26.** 10, 100

Write each fraction in simplest form.

27. $\frac{30}{50}$ **28.** $\frac{18}{27}$ **29.** $\frac{16}{42}$ **30.** $\frac{25}{100}$

🖊 **Test Prep**   Choose the correct letter for the answer.

Clara pays $15 per week for ballet lessons. During the first month, She spent more than $25 for a pair of tights and more than $40 for ballet shoes.

31. Which number in the paragraph is an exact number?
(1-3)

A $15   **B** $25   **C** $40   **D** All of these

LESSON 4-9

Relating Fractions and Decimals

California Content Standard *Number Sense 1.2 (Gr. 5)(▪▬): Find decimal and percent equivalents for common fractions and explain why they represent the same value . . ..*

Math Link You know how to compare fractions, and you know how to compare decimals. Now you will learn how to write a fraction as a decimal and a decimal as a fraction.

Example 1

You ski 0.7 mile and your friend skis $\frac{3}{4}$ ($\frac{4}{6}$) mile. Who skis farther?

To help you compare 0.7 and $\frac{3}{4}$, write $\frac{3}{4}$ as a decimal.

To write a fraction as a decimal, divide the numerator by the denominator.

$$\frac{3}{4} = 4\overline{)3.00}\;\;\;^{0.75}$$

Since 0.75 > 0.7, your friend skis farther.

Example 2

Write 0.65 as a fraction in simplest form.

Step 1 Use what you know about place value to write 0.65 as a fraction.	**Step 2** Write the fraction in simplest form.
$0.65 = \frac{65}{100}$	$\frac{65 \div 5}{100 \div 5} = \frac{13}{20}$

hundredths place

$0.65 = \frac{13}{20}$

More Examples

A. Write $3\frac{4}{5}$ as a decimal.

$$\frac{4}{5} = 5\overline{)4.0}\;\;\;^{0.8}$$

$3\frac{4}{5} = 3 + 0.8 = 3.8$

B. Write $\frac{1}{3}$ as a decimal.

$$3\overline{)1.00}\;\;\;^{0.33}$$
$$\underline{-9}$$
$$10$$

The remainder is always 1. The decimal repeats.

$\frac{1}{3} \approx 0.33$

$\frac{1}{3}$ is approximately 0.33.

Additional Standards: *Mathematical Reasoning 3.3 (See p. 131.)*

Guided Practice *For another example, see Set G on p. 163.*

Write each fraction as a decimal and each decimal as a fraction in simplest form.

1. $\dfrac{2}{5}$

2. $\dfrac{1}{8}$

3. $4\dfrac{3}{20}$

4. 0.6

5. 0.08

6. Mental Math One recipe calls for 2.5 cups of flour. Another recipe calls for $2\dfrac{1}{4}$ cups of flour. Which recipe uses more flour?

Independent Practice *For more practice, see Set G on p. 165.*

Write each fraction as a decimal and each decimal as a fraction in simplest form.

7. $\dfrac{3}{4}$

8. $3\dfrac{1}{8}$

9. 0.12

10. 0.55

11. 4.87

12. Thomas drove $85\dfrac{4}{5}$ miles to get to summer camp. Lisa drove 45.7 miles to her grandmother's home to spend the night and then 39.4 miles on to camp. Who drove farther? Explain your answer.

13. Mental Math Explain how to find decimals equal to $\dfrac{1}{4}$ and $\dfrac{3}{4}$ using parts of a dollar.

14. To use a computer to write music, you need to write notes as decimals. What decimals are used for a half note, quarter note, eighth note, and sixteenth note?

Mixed Review

15. A certain cell triples every day. If you begin with one cell, at the end of one day there are 3 cells. At the end of 2 days, there are 3^2 or 9 cells, and so on. After 4 days, how many cells will there be?

16. Write $\dfrac{5}{9}$ and $\dfrac{1}{6}$ as fractions with the same denominator.

Compare. Write <, >, or = for each ⬤.

17. $\dfrac{7}{8}$ ⬤ $\dfrac{9}{16}$

18. $\dfrac{5}{3}$ ⬤ $\dfrac{11}{6}$

19. $2\dfrac{1}{7}$ ⬤ $\dfrac{13}{7}$

Test Prep Choose the correct letter for each answer.

20. Algebra Solve $x - 2.4 = 1.8$.
(1-12)

  A 0.6   **B** 1.3   **C** 4.2   **D** 4.32   **E** NH

21. Which number is divisible by 9?
(4-2)

  F 27,723   **G** 6,543   **H** 72,817   **J** 92,036   **K** NH

LESSON

4-10

Understand
Plan
Solve
Look Back

Problem-Solving Application:
Using Fractions and Decimals

California Content Standard *Mathematical Reasoning 2.7): Make precise calculations and check the validity of the results from the context of the problem.*

Warm-Up Review

Compare. Write $<$, $>$, or $=$ for each ●.

1. $\frac{2}{3}$ ● $\frac{5}{6}$

2. $\frac{5}{9}$ ● $\frac{3}{5}$

3. $\frac{1}{4}$ ● 0.3

4. A baker sells 2.5 dozen rolls and $2\frac{1}{4}$ dozen bagels. How many more rolls than bagels did the baker sell?

The drawing at the right shows the floor plan of the Visitor's Center gift shop. The new manager is planning to rearrange the displays. She plans to use $\frac{1}{4}$ of the total space for postcards, $\frac{1}{3}$ for T-shirts, $\frac{1}{4}$ for hats, and $\frac{1}{6}$ for posters. Which display spaces will change and how?

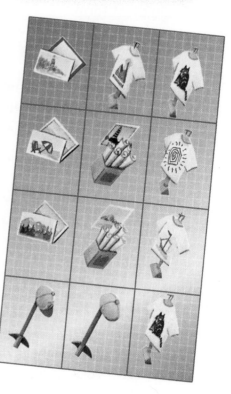

Understand

What do you need to find?

You need to know what fraction of the space is currently being used for each item and what fraction of the space each item will be given.

Plan

How can you solve the problem?

You can make a table to organize your information. Show the current display space, the planned space, and the comparison between the two.

Solve

The current space for T-shirts is greater than the planned space, so the space for T-shirts will decrease.

The current space for hats is less than the planned space, so the space for hats will increase.

The spaces for postcards and for posters will stay the same.

Item	Current Space	Planned Space	Comparison
Postcards	$\frac{1}{4}$	$\frac{1}{4}$	$\frac{1}{4} = \frac{1}{4}$
T-shirts	$\frac{5}{12}$	$\frac{1}{3} = \frac{4}{12}$	$\frac{5}{12} > \frac{1}{3}$
Hats	$\frac{1}{6} = \frac{2}{12}$	$\frac{1}{4} = \frac{3}{12}$	$\frac{1}{6} < \frac{1}{4}$
Posters	$\frac{1}{6}$	$\frac{1}{6}$	$\frac{1}{6} = \frac{1}{6}$

Look Back

How was understanding fractions useful in interpreting the floor plan diagram?

156   *Additional Standards: Mathematical Reasoning 2.2 (✎) (See p. 131.)*

Guided Practice

Use the prices shown at the right for Exercises 1–3.

1. What could you buy for exactly $20?

2. You have $50. Can you buy 4 hats and 5 posters? Explain.

3. You buy 2 T-shirts and pay with $40. How many hats can you buy with the change?

Independent Practice

Crystal Falls Park

22.75 miles

Cape Ernie Vistor's Center

22.9 miles

Castle Rock Lighthouse

22.3 miles

22.5 miles

Boathouse Restaurant

White Sands Beach

4. Which tourist attraction is closer to the Cape Ernie Visitor's Center—Crystal Falls Park or Castle Rock Lighthouse? How much closer is it?

5. You leave Castle Rock Lighthouse, pass the Visitor's Center, and continue on to the Boathouse Restaurant. Then you return to the Visitor's Center. How far do you travel?

Mixed Review

Use the table at the right for Exercises 6 and 7.

6. Paula tracked the diving habits of a whale on a chart like the one shown at the right. If the pattern continues, at what time will the whale come up from its sixth dive?

7. How much time did it take the whale to complete 4 dives?

Dive	Down	Up
1	8:00	8:05
2	8:06	8:11
3	8:12	8:17
4	8:18	8:23

(Use Homework Workbook 4-10.)

Diagnostic Checkpoint

Complete. For Exercises 1–4, use the words from the Word Bank.

Word Bank

base

composite number

equivalent fractions

exponent

improper fraction

least common denominator

mixed number

prime factorization

prime number

1. A _____ is a whole number greater than one with exactly two factors, itself and one.
(4-2)

2. You can use an _____ to tell how many times a number is used in a factorization.
(4-1)

3. You can make a factor tree to find the _____ of a composite number.
(4-2)

4. A _____ is a whole number greater than one that has more than two factors.
(4-2)

Write each fraction in simplest form.

5. $\dfrac{18}{14}$
(4-8)

6. $\dfrac{16}{36}$
(4-7)

7. $\dfrac{22}{24}$
(4-7)

8. $\dfrac{16}{100}$
(4-7)

9. $\dfrac{48}{114}$
(4-7)

Use the least common denominator to write like fractions.

10. $\dfrac{2}{9}, \dfrac{1}{4}$
(4-7)

11. $\dfrac{9}{2}, \dfrac{10}{7}$
(4-7)

12. $\dfrac{4}{5}, \dfrac{5}{8}$
(4-7)

13. $\dfrac{4}{9}, \dfrac{1}{6}, \dfrac{5}{12}$
(4-7)

14. $\dfrac{3}{5}, \dfrac{1}{6}, \dfrac{2}{3}$
(4-7)

In Exercises 15–18, write >, <, or = for each ⬤.

15. $\dfrac{2}{7}$ ⬤ $\dfrac{1}{3}$
(4-8)

16. $\dfrac{5}{8}$ ⬤ $\dfrac{3}{5}$
(4-8)

17. $\dfrac{5}{9}$ ⬤ $\dfrac{4}{7}$
(4-8)

18. $\dfrac{8}{9}$ ⬤ $\dfrac{7}{8}$
(4-8)

In Exercises 19–22, arrange in order from least to greatest.

19. $\dfrac{5}{7}, \dfrac{3}{8}, \dfrac{1}{2}$
(4-8)

20. $\dfrac{4}{9}, \dfrac{1}{3}, \dfrac{5}{6}$
(4-8)

21. $\dfrac{2}{5}, \dfrac{1}{2}, \dfrac{4}{9}$
(4-8)

22. $5\dfrac{3}{4}, 5\dfrac{11}{16}, 6$
(4-8)

Write each improper fraction as a mixed number and each mixed number as an improper fraction.

23. $\dfrac{44}{12}$
(4-8)

24. $\dfrac{31}{8}$
(4-8)

25. $5\dfrac{7}{8}$
(4-8)

26. $6\dfrac{2}{5}$
(4-8)

Write each fraction as a decimal and each decimal as a fraction in simplest form.

27. $\dfrac{16}{25}$
(4-9)

28. $\dfrac{5}{100}$
(4-9)

29. 0.55
(4-9)

30. 0.125
(4-9)

31. The distance from Waldo Station to Litchfield is $8\dfrac{1}{2}$ miles. The distance from Waldo Station to Monroe is 8.6 miles. Which town is farther from Waldo Station?
(4-10)

Chapter 4 Test

Evaluate.

1. 20^1

2. 0.3^3

3. $(n - 6)^5$ when $n = 8$

Use exponents to write the prime factorization.

4. 180

5. 175

6. 91

Find the greatest common factor for each set of numbers.

7. 8, 12

8. 7, 21

9. 10, 15, 20

Find the least common multiple for each set of numbers.

10. 4, 20

11. 16, 6

12. 9, 12

Arrange in order from least to greatest and place them on a number line.

13. $\frac{7}{8}, \frac{5}{6}, \frac{3}{4}$

14. $3\frac{3}{10}, 3\frac{4}{5}, 3\frac{1}{4}$

Write each improper fraction as a mixed number and each mixed number as an improper fraction.

15. $\frac{15}{7}$

16. $\frac{52}{6}$

17. $2\frac{7}{8}$

18. $5\frac{4}{9}$

Write each fraction as a decimal and each decimal as a fraction in simplest form.

19. $\frac{18}{20}$

20. $\frac{2}{25}$

21. 0.88

22. 0.25

23. At the opening of a new campsite, every third visitor wins a free cap. Every fifth visitor wins a T-shirt. Every tenth visitor wins a poster. Which visitors win all three prizes?

24. A dog kennel contains 48 dog pens. Half of the pens can hold 3 dogs each, $\frac{1}{4}$ of the pens can hold 2 dogs each, and the remaining pens hold only 1 dog each. Is it reasonable to say that the kennel can hold 100 dogs? Explain your answer.

25. A four-digit number contains all odd numbers. The two middle digits are the same number. Their sum is 14. The first digit is 4 less than the second digit. The fourth digit is the first digit to the second power. What is the four-digit number?

Multiple-Choice
Chapter 4 Test

Choose the correct letter for each answer.

1. Evaluate $3 + n^2$ when $n = 5$.

   A   60

   B   54

   C   28

   D   0

   E   NH

2. Which fraction is equivalent to $\frac{33}{60}$?

   F $\frac{1}{3}$

   G $\frac{27}{60}$

   H $\frac{11}{20}$

   J $\frac{9}{10}$

3. Liberty Bus Lines operates tours numbered 19, 39, 41, 51, 73, and 288. Only tours with prime numbers leave from Grand Station. Which tours do *not* leave from Grand Station?

   A   19, 39

   B   41, 51, 288

   C   19, 41, 51, 73

   D   39, 51, 288

4. Which of the following is equivalent to 0.35?

   F $\frac{35}{1,000}$ J $\frac{3}{5}$

   G $\frac{1}{3}$ K   NH

   H $\frac{7}{20}$

5. Which shows the following mixed numbers in order from least to greatest?

   $$4\frac{3}{4}, 4\frac{1}{2}, 4\frac{1}{4}, 4\frac{1}{8}$$

   A $4\frac{1}{2}, 4\frac{1}{4}, 4\frac{1}{8}, 4\frac{3}{4}$

   B $4\frac{1}{8}, 4\frac{3}{4}, 4\frac{1}{2}, 4\frac{1}{4}$

   C $4\frac{1}{4}, 4\frac{1}{2}, 4\frac{3}{4}, 4\frac{1}{8}$

   D $4\frac{1}{8}, 4\frac{1}{4}, 4\frac{1}{2}, 4\frac{3}{4}$

6. During the week, $\frac{3}{8}$ of the passengers go to Monroe, $\frac{1}{10}$ go to Litchfield, $\frac{1}{8}$ go to Mayville, and $\frac{2}{5}$ go to Lawndale. Where do most passengers go?

   F   Monroe   H   Mayville

   G   Litchfield   J   Lawndale

7. 612 is divisible by which numbers?

   A   2, 3, 4, 6, 9   C   2, 7, 8, 9

   B   2, 4, 5   D   2, 10, 15

8. Ryan traveled 4.2 miles on his bike, 4.2 miles in a car, 4.2 miles on his skates, and then 4.2 miles on foot. Which expression represents how far Ryan traveled?

   F $4.2 \times 4.2 \times 4.2$ H $4 + 4.2$

   G 4.2^4 J 4×4.2

9. What is the greatest common factor of 36 and 40?

A 2

B 4

C 40

D 360

10. Which shows the prime factorization of 20?

F $5 + 5 + 5 + 2 + 3$

G $2 \times 2 \times 3 \times 5$

H 20, 40, 60, 80

J $2 \times 2 \times 5$

11. 12 is the least common multiple of which set of numbers?

A 4, 2, 1, 0

B 24 and 48

C 4, 3, 1, 6

D 12 and 16

12. Which of the following show mixed numbers $9\frac{5}{8}$ and $6\frac{9}{10}$ as improper fractions?

F $\frac{77}{8}$ and $\frac{69}{10}$

G $\frac{77}{5}$ and $\frac{60}{9}$

H $\frac{22}{8}$ and $\frac{67}{10}$

J $\frac{67}{8}$ and $\frac{51}{10}$

13. What is the least common multiple of 50, 75, and 100?

A 25

B 200

C 300

D 500

E NH

14. Which clue describes the number 80,224?

F The digits are all even.

G The sum of the digits is odd.

H The digits are all divisible by 4.

J The difference between the first and last digits is 2.

15. To write $\frac{18}{54}$ in simplest form, divide both the numerator and the denominator by which number?

A 3

B 6

C 18

D 54

E NH

16. Which of the following is equivalent to $\frac{3}{8}$?

F 0.125

G 0.375

H 0.38

J 0.4

K 0.5

Reteaching

Set A *(pages 132–134)*

Use exponents to write
2 × 2 × 2 × 2 × 2.
Then evaluate.

$$2 \times 2 \times 2 \times 2 \times 2$$

$$\underbrace{}$$

5 factors

exponent

2^5

base

$2^5 = 32$

Remember an exponent shows how many times a number is used as a factor.

Use exponents to write each expression and then evaluate.

1. 6×6

2. $11 \times 11 \times 11$

3. $5 \times 5 \times 5 \times 5$

4. $0.2 \times 0.2 \times 0.2$

Set B *(pages 135–137)*

Is 93 divisible by 2, 3, 4, 5, 6, 9, or 10?
Since the last digit of 93 is 3, 93 is not divisible by 2, 5, or 10. Since 93 is not divisible by 2, it is not divisible by 4 or 6. Since the sum of the digits in 93 is 12 and 12 is divisible by 3, 93 is divisible by 3. The sum of the digits, 12, is not divisible by 9 so 93 is not divisible by 9.

Remember *divisible* means having no remainder after dividing. Remember to use the divisibility rules.

Tell if each number is divisible by 2, 3, 4, 5, 6, 9, or 10.

1. 212 **2.** 69

3. 324 **4.** 50

Set C *(pages 140–141)*

Find the greatest common factor (GCF) of 30 and 10.
List the factors of 30 and 10.
30: 1, 2, 3, 5, 6, ⑩, 15, 30
10: 1, 2, 5, ⑩
The greatest common factor is 10.

Remember when finding the GCF, list the factors from least to greatest.

Find the greatest common factor (GCF).

1. 24, 36 **2.** 48, 112

3. 90, 162 **4.** 88, 154

Set D *(pages 144–145)*

Find the least common multiple of 4 and 9.

List the multiples of 4 and 9.

4: 4, 8, 12, 16, 20, 24, 28, 32, <u>36</u>
9: 9, 18, 27, <u>36</u>, 45, 54

The least common multiple is 36.

Remember to list multiples of the given numbers and select the smallest multiple common to all numbers given.

Find the least common multiple (LCM).

1. 10, 11 **2.** 4, 3, 2

3. 6, 15 **4.** 9, 7

Set E *(pages 148–150)*

Write $\frac{6}{7}$ and $\frac{1}{3}$ as equivalent fractions.

Find the LCM of the denominators.

7: 7, 14, <u>21</u>, 28

3: 3, 6, 9, 12, 15, 18, <u>21</u>, 24

Write equivalent fractions.

$\frac{6}{7} = \frac{6 \times 3}{7 \times 3} = \frac{18}{21}$

$\frac{1}{3} = \frac{1 \times 7}{3 \times 7} = \frac{7}{21}$

Remember two fractions with the same value are equivalent fractions.

Write equivalent fractions with the same denominator.

1. $\frac{6}{4}$, $\frac{16}{20}$ **2.** $\frac{8}{9}$, $\frac{2}{4}$

3. $\frac{7}{12}$, $\frac{2}{3}$ **4.** $\frac{1}{7}$, $\frac{3}{8}$

5. $\frac{3}{5}$, $\frac{7}{3}$ **6.** $\frac{7}{16}$, $\frac{5}{32}$

Set F *(pages 151–153)*

Compare. Write <, >, or = for the 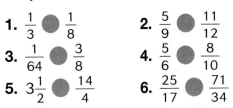**.**

$$\frac{2}{3} \quad \bullet \quad \frac{3}{6}$$

The LCM of 3 and 6 is 6. $\frac{2 \times 2}{3 \times 2} = \frac{4}{6}$

Now compare $\frac{4}{6}$ and $\frac{3}{6}$.

Since $\frac{4}{6} > \frac{3}{6}$, $\frac{2}{3} > \frac{3}{6}$.

Remember when comparing fractions, write equivalent fractions with the same denominator.

Compare. Write <, >, or = for each ●**.**

1. $\frac{1}{3}$ ● $\frac{1}{8}$ **2.** $\frac{5}{9}$ ● $\frac{11}{12}$

3. $\frac{1}{64}$ ● $\frac{3}{8}$ **4.** $\frac{5}{6}$ ● $\frac{8}{10}$

5. $3\frac{1}{2}$ ● $\frac{14}{4}$ **6.** $\frac{25}{17}$ ● $\frac{71}{34}$

Set G *(pages 154–155)*

Write $\frac{6}{8}$ as a decimal and write 0.14 as a fraction in simplest form.

$$\frac{6}{8} = 8\overline{)6.00} = 0.75$$
$$0.75$$
$$\underline{56}$$
$$40$$
$$\underline{-40}$$
$$0$$

$$0.14 = \frac{14}{100} = \frac{7}{50}$$

Remember to write a fraction as a decimal, divide the numerator by the denominator. To write a decimal as a fraction, use what you know about place value and simplify.

Write each fraction as a decimal and each decimal as a fraction in simplest form.

1. $\frac{4}{5}$ **2.** 0.68

3. 0.22   **4.** $\frac{3}{8}$

More Practice

Set A (pages 132–134)

Use exponents to write each expression.

1. 5×5 **2.** $10 \times 10 \times 10$ **3.** $2 \times 2 \times 2 \times 2$ **4.** $1 \times 1 \times 1 \times 1$

Evaluate.

5. 2^9 **6.** 5^5 **7.** 3^5 **8.** 12^3 **9.** 0^9

10. Every half hour a microbe splits and becomes two microbes. How many microbes will there be after three hours?

Set B (pages 135–137)

Tell if each number is divisible by 2, 3, 4, 5, 6, 9, 10, or none of these.

1. 78   **2.** 205   **3.** 97   **4.** 450

Write the prime factorization of each number. Use exponents.

5. 45   **6.** 84   **7.** 200   **8.** 150   **9.** 58

10. If there are 120 band members, can they line up in equal rows of 6 or equal rows of 9?

Set C (pages 140–141)

Find the greatest common factor for each set of numbers.

1. 5, 10   **2.** 21, 33   **3.** 12, 20   **4.** 14, 28, 49

5. Twenty-five tourists had their pictures taken by a photographer. Twenty tourists bought pictures. Is it true that $\frac{4}{5}$ of the tourists bought pictures?

Set D (pages 144–145)

Find the least common multiple for each set of numbers.

1. 5, 9   **2.** 9, 10   **3.** 6, 20   **4.** 2, 4, 6   **5.** 3, 6, 8

6. It takes Connie 5 minutes to swim one lap in the pool. It takes Joan 6 minutes. If they start together, after how many minutes will they both be at their starting point?

Set E (pages 148–150)

Write each fraction in simplest form.

1. $\frac{8}{10}$ **2.** $\frac{21}{28}$ **3.** $\frac{11}{22}$ **4.** $\frac{26}{32}$ **5.** $\frac{18}{63}$

Write the LCD for each set of fractions.

6. $\frac{3}{5}, \frac{1}{6}$ **7.** $\frac{9}{10}, \frac{3}{8}$ **8.** $\frac{5}{7}, \frac{3}{4}$ **9.** $2\frac{4}{9}, 1\frac{2}{3}$

10. Sarah has 25 postcards to mail. Of these, $\frac{1}{5}$ need stamps. If Sarah has 6 stamps, does she have enough?

Set F (pages 151–153)

Write each improper fraction as a mixed number or as a whole number. Write each mixed number as an improper fraction.

1. $\frac{23}{4}$ **2.** $\frac{9}{7}$ **3.** $\frac{12}{5}$ **4.** $\frac{18}{3}$ **5.** $\frac{25}{4}$

6. $\frac{53}{4}$ **7.** $6\frac{1}{2}$ **8.** $2\frac{3}{5}$ **9.** $2\frac{4}{9}$ **10.** $3\frac{5}{8}$

Compare. Write $<$, $>$, or $=$ for each .

11. $\frac{5}{8}$ ⬤ $\frac{4}{5}$ **12.** $\frac{3}{7}$ ⬤ $\frac{6}{14}$ **13.** $\frac{2}{3}$ ⬤ $\frac{3}{6}$ **14.** $\frac{7}{8}$ ⬤ $\frac{3}{4}$

Order from least to greatest.

15. $\frac{3}{7}, \frac{1}{3}, \frac{1}{5}$ **16.** $\frac{2}{3}, \frac{4}{5}, \frac{1}{2}$ **17.** $2\frac{3}{5}, 2\frac{5}{8}, 2\frac{1}{4}$

18. You have 5 oranges cut into thirds. How many friends could be given 2 pieces each if you save 1 piece for yourself?

Set G (pages 154–155)

Write each fraction as a decimal.

1. $\frac{3}{4}$ **2.** $\frac{27}{100}$ **3.** $\frac{6}{25}$ **4.** $7\frac{11}{20}$ **5.** $4\frac{3}{10}$

Write each decimal as a fraction in simplest form.

6. 0.4   **7.** 0.48   **8.** 0.01   **9.** 0.64   **10.** 0.875

11. Gina skied 2.8 miles in 5 minutes. Ronnie skied $2\frac{7}{8}$ miles in the same time. Who skied faster?

Problem Solving: Preparing for Tests

Choose the correct letter for each answer.

1. A magazine reporter found that of 350 readers, 2 out of 7 wanted more articles on sports. How many of these readers do NOT want more articles on sports?

   A   50

   B   100

   C   140

   D   250

   Tip

   Look at the facts that are given. Make sure your answer makes sense compared to those facts.

   MORE SPORTS   OK AS IS

2. Irma works more than 1 hour but fewer than 4 hours a day for 5 days a week at an after-school job. She earns $5.25 per hour. Which of these is a reasonable amount for Irma to expect to earn in 1 month?

   F $75

   G $100

   H $300

   J $800

   Tip

   Make a Table using 1, 2, 3, and 4 hours each day.

3. Angela used her computer to send an e-mail message to each of 3 friends. Each of them sent the message to 2 people. Then each of those people sent the message to 4 more people. How many people altogether read Angela's message?

   A   9

   B   21

   C   24

   D   33

   Tip

   Use one of the strategies to solve this problem.
   - *Find a Pattern*
   - *Draw a Diagram*
   - *Use Logical Reasoning*

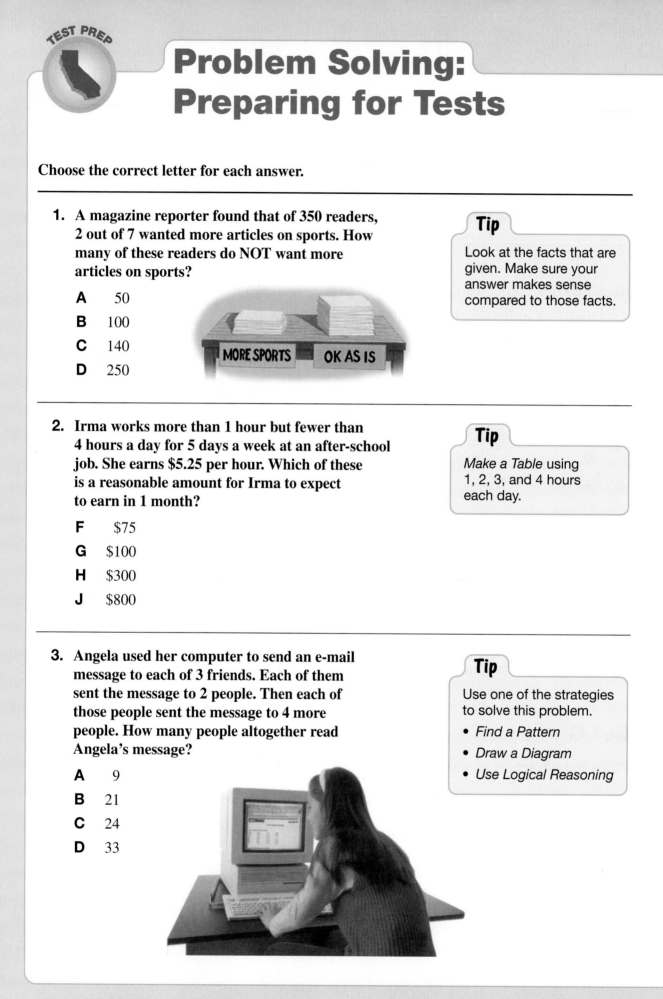

4. Volunteers serve about 370 meals a month. If lunch and dinner are served every day, what is a good estimate for the number of meals served each year?

   F   Fewer than 3,000

   G   Between 3,000 and 3,500

   H   Between 3,500 and 4,500

   J   Between 5,000 and 6,000

5. A plane flies 789 miles in about 3 hours. Which is the best estimate of how far it can fly in 5 hours?

   A   Less than 800 miles

   B   Between 800 and 1,000 miles

   C   Between 1,000 and 2,000 miles

   D   About 3,000 miles

6. Which is the best interpretation of the information shown on this graph?

   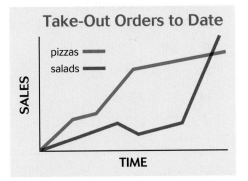

   Take-Out Orders to Date

   pizzas ——
   salads ——

   SALES

   TIME

   F   At present, salad sales are greater than pizza sales.

   G   Pizza sales are increasing, and salad sales are decreasing.

   H   Both pizzas and salads are decreasing.

   J   At present, more pizzas are sold than salads.

7. A survey showed that 72 people owned videotape players. This was more than $\frac{1}{3}$ of the people in the survey. Of the people surveyed, $\frac{1}{8}$ owned CD players. Which of these is a reasonable number of people in the survey?

   A   24   C   200

   B   25   D   250

8. A diagonal is a line segment that connects 2 vertices of a polygon and is not a side. Diane made a design by drawing the rest of the diagonals on a pentagon like this one. What shape was her design?

   F   Star

   G   Triangle

   H   Circle

   J   The letter A

9. Ann has $1.70 in her pocket. She has only dimes and quarters. Which number sentence could represent T, the total value of the coins?

   A $T = (2 \times 0.10) + (2 \times 0.25)$

   B $T = (2 \times 0.10) + (6 \times 0.25)$

   C $T = (6 \times 0.10) + (6 \times 0.25)$

   D $T = (8 \times 0.10) + (8 \times 0.25)$

10. A restaurant cuts pizzas into 8 equal slices. One night it sold 50 slices of pizza. How many pizzas did it cut?

    F   6

    G   7

    H   48

    J   50

Multiple-Choice Cumulative Review

Choose the correct letter for each answer.

Number Sense

1. Which fraction is equivalent to $\frac{9}{12}$?

A $\frac{2}{3}$ **C** $\frac{7}{10}$

B $\frac{4}{6}$ **D** $\frac{6}{8}$

2. Mark wants to arrange the drill bits in his toolbox by diameter in groups from least to greatest. He has $\frac{1}{4}$-inch, $\frac{1}{8}$-inch, and $\frac{1}{2}$-inch bits. Which list shows the order in which he should put them?

F $\frac{1}{8}, \frac{1}{4}, \frac{1}{2}$ **H** $\frac{1}{4}, \frac{1}{8}, \frac{1}{2}$

G $\frac{1}{2}, \frac{1}{8}, \frac{1}{4}$ **J** $\frac{1}{2}, \frac{1}{4}, \frac{1}{8}$

3. Which expression shows 18 as a product of prime factors?

A 2×9

B 3×6

C $2 \times 3 \times 3$

D 1×18

4. What decimal number does this model represent?

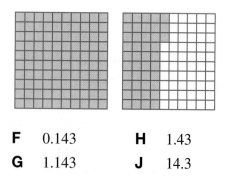

F 0.143   **H** 1.43

G 1.143   **J** 14.3

Algebra and Functions

5. Which number is missing from this pattern?

$10 \times 1 = 10$
$10 \times 10 = 100$
$10 \times 100 = 1,000$
$10 \times \blacksquare = 10,000$

A   1,000

B   10,000

C   100,000

D   1,000,000

6. Jack estimates that he passes by the same corner an average of 12 times a week. Which number sentence should you use to find out how many times Jack passes that corner in a year?

F $365 \div 12 = x$

G $12 \times (52 + 7) = x$

H $52 \times 12 = x$

J $52 \times (12 \times 7) = x$

7. The following points are plotted on a coordinate plane

$(0, 0), (1, 2), (2, 4), (3, 6)$

If the same pattern is continued, which would be the next point plotted?

A $(3, 7)$

B $(4, 7)$

C $(4, 8)$

D $(4, 10)$

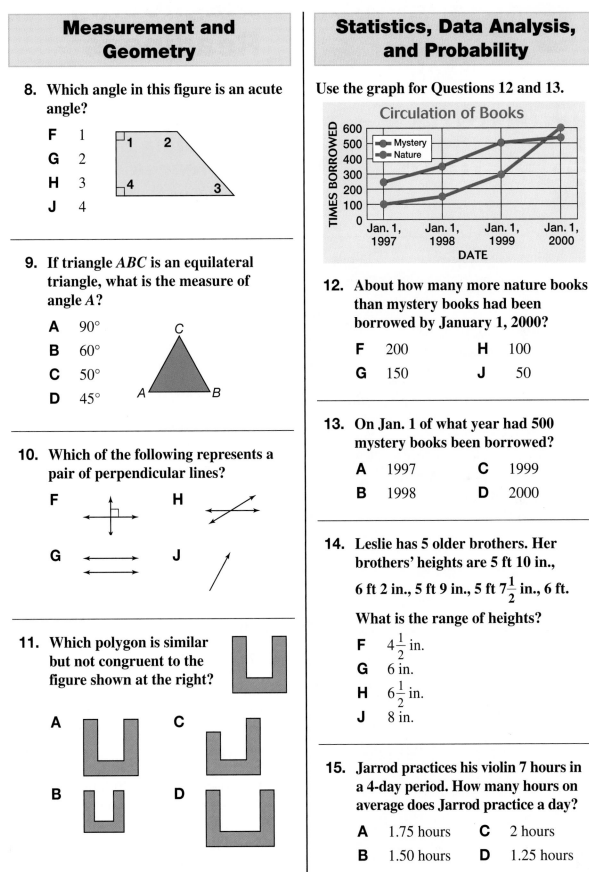

Measurement and Geometry

8. Which angle in this figure is an acute angle?

F 1
G 2
H 3
J 4

9. If triangle *ABC* is an equilateral triangle, what is the measure of angle *A*?

A 90°
B 60°
C 50°
D 45°

10. Which of the following represents a pair of perpendicular lines?

F

H

G

J

11. Which polygon is similar but not congruent to the figure shown at the right?

A

C

B

D

Statistics, Data Analysis, and Probability

Use the graph for Questions 12 and 13.

Circulation of Books

12. About how many more nature books than mystery books had been borrowed by January 1, 2000?

F 200   **H** 100
G 150   **J** 50

13. On Jan. 1 of what year had 500 mystery books been borrowed?

A 1997   **C** 1999
B 1998   **D** 2000

14. Leslie has 5 older brothers. Her brothers' heights are 5 ft 10 in., 6 ft 2 in., 5 ft 9 in., 5 ft $7\frac{1}{2}$ in., 6 ft.

What is the range of heights?

F $4\frac{1}{2}$ in.
G 6 in.
H $6\frac{1}{2}$ in.
J 8 in.

15. Jarrod practices his violin 7 hours in a 4-day period. How many hours on average does Jarrod practice a day?

A 1.75 hours   **C** 2 hours
B 1.50 hours   **D** 1.25 hours

Fraction Operations

Diagnosing Readiness

In Chapter 5, you will use these skills:

Ⓐ Estimating Sums and Differences

(pages 12–19)

Estimate the following.

1. $1,987 + 2,103 - 669$

2. $103 + 987 - 482$

3. $10.784 + 21.34$

4. $89.34 - 67.87 - 2.07$

5. $73,924 - 22,821$

6. Lola's mom purchased a new couch for $1,279.36, a loveseat for $1,023.99, and a chair for $923.77. About how much money did Lola's mom spend?

Ⓑ Estimating Products

(pages 52–54)

Estimate.

7. $18 \times 21 \times 9$

8. 88.2×3.8

9. $5.3 \times 21 \times 2.9$

10. 519×9.8

11. There were 87 students at the pep rally. The football stadium holds about 10 times that number of people. About how many people does the stadium hold?

C Simplifying Fractions

(pages 148–150)

Write each fraction in lowest terms.

12. $\frac{36}{252}$ **13.** $\frac{40}{72}$

14. A farmer has 54 cows, including 18 dairy cows. Simplify $\frac{18}{54}$.

D Writing Mixed Numbers as Improper Fractions and Improper Fractions as Mixed Numbers

(pages 151–153)

Write each mixed number as a improper fraction and each improper fraction as a mixed or whole number.

15. $31\frac{1}{2}$ **16.** $2\frac{3}{4}$

17. $\frac{11}{7}$ **18.** $\frac{71}{10}$

19. How many quarter-inch pieces of ribbon can be cut from a piece of ribbon $9\frac{1}{4}$ inches long? Use an improper fraction to help you decide.

E Writing Equivalent Fractions

(pages 148–150)

Determine if the fractions in each set are equivalent.

20. $\frac{15}{18}$ and $\frac{30}{48}$ **21.** $\frac{8}{12}$ and $\frac{48}{72}$

22. On a necklace, $\frac{8}{32}$ of the links are gold. On a bracelet, $\frac{4}{8}$ of the links are silver. Are $\frac{8}{32}$ and $\frac{4}{8}$ equivalent?

F Solving Addition and Subtraction Equations

(pages 30–31)

Solve for x.

23. $x - 7 = 103$ **24.** $16 = 8 + x$

25. If Sue had 8 more scarves, she would have a total of 22 scarves. How many scarves does she have?

G Finding the Least Common Denominator

(pages 148–150)

Write the fractions with their least common denominator.

26. $\frac{1}{6}$ and $\frac{4}{7}$ **27.** $\frac{4}{5}, \frac{1}{4},$ and $\frac{6}{10}$

28. Scott ran $\frac{7}{10}$ of a mile, Natalie ran $\frac{4}{6}$ of a mile. Who ran farther?

To the Family and Student

Looking Back	Chapter 5	Looking Ahead
In Grade 5, students learned how to add, subtract, multiply, and divide fractions.	In this chapter, students will add, subtract, multiply, and divide fractions to solve equations containing fractions.	In Chapter 9, students will develop an understanding of how fractions relate to percents.

Math and Everyday Living

Opportunities to apply the concepts of Chapter 5 abound in everyday situations. During the chapter, think about how manipulating fractions can be used to solve a variety of real-world problems. The following examples suggest just a few of the many situations that could launch a discussion about fractions.

Math in the Kitchen For a taco recipe, you need $2\frac{3}{4}$ cups of shredded cheese. You already have $1\frac{2}{3}$ cups of cheese shredded. How many more cups of cheese do you need to shred?

Math and Home Improvement You and your family need to paint the interior of your home. You estimate that you'll need $\frac{1}{4}$ gallon of paint for the bathroom, $1\frac{1}{2}$ gallons for the family room, and $1\frac{1}{2}$ gallons for the master bedroom. How much paint will you need in all?

Math in the Car When you and your family leave your house in the morning, the car's gas tank is $\frac{3}{4}$ full. By the end of the day, the tank is only $\frac{1}{4}$ full. What fraction of the tank was used during the day?

Math and the Stock Market

Stock	PECO	DAINC
High (year)	$42\frac{3}{4}$	$21\frac{1}{8}$
Low (year)	$36\frac{7}{8}$	$16\frac{1}{3}$
Close (today)	$40\frac{1}{8}$	$19\frac{2}{3}$
Net Change	$\frac{1}{2}$	$\frac{3}{8}$

Your family owns PECO and DAINC stock. What is the difference in PECO's low and high price for the year?

Math and Real Estate Two years ago, your family decided to sell off $\frac{2}{5}$ of a 60-acre farm. This year they sold off $\frac{1}{3}$ of the remaining acreage. How much did your family sell in all?

Math and Construction

A concrete crew can pave $\frac{3}{8}$ of the sidewalk in front of your home in one day. If the sidewalk is 200 feet long, how many days will it take the crew to pave the entire sidewalk?

Math on the Job You create a weekly schedule for the library volunteers. Use the schedule below to find out how many hours per week each volunteer works.

Name	Days	Hours per Day
Marin	6	$3\frac{1}{2}$
Clara	2	$6\frac{1}{3}$
Julia	3	$4\frac{2}{3}$
Beau	3	$8\frac{1}{4}$
Gray	4	$2\frac{5}{6}$

California Content Standards in Chapter 5 Lessons*

Number Sense	Teach and Practice	Practice
2.0 Students calculate and solve problems involving addition, subtraction, multiplication, and division.		5-2, 5-3, 5-4, 5-5, 5-7, 5-8, 5-9, 5-10, 5-11
2.1 Solve problems involving addition, subtraction, multiplication, and division of positive fractions and explain why a particular operation was used for a given situation.	5-2, 5-7	5-4, 5-5, 5-8, 5-10, 5-11
2.2 Explain the meaning of multiplication and division of positive fractions and perform the calculations.	5-8	5-7, 5-10
2.4 (🔑) Determine the least common multiple and the greatest common divisor of whole numbers; use them to solve problems with fractions (e.g., to find a common denominator, to add two fractions, or to find the reduced form for a fraction).	5-4	5-10

Algebra and Functions	Teach and Practice	Practice
1.1 (🔑) Write and solve one-step linear equations in one variable.	5-5, 5-10, 5-11	

Mathematical Reasoning	Teach and Practice	Practice
1.1 Analyze problems by identifying relationships, distinguishing relevant from irrelevant information, identifying missing information, sequencing and prioritizing information, and observing patterns.		5-1, 5-3, 5-7, 5-11
1.3 Determine when and how to break a problem into simpler parts.	5-3	5-9
2.0 Students use strategies, skills, and concepts in finding solutions.	5-1, 5-6	
2.1 Use estimation to verify the reasonableness of calculated results.		5-2, 5-7
2.2 Apply strategies and results from simpler problems to more complex problems.	5-9	
2.4 Use a variety of methods such as words, numbers, symbols, charts, graphs, tables, diagrams, and models to explain mathematical reasoning.		5-3
3.2 Note the method of deriving the solution and demonstrate a conceptual understanding of the derivation by solving similar problems.		5-9

* The symbol (🔑) indicates a key standard as designated in the Mathematics Framework for California Public Schools. Full statements of the California Content Standards are found at the beginning of this book following the Table of Contents.

Estimating Sums and Differences

Warm-Up Review

Estimate.

1. $4.2 + 3.9$

2. $3.24 - 0.65$

3. $10.88 - 8.29$

4. $0.99 + 86$

5. Jordan grew 1.75 inches one year, 2.25 inches the next, and 2 inches the third. Estimate the mean amount he grew per year.

Math Link You know how to estimate when adding and subtracting decimals. Now you will learn how to estimate when adding and subtracting mixed numbers.

Example 1

Bonsai trees originated in China about 1,000 years ago. About how much taller is the sneaker than the tree?

Estimate: $5\frac{15}{16} - 4\frac{5}{8}$

You can round each number to estimate.

Use the number line to help you round.

$5\frac{15}{16}"$ $4\frac{5}{8}"$

$4\frac{5}{8}"$ $5\frac{15}{16}"$

Step 1 Look at the number line above.	**Step 2** Round each number to the nearest whole number.	**Step 3** Subtract.
$5\frac{15}{16}$ is closer to 6 than to 5.	$5\frac{15}{16} - 4\frac{5}{8}$	$6 - 5 = 1$
$4\frac{5}{8}$ is closer to 5 than to 4.	$6 \quad - \quad 5$	

The sneaker is about 1 inch taller than the bonsai tree.

Example 2

Is $5\frac{3}{8}$ a reasonable answer for $3\frac{3}{8} + 1\frac{5}{8} + 2\frac{3}{8}$?

Estimate by finding a range: $3 + 1 + 2 = 6$
$4 + 2 + 3 = 9$

The answer should be between 6 and 9, so $5\frac{3}{8}$ is not a reasonable answer.

Additional Standard: Mathematical Reasoning 1.1 (See p. 173.)

Guided Practice
For another example, see Set A on p. 206.

Estimate.

1. $2\frac{2}{3} + \frac{3}{4}$ **2.** $1\frac{7}{8} + 2\frac{1}{4}$ **3.** $4\frac{1}{10} - 2\frac{11}{12}$ **4.** $3\frac{9}{10} - 1\frac{1}{3}$

5. During a camping trip, Karyn hiked a total of $17\frac{1}{2}$ miles. On Saturday, the last day of the trip, she hiked $2\frac{1}{4}$ miles in the morning and $3\frac{1}{2}$ miles in the afternoon. Estimate how much she hiked before Saturday.

Independent Practice
For more practice, see Set A on p. 208.

Estimate.

6. $4\frac{7}{8} + 19\frac{2}{7}$ **7.** $1\frac{9}{10} + \frac{1}{6}$ **8.** $16\frac{7}{16} - 3\frac{4}{5}$ **9.** $5\frac{4}{5} + 6\frac{1}{12}$

10. $2\frac{5}{6} - \frac{1}{4}$ **11.** $5\frac{2}{3} + 7\frac{9}{10}$ **12.** $\frac{5}{8} + 9\frac{1}{10}$ **13.** $18\frac{3}{8} - 5\frac{4}{5}$

Use the map for Exercises 14–18.

The map shows four hiking trails. The length of each hiking trail is shown in miles.

14. About how much shorter is Trail A than Trail B?

15. If you hiked Trail D in the morning and Trail C in the afternoon, about how far would you hike?

Trail Map

Trail D $1\frac{7}{10}$ mi

North

Trail C $6\frac{1}{8}$ mi

Trail A $3\frac{3}{4}$ mi   Start

Trail B $7\frac{2}{3}$ mi

Mixed Review

16. Which trail is the longest? the shortest?

Use a decimal to represent the length

17. of Trail D.   **18.** of Trail A.

Test Prep   Choose the correct letter for each answer.

Use the stem-and-leaf plot at the right for Exercises 19 and 20.

19. Find the median.
(3-3)

    A 10   **B** 44   **C** 46   **D** 83

20. Find the mode.
(3-3)

    F 10   **G** 44   **H** 46   **J** 83

Number of CDs Owned	
Stem	Leaves
1	003
2	56
4	147
6	358
9	13

(Use Homework Workbook 5-1.) **175**

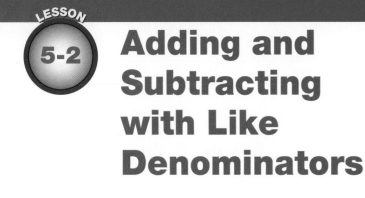

Adding and Subtracting with Like Denominators

Warm-Up Review

Express each fraction or mixed number in simplest form.

1. $\frac{8}{10}$ 2. $1\frac{6}{8}$

3. $\frac{9}{12}$ 4. $\frac{8}{24}$

5. $\frac{10}{15}$ 6. $3\frac{12}{15}$

7. John has $2\frac{1}{4}$ yards of red cloth, $3\frac{3}{4}$ yards of blue cloth, and $2\frac{2}{3}$ yards of yellow cloth. About how much cloth does he have to use for a red and blue banner?

California Content Standard *Number Sense 2.1: Solve problems involving addition, subtraction, . . . of positive fractions . . ..*

Math Link You know how to estimate sums and differences of fractions and mixed numbers. Now you will learn how to find the exact sum or difference of these numbers.

Example 1

Find $\frac{3}{8} + \frac{1}{8}$.

Step 1 Add the numerators. Use the common denominator.	**Step 2** Simplify if possible.
$\frac{3}{8} + \frac{1}{8} = \frac{4}{8}$ $\frac{3}{8} + \frac{1}{8} = \frac{1}{2}$	$\frac{3}{8} + \frac{1}{8} = \frac{4}{8} = \frac{1}{2}$

Here's WHy It Works

The fraction strips show 3 eighths + 1 eighth = 4 eighths. The fractions have like denominators.

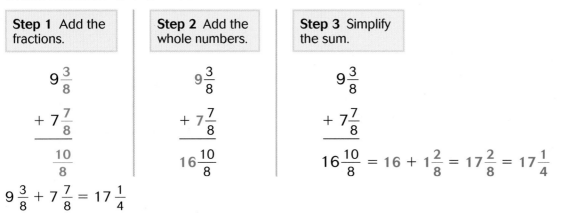

Example 2

Find $9\frac{3}{8} + 7\frac{7}{8}$.

Estimate first. Round each fraction to the nearest whole number: $9 + 8 = 17$

Step 1 Add the fractions.	**Step 2** Add the whole numbers.	**Step 3** Simplify the sum.
$9\frac{3}{8}$ $+ 7\frac{7}{8}$ $\overline{\frac{10}{8}}$	$9\frac{3}{8}$ $+ 7\frac{7}{8}$ $\overline{16\frac{10}{8}}$	$9\frac{3}{8}$ $+ 7\frac{7}{8}$ $\overline{16\frac{10}{8}} = 16 + 1\frac{2}{8} = 17\frac{2}{8} = 17\frac{1}{4}$

$9\frac{3}{8} + 7\frac{7}{8} = 17\frac{1}{4}$

Since $17\frac{1}{4}$ is close to 17, the answer is reasonable.

Additional Standards: Number Sense 2.0; Mathematical Reasoning 2.1 (See p. 173.)

Example 3

Find $\dfrac{7}{10} - \dfrac{3}{10}$.

Step 1 Subtract the numerators. Use the common denominator.

$$\dfrac{7}{10} - \dfrac{3}{10} = \dfrac{4}{10}$$

Step 2 Simplify if possible.

$$\dfrac{7}{10} - \dfrac{3}{10} = \dfrac{4}{10} = \dfrac{2}{5}$$

$$\dfrac{7}{10} - \dfrac{3}{10} = \dfrac{2}{5}$$

Example 4

Carmine has $4\dfrac{1}{4}$ cups of tomatoes. He will use $2\dfrac{3}{4}$ cups to make salsa. How many cups of tomatoes will be left?

To find out, subtract $4\dfrac{1}{4} - 2\dfrac{3}{4}$.

Estimate first: $4 - 3 = 1$

Step 1 You need to rename before you subtract because $\dfrac{1}{4} < \dfrac{3}{4}$.

$$4\dfrac{1}{4} = 3\dfrac{4}{4} + \dfrac{1}{4} = \quad\quad 3\dfrac{5}{4}$$
$$-\ 2\dfrac{3}{4} \quad\quad\quad\quad\quad -\ 2\dfrac{3}{4}$$

Step 2 Subtract the fractions and then the whole numbers. Simplify if possible.

$$3\dfrac{5}{4}$$
$$-\ 2\dfrac{3}{4}$$
$$\overline{1\dfrac{2}{4} = 1\dfrac{1}{2}}$$

There will be $1\dfrac{1}{2}$ cups of tomatoes left.

Since $1\dfrac{1}{2}$ is close to 1, the answer of $1\dfrac{1}{2}$ is reasonable.

More Examples

A. $3\dfrac{3}{8}$
$+\ 6\dfrac{5}{8}$
$\overline{9\dfrac{8}{8} = 9 + 1 = 10}$

B. $12\dfrac{5}{9}$
$\dfrac{8}{9}$
$+\ 9\dfrac{2}{9}$
$\overline{21\dfrac{15}{9} = 21 + 1\dfrac{6}{9} = 22\dfrac{6}{9} = 22\dfrac{2}{3}}$

C. $9\quad = 8\dfrac{5}{5}$
$-\ 2\dfrac{3}{5} = 2\dfrac{3}{5}$
$\overline{\quad\quad\quad 6\dfrac{2}{5}}$

Guided Practice *For another example, see Set B on p. 206.*

Add or subtract. Write each answer in simplest form.

1. $\dfrac{11}{15} - \dfrac{4}{15}$ 　　**2.** $\dfrac{1}{8} + \dfrac{3}{8}$ 　　**3.** $\dfrac{7}{8} - \dfrac{5}{8}$ 　　**4.** $\dfrac{7}{12} - \dfrac{3}{12}$ 　　**5.** $\dfrac{8}{9} - \dfrac{2}{9}$

Estimate first. Check that your answer is reasonable.

6. $4\dfrac{1}{3} - 2\dfrac{2}{3}$ 　　**7.** $8\dfrac{6}{8} + 4\dfrac{7}{8}$ 　　**8.** $3\dfrac{6}{7} + 1\dfrac{5}{7}$ 　　**9.** $6 - 4\dfrac{3}{4}$

10. Carmine has $\dfrac{3}{4}$ cup of chopped bell pepper. How much more does the recipe below call for?

Independent Practice *For more practice, see Set B on p. 208.*

Add or subtract. Write each answer in simplest form.

11. $\dfrac{7}{8} - \dfrac{3}{8}$ 　　**12.** $\dfrac{7}{11} + \dfrac{2}{11}$ 　　**13.** $\dfrac{3}{5} - \dfrac{2}{5}$ 　　**14.** $\dfrac{7}{9} + \dfrac{1}{9}$ 　　**15.** $\dfrac{8}{15} + \dfrac{11}{15}$

Estimate first. Check that your answer is reasonable.

16. $7\dfrac{1}{3} - 3\dfrac{2}{3}$ 　　**17.** $21\dfrac{7}{9} + 13$ 　　**18.** $10 - 7\dfrac{5}{6}$ 　　**19.** $15\dfrac{7}{8} + 4\dfrac{5}{8}$

Use the recipe for Exercises 20–22.

20. How many more cups of tomatoes are called for than cups of onions? Did you add or subtract to find the answer?

21. Sean is looking for two ingredients that when combined total 6 cups or more. Which ones might he choose? Did you add or subtract to find the answer?

Mixed Review

22. Math Reasoning Can the ingredients for the salsa recipe be mixed together in a bowl that holds 7 cups? Explain your answer.

Spicy Salsa

$4\frac{1}{4}$ cups fresh diced tomatoes

$\frac{3}{4}$ cup diced onion

$1\frac{1}{4}$ cups chopped bell pepper

$1\frac{3}{4}$ cups water

4 chili peppers

1 tsp. oregano

2 tsp. olive oil

✎ Test Prep　Choose the correct letter for each answer.

23. Algebra Solve $h - 4.6 = 5.4$ for h.
(1-12)

    A $h = 0.8$ 　　**C** $h = 10$

    B $h = 1.2$ 　　**D** $h = 24.84$

24. $\dfrac{1}{4} =$
(4-9)

    F 2.5 　　**H** 0.75

    G 1.4 　　**J** 0.25

Multiple-Choice Cumulative Review

Choose the correct letter for each answer.

1. Jim painted an ivy pattern on the kitchen wall. He put 3 leaves in the top row, 5 in the second row, and 7 in the third row. The next four rows had 11, 13, 15, and 19 leaves. If he continues this pattern, how many leaves will be in the *twelfth* row?

   A 23 leaves

   B 27 leaves

   C 31 leaves

   D 35 leaves

2. Which number sentence is NOT true?

   F $\frac{3}{8} > \frac{1}{4}$

   G $\frac{1}{2} = \frac{6}{12}$

   H $\frac{3}{4} < \frac{7}{8}$

   J $\frac{4}{5} > \frac{9}{10}$

3. Which are all of the prime numbers between 64 and 81?

   A 67, 69, 73, 79

   B 67, 71, 73, 79

   C 69, 73, 77, 79

   D 71, 73, 77, 81

4. Find $\frac{11}{12} + \frac{2}{12} + \frac{3}{12}$.

   F $\frac{1}{3}$ **H** $1\frac{1}{3}$

   G $\frac{4}{9}$ **J** $1\frac{7}{12}$

Use the graph for Questions 5–7.

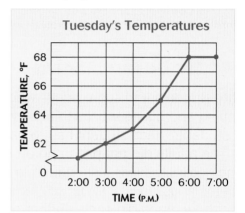

5. In what time interval did the temperature rise the most?

   A 2:00 – 3:00 P.M.

   B 3:00 – 4:00 P.M.

   C 4:00 – 5:00 P.M.

   D 5:00 – 6:00 P.M.

6. Which of the following is the best estimate for the temperature at 3:30 P.M.?

   F 63°F   **H** 61.5°F

   G 62.5°F   **J** 60.5°F

7. What was the change in temperature from 3:00 P.M. to 5:00 P.M.

   A 4°

   B 3.5°

   C 3°

   D 2.5°

Problem-Solving Skill:
Multistep Problems

California Content Standard *Mathematical Reasoning 1.3: Determine when and how to break a problem into simpler parts.*

Read for Understanding

Eighty students and some adults went on a three-day camping and hiking trip. Each adult was responsible for five students. Each student had to pay $120 to go on the trip. The adults did not pay to go on the trip. The amount of money collected was just enough to cover expenses for students and adults. If expenses for adults and students were the same, how much did each student contribute to the adults' expenses? What steps are needed to solve this problem?

1 How many students went on the trip?

2 For how many students was each adult responsible?

Think and Discuss

MATH FOCUS

Multistep Problems

Sometimes you need to find the answer to one or more questions before you can find the solution to a problem.

Reread the first paragraph on the page.

3 How many adults went on the trip? Explain how you know.

4 How many people went on the camping trip? Explain how you know.

5 How much money was collected? Explain how you know.

6 What is the cost per person? Explain how you know.

7 Subtract the cost per person from the amount each student paid to find how much each student contributed to the adults expenses.

Additional Standards: *Number Sense 2.0; Mathematical Reasoning 1.1, 2.4 (See p. 173.)*

Guided Practice

The pictures at the right show the departure time for campers as well as the time they spent at lunch and rest stops. The total driving time was $7\frac{1}{2}$ hours.

1. What steps do you need to follow to find when the bus will reach the campsite?

   a. Find the total number of hours driving, resting, and eating to the departure time.

   b. Add the number of stops the bus made to the departure time.

   c. Find the total number of hours driving and subtract the time spent on eating and resting. Add this total to the departure time.

2. Which statement best describes the time that the bus arrived at the campsite?

   a. 3:30 P.M., because they left at 8:00 A.M. and drove $7\frac{1}{2}$ hours

   b. 12:00 noon, because they left at 8:00 A.M. and made 4 stops

   c. 6:30 P.M., because they left at 8:00 A.M., made 3 hours worth of stops, and traveled for $7\frac{1}{2}$ hours

Independent Practice

Adults carried large backpacks that weighed $21\frac{5}{8}$ pounds each. The students carried smaller backpacks, which were $8\frac{1}{2}$ pounds lighter than those carried by the adults. Each person also carried a canteen weighing $1\frac{1}{4}$ pounds.

3. Which of these questions do you need to answer before you can find how much weight each student carried?

   a. How much did a small backpack weigh?

   b. How much more did a large backpack weigh than a small backpack?

   c. How many students went on the hike?

4. **Math Reasoning** How much weight did each student carry?

DEPARTURE

REST STOP $\frac{5}{6}$ h

LUNCH STOP $1\frac{1}{3}$ h

REST STOP $\frac{5}{6}$ h

ARRIVAL

Adding and Subtracting with Unlike Denominators

California Content Standard *Number Sense 2.4 (🔑): Determine the least common multiple . . . of whole numbers; use them to solve problems with fractions (e.g., to find a common denominator to add two fractions and to find the reduced form for a fraction).*

Math Link You can use what you know about finding the least common multiple to add and subtract fractions with unlike denominators.

Before you can add or subtract fractions with unlike denominators, you have to write equivalent fractions with like denominators. The **least common denominator** (LCD) is the least common multiple of the denominators of two or more fractions.

Warm-Up Review

Give the least common multiple for each pair of numbers.

1. 9, 6   **2.** 10, 7

3. 10, 15   **4.** 16, 28

5. A kitten weighed $1\frac{7}{8}$ pounds at birth. It lost $\frac{3}{8}$ pound and then gained $\frac{5}{8}$ pound. How much did it weigh then?

Word Bank

Least common denominator (LCD)

Example 1

Find $\frac{3}{4} - \frac{1}{3}$.

Step 1 Find the least common denominator (LCD) of the fractions.

$$\frac{3}{4}$$
$$-\frac{1}{3}$$

The LCD is 12.

Step 2 Write equivalent fractions.

$$\frac{3 \times 3}{4 \times 3} = \frac{9}{12}$$
$$-\frac{1 \times 4}{3 \times 4} = -\frac{4}{12}$$

Step 3 Subtract. Simplify, if possible.

$$\frac{9}{12}$$
$$-\frac{4}{12}$$
$$\frac{5}{12}$$

Example 2

Find $\frac{5}{12} + \frac{2}{15}$.

Step 1 Find the LCD.

$12 = 2 \times 2 \times 3$
$15 = \qquad 3 \times 5$

$2 \times 2 \times 3 \times 5 = 60$

Step 2 Write equivalent fractions.

$$\frac{5 \times 5}{12 \times 5} = \frac{25}{60}$$
$$\frac{2 \times 4}{15 \times 4} = \frac{8}{60}$$

Step 3 Add. Simplify, if possible.

$$\frac{25}{60}$$
$$+\frac{8}{60}$$
$$\frac{33}{60} = \frac{11}{20}$$

Additional Standards: Number Sense 2.0, 2.1 (See p. 173.)

Example 3

Students at an agricultural school planted two rows of corn. The first row of corn was given experimental plant food. The second row of corn was not given any plant food. The graph at the right shows growth over a five-week period. How many inches did the experimental plants grow during Weeks 4 and 5?

To find out, add $8\frac{2}{3} + 10\frac{3}{4}$.

Estimate first, using a range: $8 + 10 = 18$
$9 + 11 = 20$

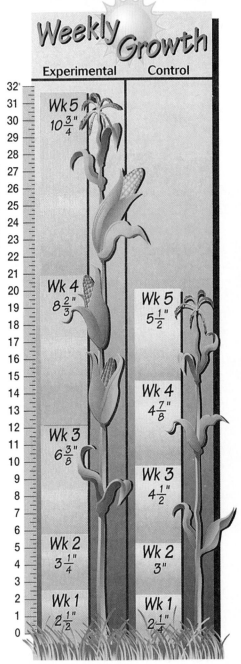

Step 1 Write equivalent fractions, using the LCD.	Step 2 Add. Simplify, if possible.
$8\frac{2}{3} = \quad 8\frac{8}{12}$ $+ 10\frac{3}{4} = + 10\frac{9}{12}$	$8\frac{8}{12}$ $+ 10\frac{9}{12}$ $18\frac{17}{12} = 18 + 1\frac{5}{12} = 19\frac{5}{12}$

The plants grew $19\frac{5}{12}$ inches.

The answer is reasonable because $19\frac{5}{12}$ is between 18 and 20.

Example 4

During Week 3, how many more inches did the experimental plants grow than the control plants?

To find out, subtract $6\frac{3}{8} - 4\frac{1}{2}$.

Estimate first: $6 - 5 = 1$

Step 1 Write equivalent fractions, using the LCD.	Step 2 Rename if you cannot subtract.	Step 3 Subtract. Simplify, if possible.
$6\frac{3}{8} = \quad 6\frac{3}{8}$ $- 4\frac{1}{2} = - 4\frac{4}{8}$	Rename $6\frac{3}{8}$. $6\frac{3}{8} = 5 + \frac{8}{8} + \frac{3}{8} = 5\frac{11}{8}$	$5\frac{11}{8}$ $- 4\frac{4}{8}$ $1\frac{7}{8}$

The experimental plants grew $1\frac{7}{8}$ inches more. The answer is reasonable because $1\frac{7}{8}$ is close to the estimate of 1.

More Examples

A.

$6\dfrac{9}{10} = 6\dfrac{18}{20}$

$4\dfrac{3}{4} = 4\dfrac{15}{20}$

$+\ 2\dfrac{2}{5} = 2\dfrac{8}{20}$

$12\dfrac{41}{20} = 12 + 2 + \dfrac{1}{20}$

$= 14\dfrac{1}{20}$

B.

$40\dfrac{1}{7} = \quad 40\dfrac{3}{21} = \quad 39\dfrac{24}{21}$

$-\ 15\dfrac{2}{3} = -\ 15\dfrac{14}{21} = -\ 15\dfrac{14}{21}$

$24\dfrac{10}{21}$

Guided Practice   *For another example, see Set C on p. 206.*

Add or subtract. Write each answer in simplest form.

1. $\dfrac{8}{9} + \dfrac{4}{15}$

2. $\dfrac{1}{9} + \dfrac{1}{6} + \dfrac{1}{30}$

3. $\dfrac{1}{2} - \dfrac{1}{10}$

4. $\dfrac{7}{8} - \dfrac{9}{32}$

Estimate first. Check that your answer is reasonable.

5. $9\dfrac{1}{4}$

$+\ 2\dfrac{1}{3}$

6. $6\dfrac{13}{15}$

$+\ 4\dfrac{2}{33}$

7. $12\dfrac{3}{8}$

$-\ 3\dfrac{7}{10}$

8. $6\dfrac{1}{7}$

$-\ 4\dfrac{2}{3}$

Use the graph at the right for Exercises 9–11.

9. A second plant-food experiment was carried out on pea plants. The double line graph at the right shows the results of the experiment. How much taller were the experimental plants than the control plants at the end of two weeks?

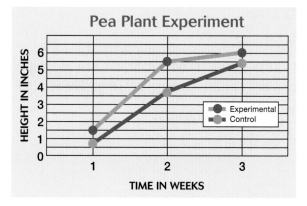

10. How much taller were the control plants at the end of three weeks than at the end of one week?

11. Which plants grew the most from Week 1 to Week 2?

Independent Practice   *For more practice, see Set C on p. 208.*

Add or subtract. Write each answer in simplest form.

12. $\dfrac{9}{20}$

$-\ \dfrac{2}{15}$

13. $\dfrac{7}{8}$

$-\ \dfrac{19}{32}$

14. $\dfrac{43}{48}$

$+\ \dfrac{1}{72}$

15. $\dfrac{3}{16}$

$+\ \dfrac{5}{24}$

Estimate first. Check that your answer is reasonable.

16. $2\frac{5}{16}$
$+ 1\frac{1}{4}$

17. $3\frac{5}{6}$
$- 1\frac{1}{3}$

18. $9\frac{1}{2}$
$- 4\frac{7}{8}$

19. $6\frac{2}{30}$
$+ 4\frac{3}{50}$

20. $6\frac{3}{8}$
$- 1\frac{1}{6}$

21. $5\frac{1}{15}$
$+ 9\frac{7}{30}$

22. $4\frac{9}{16}$
$- 1\frac{5}{8}$

23. 8
$- 7\frac{3}{5}$

24. A fruit salad recipe uses $4\frac{3}{8}$ cups of oranges, $2\frac{3}{4}$ cups of apples, and $3\frac{1}{3}$ cups of peaches. How many more cups of oranges does it use than cups of apples?

25. **Mental Math** Explain how you could add $\frac{2}{5} + \frac{4}{15} + \frac{3}{5}$ mentally.

26. **Math Reasoning** If you add two fractions that are each less than $\frac{1}{2}$, will you ever get a sum greater than 1? Explain your answer.

27. **Math Reasoning** When you subtract a mixed number from a whole number, will the difference be a mixed number, a fraction, or a whole number? Explain.

Mixed Review

28. Look at the graph "Pea Plant Experiment" on page 184. If the graph was drawn with a vertical scale of 1 inch rather than $\frac{1}{2}$ inch, what impression would the graph give?

Estimate.

29. $1\frac{7}{8} + 10\frac{3}{4}$

30. $14\frac{1}{2} + 2\frac{1}{8}$

31. $8\frac{1}{3} - 3\frac{11}{12}$

32. $17\frac{3}{10} - 5\frac{7}{10}$

Add or subtract. Write each answer in simplest form.

33. $3 + 8\frac{5}{6} + 2\frac{1}{6}$

34. $7\frac{7}{10} - 2\frac{9}{10}$

35. $8\frac{1}{4} + 7\frac{3}{4} + 1\frac{3}{4}$

36. $7 - \frac{3}{8}$

Test Prep Choose the correct letter for each answer.

37. **Algebra** Evaluate $3a + (4b - 5c)$
(1-10) for $a = 12$, $b = 7$, and $c = 4$.

   A 25
   B 44
   C 63
   D 305

38. Evaluate 5^3.
(4-1)

   F 243
   G 125
   H 15
   J 8

Solving Addition and Subtraction Equations

Algebra

California Content Standard *Algebra and Functions 1.1 (🔑): Write and solve one-step linear equations in one variable.*

Math Link You know how to solve equations with whole numbers and decimals. Now you will solve equations with fractions.

Example 1

The miniature barrel cactus at the right grows in Mexico.

One day the bloom was $\frac{1}{2}$ inch tall. Then it grew to a height of $\frac{3}{4}$ inch. How much did it grow to reach the new height?

You can write an equation to solve the problem.

Let x represent the amount of growth.

$$\frac{1}{2} + x = \frac{3}{4}$$
To undo addition, subtract $\frac{1}{2}$ from *both* sides.

$$\frac{1}{2} + x - \frac{1}{2} = \frac{3}{4} - \frac{1}{2}$$

$$\frac{1}{2} + x - \frac{1}{2} = \frac{3}{4} - \frac{2}{4}$$
Write the fractions with their LCD.

$$x = \frac{1}{4}$$

The cactus grew $\frac{1}{4}$ inch.

Warm-Up Review

Solve each equation.

1. $m - 87 = 97$

2. $a + 13 = 41$

3. $d + 3 = 6.2$

4. Shauna spent $1\frac{2}{3}$ hours practicing and $1\frac{3}{4}$ hours doing homework. She has $5\frac{1}{2}$ hours after school until bedtime. How much free time does she have?

Example 2

Solve $m - 3\frac{2}{3} = 18\frac{3}{5}$.

$$m - 3\frac{2}{3} + 3\frac{2}{3} = 18\frac{3}{5} + 3\frac{2}{3}$$
To undo subtraction, add $3\frac{2}{3}$ to each side.

$$m - 3\frac{2}{3} + 3\frac{2}{3} = 18\frac{9}{15} + 3\frac{10}{15}$$
Write the fractions with their LCD.

$$m = 21\frac{19}{15}$$
Add.

$$m = 22\frac{4}{15}$$
Simplify.

Check:

$$m - 3\frac{2}{3} = 18\frac{3}{5}$$
Write the equation.

$$22\frac{4}{15} - 3\frac{2}{3} \stackrel{?}{=} 18\frac{3}{5}$$
Replace m with $22\frac{4}{15}$.

$$21\frac{19}{15} - 3\frac{10}{15} \stackrel{?}{=} 18\frac{9}{15}$$
Subtract.

$$18\frac{9}{15} = 18\frac{9}{15}$$
The answer checks.

 Additional Standards: Number Sense 2.0, 2.1 (See p. 173.)

Guided Practice *For another example, see Set D on p. 206.*

Solve each equation.

1. $n + \dfrac{3}{5} = 1$ **2.** $2\dfrac{1}{3} = x + 2\dfrac{1}{18}$ **3.** $a - \dfrac{5}{6} = \dfrac{1}{16}$ **4.** $y + 2\dfrac{1}{18} = 3\dfrac{1}{4}$

Write an equation. Then solve.

5. Sonja walked $\dfrac{3}{4}$ mile farther than Duane did. If Sonja walked $\dfrac{9}{10}$ mile, how far did Duane walk?

Independent Practice *For more practice, see Set D on p. 208.*

Solve each equation.

6. $x - 6\dfrac{1}{4} = 3$ **7.** $d - 5 = 8\dfrac{1}{6}$ **8.** $12\dfrac{2}{5} = x - \dfrac{11}{15}$ **9.** $c + 2\dfrac{1}{2} = 7\dfrac{3}{4}$

Write an equation. Then solve.

10. At the end of the school year, Aaron's height was $62\dfrac{1}{2}$ inches. During the school year, he had grown $2\dfrac{1}{2}$ inches. What was his height at the beginning of the school year?

11. Jack cut $8\dfrac{3}{16}$ feet off the beanstalk. The beanstalk is now $1\dfrac{12}{16}$ feet tall. How high was the beanstalk before it was cut?

Mixed Review

12. Math Reasoning Explain how you could use addition properties to find $3\dfrac{1}{5} + 15\dfrac{3}{5}$ mentally.

Estimate first. Check that your answer is reasonable.

13. $8\dfrac{3}{5} + 6\dfrac{2}{5}$ **14.** $13\dfrac{5}{12} - 9\dfrac{11}{12}$ **15.** $12\dfrac{7}{12} - 7\dfrac{3}{8}$ **16.** $12\dfrac{5}{18} + 9\dfrac{1}{24}$

Test Prep   Choose the correct letter for each answer.

Miranda put 10.4 gallons of gas in her car and paid $19.66. She thinks she uses about a half gallon of gas each day.

17. Which number in the paragraph is
(1-3) an estimate?

    A Gallons of gas Miranda bought

    B Amount Miranda paid

    C Gallons of gas Miranda uses

    D All are exact.

18. How many days can Miranda drive
(2-5) on 10.4 gallons of gas?

    F About 5 days

    G About 10 days

    H About 15 days

    J About 20 days

Diagnostic Checkpoint

Estimate.

1. $3\frac{5}{9} - 2\frac{1}{8}$
(5-1)

2. $9\frac{1}{3} + 8\frac{5}{6}$
(5-1)

3. $\frac{7}{11} + 7\frac{1}{16}$
(5-1)

4. $22\frac{6}{14} + 4\frac{1}{4}$
(5-1)

5. $6\frac{4}{5} + 7\frac{11}{12}$
(5-1)

6. $15\frac{1}{13} - 4\frac{9}{12}$
(5-1)

7. $10\frac{3}{20} - 6\frac{9}{13}$
(5-1)

8. $78\frac{16}{19} - 41$
(5-1)

Add or subtract. Write each answer in simplest form.

9. $15\frac{1}{10}$
(5-2)
$+ 3\frac{3}{10}$

10. $4\frac{13}{15}$
(5-2)
$- 2\frac{1}{15}$

11. $3\frac{2}{3}$
(5-2)
$+ 7\frac{1}{3}$

12. $6\frac{3}{5}$
(5-2)
$- 4\frac{2}{5}$

13. $6\frac{11}{12}$
(5-2)
$- 3\frac{1}{12}$

14. $\frac{9}{8} + \frac{6}{8}$
(5-2)

15. $\frac{21}{60} + \frac{18}{60}$
(5-2)

16. $4 - 2\frac{1}{4}$
(5-2)

17. $\frac{11}{13} + \frac{2}{13}$
(5-2)

18. $\frac{2}{3}$
(5-4)
$+ \frac{1}{9}$

19. $\frac{9}{10}$
(5-4)
$- \frac{3}{4}$

20. $7\frac{3}{5}$
(5-4)
$+ 5\frac{2}{3}$

21. $3\frac{3}{5}$
(5-4)
$+ 5\frac{3}{4}$

22. $8\frac{7}{12}$
(5-4)
$- 3\frac{1}{4}$

23. $\frac{17}{20} - \frac{3}{10}$
(5-4)

24. $\frac{11}{12} + \frac{5}{6}$
(5-4)

25. $4\frac{1}{8} + 3\frac{5}{6}$
(5-4)

26. $2\frac{1}{2} + 1\frac{1}{3}$
(5-4)

Solve each equation.

27. $x - 6 = 3\frac{1}{4}$
(5-5)

28. $a + 5 = 8\frac{1}{5}$
(5-5)

29. $12\frac{1}{5} = x - \frac{1}{5}$
(5-5)

30. $y + 2 = 7\frac{1}{2}$
(5-5)

31. $9\frac{1}{2} = x + 1\frac{1}{2}$
(5-5)

32. $c + \frac{2}{3} = 1\frac{2}{3}$
(5-5)

33. $d + \frac{5}{8} = 6\frac{5}{8}$
(5-5)

34. $n - 3 = 4\frac{1}{5}$
(5-5)

35. Lynda mows lawns to make money. It took her 10 hours to
(5-3)
mow 4 lawns. She spent $2\frac{3}{4}$ hours on each of two lawns and
$1\frac{1}{4}$ hours on the third lawn. How many hours did she spend on
the fourth lawn?

36. Jeff walked $\frac{1}{2}$ of a mile. Fred walked $\frac{11}{12}$ of a mile. Who walked
(5-3)
farther? How many miles farther?

37. Colleen has a mixing bowl that holds 7 cups. She puts in
(5-3)
$2\frac{1}{4}$ cups of carrots and $\frac{3}{4}$ cup of onions. How many more cups
of vegetables can the bowl hold?

Multiple-Choice Cumulative Review

Choose the correct letter for each answer.

1. Which number is the least common multiple of 6 and 15?

   A   3   C   30   E   NH

   B   21   D   60

2. Maria is saving for a new computer. This chart shows the amount of money in Maria's savings account.

Week	1	2	3	4	5
Dollars	$55	$56	$59	$64	$71

   If Maria's savings continue in this pattern, how much money will be in her account at the end of 8 weeks?

   F $102   H $104

   G $103   J $105

3. The distance from Allison's house to Ted's house is $6\frac{7}{8}$ miles. To Jay's house it is $5\frac{11}{12}$ miles. How much farther is it to Ted's house?

   A $12\frac{1}{12}$ miles   C $\frac{23}{24}$ mile

   B $1\frac{3}{24}$ miles   D $\frac{1}{8}$ mile

4. By which group of numbers is 5,490 divisible?

   F   2, 3, 4, 10

   G   2, 3, 5, 6, 9, 10

   H   2, 5, 8, 9, 10

   J   2, 4, 6, 8, 10

   K   NH

5. Lee earns $15 per yard for mowing lawns and $5 per yard for trimming bushes. If Lee mows 3 yards and trims the bushes at 2 of them, how much money will she earn?

   A $45   C $55

   B $50   D $60

6. Which is the greatest common factor of 75 and 100?

   F   5   H   25   K   NH

   G   15   J   50

7. Which of the following statements is true?

   A $\frac{2}{3} + \frac{8}{9} < \frac{5}{8} + \frac{4}{8}$

   B $1 + \frac{7}{9} > \frac{11}{12}$

   C $\frac{10}{11} + \frac{2}{15} < \frac{10}{11} - \frac{5}{6}$

   D $\frac{4}{3} - \frac{3}{7} < \frac{1}{2}$

8. A decorative wreath contains 56 ruby-red plastic berries. A company made 1,825 wreaths. How many berries did they use?

   F   102,200 berries

   G   102,000 berries

   H   91,250 berries

   J   1,763 berries

Estimating Products

Warm-Up Review

Estimate first. Then multiply.

1. 48.2×3.56

2. 41.8×7.6

3. You earned $8.50 an hour for 4.5 hours and $7.50 an hour for 2.5 hours. How much did you earn in all?

California Content Standard *Mathematical Reasoning 2.0: Students use strategies, skills, and concepts in finding solutions.*

Math Link You know how to estimate when multiplying decimals. Now you will learn how to estimate when multiplying fractions and mixed numbers.

Example 1

Lee and some friends have a delivery service. Stores pay them to deliver packages by bicycle to customers.

Lee figures that the average distance he travels each hour is $4\frac{7}{8}$ miles. Last week Lee worked $18\frac{1}{4}$ hours. About how far did he travel?

Use rounding to estimate the product $4\frac{7}{8} \times 18\frac{1}{4}$.

Step 1 Round each mixed number to the nearest whole number.	**Step 2** Multiply the whole numbers.
$4\frac{7}{8} \times 18\frac{1}{4}$ ↓ ↓ 5 × 18	$5 \times 18 = 90$

Lee traveled about 90 miles.

Example 2

Use compatible numbers to estimate the product $\frac{1}{6} \times 53$.

Step 1 Change the whole number to the nearest number that is a multiple of the denominator of the fraction.	**Step 2** Simplify, then multiply.
$\frac{1}{6} \times 53$ $\frac{1}{6} \times 54$	$\frac{1}{\overset{}{6}} \times \overset{9}{\cancel{54}} = 1 \times 9 = 9$

$\frac{1}{6} \times 53$ is about 9.

Guided Practice *For another example, see Set E on p. 207.*

Estimate.

1. $12\frac{7}{8} \times 4\frac{2}{7}$ **2.** $\frac{1}{4} \times 122$ **3.** $\frac{1}{6} \times 177$ **4.** $49\frac{3}{4} \times 1\frac{5}{6}$ **5.** $\frac{3}{5} \times 219$

6. Dean works an average of $5\frac{3}{4}$ hours per day. Last week, he worked $4\frac{1}{4}$ days. About how many hours did he work?

Independent Practice *For more practice, see Set E on p. 209.*

Estimate.

7. $1\frac{5}{8} \times 120$ **8.** $3\frac{1}{8} \times 7\frac{5}{6}$ **9.** $\frac{7}{8} \times 245$ **10.** $5\frac{1}{3} \times 19\frac{1}{7}$ **11.** $\frac{3}{8} \times 162$

12. A store ordered 68 bags of onions. Each bag weighed about $4\frac{3}{4}$ pounds. Estimate the total weight of the shipment.

13. Math Reasoning Is 100 a reasonable estimate for the product of $1\frac{1}{3}$ and 120? Explain.

Mixed Review

Use the diagram for Exercises 14 and 15.

14. Estimate the total height of the three bonsai trees whose heights are given.

15. If Amanda is $62\frac{1}{2}$ inches tall, about how tall is the fourth tree?

16. $9\frac{3}{25} + 6\frac{7}{30}$

17. $9\frac{3}{18} - 7\frac{11}{12}$

Algebra Solve each equation.

18. $z - 38\frac{4}{5} = 102\frac{11}{15}$

19. $t - 20 = 99\frac{3}{7}$

$20\frac{5}{8}''$

$62\frac{1}{2}''$

$15\frac{7}{8}''$

$13\frac{7}{16}''$

> **Test Prep**   Choose the correct letter for each answer.

20. Which number is greatest?
(1-2)

   A 0.068   **B** 0.0068   **C** 0.68   **D** 0.6

21. 12.03×7
(2-2)

   F 8.421   **G** 8.0421   **H** 8.4021   **J** 842.1   **K** NH

Multiplying Fractions and Mixed Numbers

California Content Standard *Number Sense 2.1: Solve problems involving . . . multiplication . . . of positive fractions. . . .*

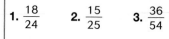

Warm-Up Review

Simplify each fraction.

1. $\frac{18}{24}$ 2. $\frac{15}{25}$ 3. $\frac{36}{54}$

Write each mixed number as an improper fraction.

4. $4\frac{1}{6}$ 5. $7\frac{2}{3}$ 6. $1\frac{7}{8}$

7. A rectangular garden is $12\frac{1}{2}$ feet wide and 18 feet long. What is the distance around the garden?

Math Link You know how to multiply whole numbers and decimals. Now you will learn how to multiply fractions and mixed numbers.

Example 1

Multiply $\frac{1}{6} \times \frac{4}{5}$.

Step 1 Multiply numerators. Then multiply denominators.

Step 2 Simplify, if possible.

$$\frac{1}{6} \times \frac{4}{5} = \frac{1 \times 4}{6 \times 5} = \frac{4}{30}$$

$$\frac{4 \div 2}{30 \div 2} = \frac{2}{15}$$

Here's WHY It Works

$\frac{4}{5}$ of the squares are shaded blue.

$\frac{1}{6}$ of the blue squares are shaded black.

$\frac{4}{30}$ of the squares are shaded blue and black.

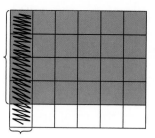

Example 2

Pat and Luna received an order from a local store for $5\frac{1}{2}$ sets of large buttons. If it takes $1\frac{1}{3}$ sheets of paper to make a set of large buttons, how many sheets of paper will they need?

To find out, multiply $5\frac{1}{2} \times 1\frac{1}{3}$.

Estimate first: $6 \times 1 = 6$

Step 1 Write each mixed number as an improper fraction.

Step 2 Look for common factors and simplify.

Step 3 Multiply. Simplify, if possible.

$$5\frac{1}{2} \times 1\frac{1}{3} = \frac{11}{2} \times \frac{4}{3}$$

$$\frac{11}{\underset{1}{2}} \times \frac{\overset{2}{4}}{3} = \frac{11}{1} \times \frac{2}{3}$$

$$\frac{11}{1} \times \frac{2}{3} = \frac{22}{3} = 7\frac{1}{3}$$

They will need $7\frac{1}{3}$ sheets of paper.

Additional Standards: Number Sense 2.0, 2.2; Mathematical Reasoning 1.1, 2.1 (See p. 173.)

Guided Practice   *For another example, see Set F on p. 207.*

Multiply. Write each answer in simplest form.

1. $\dfrac{3}{10} \times \dfrac{4}{15}$ **2.** $\dfrac{11}{12} \times \dfrac{48}{55}$ **3.** $5\dfrac{5}{6} \times 2\dfrac{4}{7}$ **4.** $3\dfrac{4}{7} \times 1\dfrac{2}{5}$

5. Luna's vest had $2\dfrac{2}{3}$ dozen buttons pinned to it. Pat pinned $2\dfrac{1}{4}$ times as many buttons to his jacket. How many buttons did Pat have?

Independent Practice   *For more practice, see Set F on p. 209.*

Multiply. Write each answer in simplest form.

6. $\dfrac{8}{35} \times \dfrac{7}{40}$ **7.** $6 \times \dfrac{15}{27}$ **8.** $\dfrac{7}{8} \times 1\dfrac{5}{6}$ **9.** $2\dfrac{1}{4} \times \dfrac{1}{3}$

10. $2\dfrac{3}{10} \times \dfrac{9}{11}$ **11.** $4 \times 3\dfrac{3}{8}$ **12.** $3\dfrac{1}{3} \times 4\dfrac{1}{4}$ **13.** $\dfrac{7}{10} \times \dfrac{5}{21}$

14. Math Reasoning How could you use the distributive property to multiply 8 times $3\dfrac{1}{2}$ mentally?

15. Beans take up $\dfrac{3}{8}$ of a garden. Lima beans take up $\dfrac{2}{3}$ of the bean patch, and green beans take up the remaining $\dfrac{1}{3}$. What fraction of the garden is planted in lima beans? in green beans?

16. The rest of the garden is planted in corn. How much of the garden is planted in corn?

17. Mental Math
Compare. $\dfrac{2}{3} \times \dfrac{3}{2} \bullet \dfrac{5}{6} \times \dfrac{6}{5}$

Mixed Review

18. Math Reasoning Tom walks his dog in a park every third day. Alice jogs in the park every fourth day. They both arrive at the park entrance at 8 A.M. If they meet there on Monday, on what day will they meet there again?

Test Prep   Choose the correct letter for each answer.

19. Algebra Solve $x - \dfrac{5}{18} = \dfrac{11}{24}$.
(5-5)

A $x = \dfrac{13}{72}$ **C** $x = \dfrac{7}{8}$

B $x = \dfrac{2}{9}$ **D** $x = \dfrac{53}{72}$

20. Algebra Solve $n + 2\dfrac{7}{8} = 5\dfrac{3}{20}$.
(5-5)

F $n = 2\dfrac{11}{40}$ **H** $n = 3\dfrac{3}{4}$

G $n = 2\dfrac{1}{4}$ **J** $n = 3\dfrac{29}{40}$

Use Homework Workbook 5-7.   **193**

LESSON 5-8

Dividing Fractions and Mixed Numbers

California Content Standard *Number Sense 2.2: Explain the meaning of . . . division of positive fractions and perform the calculations.*

Math Link You know how to multiply fractions and mixed numbers. Now you will use the same skills to divide fractions and mixed numbers.

Example 1

Several students use salt dough to make storyteller dolls.

How many dolls can they make using the amounts in the recipe at the right if one doll takes $\frac{3}{4}$ pound of dough? To find out, divide $3 \div \frac{3}{4}$.

To divide fractions, multiply the dividend by the reciprocal of the divisor. Two numbers are **reciprocals** if their product is 1.

SALT DOUGH RECIPE

(MAKES 3 POUNDS OF DOUGH)

Ingredients

4   cups flour (any kind except self-rising)
1½ cup warm water
1   cup salt

Step 1 Since $\frac{3}{4} \times \frac{4}{3} = 1$, the reciprocal of $\frac{3}{4}$ is $\frac{4}{3}$. Rewrite as a multiplication exercise.

$$3 \div \frac{3}{4} = 3 \times \frac{4}{3}$$

Step 2 Multiply.

$$\frac{\cancel{3}^{1}}{1} \times \frac{4}{\cancel{3}_{1}} = \frac{1}{1} \times \frac{4}{1} = 4$$

> **Word Bank**
>
> reciprocal

They can make 4 dolls.

Example 2

Divide $6\frac{3}{4} \div 1\frac{1}{8}$.

Step 1 Write each mixed number as an improper fraction.

$$6\frac{3}{4} \div 1\frac{1}{8} = \frac{27}{4} \div \frac{9}{8}$$

Step 2 Multiply the dividend by the reciprocal of the divisor.

$$\frac{27}{4} \div \frac{9}{8} = \frac{\cancel{27}^{3}}{\cancel{4}_{1}} \times \frac{\cancel{8}^{2}}{\cancel{9}_{1}} = \frac{6}{1} = 6$$

   Additional Standards: Number Sense 2.0, 2.1 (See p. 173.)

Guided Practice *For another example, see Set G on p. 207.*

Divide. Write each answer in simplest form.

1. $\dfrac{2}{3} \div 16$ **2.** $\dfrac{36}{77} \div \dfrac{9}{14}$ **3.** $3\dfrac{3}{8} \div 2\dfrac{1}{4}$ **4.** $7\dfrac{1}{4} \div 3$

5. Large storyteller dolls take $\dfrac{7}{8}$ pound of salt dough, and small dolls take $\dfrac{3}{8}$ pound of dough. The recipe makes 3 pounds of dough. The students double the recipe. How many large dolls can they make?

Independent Practice *For more practice, see Set G on p. 209.*

Divide . Write each answer in simplest form.

6. $\dfrac{5}{6} \div \dfrac{5}{8}$ **7.** $9 \div \dfrac{36}{37}$ **8.** $4\dfrac{1}{2} \div 2\dfrac{7}{10}$ **9.** $44 \div 1\dfrac{5}{6}$

10. $15 \div 4\dfrac{1}{2}$ **11.** $4\dfrac{2}{3} \div 3\dfrac{1}{2}$ **12.** $2\dfrac{3}{4} \div \dfrac{1}{4}$ **13.** $6\dfrac{2}{5} \div 4$

14. Marcus and Tom are making some large puppets with red fronts and yellow backs. Each front takes $\dfrac{7}{8}$ yard of cloth, and each back takes $1\dfrac{1}{4}$ yards. They have $4\dfrac{2}{3}$ yards of red cloth and $5\dfrac{7}{8}$ yards of yellow cloth. How many puppets can they make?

Mixed Review

15. Amy had 36 trading cards. She gave $\dfrac{1}{4}$ of her cards to Jon and $\dfrac{1}{6}$ of her cards to Katy. How many cards did she have left?

16. $4\dfrac{8}{9} + 6\dfrac{1}{5} + 2\dfrac{4}{5}$ **17.** $3\dfrac{1}{3} \times 2\dfrac{1}{5}$ **18.** $\dfrac{5}{6} \times 4\dfrac{1}{2}$

19. Estimate $\dfrac{9}{10} \times 5\dfrac{10}{12}$.   **20.** Estimate $\dfrac{2}{3} \times 29$.

Test Prep   **Choose the correct letter for each answer.**

Use the graph at the right for Exercises 21 and 22.

21. How many more students like blue than like red?
(1-13)

     A 3   **B** 4

     C 5   **D** 6

22. What color had the greatest range
(1-13) in students' preferences?

     F Orange   **H** Green

     G Blue   **J** Yellow

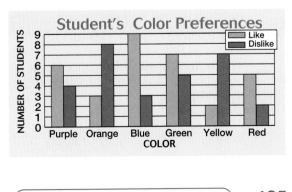

Problem-Solving Strategy:

Solve a Simpler Problem

Warm-Up Review

1. $\frac{1}{2}$ of 24,000

2. $\frac{1}{3}$ of 150,000

3. One fourth of the 800 students in Steward School brought their lunch. How many students did not bring their lunch?

California Content Standard *Mathematical Reasoning 2.2: Apply strategies and results from simpler problems to more complex problems.*

Example

Erica's Lawn and Garden Service maintains the city park shown at the right. One half of the park is grass, and one half is a flower garden. One fourth of the flower garden is roses. What is the area of the park?

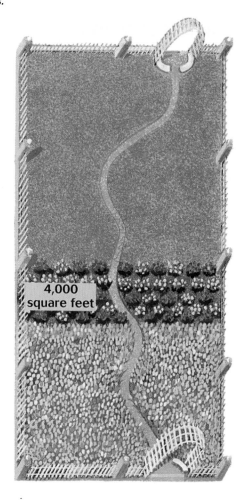

4,000 square feet

Understand

What do you need to find?

You need to find the area of the park.

Plan

How can you solve the problem?

You can **solve a simpler problem**.
Use simpler numbers to solve a similar problem.

Solve

Roses take up 4,000 square feet. Since 4,000 is 4 × 1,000, use the simpler number 4 to represent the area covered by roses.

One fourth of the flower garden is roses. So the total area of the flower garden is 4 times the area of the roses. The total flower-garden area can be represented by 4 × 4, or 16. Since the area of the flower garden is one half of the area of the park, the area of the park can be represented as 2 × 16, or 32.

The actual area of the park is 32 × 1,000, or 32,000, square feet.

Look Back

Why is it necessary to multiply 32 by 1,000 to find the actual area of the park?

Additional Standards: Number Sense 2.0; Mathematical Reasoning 1.3, 3.2 (See p. 173.)

Guided Practice

1. Erica is planting shrubs that will cover $\frac{1}{4}$ of each of the three house lots shown at the right. How many square feet will be covered with shrubs?

   Lot A: 28,000 square feet

   Lot B: 32,000 square feet

   Lot C: 36,000 square feet

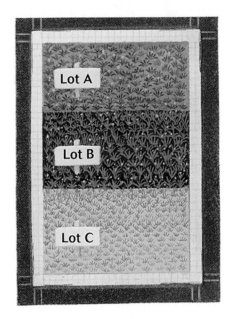

Lot A

Lot B

Lot C

Independent Practice

2. A roll of weed-blocking material covered 480 square feet. If $\frac{1}{8}$ of the material was used on Mr. Jackson's landscaping, $\frac{1}{4}$ on Ms. Knight's landscaping, and $\frac{5}{8}$ on landscaping at the school, how many more square feet of weed-blocking material was used on Ms. Knight's landscaping than on Mr. Jackson's?

3. A parcel of land with an area of 24,000 square feet is to be divided into 3 lots. The first lot will take $\frac{2}{3}$ of the parcel. The area of the second lot will be equal to the area of the third lot. Find the area of each lot.

Mixed Review

Try these or other strategies to solve each problem.
Tell which strategy you used.

Problem-Solving Strategies

- *Make a Graph*
- *Use Logical Reasoning*
- *Work Backward*
- *Find a Pattern*

4. When Ed planted six rows of mums, he made the first row 48 feet long, the second row 24 feet long, and the third row 12 feet long. If he continued this pattern, what were the lengths of the fourth, fifth, and sixth rows?

5. Karyn enjoys reading nature books. Half of her books are about birds. One fourth are about wildflowers, and the remaining 2 are about wildlife. How many nature books does she have?

Solving Equations Using Fractions

Algebra

Warm-Up Review

Solve each equation.

1. $4n = 36$

2. $y \div 3 = 6$

3. $\frac{x}{6} = 7$

4. Teresa went to her grandmother's farm. Her family drove $2\frac{1}{2}$ hours before lunch and $1\frac{3}{4}$ hours after lunch. How fast did they drive?

California Content Standard *Algebra and Functions 1.1(🔑): Write and solve one-step linear equations in one variable.*

Math Link You know how to solve equations using multiplication and division of whole numbers. Now you will learn how to solve equations by using multiplication and division of fractions.

Example 1

Ryan is using planks to build a boat dock that is $22\frac{1}{2}$ feet long. Each plank is $\frac{3}{4}$ of a foot wide and 4 feet long. The dock will be built so that the planks are right next to each other and parallel to the shore. How many planks does Ryan need?

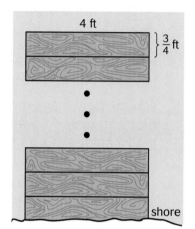

4 ft

$\frac{3}{4}$ ft

shore

You can write an equation to solve the problem.

Let n be the number of planks needed.

$$\frac{3}{4}n = 22\frac{1}{2}$$

$$\frac{3}{4} \cdot n = 22\frac{1}{2}$$

A centered dot can be used as a multiplication symbol.

$$\frac{4}{3} \cdot \frac{3}{4}n = \frac{4}{3} \cdot 22\frac{1}{2}$$

Since n is multiplied by $\frac{3}{4}$, divide each side by $\frac{3}{4}$. To divide by $\frac{3}{4}$, multiply both sides of the equation by the reciprocal of $\frac{3}{4}$, which is $\frac{4}{3}$.

$$1 \cdot n = \frac{4}{\overset{2}{\cancel{3}}} \cdot \frac{\overset{15}{\cancel{45}}}{\underset{1}{\cancel{2}}}$$

$$n = \frac{30}{1} = 30$$

Ryan needs 30 planks.

Here's WHY It Works

Reciprocals have a product of 1.

$$\frac{4}{3} \cdot \frac{3}{4}n = 1 \cdot n = n$$

The variable, n, is left by itself.

Example 2

$$1\frac{2}{7}n = 1\frac{17}{28}$$

$$\frac{9}{7}n = \frac{45}{28}$$ Write as improper fractions.

$$\frac{7}{9} \cdot \frac{9}{7}n = \frac{\overset{1}{\cancel{7}}}{\underset{1}{\cancel{9}}} \cdot \frac{\overset{5}{\cancel{45}}}{\underset{4}{\cancel{28}}}$$ Multiply both sides by the reciprocal of $\frac{9}{7}$, which is $\frac{7}{9}$.

$$n = \frac{5}{4} = 1\frac{1}{4}$$

Check:

$$1\frac{2}{7}n = 1\frac{17}{28}$$ Write the equation.

$$1\frac{2}{7} \times 1\frac{1}{4} \overset{?}{=} 1\frac{17}{28}$$ Replace n with $1\frac{1}{4}$.

$$\frac{9}{7} \times \frac{5}{4} \overset{?}{=} 1\frac{17}{28}$$ Multiply.

$$1\frac{17}{28} = 1\frac{17}{28}$$ The answer checks.

Additional Standards: Number Sense 2.0, 2.1, 2.2, 2.4 (🔑) (See p. 173.)

Guided Practice *For another example, see Set H on p. 207.*

Solve each equation. Write each answer in simplest form.

1. $\frac{2}{5}x = \frac{4}{15}$

2. $\frac{3}{14}n = \frac{3}{16}$

3. $\frac{6}{7}a = 16$

4. $\frac{3}{25}c = 2\frac{3}{10}$

5. It takes $1\frac{1}{4}$ hours to bake a ceramic sculpture. If only one sculpture can be baked at a time, how many can be baked in 10 hours? Use the equation $1\frac{1}{4}x = 10$ to solve.

Independent Practice *For more practice, see Set H on p. 209.*

Solve each equation. Write each answer in simplest form.

6. $\frac{3}{16}x = \frac{3}{4}$

7. $\frac{12}{23}d = \frac{16}{69}$

8. $\frac{3}{5}e = \frac{30}{55}$

9. $\frac{15}{9}y = \frac{5}{27}$

10. Karyn put 30 dolls on display. This was $1\frac{1}{2}$ times as many as she had last year. How many dolls did she have last year? Use the equation $1\frac{1}{2}d = 30$.

11. Amy and Jason make hand puppets. They need $1\frac{1}{8}$ yards of cloth for each puppet. If they have $6\frac{3}{4}$ yards of cloth, how many puppets can they make? Use the equation $1\frac{1}{8}p = 6\frac{3}{4}$ to solve.

Mixed Review

12. Math Reasoning Test each of the numbers in the table at the right for divisibility by 2, 3, 4, 6, and 12. Write *yes* or *no*. Make a conjecture about the divisibility rule for 12.

Number	Divisible by				
	2	3	4	6	12
240	yes	yes	yes	yes	yes
450					
1,524					
2,118					

13. $3\frac{1}{8} \times \frac{3}{5}$

14. $3\frac{1}{4} \times \frac{12}{13}$

15. $7\frac{1}{2} \div 4\frac{1}{6}$

16. $6\frac{3}{5} \div 2\frac{1}{5}$

Test Prep Choose the correct letter for each answer.

17. Algebra According to the distributive property, $4(3+5) =$
(2-1)

    A $(4 \times 3) + (4 \times 5)$.

    B $12 + 5$.

    C $(4 + 3) \times (4 + 5)$.

    D $3 + 20$.

18. Algebra According to the associative property of addition,
(1-4) $4 + (a + 7) =$

    F $4a + 28$ **G** $4 + (7 + a)$ **H** $(a + 7) + 4$ **J** $(4 + a) + 7$

LESSON
5-11

Understand
Plan
Solve
Look Back

Problem-Solving Application:

Using Fractions and Mixed Numbers

Algebra

Warm-Up Review

1. $5 \times 1\frac{2}{5}$

2. $\frac{1}{3} \times 4\frac{1}{2}$

3. $\frac{3}{4} \div 1\frac{7}{8}$

4. $\frac{5}{8} \div 1\frac{2}{3}$

5. Marcus worked $12\frac{1}{2}$ hours a week, 4 weeks a month, for $2\frac{1}{4}$ months. How many hours did he work?

California Content Standard *Algebra and Functions 1.1(🔑): Write and solve one-step linear equations in one variable.*

Example 1

How many shares of BR stock can you buy for $247? How much will your stock be worth if the price goes up $\frac{1}{2}$ point ($0.50)?

Understand

What do you need to know?

You need to know the price of one share of BR stock today.

STOCK TABLE

Company	Price of One Share (in dollars)	Price Change From Yesterday (in dollars)
GSO	43 ½	-1
TRP	25 ¼	+⅛
BR	9 ½	+½
CK	7 ¼	-¼
LGA	13	no change

Plan

How can you solve the problem?

You can write an equation to find the number of shares you can buy. Then you can write another equation to find the value of those shares if the price goes up.

▲ Stock prices are expressed with fractions instead of cents, so 43½ means $43.50.

Solve

First find out how many shares you can buy.

$$s = 247 \div 9\frac{1}{2}$$
$$s = 247 \div \frac{19}{2}$$
$$s = 247 \times \frac{2}{19} = 26$$

You can buy 26 shares of BR stock.

Then find the value of your shares if the price goes up $\frac{1}{2}$ point.

$$v = \left(9\frac{1}{2} + \frac{1}{2}\right) \times 26$$
$$v = 10 \times 26$$
$$v = 260$$

Your stock will be worth $260.

Look Back

Suppose the stock dropped $\frac{1}{2}$ point instead of going up. What would your stock be worth?

Additional Standards: Number Sense 2.0, 2.1 (🔑); Mathematical Reasoning 1.1 (See p. 173.)

Example 2

How many shares of CK stock could you buy for the cost of one share of GSO stock?

$$7\frac{1}{4}s = 43\frac{1}{2}$$

$$\frac{29}{4}s = \frac{87}{2}$$

$$\frac{4}{29} \cdot \frac{29}{4}s = \frac{\overset{2}{\cancel{4}}}{\underset{1}{\cancel{29}}} \cdot \frac{\overset{3}{\cancel{87}}}{\underset{1}{\cancel{2}}} = \frac{6}{1} = 6$$

You could buy 6 shares of CK stock for the cost of one share of GSO stock.

Guided Practice

Use the stock table on page 200 for Exercises 1–6.

1. Last year, the Johnsons bought 30 shares of TRP stock at $29\frac{1}{2}$ per share. What is their stock worth now? How much money did they make or lose?

2. Which company had the greatest price increase of one share from the previous day? Which stock showed no change in price?

Independent Practice

3. If you own 4 shares of GSO, what is it worth today?

4. **Math Reasoning** Kyle wants to buy 8 shares of GSO, 5 shares of BR, and 10 shares of LGA. Will $550 be enough to buy all the stock? Explain.

5. Yesterday the Kellers bought 18 shares of stock for $783. Which company's stock did they buy?

6. Lee spent $275 on stocks today. He bought shares of LGA stock and CK stock. If he purchased 10 shares of LGA, how many shares of CK did he buy?

Mixed Review

7. Amanda paid $24.00 for pots. She bought both round pots and square pots. Round pots cost $4.00 each, and square pots cost $6.00. How many of each did she buy?

8. One day Erica earned one half of her income weeding gardens, one fourth mowing lawns, and the rest planting shrubs. If she earned $30 planting shrubs, how much did she earn that day?

Diagnostic Checkpoint

Complete. For Exercises 1–3 use the words from the Word Bank.

Word Bank

compatible numbers

least common denominator

reciprocal

simplest form

1. Two numbers are _____ if their
(5-8)   product is 1.

2. You can use _____ when estimating
(5-6)   the product of a fraction and a whole number.

3. When adding or subtracting fractions with unlike denominators,
(5-4)   write them with their _____ .

Estimate.

4. $3 \times 2\frac{1}{6}$
(5-6)

5. $5\frac{1}{5} \times 6\frac{7}{8}$
(5-6)

6. $\frac{1}{2} \times \frac{7}{8}$
(5-6)

7. $\frac{7}{8} \times \frac{11}{12}$
(5-6)

8. $27 \times \frac{3}{5}$
(5-6)

9. $\frac{7}{8} \times 30$
(5-6)

10. $\frac{5}{9} \times 17$
(5-6)

11. $13 \times \frac{5}{6}$
(5-6)

Multiply or divide. Write each answer in simplest form.

12. $\frac{1}{3} \times \frac{5}{6}$
(5-7)

13. $\frac{2}{3} \times 6$
(5-7)

14. $4 \times \frac{3}{10}$
(5-7)

15. $\frac{2}{3} \times 5$
(5-7)

16. $1\frac{3}{7} \times \frac{3}{4}$
(5-7)

17. $\frac{3}{10} \times \frac{6}{10}$
(5-7)

18. $\frac{5}{8} \times \frac{3}{4}$
(5-7)

19. $\frac{5}{8} \times 2$
(5-7)

20. $10 \div 3\frac{3}{5}$
(5-8)

21. $3\frac{1}{4} \div \frac{1}{2}$
(5-8)

22. $5\frac{1}{6} \div 5\frac{2}{3}$
(5-8)

23. $7\frac{3}{5} \div 19$
(5-8)

24. $4\frac{1}{5} \div 2\frac{1}{3}$
(5-8)

25. $18 \div \frac{1}{3}$
(5-8)

26. $\frac{5}{6} \div 10$
(5-8)

27. $3\frac{3}{4} \div \frac{5}{8}$
(5-8)

Solve each equation.

28. $1\frac{3}{7}x = 1$
(5-10)

29. $1\frac{1}{5}y = 6$
(5-10)

30. $\frac{4}{9}n = \frac{2}{9}$
(5-10)

31. $\frac{5}{8}a = \frac{1}{6}$
(5-10)

32. A 120,000-acre farm is divided into 4 areas. Area A is $\frac{1}{6}$ of the farm
(5-9)   and is used for corn. Area B is $\frac{2}{4}$ of the farm and is used for peas.
    Area C is $\frac{1}{4}$ of the farm and is used for beans. Area D is $\frac{1}{12}$ of the
    farm and is used for fruit trees. Find the area of each lot.

33. Sharon bought 70 shares of PGR stock last week at $\$55\frac{3}{4}$ per share.
(5-11)   Today the stock is valued at $\$59\frac{5}{8}$ per share. What is her stock
    worth now? How much money did she make or lose?

Chapter 5 Test

Estimate.

1. $3\frac{17}{20} + 5\frac{1}{8}$ **2.** $14\frac{5}{8} - 13\frac{7}{8}$ **3.** $3\frac{6}{7} \times 2\frac{4}{5}$ **4.** $4\frac{1}{5} \times 7\frac{7}{8}$

Add or subtract. Write each answer in simplest form.

5. $6 + 9\frac{3}{5}$ **6.** $\frac{2}{3} - \frac{2}{5}$ **7.** $7\frac{3}{10} + 4\frac{1}{2}$

8. $\frac{11}{12} - \frac{7}{12}$ **9.** $6\frac{3}{4} + 7\frac{3}{4}$ **10.** $5 - 2\frac{3}{8}$

Multiply or divide. Write each answer in simplest form.

11. $1\frac{1}{8} \times 2\frac{1}{3}$ **12.** $\frac{3}{4} \times \frac{8}{9}$ **13.** $4\frac{1}{3} \div 6\frac{1}{2}$

14. $3\frac{4}{7} \times 4\frac{1}{5}$ **15.** $5 \div \frac{1}{5}$ **16.** $2\frac{2}{5} \div 3\frac{3}{5}$

Solve each equation. Write each answer in simplest form.

17. $3\frac{1}{5} + x = 5\frac{2}{15}$ **18.** $y - 1\frac{3}{10} = 4\frac{5}{6}$ **19.** $m - \frac{1}{45} = 6\frac{7}{10}$

20. $\frac{2}{7}c = 2$ **21.** $\frac{5}{8}n = 40$ **22.** $2\frac{2}{5}a = 3\frac{3}{5}$

23. A developer owns 78 acres of land. He divides the land into 3 parcels as shown at the right. Homes will be built on $\frac{1}{6}$ of parcel A, $\frac{1}{4}$ of parcel B, and parcel C will remain untouched. How much land will not be used for homes on the three parcels combined?

Parcel A
36 acres
Parcel B
24 acres
Parcel C
18 acres

24. Michael wants to buy 14 shares of TWX stock for himself, 10 shares for his wife, and 6 shares for his son. TWX stock is selling for $\$14\frac{3}{8}$ per share. Will $400.00 be enough to buy all of the stock? Explain your answer.

Write an equation. Then solve.

25. Dwight grew 2 inches during the summer. At the end of the summer he was $54\frac{1}{4}$ inches tall. What was his height at the beginning of the summer?

Multiple-Choice Chapter 5 Test

Choose the correct letter for each answer.

1. Select the best estimate of $9\frac{7}{8} + \frac{27}{50}$.

   A $1\frac{1}{2}$ C 10

   B 9   D 40

2. After a plant grew $\frac{1}{2}$ inch, it was $6\frac{1}{2}$ inches tall. What was the height before it grew $\frac{1}{2}$ inch? Which equation would you use to find the answer?

   F $x + \frac{1}{2} = 6\frac{1}{2}$

   G $x - \frac{1}{2} = 6\frac{1}{2}$

   H $x + 6\frac{1}{2} = \frac{1}{2}$

   J $6\frac{1}{2} + \frac{1}{2} = x$

3. Each puppet show was to run for $1\frac{1}{8}$ hours, including a rest period. How many shows could the students perform in $4\frac{1}{2}$ hours?

   A 6 shows   C 4 shows

   B 5 shows   D 3 shows

4. Which of the following gives an estimate of 64?

   F $8\frac{10}{12} \times 9\frac{3}{4}$ J $16\frac{1}{8} \times 2\frac{1}{3}$

   G $31\frac{9}{11} \times 2\frac{1}{8}$ K NH

   H $14\frac{9}{11} \times 4\frac{5}{6}$

5. On a two-day hike Denise walked $4\frac{2}{5}$ miles and $4\frac{7}{10}$ miles. Tommy walked $3\frac{1}{2}$ miles and $4\frac{1}{4}$ miles. How much farther did Denise walk?

   A $2\frac{1}{10}$ miles   C $1\frac{2}{3}$ miles

   B $1\frac{5}{6}$ miles   D $1\frac{7}{20}$ miles

Use the picture for Questions 6 and 7.

$62\frac{1}{2}$ oz $8\frac{1}{3}$ oz

6. Yolanda made lemonade to sell at the county fair. On the first day, she made 40 pitchers of lemonade. How many ounces of lemonade did she make?

   F 1.56 ounces

   G $102\frac{1}{2}$ ounces

   H 333 ounces

   J 2,500 ounces

7. How many glasses could Yolanda fill from one pitcher of lemonade?

   A 10 glasses

   B 8 glasses

   C 7 glasses

   D 6 glasses

8. The floor area of a 120-square-foot moving van is separated into 3 sections. The first section, to be used for furniture, will take up $\frac{1}{2}$ of the floor area of the van. The second section will contain the boxes, and the third section will be used for yard equipment. The second section takes up $\frac{3}{8}$ of the floor area. What is the floor area taken up by the third section?

   F   15 feet^2

   G   30 feet^2

   H   45 feet^2

   J   60 feet^2

---

9. Solve for x.

$$9\frac{2}{11}x = \frac{6}{22}$$

   A $x = \frac{3}{101}$

   B $x = \frac{3}{100}$

   C $x = 2\frac{1}{4}$

   D $x = 2\frac{1}{2}$

---

10. Linda ran $5\frac{1}{6}$ miles the first week and $3\frac{1}{3}$ miles the second week. She doubled her second week's distance the third week. What is the total number of miles she ran in 3 weeks?

   F $8\frac{1}{2}$ miles

   G $8\frac{2}{3}$ miles

   H $11\frac{5}{6}$ miles

   J $15\frac{1}{6}$ miles

Use the table for Questions 11–13.

Company	Open	Close
Fast Track RR	$22\frac{1}{8}$	$22\frac{3}{4}$
HiFly Airways	$44\frac{7}{8}$	$46\frac{1}{4}$
Blue Cab, Inc.	$19\frac{3}{4}$	$19\frac{7}{8}$
City Line Bus Co.	37	$41\frac{1}{8}$
Leisure Boats, Inc.	$76\frac{1}{2}$	$77\frac{3}{8}$

11. Gail purchased 40 shares of HiFly Airways stock when the market first opened and then sold all her shares at the close. How much money did Gail make or lose?

   A $55.00 profit

   B $55.00 loss

   C $95.00 profit

   D $95.00 loss

---

12. Which stock had the greatest gain between the market opening and closing?

   F   HiFly Airways

   G   Blue Cab, Inc.

   H   City Line Bus Co.

   J   Leisure Boats, Inc.

---

13. When the market opened, Shawn purchased 60 shares of Blue Cab, Inc., 10 shares of Leisure Boats, Inc., and 12 shares of Fast Track RR. How much money did Shawn spend?

   A $460.50

   B $1,527.00

   C $2,215.50

   D $4,605.00

Reteaching

Set A (pages 174–175)

Estimate $6\frac{7}{8} - 2\frac{1}{3}$.

$6\frac{7}{8}$ rounds to 7. $2\frac{1}{3}$ rounds to 2.

$7 - 2 = 5$

The estimate of $6\frac{7}{8} - 2\frac{1}{3}$ is 5.

Remember to round each number.

Estimate.

1. $9\frac{7}{9} - 3\frac{5}{6}$

2. $14\frac{8}{11} + 10\frac{9}{12}$

3. $13\frac{1}{8} + 9\frac{2}{3}$

4. $6\frac{5}{8} - 5\frac{6}{7}$

Set B (pages 176–178)

Add.

$6\frac{7}{11} + 4\frac{8}{11}$

Add the whole numbers:

$6 + 4 = 10$

Add the fractions:

$\frac{7}{11} + \frac{8}{11} = \frac{15}{11} = 1\frac{4}{11}$

Add: $10 + 1\frac{4}{11} = 15\frac{4}{11}$

Remember when adding and subtracting with like denominators, add the numerators and simplify.

Add or subtract. Write each answer in simplest form.

1. $2\frac{5}{9} - \frac{8}{9}$

2. $16 - 8\frac{3}{8}$

3. $9\frac{5}{7} + 10\frac{3}{7}$

4. $3\frac{3}{4} - 1\frac{1}{4}$

5. $5\frac{5}{6} + 9$

6. $4\frac{1}{12} + 5\frac{7}{12}$

Set C (pages 182-185)

Subtract.

$$5\frac{3}{10} = 5\frac{3}{10} = 4\frac{13}{10}$$
$$-3\frac{1}{2} = -3\frac{5}{10} = 3\frac{5}{10}$$
$$\overline{\phantom{-3\frac{1}{2} = -3\frac{5}{10} =}\; 1\frac{8}{10} = 1\frac{4}{5}}$$

Remember to find the least common denominator (LCD) of fractions with unlike denominators. Write equivalent fractions before adding or subtracting.

Add or subtract. Write each answer in simplest form.

1. $2\frac{1}{2} + 1\frac{1}{3}$

2. $6\frac{3}{4} + 2\frac{3}{8}$

3. $8\frac{1}{2} - 2\frac{2}{3}$

4. $6\frac{3}{9} - 1\frac{1}{6}$

Set D (pages 186–187)

Solve $x + \frac{2}{3} = 4\frac{1}{3}$. Subtract $\frac{2}{3}$ from each side of the equation.

$x + \frac{2}{3} - \frac{2}{3} = 4\frac{1}{3} - \frac{2}{3}$

$x = 4\frac{1}{3} - \frac{2}{3}$ Subtract.

$x = 3\frac{2}{3}$

Remember to use the inverse properties of addition and subtraction.

1. $x - 6\frac{1}{4} = 3\frac{1}{4}$

2. $12\frac{1}{3} = n + \frac{1}{5}$

3. $a + 3\frac{5}{8} = 8$

4. $\frac{5}{12} = c - \frac{3}{4}$

Set E (pages 190–191)

Estimate $\frac{1}{8} \times 65$.

$\frac{1}{8} \times 65$ Change 65 to the nearest number compatible with 8.

$\frac{1}{8} \times 64$

$\frac{1}{\cancel{8}} \times \cancel{64}^{8} = 1 \times 8 = 8$ Simplify and multiply.

$\frac{1}{8} \times 65$ is about 8.

Remember that you can use rounding or compatible numbers when estimating products.

Estimate.

1. $2\frac{3}{4} \times 8\frac{9}{11}$ **2.** $\frac{3}{4} \times 245$

3. $\frac{5}{6} \times 304$ **4.** $7\frac{1}{3} \times 6\frac{4}{5}$

Set F (pages 192-193)

Multiply $3\frac{2}{3} \times 2\frac{1}{11}$.

$3\frac{2}{3} \times 2\frac{1}{11}$ Write mixed numbers as improper fractions.

$\frac{11}{3} \times \frac{23}{11}$

$\frac{\cancel{11}^{1}}{3} \times \frac{23}{\cancel{11}^{1}} = \frac{1 \times 23}{3 \times 1} = \frac{23}{3} = 7\frac{2}{3}$ Simplify and multiply.

Remember when multiplying fractions to write each mixed number as an improper fraction, then multiply the numerators and the denominators.

1. $\frac{3}{4} \times 1\frac{3}{7}$ **2.** $3\frac{1}{3} \times 6\frac{2}{7}$

3. $\frac{5}{8} \times \frac{4}{15}$ **4.** $2\frac{1}{4} \times 2\frac{1}{3}$

Set G (pages 194–195)

Divide $\frac{8}{9} \div \frac{2}{11}$.

$\frac{8}{9} \times \frac{11}{2}$ Rewrite as multiplication.

                    Multiply.

$\frac{\cancel{8}^{4}}{9} \times \frac{11}{\cancel{2}^{1}} = \frac{4 \times 11}{9 \times 1} = \frac{44}{9} = 4\frac{8}{9}$

Remember when dividing fractions, multiply by the reciprocal of the divisor. Two numbers are reciprocals if their products are one.

1. $2 \div \frac{1}{8}$ **2.** $\frac{7}{8} \div \frac{5}{16}$

3. $2\frac{1}{2} \div 5$ **4.** $1\frac{3}{4} \div 1\frac{1}{3}$

5. $1\frac{1}{2} \div 2\frac{2}{3}$ **6.** $3\frac{3}{8} \div 2\frac{1}{4}$

Set H (pages 198–199)

Solve $2\frac{1}{4}x = 1\frac{1}{8}$.

$\frac{9}{4}x = \frac{9}{8}$ Write the mixed numbers as improper fractions.

$\frac{4}{9} \cdot \frac{9}{4}x = \frac{4}{9} \cdot \frac{9}{8}$ Multiply both sides by the reciprocal of $\frac{9}{4}$.

$\frac{4}{9} \cdot \frac{9}{4}x = \frac{\cancel{4}^{1}}{\cancel{9}^{1}} \cdot \frac{\cancel{9}^{1}}{\cancel{8}^{2}}$ Simplify.

$x = \frac{1}{2}$

Remember to use reciprocals when solving equations involving fractions.

Solve each equation.

1. $\frac{1}{6}x = \frac{2}{9}$ **2.** $4n = \frac{2}{15}$

3. $2\frac{3}{4}y = \frac{3}{20}$ **4.** $\frac{2}{3}c = \frac{1}{9}$

5. $1\frac{1}{2}n = \frac{2}{3}$ **6.** $\frac{5}{8}a = 2\frac{1}{2}$

More Practice

Set A (pages 174–175)

Estimate each sum or difference.

1. $1\frac{7}{8} + 2\frac{13}{14}$ **2.** $4\frac{1}{2} + 4\frac{5}{8}$ **3.** $18\frac{1}{9} - 2\frac{11}{12}$ **4.** $26 - 5\frac{7}{8}$ **5.** $2\frac{3}{6} + 4\frac{1}{5}$

6. $3\frac{5}{8} - 2\frac{1}{6}$ **7.** $15\frac{2}{3} + 1\frac{9}{10}$ **8.** $2\frac{2}{3} + 5\frac{1}{10}$ **9.** $7\frac{7}{8} + 4\frac{4}{5}$ **10.** $10\frac{11}{12} - \frac{9}{10}$

11. Rosemary has a plant that was $2\frac{3}{8}$ in. tall. The next month it was $3\frac{7}{8}$ in. tall. About how many inches did it grow in that month?

Set B (pages 176–178)

Add or subtract. Write each answer in simplest form.

1. $7\frac{3}{8} - 1\frac{7}{8}$ **2.** $6\frac{11}{12} - 4\frac{7}{12}$ **3.** $8\frac{1}{4} + 2\frac{1}{4}$ **4.** $16\frac{2}{3} + 4\frac{2}{3}$

5. Andrea and Rick planted seeds in a tray. Andrea used $\frac{7}{16}$ of the tray and Rick used $\frac{5}{16}$ of the tray. What fraction of the tray did they use altogether?

Set C (pages 182–185)

Add or subtract. Write each answer in simplest form.

1. $\frac{5}{6} - \frac{1}{3}$ **2.** $\frac{1}{2} + \frac{1}{8}$ **3.** $6\frac{3}{4} - 3\frac{7}{8}$ **4.** $7\frac{2}{3} + 3\frac{4}{5}$

5. $12 - 11\frac{5}{6}$ **6.** $4\frac{5}{8} + \frac{3}{8}$ **7.** $7\frac{5}{12} - 6\frac{2}{3}$ **8.** $3\frac{3}{4} + 2\frac{3}{10}$

9. Brian has $\frac{1}{8}$ cup of rhubarb, $1\frac{1}{2}$ cup of apples, and $2\frac{1}{4}$ cups of cherries. He needs $4\frac{1}{4}$ cups of fruit. Does he have enough fruit? Explain how you know.

Set D (pages 186–187)

Solve each equation.

1. $y - \frac{3}{8} = 1$ **2.** $x - \frac{1}{6} = \frac{8}{9}$ **3.** $r + \frac{9}{16} = 2\frac{3}{4}$ **4.** $\frac{9}{10} + m = 1\frac{1}{2}$

5. $c - 1\frac{1}{6} = 2\frac{3}{10}$ **6.** $5\frac{1}{3} + y = 10$ **7.** $n - 2\frac{1}{2} = 4\frac{3}{4}$ **8.** $1\frac{1}{2} = a + 1\frac{1}{2}$

9. Derek grew $2\frac{3}{8}$ inches over the past year. He is now $54\frac{1}{4}$ inches tall. How tall was Derek last year? Write and solve an equation.

Set E (pages 190–191)

Estimate.

1. $\frac{7}{10} \times 102$

2. $2\frac{7}{8} \times 3\frac{1}{3}$

3. $7\frac{7}{8} \times 6\frac{1}{3}$

4. $50 \times \frac{1}{8}$

5. $5\frac{7}{9} \times 1\frac{5}{7}$

6. $63 \times \frac{7}{8}$

7. $3\frac{1}{8} \times 15\frac{2}{3}$

8. $9\frac{1}{7} \times 7\frac{3}{4}$

9. Jack and Pat spent $20\frac{1}{4}$ hours making pins. It took them $2\frac{3}{4}$ times as long to sell the pins. About how many hours did they spend selling pins?

Set F (pages 192–193)

Multiply. Write each answer in simplest form.

1. $3\frac{2}{5} \times 1\frac{3}{17}$

2. $\frac{6}{7} \times \frac{7}{8}$

3. $\frac{5}{8} \times 3\frac{3}{5}$

4. $6\frac{1}{3} \times 1\frac{2}{19}$

5. $2\frac{5}{8} \times 3\frac{1}{3}$

6. $1\frac{2}{9} \times 6$

7. $\frac{5}{12} \times \frac{3}{10}$

8. $3\frac{3}{4} \times 4\frac{1}{2}$

9. At the county fair, Luna sold four times as many pins as Pat did. If Pat sold $4\frac{1}{2}$ dozen pins, how many pins did Luna sell?

Set G (pages 194–195)

Divide. Write each answer in simplest form.

1. $3 \div \frac{1}{2}$

2. $6 \div \frac{3}{4}$

3. $\frac{5}{6} \div \frac{1}{12}$

4. $\frac{4}{5} \div \frac{4}{7}$

5. $7\frac{1}{2} \div 3\frac{3}{4}$

6. $6\frac{1}{4} \div 6\frac{2}{3}$

7. $8\frac{1}{2} \div 4$

8. $2\frac{2}{3} \div 6\frac{2}{5}$

9. To make a set for a stage, you bought a piece of lumber 10 feet long. How many floorboards $2\frac{1}{4}$ feet long can you cut from this piece of lumber?

Set H (pages 198–199)

Solve each equation. Write each answer in simplest form.

1. $\frac{3}{8}x = \frac{2}{8}$

2. $\frac{7}{15}n = \frac{7}{10}$

3. $\frac{11}{12}y = \frac{2}{3}$

4. $\frac{8}{10}a = 40$

5. $1\frac{1}{2}m = 6$

6. $1\frac{1}{5}b = 18$

7. $2\frac{1}{4}c = 2\frac{1}{3}$

8. $7\frac{1}{3}d = 1\frac{5}{6}$

9. It takes $\frac{5}{6}$ of an hour to make a hat. How many hours does it take to make 30 hats?

Problem Solving: Preparing for Tests

Choose the correct letter for each answer.

1. Every 8 seconds a warning signal on a buoy in a harbor sounds twice. Another signal sounds once every 12 seconds. If the two signals start at the same time, how often do they sound at the same time?

   Tip
   You can *Draw a Diagram* to solve this problem.

   A   Every 12 seconds
   B   Every 24 seconds
   C   Every 48 seconds
   D   Every 72 seconds

2. Tina's age, t, is $1\frac{1}{2}$ times Mark's age, m. Which expression shows the sum of their ages?

   Tip
   The equation $t = \frac{3}{2}m$ shows Tina's age in terms of Mark's age.

   F $\frac{3}{2}m$
   G $\frac{2}{3}m$
   H $m + \frac{3}{2}m$
   J $t + \frac{1}{2}t$

3. In one 5-day period, Sam practiced the clarinet $1\frac{1}{4}$ hours, 2 hours, $2\frac{3}{4}$ hours, $\frac{3}{4}$ hour, and $1\frac{1}{2}$ hours. What was the total number of hours that Sam spent practicing the clarinet during the 5 days?

   Tip
   Estimation can help you eliminate answer choices in this problem.

   A $6\frac{1}{4}$ hours

   B $7\frac{1}{2}$ hours

   C $8\frac{1}{4}$ hours

   D $8\frac{1}{2}$ hours

4. Jo's shop had weekly sales of 100, 80, 110, 90, 120, and 100 large baskets. If the sales pattern for large baskets continues, about how many will Jo sell next week?

F   90 baskets

G   110 baskets

H   130 baskets

J   150 baskets

5. Irma had $72. She bought 2 tote bags for $18.79 each and an umbrella for $5.73. She gave the clerk $60. How much change did she get?

A $16.69

B $25.48

C $28.69

D $43.31

6. Karla bought $2\frac{1}{8}$ pounds of oranges, $3\frac{3}{4}$ pounds of grapes, $5\frac{1}{2}$ pounds of potatoes, and $1\frac{3}{4}$ pounds of lettuce. Which is the best estimate of the number of pounds of *fruit* she bought?

F   14 pounds

G   12 pounds

H   11 pounds

J   6 pounds

7. Gina has scores of 85, 95, and 80 on three math tests. Which score will give her an average *greater than* 85 for four math tests?

A   65   C   75

B   70   D   85

8. Nick bought $3\frac{1}{4}$ yards of fabric. He used 18 inches. Which of these is reasonable for the amount of fabric Nick has left?

F   About 60 inches

G   About 100 inches

H   About 110 inches

J   About 120 inches

Use this graph for Questions 9 and 10.

The graph shows the money two people earned each month for six months.

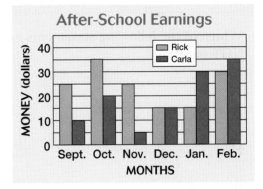

9. Based on the graph, which is true?

A   Both people earned less in October than in September.

B   Both people earned less in December than in January.

C   Both people earned more in December than in November.

D   Both people earned more in February than in January.

10. Which is the best estimate of the amount of money each person earned *after* December 31?

F   Less than $100

G   Between $100 and $150

H   Between $150 and $175

J   Between $175 and $200

211

Multiple-Choice Cumulative Review

Choose the correct letter for each answer.

Number Sense

1. What is 32.965 rounded to the nearest tenth?

   A   30

   B   32.9

   C   32.97

   D   33.0

2. Which of the following statements is NOT true?

   F $\frac{3}{4} > \frac{1}{2}$

   G $\frac{5}{8} < \frac{3}{4}$

   H $\frac{5}{8} > \frac{1}{2}$

   J $\frac{7}{8} < \frac{3}{4}$

3. Which fraction is equivalent to $\frac{2}{3}$?

   A $\frac{10}{12}$

   B $\frac{10}{15}$

   C $\frac{9}{15}$

   D $\frac{4}{12}$

4. What is the least common multiple of 6 and 9?

   F   3

   G   18

   H   36

   J   54

5. What is the difference between 71.4 and 37.7?

   A   43.7   C   37.3

   B   43.1   D   33.7

6. Rose sorted buttons into a tray with 6 equal sections. She put skirt buttons in 2 sections, jacket buttons in 1 section, and blouse buttons in 3 sections. How much more of the tray held blouse buttons than jacket buttons?

   F $\frac{1}{6}$ of the tray   H $\frac{1}{2}$ of the tray

   G $\frac{1}{3}$ of the tray   J $\frac{5}{6}$ of the tray

7. What is the sum of $\frac{5}{6}$ and $\frac{2}{3}$?

   A $1\frac{1}{2}$ C $1\frac{1}{6}$

   B $1\frac{1}{3}$ D $\frac{7}{9}$

8. On Wednesday, Joe and Fred ate $\frac{1}{2}$ of a pizza. On Thursday, they ate $\frac{1}{3}$ of the pizza. Which picture shows how much was left?

   F   H

   G   J

Algebra and Functions

9. Which is the next number in this pattern?

$$2, 5, 11, 23, 47, \ldots$$

A	59	**C**	95
B	71	**D**	107

10. Which point best represents the ordered pair (4, 2)?

F *P*
G *Q*
H *R*
J *S*
K NH

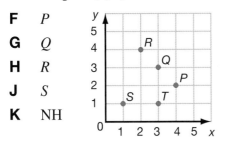

11. Maria is putting boxes on shelves. She put 4 boxes on the top shelf, 7 boxes on the next shelf down, 11 boxes on the next shelf, and 16 boxes on the fourth shelf. If she continues this pattern, how many boxes will be on the next shelf?

A 16 boxes

B 18 boxes

C 20 boxes

D 22 boxes

12. Which point represents the number 3.25 on the number line?

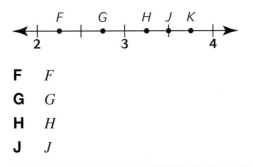

F *F*

G *G*

H *H*

J *J*

Measurement and Geometry

13. The perimeter of a rectangular patio is 72 feet. How many yards is this?

A 9 yards

B 14 yards

C 16 yards

D 24 yards

14. Heather saw an alligator that was 96 inches long. How many feet long was the alligator?

F 6.5 feet

G 8 feet

H 8.5 feet

J 9 feet

15. Mr. Diaz wants to put a fence around a square area of lawn to create a play area for his children. Each side of the play area is to be 4.5 yards long. Which equation can be used to find out how many yards of fencing, *f*, he will need?

A $4.5 + 4.5 = f$

B $4 \times 4.5 = f$

C $2 \times 4.5 = f$

D $4(4.5 \div 4.5) = f$

16. A jar holds 8 cups of water. How many quarts is this?

F 16 quarts

G 6 quarts

H 4 quarts

J 2 quarts

CHAPTER 6

Positive and Negative Numbers

Diagnosing Readiness

In Chapter 6, you will use these skills:

Ⓐ Comparing and Ordering Fractions, Decimals, and Whole Numbers

(pages 6–7, 150–153)

Write the numbers in each set from least to greatest.

1. 27, 0.273, 270.89, 0.22

2. 0.125, 0.85, 0.32, 0.07

3. $\dfrac{6}{2}, \dfrac{3}{8}, \dfrac{12}{9}, \dfrac{39}{10}$

4. 1.0067, 1.0632, 1.0007, 1.00031

Ⓑ Adding and Subtracting Whole Numbers and Decimals

(pages 14–19)

Find each sum or difference.

5. 2,118 + 72 + 390

6. 0.08737 − 0.0062

7. Danny's car has been driven 63,086 miles. He plans to drive the car another 19,000 miles before he sells it. How many miles will the car have been driven when Danny sells the car?

C Writing Expressions

(pages 28–29)

Write each phrase as an expression.

8. 18.3 less than x

9. x divided by 13

10. Forty-five times the sum of x and 0.3

11. Evan has y dollars. He spends 75 cents for lunch. How much does he have left?

D Multiplying and Dividing Whole Numbers and Decimals

(pages 52–54, 58–63)

Find each product or quotient.

12. $43 \times 2 \times 18$

13. $4 \times 18 \times 6 \times 0.5$

14. $0.2072 \div 0.37$

15. $304,500 \div 875$

16. Jackie purchased 16 rolls of wrapping paper. Each roll cost $4.43. How much did she pay altogether?

E Solving Addition and Subtraction Equations

(pages 30–31, 186–187)

Solve for x.

17. $x + 27 = 63$

18. $x - 94 = 7.02$

19. Carl needs $\frac{3}{4}$ cup of flour for his recipe. He only has $\frac{1}{3}$ cup. Write and solve an equation to determine how much more flour Carl needs.

F Solving Multiplication and Division Equations

(pages 68–69, 198–199)

Solve.

20. $\frac{x}{6} = 1$

21. $8 = \frac{s}{9}$

22. $4t = 480$

23. $2r = 1,022$

24. Phil wants to separate his lizards into three tanks so there are 8 lizards in each tank. How many lizards does Phil have?

To the Family and Student

Looking Back

In Grade 5, students used number lines to compare and order positive and negative numbers.

Chapter 6

In this chapter, students will learn how to add, subtract, multiply, and divide integers.

Looking Ahead

In Chapter 10, students will learn how to graph equations involving integers.

Math and Everyday Living

Opportunities to apply the concepts of Chapter 6 abound in everyday situations. During the chapter, think about how positive and negative numbers can be used to solve a variety of real-world problems. The following examples suggest just several of the many situations that could launch a discussion about positive and negative numbers.

Math in the House Your family decides to hire a builder to build a new house. Part of the construction will include digging a basement. The construction crew will dig a hole 15-ft deep by 42-ft wide and 27-ft long. Express the depth of the basement as an integer.

Math and the Community Every winter the volunteers at the community swimming pool have to drain the entire pool. If they empty the pool at the rate of 22 gallons per minute, what is the change in the water volume after 20 minutes?

Math and Chemistry Chlorine and Iodine, two chemicals found in seawater, have extremely different freezing points. The freezing point of chlorine is about ⁻100°C. The freezing point of Iodine is about 114°C. Determine the difference between the freezing points.

Math and Money Your family files two separate federal tax returns this year. At the end of the 1040 form on the first tax return it reads that a tax payment of $6,337 is due from the taxpayer to the Internal Revenue Service. At the end of the 1040 form of the second tax return it reads that a tax refund of $4,829 is owed to the taxpayer from the Internal Revenue Service. Write an equation to show the total amount owed or due to the taxpayer from the two tax returns.

Math and The Earth Asia contains both the highest point in elevation and the lowest point below sea level on land. Mount Everest in Nepal-Tibet reaches a height of 29,028 feet. The Dead Sea in Israel-Jordan measures 1,312 feet below sea level. What is the change in height between the peak of Mount Everest and the deepest point of the Dead Sea?

Math in the Office You go to a government building to obtain a copy of your original birth certificate. You find a parking spot on the second level below the street. The office of Vital Statistics is located on the 5th floor. The first floor is at street level. How many floors do you have to travel to get your birth certificate? In what direction must you go?

While you are at the building you decide to have your passport made. Passports are processed on the 7th floor. After you are finished, how many floors do you have to travel to get to your car? What direction must you go?

Math and Banking Your family purchases groceries for $63.57, using a debit card. Later that day, $50 is deposited in the bank. What is the net change in the account balance?

California Content Standards in Chapter 6 Lessons*

Number Sense	Teach and Practice	Practice
1.1 Compare and order positive and negative fractions, decimals, and mixed numbers and place them on a number line.	6-1	
2.3 Solve addition, subtraction, multiplication, and division problems, including those arising in concrete situations, that use positive and negative integers and combinations of these operations.	6-2, 6-3, 6-5, 6-6, 6-10	6-4, 6-7, 6-8, 6-9

Algebra and Functions	Teach and Practice	Practice
1.1 Write and solve one-step linear equations in one variable.	6-8, 6-9	6-10
1.2 Write and evaluate an algebraic expression for a given situation, using up to three variables.	6-4, 6-7	
1.3 Apply algebraic order of operations and the commutative, associative, and distributive properties to evaluate expressions and justify each step in the process.		6-7

Statistics, Data Analysis, and Probability	Teach and Practice	Practice
1.1 Compute the range, mean, median, and mode of data sets.		6-6

Mathematical Reasoning	Teach and Practice	Practice
1.1 Analyze problems by identifying relationships, distinguishing relevant from irrelevant information, identifying missing information, sequencing and prioritizing information, and observing patterns.		6-1, 6-2, 6-4
1.2 Formulate and justify mathematical conjectures		6-3, 6-5
2.2 Apply strategies and results from simpler problems to more complex problems.		6-8
2.5 Express the solution clearly and logically by using the appropriate mathematical notation and terms and clear language; support solutions with evidence in both verbal and symbolic work.		6-9, 6-10
3.0 Students move beyond a particular problem by generalizing to other situations.		6-4, 6-9, 6-10
3.2 Note the method of deriving the solution and demonstrate a conceptual understanding of the derivation by solving similar problems.		6-9

---

* The symbol (🗝) indicates a key standard as designated in Mathematics Framework for California Public Schools. Full statements of the California Content Standards are found at the beginning of this book following the Table of Contents.

Comparing and Ordering Positive and Negative Numbers

California Content Standard *Number Sense 1.1(🔑): Compare and order positive and negative fractions, decimals, and mixed numbers and place them on a number line.*

Warm-Up Review

Compare. Use >, <, or = for each ⬤.

1. $^+2.3$ ⬤ $^+3.2$

2. $^+0.05$ ⬤ $^+0.051$

3. $^+\frac{3}{4}$ ⬤ $^+\frac{1}{2}$

4. On Monday the temperature was $^+28°F$, on Tuesday it was $^+31°F$. and on Wednesday it was colder than Tuesday. Which day was coldest?

Math Link You know how to compare and order whole numbers, decimals, and fractions. Now you will learn how to compare and order positive and negative numbers.

Example 1

When the outdoor temperature is $^-10°F$ and the wind speed is $^+5$ mph, the wind makes you feel as if the temperature were $^-15°F$.

Read $^-15$ as "negative fifteen." Similarly, read $^+15$ as "positive fifteen."

Wind Chill Table					
Wind Speed (mph) 0	**Outdoor Temperature (°F)**				
	$^-10$	0	$^+10$	$^+20$	$^+30$
$^+5$	$^-15$	$^-5$	$^+6$	$^+16$	$^+27$
$^+10$	$^-34$	$^-22$	$^-9$	$^+3$	$^+16$
$^+15$	$^-45$	$^-31$	$^-18$	$^-5$	$^+9$
$^+20$	$^-53$	$^-39$	$^-24$	$^-10$	$^+4$
$^+25$	$^-59$	$^-44$	$^-29$	$^-15$	$^+1$

Use a number line to compare $^-10$ and $^-15$.

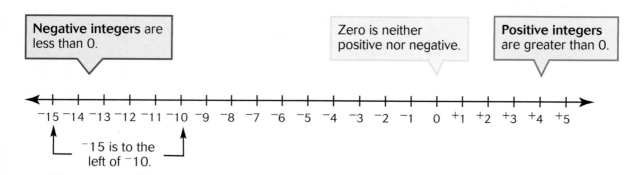

Negative integers are less than 0.

Zero is neither positive nor negative.

Positive integers are greater than 0.

$^-15$ is to the left of $^-10$.

Look at the number line. Just as with positive numbers, negative numbers increase in value when moving from left to right.

$^-15$ is to the left of $^-10$. So, $^-15 < ^-10$.

Additional Standards: Mathematical Reasoning 1.1 (See p. 217.)

Example 2

Integers consist of counting numbers, their opposites, and zero. Pairs of integers that are the same distance from 0, such as $^-2$ and $^+2$, are called **opposites**. The **absolute value** of an integer is its distance from zero on the number line. The absolute value of $^-2$ is 2, the absolute value of $^+2$ is 2.

Place $^+5$, $^-4$, $^+2$, 0, and $^-2$ on a number line. Then write them in order from least to greatest.

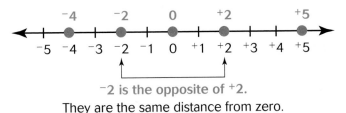

$^-2$ is the opposite of $^+2$.
They are the same distance from zero.

The numbers increase from left to right on the number line.
The numbers in order are $^-4$, $^-2$, 0, $^+2$, $^+5$.

Example 3

Place $^+2$, $^-0.5$, $^+1\frac{3}{4}$, 0, $^-2\frac{1}{4}$ and $^-3$ on a number line. Then write them in order from least to greatest.

The numbers in order from least to greatest are $^-3$, $^-2\frac{1}{4}$, $^-0.5$, 0, $^+1\frac{3}{4}$, $^+2$

Guided Practice   *For another example, see Set A on p. 248.*

Compare. Use >, <, or = for each ⬤.

1. $^+3$ ⬤ $^-2$ **2.** $^-7$ ⬤ 0   **3.** $^-4$ ⬤ $^-9$ **4.** $^+8$ ⬤ $^-2$

Place the numbers on a number line. Then write them in order from least to greatest.

5. 0, $^+5$, $^-12$, $^+15$

6. $^-5$, $^+2\frac{1}{2}$, $^-3\frac{1}{2}$, $^-2.25$, $^+1\frac{3}{4}$

Write the absolute value and opposite of each number.

7. $^-11$ **8.** $^-43$ **9.** $^+18$ **10.** $^-25$

11. Use the table on page 218. On one day the temperature is $^+20°F$ and the wind speed is $^+25$ mph. If the temperature drops to 0°F and the wind speed is $^+5$ mph, will it feel colder or warmer?

Independent Practice *For more practice, see Set A on p. 250.*

Compare. Use >, <, or = for each ⬤.

12. $^+12$ ⬤ $^-13$ **13.** $^-16$ ⬤ $^+31$ **14.** $^-44$ ⬤ 0 **15.** $^-23$ ⬤ $^-25$

Place the numbers on a number line. Write in order from least to greatest.

16. $^+5, ^+3, ^-1$ **17.** $^-6, ^+4.5, ^-5.5, ^+3.5$ **18.** $^-1.75, ^+2\frac{1}{3}, ^+1\frac{1}{4}, ^-\frac{1}{2}$

Use the number line below for Exercises 19–24.
Write the number that represents each point.

19. B   **20.** C   **21.** D   **22.** A   **23.** E   **24.** F

25. Use the table on page 218. On Monday the temperature was $^+30°F$ and the wind speed was $^+20$ mph. On Tuesday the temperature was $^+20°F$ and the wind speed was $^+5$ mph. On which day did it feel colder?

Mixed Review

Use the table at the right for Exercises 26 and 27.

26. During which week was the temperature difference between Miami and Boston the greatest?

27. Find the mean and median temperature for Miami for the 5 weeks.

28. Algebra Solve. $5x = \frac{5}{9}$

29. $\frac{5}{9} \div \frac{1}{3}$ **30.** $1\frac{1}{4} \div \frac{5}{8}$ **31.** $2\frac{3}{4} \div 5\frac{1}{2}$

Mean Temperature (°F) Each Week		
Week	Miami	Boston
1	85	72
2	83	68
3	87	70
4	84	72
5	92	65

⬤ **Test Prep**   Choose the correct letter for each answer.

32. Marcus used $3\frac{1}{3}$ cups of flour to make 2 batches of muffins.
(5-8)   How much flour did Marcus use to make each batch?

A $\frac{3}{5}$ cup   **B** $1\frac{2}{3}$ cup   **C** $5\frac{1}{3}$ cup   **D** $6\frac{2}{3}$ cup   **E** NH

33. $6\frac{1}{2} \times 3$
(5-7)
F 18   **G** $18\frac{1}{2}$ **H** 19   **J** $19\frac{1}{2}$ **K** NH

Adding Integers

California Content Standard *Number Sense 2.3(🔑): Solve addition, . . . problems, including those arising in concrete situations, that use positive and negative integers . . .*

Warm-Up Review

Identify each point on the number line.

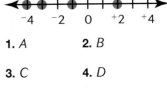

1. *A*   **2.** *B*

3. *C*   **4.** *D*

5. Your football team gained 7 yards and then lost 5 yards. How many more yards do they need in order to gain 10 yards in all?

Math Link You know how to compare and order positive and negative numbers. Now you will learn to add them.

Example 1

On the first day of a golf tournament, Jane was 2 strokes over par, or $^+2$. On the second day she was 3 strokes under par, or $^-3$. How many total strokes under or over par was she after the second day?

Find $^+2 + {}^-3$.

You can add integers using a number line. Think of walking along the number line. Use the following rule: Walk forward for positive numbers, walk backward for negative numbers.

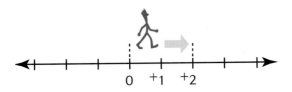

Start at zero, facing the positive numbers. Walk forward 2 steps for $^+2$.

Then walk backward 3 steps for $^-3$.

You stop at -1. $^+2 + {}^-3 = {}^-1$. Jane was 1 stroke under par.

Example 2

Find $^-2 + {}^-3$.

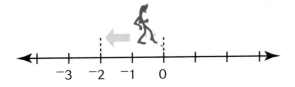

Start at zero, facing the positive integers. Walk backward 2 steps for $^-2$.

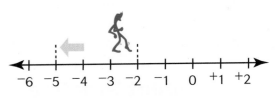

Then walk backward 3 steps for $^-3$.

You stop at $^-5$.

$^-2 + {}^-3 = {}^-5$

More Examples

A $^-3 + {}^-1$

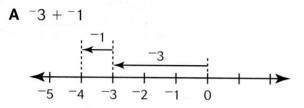

Start at zero.
Move backward 3 units.
Then move backward 1 unit.

$^-3 + {}^-1 = {}^-4$

B $^-4 + {}^+7$

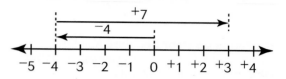

Start at zero.
Move backward 4 units.
Then move forward 7 units.

$^-4 + {}^+7 = {}^+3$

The rules for adding integers are given below.

Rules for Adding Integers

Adding Integers with the Same Sign
- Add the absolute values of the two numbers.
- The sum of two positive integers is positive.
- The sum of two negative integers is negative.

Adding Integers with Different Signs
- Subtract the number with the smaller absolute value from the number with the larger absolute value.
- The sum has the same sign as the number with the larger absolute value.

Guided Practice   *For another example, see Set B on p. 248.*

Add. Use the rules for adding integers or a number line.

1. $^+2 + {}^-7$ **2.** $^+5 + {}^+3$ **3.** $^-4 + {}^-8$ **4.** $^+9 + {}^-5$

5. $^+4 + {}^-8$ **6.** $^-2 + {}^+2$ **7.** $^-3 + {}^-6$ **8.** $^+8 + {}^-7$

9. After scoring 3 over par on the first hole of golf and 1 under par on the second hole, Jack was 1 under par on the third hole and 1 over par on the fourth hole. How many strokes is Jack under or over par after 4 holes?

10. What is the sum of a number and its opposite?

Independent Practice   *For more practice, see Set B on p. 250.*

Add. Use the rules for adding integers or a number line.

11. $^+10 + {}^-11$ **12.** $^-4 + {}^+16$ **13.** $^+7 + {}^-14$ **14.** $^-14 + {}^+8$

15. $^+30 + {}^-8$ **16.** $^-12 + {}^+2$ **17.** $^+13 + {}^-7$ **18.** $^-21 + {}^+12$

Algebra Follow the rule to complete each table.

Rule: Add ⁻4

	Input	Output
19.	⁺6	
20.	⁻9	
21.	0	
22.	⁺1	

Rule: Add ⁺3

	Input	Output
23.	⁻7	
24.	⁻12	
25.	⁺35	
26.	⁻2	

Rule: Add ⁻5

	Input	Output
27.	⁻19	
28.	⁻50	
29.	⁺28	
30.	⁺3	

31. Mental Math Find the sum of ⁻72 + ⁻6 + ⁺72.

32. With respect to par, James scored ⁻2, 0, ⁺3, and ⁻1 on the first four days of the tournament. What is his score so far with respect to par?

33. In golf, the person with the lower score is playing better. With respect to par, Cathy scored ⁻2, ⁺5, ⁻1 and Diane scored ⁻1, ⁺3, ⁻2 during a three-day tournament. Who played better at the tournament?

Mixed Review

34. Miranda had a total score of x on her last math test. She was given 3 bonus points. Write an expression that describes her total score.

Algebra Solve. Write each answer in simplest form.

35. $4y = \dfrac{2}{5}$ **36.** $\dfrac{3}{4}y = 15$ **37.** $\dfrac{1}{5}y = 7$

Write in order from least to greatest.

38. ⁺11, ⁺9, ⁻7, ⁻9   **39.** ⁺1, ⁻1, ⁺2, ⁻2.5   **40.** $^+\dfrac{1}{3}, ^-\dfrac{5}{6}, ^-0.5, 0$

41. In the Northern Hemisphere, the shortest day occurs in December, with an average of $9\dfrac{3}{4}$ hours of daylight. The longest day, in June, has an average of $14\dfrac{1}{2}$ hours of daylight. How much more daylight does the longest day have than the shortest day?

Test Prep   Choose the correct letter for each answer.

42. Which of the following is true?
(6-1)

A $-\dfrac{1}{4} > ^-0.5$ **B** $-\dfrac{1}{4} < ^-0.5$ **C** $^+\dfrac{1}{4} < ^-0.5$ **D** $-\dfrac{1}{4} > ^+0.5$

43. Algebra Solve $n - 9 = 8$
(1-12)

F $n = 1$ **G** $n = 10$ **H** $n = 16$ **J** $n = 17$

Subtracting Integers

California Content Standard *Number Sense 2.3(🔑): Solve addition, subtraction problems, . . . including those arising in concrete situations, that use positive and negative integers . . .*

Math Link In the previous lesson you added integers. Now you will learn how to subtract integers.

Warm-Up Review

Use a number line to add.

1. $^-4 + ^-8$ **2.** $^-5 + ^+3$

3. $^+2 + ^-6$ **4.** $^+1 + ^-7$

5. $^-8 + ^-3$ **6.** $^+9 + ^-9$

7. Jan studied for 95 minutes on Monday, 34 minutes on Thursday, and 47 minutes on Friday. How many more minutes did she study on Monday than on Friday?

Example 1

Find $^+7 - ^-2$.

You can subtract integers using a number line. Remember, walk forward for positive numbers, walk backward for negative numbers.

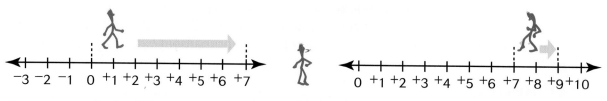

Start at zero, facing the positive numbers. Walk forward 7 steps for $^+7$.

The subtraction sign, −, means **turn around.**

Then walk backward 2 steps for $^-2$.

You stop at $^+9$.

$^+7 - ^-2 = ^+9$

Example 2

Find $^-4 - ^-6$.

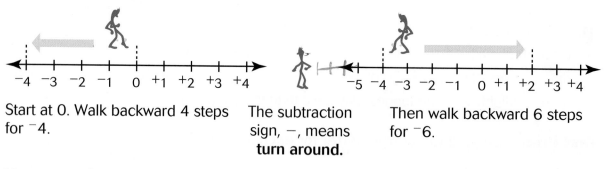

Start at 0. Walk backward 4 steps for $^-4$.

The subtraction sign, −, means **turn around.**

Then walk backward 6 steps for $^-6$.

You stop at $^+2$.

$^-4 - ^-6 = ^+2$

You can use number lines to show a very important relationship between integer addition and subtraction.

Example 3

A Find $^-5 - {}^-4$.

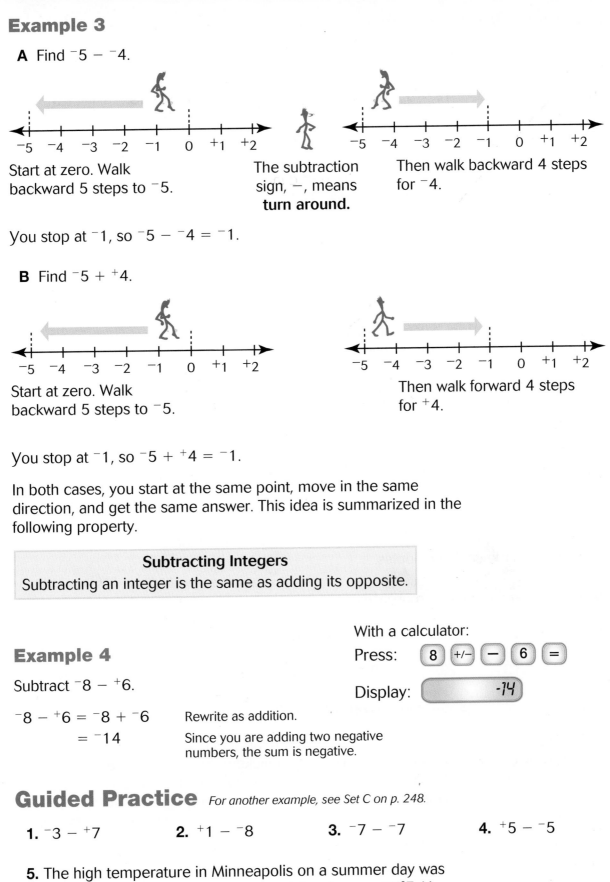

Start at zero. Walk
backward 5 steps to $^-5$.

The subtraction
sign, −, means
turn around.

Then walk backward 4 steps
for $^-4$.

You stop at $^-1$, so $^-5 - {}^-4 = {}^-1$.

B Find $^-5 + {}^+4$.

Start at zero. Walk
backward 5 steps to $^-5$.

Then walk forward 4 steps
for $^+4$.

You stop at $^-1$, so $^-5 + {}^+4 = {}^-1$.

In both cases, you start at the same point, move in the same
direction, and get the same answer. This idea is summarized in the
following property.

> **Subtracting Integers**
> Subtracting an integer is the same as adding its opposite.

Example 4

Subtract $^-8 - {}^+6$.

With a calculator:

Press: 8 [+/−] [−] 6 [=]

Display: -14

$^-8 - {}^+6 = {}^-8 + {}^-6$ Rewrite as addition.

$= {}^-14$ Since you are adding two negative
numbers, the sum is negative.

Guided Practice   *For another example, see Set C on p. 248.*

1. $^-3 - {}^+7$ **2.** $^+1 - {}^-8$ **3.** $^-7 - {}^-7$ **4.** $^+5 - {}^-5$

5. The high temperature in Minneapolis on a summer day was
$^+89°F$. The high temperature on a winter day was $^-7°F$. How
much lower was the winter temperature?

Independent Practice

For more practice, see Set C on p. 250.

6. $^-10 - ^-10$ **7.** $^+7 - ^+3$ **8.** $^+6 - ^-2$ **9.** $^-2 - ^+8$

10. $^+12 - ^-3$ **11.** $^-9 - ^+5$ **12.** $^-15 - 0$ **13.** $^-14 - ^-5$

14. $^+5 - ^-4$ **15.** $^-6 - ^+9$ **16.** $^+10 - ^-1$ **17.** $^+9 - ^+17$

18 Belukha, one of the Altai Mountains in Asia, is $^+14,783$ ft high. Death Valley is 282 ft below sea level. How much higher is Belukha than Death Valley?

19 A scuba diver was 25 feet below the surface of the water. She went down 20 more feet. How far was she below the surface of the water?

20. Math Reasoning If you subtract a negative integer from a positive integer, will your answer always be positive? Explain.

21. Algebra If a and b are integers, then $a - b = a +$ _____.

22. A new amusement park ride has a free-fall altitude change of $^-123$ feet. It replaced a ride that had a free-fall altitude change of $^-65$ feet. How much farther do you free-fall in the new ride?

Mixed Review

23. Algebra Apples cost $0.35 each. Write an expression that describes the cost of a apples.

Write in order from least to greatest.

24. 0, $^-5$, $^-2$ **25.** $^-3$, $^-4$, $^-7$ **26.** $^-4.3$, $^-4.6$, $^-3.7$ **27.** $^-0.6$, $^+\frac{2}{3}$, $^-\frac{1}{3}$

28. $^+11 + ^-13$ **29.** $^-10 + ^+2$ **30.** $^+17 + ^-19$ **31.** $^-20 + ^+4$

Test Prep   Choose the correct letter for each answer.

32. A hiker walked 50 miles during a (4-3) 3-day hike by walking 6 hours each day. Which of the following is a reasonable distance the hiker walked each hour?

   A 2 miles   **C** 4 miles

   B 3 miles   **D** 23 miles

33. A farmer collected 40 eggs from her (2-3) chickens. She packed the eggs in one-dozen cartons to sell. She kept the remaining eggs for her family. What does the remainder represent?

   F The number of cartons of eggs.

   G The number of eggs the chickens laid.

   H The number of eggs in a dozen.

   J The number of eggs the farmer kept.

(**Use Homework Workbook 6–3.**)

Multiple-Choice Cumulative Review

Choose the correct letter for each answer.

1. What is the value of the expression when $b = 6\frac{3}{8}$?

$$12\frac{3}{8} - b + 2\frac{1}{8}$$

A $8\frac{1}{8}$ D $8\frac{19}{24}$

B $8\frac{3}{8}$ E NH

C $8\frac{5}{8}$

Use the graph for Questions 2 and 3.

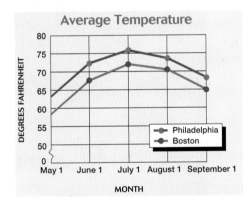

Average Temperature

2. Between which two days did Boston have the greatest increase in temperature?

F June 1 and July 1

G August 1 and September 1

H May 1 and June 1

J July 1 and August 1

3. The record low in Philadelphia last winter was $^-22°F$. What is the difference between the record low and the average temperature on July 1 in Philadelphia?

A 51°F   C 75°F

B 54°F   D 98°F

4. What is the least common multiple of 6, 3, 8, and 2?

F 2

G 12

H 24

J 288

K NH

5. A parade route was extended 1.8 miles so that more people could view it. If the new route is 7.9 miles, how long was the original route?

A 4.39 miles

B 6.1 miles

C 9.7 miles

D 14.22 miles

6. Which of the following has the greatest sum?

F $^-100 + {}^-45$

G $^+33 + {}^-92$

H $^+50 + {}^-86$

J $^+45 + {}^-22$

7. In your vacation photo album, $\frac{2}{3}$ of the 126 pictures are from your vacation to the beach. How many pictures are from other places than the beach?

A 42   C 60

B 57   D 84

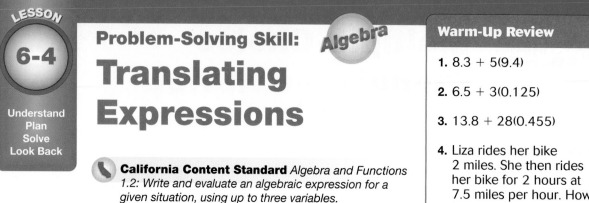

LESSON 6-4

Understand
Plan
Solve
Look Back

Problem-Solving Skill: *Algebra*
Translating Expressions

California Content Standard *Algebra and Functions 1.2: Write and evaluate an algebraic expression for a given situation, using up to three variables.*

Warm-Up Review

1. $8.3 + 5(9.4)$

2. $6.5 + 3(0.125)$

3. $13.8 + 28(0.455)$

4. Liza rides her bike 2 miles. She then rides her bike for 2 hours at 7.5 miles per hour. How far did she ride in all?

Read for Understanding

Lily has learned how water pressure and air pressure affect divers.

As a diver descends, the water pressure increases $^+0.445$ pounds per square inch (psi) every foot below the water's surface. The total pressure a diver feels also includes an additional $^+14.7$ psi, which is caused by the weight of the air pressing down on the water's surface.

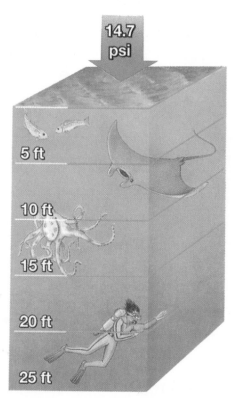

❶ How much does water pressure increase as a diver descends?

❷ How much additional pressure is caused by the weight of the air on the surface?

❸ What makes up the total pressure on a diver?

Think and Discuss

MATH FOCUS

Translating and Using Expressions

Mathematical expressions use variables and numbers. They are part of the language of symbols used in algebra. Writing and translating expressions can help you solve problems.

▲ **Science Connection** Water has weight, which creates pressure on a diver. The deeper you go, the greater the pressure becomes.

Reread the paragraphs at the top of the page.

❹ How would you find the total pressure on a diver 10 feet below the water's surface? 20 feet below the surface?

❺ Write an expression that tells you how to find the total pressure at *d* feet below the surface.

❻ Use your expression to find the total pressure on a diver at the depth $^-67$ feet.

228 *Additional Standards: Number Sense 2.3; Mathematical Reasoning 1.1, 3.0 (See p. 217.)*

Guided Practice

When Lily returns to the surface after a dive, she must be careful not to come up too fast. If the depth of her dive is less than 30 feet, she must not come up more than 1 foot each second. To be safe, she came up from a 25-foot dive at a rate of 1 foot every 2 seconds.

1. What does Lily do to come up safely?

   a. She returns to the surface faster than 1 foot per second.

   b. She returns to the surface at the rate of 1 foot per second.

   c. She returns to the surface more slowly than 1 foot per second.

2. To find out how long it will take her to reach the surface, what does Lily need to know?

   a. The time at which she starts to come back to the surface

   b. The depth at which she starts to come back to the surface

   c. The pressure at which she starts to come back to the surface

3. If you let d be the depth of the dive, which expression tells how many seconds it will take Lily to resurface?

   a. $d + 2$

   b. $2d$

   c. $30d$

Independent Practice

Lily wants to explore some undersea caves. She spent $175 for a new wet suit for the trip. The rental fee for a boat with a driver is $65 an hour. The driver charges an additional fee of $75 for equipment.

BOAT RENTAL $65.00 HOUR

FEE FOR EQUIPMENT $75.00

4. What does Lily know about the rental fee for the boat?

   a. It costs $65 for the whole day.

   b. It costs $65 for each hour.

   c. It costs $175 for the whole day.

5. What other cost does she have to consider when renting the boat?

   a. $175 for a wet suit

   b. $65 for equipment use

   c. $75 for equipment use

6. Math Reasoning Lily uses the expression $65h + 75$ to find the cost of renting a boat. Explain what each term of the expression represents.

7. How much will it cost Lily to rent the boat for 4 hours?

LESSON 6-5 Multiplying Integers

California Content Standard *Number Sense 2.3*(🔑): *Solve . . . multiplication problems, including those arising in concrete situations, that use positive and negative integers and combinations of these operations.*

Math Link You know how to add and subtract integers. Now you will learn how to multiply integers.

Example 1

Thomas and Maria are playing a game in which a player either gains or loses 2 points each turn. They have each taken 5 turns. Maria gained two points each turn and Thomas lost two points each turn. What is each player's score?

Maria's score is $^+5 \times ^+2 = ^+2 + ^+2 + ^+2 + ^+2 + ^+2 = ^+10$
Thomas's score is $^+5 \times ^-2 = ^-2 + ^-2 + ^-2 + ^-2 + ^-2 = ^-10$

When you multiply two integers, you need to know whether the product is positive or negative.

There are four cases to think about.

Case 1: The first case is like Maria's score.

$$^+5 \quad \times \quad ^+2 \quad = \quad ^+10$$
$$\downarrow \qquad\qquad \downarrow \qquad\qquad \downarrow$$

positive number	×	positive number	=	positive number

Case 2: The second case is like Thomas's score.

$$^+5 \quad \times \quad ^-2 \quad = \quad ^-10$$
$$\downarrow \qquad\qquad \downarrow \qquad\qquad \downarrow$$

positive number	×	negative number	=	negative number

Case 3: The third case is the same as the second case, because of the commutative property of multiplication.

$$^-2 \quad \times \quad ^+5 \quad = \quad ^-10$$
$$\downarrow \qquad\qquad \downarrow \qquad\qquad \downarrow$$

negative number	×	positive number	=	negative number

Case 4: To find what happens in the fourth case, complete the pattern in the table.

Look at the products:
$^-25, ^-20, ^-15, ^-10, ^-5, 0, ?, ?$

Notice that the numbers in the pattern increase by 5.

Multiplying by $^-5$
$^-5 \times ^+5 = ^-25$
$^-5 \times ^+4 = ^-20$
$^-5 \times ^+3 = ^-15$
$^-5 \times ^+2 = ^-10$
$^-5 \times ^+1 = ^-5$
$^-5 \times\ \ 0 = 0$
$^-5 \times ^-1 = ?$
$^-5 \times ^-2 = ?$

The next two numbers in the pattern are $^+5$ and $^+10$.

$$^-5 \quad \times \quad ^-2 \quad = \quad ^+10$$
$$\downarrow \qquad\qquad \downarrow \qquad\qquad \downarrow$$

negative number	×	negative number	=	positive number

Additional Standards: Mathematical Reasoning 1.2 (See p. 217.)

The table below shows the four cases presented on page 230.

First Number	Second Number	Product
positive	positive	positive
positive	negative	negative
negative	positive	negative
negative	negative	positive

These 4 cases can be combined into the two rules shown below.

> ### Rules for Multiplying Integers
> The product of two numbers with the same sign is positive.
>
> The product of two numbers with different signs is negative.

More Examples

A Find $^-12 \times ^-5$.

$$^-12 \times ^-5 = 60$$

The signs are the same, so the product is positive.

B Find $^-6 \times ^+8$.

$$^-6 \times ^+8 = ^-48$$

The signs are different, so the product is negative.

C Find $^+7 \times ^-3$.

$$^+7 \times ^-3 = ^-21$$

The signs are different, so the product is negative.

D Find $^+4 \times ^+25$.

$$^+4 \times ^+25 = ^+100$$

The signs are the same, so the product is positive.

Guided Practice *For another example, see Set D on p. 249.*

1. $^-4 \times ^+4$

2. $^+6 \times ^-5$

3. $^-9 \times ^-6$

4. $^-8 \times 0$

5. $^-10 \times ^-3$

6. $^+6 \times ^-12$

7. $^-11 \times ^+11$

8. $^+8 \times ^+9$

9. In another game, Maria loses 3 points each turn for her first four turns. What is her score?

Independent Practice *For more practice, see Set D on p. 251.*

10. $^+11 \times ^-3$

11. $^-12 \times ^-7$

12. $^-4 \times ^+9$

13. $^+8 \times ^+7$

14. $^-15 \times ^-10$

15. $^-9 \times ^+14$

16. $^-11 \times ^-16$

17. $^+6 \times ^-28$

18. $^-5 \times ^+20$

19. $^+30 \times ^-6$

20. $^-25 \times ^-7$

21. $^-12 \times ^-40$

22. Mental Math Find the product of $^-1 \times ^+1 \times ^-1 \times ^+1$.

23. Algebra Evaluate $^+2n - ^-6$ for $n = ^-10$.

Algebra Use order of operations to evaluate each expression.

24. $^-6 + ^+3 \times ^-2 + ^-1$

25. $^+9 - ^-6 + ^-5 \times ^+3$

26. **Math Reasoning** Is the product of three negative numbers positive or negative? What about the product of four negative numbers? Explain your answers.

27. A hockey player's plus-minus rating compares the number of goals scored by his or her team (plus) to the number scored by the opponents (minus) while he or she is playing. Last year, 6 members of Mario's team had a plus-minus rating of $^-17$. What was the total of their ratings?

Mixed Review

For Exercises 28 and 29, tell whether each sample is likely to be representative or biased. Identify each as random sampling, convenience sampling, or responses to a survey.

The staff of the school newspaper conducted a poll to determine whether students prefer to spend money raised during a drive on new computers or on athletic equipment.

28. The newspaper staff asks students attending last week's football game.

29. The newspaper staff passes out questionnaires during a school assembly and asks students to leave them in drop boxes.

30. $^-12 + ^+5$ 31. $^-7 - ^-5$ 32. $^+10 + ^+6$ 33. $^-15 - ^+15$

Algebra Use order of operations to evaluate each expression.

34. $36 - 4 \times 8 + 3$ 35. $52 - 12 + 10 \times 2$ 36. $\frac{1}{4} + \frac{3}{4} \times \frac{1}{6}$

Test Prep Choose the correct letter for each answer.

37. How many more students at Washington School watch music videos than students at West Windsor School?
(2-8)

    A 50   **C** 200

    B 100   **D** 250

Music Video Watchers per School	
West Windsor	🧍🧍🧍🧍🧍
Washington	🧍🧍🧍🧍🧍🧍
Franklin	🧍🧍🧍
Lafayette	🧍🧍🧍🧍🧍🧍🧍🧍

🧍 = 100 students

38. How many more students at Franklin and Lafayette Schools combined watch music videos than students at Washington School?
(2-8)

    F 50   **H** 300

    G 200   **J** 500

Diagnostic Checkpoint

Compare. Use >, <, or = for each ⬤.

1. $^+3$ ⬤ $^-5$
(6-1)

2. $^-9$ ⬤ 0
(6-1)

3. $^-2$ ⬤ $^-1$
(6-1)

4. $-\dfrac{7}{9}$ ⬤ $-\dfrac{8}{9}$
(6-1)

5. $-\dfrac{10}{21}$ ⬤ $\dfrac{-12}{21}$
(6-1)

6. $^-17$ ⬤ $^+5$
(6-1)

7. $^-1$ ⬤ $^-1$
(6-1)

8. $^-3.85$ ⬤ $^-3.58$
(6-1)

Write in order from least to greatest.

9. $^-5, 0, ^-3, ^-2, ^+4$
(6-1)

10. $^+5, ^+7, ^-6, ^-4$
(6-1)

11. $^-9.9, ^+0.6, ^-3.3, ^+0.4, ^+0.1, ^-0.2$
(6-1)

Add or subtract.

12. $^+8 + ^-7$
(6-2)

13. $^-9 + ^-3$
(6-2)

14. $^-6 - ^+9$
(6-3)

15. $^+11 - ^-3$
(6-3)

16. $^-5 - ^-3$
(6-3)

17. $^-2 + ^+2$
(6-2)

18. $^-2 - ^+2$
(6-3)

19. $^+7 + ^-4$
(6-2)

20. $^-10 - ^-9$
(6-3)

21. $^+11 - ^-8$
(6-3)

22. $^+18 - ^+4$
(6-3)

23. $^-15 - ^-15$
(6-3)

Find the product.

24. $^-15 \times ^-4$
(6-5)

25. $^+14 \times ^-8$
(6-5)

26. $^-9 \times ^-4$
(6-5)

27. $^+4 \times ^+16$
(6-3)

28. $^-22 \times ^+6$
(6-5)

29. $^+7 \times ^-22$
(6-5)

30. $^-70 \times ^-2$
(6-5)

31. $^-8 \times ^-9$
(6-5)

Solve.

32. Death Valley is 282 ft below sea level. A hot-air balloon flying
(6-2) over this desert is 200 ft above sea level. How many feet above Death Valley is the balloon?

33. At 6:00 A.M. you check the thermometer. It reads $^-18°F$. At
(6-3) noon the thermometer shows that the temperature has risen to 23°F. How many degrees did the temperature rise?

34. Chester deposits $3,250 into his checking account on the 10th of every
(6-4) month. On the 15th of each month, $319 is automatically deducted from his account to pay his car payment. Write an expression to show the amount of money Chester has in his account on the 16 TH of the month if he had x dollars in his account at the beginning of the month.

35. Is the product of two negative integers greater than or less
(6-5) than zero? Explain.

Dividing Integers

California Content Standard *Number Sense 2.3*(🔑)*: Solve . . . division problems, including those arising in concrete situations, that use positive and negative integers and combinations of these operations.*

Warm-Up Review

1. $^-5 \times {}^+4$ 2. $^-6 \times {}^-7$

3. $^-8 \times {}^-11$ 4. $^+12 \times {}^+3$

5. The temperature dropped 1.5° in one minute, 2.5° the next minute, and 5° the third minute. Find the mean drop in temperature per minute.

Math Link You can use what you know about multiplying integers to help you understand how to divide integers.

Remember that multiplication and division are inverse operations. They "undo" each other. This relationship tells us how to find the sign of the quotient when dividing integers.

		Examples			
Sign of dividend	Sign of divisor	Division fact	Related multiplication fact	Quotient n	Sign of quotient
+	+	$^+15 \div {}^+3$	$^+3n = {}^+15$	$^+5$	+
−	−	$^-15 \div {}^-3$	$^-3n = {}^-15$	$^+5$	+
+	−	$^+15 \div {}^-3$	$^-3n = {}^+15$	$^-5$	−
−	+	$^-15 \div {}^+3$	$^+3n = {}^-15$	$^-5$	−

The rules for dividing integers are similar to the rules for multiplying integers.

> **Rules for Dividing Integers**
> The quotient of two numbers with the same sign is positive.
> The quotient of two numbers with different signs is negative.

Example

A submarine dives 210 feet in 3 dives. What is the average change in depth per dive?

The total change in depth is $^-210$ feet. Divide by $^+3$ to find the mean.

Total depth of dives		Number of dives		Mean change in depth per dive
$^-210$	÷	$^+3$	=	n

$$^-70 = n$$

The average change in depth per dive is $^-70$ feet.

Here's WHY It Works

To find $^-210 \div {}^+3 = n$ use a related multiplication fact:

$$^+3n = {}^-210$$

The product is negative. Because of the rules for multiplying integers, one of the factors must be negative. Since $^+3$ is positive, n must be negative. So, $^-210 \div {}^+3 = {}^-70$.

🔑 *Additional Standards: Statistics, Data Analysis, and Probability 1.1 (See p. 217.)*

Guided Practice For another example, see Set E on p. 249.

1. $\dfrac{-35}{+7}$ 　　　　2. $\dfrac{-75}{-3}$ 　　　　3. $^-120 \div {}^+4$ 　　　　4. $^+560 \div {}^-8$

5. A company lost the following amounts in four days: $1,230; $2,570; $805; $415. What was the company's average loss per day for the four days?

Independent Practice For more practice, see Set E on p. 251.

6. $\dfrac{-64}{+4}$ 　　　7. $\dfrac{-280}{+7}$ 　　　8. $\dfrac{-350}{-50}$ 　　　9. $\dfrac{+500}{-25}$

10. $^+360 \div {}^-9$ 　　　11. $^-32 \div {}^-4$ 　　　12. $^+51 \div {}^-3$ 　　　13. $^-95 \div {}^+5$

Use the data in the table below for Exercises 14–15.

Sun.	Mon.	Tues.	Wed.	Thurs.	Fri.	Sat.
$^-5$°F	$^-7$°F	$^-1$°F	$^+2$°F	$^+3$°F	$^-2$°F	$^-4$°F

14. Find the average temperature for the week.

15. Find the median temperature for the week.

16. **Mental Math** Is the quotient $^-238 \div {}^+34$ greater than or less than zero?

Mixed Review

17. Which measure of central tendency, mean, median, or mode, is *not* appropriate to indicate the typical temperature for the week using the data in the table above? Explain your answer.

18. $^+2 - {}^+9$ 　　　19. $^-2 - {}^+12$ 　　　20. $^-13 - {}^-4$ 　　　21. $^-5 - {}^+6$

22. $^+8 \times {}^-9$ 　　　23. $^-10 \times {}^-4$ 　　　24. $^-7 \times {}^+7$ 　　　25. $^-2 \times {}^-2 \times {}^-2$

Test Prep Choose the correct letter for each answer.

26. **Algebra** It costs $5 to join a video
(6-4)　club and then $2 to rent each video. Which expression gives the total cost of joining and renting v videos?

　　A $^+2 + {}^+5v$ 　　**C** $^+5 + v$

　　B $(^+5 + {}^+2)v$ 　　**D** $^+5 + {}^+2v$

27. **Algebra** Which equations are true?
(6-5)
　　I. $^-10 \times {}^+2 = {}^+20$
　　II. $^-10 \div {}^-2 = {}^+5$
　　III. $^+10 \times {}^-2 = {}^-20$
　　IV. $^-10 \div {}^+2 = {}^-5$

　　F Only I 　　　　**H** Only II, III, and IV

　　G Only II and III 　　**J** I, II, III, and IV

Expressions with Integers

Algebra

Warm-Up Review

Write each phrase as an expression.

1. 8 less than *n*

2. 3 more than the product of 2 and *k*

3. 4 times the difference of *x* and 4

4. Jim is atop a hill 50 feet above sea level. He descends the hill at a rate of 1.5 feet per second. Write an expression for his height above sea level after *t* seconds.

California Content Standard *Algebra and Functions 1.2: Write and evaluate an algebraic expression for a given situation, using up to three variables.*

Math Link You have written and evaluated expressions in previous chapters. In this lesson you will work with expressions that use integers.

Negative numbers, such as $^-200$, are always written with a negative ($^-$) sign. Positive numbers, such as $^+100$, are usually written without the positive ($^+$) sign. From now on, positive numbers will be written without a positive sign.

Example 1

While hiking, Addie and her family started at an altitude of 500 feet above sea level and descended at a rate of 200 feet per hour. Write an expression for their altitude after *h* hours. Evaluate the expression to find their altitude after 3 hours.

Starting altitude	Descent each hour	Number of hours
↓	↓	↓
500 $-$	200 $\times$	*h*

Now, evaluate the expression for $h = 3$.

$500 - 200h$
$500 - 200(3)$ Substitute 3 for *h*.
$500 - 600$ Use the order of operations. Multiply first.
$500 + {}^-600$ Subtracting 600 is the same as adding $^-600$.
$^-100$ Add. The signs are different and $^-600$ is farther from zero than 500, so the sum is negative.

After 3 hours their altitude is $^-100$ feet, or 100 feet below sea level.

Example 2

Complete the table.

n	5 − 3*n*
2	
$^-1$	
$^-4$	

$5 - 3(2) = 5 - 6 = {}^-1$

$5 - 3(^-1) = 5 - {}^-3 = 5 + 3 = 8$

$5 - 3(^-4) = 5 - {}^-12 = 5 + 12 = 17$

n	5 − 3*n*
2	$^-1$
$^-1$	8
$^-4$	17

 Additional Standards: Number Sense 2.3; Algebra and Functions 1.3 (See p. 217.)

Guided Practice *For another example, see Set F on p. 249.*

Complete each table.

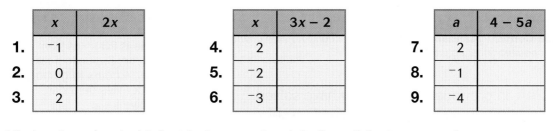

	x	2x
1.	⁻1	
2.	0	
3.	2	

	x	3x − 2
4.	2	
5.	⁻2	
6.	⁻3	

	a	4 − 5a
7.	2	
8.	⁻1	
9.	⁻4	

10. A submarine is 10 feet below sea level. It dives 8 feet a second. Write an expression to describe the submarine's position after *s* seconds. Evaluate the expression to find the submarine's position after 30 seconds.

Independent Practice *For more practice, see Set F on p. 251.*

Complete each table.

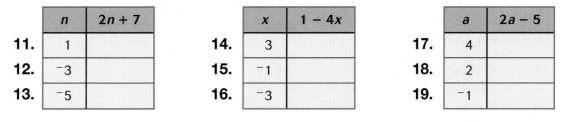

	n	2n + 7
11.	1	
12.	⁻3	
13.	⁻5	

	x	1 − 4x
14.	3	
15.	⁻1	
16.	⁻3	

	a	2a − 5
17.	4	
18.	2	
19.	⁻1	

20. Math Reasoning Will the expression 4 − 2n have a positive or a negative value when *n* is negative? Explain your answer.

Mixed Review

21. A hot air balloon was one mile above the ground when it started to ascend $\frac{1}{8}$ of a mile a minute. How high was the balloon after 5 minutes?

22. ⁻5 × 8

23. ⁻2 × ⁻16

24. $\frac{-18}{2}$

25. ⁻56 ÷ ⁻7

26. ⁻100 ÷ ⁻4

27. 9 × ⁻11

28. ⁻5 × ⁻25

29. 36 ÷ ⁻12

🖊 Test Prep Choose the correct letter for each answer.

30. Jack ran 5 laps of the track in 8.5 minutes. What was his
(2-7) average time per lap?

   A 0.17 min   **B** 1.7 min   **C** 17 min   **D** 19 min

31. Which of the following is the best estimate of $3\frac{1}{3} \times \frac{8}{9}$?
(5-6)

   F 1   **G** 3   **H** 5   **J** 7

LESSON 6-8 Equations with Integers

Algebra

Warm-Up Review

Solve each equation.

1. $n - 4 = 7$ 2. $x + 5 = 17$

3. $4x = 40$ 4. $\frac{n}{6} = 3$

5. Mia is 28 miles from home. Suppose it takes her 4 hours to go home at x miles per hour. Solve for x.

California Content Standard *Algebra and Functions 1.1 (⟜): Write and solve one-step linear equations in one variable.*

Math Link In previous chapters, you have solved equations. In this lesson you will learn how to solve equations involving integers.

The properties of equality that you have been using to solve equations with whole numbers, decimals, and fractions also apply to solving equations with integers.

Example 1

Over three hours, the temperature dropped a total of 36°F.
Solve $3t = {}^-36$ to find the average change in temperature per hour.

Let t = the average change per hour.

number of hours		average change per hour		total change in temperature
↓		↓		↓
3	×	t	=	$^-36$

$3t = {}^-36$

$\dfrac{3t}{3} = \dfrac{^-36}{3}$ Divide each side by 3.

$t = {}^-12$ Negative divided by positive is negative.

Check: $3t = {}^-36$ Replace t with $^-12$.

$3 \times {}^-12 \overset{?}{=} {}^-36$ Multiply.

$^-36 = {}^-36$ The answer checks.

The average change in temperature was $^-12$°F per hour.

Example 2

$n + 12 = 4$

$n + 12 - 12 = 4 - 12$ Subtract 12 from both sides.

$n + 0 = 4 + {}^-12$ Change subtraction to addition.

$n = {}^-8$ Add.

Check: $n + 12 = 4$ Replace n with $^-8$

$^-8 + 12 \overset{?}{=} 4$ Add.

$4 = 4$ The answer checks.

Example 3

$\dfrac{a}{15} = {}^-3$

$15 \times \dfrac{a}{15} = {}^-3 \times 15$ Multiply both sides by 15.

$a = {}^-45$ Negative times positive is negative.

Check: $\dfrac{a}{15} = {}^-3$ Replace a with $^-45$.

$\dfrac{^-45}{15} \overset{?}{=} {}^-3$ Divide.

$^-3 = {}^-3$ The answer checks.

238 *Additional Standards: Number Sense 2.3 (⟜); Mathematical Reasoning 2.2 (See p. 217.)*

Guided Practice *For another example, see Set G on p. 249.*

1. $\dfrac{x}{^-10} = 12$ **2.** $^-8d = ^-104$ **3.** $t - 17 = ^-35$ **4.** $r + 56 = ^-20$

5. After Marcus spent \$25 for a pair of blue jeans, he was \$8 in debt. Use the equation $n - 25 = ^-8$ to find how much money Marcus had before he bought the blue jeans.

Independent Practice *For more practice, see Set G on p. 251.*

6. $n - 15 = ^-9$ **7.** $p - 93 = 12$ **8.** $a + 70 = 55$ **9.** $s + 9 = ^-28$

10. $^-3c = 42$ **11.** $\dfrac{m}{^-12} = ^-6$ **12.** $6h = ^-48$ **13.** $\dfrac{w}{6} = ^-1$

14. The temperature dropped 30° in 5 hours. Use the equation $5d = ^-30$ to find the average temperature change per hour.

15. Math Reasoning Without solving, tell whether each variable is greater than, less than, or equal to 95.

a. $k - 10 = 95$ **b.** $n + ^-2 + 2 = 95$ **c.** $p + 40 = 95$

Mixed Review

16. Carole had \$50 to spend on aquarium supplies. She spent $\dfrac{1}{5}$ of the total for plants. Then she spent $\dfrac{1}{2}$ of what she had left on fish. How much did she spend on plants and fish?

17. $^-12 \div 2$ **18.** $\dfrac{-52}{^-13}$ **19.** $\dfrac{70}{^-14}$ **20.** $^-80 \div ^-10$

Complete each table.

x	x − 5
21. ⁻3	
22. ⁻1	
23. 1	

x	2x + 3
24. 3	
25. ⁻2	
26. 4	

n	6 − 4n
27. 4	
28. 0	
29. ⁻1	

Test Prep Choose the correct letter for each answer.

30. Which of the following is true?
(4-8)

A $\dfrac{1}{4} > \dfrac{1}{3}$ **B** $2\dfrac{1}{2} < 2\dfrac{3}{7}$ **C** $\dfrac{1}{8} > \dfrac{1}{7}$ **D** $3\dfrac{1}{5} < \dfrac{17}{5}$

31. Evaluate 2^5.
(4-1)

F 10 **G** 16 **H** 32 **J** 64 **K** NH

Problem-Solving Strategy:

Write an Equation  *Algebra*

California Content Standard *Algebra and Functions 1.1: Write and solve one-step linear equations in one variable.*

Warm-Up Review

Solve each equation.

1. $x - 9 = 5$

2. $^-2n = 24$

3. $x + 11 = ^-4$

4. $\frac{n}{^-3} = ^-7$

5. An insect is 8 inches above the ground and a bird is 50 inches above the insect. How far above the ground is the bird?

Example

In the picture at the right, a kingfisher hovers over his prey. How far above the water is the bird?

Understand

What do you need to find?

You need to find the distance between the bird and the water.

Plan

How can you solve the problem?

You can write a subtraction equation to represent the distance between the fish and the bird.

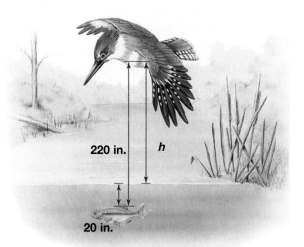

220 in.   *h*

20 in.

Solve

Write an equation. Let *h* represent the height of the bird above the water.

bird above   fish below   total
water   water   distance

$$h \quad - \quad ^-20 \quad = \quad 220$$

$$h - {}^-20 = 220 \qquad \text{Rewrite subtraction as addition.}$$
$$h + 20 = 220 \qquad \text{Add the opposite of 20 to both sides.}$$
$$h + 20 + {}^-20 = 220 + {}^-20 \qquad \text{Add.}$$
$$h + 0 = 200$$
$$h = 200$$

The bird is 200 inches above the water.

Look Back

The fish is 20 inches below water level and the bird is 200 inches above the water. $200 - {}^-20 = 220$. The answer is correct.

Additional Standards: Number Sense 2.3; Mathematical Reasoning 2.5, 3.0, 3.2 (See p. 217.)

Guided Practice

Write an equation to solve each problem. Then solve the problem.

1. A diver was 50 feet below the surface of the water. She rose to 20 feet below the surface. How many feet did she rise?

2. Bill separates 108 fish equally into nine fish bowls. How many fish will be in each bowl?

Independent Practice

Write an equation to solve each problem. Then solve the problem.

3. A pelican sat on top of a 10-foot pole that was on a dock 3 feet above the water. The pelican dove to a depth of 5 feet below the surface of the water. What was the total distance the pelican traveled?

4. Four friends have a debt of $96. They decide to equally share the debt among themselves. Find each friend's debt.

5. The stock market fell 165 points in 3 hours. What is the average change each hour?

Mixed Review

Try these or other strategies to solve each problem. Tell which strategy you used.

Problem-Solving Strategies

- *Work Backward*
- *Find a Pattern*
- *Solve a Simpler Problem*
- *Write an Equation*

6. Acme makes wagons, bicycles, and tricycles. Last week they made as many wagons as tricycles, and half as many bicycles as wagons. If they used 400 wheels, how many of each vehicle did they make?

7. George needs 42 apples for a science project. Each day he brings home 7 apples, but every night his sisters and brother eat 3 of them. On which day will he have 42 apples?

8. Tony spent exactly $8.00 on lunch for 7 days. Lunches cost $1.10 without milk and $1.25 with milk. How many lunches with milk did he buy?

LESSON

6-10

Understand
Plan
Solve
Look Back

Problem-Solving Application:
Using Integers

Algebra

California Content Standard *Number Sense 2.3 ( ): Solve addition, subtraction, multiplication, and division problems, including those arising in concrete situations, that use positive and negative integers and combinations of these operations.*

Warm-Up Review

Fill in the blanks.

1. Positive × Negative = ____.

2. Negative + Negative = ____.

3. Negative × Negative = ____.

4. Negative ÷ Positive = ____.

5. Positive − Negative = ____.

Example

In the first quarter of the football game the Redhawks gained 7 yards on the first play and then lost 10 yards. On the third play they gained 8 yards. How many yards had the Redhawks gained or lost by the end of three plays?

Understand

What do you need to find?

You need to find the total number of yards gained or lost by the end of the three plays.

Plan

How can you solve the problem?

You can write an equation. Add the yards gained ($^+$) and the yards lost ($^-$).

Solve

Let y represent the number of yards gained or lost by the end of 3 plays.

$y = {}^+7 + {}^-10 + {}^+8$
$y = {}^+15 + {}^-10$
$y = {}^+5$

The Redhawks had gained 5 yards after the three plays.

Look Back

How could you draw a diagram to check if the answer is reasonable?

REDHAWKS

— Redhawks + (left side)

+ Bulldogs − (right side)

10
20
30
40
50
40
30
20
10

BULLDOGS

Additional Standards: Algebra and Functions 1.1; Mathematical Reasoning 2.5, 3.0 (See p. 217.)

Guided Practice

Write an equation for each problem. Then solve the problem.

1. The Bulldogs lost 12 yards on the first play, gained 5 yards on the second play, and lost 3 yards on the third play. How many yards had the Bulldogs gained or lost by the end of the 3 plays?

2. The difference between the highest and lowest temperatures in North Dakota is 181°F. If the highest temperature is 121°F, what is the lowest temperature?

Independent Practice

Write an equation for each problem. Then solve the problem.

3. Andy and his parents want to explore a cave passage whose elevation is ⁻56 feet. They plan to descend at a rate of 8 feet per minute. How long will it take them to reach the passage?

4. The Redhawks gained 9 yards on the first play. After the second play the Redhawks had lost a total of 5 yards during the two plays. Did they gain or lose yards on the second play? How many?

5. The difference between the highest and lowest temperatures ever recorded in California is 179°F. If the lowest temperature is ⁻45°F, what is the highest temperature?

6. In Friday's game, Carlos lost 4 yards on each of three consecutive plays. On the next two plays he gained 3 yards and 5 yards. How many yards had he gained or lost?

7. Marisa's father told her the temperature had dropped 20 degrees to ⁻12° since she had gotten home from school. What was the temperature when Marisa got home from school?

Mixed Review

8. In a football game, from their 35-yard line, the Redhawks kicked the ball a distance of 40 yards toward the Bulldogs' goal line. On what yard line did the Bulldogs get the ball?

9. In 1998, movie ticket prices were twice the 1990 prices. The price fell $0.50 in 1999 and then rose $1.25 to $8.25 in 2000. How much were tickets in 1990?

Diagnostic Checkpoint

Write the missing word that completes each sentence.

1. You can solve an equation by using ___?___.
(1-12)

2. One way to subtract an integer is to add its ___?___.
(6-3)

3. ___?___ are numbers greater than zero.
(6-1)

Word Bank

absolute value
integers
inverse operations
opposite
negative numbers
positive numbers

Find each quotient.

4. $^-27 \div ^-3$
(6-6)

5. $^-8 \div ^+2$
(6-6)

6. $^+72 \div ^-9$
(6-6)

7. $^+180 \div ^+3$
(6-6)

8. $^-36 \div ^+6$
(6-6)

9. $^-67 \div ^+67$
(6-6)

10. $0 \div ^-8$
(6-6)

11. $^-12 \div ^-4$
(6-6)

Complete each table.

12. (6-7)

x	$3x - 4$
$^-1$	
0	
$^+2$	
$^+3$	

13. (6-7)

y	$2 - 5y$
$^-2$	
$^-1$	
$^+1$	
$^+3$	

14. (6-7)

b	$7 - 8b$
$^+4$	
$^+1$	
$^-3$	
$^-5$	

Solve each equation.

15. $z - ^-3 = 5$
(6-8)

16. $^-8m = 96$
(6-8)

17. $t - 5 = ^-7$
(6-8)

18. $^-9w = ^-90$
(6-8)

19. $b \div ^-16 = 3$
(6-8)

20. $x + ^-6 = ^-5$
(6-8)

21. $s \div 4 = ^-12$
(6-8)

22. $10x = ^-70$
(6-8)

23. $t + 9 = ^-11$
(6-8)

Write an equation to solve each problem.

24. Kent's most profitable stock dropped 2 points to an all time low value of 22. Find the value before the decrease.
(6-9)

25. An airplane was flying 14,211 meters high. It dropped 920 meters, then rose 112 meters, and then dropped 87 meters. What is its new altitude?
(6-10)

Chapter 6 Test

1. Plot the following points on a number line. Then order them from least to greatest.

$^-6, ^+3, ^-1.5, ^-\frac{2}{3}, ^+1, ^+3.5, ^-4.6$

```
←++++++++++++++++→
 ¯6   ¯4   ¯2   0   ⁺2   ⁺4   ⁺6
```

Find each answer.

2. $^-7 + ^+4$

3. $^+18 \div ^-6$

4. $^-15 - ^-22$

5. $^-12 \times ^-72$

6. $^+15 + ^-30$

7. $0 \div ^-72$

8. $^-10 \times ^-51$

9. $^-21 - ^-17$

10. $^+55 \times ^-6$

11. $^+28 \div ^-2$

12. $^-77 \div ^-7$

13. $^+44 + ^-6$

Complete each table.

14.

x	2 − 3x
¯4	
¯2	
⁺1	

15.

s	5s + 4
¯1	
0	
⁺1	

16.

t	x − 6
¯5	
¯3	
⁺4	

Solve each equation.

17. $n - ^-6 = 32$

18. $b \div ^-8 = 55$

19. $^-24m = 120$

20. $5s = ^-75$

21. $t + ^-13 = 25$

22. $x - 11 = ^-16$

Use the following information for Exercises 23–24.

Some scientists explored a man-made pond. They created a profile of the bottom of the pond at the right to use in their research.

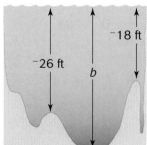

¯18 ft
¯26 ft
b

23. Evaluate the expression $(^-26 + b + ^-18) \div 3$ for $b = ^-31$ feet to find the average depth of the pond.

24. One of the scientists was 22 feet below the surface of the water. She then rose to 5 feet below the surface. Let d be the distance the scientist rose. Write and solve an equation to show how many feet the scientist rose.

25. The temperature at noon was 12°F. The temperature had dropped 15° by midnight and dropped another 5° by 6:00 A.M. What was the temperature at 6:00 A.M.?

Multiple-Choice
Chapter 6 Test

Choose the correct letter for each answer.

1. Select the set of numbers that is ordered from least to greatest.

    A $^+1, -\frac{1}{2}, -\frac{1}{8}, 0, ^+6$

    B $^-6, ^-17, 0, ^+1.67, ^+11.3$

    C $^-12, ^-7, ^-2.5, 0, ^+3$

    D $^-1.7, ^-2.2, ^-3.7, 0, ^+1.8$

    E   NH

2. The product of an integer greater than zero and an integer less than zero

    F   is a negative integer.

    G   is zero.

    H   is a positive integer.

    J   can be positive or negative.

3. $^-288 \div 3$

    A $^+864$

    B $^+96$

    C $^-96$

    D $^-864$

    E   NH

4. $^+36 + ^-43$

    F $^-79$

    G $^-7$

    H $^+7$

    J $^+79$

    K   NH

Use the table for Questions 5–7.

Above and Below Sea Level	
Place	Elevation (ft)
Death Valley	−282
Salton Sea	−235
Foraker	17,400
Mt. St. Elias	18,008
Mt. McKinley	20,320

5. Which mountain is 18,290 feet higher than Death Valley?

    A   Foraker

    B   Mt. St. Elias

    C   Mt. McKinley

    D   Impossible to know

6. Which is the closest to sea level?

    F   Death Valley

    G   Salton Sea

    H   Foraker

    J   Mt. McKinley

7. What is the difference in elevation between Mt. St. Elias and Salton Sea?

    A   17,773 feet

    B   18,213 feet

    C   18,243 feet

    D   18,290 feet

8. An airplane is descending 168 feet per minute. Which expression best describes the change in the airplane's altitude over the past h minutes?

   F $\quad ^-168 \times (^-h)$

   G $\quad ^+168h$

   H $\quad ^-168h$

   J $\quad ^-168 \div ^-h$

---

9. Subtract $^-2$ from the product of 18 and $^-3$.

   A $\quad ^-56$

   B $\quad ^-52$

   C $\quad ^+52$

   D $\quad ^+56$

   E $\quad$ NH

---

10. Select the point that describes $^-6 - {}^-2$.

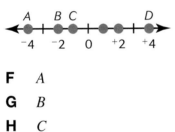

   F $\quad A$

   G $\quad B$

   H $\quad C$

   J $\quad D$

   K $\quad$ NH

---

11. Which statement is true?

   A $\quad ^+5 < {}^+2$

   B $\quad ^-5 > {}^-4$

   C $\quad ^+9 < {}^-10$

   D $\quad ^-6 < {}^-1$

---

12. The Cougar football team has only 3 minutes left to score a touchdown to win the game against the Mustangs. On the first play, the Cougars were penalized 10 yards. On the second play, the Cougars lost 6 yards. On the third play the Cougars gained 11 yards. How many yards did the Cougars gain $(+)$ or lose $(-)$ in the 3 plays?

   F $\quad ^-3$ yards

   G $\quad ^+3$ yards

   H $\quad ^-5$ yards

   J $\quad ^+5$ yards

---

13. Before the Mustang's first play, they needed 6 yards to score a touchdown. On the first play the Mustangs gained 3 yards. On the second play they lost 12 yards. On the third play they gained 9 yards. How many yards do they need on their fourth play to score a touchdown?

   A $\quad$ 0 yards

   B $\quad$ 2 yards

   C $\quad ^-2$ yards

   D $\quad$ 6 yards

---

14. Which statement is false?

   F $\quad ^-3 \times {}^-12 = {}^+36$

   G $\quad ^-37 - {}^+2 = {}^+39$

   H $\quad ^-9 = {}^-81 \div {}^+9$

   J $\quad ^-22 + {}^-15 - 7 = {}^-44$

Reteaching

Set A *(pages 218–220)*

Write ⁻4, ⁻1.3, 3, 1.6, 0.5, ⁻2 in order from least to greatest.

Locate the numbers on a number line.

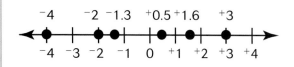

Write the numbers from left to right.

⁻4, ⁻2, ⁻1.3, 0.5, 1.6, 3

Remember negative numbers are less than zero. Zero is neither (+) nor (−) and positive numbers are greater than zero.

Compare. Use >, <, or = for each ⬤.

1. ⁻2.5 ⬤ ⁻2   **2.** 1.7 ⬤ ⁻1.6

3. 0 ⬤ ⁻6   **4.** ⁻17 ⬤ ⁻20

Write in order from least to greatest.

5. 15, 13.7, ⁻6, ⁻1, 5

6. ⁻2, ⁻3, ⁻7, 7, $\frac{1}{2}$

Set B *(pages 221–223)*

Use a number line to add ⁻3 + ⁺1.

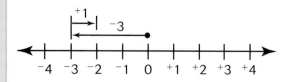

Start at 0, move 3 to the left. Then move 1 to the right.

So, ⁻3 + ⁺1 = ⁻2.

Remember when adding two negative numbers the sum is negative. When adding a positive number and a negative number, the sum has the same sign as the number that is farther from zero on the number line.

1. ⁻5 + ⁺7   **2.** ⁺11 + ⁻4

3. ⁻3 + ⁻9   **4.** ⁻4 + ⁻3

5. ⁻1 + ⁻8   **6.** ⁻13 + ⁺13

7. ⁺10 + ⁻14   **8.** ⁻11 + ⁻15

Set C *(pages 224–226)*

Subtract ⁻7 − ⁺5.

⁻7 − ⁺5 = ⁻7 + (⁻5)
     = ⁻12

Add the opposite of ⁺5 to ⁻7.

Remember to subtract an integer, add its opposite.

1. ⁻10 − ⁺3   **2.** ⁺8 − ⁺8

3. ⁺3 − ⁺7   **4.** 0 − ⁻3

5. ⁺19 − ⁻12   **6.** ⁻35 − ⁻9

Set D *(pages 230–232)*

Find the product of $^-11 \times {}^-16$.

The signs are both negative so the product is positive.

$^-11 \times {}^-16 = {}^+176$

Remember when multiplying integers:
positive × positive = positive,
positive × negative = negative,
negative × positive = negative,
negative × negative = positive.

1. $^-9 \times {}^-12$ 2. $^-30 \times {}^+5$

3. $^+7 \times {}^-20$ 4. $^-2 \times 0$

5. $^+12 \times {}^-15$ 6. $^-25 \times {}^-6$

Set E *(pages 234–235)*

Find $^-18 \div {}^+6$

The quotient of two numbers with different signs is negative.

$^-18 \div {}^+6 = {}^-3$

Remember the rules for dividing integers: the quotient of two numbers with the same sign is positive, the quotient of two numbers with different signs is negative.

1. $^-21 \div {}^-7$ 2. $^-64 \div {}^+8$

3. $^-65 \div {}^+5$ 4. $^-72 \div {}^-3$

Set F *(pages 236–237)*

Complete the table.

b	$^-8 + 2b$	
0	$^-8$	$^-8 + 2 \times 0 = {}^-8$
$^-2$	$^-12$	$^-8 + 2 \times (^-2) = {}^-12$
$^+2$	$^-4$	$^-8 + 2 \times 2 = {}^-4$

Remember to substitute the value of the variable in the expression.

Complete each table.

1.
x	$4x$
$^-1$	
$^-2$	
0	

2.
y	$^-2 - 6y$
$^-2$	
0	
1	

Set G *(pages 238–239)*

Solve the equation $^-6 + m = 15$.

$$^-6 + m = {}^-15$$
$$^-6 - {}^-6 + m = {}^-15 - {}^-6$$
$$^-6 + 6 + m = {}^-15 + 6$$
$$m = {}^-9$$

Remember to use the rules for adding, subtracting, multiplying, and dividing integers when solving equations.

1. $m + 2 = {}^-14$ 2. $\dfrac{x}{^-3} = {}^-21$

3. $s \div {}^-3 = 6$ 4. $y - 10 = {}^-12$

More Practice

Compare. Use >, <, or = for each ⬤.

1. ⁻5 ⬤ ⁻6
2. 0 ⬤ ⁺7
3. $\frac{+3}{5}$ ⬤ $\frac{-9}{8}$
4. ⁻6 ⬤ 0

5. ⁻19 ⬤ ⁻21
6. ⁻6 ⬤ ⁻1
7. ⁺2 ⬤ ⁻2
8. 0 ⬤ ⁻12

Write in order from least to greatest.

9. ⁺5, ⁻7, ⁻2
10. ⁻8, 0, ⁻9
11. ⁻6, ⁻8, ⁺1
12. ⁺8, ⁻8, ⁻2

13. On Monday, the temperature was ⁻15°F, and on Tuesday, the temperature was ⁻10°F. Which day was colder?

Set B *(pages 221–223)*

Add.

1. ⁺7 + ⁻3
2. ⁻6 + ⁻3
3. ⁻6 + ⁺9
4. ⁺5 + ⁻2

5. 0 + ⁻1
6. ⁺4 + ⁻4
7. ⁻5 + ⁻8
8. ⁺6 + ⁻5

9. ⁺12 + ⁻29
10. ⁻80 + ⁻20
11. ⁺45 + ⁻43
12. ⁻16 + ⁺19

13. After the ninth hole, Rick's golf card showed that his score was 4 under par. After the tenth hole, the card showed Rick's score was par. If 5 strokes is par for the tenth hole, how many strokes did Rick use on the tenth hole?

Set C *(pages 224–226)*

Subtract.

1. ⁻4 − ⁻2
2. ⁻7 − ⁺3
3. ⁺7 − ⁻3
4. ⁺3 − ⁻3

5. ⁻3 − ⁺3
6. ⁺8 − ⁻4
7. ⁻5 − 0
8. 0 − ⁺6

9. ⁻41 − ⁺51
10. ⁺32 − ⁻25
11. ⁺14 − ⁺18
12. ⁻23 − ⁻23

13. You are 120 feet over the ocean in a hot-air balloon. Your friend is scuba diving directly beneath you. She is 25 feet below the surface of the ocean. How far apart are you?

Set D *(pages 230–232)*

Find each product.

1. $^-13 \times {}^+5$ **2.** $^-8 \times {}^+12$ **3.** $^-1 \times {}^-1$ **4.** $0 \times {}^-6$

5. Every minute, Joel's hot-air balloon descends 17 feet. If this continues for 8 minutes, what is the change in height?

Set E *(pages 234–235)*

Find each quotient.

1. $^-20 \div {}^-2$ **2.** $^-8 \div {}^-4$ **3.** $^+500 \div {}^+10$ **4.** $^+625 \div {}^-25$

5. The price of XYZ stock changed $^-27$ points in nine days. Determine the average daily change of XYZ stock.

Set F *(pages 236–237)*

Complete each table.

1.

b	$2b + 18$
$^-6$	
$^-2$	
$^+4$	

2.

a	$6a - 7$
$^-8$	
$^-7$	
$^+8$	

3.

n	$10n - 30$
$^+6$	
$^+5$	
$^-1$	

4. A miner was 40 feet below the surface of the Earth. He then descended 30 feet every b minutes. Write an expression to describe the miner's location after b minutes. Evaluate the expression to find the miner's location after 6 minutes.

Set G *(pages 238–239)*

Solve each equation.

1. $t - 11 = {}^-38$ **2.** $51 = {}^-3x$ **3.** $3b = -21$ **4.** $^-5n = 30$

5. $\dfrac{s}{^-4} = 80$ **6.** $^-4x = {}^-48$ **7.** $s - 2 = {}^-8$ **8.** $t + 19 = {}^-31$

9. A weather forecaster recorded temperatures on a cold day. The first reading was 15°F and the last was $^-2$°F. What was the change in temperature?

Choose the correct letter for each answer.

1. **Starting Monday, December 1, the temperature went down 2°F each day until Friday. What was the temperature on Saturday?**

   A ⁻0.5°F

   B ⁻2.5°F

   C ⁻3°F

   D NH

   > **Tip**
   >
   > First decide if a problem has enough information to answer the question.

2. **Pete is older than Joan, but younger than Vic. Sam is older than Pete. Which of these is a reasonable conclusion?**

   F Sam is older than Joan.

   G Joan is older than Sam.

   H Vic is older than Sam.

   J Sam is older than Vic.

   > **Tip**
   >
   > Use *Logical Reasoning* to help you solve this problem.

3. **The table shows how the price of a stock changed over a five-day period.**

Change in Stock Price					
Day	Mon.	Tues.	Wed.	Thurs.	Fri.
Price Change	0	⁻1	⁻3	⁺3	⁺4

   What was the range of the price changes?

   A 2

   B 3

   C 5

   D 7

   > **Tip**
   >
   > Negative integers represent a decrease in the value of the stock.

4. Trudy's class is making 100 magnetic compasses. For each compass, they need a piece of metal wire $8\frac{7}{8}$ centimeters long. Which is a good estimate of the total amount of wire the class needs?

F 600 cm   **H** 800 cm

G 750 cm   **J** 900 cm

5. Carrie is practicing for a long-distance race. Over the last 7 months, her practice runs have averaged 3, 6, 9, 13, 17, 22, and 27 kilometers. If this pattern continues, what is a reasonable goal for an average distance for her practice runs for the next month?

A 27 km

B 29 km

C 30 km

D 33 km

6. The price of a stock went down two points per day for 5 days. In which equation does *n* equal the total change in the value of the stock?

F $5 \times {}^-2 = n$ **H** ${}^-5n = {}^-2$

G ${}^-5 \times {}^-2 = n$ **J** $5n = {}^-2$

7. Tasha owes Gabe $37.00. She also owes her mom $52.11. She earned $8.25 babysitting and gave her earnings to Gabe. Which expression could be used to find how much money Tasha needs to pay off her debt?

A $(37 + 52.11) + 8.25$

B $({}^-37 + 8.25) + 52.11$

C $(8.25 + 37) - 52.11$

D $(52.11 + 37) - 8.25$

8. The graph below shows the hours worked in the school library by 4 students in 1 week.

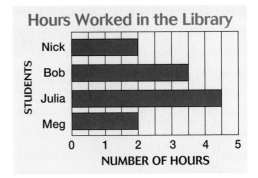

Hours Worked in the Library

Julia works the same number of hours each week. How many hours did Julia work in 4 weeks?

F 5 hours   **H** 16 hours

G 9 hours   **J** 18 hours

9. Mark planted a variety of flower bulbs over a period of 8 weeks. The chart shows how many bulbs he planted each week for the first 5 weeks.

Week	1	2	3	4	5
Number	15	30	20	35	25

If Mark continues in this pattern, how many bulbs will he plant in the *eighth* week?

A 60   **C** 50

B 55   **D** 45

10. At the start of the dogsled race, the temperature was ${}^-2°$F. By the end of the race, the temperature had increased $12°$F. What was the temperature at the end of the race?

F ${}^-14°$F

G ${}^-10°$F

H ${}^+10°$F

J ${}^+18°$F

Multiple-Choice Cumulative Review

Choose the correct letter for each answer.

Number Sense

1. Which integer describes a loss of 15 dollars?

   A $^+1,500$

   B $^+15$

   C $^-15$

   D $^-1,500$

2. Which number sentence is true?

   F $^-3 < ^-2$

   G $^+4 = ^-4$

   H $^-1 > 0$

   J $0 < ^-10$

3. Which set of numbers is in order from *greatest* to *least*?

   A $^-1, ^+2, 0, ^-3$

   B $0, ^-1, ^+2, ^-3$

   C $^-3, ^+2, ^-1, 0$

   D $^+2, 0, ^-1, ^-3$

4. Nick helps out at a day-care center. There are 16 three-year-olds, 12 four-year-olds, and 8 five-year-olds at the center. Nick wants to divide the children into groups so that each group has the same number of children of each age. What is the greatest number of groups Nick can make?

   F 2 groups

   G 4 groups

   H 6 groups

   J 8 groups

5. What is the sum of $^+6$ and $^-8$?

   A $^-14$

   B $^-2$

   C $^+2$

   D $^+14$

6. The temperature dropped 6 degrees and then rose 11 degrees. What was the total change in temperature?

   F $^-17$ degrees

   G $^-5$ degrees

   H $^+5$ degrees

   J $^+17$ degrees

7. Which of the following has the greatest sum?

   A $\frac{11}{12} + \frac{3}{4}$

   B $\frac{5}{7} + 3$

   C $^-3 + 7$

   D $\frac{5}{2} + \frac{3}{4}$

8. Evaluate $16 - 2 \times 4 + 1$.

   F 70

   G 57

   H 9

   J 7

   K NH

Algebra and Functions

9. Ronnie scored twice as many points in basketball games this week as he did last week. If the number of points he scored this week is *p*, which expression could be used to find how many points he scored last week?

A $2 \times p$

B $p + 2$

C $p \div 2$

D $p - 2$

10. Which point represents ⁻1.5 on the number line?

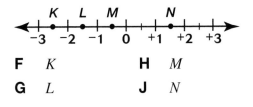

F *K*

G *L*

H *M*

J *N*

Use the graph below to answer Questions 11 and 12.

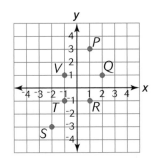

11. Which ordered pair is represented by point *P*?

A (⁺3, ⁺1)

B (⁻1, ⁻3)

C (⁺1, ⁺2)

D (⁺1, ⁺3)

12. Which point on the graph represents the ordered pair (⁻1, ⁺1)?

F *V*

G *T*

H *R*

J *Q*

Statistics, Data Analysis, and Probability

13. What is the mode for the following set of data: 105, 100, 96, 100, 98, 101, 100, 103?

A 105

B 100

C 96

D 9

14. Three boys are 57 in., 58 in., and 62 in. tall. Which of the following is the average height of the 3 boys?

F 55 inches

G 58 inches

H 59 inches

J 62 inches

Use the graph to answer Questions 15 and 16.

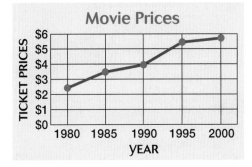

15. Which 5-year period showed the smallest price increase?

A 1980–1990

B 1985–1990

C 1990–1995

D 1995–2000

16. How much more would you have paid for a movie ticket in 1990 than 1985?

F $1.25

G $1.00

H $0.50

J $0.25

CHAPTER

7

Measurement and Geometry

Diagnosing Readiness

In Chapter 7, you will use these skills:

Ⓐ Multiplying and Dividing Whole Numbers, Fractions, and Decimals

(pages 52–54, 58–61, 192–195)

1. 2.54×73

2. $4\frac{1}{2} \div 28$

3. $122{,}364 \div 2{,}000$

4. $6\frac{1}{2} \times 1\frac{1}{3}$

5. A container holds 128 ounces of juice. How many ounces are left over if eight 16-ounce cups are filled with juice?

Ⓑ Comparing Quantities

(Grade 5)

Determine which is larger.

6. A swimming pool or a bathtub

7. A cup of tea or a gallon of paint

8. The length of a bed or the width of a book

9. The length of a pencil or the width of a chalkboard

10. The width of a TV screen or the height of a can of soup

ⓒ Patterns

(pages 22–23)

Find the next two items in each pattern.

11. $\frac{1}{4}, \frac{1}{40}, \frac{1}{400}, \frac{1}{4,000}$

12. $12\frac{1}{2}, 12\frac{1}{4}, 12\frac{1}{8}, 12\frac{1}{16}$

13. 0.75, 1.5, 2.25, 3

14.

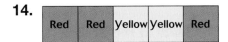

| Red | Red | Yellow | Yellow | Red |

ⓓ Solving Equations

(pages 30–31, 198–199)

Solve for x.

15. $165 + x = 360$

16. $180 - 75 = x$

17. $3\frac{1}{2}x = 14$

18. $5x = 3.5$

19. Jeremy has already saved $50. He wants to buy a portable CD player for $89. Write and solve an equation to find out how much more he needs to save.

ⓔ Writing Expressions

(pages 28–29)

Write an expression for each phrase.

20. 9 less than x

21. 6 more than y

22. 27 divided by a

23. 7 times b

24. Nicholas made 3 more paintings this week than last week. Last week he made 3 paintings. How many did he make this week?

ⓕ Elapsed Time

(Grade 5)

Find the time of the following.

25. 10:30 A.M. to 6:45 P.M.

26. $3\frac{1}{2}$ hours before noon.

27. 10:45 P.M. to 3:20 A.M.

28. $1\frac{1}{4}$ hours after 8:15 P.M.

29. It takes Joannie 25 minutes to prepare a pot pie and 50 minutes to bake it. If she plans to serve dinner at 6:30 P.M., what time does she need to start preparing the pot pie?

To the Family and Student

Looking Back

In Grade 5, students learned to measure using customary units of measure and metric units of measure.

Chapter 7

Measurement and Geometry

In this chapter, students will convert between customary and metric units of measure. They will also learn about basic figures in geometry.

Looking Ahead

In Chapter 12, students will apply their knowledge of measurement and geometry to help them find the perimeter, area, and volume of geometric figures.

Math and Everyday Living

Opportunities to apply the concepts of Chapter 7 abound in everyday situations. During the chapter, think about how measurement and geometry can be used to solve a variety of real-world problems. The following examples suggest just a few of the many situations that could launch a discussion about measurement and geometry.

Math in the Laundry Room Occasionally, the washing machine in your house becomes unbalanced and needs to be re-leveled. If your laundry room floor is perfectly level, what kind of angle should be formed between the floor and the side of the machine?

Math on the Clock At your 6:00 P.M. dinner hour, you notice that the minute hand on the 12 and the hour hand on the 6 form a 180° angle.

Provide an example of the time when the hands on the clock form a 90° angle.

Math on the Treadmill You are entering a 5-mile walk for charity. To prepare, you walk $2\frac{1}{2}$ miles daily. What is the difference between your training distance and the length of the charity walk?

Math at Home Suppose you always use 250 liters of water for a bath and your shower uses 15 liters of water per minute. What is the greatest whole number of minutes you can shower and still use less water than you would use taking a bath?

Math on the Telephone You realize at 8:30 P.M. that you want to call your cousin on the East Coast. You know she goes to bed at 10:00 P.M. If you are calling her from California, will she be awake? Explain.

Math at the Grocery Store You need one gallon of orange juice for the soccer team. At the grocery store you bought three 12-ounce cans of frozen orange juice. Each 12-ounce can makes 48 ounces of juice. Will you have enough juice if you buy 3 cans of frozen juice? Explain.

Math in Nature In hopes of finding a good-luck charm, you look in your yard for a 4-leaf clover. Among the many 3-leaf clovers, you find a 4-leaf clover. How many lines of symmetry does a 4-leaf clover have? How many does a 3-leaf clover have?

California Content Standards in Chapter 7 Lessons*

Algebra and Functions	Teach and Practice	Practice
1.1 (🔑) Write and solve one-step linear equations in one variable.		7-6, 7-7, 7-8
1.2 Write and evaluate an algebraic expression for a given situation, using up to three variables.		7-9
2.1 Convert one unit of measurement to another (e.g., from feet to miles, from centimeters to inches).	7-1, 7-2, 7-3	
3.2 Express in symbolic form simple relationships arising from geometry.		7-6, 7-7, 7-8

Measurement and Geometry	Teach and Practice	Practice
1.0 Students deepen their understanding of the measurement of plane and solid shapes and use this understanding to solve problems.		7-5
2.0 Students identify and describe the properties of two-dimensional figures.		7-7, 7-8, 7-10
2.1 (Grade 5) (🔑) Measure, identify, and draw angles . . . by using appropriate tools	7-5	
2.1 Identify angles as vertical, adjacent, complementary, or supplementary and provide descriptions of these terms.	7-6	
2.2 (🔑) Use the properties of complementary and supplementary angles and of the angles of a triangle to solve problems involving an unknown angle.	7-6	7-7
2.3 Draw quadrilaterals and triangles from given information about them (e.g., a quadrilateral having equal sides but no right angles, a right isosceles triangle).	7-7, 7-8	7-10
3.2 (Grade 7) Understand . . . simple figures . . . and determine their images under translations and reflections.	7-10	

Mathematical Reasoning	Teach and Practice	Practice
1.0 Students make decisions about how to approach problems.		7-1, 7-11
1.1 Analyze problems by identifying relationships . . . and observing patterns.	7-4	7-9
1.2 Formulate and justify mathematical conjectures based on a general description of the mathematical question or problem posed.	7-9	
2.0 Students use strategies, skills, and concepts in finding solutions.	7-11	
2.2 Apply strategies and results from simpler problems to more complex problems.		7-8
2.4 Use a variety of methods, such as words, numbers, symbols, charts, graphs, tables, diagrams, and models, to explain mathematical reasoning.	7-9	7-7
3.0 Students move beyond a particular problem by generalizing to other situations.		7-4, 7-9, 7-11
3.1 Evaluate the reasonableness of the solution in the context of the original situation.		7-2
3.2 Note the method of deriving the solution and demonstrate a conceptual understanding of the derivation by solving similar problems.		7-9
3.3 Develop generalizations of the results obtained and the strategies used and apply them in new problem situations.		7-4

* The symbol (🔑) indicates a key standard as designated in the Mathematics Framework for California Public Schools. Full statements of the California Content Standards are found at the beginning of this book following the Table of Contents.

LESSON 7-1

Customary Units of Measurement

California Content Standard *Algebra and Functions 2.1: Convert from one unit of measurement to another (e.g., from feet to miles . . . .).*

Warm-Up Review

1. $168 \times \frac{3}{4}$

2. $3\frac{1}{4} \times 12$

3. $1\frac{1}{2} \times 5,280$

4. $78 \div 8$

5. A garden is $\frac{3}{5}$ as wide as it is long. If the garden is 120 feet long, how wide is it?

Math Link You know how to multiply and divide. Now you will use these skills to change from one unit of customary measurement to another.

The customary system of measurement is widely used in the United States. Some relationships between customary units are shown in the following tables.

Customary Units of Length
1 foot (ft) = 12 inches (in.)
1 yard (yd) = 36 inches
1 yard = 3 feet
1 mile (mi) = 5,280 feet
1 mile = 1,760 yards

Customary Units of Weight
1 pound (lb) = 16 ounces (oz)
1 ton (T) = 2,000 pounds

Customary Units of Capacity
1 cup (c) = 8 fluid ounces (fl oz)
1 pint (pt) = 2 cups
1 quart (qt) = 2 pints
1 gallon (gal) = 4 quarts

Example 1

Find the width of the tennis court in yards and in inches.

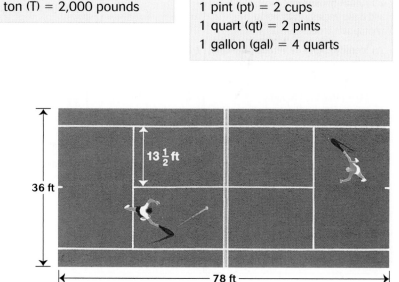

Change 36 feet to yards.
A foot is a smaller unit than a yard.

> To change from a smaller unit to a larger unit, divide.

36 ft = ■ yd

36 ÷ 3 = 12 | 3 ft = 1 yd |

36 ft = 12 yd

The width is 12 yards.

Change 36 feet to inches.
A foot is a larger unit than an inch.

> To change from a larger unit to a smaller unit, multiply.

36 ft = ■ in.

36 × 12 = 432 | 1 ft = 12 in. |

36 ft = 432 in.

The width is 432 inches.

  Additional Standard: Mathematical Reasoning 1.0 (See p. 259.)

Example 2

Find the weight of a 20-ounce basketball in pounds.

An ounce is a smaller unit than a pound, so divide.

20 oz = ■ lb

16 oz = 1 lb

20 ÷ 16 = 1 R4

20 oz = 1 lb 4 oz,
    or $1\frac{1}{4}$ lb

4 oz = $\frac{1}{4}$ lb

Example 3

For a marathon, $21\frac{1}{2}$ quarts of water was bottled in pint containers. How many pints is this?

A quart is a larger unit than a pint, so multiply.

$21\frac{1}{2}$ qt = ■ pt

1 qt = 2 pt

$21\frac{1}{2} \times 2 = 43$

$21\frac{1}{2}$ qt = 43 pt

More Examples

A. 9 yd 2 ft = ■ in.

$(9 \times 36) + (2 \times 12) = 348$

9 yd 2 ft = 348 in.

1 yd = 36 in.
1 ft = 12 in

B. $1\frac{1}{4}$ T = ■ lb

$1\frac{1}{4} \times 2,000 = \frac{5}{4} \times 2,000 = 2,500$

$1\frac{1}{4}$ T = 2,500 lb

1T = 2,000 lb

C. 21 qt = ■ gal

21 ÷ 4 = 5 R1

21 qt = 5 gal 1 qt, or $5\frac{1}{4}$ gal

4 qt = 1 gal

Word Bank
inch
foot
yard
mile
ounce
pound
ton
fluid ounce
cup
pint
quart
gallon

Guided Practice   *For another example, see Set A on p. 292.*

Complete.

1. 1 yd = ■ in., so 3 yd = ■ in.

2. 1 ft = ■ in., so $\frac{1}{3}$ ft = ■ in.

3. 12 in. = ■ ft, so 6 in. = ■ ft

4. 1 lb = ■ oz, so $\frac{1}{4}$ lb = ■ oz

5. 12 oz = ■ lb

6. 1 gal = ■ pt

7. 5 c = ■ pt

8. $10\frac{1}{2}$ lb = ■ oz

9. 9 qt = ■ gal

10. 1 pt = ■ fl oz

11. Math Reasoning Explain how you would change 6 gallons to fluid ounces.

12. A tennis ball can weigh as little as 2 ounces. What fraction of a pound is this?

Independent Practice
For more practice, see Set A on p. 295.

Complete.

13. 3 mi = ■ yd

14. 5,000 lb = ■ T

15. 32 pt = ■ gal

16. $\frac{1}{2}$ lb = ■ oz

17. $2\frac{1}{4}$ qt = ■ c

18. $4\frac{1}{3}$ yd = ■ ft

19. 5 yd 2 in. = ■ in.

20. 48 in. = ■ yd ■ ft

21. $\frac{1}{2}$ T = ■ lb

22. 3 ft 4 in. = ■ in.

23. 56 fl oz = ■ pt

24. 15 qt = ■ gal

25. 8 ft = ■ yd

26. $1\frac{1}{2}$ mi = ■ ft

27. 75 oz = ■ lb

28. Use the drawing shown with Example 1. Find the length of the tennis court in yards.

29. Grapefruit juice in a 1-pint 4-ounce bottle costs $0.78, and the same juice in a 10-ounce bottle costs $0.49. What is the difference in the price per fluid ounce?

30. Math Reasoning Explain why you multiply to change from a larger unit to a smaller unit.

31. Math Reasoning Explain why you divide to change from a smaller unit to a larger unit.

Mixed Review

32. Luis hiked two miles in $\frac{1}{2}$ hour. He stopped for 5 minutes to take pictures and took 30 minutes to eat. Estimate the total time in hours he spent on the trail.

Algebra Evaluate each expression.

33. $7 - 4n$ for $n = {}^-2$

34. $5a - 16$ for $a = 2$

Algebra Solve each equation.

35. $c + 19 = {}^-78$

36. ${}^-2t = 36$

37. $x - 8 = {}^-12$

38. $\frac{p}{21} = {}^-7$

Test Prep Choose the correct letter for each answer.

39. $3\frac{3}{4} \div \frac{1}{8}$
(5-8)

A $\frac{15}{32}$

C 6

B $24\frac{3}{4}$

D 30

40. ${}^-4 - {}^-19 =$
(6-2)

F $^-23$

H $^-15$

G 15

J 23

Metric Units of Measurement

California Content Standard *Algebra and Functions 2.1: Convert one unit of measurement to another.*

Warm-Up Review

1. 100×0.35

2. $568 \div 100$

3. $0.69 \times 1,000$

4. $87 \div 1,000$

5. The cost of film was $3.99. Developing the film cost $4.29. How many rolls of film did you buy and develop if the total cost was $24.84?

Math Link You know how to multiply and divide by 10, 100, and 1,000. Now you will use these skills to change from one unit of metric measure to another.

The metric system of measurement is used in most of the world. The **meter** is the basic unit of length in the **metric** system.

The chart below shows how metric units of length are related to the meter, and how to change from one unit to another.

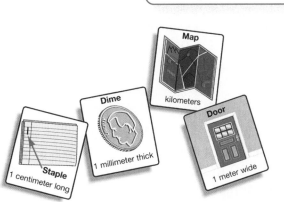

Map
kilometers
Dime
1 millimeter thick
Door
1 meter wide
Staple
1 centimeter long

$\times 10 \quad \times 10 \quad \times 10 \quad \times 10 \quad \times 10 \quad \times 10$

kilometer	hectometer	dekameter	meter	decimeter	centimeter	millimeter
km	hm	dam	m	dm	cm	mm
1 km = 1,000 m	1 hm = 100 m	1 dam = 10 m		1 dm = 0.1 m	1 cm = 0.01 m	1 mm = 0.001 m

$\div 10 \quad \div 10 \quad \div 10 \quad \div 10 \quad \div 10 \quad \div 10$

Example 1

In the 1996 Olympics, the United States won the 1,600-meter relay. How many kilometers is this?

A meter is a smaller unit than a kilometer.

To change from a smaller unit to a larger unit, divide.

1,600 m = ■ km

1,600 ÷ 1,000 = 1.6

1,600 m = 1.6 km

1,600 meters equal 1.6 kilometers.

1,000 m = 1 km

Example 2

Stefka Kostadinova won a gold medal in 1996 with a high jump of 2.05 meters. How many centimeters is this?

A meter is a larger unit than a centimeter.

To change from a larger unit to a smaller unit, multiply.

2.05 m = ■ cm

2.05 × 100 = 205

2.05 m = 205 cm

2.05 meters equal 205 cm.

1 m = 100 cm

The **gram** is the basic unit of mass in the metric system. A large paperclip weighs about 1 gram. The **liter** is the basic unit of capacity.

These charts show how the metric units of mass and capacity are related.

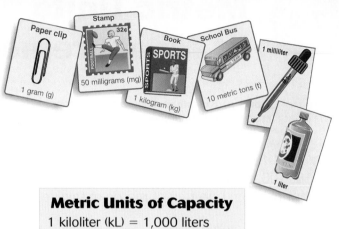

Metric Units of Mass

1 gram (g) = 1,000 milligrams (mg)
1 kilogram (kg) = 1,000 grams
1 metric ton (t) = 1,000 kilograms

Metric Units of Capacity

1 kiloliter (kL) = 1,000 liters
1 liter (L) = 1,000 milliliters (mL)

Example 3

Shot-put is a track-and-field event. The women's shot has a mass of 4,000 grams. How many kilograms is this?

A gram is a smaller unit than a kilogram, so divide.

4,000 g = ■ kg
4,000 ÷ 1,000 = 4   1 kg = 1,000 g
4,000 g = 4 kg

The woman's shot has a mass of 4 kg.

Example 4

An ice hockey rink may hold as much as 30 kiloliters of water. How many liters of water is this?

A kiloliter is a larger unit than a liter, so multiply.

30 kL = ■ L
30 × 1,000 = 30,000   1 kL = 1,000 L

An ice hockey rink can hold 30,000 L of water.

Guided Practice   *For another example, see Set B on p. 292.*

Choose the most reasonable unit of metric measure.

1. mass of a bowling ball   **2.** length of a golf tee   **3.** capacity of a sink

4. distance to the next town **5.** length of a room   **6.** mass of a pinch of salt

Complete.

7. ■ kL = 4,250 L   **8.** ■ dm = 1 m   **9.** 2,500 mm = ■ m

10. 6.5 L = ■ mL   **11.** 3 km = ■ m   **12.** ■ g = 0.001 kg

13. Math Reasoning Which do you think is easier, changing from one unit of customary measure to another or changing from one unit of metric measure to another? Explain why.

Independent Practice *For more practice, see Set B on p. 295.*

Choose the most reasonable unit of metric measure.

14. Mass of a car

15. Thickness of a magazine

16. Capacity of a spoon

17. Height of a tree

18. Distance to the moon

19. Mass of a penny

Complete.

20. ■ hm = 1,200 m

21. 35 cm = ■ mm

22. ■ cm = 7.6 dm

23. 6.7 km = ■ m

24. 125 m = ■ km

25. 12 dam = ■ cm

26. 575 mg = ■ g

27. 1.6 t = ■ kg

28. ■ g = 4,700 mg

29. 7.5 g = ■ mg

30. ■ g = 0.02 kg

31. 1.75 kL = ■ L

32. 15 L = ■ kL

33. 8,000 mL = ■ L

34. 400 mL = ■ L

35. The 100-meter run, the 400-meter run, the 110-meter hurdles, and the 1.5-kilometer run are four track events in the decathlon. Find the total distance in kilometers for these four events.

36. The Hotel Fairmount in San Antonio, Texas, was moved 5 blocks. It had a mass of 1,454,545 kilograms. To the nearest tenth, how many metric tons is this?

Mixed Review

37. Lois had $3.00 in her purse and $0.20 in her pocket. She spent $1.35 of the money on a snack and $0.35 on a phone call. Then her friend gave her $0.45. How much money does Lois have now?

Algebra Solve each equation.

38. $x - 7 = {}^-4$

39. ${}^-8n = {}^-40$

40. $y + {}^-3 = {}^-21$

Complete.

41. 10 yd = ■ ft

42. 5 qt = ■ pt

43. 56 oz = ■ lb

🔖 **Test Prep**   Choose the correct letter for each answer.

44. Which number is divisible by 6?
<small>(4-2)</small>

   A 1,115

   B 4,772

   C 2,526

   D 6,135

45. Which of the following is true?
<small>(6-1)</small>

   F ${}^-8 > {}^-5$

   G ${}^-0.6 > 0.38$

   H ${}^-0.5 < {}^-0.6$

   J ${}^-0.25 < {}^-0.125$

Converting Between Measurement Systems

 California Content Standard *Algebra and Functions 2.1: Convert from one unit of measurement to another (e.g., . . . from centimeters to inches).*

Math Link You know how to convert units within the customary and within the metric systems of measurement. Now you will convert units between systems.

Example 1

Find the length of the line segment in inches and in centimeters.

The segment is about $2\frac{1}{2}$ inches long and about 6.5 centimeters long.

You can convert between customary and metric measures using the table at the right. Only the equivalent for inches and centimeters is exact. All the other equivalents are approximate. $\approx$ is read "is approximately equal to."

Example 2

Convert $2\frac{1}{2}$ inches to centimeters.

1 in. = 2.54 cm	An inch is larger than a centimeter.
2.5 in. = ■ cm	Write $2\frac{1}{2}$ as 2.5.
$2.5 \times 2.54 = 6.35$	To change from a larger unit to a smaller unit, multiply.
2.5 in. = 6.35 cm	

Example 3

Convert 5 pounds to kilograms.

1 kg $\approx$ 2.2 lb	
5 lb $\approx$ ■ kg	A pound is less than a kilogram.
$5 \div 2.2 \approx 2.27$	To change from a smaller unit to a larger unit, divide.
5 lb $\approx$ 2.3 kg	

Customary and Metric Unit Equivalents

Length
1 in. = 2.54 cm
1 m $\approx$ 39.37 in.
1 m $\approx$ 1.09 yd
1 mi $\approx$ 1.61 km

Weight and Mass
1 oz $\approx$ 28.35 g
1 kg $\approx$ 2.2 lb
1 metric ton (t) $\approx$ 1.102 tons (T)

Capacity
1 L $\approx$ 1.06 qt
1 gal $\approx$ 3.79 L

Guided Practice *For another example, see Set C on p. 292.*

Complete. Round to the nearest tenth.

1. 7.4 m ≈ ■ in.

2. 4 qt ≈ ■ L

3. 545 g ≈ ■ oz

4. A room is 4 meters long. About how many feet is this?

5. Draw a segment that is 4.5 centimeters long. About how many inches is this?

Independent Practice *For more practice, see Set C on p. 295.*

Complete. Round to the nearest tenth.

6. 6 in. ≈ ■ cm

7. 5 kg ≈ ■ lb

8. 4 L ≈ ■ qt

9. 10 mi ≈ ■ km

10. 3 t ≈ ■ T

11. 2 L ≈ ■ gal

12. 11.6 cm ≈ ■ in.

13. $5\frac{1}{4}$ lb ≈ ■ kg

14. 9.8 km ≈ ■ mi

15. Draw a segment that is $\frac{3}{4}$ inch long. About how many centimeters is this?

16. Math Reasoning You know that 1 L ≈ 1.06 quarts. Explain how you would convert one pint to liters.

17. Rewrite the recipe at the right using liters as the unit of measure for each ingredient.

Fruity Surprise Punch

46 fluid ounces of pineapple juice

1 quart orange juice

32 fluid ounces cranberry juice

2 cups apple juice

Mixed Review

18. In the recipe at the right, how many quarts of pineapple juice are used?

Complete.

19. 5 yd 2 ft = ■ in.

20. 2,500 mm = ■ m

21. 7 c = ■ qt

Test Prep Choose the correct letter for each answer.

22. Algebra ⁻15 + ⁻28
(6-2)

   A ⁻43   **C** ⁻13

   B 13   **D** 43

23. $\frac{5}{8}$ =
(4-7)

   F $\frac{10}{48}$ **H** $1\frac{3}{8}$

   G 0.625   **J** 1.6

LESSON

7-4

Understand
Plan
Solve
Look Back

Problem-Solving Skill:

Spatial Reasoning

Warm-Up Review

Find the next three numbers in each pattern.

1. 0, 2, 6, 12, ■, ■, ■

2. 1, 3, 9, 27, ■, ■, ■

3. 1, $\frac{1}{2}$, $\frac{1}{4}$, $\frac{1}{8}$, ■, ■, ■

4. 0.5, 1, 2, 4, ■, ■, ■

5. Joe has a 3-quart container and a $\frac{1}{2}$-gallon container. Which container holds more?

California Content Standard *Mathematical Reasoning 1.1: Analyze problems by identifying relationships, . . . and observing patterns.*

Read for Understanding

Todd's pinwheel has 4 vanes that rotate around a point. Shown below are three different views of his pinwheel turning.

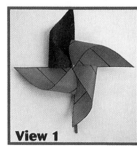

View 1

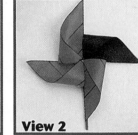

View 2

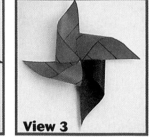

View 3

1 How are the vanes similar? How are they different?

2 How does View 2 differ from View 1?

3 How does View 3 differ from View 2? from View 1?

Think and Discuss

MATH FOCUS

Spatial Reasoning

Spatial reasoning is mentally picturing objects in different positions and in different ways. You can use spatial reasoning when it is not practical to use actual objects.

4 Suppose the pattern continues. How many more views will there be before the pinwheel looks as it does in View 1?

5 How does being able to turn the pinwheel mentally help you answer Exercise 4? Explain.

268

 Additional Standards: Mathematical Reasoning 3.0, 3.3 (See p. 259.)

Guided Practice

Joan drew the shapes below on folded paper. Then she cut them out and unfolded them.

①   ②   ③   ④

1. Which figure below shows Shape 2 unfolded?

a. 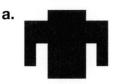 b. 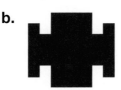 c.

2. Which shape looks like this figure when unfolded?

   a. Shape 1

   b. Shape 2

   c. Shape 3

3. Which shape might look like this figure if it was folded again horizontally?

   a. Shape 1

   b. Shape 2

   c. Shape 3

Independent Practice

Amaro made the design shown below. When he was finished, he noticed that the figure was made up of squares and triangles.

4. How many squares are in the design?

   a. 3 squares

   b. 4 squares

   c. 7 squares

5. How many triangles are in the design?

   a. 8 triangles

   b. 16 triangles

   c. 32 triangles

6. Math Reasoning How many $\frac{1}{4}$ turns of Amaro's design are needed before the design looks as it does now?

7. Math Reasoning Suppose Amaro wants to change his design to include more triangles. Explain how he could do this.

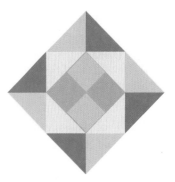

Classifying and Measuring Angles

California Content Standard *Measurement and Geometry 2.1(Gr.5)* (🔑): *Measure, identify, and draw angles by using appropriate tools . . . .*

Math Link You can use what you know about figures to draw, measure, and classify angles.

You can see examples of basic geometric ideas, such as **angles**, all around you. Angles are formed by two rays with a common endpoint called a **vertex**.

Example 1

Name the following geometric figures shown in the photo.
Point: *A*, center of Ferris wheel
Line: $\overleftrightarrow{EF}$, two spokes lined up
Line segment: $\overline{AD}$, spoke
Ray: $\overrightarrow{AF}$, spoke extended
Angle: ∠*BAC*, angle formed by two spokes

A **protractor** is an instrument used to measure and draw angles.

Example 2

Find the measure of ∠*AOB* and ∠*COD*.

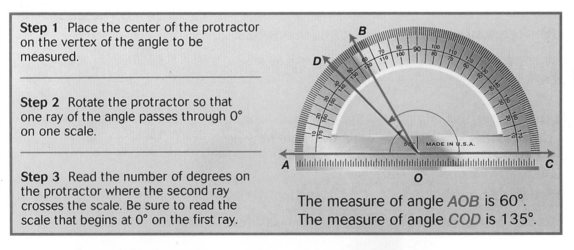

Step 1 Place the center of the protractor on the vertex of the angle to be measured.
Step 2 Rotate the protractor so that one ray of the angle passes through 0° on one scale.
Step 3 Read the number of degrees on the protractor where the second ray crosses the scale. Be sure to read the scale that begins at 0° on the first ray.

The measure of angle *AOB* is 60°.
The measure of angle *COD* is 135°.

Word Bank

point
line
line segment
ray
angle
vertex
plane
protractor
congruent
right angle
obtuse angle
acute angle
straight angle

Additional Standard: Measurement and Geometry 1.0 (See p. 259.)

Example 3

Draw an angle that measures 120°.

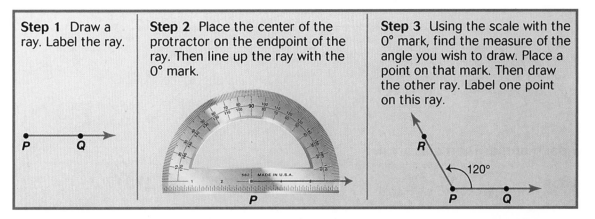

Step 1 Draw a ray. Label the ray.

Step 2 Place the center of the protractor on the endpoint of the ray. Then line up the ray with the 0° mark.

Step 3 Using the scale with the 0° mark, find the measure of the angle you wish to draw. Place a point on that mark. Then draw the other ray. Label one point on this ray.

The measure of angle *RPQ* is 120°. This can be written as m∠*RPQ* = 120°.

Angles are classified according to their measure.

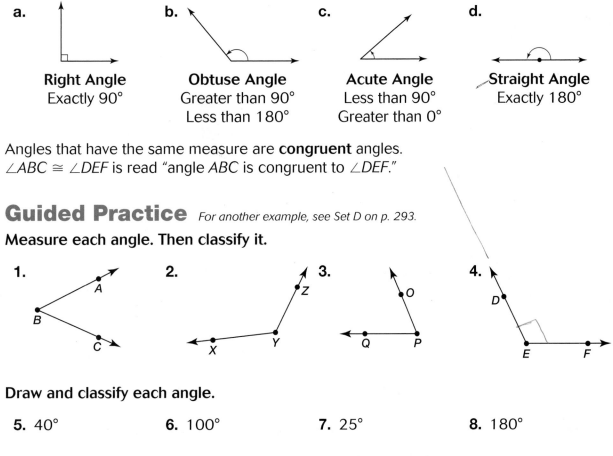

a. Right Angle
Exactly 90°

b. Obtuse Angle
Greater than 90°
Less than 180°

c. Acute Angle
Less than 90°
Greater than 0°

d. Straight Angle
Exactly 180°

Angles that have the same measure are **congruent** angles.
∠*ABC* ≅ ∠*DEF* is read "angle *ABC* is congruent to ∠*DEF*."

Guided Practice   *For another example, see Set D on p. 293.*

Measure each angle. Then classify it.

1.   2.   3.   4.

Draw and classify each angle.

5. 40°   **6.** 100°   **7.** 25°   **8.** 180°

9. What type of angle is formed by the hour and minute hand at 3:00?

Independent Practice
For more practice, see Set D on p. 296.

Measure each angle. Then classify it.

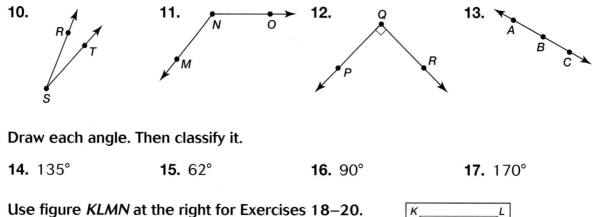

10.

11.

12.

13.

Draw each angle. Then classify it.

14. 135°   **15.** 62°   **16.** 90°   **17.** 170°

Use figure *KLMN* at the right for Exercises 18–20.

18. Name two angles that appear to be right.

19. Name two angles that appear to be acute.

20. Name an angle that appears to be congruent to ∠*KML* and that has vertex *M*.

21. Math Reasoning Suppose you did not have a protractor. How could you draw an angle that has a measure of about 45°?

Mixed Review

Algebra Complete.

22. Karen needs 5 paper tableclothes, each 3 feet 10 inches long to cover tables for the school picnic. Will an 18-foot roll contain enough paper? Explain.

23. 0.5 kL = ■ L   **24.** 30 mg = ■ g   **25.** 1 km = ■ m

26. 1 mi ≈ 1.6 km, so 15 mi ≈ ■ km.   **27.** 1 L ≈ 1.06 qt, so 3 L ≈ ■ qt.

Test Prep   Choose the correct letter for each answer.

28. A slice of bread contains
(7-2)   about 100 ___?___ of salt.

    A kg   **C** g

    B L   **D** cm

29. The baseball was hit 100 ___?___
(7-2)   into left field.

    F mm   **H** cm

    G m   **J** km

Diagnostic Checkpoint

Choose the most reasonable customary unit of measure.

1. Weight of a dump truck
(7-1)

2. Distance a tennis ball is hit
(7-1)

3. Capacity of a juice glass
(7-1)

4. Length of a calculator
(7-1)

Choose the most reasonable metric unit of measure.

5. Width of an eraser
(7-2)

6. Distance of a marathon
(7-2)

7. Mass of an apple
(7-2)

8. Capacity of a large bottle of bleach
(7-2)

Complete.

9. 8 mi = ■ yd
(7-1)

10. 19 pt = ■ qt
(7-1)

11. 24,000 lb = ■ T
(7-1)

12. 2,640 ft = ■ mi
(7-1)

13. 6.2 cm = ■ mm
(7-2)

14. ■ km = 942 m
(7-2)

15. ■ hm = 64 dm
(7-2)

16. 24,023 mm = ■ km
(7-2)

17. ■ dam = 25 m
(7-2)

Complete. Round to the nearest tenth.

18. 18 oz ≈ ■ g
(7-3)

19. 84 mi ≈ ■ km
(7-3)

20. 340 in. = ■ cm
(7-3)

Use a protractor to measure or draw each angle. Then classify it.

21.
(7-5)

22.
(7-5)

23. 116°
(7-5)

24. 33°
(7-5)

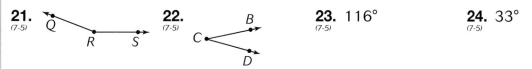

25. Sammy folded the figure to the right in half. Sketch what Sammy's figure looks like.
(7-4)

26. Kelly bought boxes of tomatoes weighing 4 pounds 9 ounces, 3 pounds 8 ounces, and 4 pounds 7 ounces. Find the total weight of the tomatoes.
(7-1)

27. How many squares are in the figure at the right?
(7-4)

Angle Pairs

Algebra

Warm-Up Review

Use a protractor to measure each angle.

1. $\angle NAP$ **2.** $\angle NAM$

3. Find the sum of the angle measures.

Math Link You know how to measure and classify angles. Now you will learn about angle pairs.

You can use the following relationships to find the measure of some angles.

Two angles are **vertical angles** if they are formed by intersecting lines and have no sides in common. Vertical angles are congruent.

Two angles are **supplementary angles** if the sum of their measures equals 180°.

Two angles are **complementary angles** if the sum of their measures equals 90°.

Two angles are **adjacent angles** if they have a common vertex and a common side. Adjacent angles do not overlap.

Example 1

Find the measure of $\angle GEJ$ in the figure at the right.

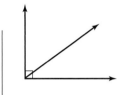

$\angle GEJ$ and $\angle FEH$ are vertical angles, so $m\angle GEJ = m\angle FEH = 147°$.

Example 2

Find $m\angle AOC$.

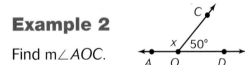

$\angle AOC$ and $\angle COD$ are adjacent, supplementary angles and $m\angle COD = 50°$. You can write and solve this equation to find $m\angle AOC$.

$$m\angle AOC + m\angle COD = 180°$$
$$x + 50 = 180$$
$$x = 130$$

$$m\angle AOC = 130°$$

Example 3

Find $m\angle KLM$.

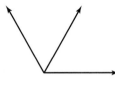

$\angle KLM$ and $\angle MLN$ are adjacent, complementary angles and $m\angle MLN = 25°$. You can write and solve this equation to find $m\angle KLM$.

$$m\angle KLM + m\angle MLN = 90°$$
$$y + 25 = 90$$
$$y = 65$$

$$m\angle KLM = 65°$$

Guided Practice For another example, see Set E on p. 293.

Find the measure of the angle labeled with a letter.

1.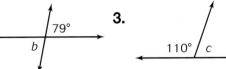
a
$35°$

2.
$79°$
b

3.
$110°$ c

4.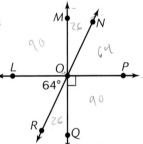
d
$50°$
$130°$

5. Draw an angle with a measure of 120°. Then draw an adjacent, supplementary angle and give its measure.

6. Draw an angle with a measure of 45°. Then draw an adjacent, complementary angle and give its measure.

7. Math Reasoning Two angles are congruent and supplementary. What are their measures?

Independent Practice For more practice, see Set E on p. 296.

Find the measure of an angle that is supplementary to an angle with each measure.

8. 145°   **9.** 53°   **10.** 110°   **11.** 17°

Find the measure of an angle that is complementary to an angle with each measure.

12. 42°   **13.** 20°   **14.** 65°   **15.** 1°

Find the measure of each angle in the figure at the right.

16. ∠MON   **17.** ∠NOP   **18.** ∠ROM   **19.** ∠ROQ

Mixed Review

20. Janie drove 300 kilometers on 12 gallons of gasoline. How many miles did she drive? How many liters of gasoline did she use?

21. Use a protractor to measure the angle at the right. Then classify it.

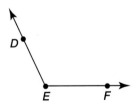
D
E F

Test Prep   Choose the correct letter for the answer.

22. Algebra A submarine was 20 feet below sea level when it
(6-7) started to dive. It dove 5 feet per second. Which expression
gives the submarine's position after s seconds?

  A ⁻5 − 20s **B** 5 − 20s **C** 20 − 5s **D** ⁻20 − 5s

Use Homework Workbook 7-6. **275**

Triangles

California Content Standard *Measurement and Geometry 2.3: Draw . . . triangles from information about them (e.g., . . . a right isosceles triangle).*

Warm-Up Review

1. Measure each angle of the triangle.

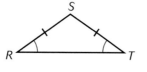

2. Find the sum of the measures of the angles of the triangle.

Math Link You know how to classify angles. Now you will learn how to classify triangles.

You can name the triangle at the right △RST. The slashes show congruent sides and the arcs show congruent angles.

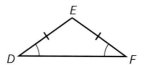

△RST and △DEF are **congruent triangles.** They have the same shape and the same size.

The following table shows how you can classify triangles.

Classified by Side Measures		Classified by Angle Measures	
Description	Example	Description	Example
Equilateral Three sides have the same length.		**Acute** All angles are acute.	
Isosceles Two sides have the same length.		**Right** There is one right angle.	
Scalene No two sides have the same length.		**Obtuse** There is one obtuse angle.	

Example 1

Classify each triangle according to side measures and according to angle measures.

a.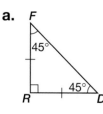

△DRF has one right angle and two congruent sides. It is an isosceles right triangle.

b.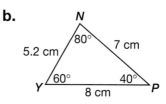

△YNP has no congruent sides and all acute angles. It is a scalene acute triangle.

Additional Standards: Algebra and Functions 1.1(➥), 3.2; Measurement and Geometry 2.0; Mathematical Reasoning 2.4 (See p. 259.)

Example 2

Find the sum of the angle measures for the two triangles in Example 1. What do you notice?

Sum of angle measures of △DRF =

$m\angle D + m\angle R + m\angle F =$
$45° + 90° + 45° = 180°$

Sum of angle measures of △YNP =

$m\angle Y + m\angle N + m\angle P =$
$60° + 80° + 40° = 180°$

The sum of the angle measures for each triangle is 180°.

The sum of the angle measures of any triangle is 180°.

Word Bank

congruent triangles
equilateral triangle
isosceles triangle
scalene triangle
acute triangle
right triangle
obtuse triangle

Example 3

Find $m\angle K$.

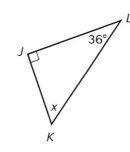

$m\angle K + m\angle J + m\angle L = 180°$
$x + 90 + 36 = 180$
$x + 126 = 180$
$x = 54$

$m\angle K = 54°$

Example 4

Use a ruler and a protractor to draw △GKH with $KH = 4$ cm, $m\angle K = 30°$, and $m\angle H = 60°$.

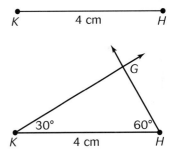

Step 1 Draw a 4-cm segment. Label it *KH*.

Step 2 Draw a 30° angle with vertex *K* and side *KH*.

Step 3 Draw a 60° angle with vertex *H* and side *KH*. Extend the sides until they meet. Label the point G.

Guided Practice   *For another example, see Set F on p. 293.*

Classify each triangle in two ways.

Algebra Find the measure of the third angle of each triangle.

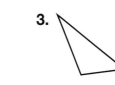

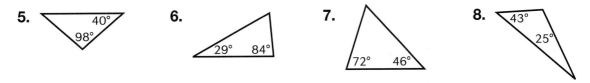

9. Draw △ABC with $AB = 3$ cm, $AC = 2$ cm, and $m\angle A = 100°$.

Independent Practice For more practice, see Set F on p. 296.

Classify each triangle in two ways.

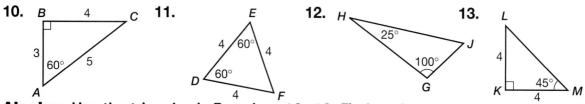

10. B 4 C

3
60° 5
A

11. E
4 60° 4
D 60°
4 F

12. H
25°
J
100°
G

13. L

4

K 45° M
4

Algebra Use the triangles in Exercises 10–13. Find each missing angle measure.

14. m∠C in △ABC   **15.** m∠F in △DEF   **16.** m∠J in △JGH   **17.** m∠L in △KLM

18. Draw △PQR with PQ = 3 cm, m∠P = 35°, m∠Q = 70°

19. Draw △STU with m∠T = 80°, TU = 2 cm, TS = 2 cm

Math Reasoning Sketch each triangle or explain why it cannot be done.

20. Isosceles, obtuse   **21.** Equilateral, obtuse   **22.** Scalene, right

23. The diagram at the right shows a truss that might be used to support a bridge. Write the missing angle measures for the truss.

Mixed Review

Classify each angle in the diagram above.

24. ∠QRX   **25.** ∠QXY   **26.** ∠YRQ

27. Mental Math An angle has a measure of 30°. What is the measure of an angle complementary to it?

28. Two angles are supplementary. The measure of one angle is twice the measure of the other. What are the angle measures?

Test Prep   Choose the correct letter for each answer.

29. The width of a tennis court for a doubles game is 36 feet. If the
(7-1) length of the back court is half this width, what is the length of the back court in yards?

   A $1\frac{1}{2}$ yd   **B** 6 yd   **C** 18 yd   **D** 54 yd

30. Algebra Solve. 1.2 y = 1,200
(2-7)

   F y = 10   **G** y = 100   **H** y = 1,000   **J** y = 10,000

LESSON 7-8

Quadrilaterals

Algebra

California Content Standards *Measurement and Geometry 2.3: Draw quadrilaterals . . . from information about them (e.g., a quadrilateral having equal sides but no right angles, . . .).*

Math Link You know how to classify and draw triangles and how to find a missing angle measure in a triangle. Now you will learn how to classify, draw, and find missing angle measures in quadrilaterals.

Quadrilaterals are polygons with four sides and four angles. Quadrilaterals are named according to the special properties of their sides and angles.

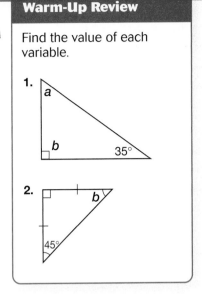

Warm-Up Review

Find the value of each variable.

1.

2.

Word Bank

quadrilateral
trapezoid
parallelogram
rhombus
rectangle
square
diagonal

Quadrilaterals

Description	Example
A **trapezoid** has one pair of parallel sides. ‖ means "is parallel to."	Trapezoid $\overline{AB} \parallel \overline{DC}$
A **parallelogram** has two pairs of parallel sides. Opposite sides and opposite angles are congruent.	Parallelogram $\overline{EF} \parallel \overline{HG}$ $\overline{EH} \parallel \overline{FG}$
A **rhombus** is a parallelogram with all sides congruent.	Rhombus
A **rectangle** is a parallelogram with four right angles.	Rectangle
A **square** is a rectangle with four congruent sides.	Square

Example 1

Classify the shape of the bicycle crossing sign, using as many names as possible from the table above.

The shape is a quadrilateral, a parallelogram, a rhombus, a rectangle, and a square.

 Additional Standards: Algebra and Functions 1.1(🔑), 3.2; Measurement and Geometry 2.0; Mathematical Reasoning 2.2 (See p. 259.)

279

The **diagonal** of a polygon is a segment that joins one vertex to another, but is not a side of the polygon.

In a quadrilateral, a diagonal divides the quadrilateral into two triangles. Since the angle measure of any triangle is 180°, the angle measure of any quadrilateral is 2 × 180°, or 360°.

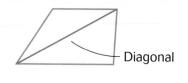
Diagonal

Example 2

Find m∠Y in the quadrilateral VWXY at the right.

$$m\angle Y + m\angle V + m\angle W + m\angle X = 360°$$
$$y + 115 + 90 + 90 = 360$$
$$y + 295 = 360$$
$$y = 65$$

m∠Y = 65°

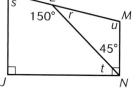

Example 3

Find the missing angle measures in quadrilateral JKMN.

a. Find m∠r.

∠r and the 150° angle are supplementary.

$$r + 150 = 180$$
$$r = 30$$

So m∠r = 30°.

b. Find m∠t.

∠t and the 45° angle are complementary.

$$t + 45 = 90$$
$$t = 45$$

So m∠t = 45°.

c. Find m∠u.

You found that m∠r = 30°, so you now know two angle measures in △LMN. Find m∠u.

$$u + 30 + 45 = 180$$
$$u + 75 = 180$$
$$u = 105$$

So m∠u = 105°.

d. Find m∠s.

You found that m∠t = 45°, so you now know three angle measures in quadrilateral JKLN. Find m∠s.

$$s + 150 + 45 + 90 = 360$$
$$s + 285 = 360$$
$$s = 75$$

So m∠s = 75°.

Guided Practice   For another example, see Set G on p. 294.

Algebra Find each missing angle measure, *n*. Then classify the polygon. Use as many names as possible.

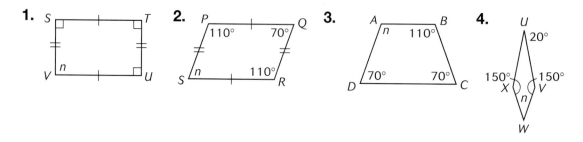

5. Draw a quadrilateral having no parallel sides or explain why it cannot be done.

Independent Practice   *For more practice, see Set G on p. 297.*

Find each missing angle measure, *n*. Then classify the polygon. Use as many names as possible.

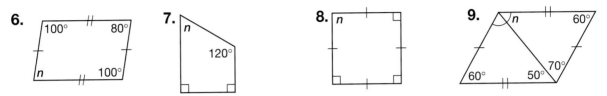

6. 100° 80° *n* 100°

7. *n* 120°

8. *n*

9. *n* 60° 70° 60° 50°

Sketch and classify each quadrilateral in Exercises 10–13.

10. A figure that is both a rectangle and a rhombus

11. A quadrilateral that is not a rectangle, with two right angles

12. A parallelogram with all sides the same length

13. A quadrilateral in the shape of a checkers game board

Use parallelogram *WXYZ* at the right. Find the measure of each angle.

X *h* 35° *y* *g* 85° *b* *a* *c* 125° *f* 35° *e* *d* W Z

14. m∠*a*

15. m∠*h*

16. m∠*e*

Mixed Review

17. Algebra Suppose the measure of angle *E* in triangle *DEG* is 90°. If the measure of angle *G* is half the measure of angle *D*, what is the measure of angle *D*?

Find the measure of each angle in the figure at the right.

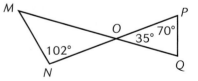

M P O 35° 70° 102° N Q

18. ∠*MON*

19. ∠*PQO*

20. ∠*NMO*

Test Prep   Choose the correct letter for each answer.

21. Algebra Solve *n* + 17 = 5.
(6-8)

   A *n* = ⁻22   **B** *n* = ⁻12   **C** *n* = 12   **D** *n* = 22

22. Algebra Solve $4\frac{1}{2}x = 24$.
(5-10)

   F $x = 5\frac{1}{3}$ **G** $x = 19\frac{1}{2}$ **H** $x = 28\frac{1}{2}$ **J** $x = 108$

Understand
Plan
Solve
Look Back

Problem-Solving Strategy:
Make a Table

 California Content Standard *Mathematical Reasoning 2.4: Use a variety of methods, such as words, numbers, . . . tables, diagrams, and models, to explain mathematical reasoning. Also, Mathematical Reasoning 1.2.*

Example

How many diagonals can be drawn from one vertex of a polygon with *n* sides?

Understand

What do you need to find?

You need to find the number of diagonals that can be drawn from one vertex.

Plan

How can you solve the problem?

You can make a table and then look for a pattern in the number of diagonals that can be drawn when the number of sides, *n*, is 4, 5, 6, and so on.

Solve

Draw a diagram for several polygons and record your results in a table.

Number of sides	4	5	6	7
Number of diagonals from one vertex	1	2	3	4

For each, the number of diagonals from one vertex of a polygon with *n* sides is 3 less than *n*, or $n - 3$.

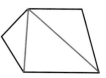

Look Back

How many diagonals can be drawn from one vertex of a polygon with 100 sides?

Guided Practice

1. Copy the table used in the Solve step above. Add another row labeled "Number of triangles formed by the diagonals from one vertex." Complete the row.

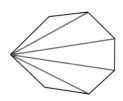

  Additional Standards: Algebra and Functions 1.2; Mathematical Reasoning 1.1, 3.0, 3.2 (See p. 259.)

2. Add a fourth row to your table. Label it "Sum of the angle measures in each polygon." Complete the row.

3. Compare the number of sides in a polygon and the sum of the angle measures. Make a conjecture about the number of sides and the angle measure. Use your conjecture to find the sum of the angle measures in a 12-sided polygon.

Independent Practice

Suppose square tables are placed end to end and one person can sit on each available side as shown at the right.

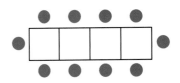

4. How many people can sit around one table? two tables? three tables? four tables?

5. How are the number of tables and the number of people seated on the longer sides related? How many additional people are there?

6. Make a conjecture about the number of tables and the number of people that can be seated. Find the number of people that could be seated around 25 tables.

7. Suppose the tables placed end to end are rectangular, that two people can sit on each available side, and that one person can sit at each end. Answer the questions in Exercise 6 for this situation.

Mixed Review

Try these or other strategies to solve each problem. Tell which strategy you used.

> ### Problem-Solving Strategies
>
> - *Use Logical Reasoning*
> - *Find a Pattern*
> - *Make a Table*
> - *Write an Equation*

8. A soccer ball weighs more than a football. A basketball weighs more than a softball. A football weighs less than a basketball. The weight of a soccer ball is between that of a football and a basketball. Which ball weighs the most?

9. An ice-hockey rink is 200 feet long. Suppose hockey sticks each 4 ft 6 in. long are placed end to end along the ice. How many hockey sticks are needed to create a line from one end of the rink to the other?

Transformations

California Content Standard *Measurement and Geometry 3.2 (Gr. 7): Understand . . . simple figures, . . . and determine their images under translations and reflections.*

Math Link You have worked with geometric figures. Now you will identify translations, rotations, and reflections of these figures.

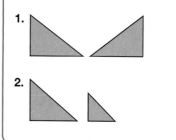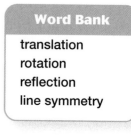
Example 1

For each example below, trace Figure I. Move the tracing paper to fit exactly on Figure II. Try to not lift the tracing paper from the page unless you have to. Tell how you had to move Figure I to change its position to Figure II.

Word Bank

- translation
- rotation
- reflection
- line symmetry

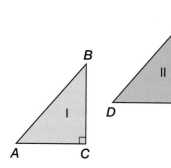

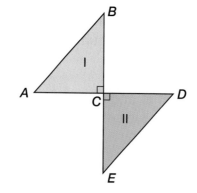

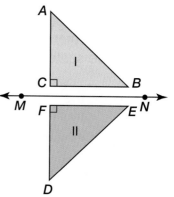

A change in position resulting from a *slide* is called a **translation.**

A change in position resulting from a *turn* is called a **rotation.**

A change in position resulting from a *flip* is called a **reflection.**

Example 2

A figure has **line symmetry** if it can be folded along a line so that both sides match.

How many lines of symmetry does each figure have?

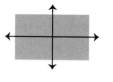

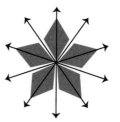

2 lines of symmetry   4 lines of symmetry   5 lines of symmetry

 Additional Standards: Measurement and Geometry 2.0, 2.3 (See p. 259.)

Guided Practice *For more practice, see Set H on p. 294.*

Trace Figure I. Move the tracing paper to fit exactly onto Figure II.
Use *translation, rotation,* and *reflection* to describe the motions used.

1.   **2.**   **3.**

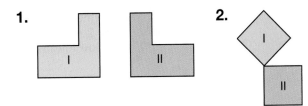

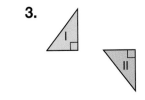

4. Sketch a triangle with exactly three lines of symmetry.

Independent Practice *For another example, see Set H on p. 297.*

Trace Figure I. Move the tracing paper to fit exactly onto Figure II.
Use *translation, rotation,* and *reflection* to describe the motions used.

5.   **6.**   **7.**

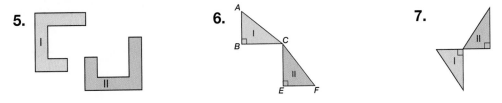

Sketch a polygon that has exactly the number of lines of symmetry given.

8. 0   **9.** 1   **10.** 2   **11.** 4

Mixed Review

12. You have 75 daffodil and tulip bulbs. There are 23 more tulip than daffodil bulbs. How many tulip bulbs do you have?

Classify each polygon. Use as many names as you can.

13.   **14.**   **15.**

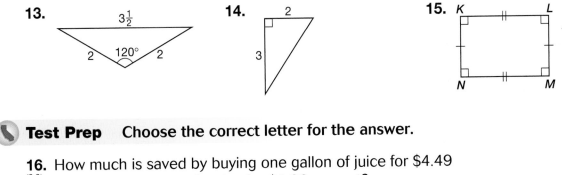

Test Prep   Choose the correct letter for the answer.

16. How much is saved by buying one gallon of juice for $4.49
(2-2)   instead of four quart bottles for $1.39 a quart?

     A $0.57   **B** $0.82   **C** $1.07   **D** $3.10

LESSON

7-11

Understand
Plan
Solve
Look Back

Problem-Solving Application:

Using Time Zones

California Content Standard *Mathematical Reasoning 2.0: Students use strategies, skills, and concepts in finding solutions.*

Warm-Up Review

Find each elapsed time.

1. 8:28 A.M. to 11:52 A.M.

2. 10:53 A.M. to 1:07 P.M.

3. Karl was in the dentist's office from 2:49 P.M. to 4:07 P.M. How long was he there?

Example

At 9:00 A.M. Hawaii time, ice skaters on tour leave Honolulu, Hawaii, for Chicago, Illinois. Their flight takes 8 hours. What will the time be in Chicago when they arrive?

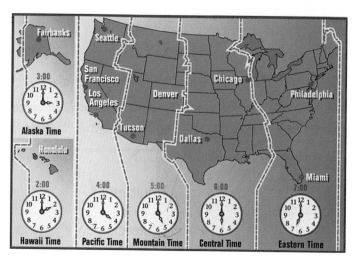

Understand

What do you know?

You know that it is 9:00 A.M. in Honolulu when the plane departs and that the flight takes 8 hours.

Plan

How can you solve the problem?

You can use logical reasoning to solve the problem. First use the map to find out what time it is in Chicago when it is 9:00 A.M. in Honolulu. Then use this information and the flying time to determine what time it will be in Chicago when the skaters arrive.

Solve

You can tell from the map that if it is 2:00 in Honolulu, then it is 6:00 in Chicago. So the time in Chicago is 4 hours later than the time in Honolulu.

If it is 9:00 A.M. in Honolulu, then it is 1:00 P.M. in Chicago. If the plane leaves Honolulu at 1 P.M. Chicago time, then it arrives at 9:00 P.M. Chicago time.

Look Back

Suppose the plane had left Honolulu at 12 noon Hawaii time. What time would it have been in Chicago when it landed?

Additional Standards: Mathematical Reasoning 1.0, 3.0 (See p. 259.)

Guided Practice

1. From Philadelphia, the skaters will travel to Seattle for their last performance of the tour. The flight is scheduled to leave Philadelphia at 11:00 P.M. Eastern Time. Arrival will be 1:50 A.M. Pacific Time. How long is the flight?

2. What time is it in Philadelphia when the plane lands in Seattle?

Independent Practice

3. A basketball game starts at 8:00 P.M. in Los Angeles and will be broadcast live in Miami. What will the time be in Miami when the game begins?

4. A sales manager has to catch a flight to Chicago that leaves 1 hour 30 minutes after a meeting in San Francisco ends. The meeting ends at 11:00 A.M. The flight takes 4 hours 45 minutes. What time will it be in Chicago when the plane arrives?

5. During Daylight Savings Time, most states set their clocks ahead one hour, but Arizona does not. If it is 12 noon, Eastern Daylight time in Miami, what time is it in Tucson, Arizona?

6. Complete the table below.

Flight Schedule				
Departure		Arrival		Length of Flight
City	Time	City	Time	
Los Angeles	10:47 A.M.	Chicago	5:02 P.M.	
Miami	10:24 A.M.	San Francisco		5 hr 52 min

Mixed Review

7. Once a year Sportsway has a clearance sale. During the first hour of the sale, 5 people entered the store. The second hour, 3 times as many people entered, and none left. The third hour twice as many people entered as entered the second hour and none left. If 60 more people entered during the fourth hour and none left, how many people were in the store at the end of the fourth hour?

8. For a bulletin-board display, Laurie is putting one picture in the first row, 3 in the second row, 6 in the third row, and 10 in the fourth row. If the pattern continues, how many pictures will she need for ten rows?

Diagnostic Checkpoint

Complete. For Exercises 1–3, use words from the Word Bank.

1. A figure that has two parallel sides with opposite sides and opposite angles congruent is a(n) _____.
(7-8)

2. A(n) _____ has three sides the same length.
(7-7)

3. Two angles are _____ when the sum of their measures is 180°.
(7-6)

Find both the complement and the supplement of each angle measure.

4. 13°
(7-6)

5. 87°
(7-6)

6. 50°
(7-6)

7. 68°
(7-6)

Classify each triangle in two ways.

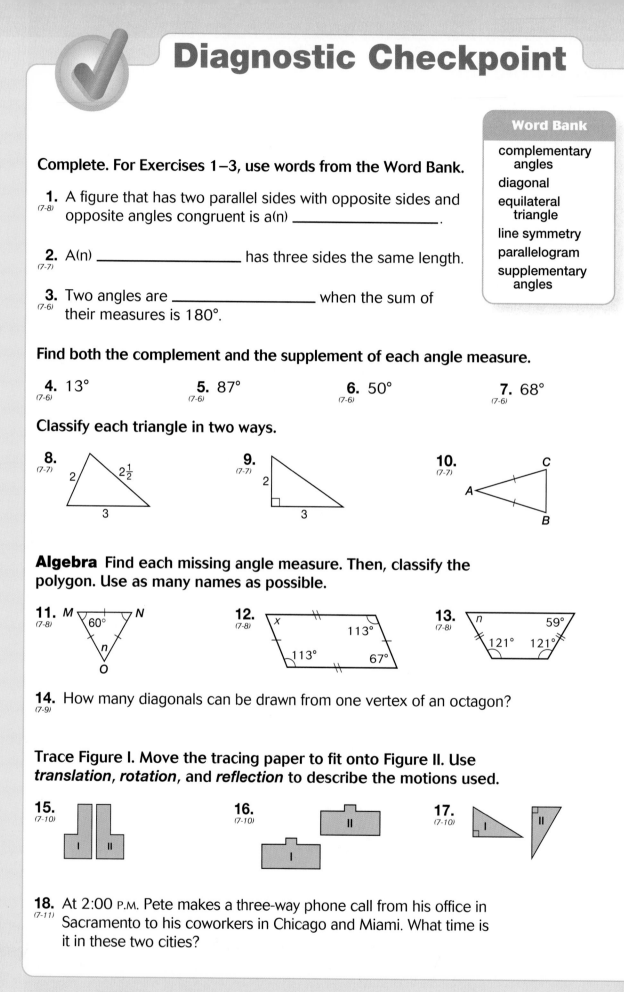

8. (7-7)

2 $2\frac{1}{2}$ 3

9. (7-7)

2 3

10. (7-7)

C A B

Algebra Find each missing angle measure. Then, classify the polygon. Use as many names as possible.

11. M N
(7-8)
$60°$
n
O

12. (7-8)
x
$113°$
$113°$
$67°$

13. (7-8)
n
$59°$
$121°$ $121°$

14. How many diagonals can be drawn from one vertex of an octagon?
(7-9)

Trace Figure I. Move the tracing paper to fit onto Figure II. Use *translation*, *rotation*, and *reflection* to describe the motions used.

15. (7-10)
I II

16. (7-10)
II I

17. (7-10)
I II

18. At 2:00 P.M. Pete makes a three-way phone call from his office in Sacramento to his coworkers in Chicago and Miami. What time is it in these two cities?
(7-11)

Chapter 7 Test

Complete.

1. 2.8 L = ■ mL

2. 10 gal ≈ ■ L

3. 9 mi = ■ yd

4. 68 cm ≈ ■ in.

5. 8,234 g = ■ kg

6. ■ gal = 41 qt

Use the figure at the right for Exercises 7–11.

7. If m∠JAB = 68°, what is the measure of its complement?

8. Classify ∠JAI.

9. Is $\overrightarrow{BF}$ a line or a ray?

10. If m∠ACH = 68°, what is the measure of its supplement?

11. What is the measure of ∠ABD?

12. How many triangles are in the design at the right?

Classify each polygon. Use as many names as possible.

13.

14.

15.

16.

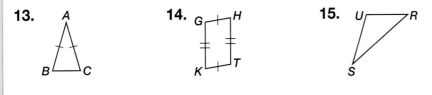

Use the figures at the right to answer Exercises 17 and 18.

17. Tell whether the change in the position of Figure I to Figure II is a result of a translation, rotation, or reflection.

18. How many lines of symmetry does Figure I have?

19. How many diagonals can be drawn from one vertex of a six-sided figure?

20. Alex phoned Shana from his home in California at 5:30 P.M. Shana, who happened to be in Miami, told him it was 8:30 P.M. If Shana calls Alex back at 11:00 P.M. her time, what time is it in California?

Multiple-Choice
Chapter 7 Test

Choose the correct letter for each answer.

1. **A basketball weighs from 20 to 22 ounces. What is the least that 12 basketballs could weigh in pounds?**

   A   12 pounds

   B   15 pounds

   C   16 pounds

   D $16\frac{1}{2}$ pounds

2. **Which describes the length of the tablecloth you should buy to cover a rectangular table of length 96 inches?**

   F   No longer than 38 cm

   G   More than 244 cm

   H   Shorter than 192 cm

   J   Exactly 150 cm

3. **Which best describes the name and symbol for the figure?**

   L •————————• S

   A   Point L

   B   Line LS; $\overleftrightarrow{LS}$

   C   Line segment LS; $\overline{LS}$

   D   Ray LS; $\overrightarrow{LS}$

4. **Classify a 116° angle.**

   F   Right angle

   G   Obtuse angle

   H   Acute angle

   J   Straight angle

Use the design shown below for Questions 5 and 6.

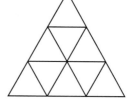

5. **How many triangles are in the design?**

   A   9 triangles

   B   10 triangles

   C   12 triangles

   D   13 triangles

6. **Which figure is *not* in the design?**

   F   Equilateral triangle

   G   Rhombus

   H   Square

   J   Trapezoid

7. **Jan drinks eight 250-mL glasses of water each day. How many liters of water does Jan drink each day?**

   A   1 L

   B   1.5 L

   C   2 L

   D   2.5 L

Use the figure for Questions 8 and 9.

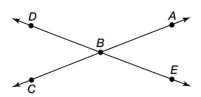

8. Which angle is the supplement of ∠*EBC*?

F   ∠*ABD*

G   ∠*EBA*

H   ∠*DBA*

J   ∠*CBA*

---

9. Name a pair of vertical angles.

A   ∠*DBA* and ∠*CBE*

B   ∠*DBC* and ∠*EBC*

C   ∠*ABD* and ∠*ABE*

D   ∠*CBA* and ∠*DBE*

---

10. Which best describes the triangle?

F   Obtuse and scalene

G   Acute

H   Right

J   Equilateral and acute

---

11. How many diagonals can be drawn from one vertex of a nonagon, a nine-sided figure?

A   4 diagonals

B   6 diagonals

C   8 diagonals

D   10 diagonals

---

12. Which best describes a rhombus with right angles?

F   Parallelogram

G   Trapezoid

H   Rectangle

J   Square

---

13. When it is 7:00 P.M. in Philadelphia it is 4:00 P.M. in Seattle. If Curtis leaves Seattle on a 5-hour non-stop flight to Philadelphia at noon Seattle time, what time will it be in Philadelphia when he arrives?

A   2:00 P.M.   C   8:00 P.M.

B   11:00 A.M.   D   6:00 P.M.

---

14. Which best describes the change in position from Figure I to Figure II?

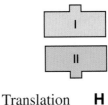

F   Translation   H   Reflection

G   Rotation   J   Flip

---

15. How many lines of symmetry does a square have?

A   1 line of symmetry

B   2 lines of symmetry

C   4 lines of symmetry

D   6 lines of symmetry

Reteaching

Set A (pages 260–262)

Complete. 616 yd = ■ mi

$$1{,}760 \text{ yd} = 1 \text{ mi}$$
$$616 \text{ yd} = ■ \text{ mi}$$
$$616 \div 1{,}760 = 0.35 \quad \textbf{Divide.}$$
$$616 \text{ yd} = 0.35 \text{ miles}$$

Remember when changing from a smaller unit to a larger unit, divide. When changing from a larger unit to a smaller unit, multiply.

Complete.

1. 7 pt = ■ fl oz   **2.** $3\frac{1}{4}$ lb = ■ oz

3. 300 in. = ■ yd   **4.** 17 pt = ■ qt

5. 3 mi = ■ ft   **6.** 2.5 T = ■ lb

7. 6 qt = ■ gal   **8.** 84 fl oz = ■ c

Set B (pages 263–265)

Complete. 2.7 kg = ■ g

$$1 \text{ kg} = 1{,}000 \text{ g}$$
$$2.7 \text{ kg} = ■ \text{ g}$$
$$1{,}000 \times 2.7 = 2{,}700 \quad \textbf{Multiply.}$$
$$2.7 \text{ kg} = 2{,}700 \text{ g}$$

Remember the metric system is based on powers of ten.

Complete.

1. 75 mg = ■ g   **2.** 9.4 L = ■ mL

3. 800 t = ■ kg   **4.** 900 cm = ■ km

5. ■ mg = 7 g   **6.** ■ kL = 4,400 mL

7. ■ dam = 80 m   **8.** ■ dm = 6 hm

Set C (pages 266–267)

Complete. 77 gal ≈ ■ L

$$1 \text{ gal} \approx 3.79 \text{ L}$$
$$77 \times 3.79 \approx 291.83 \quad \textbf{Multiply.}$$
$$77 \text{ gal} \approx 291.83 \text{ L}$$

Remember to use the conversion equivalents when converting units from one measurment system to another.

Complete.

1. ■ in. ≈ 62 m   **2.** 16 qt ≈ ■ L

3. 18 oz ≈ ■ g   **4.** 43 t ≈ ■ T

5. 14 lb ≈ ■ kg   **6.** 16 cm ≈ ■ in.

7. ■ m ≈ 393.7 in.   **8.** 30 km ≈ ■ mi

Set D *(pages 270–272)*

Classify an angle with measure 78° and an angle with measure 124°.

78° is less than 90° and greater than 0°.
An angle with measure 78° is an acute angle.

124° is greater than 90° but less than 180°.

An angle with measure 124° is an obtuse angle.

Remember angles with measures of 90° are right angles.

Classify each angle.

1. 105°   **2.** 3°

3. 175°   **4.** 90°

5. 180°   **6.** 89°

Set E *(pages 274–275)*

Find both the complement and supplement of 76°.

Complement: $90° = 76° + x$
$$90° - 76° = x$$
$$14° = x$$

Supplement: $180° = 76° + x$
$$180° - 76° = x$$
$$104° = x$$

Remember two angles are supplementary angles when the sum of their measures is 180°. Two angles are complementary angles when the sum of their measures is 90°.

Find both the complement and supplement of each angle measure.

1. 2°   **2.** 16°

3. 85°   **4.** 57°

5. 61°   **6.** 33°

Set F *(pages 276–278)*

Classify the triangle according to side measures and angle measures.

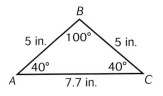

△ABC has 2 congruent sides, and 1 obtuse angle.

It is an isosceles obtuse triangle.

Remember you can classify triangles by their side or angle measures.

Classify each triangle in two ways.

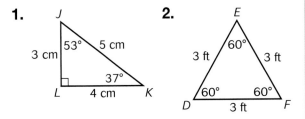

1.   **2.**

Reteaching (continued)

Set G (pages 279–281)

Classify the polygon and solve for the missing measures.

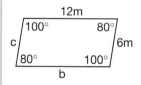

The figure has two sets of parallel sides, and opposite angles are congruent. The figure is a parallelogram.

$c = 6$ m and $b = 12$ m

Remember quadrilaterals are polygons with four sides and four angles. You can classify them according to the measure of the sides and angles. The sum of the angles in a quadrilateral is 360°.

Classify each polygon and solve for the missing measures.

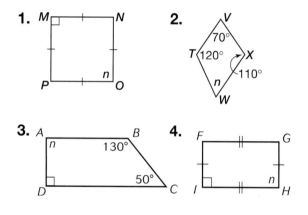

Set H (pages 284–285)

Describe the change in position from Figure I to Figure II.

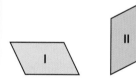

A change in position resulting from a turn is called a rotation.

Remember a change in position is typically called a translation, rotation, or reflection.

Describe the change in position from Figure I to Figure II.

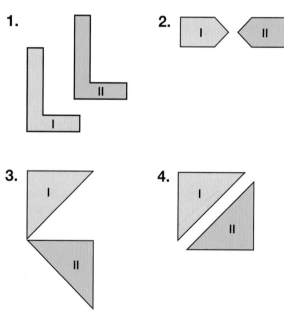

More Practice

Set A *(pages 260–262)*

Choose the most reasonable customary unit of measure for each.

1. length of a baseball bat
2. weight of a dog
3. length of a gymnasium
4. capacity of a bath tub

Complete.

5. 22 ft = ▦ in.
6. 37 mi = ▦ yd
7. 30 T = ▦ lb

8. 2 yd = ▦ in.
9. 13 lb = ▦ oz
10. 11 pt = ▦ qt

11. During his career, a pro football player ran 16,207 yards. How many feet is this? How many miles?

Set B *(pages 263–265)*

Choose the most reasonable metric unit of measure for each.

1. distance walked in $3\frac{1}{2}$ hours
2. the mass of a bowling ball
3. capacity of a soup spoon
4. the length of a seed

Complete.

5. 3 m = ▦ cm
6. 225 L = ▦ kL
7. 17 t = ▦ kg

8. ▦ kg = 650 g
9. 12 cm = ▦ mm
10. ▦ mL = 9 L

11. Thirty men have a mass of 105 kg each. Can they cross a bridge together if the bridge holds no more than 3 t? Explain.

Set C *(pages 266–267)*

Complete. Round to the nearest tenth.

1. ▦ in. ≈ 12 cm
2. 17 t ≈ ▦ T
3. ▦ mi ≈ 30 km

4. 16 oz ≈ ▦ g
5. ▦ m ≈ 600 in.
6. 75 gal ≈ ▦ L

7. 40 L ≈ ▦ qt
8. 64 mi ≈ ▦ km
9. 75 kg ≈ ▦ lb

10. Each of 6 cars weighs $1\frac{3}{4}$ tons. What is the total weight of the cars in metric tons? Round your answer to the nearest tenth.

More Practice (continued)

Set D (pages 270–272)

Measure each angle. Then classify it.

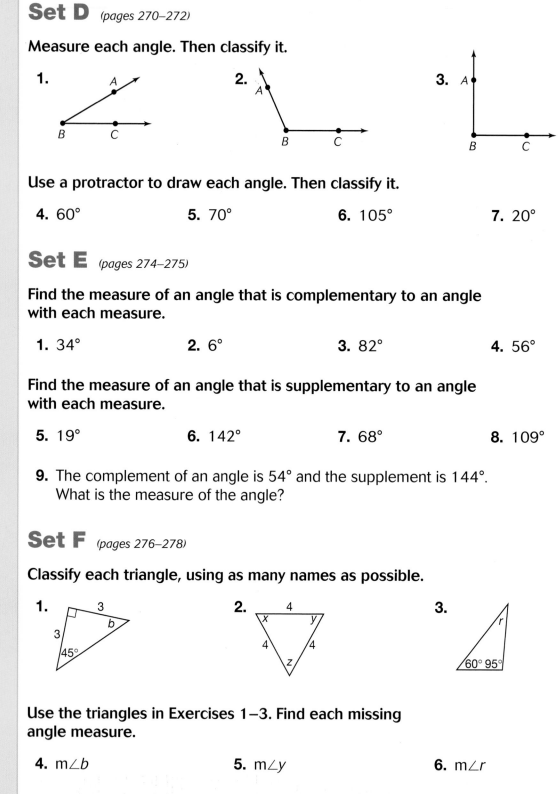

1.

2.

3.

Use a protractor to draw each angle. Then classify it.

4. 60°   **5.** 70°   **6.** 105°   **7.** 20°

Set E (pages 274–275)

Find the measure of an angle that is complementary to an angle with each measure.

1. 34°   **2.** 6°   **3.** 82°   **4.** 56°

Find the measure of an angle that is supplementary to an angle with each measure.

5. 19°   **6.** 142°   **7.** 68°   **8.** 109°

9. The complement of an angle is 54° and the supplement is 144°. What is the measure of the angle?

Set F (pages 276–278)

Classify each triangle, using as many names as possible.

1.   2.   3.

Use the triangles in Exercises 1–3. Find each missing angle measure.

4. m∠b   **5.** m∠y   **6.** m∠r

7. Lynda drew a triangle with sides that are 2 inches, 5 inches, and 5 inches long. How would you classify her triangle?

Set G *(pages 279–281)*

Find the measure of each missing angle. Then, classify the polygon. Use as many names as possible.

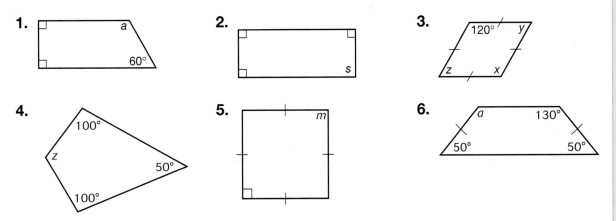

1. a 60°

2. s

3. 120° y z x

4. 100° z 50° 100°

5. m

6. a 130° 50° 50°

7. Bob labeled a drawing as a rectangle and a rhombus. Ron called it a square. Could both be correct? Explain your answer.

Set H *(pages 284–285)*

Describe each change in position from Figure I to Figure II. Use the terms *reflection*, *rotation*, and *translation*.

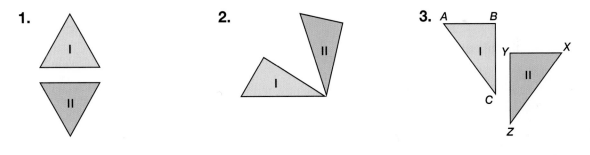

1. I II

2. II I

3. A B I Y X II C Z

Is the green line a line of symmetry? Write *yes* or *no*.

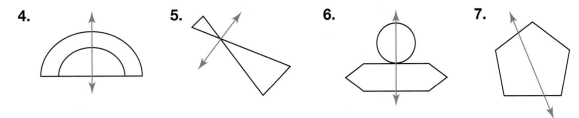

4.

5.

6.

7.

8. How many lines of symmetry can be drawn on Figure I in Exercise 1 above?

Problem Solving: Preparing for Tests

Choose the correct letter for each answer.

1. **Jules is numbering raffle tickets. The first 6 ticket numbers are 6,135; 6,118; 6,101; 6,084; 6,067; and 6,050. If he continues this pattern, what is the number of the *tenth* ticket?**

   Tip

   Try using the *Find a Pattern* strategy for this problem.

   A 5,067

   B 5,982

   C 5,999

   D 6,001

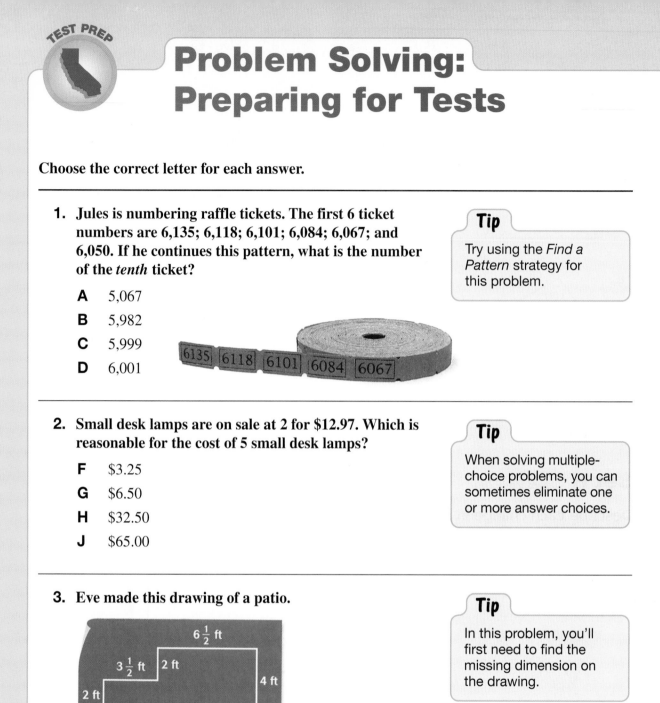

2. **Small desk lamps are on sale at 2 for $12.97. Which is reasonable for the cost of 5 small desk lamps?**

   Tip

   When solving multiple-choice problems, you can sometimes eliminate one or more answer choices.

   F $3.25

   G $6.50

   H $32.50

   J $65.00

3. **Eve made this drawing of a patio.**

   Tip

   In this problem, you'll first need to find the missing dimension on the drawing.

   $6\frac{1}{2}$ ft

   $3\frac{1}{2}$ ft   2 ft

   4 ft

   2 ft

   Later Eve decided to make the sides of the patio $1\frac{1}{2}$ times as long as those shown on the drawing. What was the length of the *longest* side of the new patio?

   A $9\frac{3}{4}$ ft

   B 10 ft

   C $11\frac{1}{2}$ ft

   D 15 ft

4. Anne cut out a cardboard pattern of a polygon having two right angles. Which of these could NOT be the shape Anne cut out?

F Pentagon

G Triangle

H Parallelogram

J Trapezoid

---

5. The sum of two angles of a triangle is 80°. Which equation could you use to find the measure, *n*, of the third angle in this triangle?

A $(2 \times 80) + 2n = 180$

B $(2 \times 80) \div n = 180$

C $80 + 2n = 180$

D $180 - 80 = n$

---

6. Mike and Angela jogged from their home to the mall and back home again. This graph shows their times and distances.

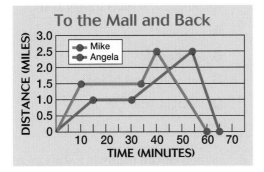

Choose the best interpretation of the graph.

F Angela stopped to rest for a longer time than Mike did.

G Angela got to the mall first.

H Angela got home first.

J Mike got home first.

---

7. Kate is designing a square metal hot plate. She starts with a square 8.2 centimeters on each side. Then she increases each side length by 0.5 centimeter. Which number sentence shows the area of the new square?

A $A = (8.2)^2$

B $A = (8.2 + 0.5)^2$

C $A = (8.2)^2 + (0.5)^2$

D $A = (8.2)^2 + (2 \times 0.5)$

---

8. One milliliter (mL) equals one thousandth of a liter (L). A scientist used about one-third of a 1.8-liter solution. Which is the best estimate of how much she used?

F 1,800 mL

G 1,200 mL

H 600 mL

J 0.6 mL

---

9. A photograph is 8 inches by 10 inches. The mat around the photo is 2 inches wide, and the frame is $1\frac{1}{4}$ inches wide. What are the dimensions of the framed photograph?

A 10 inches by 12 inches

B 11 inches by 14 inches

C $11\frac{1}{4}$ inches by $13\frac{1}{4}$ inches

D $14\frac{1}{2}$ inches by $16\frac{1}{2}$ inches

---

10. Betty and Roger have numbered ticket stubs. The numbers each have four digits. Roger's number is 1,455. If the sum of the two numbers is 6,886, which of these must be Betty's number?

F 5,431   **H** 4,135

G 5,413   **J** 3,451

Multiple-Choice Cumulative Review

Choose the correct letter for each answer.

Number Sense

1. A golden retriever weighs 3 times as much as a terrier. If the retriever weighs 75 pounds, how much does the terrier weigh?

  A 15 pounds

  B 25 pounds

  C 50 pounds

  D 225 pounds

2. Gretchen read 130 pages of a book the first week and another 241 the next week. For 3 weeks after that, she read 124 pages each week. How many pages did she read in the 5 weeks?

  F 459 pages   **H** 502 pages

  G 495 pages   **J** 743 pages

3. An average of 680 people visit a local zoo each day. Which is the best estimate of how many people visit the zoo in a month?

  A 15,000 people

  B 21,000 people

  C 27,000 people

  D 210,000 people

4. What is the sum of $\frac{3}{8} + \frac{5}{6}$?

  F $\frac{5}{16}$ **J** $1\frac{5}{24}$

  G $\frac{4}{7}$ **K** NH

  H $\frac{8}{14}$

Measurement and Geometry

5. Which is the measure of an acute angle?

  A 180°

  B 120°

  C 90°

  D 60°

6. Look at the triangle below. What is the measure of ∠*x*?

  F 30°

  G 45°

  H 60°

  J 90°

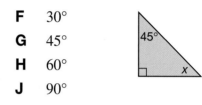

7. A figure has one right angle and two 45° angles. Which figure is it?

  A Square

  B Rhombus

  C Equilateral triangle

  D Right triangle

8. Which of the following statements is *NOT* true?

  F A square is a rectangle.

  G A rectangle is a quadrilateral.

  H A square is a rhombus.

  J A trapezoid is a parallelogram.

Measurement and Geometry

9. How many feet are in $2\frac{1}{2}$ miles? (1 mile = 5,280 ft)

   A   1,320 ft

   B   4,400 ft

   C   10,560 ft

   D   13,200 ft

10. It costs $3.00 to ship a box weighing up to 2 pounds and $0.48 for each additional ounce over 2 pounds. How much would it cost to ship a box weighing 3 pounds 3 ounces? (1 lb = 16 oz)

   F $12.12   **H** $7.44

   G $9.12   **J** $6.48

11. An Olympic-size swimming pool is 50 meters long. How many kilometers long is this? (1 km = 1,000 m)

   A   0.005 km

   B   0.05 km

   C   0.5 km

   D   5 km

12. A floor puzzle measures 12 feet long and 9 feet wide. Half of the puzzle is a design of many squares. What is the perimeter of the puzzle in yards? ($A = l \times w$)

   F   12 yards

   G   14 yards

   H   21 yards

   J   42 yards

Statistics, Data Analysis, and Probability

13. Samantha received the following scores on her math quizzes: 88, 85, 92, 89, 94, 92. What was her mean score?

   A   89   **C**   91

   B   90   **D**   92

14. Tim studied for 45 minutes on Monday, 1 hour 30 minutes on Tuesday, and 1 hour on Wednesday. What was the average amount of time he spent studying?

   F   1 hr 30 min   **H**   1 hr

   G   1 hr 5 min   **J**   45 min

Use the graph for Questions 15 and 16.

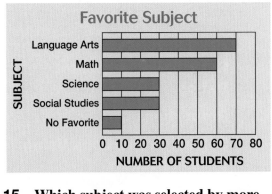

15. Which subject was selected by more than twice the number who selected science?

   A   Language Arts   **C**   Social Studies

   B   Math   **D**   No Favorite

16. How many more students chose math than social studies as their favorite subject?

   F   90 more   **H**   30 more

   G   70 more   **J**   20 more

CHAPTER

8

Ratio and Proportion

Diagnosing Readiness

In Chapter 8, you will use these skills:

Ⓐ Equivalent Fractions
(pages 148–150)

Write three fractions equivalent to the following fractions.

1. $\frac{11}{12}$ 2. $\frac{6}{8}$

3. $\frac{1}{3}$ 4. $\frac{5}{9}$

5. $\frac{20}{90}$ 6. $\frac{30}{105}$

7. Josh drinks $\frac{1}{2}$ cup of milk. Liz drinks $\frac{5}{8}$ cup, and James drinks $\frac{2}{3}$ cup. Who drank the most milk?

Ⓑ Multiplying Fractions and Mixed Numbers
(pages 192–193)

Find the product.

8. $\frac{1}{3} \times \frac{1}{7}$ 9. $\frac{3}{8} \times \frac{2}{5}$

10. $3\frac{1}{8} \times 8$ 11. $\frac{9}{16} \times 1\frac{1}{2}$

12. $5 \times \frac{5}{15}$ 13. $\frac{6}{8} \times \frac{8}{6}$

14. Mr. South earns $17.00 per hour. On Saturdays he makes $1\frac{1}{2}$ times his regular rate. What is his rate on Saturdays?

C Multiplying and Dividing Whole Numbers and Decimals

(pages 52–54, 58–63)

15.
$$\begin{array}{r} 810 \\ \times\ \ 22 \\ \hline \end{array}$$

16.
$$\begin{array}{r} 0.7642 \\ \times\ \ \ \ \ 16 \\ \hline \end{array}$$

17.
$$\begin{array}{r} 9.03 \\ \times\ \ 2.6 \\ \hline \end{array}$$

18.
$$\begin{array}{r} 21.3 \\ \times\ 0.08 \\ \hline \end{array}$$

19. $7\overline{)0.00014}$ **20.** $70\overline{)8.4}$

21. Find the cost of 12 pounds of apples at \$1.39 per pound.

D Solving Multiplication and Division Equations

(pages 68–69)

Solve.

22. $8 = b \div 9$ **23.** $9x = 81.81$

24. $14.6t = 73$ **25.** $\dfrac{s}{6} = 0.1$

26. A remote control costs $\dfrac{1}{10}$ the price of a television. The television costs \$429.50. How much does the remote control cost?

E Angle Measures in Triangles

(pages 276–278)

Determine the missing angle.

27.    **28.**

F Congruent Triangles

(pages 276–278)

Is the pair of triangles congruent?

29.

30.

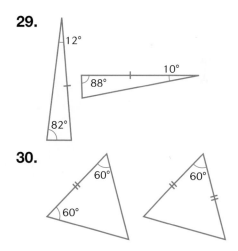

G Units of Measure

(pages 260–262)

31. 4 yd = _____ in.

32. 6 yd = _____ ft

33. Casey has fabric 8 yards long. How many pieces, each 8 inches long, can be cut from it?

To the Family and Student

| Looking Back | Chapter 8 | Looking Ahead |

Ratio and Proportion

In Grade 5, students were introduced to ratios and learned how to identify equivalent ratios.

In this chapter, students will learn how to use, write, and solve ratios and proportions.

In Chapter 9, students will learn how to use ratios and proportions to solve percent problems.

Math and Everyday Living

Opportunities to apply the concepts of Chapter 8 abound in everyday situations. During the chapter, think about how ratios and proportions can be used to solve a variety of real-world problems. The following examples suggest just several of the many situations that could launch a discussion about ratios and proportions.

Math and Quilting A quilt that has been in your family for years has a 6-square block pattern shown below.

Red	Blue	Red
Gold	Tan	Gold

The quilt contains 120 blocks. How many gold squares are on the quilt?

Math and Technology You scan your 4-inch by 6-inch family photo into the computer. When you enlarge a photo on your computer screen, the computer maintains the proportion of the original photo. So, if you enlarge the shorter side to 10 inches, what will the longer side measure?

Math and Reading Your school, built in 1994, averages 197 graduates each year. Typically $\frac{2}{3}$ of the graduates are 14 years old. About how many graduates are 14 years old? What information was not necessary for you to solve the problem?

Math on the Trail During a 20-mile hike, you maintain a pace of 4 miles per hour. Your cousin's pace is 2.5 miles per hour, and your friend's pace is 3 miles per hour. About how many hours will it take each of you to finish the hike?

Math at the Grocery Store You want to buy the most economical bag of dog food for your two pet dogs. You notice the different prices for the different sizes of dog food. Which bag has the least expensive unit price?

Dog Food	
2 pound	$3.99
5 pound	$5.44
15 pound	$9.87
27 pound	$19.99

Math and Photography With your digital camera, you can take 240 photos using one disk. How many photos can you take using 4 of the same type of disk?

California Content Standards in Chapter 8 Lessons*

Number Sense	Teach and Practice	Practice
1.0 Students solve problems involving . . . proportions		8-2
1.2 (🔑) Interpret and use ratios in different contexts (e.g., batting averages, miles per hour) to show the relative sizes of two quantities, using appropriate notations (a/b, a to b, a:b)	8-1	8-3, 8-4, 8-5, 8-6
1.3 (🔑) Use proportions to solve problems (e.g., determine the value of N if $\frac{4}{7} = \frac{N}{21}$, find the length of a side of a polygon similar to a known polygon). Use cross-multiplication as a method for solving such problems, understanding it as the multiplication of both sides of an equation by a multiplicative inverse.	8-2, 8-3, 8-8, 8-9, 8-10	8-5, 8-6

Algebra and Functions	Teach and Practice	Practice
1.1 Write and solve one-step linear equations in one variable. $6y - 2 = 10$. What is y?		8-3
2.2 (🔑) Demonstrate an understanding that rate is a measure of one quantity per unit value of another quantity.	8-5	8-6
2.3 Solve problems involving rates, average speed, distance, and time.	8-6	8-5, 8-10

Mathematical Reasoning	Teach and Practice	Practice
1.1 Analyze problems by identifying relationships, distinguishing relevant from irrelevant information, identifying missing information, sequencing and prioritizing information, and observing patterns.	8-4	8-1, 8-2, 8-5
2.2 Apply strategies and results from simpler problems to more complex problems.		8-10
2.4 Use a variety of methods, such as words, numbers, symbols, charts, graphs, tables, diagrams, and models, to explain mathematical reasoning.	8-7	8-8, 8-9
3.0 Students move beyond a particular problem by generalizing to other situations.		8-4
3.1 Evaluate the reasonableness of the solution in the context of the original situation.		8-10
3.2 Note the method of deriving the solution and demonstrate a conceptual understanding of the derivation by solving similar problems.		8-7, 8-9, 8-10

Statistics, Data Analysis, and Probability	Teach and Practice	Practice
3.1 (🔑) Represent all possible outcomes for compound events in an organized way (e.g., tables, grids, tree diagrams) and express the theoretical probability of each outcome.		8-7

* The symbol (🔑) indicates a key standard as designated in Mathematics Framework for California Public Schools. Full statements of the California Content Standards are found at the beginning of this book following the Table of Contents.

Ratios and Equivalent Ratios

California Content Standard *Number Sense 1.2* (🔑): *Interpret and use ratios in different contexts (e.g., batting averages, miles per hour) to show the relative sizes of two quantities, using appropriate notations (a/b, a to b, a:b).*

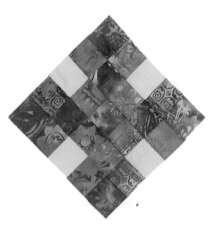

Warm-Up Review

Find each missing number.

1. $\frac{2}{7} = \frac{\blacksquare}{21}$ 2. $\frac{15}{18} = \frac{5}{\blacksquare}$

3. $\frac{6}{\blacksquare} = \frac{3}{14}$ 4. $\frac{\blacksquare}{12} = \frac{3}{4}$

5. Find the next two equivalent fractions.

$\frac{8}{18}, \frac{12}{27}, \frac{16}{36}, \frac{\blacksquare}{\blacksquare}, \frac{\blacksquare}{\blacksquare}$

Math Link You have compared numbers. Now you will learn how to use ratios to compare two quantities.

Example 1

The photo at the right shows a piece of a quilt called a block. Compare the number of turquoise squares to the number of purple squares.

A **ratio** is a comparison of two quantities.

number of turquoise squares ⟶ 12
number of purple squares ⟶ 9

The ratio of turquoise to purple squares is 12 to 9.

There are three ways to write a ratio.

12 to 9 $\frac{12}{9}$ 12:9

Example 2

There are 81 purple squares in the entire quilt.

Find the number of turquoise squares in the entire quilt.

In one block ⟶ turquoise ⟶ $\frac{12}{9}$ ⟵ purple

In the quilt ⟶ turquoise ⟶ $\frac{?}{81}$ ⟵ purple

You can use **equivalent ratios** to find the number of turquoise squares.

When both terms of a ratio are multiplied or divided by a number other than zero, the result is an **equivalent ratio**.

first term ⟶ $\frac{12}{9} = \frac{12 \times 9}{9 \times 9} = \frac{108}{81}$ ⟵ second term

There are 108 turquoise squares in the quilt.

Word Bank

ratio
equivalent ratio

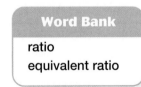
Additional Standards: Mathematical Reasoning 1.1 (See p. 305.)

Guided Practice *For another example, see Set A on p. 334.*

Are the ratios equivalent? Write = or ≠ in place of ●.

1. 5:8 ● 15:24

2. $\dfrac{3}{12}$ ● $\dfrac{9}{36}$

3. $\dfrac{4}{6}$ ● $\dfrac{16}{20}$

4. 9 to 8 ● 45 to 40

5. A quilt block has 4 yellow squares and 9 purple squares. There are 81 purple squares in the quilt. How many yellow squares are in the quilt?

Independent Practice *For more practice, see Set A on p. 336.*

Are the ratios equivalent? Write = or ≠ in place of ●.

6. 15:12 ● 5:6

7. $\dfrac{4}{10}$ ● $\dfrac{2}{5}$

8. $\dfrac{12}{9}$ ● $\dfrac{4}{3}$

9. $\dfrac{3}{16}$ ● $\dfrac{12}{4}$

Find the number that makes the ratios equivalent.

10. 14:7 = ■:14

11. $\dfrac{■}{7} = \dfrac{30}{42}$

12. 4:3 = ■:12

13. 5 to ■ = 25 to 35

14. A club has 16 members. Seven are in sixth grade and 9 are in seventh grade. Write the ratio of sixth-grade members to seventh-grade members three ways.

Mixed Review

15. Jan goes to the swimming pool every third day. Gil goes to the same pool every fifth day. Both are at the pool on the same day. In how many days will they both be at the pool again?

16. Find the measure of ∠DCB in the polygon at the right.

17. Trace polygon *ABCD* at the right. Draw as many lines of symmetry as possible.

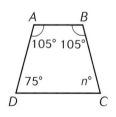

Test Prep Choose the correct letter for each answer.

18. A piece of pipe for the city sewer is 38 feet long. How many
(7-1) yards is that?

A $1\dfrac{1}{18}$ yd
B $3\dfrac{1}{6}$ yd
C $12\dfrac{2}{3}$ yd
D 38 yd

19. A fruit drink has 80 milligrams of sodium. How many grams is that?
(7-2)

F 80 g
G 8 g
H 0.8 g
J 0.08 g

Use Homework Workbook 8-1. 307

8-2

Proportions

California Content Standard *Number Sense 1.3 (🔑): Use proportions to solve problems (e.g., determine the value of N if $\frac{4}{7} = \frac{N}{21}$). . ..*

Math Link You know how to find equivalent ratios. Now you will learn how to use ratios to compare two quantities.

Example 1

The Photography Club makes prints from negatives for the yearbook. Prints are 105 millimeters by 69 millimeters. Negatives are 35 millimeters by 23 millimeters. Are the sides of a print proportional to the sides of a negative?

To find out, write two ratios and test to see if they form a **proportion.**

A proportion is an equation stating that two ratios are equivalent.

Order is important when you write the ratios to test for a proportion.

Word Bank

proportion

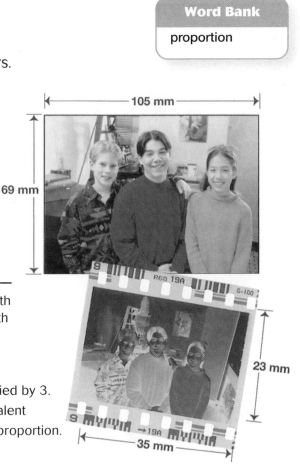

Negative   Print

length → $\frac{35 \text{ mm}}{23 \text{ mm}}$ $\overset{?}{=}$ $\frac{105 \text{ mm}}{69 \text{ mm}}$ ← length
width →   ← width

Now see if you have formed a proportion. Use equivalent ratios.

$\frac{35}{23} = \frac{35 \times 3}{23 \times 3} = \frac{105}{69}$ Both terms are multiplied by 3. $\frac{35}{23}$ and $\frac{105}{69}$ are equivalent ratios, so they form a proportion.

Equivalent Ratios

The sides of the print are proportional to the sides of the negative.

Example 2

Find the missing number in the proportion $\frac{15}{35} = \frac{n}{7}$. Use equivalent ratios.

$\frac{15}{35} = \frac{15 \div 5}{35 \div 5} = \frac{3}{7}$

$n = 3$

Additional Standards: Number Sense 1.0; Mathematical Reasoning 1.1 (See p. 305.)

Guided Practice
For another example, see Set B on p. 334.

Tell whether each pair of ratios can form a proportion.

1. $\dfrac{4}{5}, \dfrac{12}{15}$

2. $\dfrac{3}{8}, \dfrac{9}{21}$

3. $\dfrac{2}{3}, \dfrac{18}{27}$

4. $\dfrac{5}{8}, \dfrac{40}{64}$

Write a proportion and solve.

5. You are enlarging a print that is 5 inches wide and 7 inches long. If the width of the enlargement is 15 inches, what is the length?

Independent Practice
For more practice, see Set B on p. 336.

Tell whether each pair of ratios can form a proportion.

6. $\dfrac{2}{3}, \dfrac{8}{12}$

7. $\dfrac{3}{5}, \dfrac{15}{25}$

8. $\dfrac{8}{15}, \dfrac{2}{5}$

9. $\dfrac{9}{16}, \dfrac{3}{5}$

Find the missing number in each proportion.

10. $\dfrac{2}{3} = \dfrac{n}{21}$

11. $\dfrac{1}{n} = \dfrac{4}{72}$

12. $\dfrac{5}{n} = \dfrac{15}{24}$

13. $\dfrac{2}{7} = \dfrac{n}{21}$

Write a proportion and solve.

14. You are reducing a print that is 10 inches wide and 12 inches long. If the length of the reduction is 6 inches, what is the width?

15. Mental Math If two rolls of film cost $8.00, how much do four rolls of film cost?

Mixed Review

A basket has 8 apples and 4 oranges. Write each ratio three ways.

16. apples to fruit

17. oranges to apples

Trace Figure I. Move the tracing paper to fit exactly onto Figure II. Use *translation*, *rotation*, and *reflection* to describe the motions used.

18.   **19.**   **20.**

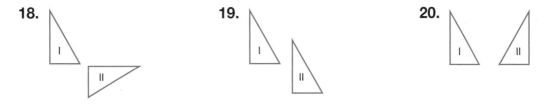

Test Prep   Choose the correct letter for each answer.

21. Algebra Solve. $n + 11 = 42$
(6-8)

    A $n = {}^-31$ **C** $n = 31$

    B $n = 20$ **D** $n = 53$

22. Solve. $t - {}^-2 = {}^-8$
(6-8)

    F $t = {}^-10$ **H** $t = {}^-6$

    G $t = {}^-8$ **J** $t = 10$

Use Homework Workbook 8-2.

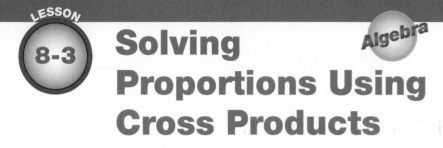

LESSON 8-3 Solving Proportions Using Cross Products

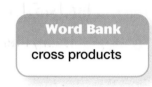 Algebra

Warm-Up Review

Find the number that makes the ratios equivalent.

1. $\dfrac{10}{6} = \dfrac{n}{3}$ 2. $\dfrac{8}{n} = \dfrac{2}{7}$

3. $\dfrac{n}{9} = \dfrac{22}{18}$ 4. $\dfrac{8}{9} = \dfrac{24}{n}$

5. A tree grew from 2.5 feet to 4.25 feet in 5 years. What was the average yearly growth of the tree?

California Content Standard *Number Sense 1.3 (🔑): Use proportions to solve problems. . . . Use cross multiplication as a method for solving such problems, understanding it as the multiplication of both sides of an equation by a multiplicative inverse.*

Math Link You know how to find the missing number in a proportion using equivalent ratios. Now you will learn how to find the missing number using cross products.

In a proportion, the cross products are equal. If the cross products are equal, the ratios form a proportion.

Word Bank

cross products

Example 1

Tell whether the ratios $\dfrac{6}{18}$ and $\dfrac{4}{12}$ form a proportion.

$\dfrac{6}{18} \diagtimes \dfrac{4}{12}$ 6×12 and 18×4 are **cross products**.

$6 \times 12 = 18 \times 4$

$72 = 72$

The cross products are equal. The ratios form a proportion.

Example 2

Find the missing number in the proportion.

$\dfrac{7}{1.2} = \dfrac{n}{3}$

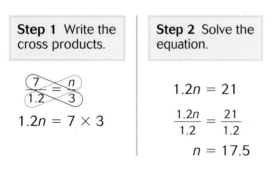

Step 1 Write the cross products.	**Step 2** Solve the equation.
$\dfrac{7}{1.2} \diagtimes \dfrac{n}{3}$	$1.2n = 21$
$1.2n = 7 \times 3$	$\dfrac{1.2n}{1.2} = \dfrac{21}{1.2}$
	$n = 17.5$

The missing number in the proportion is 17.5.

Here's WHY It Works

Finding the cross products is the same as multiplying both sides of the proportion by 3 and then multiplying both sides by 1.2.

$$\dfrac{7}{1.2} = \dfrac{n}{3}$$

$$3 \times \dfrac{7}{1.2} = \dfrac{n}{3} \times 3$$

$$\dfrac{3 \times 7}{1.2} = n$$

$$1.2 \times \dfrac{3 \times 7}{1.2} = n \times 1.2$$

$$3 \times 7 = 1.2n$$

310

Additional Standards: Number Sense 1.2 (🔑); Algebra and Functions 1.1 (See p. 305.)

Guided Practice *For another example, see Set C on p. 334.*

Find the missing number in each proportion.

1. $\dfrac{6}{9} = \dfrac{8}{n}$

2. $\dfrac{9}{15} = \dfrac{n}{10}$

3. $\dfrac{8.5}{3.2} = \dfrac{n}{8}$

4. $\dfrac{2.6}{n} = \dfrac{4}{4.8}$

Tell whether each pair of ratios form a proportion.

5. $\dfrac{4}{10}, \dfrac{6}{15}$

6. $\dfrac{6}{9}, \dfrac{9}{12}$

7. $\dfrac{6}{8}, \dfrac{9}{12}$

8. $\dfrac{6}{10}, \dfrac{9}{15}$

9. Three boxes of cereal cost $10.50. What does one box cost?

Independent Practice *For more practice, see Set C on p. 336.*

Find the missing number in each proportion.

10. $\dfrac{2}{10} = \dfrac{n}{15}$

11. $\dfrac{8}{6} = \dfrac{12}{n}$

12. $\dfrac{5}{2} = \dfrac{6}{n}$

13. $\dfrac{n}{2} = \dfrac{15}{5}$

Tell whether each pair of ratios form a proportion.

14. $\dfrac{4}{11}, \dfrac{11}{33}$

15. $\dfrac{8}{14}, \dfrac{12}{21}$

16. $\dfrac{6}{15}, \dfrac{8}{20}$

17. $\dfrac{35}{4}, \dfrac{28}{3}$

Write a proportion and solve.

18. Use the table at the right. Juan expects to bat 32 times in June. How many hits does he need to keep the same batting average (ratio of hits to times at bat) he had in May?

Batting Record				
Player	May		June	
	AB	H	AB	H
Juan	24	9	32	?
Cindy	25	10	30	
George	20	6	21	

Mixed Review

Use the table for Exercises 19 and 20. Write each ratio 3 ways.

19. Cindy's hits to her times at bat in May.

20. All three players' hits to their times at bat in May.

Find the missing number in each proportion.

21. $\dfrac{14}{32} = \dfrac{7}{n}$

22. $\dfrac{64}{11} = \dfrac{n}{121}$

23. $\dfrac{n}{45} = \dfrac{8}{15}$

Test Prep Choose the correct letter for each answer.

24. The temperature dropped 20° to ⁻8°F. Which equation could be
(6-9) used to find the temperature before it dropped?

A $t - 20 = {}^{-}8$ **C** $t + 20 = {}^{-}8$ **B** $t = {}^{-}8 - 20$ **D** $t = 20 - ({}^{-}8)$

25. $13.34 + 32.01 + 36.8$
(1-6)

F 82.24 **G** 82.15 **H** 81.43 **J** 81.15 **K** NH

Problem-Solving Skill:

Too Much or Too Little Information

Warm-Up Review

A garden has 6 daffodils, 5 tulips, and 4 dandelions. Write each ratio 3 ways.

1. daffodils to tulips

2. dandelions to daffodils

3. tulips to all flowers

California Content Standard *Mathematical Reasoning 1.1: Analyze problems by identifying relationships, distinguishing relevant from irrelevant information, identifying missing information . . ..*

Read for Understanding

Lisa has 600 stamps in her collection as shown in the table at the right. Her uncle plans to give her some more airplane stamps.

❶ How many stamps does Lisa have?

❷ How many flower stamps does she have?

Lisa's Stamp Collection

Type of Stamp	Number of Stamps
Flowers	83
Women	57
Airplanes	60
Presidents	120
Animals	114
Others	166

Think and Discuss

MATH FOCUS

Too Much or Too Little Information

If a problem contains too much information, you must decide what to use to solve the problem. You also need to know if there is too little information to solve the problem.

Reread the paragraph at the top of the page.

❸ Is there enough information to find the ratio of airplane stamps to the total stamps Lisa has now? Explain.

❹ Is there enough information to find the ratio of airplane stamps to total stamps after Lisa's uncle gives her the new stamps? Explain.

❺ Why is it important to know when there is too much or too little information when solving a problem?

Additional Standards: Number Sense 1.2 (🔑); Mathematical Reasoning 3.0 (See p. 305.)

Guided Practice

Jenny has a $\frac{1}{2}$-cent Benjamin Franklin stamp printed in 1954. She also has a $10.75 American Eagle stamp. Jenny wants to compare the purchase price of the American Eagle stamp to the price of the Franklin stamp.

1. What information is needed to compare the prices?
   a. The names of both stamps
   b. The prices of both stamps
   c. The ages of both stamps

2. What information is not needed to compare the prices?
   a. The year that the Franklin stamp was printed
   b. The price of the American Eagle stamp
   c. The price of the Benjamin Franklin stamp

3. What ratio can be used to compare the price of the American Eagle stamp to the price of the Benjamin Franklin stamp?
   a. $\frac{1}{2}$
   b. $\frac{1954}{1895}$
   c. $\frac{10.75}{0.005}$

Independent Practice

James, a stamp collector, read about a block of four 24-cent stamps issued in 1918 that has an inverted image of an airplane. The last time the block of stamps was sold, a collector paid $1.1 million for it. James wondered how much profit was made by the last person to sell the stamps.

4. What does James want to know?
   a. How much money it cost to buy the stamps in 1918
   b. How much money the last person to sell the stamps made on the sale
   c. How much money the last person to buy the stamps has

5. What information does James have that will help him?
   a. The cost of the stamps in 1918
   b. The number of stamps in the block
   c. The last price paid for the stamps

6. **Math Reasoning** What other information does James need to solve the problem?

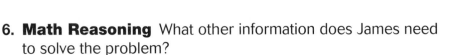

Rates

California Content Standard *Algebra and Functions
2.2 (🔑): Demonstrate an understanding that rate
is a measure of one quantity per unit of value of
another quantity.*

Warm-Up Review

Find the missing number in
each proportion.

1. $\frac{n}{20} = \frac{24}{32}$ **2.** $\frac{20}{30} = \frac{n}{45}$

3. $\frac{144}{n} = \frac{720}{125}$ **4.** $\frac{10}{n} = \frac{14}{35}$

5. You drive from home to
a cottage in the Sierra
Nevada Mountains in
4 hours. What is the ratio
of the distance you drive
to the time it takes?

Math Link You can use what you learned about ratios to
help you with rates.

A ratio is called a **rate** when the units of measure of the
quantities are different, such as miles per hour, calories
per serving, or breaths per minute. If the measure of the
second quantity in a rate is one unit, the rate is called a
unit rate. Unit rates allow you to compare rates easily.

Word Bank

rate
unit rate

Example 1

You travel 99 miles in 90 minutes. What is your average rate of
speed in miles per hour?

Step 1 Find how many hours you traveled.	**Step 2** Write a proportion.	**Step 3** Solve. You can use cross products.
There are 60 minutes in an hour. $90 \div 60 = 1.5$ hours	$\frac{99 \text{ miles}}{1.5 \text{ hours}} = \frac{r}{1 \text{ hour}}$	$1.5r = 99 \times 1$ $r = 99 \div 1.5$ $r = 66$

Your average rate of speed is 66 miles per hour.

Example 2

Reggie scored 72 points in 8 games. Robby scored 57 points in
6 games. Who scored the most points per game?

Reggie: $\frac{72 \text{ points}}{8 \text{ games}} = \frac{9 \text{ points}}{1 \text{ game}}$ Robby: $\frac{57 \text{ points}}{6 \text{ games}} = \frac{9.5 \text{ points}}{1 \text{ game}}$

Robby scored more points per game.

Guided Practice   *For another example, see Set D on p. 334.*

Find the unit rate.

1. 90 miles in 75 minutes

2. 252 miles every 9 gallons

3. 48 chairs for 6 tables

4. 96 students in 3 classrooms

*Additional Standards: Number Sense 1.2 (🔑), 1.3 (🔑); Algebra and
Functions 2.3 (🔑); Mathematical Reasoning 1.1 (See p. 305.)*

5. Your respiration rate is the number of breaths you take per minute. Laura counted 48 breaths in 3 minutes and Janna counted 34 breaths in 2 minutes. Who had the higher respiration rate?

Independent Practice *For more practice, see Set D on p. 336.*

Find the unit rate.

6. 1,800 feet for 5 seconds

7. 150 miles every 3 gallons

8. 760 calories in 8 servings

9. 18 cups for 4 people

10. **Mental Math** Suppose one hospital had 36 sets of twins out of 3,000 births. Write this information as a rate per 1,000 births.

11. Jacob did 39 situps in 30 seconds. Jordan did 59 sit-ups in 50 seconds. Find the unit rate for each. Who did more sit-ups per second?

12. The sixth-grade boys basketball team scored 56 points in their last game. There are 4 quarters in the game. How many points did they average per quarter?

13. You travel 90 kilometers in 1.2 hours. What units would you use to describe your rate?

Mixed Review

14. If 5 rolls of film cost $12.00, would it be reasonable to say that 8 rolls would cost $19.20? How do you know?

Tell whether each pair of ratios can form a proportion.

15. $\frac{7}{8}, \frac{21}{32}$

16. $\frac{14}{9}, \frac{7}{18}$

17. $\frac{15}{12}, \frac{5}{4}$

18. $\frac{18}{27}, \frac{6}{9}$

Find the missing number in each proportion.

19. $\frac{6}{10}, \frac{n}{15}$

20. $\frac{s}{3}, \frac{12}{9}$

21. $\frac{6}{n}, \frac{8}{20}$

22. $\frac{15}{10}, \frac{r}{14}$

Test Prep   Choose the correct letter for each answer.

23. Therese earned scores of 85, 91, 95, 79, 83, and 83 on six
(3-1)   exams in math class. What was her median score?

   A 83   **B** 84   **C** 86   **D** 95

24. **Algebra** Solve the equation $n + 5 = {}^-4$.
(6-8)
   F $^-9$ **G** $^-5$ **H** $^-4$ **J** $^-1$ **K** NH

Diagnostic Checkpoint

Find the missing number that makes the ratio equivalent.

1. ■ : 6 = 40:60
(8-1)

2. $\frac{9}{■} = \frac{36}{44}$
(8-1)

3. 32 to 56 = ■ to 7
(8-1)

4. $\frac{14}{21} = \frac{■}{3}$
(8-1)

5. ■ : 45 = 5 to 9
(8-1)

6. $\frac{81}{63} = \frac{9}{■}$
(8-1)

7. 5 to 3 = 60 to ■
(8-1)

8. 15 to ■ = $\frac{60}{28}$
(8-1)

9. ■ to 15 = 42 to 105
(8-1)

Find the missing number in each proportion.

10. $\frac{n}{35} = \frac{6}{7}$
(8-2)

11. $\frac{15}{n} = \frac{1}{3}$
(8-2)

12. $\frac{12}{16} = \frac{3}{n}$
(8-2)

13. $\frac{77}{33} = \frac{n}{3}$
(8-2)

14. $\frac{1.2}{n} = \frac{8}{12}$
(8-3)

15. $\frac{10}{50} = \frac{n}{20}$
(8-3)

16. $\frac{n}{9.3} = \frac{6}{8}$
(8-3)

17. $\frac{100}{110} = \frac{2}{n}$
(8-3)

18. $\frac{8}{n} = \frac{20}{25}$
(8-3)

Tell whether each pair of ratios can form a proportion.

19. $\frac{6}{7}, \frac{3}{9}$
(8-2, 3)

20. $\frac{8}{10}, \frac{16}{20}$
(8-2, 3)

21. $\frac{5}{6}, \frac{15}{18}$
(8-2, 3)

22. $\frac{1}{8}, \frac{2}{9}$
(8-2, 3)

23. $\frac{17}{21}, \frac{34}{42}$
(8-2, 3)

24. $\frac{3}{9}, \frac{6}{12}$
(8-2, 3)

25. $\frac{2.1}{12}, \frac{4.2}{8}$
(8-2, 3)

26. $\frac{7}{9}, \frac{21}{27}$
(8-2, 3)

Find the unit rate.

27. 34 points in 8 games
(8-5)

28. 146 miles in 4 hours
(8-5)

29. 16 cups for 4 people
(8-5)

30. 186 miles every 6 gallons
(8-5)

31. 348 books for 12 shelves
(8-5)

32. 30 pieces for 3 boxes
(8-5)

Solve.

33. Theo has a 1973 baseball cap from his favorite team.
(8-4) He also has a $45.25 baseball cap from his second favorite team. Theo wants to compare the purchase price of both caps to each other. What information is needed to compare the prices?

34. Jenny reduced a print that was 9 inches wide and 15 inches
(8-2) long. If the width of the reduction is 3 inches, what is the length?

35. Sarah, Ali, and Juan are going to purchase tickets to ride the
(8-3) train to San Francisco. The conductor tells them it will cost $17.25 for all three tickets. How much does one ticket cost?

Multiple-Choice Cumulative Review

Choose the correct letter for each answer.

1. Yolanda and Sid leave home at the same time. Yolanda drives at an average of 50 mph. Sid drives about 10 mph faster. Which is a reasonable distance for Yolanda to travel in $3\frac{1}{2}$ hours?

   A   Less than 100 mi

   B   About 125 mi

   C   About 175 mi

   D   About 200 mi

2. The ratio of dogs to cats at a kennel is exactly 4 to 5. If there are 36 dogs at the kennel, how many cats are at the kennel?

   F   20 cats

   G   40 cats

   H   45 cats

   J   72 cats

3. If $\frac{30}{y} = \frac{5}{6}$, what is y?

   A   25

   B   36

   C   150

   D   180

4. Tom threw a football 68 yards to score a touchdown. How many *feet* did he throw the football?

   F   300 ft   H   108 ft

   G   204 ft   J   96 ft

5. Julie bought $10\frac{1}{2}$ lb of fruit. The apples weighed $4\frac{1}{8}$ lb. Which number sentence can be used to find the weight, w, of the other fruit?

   A $w = 10\frac{1}{2} + 4\frac{1}{8}$

   B $w = 10\frac{1}{2} \times 4\frac{1}{8}$

   C $w + 4\frac{1}{8} = 10\frac{1}{2}$

   D $w - 4\frac{1}{8} = 10\frac{1}{2}$

6. Find the sum.
   $^{+}6 + {}^{-}3 + {}^{+}2 + {}^{-}1 + {}^{-}1$

   F $^{+}3$ H $^{-}2$

   G   0   J $^{-}3$

7. Subtract the sum of $^{-}94$ and 76 from 73.

   A   91

   B   55

   C $^{-}18$

   D $^{-}55$

8. The prime factors of a number are shown. What is the number?
   $$7 \times 3 \times 3 \times 2$$

   F   18

   G   126

   H   378

   J   1,134

Unit Price

Algebra

California Content Standard *Algebra and Functions 2.3: Solve problems involving rates . . ..*

Warm-Up Review

Find each unit rate.

1. 120 miles in 4 hours

2. 240 calories in 6 servings

3. 114 miles on 12 gallons

Math Link You know how to write proportions. Now you will learn how to use proportions to find unit prices.

Example

Use the data at the right. Two stores have the Alpha model rocket on sale. Which store has the better buy?

To find out, you need to know the cost of one rocket in each store. You need to find the **unit price.**

You can use a proportion to find each unit price.

Word Bank

unit price

ROCKY'S ROCKET SHOP

$$\frac{\$60.00}{12 \text{ rockets}} = \frac{n}{1 \text{ rocket}}$$
$$12 \times n = 60.00 \times 1$$
$$n = 60 \div 12$$
$$n = 5$$

The unit price is $5.00.

FLYAWAY SHOP

$$\frac{\$79.95}{15 \text{ rockets}} = \frac{n}{1 \text{ rocket}}$$
$$15 \times n = 79.95 \times 1$$
$$n = 79.95 \div 15$$
$$n = 5.33$$

The unit price is $5.33.

Rocky's Rocket Shop has the better buy.

Guided Practice   *For another example, see Set E on p. 335.*

Find the unit price. Round to the nearest cent.

1. $87.50 for 10 Alpha III rockets

2. $46.20 for 6 Tornadoes

Find each unit price. Determine the better buy.

3. 12 bananas for $1.80 or 15 bananas for $2

4. 3 tacos for $3.50 or 4 tacos for $5.00

Additional Standards: Number Sense 1.2 (━), 1.3 (━); Algebra and Functions 2.2 (━) (See p. 305.)

Independent Practice For more practice, see Set E on p. 337.

Find the unit price. Round to the nearest cent.

5. 2 launch controllers for $75.00

6. 5 notebooks for $13.95

7. $25.56 for 4 repair kits

8. 8 paint kits for $71.12

Find each unit price. Determine the better buy.

9. $31.50 for 6 posters or $27.50 for 5 posters

10. 3 video games for $68.97 or 5 video games for $109.30

11. Mental Math 10 markers for $2.00 or 5 markers for $1.10?

12. The Outlet is selling 6 T-shirts for $10. Jeans and Tees is selling 5 T-shirts for $9. Which store has the better buy?

13. Use the data on page 318. Suppose the Flyaway Shop reduces its prices and offers 15 rockets for $74.50, but the other shop keeps its prices the same. Which store has the better buy now?

Mixed Review

Write a proportion and solve.

14. Celina plays soccer on the weekends. During the month of April, she attempted 36 goals, but only scored 3 times. If she attempts 48 goals in May, how many goals must she score to keep the same ratio of goals to attempts?

Find the missing number in each proportion.

15. $\frac{9}{n} = \frac{3}{8}$
16. $\frac{8}{6} = \frac{n}{27}$
17. $\frac{n}{9} = \frac{70}{30}$
18. $\frac{2}{0.2} = \frac{10}{n}$

Find the unit rate.

19. 740 miles in 16 hours

20. 540 calories in 3 servings

Test Prep Choose the correct letter for each answer.

21. Four bowls cost $18.00. Which
(8-2) proportion can you use to find how many bowls can be purchased for $27.00?

A $\frac{4}{18} = \frac{n}{27}$ **C** $\frac{4}{27} = \frac{18}{n}$

B $\frac{4}{18} = \frac{27}{n}$ **D** $\frac{4}{n} = \frac{27}{18}$

22. Solve. $\frac{9}{21} = \frac{12}{n}$
(8-3)
F $n = 23$ **J** $n = 252$

G $n = 24$ **K** NH

H $n = 25$

Problem-Solving Strategy:

Make a List

California Content Standard *Mathematical Reasoning 2.4: Use a variety of methods, such as words, numbers, symbols, charts, graphs, tables, diagrams, and models, to explain mathematical reasoning.*

Warm-Up Review

Find each unit price.

1. $2.10 for 6 bagels

2. 2 pizzas for $10.50

3. 7 gallons for $12.53

4. You can buy 12 ounces of yogurt for $1.30 or 16 ounces of applesauce for $1.50. Which is the better buy?

Example

You know a computer password has 4 characters. The characters are R, P, 3, and J. You do not know the order of the characters. In how many ways can these 4 characters be arranged?

Understand

What do you need to find?

You need to find the number of different arrangements that can be made from the four characters.

Plan

How can you solve the problem?

You can **make a list** of the different ways to arrange the four characters. Then count the arrangements.

RP3J	PR3J
RPJ3	PRJ3
RJ3P	PJR3
RJP3	PJ3R
R3JP	P3JR
R3PJ	P3RJ
JRP3	3RPJ
JR3P	3RJP
JPR3	3JPR
JP3R	3JRP
J3RP	3PRJ
J3PR	3PJR

Solve

There are 6 ways to arrange the 4 characters beginning with R.
There are 6 ways beginning with P.
There are 6 ways beginning with J.
There are 6 ways beginning with 3.

There are 24 possible arrangements in all.

Look Back

Make sure that each arrangement is different.

320

Guided Practice

1. Jenny wants to make a necklace, using two different charms. If she can choose any of the four charms shown at the right, how many different arrangements can she choose?

Independent Practice

2. The clerk at the gift shop needs to engrave the letters R, M, and L on an ID bracelet. He forgot to ask the customer in what order the letters should be. In how many different ways could he arrange the three letters?

3. You are driving on a toll road. The toll is $0.60. You cannot use half dollars or pennies. How many different combinations of coins can you use if at least one of the coins is a quarter?

4. Three darts are thrown at and hit a target. The center ring is worth 10 points, the middle ring is worth 6 points, and the outside ring is worth 3 points. How many different total points are possible?

5. If a test has four true-or-false questions, in how many different ways could you answer the four questions?

Mixed Review

Try these or other strategies to solve each problem. Tell which strategy you used.

> ### Problem-Solving Strategies
> - *Write an Equation*
> - *Find a Pattern*
> - *Work Backward*
> - *Make a Table*

6. Ms. Cheong bought 15 postcards at a theme park. Some of the
(6-9) postcards show the rides and others show the zoo. She has 7 more cards of the rides than of the zoo. How many of each kind of postcard did she buy?

7. Four hundred people attended the county fair on the first day.
(7-9) The fair operators expect an increase of 30 people each day for the next 5 days. How many people are expected on the sixth day?

Similar Figures

Algebra

California Content Standard *Number Sense 1.3* (🔑): *Use proportions to solve problems (e.g., . . . find the length of a side of a polygon similar to a known polygon). . ..*

Math Link You know how to write and solve proportions. Now you will learn how to use proportions to find the length of a side of a polygon similar to a known polygon.

Similar figures have the same shape but not necessarily the same size.

If two figures are similar, the corresponding angles are congruent and corresponding sides are proportional.

Triangle *ABC* and triangle *DEF* are similar triangles.

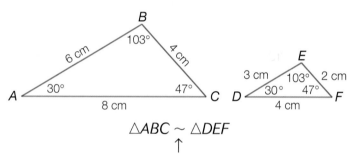

$$\triangle ABC \sim \triangle DEF$$
↑

Corresponding Angles

$\angle A \cong \angle D$
$\angle B \cong \angle E$
$\angle C \cong \angle F$

Corresponding Sides

$$\frac{AB}{DE} = \frac{6}{3} = \frac{BC}{EF} = \frac{4}{2} = \frac{AC}{DF} = \frac{8}{4} = \frac{2}{1}$$

Example

Triangle *STR* and triangle *MNP* at the right are similar triangles. Find the measure of $\angle P$ and the length of $\overline{MP}$.

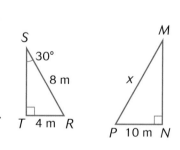

Use corresponding angles to find m$\angle R$.

$\angle P$ is congruent to $\angle R$, so their measures are equal. Find m$\angle R$.

m$\angle R$ + 30 + 90 = 180
m$\angle R$ = 60°.
m$\angle R$ = m$\angle P$ = 60°.

Use a proportion to find *MP*.
$$\frac{MP}{SR} = \frac{PN}{TR}$$
Let *x* equal the length of $\overline{MP}$.

$$\frac{x}{8} = \frac{10}{4}$$

$4x = 80$ Use cross products.

$$\frac{4x}{4} = \frac{80}{4}$$ Divide.

$x = 20$

$MP = 20$ m

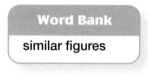

$\triangle JKL \cong \triangle MNP$

Complete each congruence statement.

1. $\overline{JK} \cong$

2. $\angle N \cong$

Word Bank

similar figures

🔑 *Additional Standards: Mathematical Reasoning 2.4*

Guided Practice *For another example, see Set F on p. 335.*

Quadrilateral *KLMN* is similar to quadrilateral *GHIJ*.
Find each measure.

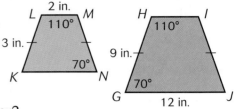

1. m∠*K*   2. *HI*   3. *KN*

4. **Math Reasoning** Are congruent triangles similar?
   Explain your answer.

Independent Practice *For more practice, see Set F on p. 337.*

Figures *ABCDEF* and *GHIJKL* are similar. Find
each measure.

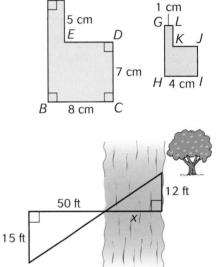

5. m∠*I*   6. *GH*   7. *AF*

8. *JI*   9. *ED*   10. *LK*

11. A surveyor needs to find the distance across
    a river. She sets up similar right triangles and
    takes the measures shown in the diagram.
    Write a proportion and solve to find *x*.

Mixed Review

12. Denise has two squares. One side of the larger square
    is 10.5 in. What is the measure of a side of the smaller
    square if one side of the larger square is three times
    that of the smaller square?

Find each unit rate.

13. 136 miles in 2 hours   14. 42 grams of fat in 5 servings

15. 4 CDs for $26   16. 5 notebooks for $4.45

Test Prep   Choose the correct letter for each answer.

17. **Algebra** Solve the equation. $x + \dfrac{1}{2} = \dfrac{5}{8}$
    (5-10)

    A $\dfrac{1}{8}$ **B** $\dfrac{5}{16}$ **C** $1\dfrac{1}{8}$ **D** $1\dfrac{1}{4}$ **E** NH

18. Lisa ran the following distances in miles: 3.5, 2.0, 3.5, 3.0, 9.5.
    (3-2)
    Which measure of central tendency is affected the most by
    the exclusion of the outlier 9.5?

    F mean   **G** median   **H** mode   **J** none are affected

8-9

Scale Drawings

Algebra

Warm-Up Review

1. $\frac{0.6}{2.4} = \frac{n}{7.2}$ 2. $\frac{18}{42} = \frac{33}{n}$

3. $\frac{24}{n} = \frac{10}{5}$ 4. $\frac{5}{7} = \frac{10}{n}$

5. Ty ran 1.2 miles on Monday and 1.5 miles on Tuesday. Sean ran 0.8 miles on Monday and 1 mile on Tuesday. Are the distances they ran proportional?

Math Link You have used ratios to compare quantities. Now you will learn now how ratios are used to compare actual lengths with lengths shown on scale drawings.

A **scale drawing** is a reduction or enlargement of an actual object. The **scale** is a ratio that compares a measure on the drawing with the actual measure.

Word Bank

scale drawing
scale

Example 1

The Concord Middle School is building a new soccer field for the soccer club. A scale drawing of the field is shown below. The length of the field on the drawing is 9.5 centimeters. What is the actual length of the field?

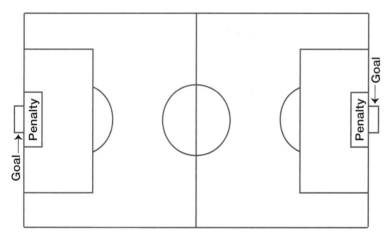

Scale: 1 centimeter = 10 meters

Step 1 Write a proportion using the scale as one of the ratios. Let *n* represent the actual length.

Step 2 Solve the proportion. Use cross products.

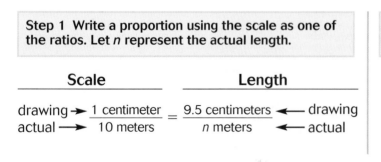

$$\frac{1}{10} = \frac{9.5}{n}$$
$$1 \times n = 10 \times 9.5$$
$$n = 95$$

The actual length of the field is 95 meters.

Example 2

You are making a scale drawing of a playground using the scale 2 centimeters = 25 meters. The actual length of the playground is 45 meters. What length should the playground be on the scale drawing?

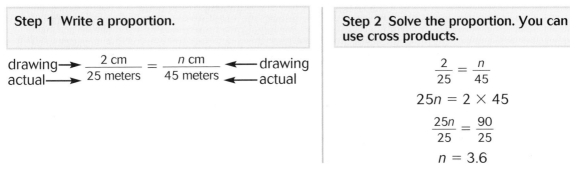

Step 1 Write a proportion.

drawing→ $\dfrac{2\ \text{cm}}{25\ \text{meters}}$ = $\dfrac{n\ \text{cm}}{45\ \text{meters}}$ ←drawing
actual→ ←actual

Step 2 Solve the proportion. You can use cross products.

$$\frac{2}{25} = \frac{n}{45}$$

$$25n = 2 \times 45$$

$$\frac{25n}{25} = \frac{90}{25}$$

$$n = 3.6$$

The length of the playground on the scale drawing should be 3.6 centimeters.

Guided Practice   *For another example, see Set G on p. 335.*

Use the scale drawing of the soccer field on page 324 to find the measures of the actual soccer field for the given lengths on the scale drawing.

1. Length of the penalty box, 1.5 cm

2. Width of the field, 5.6 cm

3. The width of the stands in the soccer field will be 62.5 meters. Using the same scale, 1 centimeter = 10 meters, find the width of the stands on the scale drawing.

Independent Practice   *For more practice, see Set G on p. 337.*

Use the scale drawing of the house at the right for Exercises 4–7. Find the measures of the actual house for the given lengths on the scale drawing.

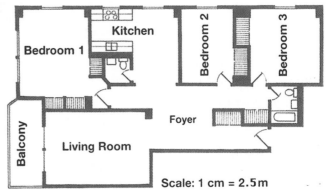

4. Width of the balcony, 0.8 cm

5. Total length of the house, 8.5 cm

6. Length of the living room, 3 cm

7. If the total width of the actual house is 12 meters, what width should be used on the scale drawing?

325

For Exercises 8–10, measure each object. Use the scale $\frac{1}{2}$ inch = 1 foot to find the actual measure.

8.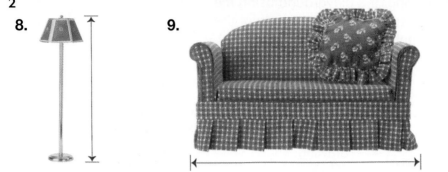

9.

10.

11. A bolt is 2.4 cm long. Find the length of an enlarged technical drawing of this bolt that uses a scale of 5 centimeters to 2 centimeters.

2.4cm

Mixed Review

12. A lap of a track is $\frac{7}{8}$ mile. Alan ran $2\frac{3}{4}$ laps on Monday and $1\frac{3}{4}$ laps on Tuesday. How far did he run in all?

13. If 6 markers cost $10 what is the unit price rounded to the nearest cent?

$\triangle DEF \sim \triangle GHJ$. **Find each measure.**

14. m∠F   15. m∠D

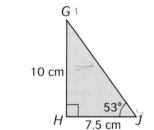

🖤 **Test Prep**   Choose the correct letter for each answer.

The figures at the right show the right-hand side of pages that are folded in half.

1   2   3   4

16. Which shape looks like this figure when unfolded?
(7-4)

   A Shape 1

   B Shape 2

   C Shape 3

   D Shape 4

17. Which shape might look like this figure if it was unfolded and then folded again horizontally?
(7-4)

   F Shape 1

   G Shape 2

   H Shape 3

   J Shape 4

Choose the correct letter for each answer.

1. Henry can solve 10 math problems in 3 minutes. He has 25 problems to solve. Which equivalent ratios can be used to find out how long this will take?

   A $\frac{10}{3} = \frac{25}{n}$

   B $\frac{3}{10} = \frac{25}{n}$

   C $\frac{n}{10} = \frac{25}{3}$

   D $\frac{3}{n} = \frac{25}{10}$

2. Diane needs to supply the team with 23 quarts of a sports drink. If it is only sold in gallons, how many gallons does she need to buy? (4 qt = 1 gal)

   F   12 gal

   G   6 gal

   H   5 gal

   J   4 gal

3. Which fraction is equivalent to $\frac{12}{40}$?

   A $\frac{3}{5}$

   B $\frac{4}{10}$

   C $\frac{1}{3}$

   D $\frac{3}{10}$

4. If $\frac{75}{y} = \frac{3}{4}$, then $y = $ ■.

   F   25

   G   50

   H   75

   J   100

5. Meg's family planted a vegetable garden. One-fourth of the garden was planted in tomatoes. The rest of the garden was divided equally between peas and carrots. How much of the garden space was planted with peas?

   A $\frac{3}{8}$ C $\frac{2}{3}$

   B $\frac{1}{2}$ D $\frac{3}{4}$

6. What is the sum of 3.45, 0.678, and 0.091?

   F   42.190   H   4.219

   G   11.140   J   1.114

7. Ralph can type about 48 words per minute. Which is the best estimate of how many words he can type in a half hour?

   A   120

   B   150

   C   1,200

   D   1,500

8. There are 12 girls in Mr. Lee's class. If the ratio of girls to boys is exactly 3 to 2, how many boys are in the class?

   F   16 boys

   G   8 boys

   H   12 boys

   J   14 boys

LESSON

8-10

Understand
Plan
Solve
Look Back

Problem-Solving Application:
Using Maps

Algebra

California Content Standard *Number Sense 1.3 (🔑): Use proportions to solve problems. . . .*

Warm-Up Review

1. $\dfrac{2.1}{n} = \dfrac{0.7}{2}$ 2. $\dfrac{10}{45} = \dfrac{4}{n}$

3. $\dfrac{n}{1.8} = \dfrac{3}{0.2}$ 4. $\dfrac{n}{18} = \dfrac{40}{45}$

5. A fruit juice drink has 31 grams of sugar. How many milligrams is this?

Example

Find the actual distance from Washington, Indiana, to Indianapolis, Indiana using the map. Round your answer to the nearest mile.

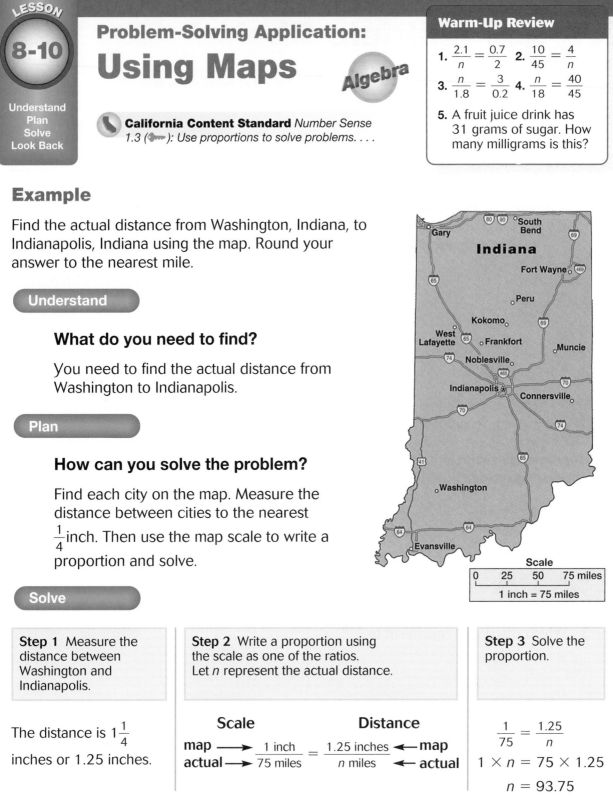

Understand

What do you need to find?

You need to find the actual distance from Washington to Indianapolis.

Plan

How can you solve the problem?

Find each city on the map. Measure the distance between cities to the nearest $\frac{1}{4}$ inch. Then use the map scale to write a proportion and solve.

Scale

| 0 | 25 | 50 | 75 miles |

1 inch = 75 miles

Solve

Step 1 Measure the distance between Washington and Indianapolis.	**Step 2** Write a proportion using the scale as one of the ratios. Let n represent the actual distance.	**Step 3** Solve the proportion.
The distance is $1\frac{1}{4}$ inches or 1.25 inches.	**Scale** **Distance** map ⟶ $\dfrac{1 \text{ inch}}{75 \text{ miles}} = \dfrac{1.25 \text{ inches}}{n \text{ miles}}$ ⟵ map actual ⟶ ⟵ actual	$\dfrac{1}{75} = \dfrac{1.25}{n}$ $1 \times n = 75 \times 1.25$ $n = 93.75$

The distance from Washington to Indianapolis is about 94 miles.

Look Back

Is a distance of 94 miles reasonable?

 Additional Standards: Algebra and Functions 2.3; Mathematical Reasoning 2.2 (See p. 305.)

Guided Practice

Use the map of Indiana on page 328 to find each actual distance. Measure to the nearest $\frac{1}{4}$ inch.

1. South Bend to Peru

2. Gary to Evansville

3. Frankfort to Indianapolis

4. Peru to Indianapolis

Independent Practice

Use the map of Massachusetts to find each actual distance. Measure to the nearest $\frac{1}{4}$ inch.

5. Newburyport to New Bedford

6. Providence to Boston

7. Lawrence to New Bedford

8. Fall River to Salem

9. Mental Math Boston to New Bedford

Find the actual distance.

10. Scale: 1 cm = 3 km
map distance: 6 cm

11. Scale: 1 inch = 10 miles
map distance: $2\frac{1}{2}$ in.

Mixed Review

Tell which strategy you used to solve each problem.

12. Anna, Ben, and Carol had a batting contest. Anna hit a ball 12 feet farther than Ben did. Carol hit a ball 180 feet, and the ball landed 6 feet short of where Ben's hit landed. How far did Anna hit the ball?

13. The Miller family paid $90 for admission to the local aquarium. The aquarium charges $12 for adults and $9 for children under 16. They bought at least one adult ticket and more tickets for children than adults. How many of each ticket did they buy?

Diagnostic Checkpoint

Choose a word from the Word Bank for each description.

1. A _____ is a comparison of two quantities.
(8-1)

2. A ratio is called a _____ when the units of measure
(8-5) of the quantities are different.

3. A _____ is an equation stating that two ratios
(8-2) are equivalent.

Word Bank
ratio
proportion
scale drawing
similar
rate
unit price

Find the unit price. Round to the nearest cent.

4. $379 for 5 keyboards
(8-6)

5. $59.97 for 3 CDs
(8-6)

Determine the better buy.

6. $46.50 for 6 model airplanes or $61.04 for 8 model airplanes
(8-6)

7. 12 books for $119.40 or 6 books for $53.34
(8-6)

8. In how many ways can the numbers 5, 6, 7, 8 be arranged?
(8-7)

Use the scale drawing to find the actual dimensions.
Measure to the nearest $\frac{1}{2}$ centimeter.

9. Length of the Picnic Bench area
(8-9)

10. Width of the Picnic Bench area
(8-9)

11. Width of the duck pond at its
(8-9) widest point

12. Length of the footpath from the
(8-9) entrance to the exit

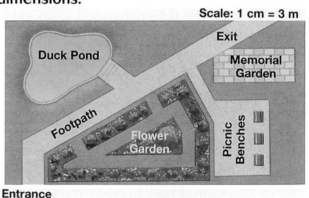

Scale: 1 cm = 3 m

Use the pair of similar figures to find each measure in Exercises 13–16.

13. measure of ∠F
(8-8)

14. measure of ∠G
(8-8)

15. measure of $\overline{GH}$
(8-8)

16. measure of $\overline{EH}$
(8-8)

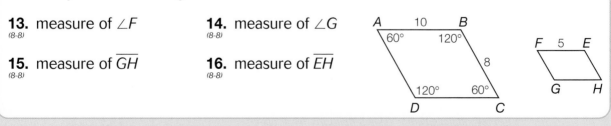

Chapter 8 Test

Are the ratios equivalent? Write = or ≠ in place of ●.

1. $\dfrac{3}{7}$ ● $\dfrac{12}{28}$

2. $\dfrac{9}{11}$ ● $\dfrac{45}{50}$

3. $\dfrac{24}{36}$ ● $\dfrac{4}{6}$

4. Tell whether the pair of ratios $\dfrac{64}{120}, \dfrac{16}{20}$ can form a proportion.

5. Find the missing number in the proportion $\dfrac{11}{12} = \dfrac{n}{36}$.

Find the unit rate or unit price.

6. 9 pounds of bananas at $3.96

7. 120 kilometers in $1\dfrac{1}{2}$ hours

8. Determine the better buy: 8 pens for $2.99 or 3 pens for $0.89.

9. Milo wants to compare Fred's batting average to his own. He knows how many times he has batted and hit, and he knows how many hits Fred has. What other information does Milo need to compare batting averages?

10. Mrs. Cantrall has 3 pictures of her children she wants to display. How many different arrangements can she make?

Use the scale drawing on the right to answer Questions 11–13.

11. What is the actual length of the store?

12. What is the actual width of the store?

13. What is the actual length of each aisle?

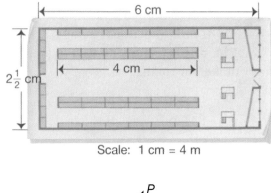

Scale: 1 cm = 4 m

Use the pair of similar figures to find each measure in Questions 14–16.

14. m∠ L

15. NM

16. m∠ P

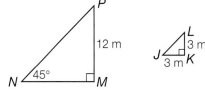

17. A map with a scale of 1 inch = 6 miles shows the distance from a convention center to a hotel as 2.8 in. What is the actual distance?

Multiple-Choice Chapter Test

Choose the correct letter for each answer.

Use the triangles below to answer Questions 1 and 2.

Triangle *ABC* is similar to Triangle *DEF*.

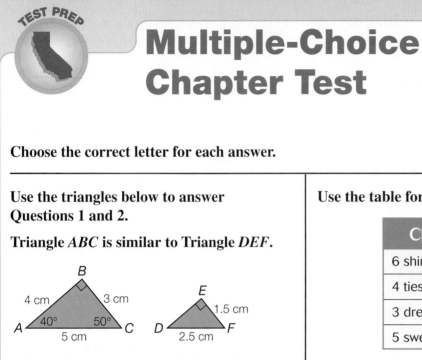

1. What is the length of side *DE*?

    A   2 cm   **C**   4 cm

    B   3 cm   **D**   8 cm

2. What is the measure of ∠*D*?

    F   20°

    G   40°

    H   50°

    J   80°

3. Tricia is making a scale model of a 350-ft building. She is using a scale of 1 in. = 20 ft. How tall should she make her model?

    A   11.5 in.   **D**   17.5 in.

    B   13.5 in.   **E**   NH

    C   15.5 in.

4. Which ratio would form a proportion with $\frac{7}{16}$?

    F $\frac{14}{34}$ **H** $\frac{21}{32}$

    G $\frac{14}{32}$ **J** $\frac{2}{3}$

Use the table for Questions 5 and 6.

Clearance!!!
6 shirts for $82.50
4 ties for $36.24
3 dresses for $48.03
5 sweaters for $59.05

5. Which article of clothing has the lowest unit price?

    A   Shirts

    B   Ties

    C   Dresses

    D   Sweaters

6. What is the unit price of the sweaters?

    F $59.05

    G $29.51

    H $11.81

    J $9.05

7. Taylor's favorite hockey player scored 5 goals in the last 4 games. How many goals did the hockey player average per game during the last 4 games?

    A   1 goal per game

    B   1.25 goals per game

    C   1.5 goals per game

    D   1.75 goals per game

Use the picture below for Questions 8 and 9.

8. Select the three different ways the ratio of blue triangles to green squares can be written.

F $\frac{2}{4}$; 2 × 4; 1 : 2

G 2 to 1; 2 to 1; 2

H 2 : 1; 2 to 1; $\frac{2}{1}$

J 4 : 2, 4 to 2; 2

9. The ratio of blue triangles to red circles is equivalent to the ratio of

A green squares to blue triangles.

B red circles to blue squares.

C blue triangles to blue squares.

D red circles to blue triangles.

10. Keena uses a map with a scale of 1 cm = 2.5 miles to figure out how many miles it is from her school to her father's office. She measures the distance as 9 cm. How many actual miles is it?

F 3.4 miles   **H** 18 miles

G 11.5 miles   **J** 22.5 miles

11. Find the missing number in the proportion $\frac{2}{3} = \frac{7}{\blacksquare}$.

A 3.5   **C** 10.5

B 6   **D** 21

Use the scale drawing for Questions 12 and 13.

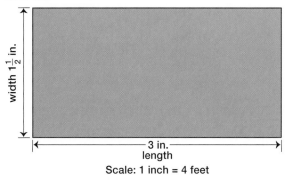

Scale: 1 inch = 4 feet

12. Which describes the actual length of the room?

F 1.5 feet   **H** 12 feet

G 2 feet   **J** 16 feet

13. Which describes the actual width of the room?

A 2.5 feet   **C** 8 feet

B 6 feet   **D** 15 feet

14. Willie forgot his 4-digit locker combination. He knows the combination has the numbers 32, 17, 6, and 8 in it. How many locker combinations can be made with these four numbers if the numbers are each used only once?

F 4   **H** 24

G 16   **J** 36

15. Jessica collects postcards and wants to compare the purchase prices of two postcards. What information is needed to compare the prices?

A The country of origin of each postcard

B The pictures on the postcards

C The prices of both postcards

D The ages of both postcards

Reteaching

Set A (pages 306–307)

Are the ratios equivalent? Write = or ≠ in place of ⬤.

$$\frac{4}{7} \bullet \frac{28}{49}$$

Multiply both terms of the first ratio by the same number to get the other ratio.

$$\frac{4}{7} = \frac{4 \times 7}{7 \times 7} = \frac{28}{49} \quad \text{So } \frac{4}{7} = \frac{28}{49}.$$

Remember when both terms of a ratio are multiplied or divided by a number other than zero, the result is an equivalent ratio.

Are the ratios equivalent? Write = or ≠ in place of ⬤.

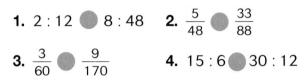

1. $2 : 12 \bullet 8 : 48$ 2. $\frac{5}{48} \bullet \frac{33}{88}$

3. $\frac{3}{60} \bullet \frac{9}{170}$ 4. $15 : 6 \bullet 30 : 12$

Set B (pages 308–309)

Tell whether $\frac{6}{16}$ and $\frac{24}{64}$ can form a proportion.

$$\frac{6}{16} = \frac{6 \times 4}{16 \times 4} = \frac{24}{64}$$

↑————— Equivalent —————↑
Ratios

Remember a proportion is an equation stating that two ratios are equivalent.

Tell whether each pair of ratios can form a proportion.

1. $\frac{7}{9}, \frac{42}{50}$ 2. $\frac{11}{18}, \frac{99}{162}$

Set C (pages 310–311)

Find the missing number in the proportion $\frac{3}{21} = \frac{n}{35}$.

$\frac{3}{21} = \frac{n}{35}$ Use cross products.

$3 \times 35 = 21 \times n$
$\quad 105 = 21n$
$\quad\quad 5 = n$

Remember in a proportion, cross products are equal.

Find the missing number in each proportion.

1. $\frac{6}{21} = \frac{n}{35}$ 2. $\frac{n}{27} = \frac{10}{45}$

3. $\frac{2}{14} = \frac{5}{n}$ 4. $\frac{3}{n} = \frac{5}{55}$

Set D (pages 314–315)

Find the unit rate of 2,235 feet in 3 seconds.

$\frac{2,235 \text{ feet}}{3 \text{ seconds}} = \frac{x \text{ feet}}{1 \text{ second}}$ Write a proportion.

$2,235 \times 1 = 3x$ Use cross products
$\frac{2,235}{3} = x$ to solve.
$\quad 745 = x$

The rate is 745 feet per 1 second.

Remember a rate is a ratio of one quantity to a different quantity. In a unit rate, the second quantity is one unit.

Find the unit rate.

1. 400 feet for 50 seconds

2. 18 gallons for 3 people

Set E (pages 318–319)

Find the unit price and determine the better buy.

   8-oz box of cereal for $2.99

   12-oz box of cereal for $3.49

Use proportions to find each unit price.

$\dfrac{\$2.99}{8\ oz} = \dfrac{n}{1\ oz}$	$\dfrac{\$3.49}{12\ oz} = \dfrac{n}{1\ oz}$
$2.99 \times 1 = 8 \times n$	$3.49 \times 1 = 12 \times n$
$2.99 \div 8 = n$	$3.49 \div 12 = n$
$0.37 = n$	$0.29 = n$
Unit price: $0.37.	Unit price: $0.29.

Better buy: 12-oz box for $3.49

Remember to compare unit prices to determine the better buy.

Find the unit price and determine the better buy.

1. $33.97 for 12 trading cards or $25.21 for 9 trading cards

2. $1.25 for 6 vitamins or $8.29 for 24 vitamins

3. $13.50 for 9 pears or $8.23 for 4 pears

Set F (pages 322–323)

Figures _ABC_ and _DEF_ are similar. Find m∠_A_ and _DE_.

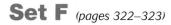
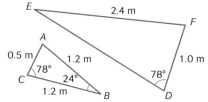

Use pairs of corresponding sides to form equivalent ratios.

$$\dfrac{1.2}{DE} = \dfrac{1.2}{2.4} \quad \text{Set the ratios equal.}$$

$$DE = 2.4 \quad \text{Solve for } DE.$$

In similar triangles, corresponding angles are congruent. So m∠ _A_ = m∠ _D_ = 78°.

Remember if two figures are similar, the corresponding angles are congruent and corresponding sides are proportional.

Figures _HJK_ and _MNO_ are similar. Find each measure.

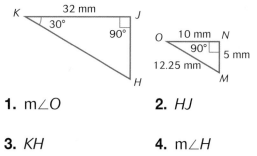

1. m∠_O_   **2.** _HJ_

3. _KH_   **4.** m∠_H_

Set G (pages 324–326)

Find the actual measure. Use the scale 2 in. = 1.5 ft.

$$\dfrac{2\ in.}{1.5ft} = \dfrac{16}{x}$$

$$2x = 16 \times 1.5$$

$$x = 24 \div 2$$

$$x = 12$$

The actual measure is 12 ft.

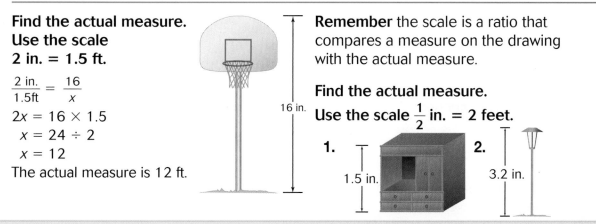

Remember the scale is a ratio that compares a measure on the drawing with the actual measure.

Find the actual measure. Use the scale $\frac{1}{2}$ in. = 2 feet.

1. 1.5 in.   **2.** 3.2 in.

More Practice

Set A *(pages 306–307)*

Are the ratios equivalent? Write = or ≠ in place of ⬤.

1. 2 : 7 ⬤ 6 : 21   **2.** $\frac{12}{5}$ ⬤ $\frac{36}{15}$ **3.** $\frac{6}{2}$ ⬤ $\frac{30}{5}$

4. What is the ratio of red triangles to green triangles?

5. If this pattern is repeated so that there are 24 red triangles, how many green triangles will there be?

Set B *(pages 308–309)*

Tell whether each pair of ratios can form a proportion.

1. $\frac{9}{8}, \frac{7}{8}$ **2.** $\frac{4}{3}, \frac{12}{9}$ **3.** $\frac{2}{11}, \frac{7}{77}$ **4.** $\frac{5}{8}, \frac{45}{70}$

Find the missing number in each proportion.

5. $\frac{1}{3} = \frac{n}{15}$ **6.** $\frac{10}{12} = \frac{5}{n}$ **7.** $\frac{n}{20} = \frac{45}{60}$ **8.** $\frac{15}{n} = \frac{30}{6}$

9. The Photography Club wants to enlarge a photograph that is 10 inches wide and 14 inches long. If the length of the larger photo is 28 inches, what is the width?

Set C *(pages 310–311)*

Find the missing number in each proportion.

1. $\frac{12}{n} = \frac{15}{10}$ **2.** $\frac{n}{21} = \frac{5}{35}$ **3.** $\frac{5}{25} = \frac{n}{15}$ **4.** $\frac{15}{45} = \frac{n}{63}$

5. $\frac{n}{20} = \frac{6}{8}$ **6.** $\frac{64}{4} = \frac{48}{n}$ **7.** $\frac{5.4}{9} = \frac{0.6}{n}$ **8.** $\frac{0.81}{n} = \frac{0.2}{2}$

9. On the test, for every 2 students who received a "B", 4 students received a "C". If 88 students received a "B", how many students received a "C"?

Set D *(pages 314–315)*

Find the unit rate.

1. 6,320 feet for 2 seconds   **2.** 324 miles every 3 gallons

3. 6 cookies for 4 people   **4.** 6 miles in 60 minutes

5. Linda flew her airplane 625 miles in 2.5 hours. About how fast was the plane traveling?

Set E *(pages 318–319)*

Find the unit price. Round to the nearest cent.

1. $5.95 for 10 disks

2. $79.95 for 3 ink cartridges

3. $38.98 for 2 dust covers

4. $6.95 for 200 sheets

Determine the better buy.

5. $79 for 16 calculators or
$139 for 32 calculators

6. $42.50 for 12 mousepads or
$35.20 for 8 mousepads

7. A catalog offered a computer game for $27.95. A computer
store sells 6 of the same games for $156.59. Which offer has
the lower unit price?

Set F *(pages 322–323)*

**Each pair of figures is similar. Give the missing side measures
and angle measures.**

1.

2.

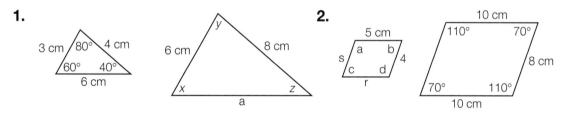

3. Are corresponding sides of similar figures congruent? Answer
yes, no, or *sometimes.* Explain.

Set G *(pages 324–326)*

**Use the scale drawing of the garden for Exercises 1 and 2.
Find the actual measures. Use the scale 1 in. = 2 ft.**

1. length of rose planter

2. width of lily planter

3. The actual dimensions of a swimming pool
are 15 ft by 10 ft. If the dimensions of a
scale drawing of the pool are 3 in. by 2 in.,
what is the scale of the drawing?

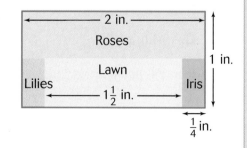

Problem Solving: Preparing for Tests

Choose the correct letter for each answer.

1. Fred has $5\frac{1}{3}$ yards of fabric that is 24 inches wide. Which is the best estimate for the amount of fabric left after Fred makes 4 square pillows 22 inches on each side?

   A Less than $\frac{1}{2}$ yd

   B About $\frac{3}{4}$ yd

   C About 1 yd

   D About $1\frac{1}{2}$ yd

> **Tip**
> Remember that each pillow must have a back and a front. Think about how many feet of fabric Fred has and about how many feet it takes to make a pillow.

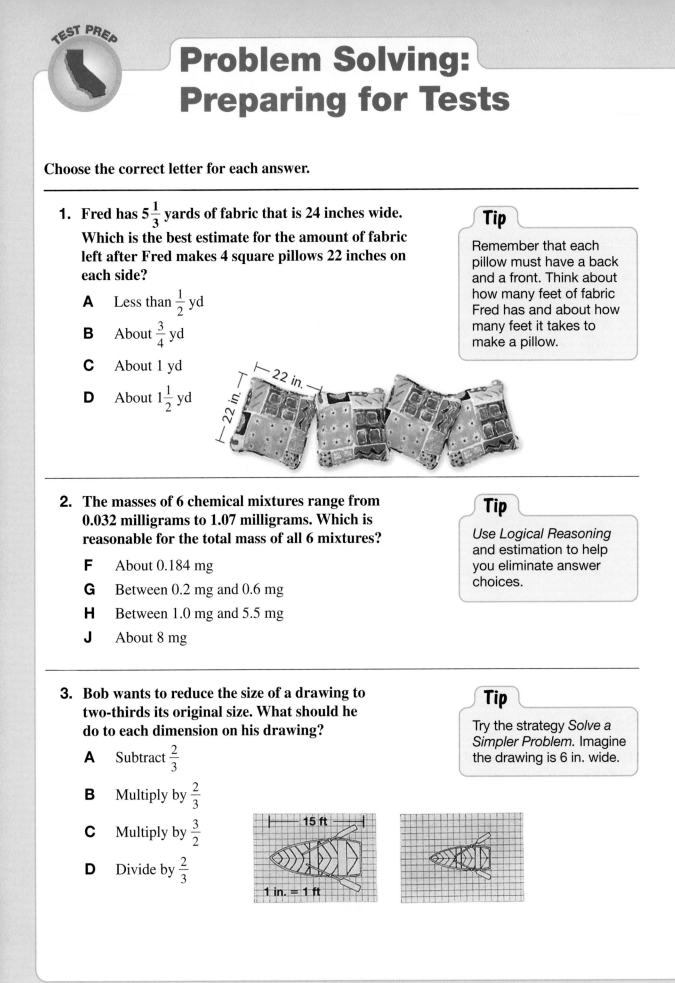

2. The masses of 6 chemical mixtures range from 0.032 milligrams to 1.07 milligrams. Which is reasonable for the total mass of all 6 mixtures?

   F About 0.184 mg

   G Between 0.2 mg and 0.6 mg

   H Between 1.0 mg and 5.5 mg

   J About 8 mg

> **Tip**
> *Use Logical Reasoning* and estimation to help you eliminate answer choices.

3. Bob wants to reduce the size of a drawing to two-thirds its original size. What should he do to each dimension on his drawing?

   A Subtract $\frac{2}{3}$

   B Multiply by $\frac{2}{3}$

   C Multiply by $\frac{3}{2}$

   D Divide by $\frac{2}{3}$

> **Tip**
> Try the strategy *Solve a Simpler Problem.* Imagine the drawing is 6 in. wide.

4. Hal made this scale drawing of a circular fountain in a courtyard. He used the scale 2 cm = 1.5 m. How wide is the actual fountain?

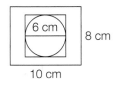

6 cm
8 cm
10 cm

F 0.5 meter

G 0.66 meter

H 3 meters

J 4.5 meters

5. Last year the population of Trudy's town increased by 8,540 people. The year before, the population decreased by 4,432 people. By about how much did the population change over the 2 years?

A Increased about 4,000 people.

B Decreased about 4,000 people.

C Decreased about 8,000 people.

D Increased about 13,000 people.

6. This graph shows a survey taken by the local library.

People Who Recycle

Paper	🧍🧍🧍🧍🧍🧍🧍🧍🧍🧍🧍
Glass	🧍🧍🧍🧍🧍
Plastic	🧍🧍🧍🧍🧍

🧍 = 500 People

About how many more people recycle paper than recycle glass and plastic combined?

F 500 people **H** 2,750 people

G 750 people **J** 5,250 people

7. Brian arranged a large number of calculators at his store. He put 89 calculators in the bottom row. The next rows had 78, 67, and 56 calculators. How many calculators will be in each of the next 5 rows of this pyramid?

A 8, 5, 3, 2, 1

B 11, 9, 7, 5, 3

C 12, 9, 6, 3, 1

D 45, 34, 23, 12, 1

8. Tom is 6 ft tall. He is $1\frac{1}{2}$ times as tall as Ben. Which number sentence can be used to find Ben's height, b?

F $b = \frac{3}{2} \times 6$

G $6 = \frac{3}{2} \times b$

H $b = 6 + \frac{3}{2}$

J $6 = b - \frac{3}{2}$

9. John ran 1.6 miles in 12 minutes. Art ran twice as fast as John. Which expression shows how many minutes it took Art to run 1.6 miles?

A 2×1.6 **C** $3.2 \div 12$

B $12 \div 1.6$ **D** $12 \div 2$

10. Last year, Ed's shop made slightly more than one-half million dollars. Which of these is reasonable for the amount of money he made?

F Less than $50,000

G More than $50,000

H Less than $500,000

J More than $500,000

Multiple-Choice Cumulative Review

Choose the correct letter for each answer.

Number Sense

1. Which fraction is greater than $\frac{5}{16}$?

   A $\frac{1}{8}$

   B $\frac{1}{5}$

   C $\frac{1}{4}$

   D $\frac{3}{8}$

2. What is 432.668 rounded to the nearest ten?

   F   432.700

   G   432.670

   H   430

   J   400

3. Which decimal is equivalent to $\frac{6}{8}$?

   A   0.45   C   0.75

   B   0.60   D   0.80

4. Which is the prime factorization of 100?

   F $2^2 \times 5^2$

   G $5^2 \times 3^2$

   H 3×25

   J 2×50

5. If you can buy 12 batteries for $10.80, how much will 15 batteries cost?

   A $10.80   C $13.50

   B $12.80   D $15.90

6. Monica is taping a television show that is 3 hours long. If she has taped $1\frac{3}{4}$ hours of the show, how much of the show is still left to be taped?

   F $2\frac{3}{4}$ hours

   G $2\frac{1}{4}$ hours

   H $1\frac{1}{4}$ hours

   J $\frac{3}{4}$ hours

7. Dave saved $124.45. Then he bought a CD player for $56.89 and 4 CDs for $9.99 each. How much did he have left?

   A $27.60

   B $57.57

   C $67.56

   D $96.85

8. Ruth rode her bike $5\frac{1}{8}$ miles on Friday, $2\frac{3}{4}$ miles on Saturday, and $3\frac{3}{8}$ miles on Sunday. How many miles did she ride in all?

   F $10\frac{1}{4}$ mi

   G $10\frac{6}{8}$ mi

   H $11\frac{1}{4}$ mi

   J $11\frac{3}{8}$ mi

Algebra and Functions

9. What is the ratio of triangles to squares in the picture below?

A 4 : 2   C 2 : 4

B 3 : 2   D 3 : 1

---

10. Which number makes the ratios equivalent?

$$10 : x = 5 : 6$$

F 8

G 12

H 15

J 30

---

11. Which point is named by the ordered pair (1, 5)?

A *L*

B *M*

C *N*

D *P*

Statistics, Data Analysis, and Probability

12. Frank is playing a game with his brother. He will win if he gets a 3 the next time he tosses a cube numbered from 1 to 6. What is the probability he will win on his next turn?

F 1 out of 3   H 3 out of 4

G 2 out of 6   J 1 out of 6

---

13. A combination for a lock is 3 single-digit numbers. The digits do not repeat. The first number is 4, and the second is 5. What is the most numbers Andy might have to try before the lock opens?

A 7   C 9

B 8   D 10

Use the information below for Questions 14 and 15.

Five sixth-graders were asked "How much of your own money do you spend each week?" The responses were

$2 $10 $5 $15 $3

14. Find the mean amount spent per week by this group.

F $4   H $6

G $5   J $7

---

15. Find the median amount spent per week by this group.

A $3   C $10

B $5   D $15

Understanding and Using Percent

Diagnosing Readiness

In Chapter 9, you will use these skills:

Ⓐ Writing Decimals and Fractions

(pages 154–155)

Write each decimal as a fraction in simplest form and each fraction as a decimal.

1. 0.60

2. 1.2

3. $\frac{5}{10}$

4. $\frac{3}{8}$

5. 0.125

6. $\frac{2}{5}$

7. Chloe plans to landscape her yard with flowers. She wants 0.25 of the flowers to be tulips. What fraction of the flowers will be tulips?

Ⓑ Simplifying Fractions

(pages 148–150)

Simplify each fraction.

8. $\frac{32}{48}$

9. $\frac{56}{64}$

10. $\frac{480}{756}$

11. $\frac{49}{700}$

12. $\frac{90}{900}$

13. $\frac{7}{42}$

14. $\frac{36}{120}$

15. $\frac{8}{10}$

16. Ryanne has 22 pairs of shoes, including 8 pairs of sandals.

Write $\frac{8}{22}$ in simplest terms.

C Multiplying and Dividing Decimals

(pages 52–54, 58–63)

17. 3.7×1.2 **18.** 0.98×125

19. 1.053×7 **20.** 24×0.30

21. 0.65×111 **22.** $298.25 \div 5$

23. $28.92 \div 1.2$ **24.** $1.86 \div 0.31$

25. The soccer league purchased 14 trophies at $12.23 each. What was the total cost?

D Using Ratios and Proportions

(pages 306–311)

Find the missing number.

26. $\frac{2}{3} = \frac{n}{15}$ **27.** $\frac{8}{9} = \frac{x}{72}$

28. $\frac{24}{32} = \frac{3}{b}$ **29.** $\frac{12}{100} = \frac{6}{y}$

30. $\frac{1000}{5} = \frac{k}{25}$ **31.** $\frac{1.5}{2.6} = \frac{3}{m}$

32. Franco enlarged a photo that was 3 in. wide by 5 in. long. If the new photo is 9 in. wide, what is the length?

E Solving Multiplication and Division Equations

(pages 68–69)

Solve each equation.

33. $0.4y = 0.08$ **34.** $b \div 7 = 3$

35. $x \div 1.2 = 18$ **36.** $98k = 882$

37. Mr. Greer wants to place 11 golf clubs in each of 23 golf bags. How many clubs will he need?

F Estimating Products

(pages 52–54)

Estimate the following products.

38. 107×23

39. 617.2×20

40. 98.7×103.2

41. 120.97×11.3

42. Your sports bottle holds 12 ounces of water. Your water cooler holds 31 times that. About how many ounces does your water cooler hold?

To the Family and Student

Looking Back

In Grade 5, students learned the relationship between decimals, fractions, and percents.

Chapter 9

Understanding and Using Percent

In this chapter, students will estimate percents and apply what they learn to problems involving sales tax, discounts, and simple interest.

Looking Ahead

In Grade 7, students will apply their knowledge of percents to problems involving compound interest.

Math and Everyday Living

Opportunities to apply the concepts of Chapter 9 abound in everyday situations. During the chapter, think about how percents can be used to solve a variety of real-world problems. The following examples suggest just several of the many situations that could launch a discussion about percent.

Math at the Mall The new running shoes you want to buy have gone on sale.

Calculate the sale price of the shoes.

Math and Your Health
You and your family discover that on the average each member of your family intakes about 80 grams of fat per day. You each commit to selecting healthier food choices to try and reduce your fat intake to only 40 grams per day. What is the percent of fat-gram reduction?

Math and Sports At a football game your family attended last Saturday, the quarterback of the winning team completed 37 passes. He attempted to complete 56 passes. What was the quarterback's percentage of completion to the nearest whole percent?

Math at the Auto Dealer

Car	Price	Rate
Red 2-dr	$6,320	6.9%
Blue 4-dr	$4,800	15%
Tan 4-dr	$5,900	12%

Your family is deciding which of the three cars to buy. You want to finance a car for 3 years. Use the simple interest formula, $I = prt$, to calculate the interest you will pay for each car. Which car has the lowest interest charges?

Math and Landscaping
What percent of your backyard needs to be mowed? Round to the nearest whole percent.

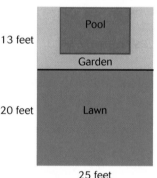

Math and the Government
You have a home-based business. You must pay approximately 15% of your earnings for self-employment taxes. Tax payments are due quarterly. About how much self-employment tax do you need to pay the government if in one quarter you earned $8,250?

California Content Standards in Chapter 9 Lessons*

Number Sense	Teach and Practice	Practice
1.0 (🔑) Students . . . solve problems involving . . . percentages.	9-2, 9-7, 9-10	9-6
1.2 (Grade 5) (🔑) Interpret percents as part of a hundred; find decimal and percent equivalents for common fractions and explain why they represent the same value.	9-1	
1.4 (🔑) Calculate given percentages of quantities and solve problems involving discounts at sales, interest earned, and tips.	9-3, 9-5, 9-8, 9-9	9-2, 9-4, 9-7, 9-10

Algebra and Functions	Teach and Practice	Practice
1.1 (🔑) Write and solve one-step linear equations in one variable.	9-6	9-7, 9-8, 9-9, 9-10
1.2 Write and evaluate an algebraic expression for a given situation, using up to three variables.		9-10
2.0 Students . . . use . . . rules to solve problems involving . . . proportions.		9-3

Mathematical Reasoning	Teach and Practice	Practice
1.3 Determine when and how to break a problem into simpler parts.		9-5
2.1 Use estimation to verify the reasonableness of calculated results.		9-9
2.2 Apply strategies and results from simpler problems to more complex problems.		9-3
2.5 Express the solution clearly and logically by using the appropriate mathematical notation and terms and clear language; support solutions with evidence in both verbal and symbolic work.		9-6
2.6 Indicate the relative advantages of exact and approximate solutions to problems and give answers to a specified degree of accuracy.	9-4	
2.7 Make precise calculations and check the validity of the results from the context of the problem.		9-7, 9-10
3.2 Note the method of deriving the solution and demonstrate a conceptual understanding by solving similar problems.		9-3, 9-7, 9-10

* The symbol (🔑) indicates a key standard as designated in Mathematics Framework for California Public Schools. Full statements of the California Content Standards are found at the beginning of this book following the Table of Contents.

Relating Fractions, Decimals, and Percents

Warm-Up Review

Write each fraction as a decimal.

1. $\frac{7}{10}$ 2. $\frac{3}{5}$

3. $\frac{1}{100}$ 4. $\frac{89}{100}$

5. Lisa was $57\frac{1}{2}$ in. tall last year. This year, she grew $3\frac{1}{4}$ in. Write Lisa's height as a decimal.

🔑 **California Content Standard** *Number Sense 1.2 (Grade 5) (🔑): Interpret percents as part of a hundred; find decimal and percent equivalents for common fractions and explain why they represent the same value.*

Math Link You know how to write a fraction as a decimal and a decimal as a fraction. Now you will learn how to write fractions and decimals as percents.

Word Bank

percent

Example 1

The art shop sells a set of 100 paints. What percent of the paints are green? How could you write the percent of green paints as a decimal? How could you write it as a fraction?

A **percent** is a special ratio that compares a number with 100. *Percent* means "per hundred."

Look at the paint set. 5 out of 100, or 5%, of the paints are green. 5% means "5 out of 100, or 5 hundredths." 5 hundredths can be written as 0.05 and $\frac{5}{100}$.

Paint Set
FOR
SALE

$$\frac{5}{100} = \frac{5 \div 5}{100 \div 5} = \frac{1}{20}$$

$$5\% = 0.05 = \frac{1}{20}.$$

Example 2

Write $1\frac{3}{4}$ as a decimal and as a percent.

$$1\frac{3}{4} = \frac{7}{4} = 7 \div 4 = 4\overline{)7.00}^{1.75}$$

To change a decimal to a percent, move the decimal point two places to the right because the decimal is multiplied by 100. Remember to write the percent (%) sign.

$$1\frac{3}{4} = 1.75 = 175\%$$

Guided Practice *For another example, see Set A on p. 372.*

Complete each table.

	Fraction	Decimal	Percent
1.			15%
2.		3.15	

	Fraction	Decimal	Percent
3.	$\frac{8}{5}$		
4.			2.7%

5. Mental Math You used $\frac{3}{5}$ of a container of paint and 4 paintbrushes. What percent of the paint did you use?

Independent Practice *For more practice, see Set A on p. 374.*

Complete each table.

	Fraction	Decimal	Percent
6.	$\frac{5}{8}$		
7.		0.095	
8.			650%

	Fraction	Decimal	Percent
9.		0.005	
10.	$\frac{3}{25}$		
11.			3%

Use the graph at the right for Exercises 12 and 13.

12. Write a fraction that describes the percent for paints.

13. Write the percent for pens and markers as a decimal and as a fraction in simplest form.

Art Shop Inventory

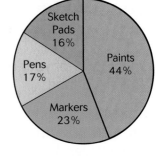

Mixed Review

14. A map has a scale of 1 inch = 50 miles. The distance on the map between two cities is $2\frac{1}{2}$ inches. What is the actual distance between the two cities?

Algebra The triangles are similar. Find each missing measure.

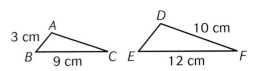

15. *AC*

16. *DE*

Test Prep   Choose the correct letter for each answer.

17. Algebra Solve $\frac{15}{x} = \frac{10}{30}$.
(8-3)

   A 5   **C** 45

   B 20   **D** 90

18. Algebra If 8 bagels cost $4.16, how much do 12 bagels cost?
(8-3)

   F $0.32   **H** $2.78

   G $0.52   **J** $6.24

Estimating Percent

California Content Standard *Number Sense 1.0 (🔑): [S]tudents solve problems involving . . . percentages.*

Warm-Up Review

Write each percent as a decimal and as a fraction in simplest form.

1. 40%   **2.** 15%

3. 16%   **4.** 75%

5. Estimate 0.3×410.

Math Link You know how to estimate fraction and decimal products. Now you will learn how to estimate with percents.

Example 1

A craft store is donating 9% of the price of each dream catcher to a school's scholarship fund. If you were to buy the dream catcher at the right, about how much money would you be contributing?

You can use rounding to estimate 9% of $19.99.

9% × $19.99

↓   ↓

10% × $20.00 =

$\quad$ $0.10 \times 20 = 2$

About $2.00 of your money will go to the scholarship fund.

Since 9% was rounded up to 10% and $19.99 up to $20.00, your estimate is greater than the exact answer. The actual amount of your donation would be slightly less than $2.00.

▲ By tradition, dream catchers are supposed to keep the good dreams with you and keep the bad dreams away.

More Examples

A. Estimate 28% of 71.

28% of 71
↓   ↓
30% of 70   Round.

$0.30 \times 70 = 21$ Write 30% as a decimal and multiply.

28% of 71 is about 21.

B. Estimate 82% of 202.

82% of 202
↓   ↓
80% of 200   Round.

$\frac{4}{5} \times 200 = 160$ Write 80% as a fraction and multiply.

82% of 202 is about 160.

🔑 *Additional Standards: Number Sense 1.4 (🔑) (See p. 345.)*

Guided Practice *For another example, see Set B on p. 372.*

Estimate.

1. 49% of 49

2. 11% of 38

3. 9% of $59.97

4. 22% of 78

5. 71% of $17.89

6. 20% of 36

7. If you were to buy a dream catcher that costs $14.99 and 9% was donated to the scholarship fund, about how much money would you be contributing?

Independent Practice *For more practice, see Set B on p. 374.*

Estimate.

8. 11% of 99

9. 22% of $31.00

10. 49% of 86

11. 5% of 199

12. 68% of $37.95

13. 89% of 6

14. Math Reasoning Suppose you estimated 17% of 199 to be 40. Is your answer greater than or less than the exact answer? Explain.

Use this information for Exercises 15 and 16.

A jewelry store sponsors a local sports team. The store donates 12% of every purchase to the team for equipment and uniforms.

15. You spent $29.95 on jewelry. About how much money is donated to the sports team?

16. Your friend bought 5 jewelry sets at $8.95 per set. About how much is donated to the sports team?

Mixed Review

17. On a scale drawing of a house, the living room is 3.5 cm long. The scale is 1 cm = 2 m. How long is the actual living room?

Write each percent as a decimal and as a fraction in simplest form.

18. 60%

19. 34%

20. 20%

21. 25%

🕐 **Test Prep**   **Choose the correct letter for the answer.**

22. Carson had a piece of material $3\frac{1}{4}$ yards long. He used
(5-4) $2\frac{2}{3}$ yards making a costume for the school play. How much material does he have left?

A $\frac{7}{12}$ yd   **B** $1\frac{5}{12}$ yd   **C** $1\frac{1}{2}$ yd   **D** $5\frac{11}{12}$ yd

Finding a Percent of a Number

Algebra

California Content Standard *Number Sense 1.4 (🔑): Calculate given percentages of quantities . . ..*

Warm-Up Review

Estimate.

1. 25% of 420

2. 11% of 560

3. Twelve eggs cost $0.89. How much do 5 dozen eggs cost?

Math Link You know how to solve a proportion. Now you will learn how to use a proportion to find a percent of a number.

Example 1

The Jeans Factory is having a sale. How much money will you save at this store if you buy a pair of jeans on sale that originally cost $60.00?

You can find out how much you will save by finding 30% of $60.00.

Write a proportion.

Let n = the amount of savings.

$$\frac{30}{100} = \frac{n}{60}$$

Use cross products to solve for n.

$$\frac{30}{100} = \frac{n}{60}$$

$30 \times 60 = 100n$

$1,800 = 100n$

$\frac{1,800}{100} = n$

$18 = n$

You will save $18.00.

Example 2

Write a proportion to find 40% of 75.

Let n = 40% of 75. Use cross products to solve for n.

$$\frac{40}{100} = \frac{n}{75}$$

$40 \times 75 = 100n$

$3,000 = 100n$

$\frac{3,000}{100} = n$

$30 = n$

30 is 40% of 75.

Additional Standards: Algebra and Functions 2.0; Mathematical Reasoning 2.2, 3.2 (See p. 345.)

Guided Practice For another example, see Set C on p. 372.

Find the percent of each number.

1. 40% of 120

2. 25% of 245

3. 120% of 60

4. 6% of 25

5. 10% of 46

6. 35% of 90

7. 45% of 50

8. 100% of 7

9. How much would you save on a $45 pair of jeans on sale for 40% off?

Independent Practice For more practice, see set C on p. 374.

Find the percent of each number.

10. 25% of 220

11. 65% of 300

12. 90% of 55

13. 160% of 70

14. 75% of 160

15. 9% of 50

16. Discount Denims sells a $60 pair of jeans at a 30% discount. Jeans Factory sells them at a 20% discount. How much more will you save at Discount Denims than at Jeans Factory?

17. Mental Math Outdoor Outfits has socks on sale for 25% off. The sale price for each pair of socks is $2.50. How many pairs of socks could you buy if you had $25.00?

Mixed Review

18. Jeans were originally developed in the United States in the mid-1800s for miners. A pair of jeans cost $0.22 in 1850. How many pairs of jeans could you buy for $2.00 in 1850?

Write each fraction as a percent.

19. $\frac{2}{25}$

20. $\frac{1}{10}$

21. $\frac{14}{20}$

22. $\frac{7}{35}$

Estimate.

23. 18% of 22

24. 56% of 72.98

25. 14% of 23

Test Prep   Choose the correct letter for each answer.

John's test scores were 85, 23, 92, 85, and 89.

26. Find John's mean test score.
(3-1)

    A 23

    B 85

    C 74.8

    D 87

27. Which statistic is affected the most by the exclusion of the outlier 23?
(3-2)

    F Mean

    G Median

    H Mode

    J None

Problem-Solving Skill:
Is an Estimate Enough?

Warm-Up Review

Find the percent of each number.

1. 82% of 43

2. 60% of 66

3. What is the discount on a $30 pair of shoes if they are marked down 25%?

California Content Standard *Mathematical Reasoning 2.6: Indicate the relative advantages of exact and approximate solutions to problems . . ..*

Read for Understanding

Jeremy went to the Western Shop, which was having a sale on hats and boots. He saw three different hat styles and was trying to decide which style to buy.

1 Which hat costs $90 before any discount is given?

2 What is the percent of discount on the Sidewinder?

3 On which hat is the 15% discount given?

The Wrangler
$90.00
Take 40% off

The Sidewinder
$75.00
Take 25% off

The Westerner
$65.00
Take 15% off

Think and Discuss

MATH FOCUS

Is an Estimate Enough?

Sometimes an estimate is all you need to solve a problem. Whether an estimate is enough or an exact answer is needed depends on the situation.

Reread the paragraph and look at the photograph at the top of the page.

4 Which hat costs the least before any discount is given? Which costs the most?

5 Does a cashier find an estimate or an exact answer for the amount of discount?

6 Can Jeremy use an estimate to decide which hat style would save him the most money?

Additional Standards: Number Sense 1.4 (✏); (See p. 345.)

Guided Practice

Ella went to the Western Shop to buy a new shirt. She has $45.00 to spend. There are three different shirt styles on sale.

1. How can Ella find the shirt style that offers the greatest savings?

    a. Estimate the savings on the styles that offer the same percent discount.

    b. Estimate the product of the regular price times the percent discount for each style.

    c. Find the greatest percent off.

2. How could Ella find the exact savings on shirt style C?

    a. Multiply $58 by 0.40.

    b. Subtract $40 from $58.

    c. Divide $58 by 0.40.

3. **Math Reasoning** Is an estimate enough for Ella to determine whether style C is still the most expensive shirt after the discount? Explain your answer.

Independent Practice

Roger is planning to see a movie about the Old West starting at 1:00 P.M. The movie runs for 1 hour and 40 minutes. Roger tells his friends to meet him at the bookstore at 2:45 P.M. The bookstore is a 15- to 20-minute walk from the movie theater.

4. Which of the following is an estimate?

    a. The running time of the movie

    b. The time that the movie ends

    c. The time needed to walk from the theater to the bookstore

5. Which expression shows the earliest time Roger could arrive at the bookstore?

    a. 100 minutes + 15 minutes

    b. 1:00 P.M. + 20 minutes

    c. 2:40 P.M. + 15 minutes

6. **Math Reasoning** Will Roger arrive at the bookstore on time? Explain how you would estimate the meeting time.

Mental Math: Finding a Percent of a Number

California Content Standard *Number Sense 1.4 (🗝): Calculate given percentages of quantities and solve problems involving . . . tips.*

Warm-Up Review

Write each percent as a decimal and as a fraction in simplest form.

1. 35%   **2.** 90%

3. 75%   **4.** 45%

5. What is the percent discount given at a half-price sale?

Math Link You have learned that proportions can be used to find a percent of a number. Now you will use mental math to calculate percents.

Example 1

After eating at their favorite restaurant, Casey and his friends owe $20.00 for their meal. They want to leave a 15% tip. How much should they leave?

To find 15% of $20.00 mentally, break apart 15% into 10% + 5%.

Find 10% of 20.00: $0.1 \times 20.00 = 2.00$

5% is one half of 10%, so 5% of 20.00 is one half of 2.00, or 1.00.

10% of $20.00 + 5% of $20.00 = 15% of $20.00

2.00   +   1.00   =   3.00

They should leave a tip of $3.00.

More Examples

Use mental math to find the percent of each number.

A. Find $33\frac{1}{3}$% of $120.

To find $33\frac{1}{3}$% of $120, write $33\frac{1}{3}$% as a fraction.

Then solve mentally.

$33\frac{1}{3}\% = \frac{1}{3}$

$\frac{1}{3}$ of 120 = 40 | 120 ÷ 3 = 40 |

$33\frac{1}{3}$% of $120 = $40.

B. Find 120% of 40.

Break apart 120% into 100% + 20%.

Then solve mentally.

100% of 40 = 40

20% of 40 = 8

120% of 40 = 40 + 8

120% of 40 = 48

Additional Standards: Mathematical Reasoning 1.3 (See p. 345.)

Guided Practice For another example, see Set D on p. 372.

Use mental math to find the percent of each number.

1. $33\frac{1}{3}$% of 90

2. 50% of $82.50

3. 15% of $160

4. 55% of 200

5. You and your friends spent $36 at a restaurant. If you want to leave a 15% tip, how much should you leave?

Independent Practice For more practice, see Set D on p. 374.

Use mental math to find the percent of each number.

6. 5% of 320

7. 150% of 160

8. 25% of 60

9. 40% of $10.50

10. 130% of 20

11. 20% of $5.50

12. 30% of $50

13. $66\frac{2}{3}$% of $9.90

14. Eileen orders a meal that costs $12.00. If she leaves a 15% tip, what does she pay altogether?

15. Math Reasoning Explain how you would use mental math to find 200% of $80.

Mixed Review

16. Shannon swam the 50-meter freestyle race in 30.6 seconds. Amy swam it in 31.4 seconds. How much faster was Shannon than Amy?

Estimate.

17. 26% of 30

18. 17% of 19

19. 63% of 102

Find the percent of each number.

20. 25% of 80

21. 100% of 500

22. 12.5% of 16

Test Prep   Choose the correct letter for each answer.

23. Which is a fair survey question?
(3-8)

    A Do you like restaurants with healthy foods best?

    B Do you like restaurants with greasy foods best?

    C What is your favorite restaurant?

    D None are fair.

24. Which would be the best graph to use to show the number of people who say they leave no tip, a 10% tip, a 15% tip, or a 20% tip?
(3-4)

    F Bar graph   **H** Stem-and-leaf plot

    G Line graph   **J** None are appropriate.

Diagnostic Checkpoint

Write each percent as a decimal or each decimal as a percent.

1. 58%
(9-1)

2. 60%
(9-1)

3. 75%
(9-1)

4. 0.35
(9-1)

5. 20%
(9-1)

6. 45%
(9-1)

7. 88%
(9-1)

8. 9%
(9-1)

9. 0.362
(9-1)

10. 200%
(9-1)

11. 0.49
(9-1)

12. 0.06
(9-1)

13. 11%
(9-1)

14. 3
(9-1)

15. 8%
(9-1)

Write each fraction or whole number as a percent or each percent
as a fraction or whole number.

16. $\frac{25}{100}$
(9-1)

17. $\frac{5}{10}$
(9-1)

18. $\frac{4}{50}$
(9-1)

19. $\frac{3}{25}$
(9-1)

20. 50%
(9-1)

21. $\frac{1}{5}$
(9-1)

22. $\frac{20}{80}$
(9-1)

23. 2
(9-1)

24. $\frac{3}{20}$
(9-1)

25. 2%
(9-1)

Find each percent.

26. 62% of 120
(9-3)

27. 10% of 1,200
(9-5)

28. $33\frac{1}{3}$% of 150
(9-5)

29. 95% of 200
(9-3)

Copy and complete.

	Percent	Fraction	Decimal
30. *(9-1)*	39%		
31. *(9-1)*		$\frac{2}{5}$	
32. *(9-1)*			0.15
33. *(9-1)*		$\frac{2}{3}$	
34. *(9-1)*	2%		

	Percent	Fraction	Decimal
35. *(9-1)*			0.32
36. *(9-1)*		$\frac{1}{8}$	
37. *(9-1)*	4%		
38. *(9-1)*		$1\frac{1}{4}$	
39. *(9-1)*			0.875

Estimate.

40. 52% of 299
(9-2)

41. 22% of 38.98
(9-2)

42. 39% of 80
(9-2)

43. 18% of 60
(9-2)

44. Mona has $19.00 to spend on new gloves. The $34 leather
(9-4) gloves are on sale for 50% off. The $25 suede gloves are on sale
for 20% off. Explain how Mona can determine the style of gloves
that she can afford.

45. Celeste bought ballet shoes for 25% off the ticketed price of
(9-5) $80.00. Use mental math to find how much Celeste saved.

Multiple-Choice Cumulative Review

Choose the correct letter for each answer.

1. Find n in $\dfrac{4}{n} = \dfrac{6}{15}$.

   A $n = 1.6$ C $n = 12$

   B $n = 10$ D $n = 22.5$

2. Find the value of a in the triangle below.

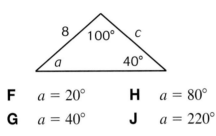

   F $a = 20°$ H $a = 80°$

   G $a = 40°$ J $a = 220°$

3. When you left home, the odometer in the car showed 456.2 miles. On the first day of your trip, you traveled 287.7 miles. What did the odometer show at the end of the day?

   A   168.5 mi   C   743.2 mi

   B   663.9 mi   D   743.9 mi

4. Solve $h - {}^-4 = 20$.

   F $h = {}^-24$

   G $h = {}^-16$

   H $h = 16$

   J $h = 24$

   K   NH

5. Onions cost 49¢ per pound and tomatoes cost 99¢ per pound. Jill bought $2\dfrac{1}{2}$ lb of onions and 5 lb of tomatoes. How much did she spend?

   A $1.23

   B $4.95

   C $6.18

   D $7.43

6. Find $6\dfrac{1}{8} \div 2\dfrac{5}{6}$.

   F $2\dfrac{1}{6}$

   G $2\dfrac{11}{68}$

   H $3\dfrac{3}{20}$

   J $17\dfrac{17}{48}$

   K   NH

7. Heather drew a triangle. The measure of the first angle is 30°. The measure of the third angle is 120°. Find the measure of the second angle.

   A   30°

   B   50°

   C   60°

   D   70°

8. Find the mean for this set of numbers: 4, 6, 7, 8, 8

   F   6.6   H   7.2

   G   7   J   8

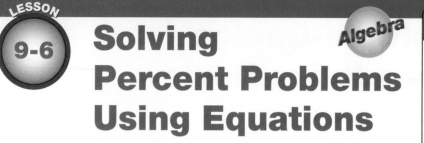

LESSON 9-6
Solving Percent Problems Using Equations

Algebra

Warm-Up Review

Find the percent of each number mentally.

1. 25% of 44

2. 75% of 44

3. 200% of 16

4. 110% of 10

5. If 10% of the 150 stamps in Greg's collection are foreign stamps, how many stamps are U.S. stamps?

California Content Standard *Algebra and Functions 1.1 (🔑): Write and solve one-step linear equations in one variable.*

Math Link You have used proportions and mental math to solve percent problems. Now you will use equations to solve problems involving percent.

Here are two things to remember when translating percent problems into equations.

1. *Of* usually means *times*.

2. Rewrite percents as decimals.

Example 1

What number is 25% of 62?

$$n = 0.25 \times 62$$
$$n = 15.5$$

15.5 is 25% of 62.

Check using cross products.

$$\frac{25}{100} \overset{?}{=} \frac{15.5}{62}$$

$$100 \times 15.5 \overset{?}{=} 25 \times 62$$

$$1{,}550 = 1{,}550$$

Example 2

15 is what percent of 75?

$$15 = p \times 75$$

$$\frac{15}{75} = \frac{p \times 75}{75}$$

$$0.2 = p$$
$$20\% = p$$

Check using cross products.

$$\frac{20}{100} \overset{?}{=} \frac{15}{75}$$

$$15 \times 100 \overset{?}{=} 20 \times 75$$

$$1{,}500 = 1{,}500$$

Guided Practice   *For another example, see Set E on p. 373.*

Write an equation and solve.

1. What number is 40% of 88?

2. What percent of 90 is 27?

3. What is 120% of 360?

4. 16 is what percent of 40?

358

Additional Standards: Number Sense 1.0 Mathematical Reasoning 2.5 (See p. 345.)

5. The sixth-grade class is having a book fair. Their order included 300 novels. So far, 180 novels have been sold. What percent of the novels have been sold?

Independent Practice For more practice, see Set E on p. 375.

Write an equation and solve.

6. What number is 5% of 60?

7. 60 is what percent of 160?

8. What percent of 12 is 9?

9. What percent of 12.5 is 5?

10. What is 25% of 200?

11. What number is 10% of 25?

12. Each side of a photo is reduced by 20%.The original size of the photo is 15 inches by 20 inches. By how many inches is the 15-inch side reduced?

13. Math Reasoning When you find what percent one number is of another, how can you tell whether the answer will be less than 100% or greater than 100%?

14. Mental Math Find 300% of 2.

15. As goalie on the soccer team, Callie allowed only 7 goals in 198 attempts. What percent of attempts were goals?

Mixed Review

In Exercises 16–17, tell whether the claim is justified by the information at the right. Explain your answers.

> Jenny read a 384-page book in 9 days.
> Roberto read a 413-page book in 7 days.

16. Roberto is a faster reader than Jenny.

17. Roberto's book had more pages than Jenny's book.

Find each percent.

18. 18% of 16.50 **19.** 47% of 58 **20.** 10% of 50 **21.** 3% of 300

Test Prep Choose the correct letter for each answer.

22. (7-2) 9,400 grams is equal to how many kilograms?

    A 0.94 kg   **C** 94 kg

    B 9.4 kg   **D** 940 kg

23. (7-2) 0.014 centimeter is equal to how many millimeters?

    F 0.0014 mm   **H** 0.14 mm

    G 0.014 mm   **J** 1.4 mm

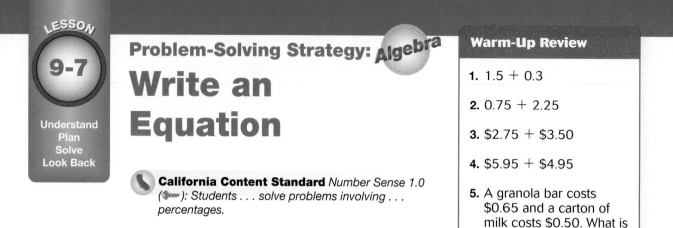

Problem-Solving Strategy: *Algebra*

Write an Equation

Warm-Up Review

1. $1.5 + 0.3$

2. $0.75 + 2.25$

3. $\$2.75 + \$3.50$

4. $\$5.95 + \$4.95$

5. A granola bar costs $0.65 and a carton of milk costs $0.50. What is the total cost?

California Content Standard *Number Sense 1.0 (🔑): Students . . . solve problems involving . . . percentages.*

Example

For lunch, Jenny had a large fruit cup, a large garden salad, and an orange juice. She left the waiter a $2.05 tip. The tip was what percent of the cost of Jenny's food?

Salad Sensations

Small Garden Salad	$3.00
Large Garden Salad	$5.50
Small Fruit Cup	$2.25
Large Fruit Cup	$3.50
Small Pasta Salad	$4.00
Large Pasta Salad	$6.50
Milk	$1.00
Orange Juice	$1.25
Cranberry Juice	$1.50

Understand

What do you need to find?

You need to find what percent of the cost of Jenny's food equals $2.05.

Plan

How can you solve the problem?

You can **write an equation**.

Solve

Let p represent the percent of the tip.

large fruit cup		large garden salad		orange juice		
p × ($\$3.50$	+	$\$5.50$	+	$\$1.25$)	=	$\$2.05$

$p \times 10.25 = 2.05$

$$\dfrac{p \times 10.25}{10.25} = \dfrac{2.05}{10.25}$$

$p = 0.2$

$p = 20\%$

The tip was 20% of the cost of Jenny's bill.

Look Back

How can you use estimation to check your answer?

Additional Standards: Number Sense 1.4 (🔑); Algebra and Functions 1.1; Mathematical Reasoning 2.7, 3.2 (See p. 345.)

Guided Practice

Write an equation for each exercise. Use the menu on page 360.

1. Jason bought a large pasta salad, a large fruit cup, and two milks. He left a $1.80 tip. The tip was what percent of the cost of Jason's food?

2. Hannah left the waitress a 20% tip for a large pasta salad and cranberry juice. How much did she spend in all?

Independent Practice

Write an equation for each exercise Use the menu on page 360.

3. Jake ordered a large garden salad and orange juice. He left a $1.35 tip for the waiter. The tip was what percent of the cost of Jake's food?

4. A group of friends ordered 3 small pasta salads. They left 7 quarters for a tip. Was the tip more or less than 15%? Explain your answer.

5. **Math Reasoning** Which is greater, a 15% tip for a small pasta salad or a 20% tip for a small fruit cup? Explain your answer.

Mixed Review

Try these or other strategies to solve each problem. Tell which strategy you used.

> ## Problem-Solving Strategies
> - *Make a List*
> - *Work Backward*
> - *Use Logical Reasoning*
> - *Solve a Simpler Problem*

6. Edna made $20 in tips on Sunday, $15 on Monday, $25 on Tuesday, $20 on Wednesday, and $30 on Thursday. If this pattern continues, how much can she expect in tips on Friday?

7. Carol, Mae, Bill, and Rick sat at different sides of a square table. Rick was on Carol's left. Bill was on Mae's right but not next to Carol. Who sat across from Rick?

8. Murray paid half as much for lunch as he paid for dinner. The total cost of both meals was $18.75. What was the cost of each meal?

9-8 Finding Sales Tax

Algebra

California Content Standard *Number Sense 1.4 (🔑): Calculate given percentages of quantities . . ..*

Warm-Up Review

Find the percent of each number.

1. 5% of $34

2. 4% of $3.50

3. 5.5% of $20

4. You give a 10% tip on a $17 taxicab fare. What is the total that you pay?

Math Link You can use what you know about percents to find sales tax.

Example

You buy a soccer ball priced at $14.69. If the rate of the sales tax is 6.5%, what is the total cost of the ball?

Step 1 Find the sales tax.

Let t = sales tax

$t = 6.5\% \times 14.69$

$t = 0.065 \times 14.69$

$t = 0.95485$

Sales tax is always rounded up to the next cent. The sales tax is $0.96.

The total cost of the soccer ball is $15.65.

Step 2 Find the total cost.

$$\begin{array}{r} \$14.69 \\ +\ 0.96 \\ \hline \$15.65 \end{array}$$

With a calculator:

Press: 6 . 5 % × 1 4 . 6 9 =

Display: 0.95485

To find the total cost,

Press: 1 4 . 6 9 + . 9 6 =

Display: 15.65

Guided Practice *For another example, see Set F on p. 373.*

Find the sales tax and the total cost. Round the sales tax up to the nearest cent.

1. cost: $19
   rate of sales tax: 8%

2. cost: $412
   rate of sales tax: 6%

3. cost: $62.50
   rate of sales tax: 5.5%

4. A basketball cost $30. The rate of sales tax was 5%. Find the total cost of the basketball.

Independent Practice
For more practice, see Set F on p. 375.

Find the sales tax and the total cost. Round the sales tax up to the nearest cent.

5. cost: $2.25
rate of sales tax: 5%

6. cost: $12.20
rate of sales tax: 4.5%

7. cost: $34.99
rate of sales tax: 6.25%

Copy and complete the table.

	Cost	Rate of Sales Tax	Sales Tax	Total Cost
8.	$25.00	5%		$26.25
9.	$100.00	8%		$108.00
10.	$20.00	5%		
11.	$15.50	10%		

12. Jeff and Frank bought two pairs of swimming goggles for $26.50. If the rate of sales tax was 6%, what was the total cost of the goggles?

13. Math Reasoning Could the key sequence below be used to find the total cost of the soccer ball in the example on page 362? Explain.

Press: (1) (0) (6) (.) (5) (%) (×) (1) (4) (.) (6) (9) (=)

Mixed Review

14. The selling price of a piano is the cost to the dealer plus 23% of that cost. Find the selling price of a piano if the dealer's cost is $6,000.

Mental Math For Exercises 15–17, find each percent mentally.

15. 80% of 100

16. 1% of 200

17. 55% of 80

18. What is 85% of 50?

19. 10 is what percent of 80?

Test Prep Choose the correct letter for each answer.

Use the stem-and-leaf plot at the right for Exercises 20 and 21.

CDs Owned

20. Find the median number of CDs owned.
(3-3)

A 10 CDs **B** 41 CDs **C** 44 CDs **D** 46 CDs

Stem	Leaves
1	0 0 3
2	5 6
4	1 4 7
6	3 5 8
9	1 3

21. Lisa owns 87 CDs. If this number is added to
(3-3) the data in the stem-and-leaf plot, what would happen to the median?

F The median would be greater.   **H** The median would stay the same.

G The median would be less.   **J** There is not enough information to tell.

9-9 Computing Discounts

California Content Standard *Number Sense 1.4 (🔑): Calculate given percentages of quantities and solve problems involving discounts at sales . . ..*

Warm-Up Review

Find the sales tax and the total cost.

1. cost: $9
   rate of sales tax: 5%

2. cost: $28
   rate of sales tax: 4.5%

3. What will be the total price of a $12,000 car, including 8% sales tax?

Math Link You can use what you know about percent to solve problems involving discounts.

Example 1

The Nature Shop had a 25% sale on kaleidoscopes. Michael bought one originally priced at $15.99. How much did he pay on sale?

Estimate first: 25% of $15.99 is about 25% of $16, or $4.

The estimated sale price is $16.00 − $4.00 = $12.00.

Step 1 Find the discount.	Step 2 Find the sale price.

Let d = the discount.
What is 25% of 15.99?

$$d = 0.25 \times 15.99$$
$$d = 3.9975$$
$$d = 3.99$$

Discounts are always rounded down.

Let s = sale price.
sale price = regular price − discount
$$s = \$15.99 - \$3.99$$
$$s = \$12$$

Michael paid $12 for the kaleidoscope.

Example 2

Another store has a $90 kaleidoscope on sale for $33\frac{1}{3}$% off. Find the discount and the sale price.

Step 1 Find the discount.	Step 2 Find the sale price.

Let d = the discount.
What is $33\frac{1}{3}$% of 90?

$$d = \frac{1}{3} \times 90$$
$$d = 30$$

Let s = the sale price.
sale price = regular price − discount
$$s = \$90 - \$30$$
$$s = \$60$$

The discount is $30 and the sale price is $60.

364

Additional Standards: Algebra and Functions 1.1; Mathematical Reasoning 2.1 (See p. 345.)

Guided Practice For another example, see Set G on p. 373.

Find the discount and the sale price.

1. regular price: $200
rate of discount: 10%

2. regular price: $56
rate of discount: 25%

3. regular price: $66
rate of discount: $33\frac{1}{3}\%$

4. Tommy bought two kaleidoscopes on sale for 20% off. If each kaleidoscope cost $29 before the sale, what did Tommy pay for both on sale?

Independent Practice For more practice, see Set G on p. 375.

Find the discount and the sale price.

5. regular price: $16
rate of discount: 25%

6. regular price: $50
rate of discount: 50%

7. regular price: $50.50
rate of discount: 15%

8. regular price: $650
rate of discount: 20%

9. regular price: $11.99
rate of discount: 10%

10. regular price: $36
rate of discount: 25%

11. Mental Math A crystal-growing kit regularly priced at $40.00 is 20% off the regular price. What is the sale price?

12. Linda bought some crystals for 15% off the regular price of $18. She bought rocks for 25% off the regular price of $22. How much did Linda spend altogether?

Mixed Review

13. Suppose you use 8 pounds of apples to make 4 pies. Write the ratio of pounds of apples to pies in three ways.

14. What percent of 212 equals 63.6?

15. 29% of what number equals $15.95?

Find the sales tax and the total cost.

16. cost: $29.95
rate of sales tax: 7%

17. cost: $100
rate of sales tax: 6.9%

18. cost: $44.50
rate of sales tax: 3%

Test Prep Choose the correct letter for each answer.

19. A store sells 8 bracelets for $26.
(8-6) Find the unit price.

A $3 each   **C** $4 each

B $3.25 each   **D** $208 each

20. If 6 rocks cost $13.50, how much do
(8-2) 9 rocks cost?

F $6.75   **H** $18.00

G $15.00   **J** $20.25

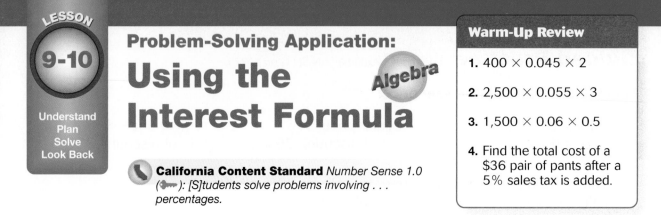

LESSON
9-10

Understand
Plan
Solve
Look Back

Problem-Solving Application:

Using the Interest Formula

Algebra

California Content Standard *Number Sense 1.0* (🔑): *[S]tudents solve problems involving . . . percentages.*

Warm-Up Review

1. $400 \times 0.045 \times 2$

2. $2,500 \times 0.055 \times 3$

3. $1,500 \times 0.06 \times 0.5$

4. Find the total cost of a $36 pair of pants after a 5% sales tax is added.

Interest is the amount of money paid for the use of money. It is a percent of the amount of money invested, borrowed, or loaned.

You put $200 in a savings account earning 5.5% simple interest per year. What is the total you will have in your account after one year?

Word Bank

interest
principal
rate of interest

Understand

What do you need to find?

You need to find the amount in your account after one year.

Plan

How can you solve the problem?

You can **use the interest formula,** $I = prt$. The **principal,** p, is the money placed in a bank or borrowed. The **rate of interest,** r, is the percent earned or charged, usually per year. The **time,** t, is how long the money is in the account or borrowed.

Solve

To find simple interest, multiply the principal, rate, and time in years.

interest = principal × rate × time

$$I = p \times r \times t$$
$$I = 200 \times 0.055 \times 1$$
$$I = \$11$$

total in   original
account = amount + interest

$$= \$200 + \$11$$
$$= \$211$$

After one year, you will have $211 in your account.

Look Back

Check the answer by multiplying $200 × 105.5%.

 Additional Standards: Number Sense 1.4 (🔑); Algebra and Functions 1.1 (🔑), 1.2, Mathematical Reasoning 2.7, 3.2 (See p. 345.)

Guided Practice

Find the interest and the total with interest.

	Principal	Yearly Rate of Interest	Time	Interest	Total with Interest
1.	$6,000	5%	5 mo		
2.	$4,500	18%	6 mo		
3.	$500	7.5%	1 yr		

4. If you want to borrow $500.00 for 6 months at 12% interest, how much money will you owe the bank? Remember, 6 months is $\frac{1}{2}$ of a year.

Independent Practice

Find the interest and the total with interest.

	Principal	Rate of Interest	Time	Interest	Total with Interest
5.	$6,500	8%	1 yr		
6.	$8,800	12%	8 mo		
7.	$2,000	5%	6 mo		
8.	$1,500	10%	9 mo		

9. Alfred earned 5% on $100 in his savings account for 1 year. Rebecca earned 3% on $200. Who earned more interest? Explain your answer.

10. Charlie put $2,000 into an account earning 5% per year. Interest is paid at the end of each year and added to the principal. How much is in Charlie's account after 2 years?

Mixed Review

Tell which strategy you used to solve each problem.

11. Art listened to an average of 6 hours of radio per day for 5 days. If he listened to 3 hours of radio for 2 days, how many hours could he have listened the other 3 days?

12. Greg sketched 100 different drawings. Of these, 65% are of animals, 15% are of plants, and the rest are of sports figures. How many of his drawings are of sports figures?

13. Kara used a coupon worth 15% off to purchase a shirt. The shirt normally costs $16. How much did she save?

Use Homework Workbook 9-10.

Diagnostic Checkpoint

Complete. For Exercises 1–3, use the words from the Word Bank.

Word Bank

discount
interest
percent
proportion
ratio

1. Money earned on a savings account is called _____.
(9-10)

2. The sale price equals the regular price minus the _____.
(9-9)

3. A _____ is a special ratio that compares a number to 100.
(9-1)

Write an equation and solve. Round to the nearest hundredth.

4. What number is 8% of 50?
(9-6)

5. 65% of what number is 20?
(9-6)

6. What percent of 15 is 7?
(9-6)

7. 16 is 60% of what number?
(9-6)

8. Kyle and his 3 brothers had a pizza delivered to their home. The pizza cost $10.00. Each person gave the delivery person a $1.50 tip. What was the percent of the tip?
(9-7)

Find the sales tax and total cost. Round the sales tax up to the nearest cent.

9. cost: $175
(9-8)
rate of sales tax: 5.5%

10. cost: $879.99
(9-8)
rate of sales tax: 4%

11. cost: $1,279
(9-8)
rate of sales tax: 8%

Find the discount and the sale price. Round the discount down to the nearest cent.

12. regular price: $120
(9-9)
rate of discount: $33\frac{1}{3}$%

13. regular price: $65
(9-9)
rate of discount: 20%

14. regular price: $29.99
(9-9)
rate of discount: 25%

Copy and complete the chart.

	Principal	Yearly Rate	Time	Interest	Total with Interest
15. (9-10)	$1,000	8.5%	9 mo		
16. (9-10)	$450	7%	1 yr		
17. (9-10)	$695	12.5%	6 mo		

Chapter 9 Test

Complete each table.

	Fraction	Decimal	Percent
1.		0.79	
2.	$\frac{7}{20}$		
3.			90%

	Fraction	Decimal	Percent
4.		0.625	
5.			56%
6.	$\frac{1}{4}$		

Find each percent.

7. 25% of 40   **8.** $33\frac{1}{3}$% of 24   **9.** 60% of 150   **10.** 130% of 80

Find the sales tax and the total cost.

11. cost: $49
rate of sales tax: 5%

12. cost: $110
rate of sales tax: 6%

Find the discount and the sale price.

13. regular price: $250
rate of discount: 25%

14. regular price: $9.80
rate of discount: 10%

Find the interest.

15. principal: $400; rate: 8%;
time: 1 year

16. principal: $1,250; rate: 5.7%;
time: 4 years

Estimate.

17. 23% of 49   **18.** 19% of 79   **19.** 8% of $82.11   **20.** 48% of 62

Write an equation and solve.

21. What percent of 240 is 96?   **22.** What is 118% of $45?

23. Laura and Andy spent $42 at a restaurant. If they want to leave a 15% tip, how much should they leave?

24. David's dinner bill was $15.00. He left a $3.00 tip. The tip was what percent of the bill?

25. Austin needs to make a quick decision regarding which vase to buy. The glass vase is 25% off $29.00. The ceramic vase is 40% off $32.00. Estimate which vase costs less.

Multiple-Choice Chapter 9 Test

Choose the correct letter for each answer.

1. Shane got $\frac{9}{10}$ of the problems right on his math quiz. What percent of problems did he get right?

   A 90%

   B 10%

   C 0.9%

   D 0.1%

2. The average test score on the history test was 45. The instructor said he wants to see a 10% increase on the next exam. Which expression can be used to find 110% of 45?

   F 110×45

   G $110 \div 45$

   H 1.1×45

   J $45 \div 1.1$

3. Deidre exercises 25 to 35 minutes every Tuesday and Friday. Afterward, she meets her mom for dinner. When she gets home, she goes to bed at 10:45 P.M. Which of the following is an estimate?

   A The days Deidre exercises

   B The length of time Deidre exercises

   C The time Deidre goes to bed

   D The person Deidre meets for dinner

4. What is 38% of 86?

   F 0.3268

   G 32.68

   H 326.8

   J 3268

   K NH

Use the advertisement for Questions 5 and 6.

SNORKEL SET 20% off
Regular price
$39.95
5% sales tax on all items

5. How much will Gina save if she buys a snorkel set on sale (not including tax)?

   A $19.98

   B $7.99

   C $2.00

   D $0.79

6. If you calculate tax on the sale price, what is the total cost of a snorkel set including the sales tax?

   A $31.96

   B $33.56

   C $35.27

   D $41.95

7. Nancy purchased two brass candlesticks on sale for 40% off. If each candlestick cost $56 before the sale, what did Nancy pay for both on sale?

F $67.20

G $56.00

H $44.80

J $33.60

8. Last year, Mr. Earp paid $810 for his car insurance. This year, he received a 25% discount because he had had no accidents. How much did Mr. Earp pay for his insurance this year?

A $600.50   **C** $608.50

B $607.50   **D** $1012.50

9. To finance a new computer, Cindy borrowed $2,150 for 12 months at 18% yearly interest. How much money will Cindy owe the bank?

F $232.20

G $387

H $2,382.2

J $2,537

10. Which of the following is true?

A $\frac{1}{2} = 0.05 = 5\%$

B $\frac{3}{4} = 0.75 = 75\%$

C $\frac{8}{10} = 0.80 = 800\%$

D $\frac{1}{3} = 0.35 = 35\%$

11. Your lunch bill is $18.11. You want to leave a tip of about 15% of the bill. What is a good estimate of the tip?

F $1.50

G $1.81

H $3.00

J $4.00

12. Jim tips his barber $3.60, which is exactly a 20% tip. What equation shows how to find the cost of Jim's haircut?

A $3.60 \times 0.20p$

B $0.20 = 3.60p$

C $3.60 = 0.20p$

D $p = 0.20 \times 3.60$

13. A baseball cap costs $25. The rate of sales tax was 7%. Find the total cost.

F $26.75

G $27.75

H $30.50

J $42.50

14. Mitch earned 8% on $1,000 in one year. Phil earned 12% on $400 in one year. Which of the following statements is true?

A Phil and Mitch had the same interest rate.

B Mitch made $80 in interest in one year.

C Mitch earned more than twice as much as Phil.

D Phil and Mitch earned the same amount of money.

Reteaching

Set A (pages 346–347)

Write 35% as a decimal and as a fraction.

35% means "35 out of 100, or 35 hundredths."

35% = 0.35

$$\frac{35}{100} = \frac{7}{20}$$

Remember that percent means "per hundred."

Complete the table.

	Fraction	Decimal	Percent
1.	$\frac{3}{20}$		
2.			9%
3.		0.125	

Set B (pages 348–349)

Estimate 42% of 312.

42% × 312 rounds to:

40% × 300

0.4 × 300 = 120

42% of 312 is about 120.

Remember that you can use rounding and fractions to estimate a percent of a number.

Estimate.

1. 53% of 58   **2.** 10% of 245

3. 74% of 21   **4.** 47% of 500

Set C (pages 350–351)

Find 85% of 52.

Write a proportion and use cross products.

$$\frac{85}{100} = \frac{n}{52}$$

85 × 52 = 100n

$$\frac{4{,}420}{100} = n$$

44.2 = n

85% of 52 is 44.2.

Remember that you can use a proportion to find a percent of a number.

Find each percent.

1. 15% of 50   **2.** 125% of 200

3. 95% of 150   **4.** 68% of 20

5. 15% of 72   **6.** 40% of 55

Set D (pages 354–355)

Use mental math to find 20% of 180.

First find 10% of 180. Then double that amount.

10% of 180 = 18

2 × 18 = 36

20% of 180 is 36.

Remember that changing percents to fractions can simplify some mental math.

Use mental math to find each percent.

1. 10% of 480   **2.** 25% of 80

3. 15% of 80   **4.** $66\frac{2}{3}$% of 30

Set E *(pages 358–359)*

Write an equation and solve to find what percent of 24 is 3.

What percent of 24 is 3?

$$n \times 24 = 3$$
$$24n = 3$$
$$\frac{24n}{24} = \frac{3}{24}$$
$$n = 0.125 = 12.5\%$$

Remember that you can write an equation to solve percent problems.

Write an equation and solve.

1. What percent of 36 is 9?

2. What is 60% of 60?

3. 8 is 25% of what number?

Set F *(pages 362–363)*

Find the sales tax and the total cost of a $29.00 shirt with a sales-tax rate of 5%.

Step 1 To find the sales tax, find 5% of 29.00.

$t = 0.05 \times 29 = 1.45$
The tax is $1.45.

Step 2 Add to find the total cost.

$29.00 + $1.45 = $30.45
The total cost is $30.45.

Remember to round sales tax up to the nearest cent.

Complete the table.

	Cost	Rate of Sales Tax	Sales Tax	Total Cost
1.	$8.00	6%		
2.	$15.50	7%		
3.	$39.59	4.5%		

Set G *(pages 364–365)*

Find the discount and the sale price of a $59.95 pair of shoes on sale for 25% off.

Step 1 To find the discount, find 25% of $59.95.

$d = 0.25 \times 59.95 = 14.9875 \approx 14.98$
The discount is $14.98.

Step 2 Subtract to find the sale price.

$59.95 − $14.98 = $44.97
The sale price is $44.97

Remember to round discounts down to the nearest cent.

Find the discount and the sale price.

1. regular price: $300
   rate of discount: 10%

2. regular price: $21.99
   rate of discount: $33\frac{1}{3}\%$

3. regular price: $9.50
   rate of discount: 20%

More Practice

Set A *(pages 346–347)*

Copy and complete.

	Percent	Decimal	Fraction
1.	70%		
2.		0.85	
3.	5%		

	Fraction	Decimal	Percent
1.		0.405	
2.			30%
3.	$\frac{5}{8}$		

4. 45% of the students in math class are boys. What fraction of the class are boys?

Set B *(pages 348–349)*

Estimate each percent.

1. 16% of 97

2. 25% of 204

3. 40% of 195

4. 75% of 208

5. 50% of 120

6. $33\frac{1}{3}$% of 190

7. Chad wants to save 10% of his earnings. He earned $68.25. About how much should he save?

Set C *(pages 350–351)*

Find each percent.

1. 100% of 35

2. 48% of 50

3. 25% of 16

4. 12% of 80

5. 107% of 620

6. 55% of 100

7. How much would you save on a $32.50 book on sale for 40% off?

Set D *(pages 354–355)*

Use mental math to find each percent.

1. 40% of 150

2. $33\frac{1}{3}$% of 150

3. 15% of 500

4. 75% of 200

5. 25% of 300

6. 250% of 10

7. Lunch cost $8.00. If you want to leave a 15% tip, how much should you leave?

Set E *(pages 358–359)*

Write an equation and solve.

1. What is 25% of 12?

2. What percent of 90 is 11.25?

3. What percent of 75 is 5?

4. What is 10% of 50?

5. What is 3% of 2?

6. 60% of what number is 33?

7. The band has 125 uniforms. Thirty-five of the uniforms need to be repaired. What percent of the uniforms need repairs?

Set F *(pages 362–363)*

Copy and complete the table.

	Cost	Rate of Sales Tax	Sales Tax	Total Cost
1.	$50.00	20%		
2.	$150.00	8%		
3.	$63.50	10%		
4.	$4.75	12.5%		
5.	$39.95	6.5%		

6. Michael bought a wallet for $17.50 and a key chain for $4.95. If the rate of sales tax was 7%, what was the total cost of his purchases?

Set G *(pages 364–365)*

Copy and complete the table.

	Regular Price	Rate of Discount	Discount	Sale Price
1.	$40	12.5%		
2.	$2,650	5%		
3.	$5,689	10%		

4. Marissa bought three shirts on sale for 15% off. The original price was $24.00 for each shirt. How much did Marissa spend, not including tax?

5. In Exercise 4, if Marissa had to pay 5% sales tax on the sale price, how much did she pay in all for three shirts?

Problem Solving: Preparing for Tests

Choose the correct letter for each answer.

1. **This graph shows Mark's progress on a bicycle trip. Which is reasonable for Mark's average speed (in miles per hour) between 2:00 P.M. and 4:00 P.M.?**

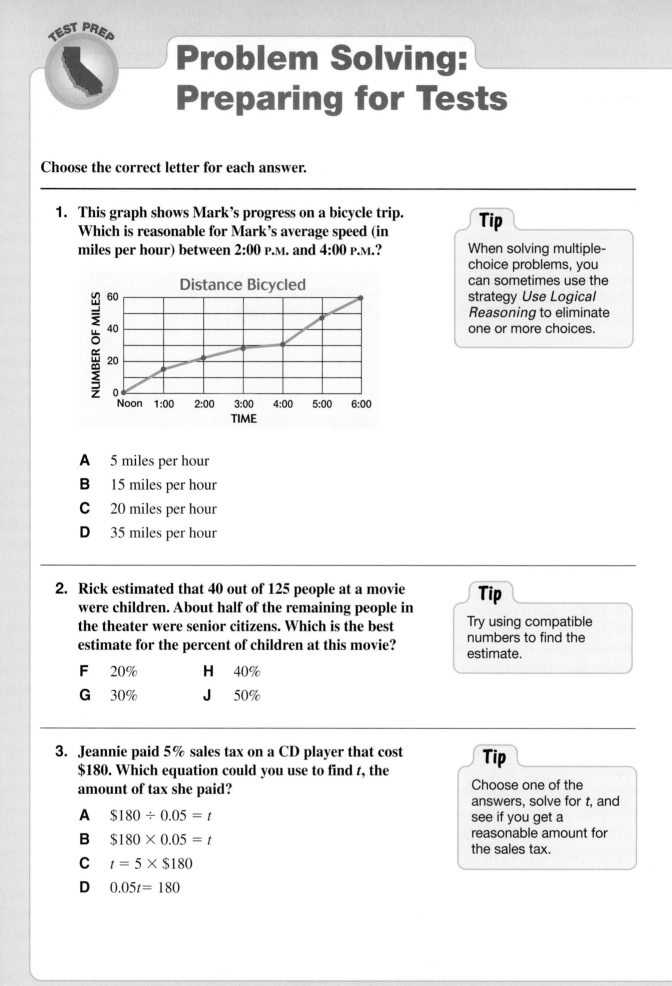

Distance Bicycled

A 5 miles per hour

B 15 miles per hour

C 20 miles per hour

D 35 miles per hour

Tip

When solving multiple-choice problems, you can sometimes use the strategy *Use Logical Reasoning* to eliminate one or more choices.

2. **Rick estimated that 40 out of 125 people at a movie were children. About half of the remaining people in the theater were senior citizens. Which is the best estimate for the percent of children at this movie?**

F 20%   **H** 40%

G 30%   **J** 50%

Tip

Try using compatible numbers to find the estimate.

3. **Jeannie paid 5% sales tax on a CD player that cost $180. Which equation could you use to find t, the amount of tax she paid?**

A $\$180 \div 0.05 = t$

B $\$180 \times 0.05 = t$

C $t = 5 \times \$180$

D $0.05t = 180$

Tip

Choose one of the answers, solve for t, and see if you get a reasonable amount for the sales tax.

4. On Sunday the temperature was 45.5°F. For the next three days, it went up 1.2°F, 2.4°F, and 3.6°F. If this pattern continues, what will the temperature be on *Friday*?

F 57.5°F   **H** 63.5°F

G 62.3°F   **J** 70.7°F

---

5. Rob is making a quilt from material that costs $1.35 per yard. These figures are part of the quilt design. Which figure is 75% *white*?

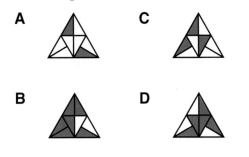

A   C

B   D

---

6. Molly needs 5.6 m of cord to make 4 pillows. The cord is sold only in 25 cm lengths. If each length costs $0.39, how much will Molly spend for the cord? (1 m = 100 cm)

F $2.18

G $8.58

H $8.97

J $17.47

---

7. The population of Westfall is 4,260. Easterly has only 1,730 people. Almost two thirds of the people in the two towns are registered to vote. More than half of the voters are women. Which is the best estimate for the number of registered voters?

A 2,000   **C** 4,000

B 3,000   **D** 6,000

---

8. A scientist believes that the number of cells in an experiment will increase in this pattern.

Day	1	2	3	4	5
Number	7	15	31	63	127

If she is right, how many cells will there be on the *seventh* day?

F 227 cells   **H** 511 cells

G 255 cells   **J** 512 cells

---

9. The amount collected for tickets to a concert was $45,000. The tickets cost between $50 and $75 each, depending on where the seats were located. Which is reasonable for the number of tickets sold?

A Fewer than 300 tickets

B Between 300 and 600 tickets

C Between 600 and 900 tickets

D Between 900 and 1,200 tickets

---

10. The graph shows the results of a survey about vacations. Which are the best estimates for the numbers of employed people and retired people represented on this graph?

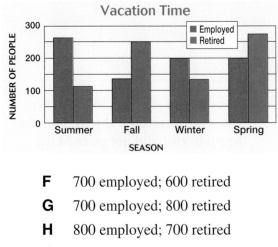

F 700 employed; 600 retired

G 700 employed; 800 retired

H 800 employed; 700 retired

J 800 employed; 900 retired

Multiple-Choice Cumulative Review

Choose the correct letter for each answer.

Number Sense

1. The length of a property's fence is 437.5479 meters. What is 437.5479 rounded to the nearest thousandth?

    A   437.0

    B   437.54

    C   437.548

    D   440

2. Which set of numbers is in order from *greatest* to *least*?

    F   0.344, 0.034, 0.434, 0.444

    G   0.444, 0.434, 0.034, 0.344

    H   0.444, 0.344, 0.0434, 0.034

    J   0.034, 0.344, 0.444, 0.434

3. On Monday, Bart went to the library. Yesterday, he read 20 pages of his 80-page book. What percent of his book did he read?

    A   10%

    B   25%

    C   50%

    D   66%

4. There are 44 students in the math club. One quarter of the students in the math club did not go to Math Field Day. What percent of the math club *did* attend Field Day?

    F   25%   H   70%

    G   50%   J   75%

Measurement and Geometry

5. Classify the figure.

    A   Quadrilateral

    B   Pentagon

    C   Hexagon

    D   Octagon

6. A ball weighs 450 grams. How many kilograms is this? (1 kg = 1,000 g)

    F   0.45 kilogram

    G   4.5 kilograms

    H   45 kilograms

    J   4,500 kilograms

7. A room is 12 feet wide by 15 feet long. What is the width of the room in yards?

    A   3 yards

    B   4 yards

    C   5 yards

    D   36 yards

8. Courtney ordered 9 crates of fruit from a supplier. Each crate weighed 15 pounds 4 ounces. How much did the 9 crates weigh in all?

    F   138 pounds 6 ounces

    G   137 pounds 4 ounces

    H   135 pounds 3 ounces

    J   132 pounds 8 ounces

Measurement and Geometry

9. Triangle *HIJ* is inscribed in triangle *DEF*. Which of the following pairs of line segments are parallel?

A $\overline{DF}$ and $\overline{HJ}$

B $\overline{DE}$ and $\overline{HI}$

C $\overline{EF}$ and $\overline{HJ}$

D $\overline{EF}$ and $\overline{IJ}$

10. Which statement is always true?

F All angles in a triangle are acute angles.

G The sum of the angles of a triangle is 180°.

H All triangles have 2 right angles.

J All triangles are similar.

11. Which of the following shows a *rotation* of the triangle?

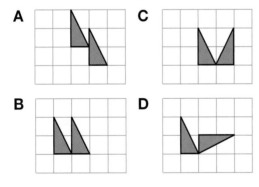

A   C

B   D

12. Figure *JKLMN* is congruent to Figure *PQRST*. Which angle is congruent to ∠*L*?

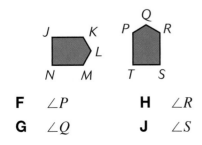

F ∠*P*   H ∠*R*

G ∠*Q*   J ∠*S*

Algebra and Functions

13. Karen made a paper chain. She first used 1 red loop, then she used 2 yellow, then 3 orange, then 2 brown, and, finally 1 purple loop. If she continues this pattern of loops in the chain, what color will the *twentieth* loop be?

A Purple

B Red

C Yellow

D Orange

14. If the ratio of girls to boys on the swim team is 3 to 4, then the team could have

F 21 girls and 28 boys.

G 28 girls and 21 boys.

H 20 girls and 15 boys.

J 16 girls and 24 boys.

15. If $352 \div x = 8$, then $x =$

A 33.

B 44.

C 66.

D 88.

16. Which point represents the number $3\frac{1}{3}$ on the number line?

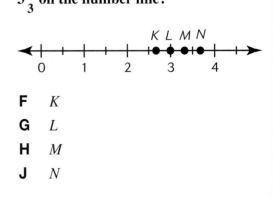

F *K*

G *L*

H *M*

J *N*

CHAPTER

10

Equations and Graphs

Diagnosing Readiness

In Chapter 10, you will use these skills:

Ⓐ Order of Operations
(pages 24–25)

Use order of operations to evaluate each expression.

1. $4 \times (5 + 7)$ **2.** $15 - 12 \div 2$

3. $36 \div (11 - 2)$ **4.** $12 - 4 + 6$

5. $(7 + 18) \div 5 + 21 \div 3$

6. Tickets to a baseball game cost $9.50 and tickets to a football game cost $15.75. Tiffany went to 4 baseball games and 2 football games. How much did she spend on tickets?

Ⓑ Evaluating Expressions
(pages 26–27, 236–237)

Evaluate each expression for $x = 9$, $y = 4$, and $z = 3$.

7. $5x - 3y$ **8.** $2x + 4y - 5z$

Complete the table.

	a	$3a - 8$
9.	4	
10.	2	
11.	⁻1	

12. The cost of one CD is $6. The cost of x number of CDs is $6x$. How much do 7 CDs cost?

C Solving Addition and Subtraction Equations

(pages 30–31, 186–187)

Solve each equation.

13. $x + 8 = 17$ **14.** $g + 79 = 300$

15. $n - 4.8 = 48$ **16.** $q + 9 = 12.1$

17. $b - \frac{1}{4} = 2\frac{1}{4}$ **18.** $3\frac{2}{5} = v + 1\frac{3}{5}$

19. The number of floats in the parade was 3 less than expected. There were 27 floats. How many floats were expected?

D Solving Multiplication and Division Equations

(pages 68–69, 198–199)

Solve each equation.

20. $9x = 900$ **21.** $x \div 5 = 100$

22. $\frac{h}{5} = 4.2$ **23.** $3.6n = 28.8$

24. $m \div 2.5 = 7.6$ **25.** $5.4y = 34.02$

26. A recipe calls for $3\frac{3}{4}$ cups of apples. Joe has b bags of apples that each hold $2\frac{1}{2}$ cups. Solve the equation $2\frac{1}{2}b = 3\frac{3}{4}$ to find how many bags of apples Joe needs to use.

E Equations with Integers

(pages 238–239)

Solve each equation.

27. $y + {}^-3 = 5$ **28.** $x - 5 = {}^-3$

29. $s + {}^-6 = 4$ **30.** $r - {}^-8 = 10$

31. $\frac{b}{7} = {}^-9$ **32.** $10h = {}^-120$

33. A hiker descended 1,200 feet in 4 hours. Solve the equation $4a = {}^-1{,}200$ to find the hiker's average change in altitude per hour.

F Positive and Negative Numbers on the Number Line

(pages 218–220)

Use the number line below for Exercises 34–37. Write the number that represents each point.

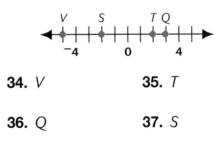

34. V **35.** T

36. Q **37.** S

38. How would you get to point V from zero on the number line?

To the Family and Student

Looking Back

In Chapters 1, 2, 5, and 6, students learned how to solve one-step linear equations in one variable.

Chapter 10

Equations and Graphs

In this chapter, students will learn how to solve and graph equations with more than one operation, such as $3x - 7 = 14$.

Looking Ahead

In Grade 7, students will learn how to solve inequalities. They will also learn how to graph functions of the form $y = mx + b$.

Math and Everyday Living

Opportunities to apply the concepts of Chapter 10 abound in everyday situations. During the chapter, think about how equations and graphs can be used to solve a variety of real-world problems. The following examples suggest just a few of the many situations that could launch a discussion about equations and graphs.

Math at the Ball Game
You see the sign below at a baseball game.

Popcorn	$2.25
Hamburger	$3.00
Juice (bottle)	$1.75

Write an expression for the cost of h boxes of popcorn and b bottles of juice. Use the expression to find the cost of 3 boxes of popcorn and 4 bottles of juice.

You have $9.75 before you buy 2 boxes of popcorn. Use the equation $1.75b + 4.50 = 9.75$ to find how many bottles of juice you can buy.

Math in the City You are at Center Fountain. How would you get to the post office?

From Center Fountain, you walk 2 blocks west and 3 blocks south. Where are you?

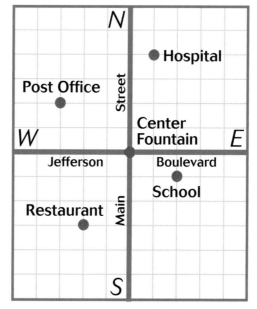

Math on the Road You live 150 miles from your grandparents' house. At 60 miles per hour, how long would it take you to drive there?

California Content Standards in Chapter 10 Lessons*

Number Sense	Teach and Practice	Practice
1.4 (🔑) Calculate given percentages of quantities and solve problems involving discounts at sales, interest earned, and tips.		10-7
2.1 Solve problems involving addition, subtraction, multiplication, and division of positive fractions and explain why a particular operation was used for a given situation.		10-6
2.3 (🔑) Solve addition, subtraction, multiplication, and division problems, including those arising in concrete situations, that use positive and negative integers and combinations of these operations.		10-3

Algebra and Functions	Teach and Practice	Practice
1.0 Students write verbal expressions and sentences as algebraic expressions and equations; they evaluate algebraic expressions, solve simple linear equations, and graph and interpret their results.	10-4, 10-5, 10-7, 10-8	10-6
1.1 (🔑) Write and solve one-step linear equations in one variable.	10-1	
1.2 Write and evaluate an algebraic expression for a given situation, using up to three variables.	10-2	10-8
1.3 Apply algebraic order of operations and the commutative, associative, and distributive properties to evaluate expressions; and justify each step in the process.		10-3
1.4 (🔑) (Grade 5) Identify and graph ordered pairs in the four quadrants of the coordinate plane.	10-4	
2.2 (🔑) Demonstrate an understanding that *rate* is a measure of one quantity per unit value of another quantity.		10-3
2.3 Solve problems involving rates, average speed, distance, and time.		10-3

Mathematical Reasoning	Teach and Practice	Practice
1.1 Analyze problems by identifying relationships, distinguishing relevant from irrelevant information, identifying missing information, sequencing and prioritizing information, and observing patterns.		10-6
2.2 Apply strategies and results from simpler problems to more complex problems.		10-1
2.3 Estimate unknown quantities graphically and solve for them by using logical reasoning and arithmetic and algebraic techniques.		10-5
2.4 Use a variety of methods, such as words, numbers, symbols, charts, graphs, tables, diagrams, and models, to explain mathematical reasoning.	10-3, 10-6	10-4, 10-5
2.5 Express the solution clearly and logically by using the appropriate mathematical notation and terms and clear language; support solutions with evidence in both verbal and symbolic work.		10-2, 10-8
3.2 Note the method of deriving the solution and demonstrate a conceptual understanding of the derivation by solving similar problems.	10-6	

* The symbol (🔑) indicates a key standard as designated in the Mathematics Framework for California Public Schools. Full statements of the California Content Standards are found at the beginning of this book following the Table of Contents.

 Equations with More Than One Operation

Algebra

California Content Standard *Algebra and Functions 1.1 (🔑): Write and solve one-step linear equations in one variable.*

Math Link You know how to solve equations using addition, subtraction, multiplication, or division. Now you will learn how to solve an equation with more than one operation.

Remember that addition and subtraction are inverse operations because they undo each other. Similarly, multiplication and division are inverse operations.

If an equation involves two operations, you use inverse operations one at a time. When you evaluate an expression using order of operations, you multiply and divide before you add and subtract. When you solve an equation with more than one operation, you *reverse* the process. So you need to undo any addition and subtraction first. Then undo any multiplication and division.

Solving Equations

1. Undo addition and subtraction first.

2. Then undo multiplication and division.

Example 1

Solve $2x - 3 = 15$. Check your answer.

$2x - 3 = 15$	Undo subtraction first.
$2x - 3 + 3 = 15 + 3$	Add 3 to **both** sides.
$2x = 18$	Undo multiplication by dividing.
$\dfrac{2x}{2} = \dfrac{18}{2}$	Divide **both** sides by 2.
$x = 9$	

Check:

$2x - 3 = 15$	Write the equation.
$2 \times 9 - 3 \stackrel{?}{=} 15$	Replace x with 9.
$18 - 3 \stackrel{?}{=} 15$	Solve.
$15 = 15$	The answer checks.

Example 2

Solve $10 - 3x = 4$. Check your answer.

$10 - 3x = 4$	Think $10 - 3x = 10 + {}^-3x$.
$10 + {}^-3x = 4$	Undo addition first.
$10 + {}^-3x - 10 = 4 - 10$	Subtract 10 from both sides.
${}^-3x = {}^-6$	Undo multiplication.
$\dfrac{{}^-3x}{{}^-3} = \dfrac{{}^-6}{{}^-3}$	Divide by ${}^-3$.
$x = 2$	

Check:

$10 - 3x = 4$	Write the equation.
$10 - 3 \times 2 \stackrel{?}{=} 4$	Replace x with 2.
$10 - 6 \stackrel{?}{=} 4$	Solve.
$10 = 10$	The answer checks.

Additional Standard: Mathematical Reasoning 2.2 (See p. 383.)

Guided Practice *For another example, see Set A on p. 406.*

Solve each equation. Check your answer.

1. $7x + 2 = 51$ **2.** $\dfrac{h}{7} + 11 = 11$ **3.** $42 = 30 - 6x$ **4.** $10 = \dfrac{t}{66} + 12$

5. Chris earns $7.50 per hour plus tips as a waiter. One evening he earned $28 in tips, for a total of $80.50. Solve the equation $7.50h + 28 = 80.50$ to find how many hours h that Chris worked.

Independent Practice *For more practice, see Set A on p. 408.*

Solve each equation. Check your answer.

6. $9h - 3 = 78$ **7.** $\dfrac{s}{4} + 118 = 15$ **8.** $200 = \dfrac{r}{2} + 214$ **9.** $10 - 20x = 50$

10. The cost for students to use the Elmtown Health Club is $355 for the first year. The cost includes an initial $25 membership fee and 12 equal monthly payments. Write and solve an equation to find, n, the amount of each monthly payment.

11. Mental Math Is the solution to the equation $^-5x = {}^-20$ greater than or less than zero? Explain your answer.

Mixed Review

12. Use the catalog ads at the right. Which store offers the best buy on a skateboard? How much can you save by buying from that store?

Find the sales tax and the total cost.

13. cost: $42
rate of sales tax: 6%

14. cost: $18.99
rate of sales tax: 5.5%

Super Sporting Goods
Zoomerang Skate Board
Regular Price $65.95
Now 20% off
Plus 3% Sales Tax
and $3.95 for shipping

Sports City
ZOOMERANG SKATE BOARD
Great Low Price $59.90
Special Sale 10% off
Sales Tax 6%
Shipping $4.50

🖊 **Test Prep** Choose the correct letter for each answer.

15. If 8 oranges cost $3, how much should 12 oranges cost?
(8-2)

  A $4.00   **B** $4.50   **C** $5.00   **D** $5.50

16. $^-6 - {}^-12 =$
(6-3)

  F $^-18$ **G** $^-6$ **H** 6   **J** 18   **K** NH

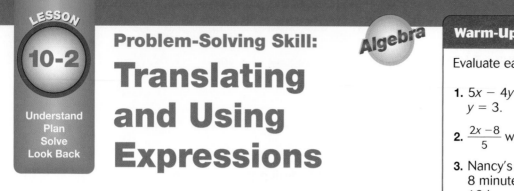

LESSON 10-2

Understand
Plan
Solve
Look Back

Problem-Solving Skill:

Translating and Using Expressions

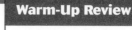 Algebra

California Content Standard *Algebra and Functions 1.2: Write and evaluate an algebraic expression for a given situation, using up to three variables.*

Read for Understanding

A zoo has different admission prices, depending on a person's age. The sign at the right shows the prices.

ZOO

ADMISSION PRICES

Adults $6.50
Children (under 14) $3.50
Seniors (over 60) $4.50

❶ What is the price for a 12-year-old?

❷ What is the price for a 65-year-old?

❸ What is the price for a 30-year-old?

❹ To find the total cost for a group to enter the zoo, what do you need to know?

Think and Discuss

MATH FOCUS

Translating and Using Expressions

Mathematical expressions use variables and numbers. Writing and evaluating expressions can help you solve problems. Some expressions use more than one variable.

Reread the paragraph and sign at the top of the page.

Let *a* represent the number of adults, *c* represent the number of children, and *s* represent the number of seniors.

❺ What expression would you use to find the total cost for a group of seniors?

❻ What expression would you use to find the total cost for a group of children under 14 and their parents? All of the parents are under 60 years of age.

❼ What expression would you use to find the cost for a group that included adults, children, and seniors?

Answer each question.

Guided Practice

Use the sign at the right for Exercises 1–3.

FARMERS' MARKET

APPLES $1.29 per pound
BANANAS $1.49 per pound
CASHEWS $4.79 per pound
PEANUTS $3.69 per pound

1. Which expression would Carly use to find the cost of a pounds of apples and b pounds of bananas?

   a. $(1.49 + 1.29) \times (a + b)$

   b. $1.49a + 1.29b$

   c. $1.29a + 1.49b$

2. How much will it cost Carly to buy 3 pounds of apples and 1 pound of bananas?

   a. $11.12

   b. $5.36

   c. $5.76

3. Which expression would you use to find the total cost of b pounds of bananas, c pounds of cashews, and p pounds of peanuts?

   a. $1.29a + 1.49b + 4.79c$

   b. $1.29b + 3.69c + 4.79p$

   c. $1.49b + 4.79c + 3.69p$

Independent Practice

Use the sign at the right for Exercises 4–7.

REFRESHMENT PRICES

Popcorn (large box)	$2.50
Granola bars	$1.50
Yogurt (cup)	$1.75
Fruit juice (carton)	$2.25

4. Which expression would Jordan use to find the total cost of p boxes of popcorn and j cartons of juice?

   a. $2.25p + 2.50j$

   b. $2.50p + 2.25j$

   c. $(2.25 + 2.50) \times (p + j)$

5. How much will it cost Jordan to buy 2 boxes of popcorn and 3 cartons of fruit juice?

   a. $11.75

   b. $12.00

   c. $12.50

6. Which expression would you use to find the cost of y yogurt cups, g granola bars, and j juice cartons?

   a. $1.75y + 1.50g + 2.25j$

   b. $2.50y + 1.75g + 2.25j$

   c. $1.50y + 2.25g + 2.50j$

7. **Math Reasoning** Tom had $10. He bought p boxes of popcorn and used the expression $10 + 2.50p$ to find the amount of money he had left. Is this right? Explain.

Solving Equations Using Tables

Algebra

California Content Standard *Mathematical Reasoning 2.4: Use a variety of methods, such as words, numbers, symbols, charts, graphs, tables, diagrams, and models, to explain mathematical reasoning.*

Math Link You know how to evaluate algebraic expressions. Now you will use this skill to use tables to solve equations.

Example 1

Mallory uses a computer to draw maps for real estate firms. Each map sells for $55. How many maps does she need to sell to earn $330?

Let m = the number of maps.
Let y = the amount earned.
The table below gives values for $y = 55m$.

Maps, m	1	2	3	4	5	6	7	8
Amount earned, y ($)	55	110	165	220	275	330	385	440

From the table, when the amount earned, y, equals 330, $m = 6$.

Mallory must sell 6 maps to earn $330.

Example 2

Christy started a business selling necklaces. She spent $225 for 50 necklaces. She sells the necklaces for $9.50 each. How many necklaces does she need to sell to make a profit of $155?

Let n = the number of necklaces Christy sells.
Let p = the amount earned after expenses (profit).
The table below gives values for $p = 9.50n - 225$.

necklaces, n	10	20	30	40	50
profit, p ($)	$^-130$	$^-35$	60	155	250

From the table, when $p = 155$, $n = 40$.

Christy needs to sell 40 necklaces to make a profit of $155.

Additional Standards: Number Sense 2.3( ); Algebra and Functions 1.3, 2.2, 2.3 (See p. 383.)

Guided Practice _For another example, see Set B on p. 406._

The equation $w = a + 4$ shows the relationship between the weight of a Great Dane puppy, w, and its age in weeks, a. The table at the right gives values for $w = a + 4$.

a (age in weeks)	0	1	2	3	4	5
w (lb)	4	5	6	7	8	9

1. How much does a Great Dane puppy weigh at birth?

2. How old is a puppy that weighs 7 pounds?

Independent Practice _For more practice, see Set B on p. 408._

The equation $t = \$0.50m + \$10$ shows the relationship between the number of miles driven, m, and the total cost, t, of renting a car. The table at the right gives values for $t = 0.50m + 10$.

m	20	40	60	80	100	120	140	160
t ($)	20	30	40	50	60	70	80	90

3. How many miles were driven if the total cost was $50?

4. What is the total cost of driving 20 miles?

5. Math Reasoning Using the table, what is a reasonable total cost of driving 50 miles? How did you decide?

6. Mental Math The ingredients for one dozen fruit bars cost $0.70. Use the equation $y = 0.70d$ to find how many dozen fruit bars can be made for $7.00.

Mixed Review

Find the discount and the sale price.

7. regular price: $49.99
rate of discount: 40%

8. regular price: $18
rate of discount: 25%

9. Solve $5x - 8 = 7$ and check your answer.

Test Prep   Choose the correct letter for each answer.

10. Brittany bought 8 pears for $3.04. What is the unit price?
(8-6)

   A $0.38   **B** $0.76   **C** $2.64   **D** $3.04

11. What is 30% of 180?
(9-3)

   F 550   **G** 54   **H** 5.4   **J** 0.54

Coordinate Graphing

10-4

Math Link You know how to graph and identify positive
and negative numbers on a number line. Now you will
learn how to graph and identify points in a plane.

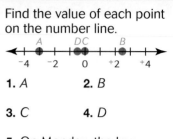
A **coordinate grid** has an *x*-axis and a *y*-axis. The two axes
meet at a point called the **origin**. You can describe a location
on a coordinate grid by using an **ordered pair**.

Word Bank

coordinate grid
x-axis
y-axis
origin
ordered pair

Example 1

Use the graph at the right. Name the
ordered pair that describes the
location of the treasure.

The first number in an ordered
pair is the number of units to
the left or right of the origin.
The treasure is 3 units to the
left of the origin.

The second number in an
ordered pair is the number of
units up or down from the
origin. The treasure is 2 units
down from the origin.

The ordered pair that locates
the treasure is (⁻3, ⁻2).

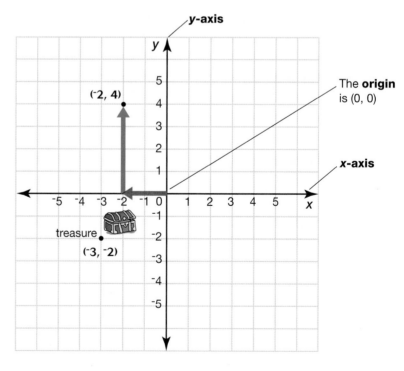

Example 2

Graph the ordered pair
(⁻2, 4) on the coordinate
grid at the right.

Begin at the origin.

Move left on the *x*-axis, since ⁻2 is a negative integer.

Then move up, since 4 is a positive integer.

You can graph equations by graphing ordered pairs that make the equation true.

Example 3

Complete the table of ordered pairs and graph the equation $y = x + 2$.

Evaluate the expression $x + 2$ for each value of x given in the table. Write that value in the y column.

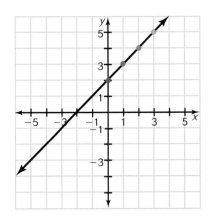

x	y	
0	2	$0 + 2 = 2$
1	3	$1 + 2 = 3$
2	4	$2 + 2 = 4$
3	5	$3 + 2 = 5$

Graph the points (0, 2), (1, 3), (2, 4), and (3, 5). Draw a line through the points.

Guided Practice For another example, see Set C on p. 406.

Write the ordered pair for each point.

1. A   **2.** B   **3.** E

Name the point for each ordered pair.

4. (⁻3, 4)   **5.** (⁻2, ⁻4)   **6.** (4, 3)

Complete the table of ordered pairs and graph each equation on a coordinate grid.

7. $y = 2x + 1$

x	y
0	
1	
2	

8. $y = 5 - x$

x	y
0	
1	
2	

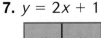
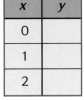

Independent Practice For more practice, see Set C on p. 408.

Write the ordered pair for each point in the coordinate grid above.

9. D   **10.** K

Name the point for each ordered pair in the coordinate grid above.

11. (⁻2, 2)   **12.** (5, 0)

Complete the table of ordered pairs and graph each equation on a coordinate grid.

13. $y = x + 1$

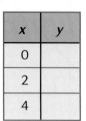

x	y
0	
2	
4	

14. $y = 4 - x$

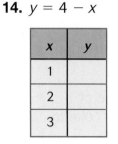

x	y
1	
2	
3	

15. $y = 2x - 2$

x	y
1	
2	
3	

Use the map at the right for Exercises 16–18.

16. Start at Town Hall. Walk 2 blocks east and 3 blocks north. Where are you?

17. Start at Town Hall. Walk 2 blocks west and 3 blocks south. Where are you?

18. From Town Hall, how would you get to the Park?

19. Math Reasoning Is the location of (⁻3, 5) the same as (5, ⁻3)? Explain.

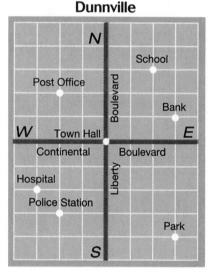

Dunnville

Mixed Review

20. During the season, Tom batted 96 times and got 36 hits. Maria batted 72 times and had the same ratio of hits to times at bat as Tom. How many hits did Maria get?

Algebra Solve each equation. Check your answer.

21. $5x - 7 = 13$

22. $4n + 15 = 31$

23. $20 = 14 + 6x$

24. Algebra The table at the right gives values for $y = 2x + 5$. If $y = 13$, what is the value of x?

x	0	2	4	6
y	5	9	13	17

Test Prep Choose the correct letter for each answer.

25. Find the mean of the following data *without* the outlier.
(2-2) 25, 20, 15, 45, 20

   A 125   **B** 80   **C** 25   **D** 20

26. Which of the following methods is most likely to select a sample
(3-6) that is representative of the population?

   F convenience sampling   **H** responses to a survey

   G random sampling   **J** none

Diagnostic Checkpoint

Solve each equation. Check your answer.

1. $9x - 5 = 58$
(10-1)

2. $\dfrac{n}{6} + 4 = 12$
(10-1)

3. $29 - 2t = 19$
(10-1)

4. $5x + 6 = 21$
(10-1)

The table at the right gives values for the equation $c = \$0.08m + \$4.50$, which shows the relationship between the number of minutes, m, and the monthly cost of long-distance telephone service.

m	c
50	$8.50
100	$12.50
150	$16.50
200	$20.50

5. How many minutes were used if the total cost was $16.50?
(10-3)

6. What is the total cost of using 200 minutes in a month?
(10-3)

Write the ordered pair for each point in the coordinate grid at the right.

7. A
(10-4)

8. G
(10-4)

9. K
(10-4)

10. M
(10-4)

11. B
(10-4)

12. H
(10-4)

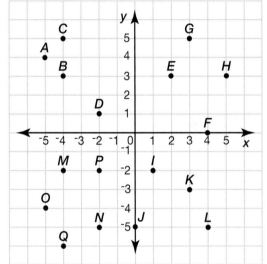

13. Write the letter of the point named by the ordered pair $(^-2, ^-5)$.
(10-4)

14. Complete the table of ordered pairs and graph the equation on a coordinate grid.
(10-4)

$y = 3x - 1$

x	y
$^-1$	
0	
1	

15. Christina is making elf costumes for a play. It takes her 7.5 hours to make a tunic and 2.5 hours to make a cap. Write an expression to represent the total time it takes Christina to make t tunics and c caps. How long would it take Christina to make 4 tunics and 5 caps?
(10-2)

Solving Equations Using Graphs

Algebra

Warm-Up Review

Evaluate each expression for $x = {}^-2$, 3, and 6.

1. $x - 4$

2. $8 - 6x$

3. $10x + 9$

4. A submarine is 100 feet below sea level before diving 8 minutes at a rate of 20 feet per minute. Find the submarine's new position.

California Content Standard *Algebra and Functions 1.0: Students . . . solve simple linear equations and graph and interpret their results. Also, Mathematical Reasoning 2.3 (See p. 383.)*

Math Link You know how to graph points in a coordinate plane. Now you will learn how to graph and solve equations by plotting points.

Example 1

When Steven got home, the temperature was 7°F. It dropped 2° an hour for the next 5 hours. How long after Steven got home was the temperature $^-2$°F?

The equation $y = 7 - 2x$ represents the relationship between the temperature, y, and the number of hours, x, since Steven got home. Make a table of ordered pairs for the equation $y = 7 - 2x$.

x	1	2	3	4	5
y	5	3	1	$^-1$	$^-3$

Plot the points on a coordinate grid and connect them. To find the value of x when $y = {}^-2$, go to $^-2$ on the y-axis. Then move across to the line. When you reach the line, move up to the x-axis.

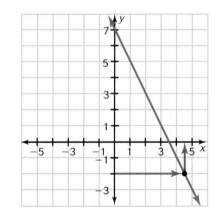

When $y = {}^-2$, x is halfway between 4 and 5. The solution to $^-2 = 7 - 2x$ is $x = 4.5$.

The temperature was $^-2$°F, 4.5 hours after Steven got home.

Example 2

Use the graph of $y = \frac{1}{2}x - 1$ at the right to solve $1 = \frac{1}{2}x - 1$.

To find the value of x when $y = 1$, go to 1 on the y-axis. Then move across to the line. When you reach the line move down to the x-axis.

When $y = 1$, $x = 4$.

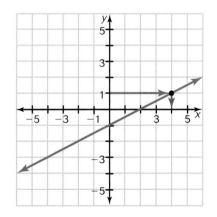

Additional Standards: Mathematical Reasoning 2.4 (See p. 383.)

Guided Practice *For another example, see Set D on p. 407.*

For Exercises 1–3, use the graph of $y = 2x - 1$ at the right to solve the equation.

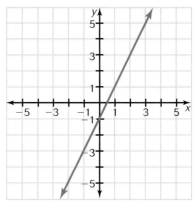

1. $3 = 2x - 1$ **2.** $-1 = 2x - 1$ **3.** $4 = 2x - 1$

4. Math Reasoning Use the graph for Example 1 on page 394. If the temperature had been dropping at the same rate for 5 hours before Steven got home, when was the temperature 11°F?

Independent Practice *For more practice, see Set D on p. 409.*

For Exercises 5–7, use the graph of $y = 3 - \frac{1}{2}x$ at the right to solve the equation.

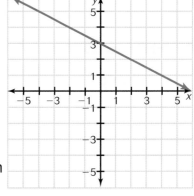

5. $4 = 3 - \frac{1}{2}x$ **6.** $2 = 3 - \frac{1}{2}x$ **7.** $1\frac{1}{2} = 3 - \frac{1}{2}x$

8. Math Reasoning The graph for Example 1 on page 394 shows all values for y and x. For example, the graph includes the point (1.54, 3.92). Does this value make sense in the situation, that is, could the temperature have been 3.92°F, 1.54 hours after Steven got home? Explain.

Mixed Review

9. Mental Math Rick bought a cap for 15% off the ticketed price of $20. How much did he save?

10. Algebra Make a table for $y = 5x + 3$ when $x = {}^{-}2, 0, 2,$ and 4. Use it to solve $^{-}7 = 5x + 3$.

11. Use grid paper to plot each point. Connect the points in the order given and name the figure formed.

$(3, 2), (0, 4), (^{-}3, 1), (^{-}2, ^{-}3), (2, ^{-}3)$

Test Prep   Choose the correct letter for each answer.

Use the triangle at the right for Questions 12 and 13.

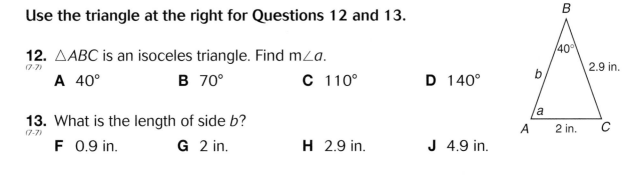

12. $\triangle ABC$ is an isoceles triangle. Find $m\angle a$.
(7-7)

   A 40°   **B** 70°   **C** 110°   **D** 140°

13. What is the length of side b?
(7-7)

   F 0.9 in.   **G** 2 in.   **H** 2.9 in.   **J** 4.9 in.

Use Homework Workbook 10-5.   **395**

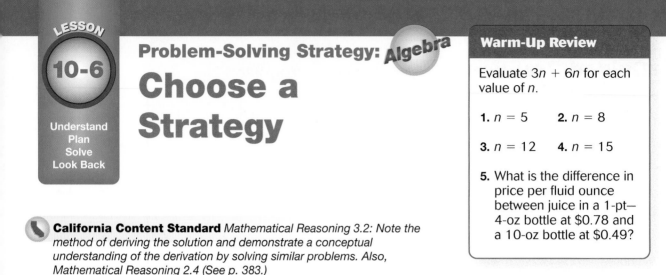

LESSON
10-6

Understand
Plan
Solve
Look Back

Problem-Solving Strategy: Algebra

Choose a Strategy

Warm-Up Review

Evaluate $3n + 6n$ for each value of n.

1. $n = 5$ **2.** $n = 8$

3. $n = 12$ **4.** $n = 15$

5. What is the difference in price per fluid ounce between juice in a 1-pt–4-oz bottle at $0.78 and a 10-oz bottle at $0.49?

California Content Standard *Mathematical Reasoning 3.2: Note the method of deriving the solution and demonstrate a conceptual understanding of the derivation by solving similar problems. Also, Mathematical Reasoning 2.4 (See p. 383.)*

Last week, the Acme Cycle Factory made twice as many tricycles as bicycles. If they used 320 wheels, how many of each kind did they make?

Understand

What do you need to know?

Bicycles have two wheels and tricycles have three wheels.

Plan

How can you solve the problem?

Choose a strategy you can use to solve the problem.

Solve

The bicycle wheels plus the tricycle wheels equals 320 wheels.

Use a Table

Number		Total Number of Wheels		
		Bicycle wheels ↓	Tricycle wheels ↓	Total wheels ↓
Bicycles	**Tricycles**			
25	50	$2 \times 25 + 3 \times 50 = 200$ (too low)		
50	100	$2 \times 50 + 3 \times 100 = 400$ (too high)		
40	80	$2 \times 40 + 3 \times 80 = 320$		

The factory made 40 bicycles and 80 tricycles.

Write an Equation

Let n be the number of bicycles. Then $2n$ is the number of tricycles, since there are twice as many.

$$(2 \times n) + (3 \times 2n) = 320$$
$$2n + 6n = 320$$
$$8n = 320$$
$$n = 40$$
$$n = 40, \text{ so } 2n = 80$$

Look Back

How can knowing more than one strategy to use be helpful in checking your work?

Additional Standards: Number Sense 2.1; Algebra and Functions 1.0; Mathematical Reasoning 1.1 (See p. 383.)

Try these or other strategies to solve each problem. Tell which strategy you used.

Problem-Solving Strategies

- *Find a Pattern*
- *Make a Graph*
- *Work Backward*
- *Make a Table*
- *Write an Equation*
- *Use Logical Reasoning*

Guided Practice

1. Grapes cost $0.75 per pound and apples cost $0.80 per pound. Chad bought $8\frac{1}{2}$ pounds of apples and some grapes. He spent $9.05. How many pounds of grapes did he buy?

2. Pat bicycled $1\frac{1}{2}$ miles on Monday. On Tuesday she rode $\frac{1}{4}$ mile more than she did on Monday. For the next three days she rode $\frac{1}{4}$ mile more than she did each previous day. How many miles had she traveled after 5 days?

Independent Practice

3. Jan goes to the swimming pool every third day. Gil goes to the same pool every fifth day. Both are at the pool on the same day. In how many days will they both be at the pool on the same day again?

4. Use the clues below to find the missing digits of the phone number 800-*jkmn*.

   Clue 1: *j*, *k*, *m*, and *n* are different.
   Clue 2: Only *m*, and *n* are prime.
   Clue 3: Only *j*, *m*, and *n* are odd.
   Clue 4: $n = 5$.

   Clue 5: $m < n$
   Clue 6: $j \times j = 1$
   Clue 7: The sum of $k + k$ is 0.

5. Trees were planted at Lafayette Park. One-fifth of the trees were damaged in a storm. There are 80 undamaged trees left. How many trees were there before the storm?

6. Don likes the roller coaster, Sue likes the Tilt-A-Whirl, and Amy likes the Whip. Don has $2.20, Sue has $1.30, and Amy has $1.90. If they combine their money, do they have enough so that each can go on their favorite ride twice?

Formulas and Variables

Algebra

California Content Standard *Algebra and Functions 1.0: Students . . . solve simple linear equations . . . and interpret their results.*

Warm-Up Review

Solve each equation. Check your answer.

1. $\frac{4}{5}x = 40$

2. $8x = 60$

3. $7 = 3n + 19$

4. You buy a pair of shoes on sale for 25% off. The shoes regularly cost $48. How much must you pay, including 5% tax?

Math Link You know how to evaluate an algebraic expression and solve an equation. Now you will learn how to use formulas.

A **formula** is a rule showing relationships among quantities. Formulas usually contain variables.

Example 1

How long will it take to travel 145 miles at a speed of 58 miles per hour?

You can use the formula $d = rt$, where d is distance, r is the rate of speed, and t is the time, to solve the problem.

Word Bank

formula

$$d = r \times t \qquad \text{Write the formula.}$$
$$145 = 58t \qquad \text{Substitute 145 for } d \text{ and 58 for } r.$$
$$\frac{145}{58} = \frac{58t}{58} \qquad \text{Divide each side by 58.}$$
$$2.5 = t$$

It will take 2.5 hours to travel 145 miles.

Example 2

The formula $g = \frac{25k}{6}$ can be used to find the percent of gold, g, in a piece of jewelry where k equals karats. Find the percent of gold in an 18-karat gold necklace.

$$g = \frac{25k}{6} \qquad \text{Write the formula.}$$
$$g = \frac{25 \times 18}{6} \qquad \text{Substitute 18 for } k.$$
$$g = \frac{25 \times \overset{3}{\cancel{18}}}{\underset{1}{\cancel{6}}} \qquad \text{Multiply.}$$
$$g = 75$$

An 18-karat gold necklace is 75% gold.

Example 3

When a team wins w games and loses ℓ games, its winning percentage, p, is given by the formula $p = \frac{w}{w + \ell}$. The value of p is always a decimal rounded to the nearest thousandth. Find the winning percentage of a volleyball team with 10 wins and 6 losses.

$$p = \frac{w}{w + \ell} \qquad \text{Write the formula.}$$
$$p = \frac{10}{10 + 6} \qquad \text{Substitute 10 for } w \text{ and 6 for } \ell.$$
$$p = \frac{10}{16} \qquad \text{Divide. If necessary, round to the nearest thousandth.}$$
$$p = 0.625$$

The volleyball team has a winning percentage of 0.625.

Additional Standard: Number Sense 1.4 (✎) (See p. 383.)

Guided Practice

For another example, see Set E on p. 407.

Use the formula $d = rt$ for Exercises 1 and 2.

1. $d = 330$ mi; $r = 55$ mph. Find t.

2. $d = 102$ km; $t = 1.2$ hr. Find r.

3. The formula $f = \$0.25 + \$0.05d$ represents the relationship between the number of days, d, a book is overdue and the amount of the fine, f. What is the fine for a book that is 10 days overdue?

4. Use the formula in Exercise 3. Ben paid an overdue book fine of $1.30. How many days was his book overdue?

Independent Practice

For more practice, see Set E on p. 409.

Use the formula $c = 22d + 10$, where c is the total cost to rent a pair of skis and d is the number of days the skis are rented. Find each missing value.

5. $d = 4$ days. Find c.

6. $c = \$142$. Find d.

7. While vacationing in Canada, Rick and Rachel saw that temperatures were given in degrees Celsius, C. Use the formula $F = \frac{9}{5}C + 32$ to find what temperature in degrees Farenheit F is equal to 25°C.

8. **Math Reasoning** Write a formula for the total cost, c, of an item with a price, p, and a 6% sales tax.

Mixed Review

9. The rate of sales tax is 6.25%. If four footballs cost $95.00, find the total cost.

10. Complete the table of ordered pairs at the right and graph the equation $y = 2 - \frac{1}{3}x$ on a coordinate grid.

x	$y = 2 - \frac{1}{3}x$
0	
3	
6	

11. Use the graph from Exercise 10 to solve the equation $3 = 2 - \frac{1}{3}x$.

Test Prep Choose the correct letter for each answer.

12. 1 gallon =
(7-1)

  A 4 cups   **C** 6 pints

  B 4 quarts   **D** 100 ounces

13. 3.5 mm =
(7-2)

  F 0.35 cm   **H** 350 cm

  G 3.5 cm   **J** 3,500 cm

LESSON

10-8

Understand
Plan
Solve
Look Back

Problem-Solving Application:
Use a Formula

Algebra

⚑ **California Content Standard**
Algebra and Functions 1.0:
Students . . . solve simple linear equations . . .

Warm-Up Review

Solve each equation.

1. $8 = 1.25x$

2. $2x - 9 = 7$

3. The Smith family paid $4.50 each for 4 movie tickets plus $10.70 for popcorn and juice. How much did they spend?

Crickets chirp faster as the temperature rises. The formula $F = \frac{c}{4} + 40$ represents the relationship between the temperature in degrees Fahrenheit, F, and the number of times a cricket chirps, c, in a minute. How many times will a cricket chirp in a minute when the temperature is 84°F?

Understand

What do you need to find?

You need to find the value of c when $F = 84$.

Plan

How can you solve the problem?

You can solve the formula for c before you substitute.

Solve

$$F = \frac{c}{4} + 40 \qquad \text{Write the formula.}$$

$$F - 40 = \frac{c}{4} + 40 - 40 \quad \text{Subtract 40 from both sides.}$$

$$F - 40 = \frac{c}{4}$$

$$4(F - 40) = \frac{c}{4} \times \frac{4}{1} \qquad \text{Multiply both sides by 4.}$$

$$4(F - 40) = c$$

Substitute 84 for F. Then solve the equation.

$$c = 4(F - 40) \qquad \text{Write the equation.}$$
$$c = 4(84 - 40) \qquad \text{Do the operation inside the parentheses first.}$$
$$c = 4 \times 44 \qquad \text{Multiply.}$$
$$c = 176$$

When the temperature is 84°, a cricket chirps 176 times a minute.

Look Back

How can you check your answer?

400

⚑ Additional Standards: Algebra and Functions 1.2 (🔑); Mathematical Reasoning 2.5 (See p. 383.)

Guided Practice

1. Use the formula given on page 400 to find how many times a cricket will chirp when the temperature is 68°F.

2. The formula $c = 1.39g$ gives the total cost c for g gallons of gasoline. Solve the formula for g. Then find the number of gallons you can buy for $20. Round your answer down to the nearest gallon.

Independent Practice

3. The formula $p = 25b - 46$ can be used to find the amount of profit, p, Stan can make selling b birdhouses. Solve the formula for b. Then find how many birdhouses Stan needs to sell in order to make a profit of $800.

4. The formula $a = \dfrac{h}{b}$ gives the batting average, a, for number of hits, h, and number of times at bat, b. Tina expects to have 40 at bats during this year's softball season. She hopes to have a batting average of 0.320. Solve the formula for h. Then find how many hits she will need to reach her goal.

5. Adam hopes to have 14 hits during this baseball season. Use the formula in Exercise 4 to find how many at bats he will need to have a batting average of 0.250.

Mixed Review

6. Using the recipe and ad at the right, find how much it will cost to prepare a vegetable salad for 12 people.

7. If the price of tomatoes changes to $0.80 a pound, how much less will it cost to prepare the salad for 12 people?

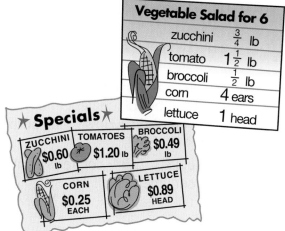

Vegetable Salad for 6	
zucchini	$\frac{3}{4}$ lb
tomato	$1\frac{1}{2}$ lb
broccoli	$\frac{1}{2}$ lb
corn	4 ears
lettuce	1 head

★ Specials ★

ZUCCHINI $0.60 lb   TOMATOES $1.20 lb   BROCCOLI $0.49 lb

CORN $0.25 EACH   LETTUCE $0.89 HEAD

8. Bank A pays 6% interest on $1,000 savings each year. Bank B pays 3% every 6 months and adds the interest to the principal for the second six months. Which account pays more in one year? Explain.

9. Gary is a deep-sea scuba diver. When rising from a very deep dive, he must stop every 20 feet and wait for 10 minutes. This helps his body adjust to the water pressure as he rises. How many times must he stop as he rises from a depth of 100 feet?

Use Homework Workbook 10-8.

Diagnostic Checkpoint

Complete. For Exercises 1–4, use the words from the Word Bank.

1. In a coordinate grid, the x-axis and the y-axis meet at a
(10-4) point called the _____.

2. You can use an _____ to describe a
(10-4) location on a coordinate grid.

3. A _____ is a rule showing relationships
(10-7) among quantities.

4. Multiplication and division are _____
(10-1) because they undo each other.

Use the graph of $y = 1 - \frac{2}{3}x$ at the right to solve each equation.

5. $3 = 1 - \frac{2}{3}x$
(10-5)

6. $^-1 = 1 - \frac{2}{3}x$
(10-5)

7. $1 = 1 - \frac{2}{3}x$
(10-5)

8. $^-3 = 1 - \frac{2}{3}x$
(10-5)

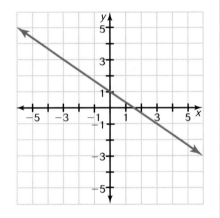

Use the formula $d = rt$ to find the missing value.

9. $d = 22.5$ miles, $r = 45$ miles per hour. Find t.
(10-7)

10. $d = 380$ kilometers, $t = 5$ hours. Find r.
(10-7)

11. There were 8 more jugglers than acrobats in the parade.
(10-6) The total number of jugglers and acrobats was 26. How many
jugglers were there? How many acrobats?

12. The formula $c = 2.54i$ converts centimeters, c, to inches, i. Zach
(10-8) is 152.4 centimeters tall. His sister Brittany is 127 centimeters
tall. How tall is each in inches? Solve the formula for i. Then solve
the problem.

13. Maya's parents are buying a car. The price, p, for the car is
(10-8) $10,000. The sales tax is 6%. Use the formula $t = p + 0.06p$
to find the total cost, t, of the car, including sales tax.

Chapter 10 Test

Solve each equation. Check your answers.

1. $6x - 11 = 31$

2. $4x + 25 = 61$

3. $19 - 7x = 12$

4. The table at the right gives values for $y = 8x - 25$. If $y = 135$, what is the value of x?

x	10	20	30
y	55	135	215

Write the ordered pair for each point in the coordinate grid at the right.

5. A

6. B

7. C

8. D

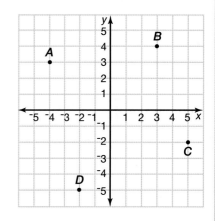

Use the formula $d = rt$ to find the missing value.

9. Find d when $r = 55$ miles per hour and $t = 5$ hours.

10. Find t when $d = 210$ kilometers and $r = 84$ kilometers per hour.

Use the graph of $y = 2 - x$ on the right to solve each equation.

11. $3 = 2 - x$

12. $^-2 = 2 - x$

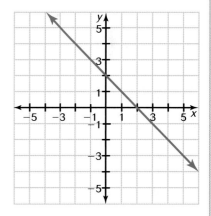

13. Write an expression to represent the total weight in an elevator holding s students with an average weight of 90 pounds and t teachers with an average weight of 150 pounds. What is the weight of 6 students and 2 teachers?

14. The formula $c = \$2r + \$5$ gives the total cost, c, for admission to an amusement park and r ride tickets. How many ride tickets can you buy if you have $35? Solve the formula for r. Then solve the problem.

15. Use the sign at the right. The McGuire family bought twice as many team photos as they did pennants. If they spent $22 on souvenirs, how many of each item did they buy?

SOUVENIRS

PROGRAMS $3.50
PENNANTS $4.00
BASEBALL $6.00
TEAM PHOTO $3.50
T-SHIRTS $12.00

Multiple-Choice Chapter 10 Test

Choose the correct letter for each answer.

1. Clarissa sells real estate. She earns $2,000 per month plus 3% commission on her sales. Last month she earned $5,750. Solve the equation $0.03s + 2,000 = 5,750$ to find Clarissa's sales s last month.

   A $s = \$112.50$

   B $s = \$125$

   C $s = \$112,500$

   D $s = \$125,000$

Use the table for Questions 2 and 3.

x	$y = 9 - 7x$
⁻2	23
0	9
2	⁻5
4	⁻19

2. Solve $^-5 = 9 - 7x$.

   F $x = {}^-2$

   G $x = 0$

   H $x = 1$

   J $x = 2$

3. Solve $^-19 = 7x + 9$.

   A $x = {}^-2$ C $x = 2$

   B $x = 0$ D $x = {}^-4$

4. Solve the equation $2x - 10 = 4$.

   F $x = {}^-3$ H $x = 7$

   G $x = 2$ J $x = 14$

Use the sign for Questions 5–7.

TICKET PRICES

BLEACHERS $5.50
GRANDSTAND $7.50
BOX SEATS $12.00

5. Which expression represents the cost of b bleacher tickets, g grandstand tickets, and x box seats?

   A $5.50b + 7.50g$

   B $5.50g + 7.50b$

   C $5.50b + 7.50g + 12x$

   D $5.50g + 7.50b + 12x$

6. How much do 3 bleacher tickets and 4 grandstand tickets cost?

   F $46.50

   G $45.50

   H $30.00

   J $16.50

7. The Lewis family spent $44.50 on bleacher and grandstand tickets. How many of each kind did they buy?

   A   3 bleacher and 3 grandstand

   B   4 bleacher and 3 grandstand

   C   3 bleacher and 4 grandstand

   D   4 bleacher and 4 grandstand

Use the coordinate grid for Questions 8 and 9.

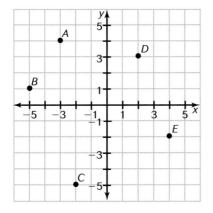

Use the graph of $y = 3x - 4$ for Questions 12 and 13.

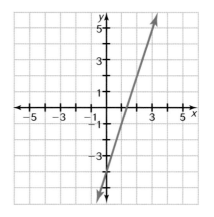

8. Which is the ordered pair for point B?

F (⁻5, 1)

G (5, ⁻1)

H (1, ⁻5)

J (⁻1, 5)

K NH

9. Which point is at (⁻2, ⁻5)?

A Point A   D Point E

B Point C   E NH

C Point D

10. Use the formula $d = rt$ to find r, the rate of speed needed to travel a distance, d, of 318 miles in 6 hours, t.

F 51 mph   H 55 mph

G 53 mph   J 60 mph

11. Solve the formula $c = 1.06p$ for p.

A $p = c + 1.06$

B $p = c - 1.06$

C $p = \dfrac{1.06}{c}$

D $p = \dfrac{c}{1.06}$

12. Use the graph to solve $5 = 3x - 4$.

F $x = 1$ J $x = 5$

G $x = 2$ K NH

H $x = 3$

13. Use the graph to solve $⁻1 = 3x - 4$.

A $x = 1$ D $x = 5$

B $x = 2$ E NH

C $x = 3$

14. Use the formula $d = rt$ to find the value of d when $r = 60$ miles per hour and $t = 4$ hours.

F 15 miles   H 64 miles

G 56 miles   J 240 miles

15. Solve the equation $5x + 15 = 50$.

A $x = 3$

B $x = 7$

C $x = 10$

D $x = 13$

Reteaching

Set A (pages 384–385)

Solve $4x + 21 = 61$.

$4x + 21 - 21 = 61 - 21$ Subtract 21 from both sides.

$$4x = 40$$
$$\frac{4x}{4} = \frac{40}{4}$$ Divide both sides by 4.

$$x = 10$$

Remember to undo addition and subtraction before you undo multiplication and division.

Solve each equation. Check your answer.

1. $9x - 15 = 12$ **2.** $\frac{n}{7} + 6 = 2$

3. $\frac{m}{4} - 3 = 6$ **4.** $58 = 8y + 18$

Set B (pages 388–389)

The table below gives values for $y = 4x - 3$. Use it to solve $5 = 4x - 3$.

x	0	1	2	3	4	5
y	-3	1	5	9	13	17

Find $y = 5$ in the table, when $y = 5$, $x = 2$.
The solution is $x = 2$.

Remember you can use a table to solve an equation.

Use the table at the left to solve each equation. Check your answer.

1. $-3 = 4x - 3$

2. $13 = 4x - 3$

3. $9 = 4x - 3$

4. $1 = 4x - 3$

Set C (pages 390–392)

Complete the table of ordered pairs and graph the equation $y = x - 2$.

x	0	1	2	3	4
y	-2	-1	0	1	2

Graph the points. Draw a line through them.

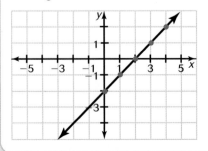

Remember you can graph an equation by graphing ordered pairs that make the equation true.

Complete the table of ordered pairs and graph each equation on a coordinate grid.

1. $y = 3 - x$

x	-1	3	5
y			

2. $y = 3x - 1$

x	-1	0	1
y			

Set D *(pages 394–395)*

Use the graph of y = x + 2 below to solve the equation ⁻1 = x + 2.

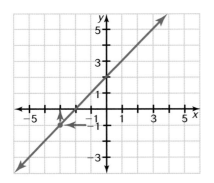

Go to ⁻1 on the *y*-axis, move across to the line, move up to the *x*-axis.
The solution is $x = ^-3$.

Remember you can use the graph of $y = x + 2$ to solve an equation like $^-1 = x + 2$ by finding the *x*-coordinate of the point where $y = ^-1$.

Use the graph at the left to solve each equation.

1. $^-2 = x + 2$ **2.** $4 = x + 2$

3. $^-3 = x + 2$ **4.** $2 = x + 2$

5. $1 = x + 2$ **6.** $3 = x + 2$

7. $0 = x + 2$ **8.** $5 = x + 2$

Set E *(pages 398–399)*

A store has T-shirts for $8 each and jeans for $35 each. There is 5% sales tax. The formula $c = 36.75j + 8.40t$ gives the total cost, c, of j jeans and t T-shirts. Use the formula to find the number of jeans purchased, j, when $c = 98.70$ and $t = 3$.

$$c = 36.75j + 8.40t$$

$98.70 = 36.75j + 8.40 \times 3$ Substitute 98.70 for c and 3 for t.

$98.70 = 36.75j + 25.20$ Multiply.

$73.50 = 36.75j$ Subtract 25.20 from both sides.

$\dfrac{73.50}{36.75} = \dfrac{36.75j}{36.75}$ Divide both sides by 36.75.

$2 = j$

The solution is $j = 2$. Two pairs of jeans were purchased.

Remember you can substitute known values into a formula and solve for the unknown value.

Use the formula $c = 36.75j + 8.40t$ to find the missing value.

1. Find c when $j = 3$ and $t = 5$.

2. Find t when $c = 78.75$ and $j = 1$.

3. Find j when $c = 107.10$ and $t = 4$.

4. Find c when $j = 4$ and $t = 7$.

5. Find j when $c = 90.30$ and $t = 2$.

6. Find t when $c = 127.05$ and $j = 3$.

7. Find c when $j = 2$ and $t = 5$.

More Practice

Set A *(pages 384–385)*

Solve each equation. Check your answer.

1. $12x - 8 = 28$ **2.** $\frac{m}{4} - 9 = 5$ **3.** $16 = 30 - 7x$ **4.** $\frac{t}{8} - 15 = 5$

5. $100 = 7x + 51$ **6.** $\frac{h}{10} + 42 = 45$ **7.** $8x + 15 = 39$ **8.** $9 - x = 4$

9. Nicole paid $21.50 to join a discount book club and get her first set of books. Membership in the club costs $9. Members can buy books for $2.50 each. Use the equation $2.50b + 9 = 21.50$ to find how many books Nicole got.

Set B *(pages 388–389)*

The table at the right gives values for $y = 15 - 8x$.
Use this table to solve each equation.

x	-2	0	2	4
y	31	15	-1	-17

1. $-1 = 15 - 8x$ **2.** $31 = 15 - 8x$ **3.** $15 = 15 - 8x$

4. Make a table for $y = 9x - 10$ when $x = 1, 2, 3, 4,$ and 5. Use it to solve $-1 = 9x - 10$.

Set C *(pages 390–392)*

Write the ordered pair for each point in the coordinate grid at the right.

1. A **2.** K **3.** O

4. E **5.** B **6.** R

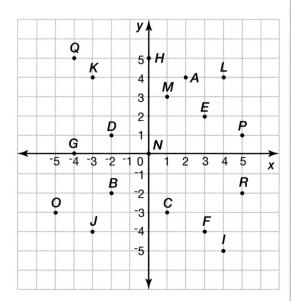

Name the point for each ordered pair in the coordinate grid at the right.

7. $(-2, 1)$ **8.** $(-4, 0)$ **9.** $(5, 1)$

Complete the table of ordered pairs and graph each equation on a coordinate grid;

10. $y = 2x - 2$

x	0	1	2	3
y				

11. $y = 2 - x$

x	-2	0	4
y			

Set D *(pages 394–395)*

Use the graph of $y = 1 - 3x$ at the right to solve each equation.

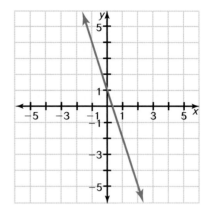

1. $4 = 1 - 3x$

2. $^-5 = 1 - 3x$

3. $^-2 = 1 - 3x$

4. $1 = 1 - 3x$

Set E *(pages 398–399)*

Use the formula $c = \$0.25m + \$25.00$, where c is the cost to rent a car and m is the number of miles it is driven. Find each missing value.

1. Find c when $m = 270$ miles.

2. Find m when $c = \$150$.

3. Find m when $c = \$71.25$.

4. Find c when $m = 875$ miles.

Use the formula $c = 2.50s + 1.75j$, where c is the total cost for s sandwiches and j cartons of juice. Find each missing value.

5. Find c when $s = 2$ and $j = 3$.

6. Find j when $c = \$16.25$ and $s = 3$.

7. Find s when $c = \$19.50$ and $j = 4$.

8. Find c when $s = 10$ and $j = 10$.

9. Use the formula $g = \dfrac{25k}{6}$ to find the percent of gold, g, in a piece of jewelry, where k is the number of karats. Find the percent of gold in a 24-karat gold ring.

10. Shannon's team has 24 wins, w, and 11 losses, ℓ. Use the formula $p = \dfrac{w}{w + \ell}$ to find the team's winning percentage, p, to the nearest thousandth.

11. Jill spends a total of $2 per day for bus fare and $2.50 per day for lunch. Some days she takes her lunch. This week, Jill has $17.50 to spend. She has to ride the bus 5 days. How many days can she buy lunch? Use the formula $c = 2b + 2.50\ell$, where c is the total cost for Jill to ride the bus b days and to eat lunch ℓ days.

Problem Solving: Preparing for Tests

Choose the correct letter for each answer.

1. Janine was cutting a 12-foot board into $\frac{3}{4}$-inch wide strips. How much of the board was left after she had cut 24 strips?

    A $9\frac{3}{4}$ ft

    B   10 ft

    C $10\frac{1}{2}$ ft

    D $11\frac{1}{4}$ ft

    E   NH

    Tip
    Notice that the answer choices are in feet.

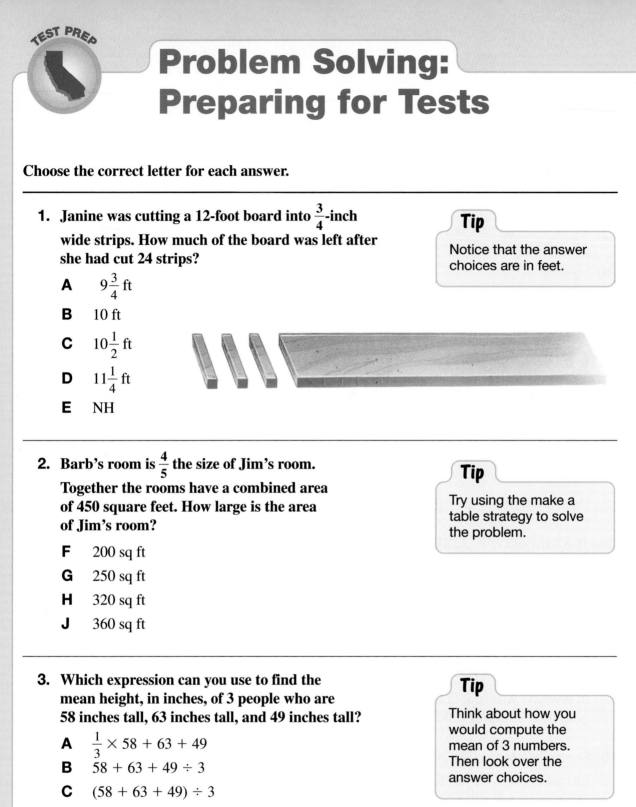

2. Barb's room is $\frac{4}{5}$ the size of Jim's room. Together the rooms have a combined area of 450 square feet. How large is the area of Jim's room?

    F   200 sq ft

    G   250 sq ft

    H   320 sq ft

    J   360 sq ft

    Tip
    Try using the make a table strategy to solve the problem.

3. Which expression can you use to find the mean height, in inches, of 3 people who are 58 inches tall, 63 inches tall, and 49 inches tall?

    A $\frac{1}{3} \times 58 + 63 + 49$

    B $58 + 63 + 49 \div 3$

    C $(58 + 63 + 49) \div 3$

    D $(58 + 63 + 49) \times 3$

    Tip
    Think about how you would compute the mean of 3 numbers. Then look over the answer choices.

4. Two years ago, a computer cost $1,950. Today, the cost of the same computer is 10% less than it was last year. If the price last year was $1,489, which is the best estimate for the price of the computer today?

F $800

G $1,000

H $1,100

J $1,350

---

5. Bill made this drawing as part of a wall mural. Which statement best describes the relationship of the two triangles?

A   They are congruent.

B   They are similar.

C   They are both right triangles.

D   One is a reflection of the other.

---

6. How many squares are in the figure shown?

F   4

G   6

H   8

J   10

---

7. Lyle collects rocks, and his sister collects shells. She has 64 shells in her collection. If Lyle gives one-third of his rock collection to his sister, she will get 37 rocks. How many rocks are in Lyle's collection?

A   37   **C**   111

B   74   **D**   148

The graph shows the percent of types of shoes sold by Shoe City. Use the graph for Questions 8 and 9.

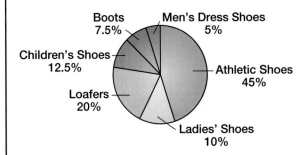

8. If Shoe City sold $200,000 worth of shoes last year, how much was from the sale of loafers?

F $40,000

G $20,000

H $10,000

J $5,000

---

9. If Shoe City sold $350,000 worth of shoes last year, how much was from the sale of boots?

A $26,250

B $26,500

C $43,750

D $44,000

---

10. Louise drew two similar triangles. The sides of the smaller triangle are half the length of the larger triangle. Two of the angles in the smaller triangle are 60° and 70°. What is the measure of the third angle in the smaller triangle?

F   40°

G   50°

H   60°

J   70°

Multiple Choice
Cumulative Review

Choose the correct letter for each answer.

Number Sense

1. An adult male has about 4.7 liters of blood in his body. During strenuous exercise the human heart may pump as much as 45 liters per minute. About how many times does the entire blood supply circulate through the heart in one minute of exercise?

   A   About 5 times

   B   About 10 times

   C   About 15 times

   D   About 20 times

2. Which is the best estimate of $3\frac{7}{8} + 2\frac{1}{16}$?

   F   2   **H**   6

   G   4   **J**   8

3. Find $9\frac{1}{2}\%$ of 8,000.

   A   680   **D**   800

   B   720   **E**   NH

   C   760

4. Find $4\frac{4}{5} \times 8\frac{3}{4}$.

   F   6

   G $32\frac{7}{20}$

   H   36

   J   42

   k   NH

Statistics Data Analysis and Probability

Use the bar graph for Questions 5 and 6.

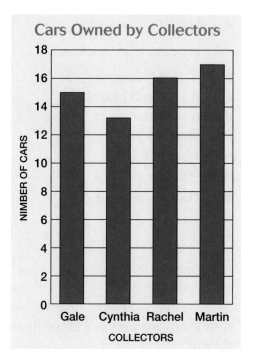

Cars Owned by Collectors

5. How many model cars would Cynthia have to add to her collection to be able to divide her collection equally among herself and three friends?

   A 1   **B** 2   **C** 3   **D** 4

6. Gale and Cynthia combine their collections. If they divide the combined collection evenly among 7 friends how many model cars does each get?

   F   4

   G   7

   H   14

   J   28

7. Which point is at $^-3$?

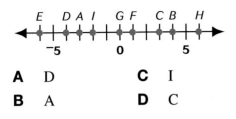

    A   D   **C**   I

    B   A   **D**   C

---

8. Which equation could be used to represent this situation?

On Thanksgiving Day, there are parades in many cities around the country. Some parades have many giant balloons. At one parade, there were 58 entries that were not giant balloons. If there was a total of 77 entries, how many were giant balloons?

    F $x + 58 = 77$

    G $x - 58 = 77$

    H $x - 77 = 58$

    J $x = 77 + 58$

---

9. Solve $a - 1 = {}^-5$.

    A $a = {}^-6$

    B $a = {}^-4$

    C $c = 4$

    D $a = 6$

---

10. Which expression represents two more than a number?

    F $n - 2$

    G $\frac{1}{2}n$

    H $n + 2$

    J $2n$

---

11. Solve $\frac{2}{3}n = 24$.

    A $n = 16$

    B $n = 24\frac{2}{3}$

    C $n = 30$

    D $n = 36$

---

12. A map has a scale of 2 centimeters = 5 kilometers. The distance between two towns on the map is 9 centimeters. What is the actual distance between the towns?

    F   about 1 kilometer

    G   3.6 kilometers

    H   20 kilometers

    J   22.5 kilometers

---

13. Ms. Thompson bought 30 oranges for $6.75. What was the unit price, rounded to nearest cent?

    A   6.75¢ each

    B   21¢ each

    C   23¢ each

    D $6.75

---

14. Two angles of a triangle have measures of 55° and 32°. Which equation could you use to find the measure of the third angle?

    F $m - 55 - 32 = 180$

    G $m + 55 + 32 = 180$

    H $m + 55 = 180 + 32$

    J $m + 55 + 32 = 360$

Probability

Diagnosing Readiness

In Chapter 11, you will use these skills:

Ⓐ Adding and Subtracting Fractions

(pages 176–178, 182–185)

1. $\frac{5}{8} + \frac{1}{8}$ **2.** $\frac{2}{3} + \frac{1}{6}$

3. $\frac{1}{2} + \frac{3}{8}$ **4.** $\frac{1}{2} + \frac{3}{16}$

5. $1 - \frac{5}{7}$ **6.** $1 - \frac{3}{5}$

7. $\frac{1}{5} - \frac{1}{10}$ **8.** $\frac{4}{7} - \frac{2}{21}$

9. Mindy ate $\frac{1}{3}$ of the pizza and Kendra ate $\frac{5}{12}$ of it. What part of the pizza was left for their little brother Austin?

Ⓑ Multiplying Fractions

(pages 192–193)

10. $\frac{1}{4} \times \frac{3}{4}$ **11.** $\frac{4}{5} \times \frac{3}{4}$

12. $\frac{1}{2} \times \frac{3}{7}$ **13.** $\frac{4}{9} \times \frac{3}{4}$

14. $\frac{1}{7} \times \frac{2}{3}$ **15.** $\frac{1}{2} \times \frac{4}{5}$

16. $\frac{5}{6} \times \frac{3}{5}$ **17.** $\frac{4}{9} \times \frac{3}{5}$

18. Juan ran $\frac{1}{3}$ of the relay race. The race was $\frac{6}{10}$ of a mile. How far did Juan run?

C Multiplying Whole Numbers

(pages 52–54)

19. $4 \times 5 \times 6$

20. $6 \times 7 \times 8$

21. $11 \times 12 \times 13$

22. $16 \times 17 \times 18$

23. Find the volume of a box that is 8 inches wide, 15 inches long, and 12 inches high.

D Relating Fractions, Decimals, and Percents

(pages 346–347)

Write each fraction or decimal as a percent.

24. $\frac{3}{5}$

25. $\frac{7}{20}$

26. 0.79

27. 0.385

Write each ratio as a percent to the nearest whole percent.

28. $\frac{3}{7}$

29. $\frac{1}{6}$

30. $\frac{5}{9}$

31. $\frac{7}{12}$

32. $\frac{1}{3}$

33. $\frac{2}{3}$

E Finding Ratios

(pages 306–307)

Write each ratio as a fraction in simplest form.

34. squares to circles

35. circles to all shapes

36. yellow shapes to blue shapes

37. red shapes to all shapes

38. yellow circles to all circles

F Finding a Percent of a Number

(pages 350–351, 354–355)

39. Find 40% of 35.

40. Find 16% of 22.

41. Find 85% of 160.

42. A shirt priced at $27 is marked 30% off. How much is the discount?

43. Sara's class ate 80% of the 50 mini-muffins she brought to the class party. How many mini-muffins were eaten?

To the Family and Student

Looking Back	Chapter 11	Looking Ahead

Looking Back

In Chapter 9, students learned how to write ratios as fractions, decimals, and percents.

$$\frac{2}{5} = 40\%$$

Chapter 11

Probability

In this chapter, students will learn how to represent probabilities as fractions, decimals, and percents.

$$P(A) = \frac{1}{4} = 0.25 = 25\%$$

Looking Ahead

In Grade 7, students will learn how to find probabilities using geometric models.

Math and Everyday Living

Opportunities to apply the concepts of Chapter 11 abound in everyday situations. During the chapter, think about how probability can be used to solve a variety of real-world problems. The following examples suggest just several of the many situations that could launch a discussion about probability.

Math in Baseball Your batting average indicates the probability that you will get a hit each time you come to bat. Find each batting average by dividing the number of hits by the times at bat. Write the answer as a decimal in thousandths.

Name	At Bats	Hits
Kevin	20	6
Tom	25	7
Karen	28	7
Lisa	15	5

Kevin's batting average is 0.300. How many hits can Kevin expect in his next 50 times at bat?

Math and Weather What is the probability it will rain tomorrow? Is it more likely to rain today or tomorrow?

Today	Tomorrow
Temperature 75°	Temperature 68°
Rain 35%	Rain 45%

Math at Home In 1998, 72% of households had air conditioners and 77% had washing machines. Based on these statistics, is your home more likely to have a washing machine or an air conditioner?

Math and News The local newspaper reports that 4 out of 5 students are involved in after-school activities. What is the probability that a student is not involved in after-school activities?

Math and Advertising A certain Saturday-morning cartoon on a local television station is projected to reach 30% of all children between the ages of 5 and 8. A toy store shows a commercial during the cartoon show. What is the probability that a 5- to 8-year-old will **not** see the commercial?

Math and Games You are playing a game with your family with a number cube labeled 1–6. You need a 4 on your next toss. What is the probability you will toss a 4?

Math in Basketball Your favorite professional basketball player shoots 89% from the free-throw line. During a game, he attempts 10 free throws. About how many free throws would you expect him to make?

California Content Standards in Chapter 11 Lessons*

	Teach	Practice
Number Sense		
1.4 Calculate given percentages of quantities and solve problems involving discounts at sales, interest earned, and tips.		11-10
2.1 Solve problems involving addition, subtraction, multiplication, and division of positive fractions and explain why a particular operation was used for a given situation.		11-3, 11-7
Statistics, Data Analysis, and Probability		
3.0 Students determine theoretical and experimental probabilities and use these to make predictions about events.	11-2, 11-10	
3.1 (🔑) Represent all possible outcomes for compound events in an organized way (e.g., . . . grids, tree diagrams) and express the theoretical probability of each outcome.	11-5, 11-6	11-9
3.2 Use data to estimate the probability of future events (e.g., batting averages or number of accidents per mile driven).	11-8, 11-10	
3.3 (🔑) Represent probabilities as ratios, proportions, decimals between 0 and 1, and percentages between 0 and 100 and verify that the probabilities computed are reasonable; know that if P is the probability of an event, $1 - P$ is the probability of an event not occurring.	11-1, 11-2,	11-3, 11-5, 11-7
3.4 Understand that the probability of either of two disjoint events occurring is the sum of two individual probabilities and that the probability of one event following another, in independent trials, is the product of the two probabilities.	11-3, 11-7	11-9
3.5 (🔑) Understand the difference between independent and dependent events.	11-9	

	Teach	Practice
Mathematical Reasoning		
2.1 Use estimation to verify the reasonableness of calculated results.		11-4, 11-10
2.4 Use a variety of methods, such as words, numbers, symbols, charts, graphs, tables, diagrams, and models, to explain mathematical reasoning		11-6
2.6 Indicate the relative advantages of exact and approximate solutions to problems	11-4	
2.7 Make precise calculations and check the validity of the results from the context of the problem.		11-10
3.1 Evaluate the reasonableness of the solution in the context of the original situation.		11-1, 11-10
3.2 Note the method of deriving the solution and demonstrate a conceptual understanding of the derivation by solving similar problems.		11-8
3.3 Develop generalizations of the results obtained and the strategies used and apply them to new problem situations.		11-2, 11-3

* The symbol (🔑) indicates a key standard as designated in the Mathematics Framework for California Public Schools. Full statements of the California Content Standards are found at the beginning of this book following the Table of Contents.

LESSON

11-1

Probability

🔑 **California Content Standard** *Statistics, Data Analysis, and Probability 3.3 (🔑): Represent probabilities as ratios . . .; know that if P is the probability of an event, 1 − P is the probability of an event not occurring.*

Math Link You learned to write a ratio comparing two quantities. Now you will learn to write a ratio to represent the probability that something will or will not happen.

The **probability** of an event is the ratio of the number of favorable outcomes to the number of all possible outcomes.

$$P = \frac{\text{number of favorable outcomes}}{\text{number of possible outcomes}}$$

The probability of an event can be any number from 0 to 1. An **impossible event** has a probability of 0. A **certain event** has a probability of 1.

Warm-Up Review

1. $1 - \frac{2}{3}$ **2.** $1 - \frac{4}{9}$

A box has 12 marbles, 4 are blue, and 5 are red. Write each ratio as a fraction in simplest form.

3. blue marbles to all the marbles

4. marbles that are not blue to all the marbles

Word Bank

probability
impossible event
certain event

Example 1

What is the probability that the spinner will land on green?

$P(\text{green}) = \dfrac{4}{8}$ ⟵ four green sections
        ⟵ eight sections in all

> Read *P*(green) as "the probability of green."

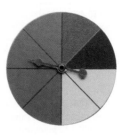

The probability of green is $\dfrac{4}{8}$, or $\dfrac{1}{2}$.

Example 2

What is the probability that the spinner will **not** land on yellow?

Find *P*(not yellow).

First find the probability that the spinner will land on yellow.

$$P(\text{yellow}) = \frac{2}{8} = \frac{1}{4}$$

$$P(\text{not yellow}) = 1 - P(\text{yellow})$$

$$= 1 - \frac{1}{4} = \frac{3}{4}$$

The probability the spinner will **not** land on yellow is $\dfrac{3}{4}$.

Here's WHY It Works

P(not yellow) means the spinner can land on any color but yellow. The favorable outcomes are landing on green, red, or blue. There are 6 sections that are not yellow.

$$P(\text{not yellow}) = \frac{6}{8} = \frac{3}{4}.$$

Each outcome is either yellow or not yellow.

$$P(\text{yellow}) + P(\text{not yellow}) = \frac{1}{4} + \frac{3}{4} = 1$$

So, *P*(not yellow) = 1 − *P*(yellow).

Example 3

Find *P* (green or red).

Since 5 sections are either green or red, *P* (green or red) $= \dfrac{5}{8}$.

418   *Additional Standard: Mathematical Reasoning 3.1 (See p. 417.)*

Guided Practice *For another example, see Set A on p. 444.*

Look at the spinner at the right. Find each probability.

1. $P(B)$ **2.** $P(B \text{ or } C)$ **3.** $P(\text{not } C)$

4. The probability of losing the big soccer match is $\frac{3}{8}$.
What is the probability that you will win?

Independent Practice *For more practice, see Set A on p. 447.*

Look at the spinner at the right. Find each probability.

5. $P(1)$ **6.** $P(\text{not } 2)$ **7.** $P(\text{odd number})$

8. $P(1 \text{ or } 4)$ **9.** $P(6)$ **10.** $P(4 \text{ or not } 4)$

Use the box of marbles at the right for Exercises 11 and 12.

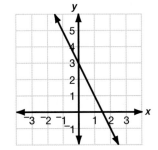

11. Mical picks a marble without looking. Mical's favorite
color is red. What is the probability that Mical will
pick a red marble?

12. Alexis picks a marble without looking. What is the
probability that Alexis will pick a large marble?

13. Math Reasoning Can a probability be greater than 1?
Explain your answer.

Mixed Review

14. Algebra While traveling in Europe, Shasta noticed the
temperature was 25°C. What was the temperature
in degrees Fahrenheit? Use the formula
$F = \frac{9}{5}C + 32$.

15. Algebra Use the graph at the right of $y = 3 - 2x$
to solve the equation $^-1 = 3 - 2x$.

Test Prep   Choose the correct letter for each answer.

16. A $39.95 dress is on sale for 25% off. What is the sale price?
(9-9)

    A $9.99   **B** $15.98   **C** $19.78   **D** $29.97

17. Algebra Solve $4x - 9 = 39$.
(10-1)

    F $x = 7\frac{1}{2}$ **G** $x = 9$ **H** $x = 12$ **J** $x = 120$

Representing Probability

Math Link You know how to write a probability as a ratio. Now you will learn how to represent probabilities in other forms.

Example 1

Joy put the letters at the right in a bag. Find the probability of choosing a vowel without looking. Write the probability as a fraction, a decimal, and a percent. Check that the probability you find is reasonable.

$$P(\text{vowel}) = \frac{\text{number of favorable outcomes}}{\text{number of possible outcomes}}$$

$$= \frac{4}{10} \quad \longleftarrow \quad \text{4 vowels}$$
$$\phantom{= \frac{4}{10}} \quad \longleftarrow \quad \text{10 letters}$$

$$= \frac{2}{5}$$

To write $\frac{2}{5}$ as a decimal, divide 2 by 5.

$$2 \div 5 = 0.4$$

To write 0.4 as a percent, move the decimal point two places to the right and add the % sign.

$$0.40 = 40\%$$

$$P(\text{vowel}) = \frac{2}{5} = 0.4 = 40\%.$$

$P(\text{vowel}) = 40\%$ is reasonable because fewer than half of the letters are vowels.

Example 2

Jason has two boxes of marbles, shown at the right. He takes a marble out of each box without looking. Is he more likely to get a red marble from Box 1 or Box 2?

$$P(\text{red from Box 1}) = \frac{3}{8} = 37.5\%$$

$$P(\text{red from Box 2}) = \frac{2}{10} = \frac{1}{5} = 20\%$$

Since $37.5\% > 20\%$, Jason is more likely to get a red marble from Box 1.

Box 1

Box 2

Additional Standard: Mathematical Reasoning 3.3 (See p. 417.)

Guided Practice *For another example, see Set B on p. 444.*

Jason chooses one marble from Box 1 on page 420 without looking. Find each probability as a fraction, a decimal, and a percent.

1. P(yellow)

2. P(blue)

3. Is Jason more likely to get a blue marble from Box 1 or Box 2 if he picks a marble from each? Explain your answer.

Independent Practice *For more practice, see Set B on p. 447.*

A marble is chosen from the box at the right without looking. Find each probability as a fraction, a decimal, and a percent. Round each decimal to the nearest hundredth and each percent to the nearest one.

4. P(green)

5. P(green or yellow)

6. P(not yellow)

7. P(marble)

8. Mental Math The letters of the word BANANA are in Bag 1 and the letters of the word APPLE are in Bag 2. A letter from each bag is drawn without looking. Is it more likely to get the letter A from Bag 1 or Bag 2? Explain your answer.

9. Nigel put the letters of the word PROPORTION in a bag and chose a letter without looking. He said that P(P, R, O, or N) $= \frac{1}{10}$. Is this probability reasonable? Explain your answer.

Mixed Review

10. You can use the formula $\$4.95 + \$0.07m$ to find the monthly cost of a long-distance telephone bill when m is the number of minutes used each month. Find the cost when $m = 316$ minutes.

You put the letters of the word YELLOW in a bag and choose a letter without looking. Find each probability as a fraction in simplest form.

11. P(not L)

12. P(L or W)

13. P(K)

14. P(Y, E, L, O, or W)

Test Prep   Choose the correct letter for each answer.

15. Ayla paid $1.33 sales tax on a purchase
(9-4)   of $29.58. What is a reasonable estimate of the sales tax she will have to pay on a purchase of $15.95?

    A $0.35   **C** $1.00

    B $0.70   **D** $1.40

16. Algebra Solve $2x - 7 = 11$.
(10-1)

    A $x = {}^-2$ **C** $x = {}^-9$

    B $x = 2$ **D** $x = 9$

Adding Probabilities

Warm-Up Review

1. $\frac{1}{2} + \frac{1}{3}$ 2. $\frac{1}{4} + \frac{1}{3}$

3. $\frac{3}{8} + \frac{1}{4}$ 4. $\frac{1}{6} + \frac{2}{3}$

5. Write the whole number that is one less than one million.

California Content Standard *Statistics, Data Analysis, and Probability 3.4: Understand that the probability of either of two disjoint events occurring is the sum of the two individual probabilities . . ..*

Math Link You know how to find the probability that an event will occur by counting outcomes. Now you will learn another way to find probabilities.

Word Bank

mutually exclusive events

Example 1

Liza and Tom have a number cube labeled with the numbers 1 through 6. They need to find the probability of tossing an even number or tossing a 5.

The two events "tossing an even number" and "tossing a 5" cannot happen at the same time. These are called **mutually exclusive events**. If one happens, the other can't happen.

You can add the two probabilities $P(\text{even})$ and $P(5)$ to find $P(\text{even or 5})$.

There are 4 favorable outcomes: 2, 4, 6, 5

There are 6 possible outcomes: 1, 2, 3, 4, 5, 6

$$P(\text{even}) + P(5) = P(\text{even or 5})$$
$$\frac{3}{6} \quad + \quad \frac{1}{6} \quad = \frac{4}{6}, \text{ or } \frac{2}{3}$$

You can add probabilities only when the events are mutually exclusive.

Example 2

Suppose you spin the spinner at the right.
Find $P(\text{article of clothing or 5-letter word})$.

These are **not** mutually exclusive events. Both events could happen at the same time. Shirt and glove are articles of clothing and they are also 5-letter words. You may not add the probabilities.

There are 5 favorable outcomes: shirt, glove, belt, horse, and daisy.

There are 8 possible outcomes: shirt, doll, glove, fish, belt, ball, daisy, horse.

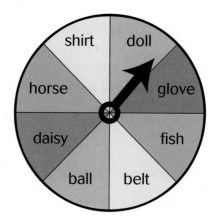

$$P(\text{clothing or 5-letter word}) = \frac{\text{number of favorable outcomes}}{\text{number of possible outcomes}}$$

$$= \frac{5}{8} = 62.5\%$$

Additional Standards: Number Sense 2.1; Statistics, Data Analysis, and Probability 3.3 ( ); Mathematical Reasoning 3.3 (See p. 417.)

Guided Practice *For another example, see Set C on p. 444.*

You toss a number cube labeled 1 through 6. Tell whether the events are mutually exclusive. Then find each probability. Express your answer as a fraction and a percent. Round to the nearest whole percent when necessary.

1. P(odd or less than 5)

2. P(4 or prime number)

3. One student is chosen from your school. Are the events that the student plays basketball and that the student plays the saxophone mutally exclusive?

Independent Practice *For more practice, see Set C on p. 447.*

A card is chosen at random from a set of 12 cards numbered 1 through 12. Tell whether the events are mutually exclusive. Then find each probability. Express your answer as a fraction and a percent. Round to the nearest whole percent when necessary.

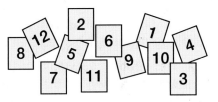

4. P(even number or 2-digit number)

5. P(multiple of 3 or multiple of 5)

6. P(1 or number greater than 8)

7. P(factor of 10 or factor of 12)

8. Math Reasoning Suppose the probability that one event will occur is $\frac{2}{5}$ and the probability that another event will occur is $\frac{2}{3}$. Is it possible that these two events are mutually exclusive? Explain your answer.

Mixed Review

9. The probability that a spinner will land on orange is $\frac{3}{5}$. What is the probability that the spinner will not land on orange?

A card is chosen without looking from a set of 12 cards numbered 1 through 12. Find each probability as a fraction, a decimal, and a percent. Round each decimal to the nearest hundredth and each percent to the nearest one.

10. P(less than 4)

11. P(not a factor of 12)

Test Prep   Choose the correct letter for the answer.

12. Which equation illustrates the distributive property?
(2-1)

A $25 \times (4 + 11) = 25 \times (11 + 4)$ **C** $6 + 19 + 6 = 6 + 6 + 19$

B $15 \times (3 + 20) = (15 \times 3) + (15 \times 20)$ **D** $0.8 \times 3 \times 100 = 0.8 \times 100 \times 3$

LESSON
11-4

Understand
Plan
Solve
Look Back

Problem-Solving Skill:
Exact or Estimated Data

California Content Standard *Mathematical Reasoning 2.6: Indicate the relative advantages of exact and approximate solutions to problems . . . .*

Read for Understanding

Jonah is at a baseball game when the notice at the right flashes on the stadium video screen. He knows that he can't count all the people in the stadium. Looking around, he sees that the stadium is about $\frac{2}{3}$ full. The seating capacity, or the number of seats in the stadium, is shown on the seating plan below.

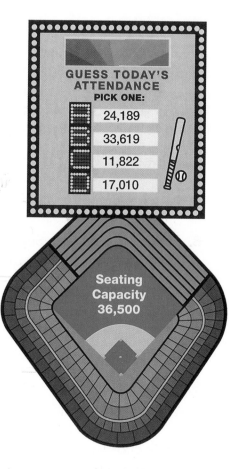

GUESS TODAY'S ATTENDANCE
PICK ONE:

24,189

33,619

11,822

17,010

Seating Capacity 36,500

1 How many seats are in the stadium?

2 About how full is the stadium?

Think and Discuss

MATH FOCUS

Exact or Estimated Data

Exact data represent an amount that can be counted. Estimated data represent an amount that has been rounded or that cannot be counted or measured.

Reread the paragraph at the top of the page.

3 Is the stadium exactly $\frac{2}{3}$ full? How do you know?

4 Will the figure for today's attendance be exact or estimated? Explain your reasoning.

5 If Jonah uses the number of seats in the stadium and his estimate that the stadium is about $\frac{2}{3}$ full, is it likely that his answer will match one of the four choices? Why or why not?

6 When solving problems, why is it important to know if data are exact or estimated?

Additional Standards: Mathematical Reasoning 2.1 (See p. 417.)

Guided Practice

Use the prices shown at the right for Exercises 1–6.

Martha's mother is taking Martha and a friend to a baseball game. She plans to buy box seats and 3 programs. She knows that they will each have some refreshments. She also plans to buy each of the young people a souvenir. She is trying to decide how much money to take to the game.

1. Should Martha's mother use an estimated amount or an exact amount to decide?

   a. Exact; she knows the prices of the tickets and programs.

   b. Estimated; she does not know exactly how much she will spend.

   c. Exact; she knows exactly what she will buy.

2. Which best describes how many programs Martha's mother plans to buy?

   a. Fewer than 3

   b. Exactly 3

   c. More than 3

3. Which data in the paragraph and in the price information at the top of the page are exact? Which data are estimated?

Independent Practice

Ms. Gomez and the 23 students in her class will use their bake-sale profits to go to a baseball game. Ms. Gomez has to order 24 grandstand tickets and rent a bus. The bus rental will be $88, and each student will have $4.00 for spending money.

4. Which of the following is exact information?

   a. 24 tickets must be ordered.

   b. The bus rental is $88.

   c. Both of the above

5. Which of the following expressions could be used to estimate the cost of the tickets?

   a. $4.00 × 25

   b. $88 × 25

   c. $8.00 × 25

6. **Math Reasoning** List the exact data that must be used to calculate the total cost of the trip. Then find the total cost of the trip.

Counting Methods

California Content Standard *Statistics, Data Analysis, and Probability 3.1 (🔑): Represent all possible outcomes of compound events in an organized way (e.g., . . . grids, tree diagrams) and express the theoretical probability of each outcome.*

Math Link You can use what you know about making tables and tree diagrams to find all possible outcomes.

Example 1

The cooking club has a sandwich luncheon. A sandwich consists of one choice of bread and one choice of filling. How many different kinds of sandwiches can be made?

Warm-Up Review

Write each ratio as a percent to the nearest whole percent.

1. $\frac{2}{3}$ **2.** $\frac{5}{9}$

3. $\frac{4}{7}$ **4.** $\frac{5}{6}$

5. Clarissa missed 3 out of 20 words on a spelling test. What percent did she get correct?

Word Bank

tree diagram

counting principle

You can draw a **tree diagram** to represent the different kinds of sandwiches.

```
           pita                        tortilla
    chicken  beef  vegetable    chicken  beef  vegetable
      1       2       3           4        5       6
```

You can represent the different types of sandwiches in a grid like the one at the right.

There are 6 different kinds of sandwiches.

	Chicken (c)	Beef (b)	Vegetable (v)
Pita (p)	pc	pb	pv
Tortilla (t)	tc	tb	tv

Additional Standards: Statistics, Data Analysis, and Probability 3.3 (🔑) (See p. 417.)

Example 2

One of each type of sandwich is prepared. You choose one without looking. Find the probability of getting a beef sandwich. Write the probability as a ratio and as a percent to the nearest whole percent.

$P(\text{beef}) = \dfrac{2}{6}$ ⟵ number of sandwiches with beef
⟵ possible number of sandwiches

$\quad\quad = \dfrac{1}{3} \approx 33\%$

The probability of getting a beef sandwich is $\dfrac{1}{3}$, or about 33%.

Example 3

If there were 3 types of bread and 4 choices of fillings, how many different kinds of sandwiches could be made?

You can use the **counting principle**.

> If there are m possible outcomes for the first event and n possible outcomes for the second event, then there are $m \times n$ possible outcomes.

possible breads	×	possible fillings		kinds of sandwiches
↓		↓		↓
3	×	4	=	12

Twelve different kinds of sandwiches could be made.

Guided Practice   *For another example, see Set D on p. 445.*

1. Use the table at the right. Draw a tree diagram to show the possible choices of sauce and pasta. How many possible choices are there?

Sauces	Pasta
alfredo	spaghetti
vegetable	fettuccini
meat	

Assume you randomly choose one of the options in Exercise 1. Find each probability as a fraction and as a percent to the nearest whole percent.

2. $P(\text{spaghetti with vegetable sauce})$ 3. $P(\text{fettuccini})$

Use the counting principle to find the number of possible outcomes, taking one from each category.

4. 5 vegetables, 7 fruits   5. 12 colors, 4 posters, 3 sizes

Independent Practice   *For more practice, see Set D on p. 448.*

6. Draw a tree diagram to show the possible outcomes of spinning the spinner and tossing the cube at the right. Assume the cube has numbers 1 through 6. How many possible outcomes are there?

Assume you spin the spinner and toss the number cube used in Exercise 6 on page 427. Find each probability as a fraction and as a percent to the nearest whole percent.

7. $P(A4)$

8. $P(3)$

9. $P(B5$ or $C1)$

Use the counting principle to find the number of possible outcomes taking one from each category.

10. 5 shirts, 4 sizes, 2 colors

11. 7 cards, 7 envelopes

Use the menu at the right for Exercises 12–15.

12. Find the number of possible choices for a meat and a vegetable.

13. Find the number of possible choices for a meat, a vegetable, and a sauce.

14. Find the probability that you will get a hamburger with ketchup when you randomly select a meat, a vegetable, and a sauce.

15. Find the probability that you will get a chicken sandwich with mustard and onions when you randomly select a meat, a vegetable, and a sauce.

meats: chicken, hamburger

vegetables: broccoli, peppers, carrots, onions

sauces: ketchup, mustard

Mixed Review

16. The probability that Brandon will ride the bus to the basketball game is $\frac{1}{4}$. The probability that his mom will take him is $\frac{1}{3}$. What is the probability he will either ride the bus or go with his mom?

You get a chicken sandwich with mustard and you select a vegetable from the menu above without looking. Find the probability as a fraction, a decimal, and a percent.

17. P(not broccoli)

18. P(carrots or onions)

Test Prep Choose the correct letter for each answer.

19. The decimal equivalent of 32.5% is
(9-1)

  A 3.25.   **B** 0.325.   **C** 0.0325.   **D** 32.5.

20. Algebra Evaluate the expression $2a + 4b$ when $a = 6$ and $b = {}^-1$.
(6-7)

  F $^-16$ **G** $^-8$ **H** 8   **J** 16

Diagnostic Checkpoint

Use the spinner below. Find each probability.

1. $P(8)$
(11-1)

2. $P(5)$
(11-1)

3. $P(9)$
(11-1)

4. $P(2 \text{ or } 5)$
(11-1)

5. $P(\text{odd or } 4)$
(11-3)

6. $P(5 \text{ or multiple of } 3)$
(11-3)

Use the spinner at the right. Write each probability as a fraction, a decimal, and a percent.

7. $P(\text{less than } 3)$
(11-2)

8. $P(\text{greater than } 5)$
(11-2)

9. $P(\text{not } 1)$
(11-2)

For Exercises 10 and 11 draw a tree diagram. Find the number of possible outcomes taking one from each category.

10.
(11-5)

Vegetable	Dip
broccoli	onion
carrots	salsa
celery	cheese

11.
(11-5)

Hat	Color
small	black
medium	white
large	

12. You randomly select one of the possible outcomes in
(11-1) Exercise 11. What is the probability that you will get a medium hat?

Use the counting principle to find the number of possible outcomes taking one from each category.

13. 5 flavors, 2 sizes
(11-5)

14. 4 salads, 4 dressings
(11-5)

15. 7 colors, 3 styles
(11-5)

You toss a number cube labeled 1 through 6. Find each probability. Express your answer as a fraction and as a percent. Round to the nearest whole percent when necessary.

16. $P(\text{even or } 1)$
(11-3)

17. $P(\text{multiple of } 3 \text{ or } 5)$
(11-3)

18. $P(6 \text{ or } 5)$
(11-3)

19. Ms. Giordino is taking her class of 32 students on a field trip to
(11-4) the aquarium. The cost per ticket is $6.00. Write and evaluate an expression that could be used to estimate the total cost of the tickets.

Permutations and Combinations

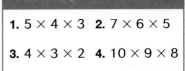
California Content Standard *Statistics, Data Analysis, and Probability 3.1 (⚷): Represent all possible outcomes for compound events in an organized way (e.g., . . . grids, . . .) . . ..*

Word Bank

permutation
combination

Math Link You know how to count possible outcomes. Now you will learn how to count the number of ways to choose things when order does and does not matter.

Example 1

Manuel wants to put two different-colored balloons on his front door. He has red, blue, yellow, green, and orange ballons. How many different arrangements can he make?

	Red (R)	Blue (B)	Yellow (y)	Green (G)	Orange (O)
Red (R)		RB	Ry	RG	RO
Blue (B)	BR		By	BG	BO
Yellow (y)	yR	yB		yG	yO
Green (G)	GR	GB	Gy		GO
Orange (O)	OR	OB	Oy	OG	

You can draw a grid to see Manuel's choices.

You can also use the counting principle.

Manuel can choose any of the 5 color choices for his first balloon. The color he chooses for his first balloon cannot be chosen for his second balloon. So he has only 4 color choices for his second balloon.

First balloon color choices		Second balloon color choices		Number of different arrangements
5	×	4	=	20

Manuel has 20 choices for selecting and arranging the two balloons.

Notice that both BR (blue and red) and RB (red and blue) appear in the grid. When the order of the items in an arrangement is important, each possible arrangement is called a **permutation**.

Example 2

Find the number of arrangements Manuel can make if he wants to put 2 different-colored balloons on his door but he does not care how they are arranged. A selection of items in which the order does not matter is a **combination**.

Each pair of balloons is listed in the grid twice, because each pair of balloons can be arranged 2 ways. If order does not matter, BR and RB are the same, so divide the number of permutations by 2.

$$\frac{20}{2} = 10$$

Manuel has 10 choices.

Additional Standard: Mathematical Reasoning 2.4 (See p. 417.)

Guided Practice *For another example, see Set E on p. 445.*

Decide whether or not order matters in each situation. Write Yes or No.

1. Choosing 5 CDs from a list of 20

2. Choosing 5 digits for a password

3. How many 3-letter permutations can be made from the letters GREAT?

4. Olga has four kinds of fruit. She wants to put three kinds in a fruit basket. How many specific arrangements (permutations) can she make?

Independent Practice *For more practice, see Set E on p. 448.*

Decide whether or not order matters in each situation. Write Yes or No.

5. Choosing 12 students for a team

6. Choosing 4 cards from a deck

Use the letters MATH. Tell how many 2-letter

7. permutations can be made.

8. combinations can be made.

9. Math Reasoning In Exercise 4, how many arrangements can Olga make if order does NOT matter?

Your school has a 10-member Math Club.

10. How many ways can two officers be selected?

11. Math Reasoning How many 2-member program committees can be formed?

Mixed Review

12. Use the table at the right. Draw a tree diagram to show the possible outcomes for a flavor and a size of yogurt. How many possible outcomes are there?

Flavor	Size
strawberry	small
lemon	medium
cherry	large
vanilla	

The numbers 1 through 8 are written on 8 cards that are placed in a bag. A card is selected from the bag without looking. Find each probability. Express your answer as a fraction and a percent.

13. P(even or greater than 4)

14. P(4 or odd)

🖊 **Test Prep**   **Choose the correct letter for the answer.**

15. Algebra Solve $\frac{5}{4} = \frac{n}{10}$.
(8-3)

   F $n = 2$ **G** $n = 7.5$ **H** $n = 8$ **J** $n = 12.5$

Independent Events

California Content Standard *Statistics, Data Analysis, and Probability 3.4: Understand . . . that the probability of one event following another, in independent trials, is the product of the two probabilities.*

Math Link You know how to find the probability that an event will occur. Now you will learn how to find the probability that two events will occur.

Warm-Up Review

Find each probability.

1. P(2 or 4)

2. P(not 2 or 4)

3. Which is greater, P(2 or 3) or P(not 2 or 3)?

Example 1

The school carnival has a spinner game. You can win a prize by spinning an A on the first spinner and then yellow on the second spinner. What is the probability of winning a prize?

Word Bank

compound event
independent event

Spinning both spinners is a compound event. A **compound event** is a combination of two or more simple events.

The outcome of the first spinner does not affect the outcome of the second spinner. The two spins are **independent events.**

To find P(A, yellow), find the probability of each event and multiply.

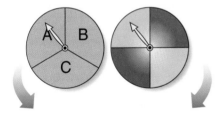

The probability of spinning an A on the first spinner and then yellow on the second spinner is denoted by P(A, yellow).

Step 1 Find each probability.	**Step 2** Multiply.

$P(A) = \frac{1}{3}$ $P(\text{yellow}) = \frac{1}{2}$ $P(A, \text{yellow}) = \frac{1}{3} \times \frac{1}{2} = \frac{1}{6}$

The probability of winning a prize is $\frac{1}{6}$, or 1 out of 6 tries.

Example 2

What is the probability of NOT winning a prize in the spinner game in Example 1?

$$P(\text{not winning}) = 1 - P(\text{winning}) = 1 - \frac{1}{6} = \frac{5}{6}$$

The probability of not winning is $\frac{5}{6}$, or 5 out of 6 tries.

Additional Standards: Number Sense 2.1; Statistics, Data Analysis, and Probability 3.3 (⬥) (See p. 417.)

Guided Practice *For another example, see Set F on p. 446.*

The duck pond is a game where players choose two ducks without looking. After picking the first duck, they replace it and pick the second duck. Use the information at the right to find each probability.

1. *P*(red, red)   **2.** *P*(green, red)

Independent Practice *For more practice, see Set F on p. 449.*

Players pick a letter from the bag without looking. They record the letter and put it back into the bag. Then they pick another letter. Use the information at the right to find each probability.

3. What is the probability of picking the letter *S* twice?

4. What is the probability of forming the word IS by choosing *I* first and *S* second?

5. Math Reasoning Do you think the probability of forming the word IS would be different if the first letter is not put back in the bag before the second letter is picked? Explain your answer.

Mixed Review

6. A restaurant offers 5 blue-plate specials, 3 beverages, and 6 desserts. How many meal choices with a special, a beverage, and a dessert are possible?

7. Sam has a choice of 3 English classes, 4 math classes, 2 science classes, and 2 history classes. How many different combinations are possible if Sam chooses one class from each category?

8. In how many ways can pictures of 5 students be placed side by side in a picture frame?

9. How many 3-person teams can be made if there are 5 people available?

Test Prep   Choose the correct letter for each answer.

10. Which number is 1,000
(1-6) more than 9,605?

   A 1,605   **C** 10,005

   B 9,705   **D** 10,605

11. Which number is 1,000
(1-7) less than 100,093?

   F 99,093   **H** 100,993

   G 99,993   **J** 909,093

Use Homework Workbook 11-7. **433**

LESSON

11-8

Understand
Plan
Solve
Look Back

Problem-Solving Strategy:
Use a Simulation

California Content Standard *Statistics, Data Analysis, and Probability 3.2: Use data to estimate the probability of future events (e.g., batting averages . . .).*

Warm-Up Review

Write each fraction as a percent.

1. $\frac{3}{4}$ 2. $\frac{4}{5}$

3. A spinner is divided into 8 congruent sections. Four sections are red, 3 are blue, and 1 is yellow. What percent of the spinner is not blue?

Example

The first 12 times you came to bat this baseball season, you got 4 hits. You usually bat 4 times per game. What is the probability that you will get at least one hit per game?

Understand

What do you need to find?

You need to find the probability that you will get at least one hit per game.

Plan

How can you solve the problem?

Your probability of getting a hit each time at bat is $\frac{4}{12}$, or $\frac{1}{3}$.

When you toss a number cube labeled 1 through 6, the probability of tossing a 1 or a 2 is also $\frac{1}{3}$. You can **use a simulation** to solve the problem. Let each toss of a number cube represent a time at bat and each toss of a 1 or 2 represent a hit.

Solve

The table shows the results of 40 tosses of a number cube labeled 1 through 6. Each row represents a game. Nine rows out of 10 contain a 1 or 2.

P(at least one hit) $= \frac{9}{10}$, or 90%.

The probability that you will get at least one hit per game is 90%.

Results of 40 Tosses			
3	2	5	3
5	2	2	3
2	2	5	2
4	4	1	4
1	6	4	2
1	3	4	5
5	4	6	5
1	6	5	5
6	6	1	2
4	1	2	3

Look Back

Is a probability of 90% reasonable? Explain your answer.

Additional Standards: Mathematical Reasoning 3.2 (See p. 417.)

Guided Practice

Use the table on page 434. Let a toss of 1 or 2 represent a hit.
Find each probability.

1. *P*(at least 2 hits per game)

2. *P*(at least 3 hits per game)

3. *P*(no hits per game)

4. *P*(exactly 2 hits per game)

Independent Practice

Use the table at the right. Find each probability.

Michelle and Ryan are evenly matched in chess; so
each time they play, each one has a 50% chance of
winning. They plan to play 5 matches each month.
Let a toss of a coin represent a match, with heads
representing wins by Michelle and tails representing
wins by Ryan. Each row represents a month of matches.

5. *P*(Michelle wins at least 1 match)

6. *P*(Michelle wins at least 2 matches)

7. *P*(Michelle wins at least 3 matches)

8. *P*(Michelle wins all the matches)

Results of 50 Tosses of a Coin				
T	H	H	H	H
T	T	H	T	T
H	T	H	H	H
H	H	H	T	H
T	T	H	H	H
H	T	T	H	H
H	H	H	H	T
H	T	T	H	T
T	T	H	H	T
T	T	H	T	H

Mixed Review

Try these or other strategies to solve each problem. Tell which
strategy you used.

Problem-Solving Strategies

- *Make a Graph*
- *Find a Pattern*
- *Work Backward*
- *Make a Table*

---

9. While playing Rocket Race, Gina
recorded her scores in a table like
the one at the right. If this pattern
continues, what will her score be for
the seventh game?

Rocket Race						
Game	1	2	3	4	5	6
Score	25	30	40	60	100	180

10. Freddy and Eileen collect video games. Freddy has 8 more
games than Eileen. Together they have a total of 44 games.
How many games does each of them have?

Dependent Events

California Content Standard *Statistics, Data Analysis, and Probability 3.5 (🔑): Understand the difference between independent and dependent events.*

Math Link You know how to find the probability of independent events. Now you will learn how to find the probability of dependent events.

Example 1

Two darts are thrown at a dart board and hit a balloon each time. Are you more likely to hit two red balloons if the first balloon is replaced before your second throw or if it is not replaced?

The probability of hitting two red balloons is a compound event.

If the balloon is replaced, the events are independent events. To find the probability, multiply the probabilities of the two events.

$P(2 \text{ red}) = P(\text{red on first}) \times P(\text{red on second})$

$$= \frac{1}{2} \times \frac{1}{2}$$

$$= \frac{1}{4} = 25\%$$

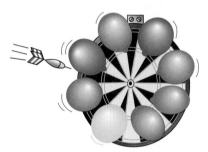

If the first balloon is **not** replaced, the outcome of the first throw affects the outcome of the second throw. The two throws are **dependent events**.

If the balloon is not replaced, the probability of hitting a red balloon on the second throw is not $\frac{1}{2}$. After a red balloon is hit, there are 3 red balloons left and 7 balloons in all.

$P(\text{red on second throw}) = \dfrac{3}{7}$ ⟵ red balloons
⟵ all balloons

$P(2 \text{ red}) = P(\text{red on first throw}) \times P(\text{red on second throw})$

$$= \frac{1}{2} \times \frac{3}{7}$$

$$= \frac{3}{14} \approx 21\%$$

$25\% > 21\%$

You are more likely to hit two red balloons if the first balloon is replaced than if it is not.

Players toss two cubes labeled 1 through 6. Find each probability.

1. $P(1, 1)$ **2.** $P(1, \text{even})$

3. $P(\text{odd}, \text{even})$

4. $P(\text{not } 1, 6)$

5. You put the letters of the word HOUSE in a bag, pick one, put it back, and then pick another one. What is the probability that you will get H twice?

> **Word Bank**
>
> dependent events

 Additional Standards: Statistics, Data Analysis, and Probability 3.1(🔑), 3.4 (See p. 417.)

Guided Practice *For another example, see Set G on p. 446.*

For Exercises 1–6, use the information to find each probability. Round to the nearest whole percent.

The letter tiles at the right are put into a bag. You select one without looking, replace it, and select another one.

1. $P(L, L)$ **2.** $P(L, O)$ **3.** $P(\text{consonant, vowel})$

The letter tiles are put into a bag. You select one without looking, do **not** replace it, and select another one.

4. $P(L, L)$ **5.** $P(L, O)$ **6.** $P(\text{consonant, vowel})$

7. Math Reasoning Your teacher selects two students to be narrators in the class play. Does the probability that you are selected involve dependent or independent events? Explain.

Independent Practice *For more practice, see Set G on p. 449.*

For Exercises 8–13, use the information at the right to find each probability.

You select one letter without looking, replace it, and select another one.

8. $P(A, A)$ **9.** $P(A, K)$ **10.** $P(\text{consonant, vowel})$

You select one letter without looking, do *not* replace it, and select another one.

11. $P(A, A)$ **12.** $P(A, K)$ **13.** $P(\text{consonant, vowel})$

14. Mental Math The probability that a certain battery will be defective is 1%. What is the probability that two batteries chosen at random will both be defective?

Mixed Review

15. How many permutations are there of the letters R, S, and T?

16. If two number cubes numbered 1 through 6 are tossed, what is the probability of tossing two 6s?

🔦 **Test Prep** Choose the correct letter for each answer.

17. Algebra Solve $\frac{2}{3}x = 6$.
(5-10)

    A $x = 6\frac{2}{3}$ **C** $x = 4$

    B $x = 5\frac{1}{3}$ **D** $x = 9$

18. Algebra Solve $n - 15 = {}^{-}3$.
(6-8)

    F $n = {}^{-}18$ **H** $n = 12$

    G $n = {}^{-}12$ **J** $n = 18$

Use Homework Workbook 11-9.

LESSON
11-10

Understand
Plan
Solve
Look Back

Problem-Solving Application:
Making Predictions

Warm-Up Review

1. Find 25% of 384.

2. Find 14% of 96.

3. Find 12.5% of 50.

4. You buy a sweater for $36. How much would you pay with sales tax if the tax rate is 4.5%?

California Content Standard *Statistics, Data Analysis, and Probability 3.2: Use data to estimate the probability of future events (e.g., . . . number of accidents . . .). Also, Statistics, Data Analysis, and Probability 3.0 (See p. 417.)*

Example

The table at the right gives data on automobile accidents and number of licensed drivers in the United States in 1998. The projected number of drivers in the United States in 2003 is 200 million. Predict how many drivers may be in accidents in 2003.

U.S. Automobile Accidents, 1998			
	Male	Female	Total
Drivers in an Accident (millions)	12.7	8.6	21.3
Licensed Drivers (millions)	93.7	91.8	185.5

Understand

What do you need to find?

You need to predict how many U.S. drivers may be in accidents in 2003.

Plan

How can you solve the problem?

Find the probability that a U.S. driver was in an accident in 1998. Multiply the probability by 200 million.

Solve

P(driver is in an accident) $= \dfrac{\text{number of drivers in accidents in 1998}}{\text{number of drivers in 1998}} = \dfrac{21.3}{185.5} \approx 11.5\%$

The probability that a U.S. driver was in an accident in 1998 was about 11.5%.

11.5% of 200 million = 0.115 × 200 million = 23 million

Approximately 23 million U.S. drivers may be in accidents in 2003.

Look Back

Is the answer reasonable?

 Additional Standards: Number Sense 1.4 (⚷); Mathematical Reasoning 2.1, 2.7, 3.1 (See p. 417.)

Guided Practice

Use the data in the table on page 438 for Exercises 1 and 2.

1. How many accidents can be expected to involve female drivers in 2003?

2. How many accidents can be expected to involve male drivers in 2003?

Independent Practice

3. Use the data in the table on page 438 to predict the number of female licensed drivers in 2003.

In 1995, 17.6 million drivers were involved in accidents. At that time, there were 177.4 million licensed drivers in the United States.

4. Find the probability a licensed driver in the United States was in an accident in 1995.

5. Use the 1995 probability to predict how many of the 185.5 million drivers would be involved in an accident in 1998.

6. **Math Reasoning** Was driving in the United States relatively safer in 1995 or 1998? Explain your answer.

7. **Math Reasoning** By what percent did the number of licensed drivers increase from 1995 to 1998?

Mixed Review

Tell which strategy you used to solve each problem.

8. You want to cut a square piece of plastic into 9 congruent squares to be used as a game. What is the least number of cuts you can use to make the squares?

9. You work for a company that wants to advertise on the radio at a time when the most sixth-grade students listen. Based on the data in the table, when should you advertise? Explain your answer.

Radio Listening Time		
Person	Morning (in minutes)	Evening (in minutes)
Sue	20	10
Phyllis	30	5
Salita	15	20
Martin	30	40
Moe	30	60
Sherry	20	15

10. Half of the 3,000 people watching a parade were sitting on the curb. One-quarter of the remaining people watched from second-story windows of nearby buildings. The rest stood and watched from the sidewalks. Is it reasonable to say there were 365 people watching from nearby buildings?

Use Homework Workbook 11-10.

Diagnostic Checkpoint

1. When one event affects another event, the two events
(11-9) are called _____.

2. A combination of two simple events is
(11-7) a(n) _____.

3. An event with a probability of 1 is
(11-1) a(n) _____.

4. Two events that cannot happen together
(11-3) are _____.

<table>
<tr><td>Word Bank</td></tr>
<tr><td>certain event</td></tr>
<tr><td>compound event</td></tr>
<tr><td>dependent events</td></tr>
<tr><td>impossible event</td></tr>
<tr><td>independent
   events</td></tr>
<tr><td>mutually exclusive
   events</td></tr>
<tr><td>probability</td></tr>
</table>

5. Does order matter when listing 6 items on a grocery list?
(11-6) Write Yes or No.

The letters of the word SCHOOL are put in a bag. You pick a letter from the bag, replace it, and then pick another letter. Find each probability.

6. $P(S, C)$
(11-7)

7. $P(O, \text{not } O)$
(11-7)

You pick a letter from a bag, but you do NOT replace the first letter before picking the second letter.

8. $P(O, O)$
(11-9)

9. $P(O, \text{not } O)$
(11-9)

Use the table at the right. Find each probability. Round to the nearest whole percent.

Two middle school basketball teams are evenly matched, so each has a 50% chance of winning each time they play each other. They usually play each other three times a year. Each row represents a year. Let heads, H, represent a win for Team A and tails, T, a win for Team B.

10. $P(\text{Team A wins all 3 games})$
(11-8)

11. $P(\text{Team B wins exactly 2 games})$
(11-8)

12. Alex had 12 hits in 40 times at bat last year. Predict how
(11-10) many hits he could expect if he has 57 at bats this year.

Results of 45 Flips of a Coin		
T	H	H
H	H	T
T	H	T
T	H	T
H	H	H
H	H	T
H	T	T
H	H	H
H	T	T
H	H	H
H	T	H
T	T	H
T	T	T
H	T	H
H	T	T

Chapter 11 Test

A bag contains 10 marbles: 1 blue, 2 red, 3 green and 4 yellow. You pick a marble from the bag without looking. For Exercises 1–10, find each probability as a fraction, a decimal to the nearest hundredth, and a percent to the nearest whole percent.

1. *P*(not red) 2. *P*(green) 3. *P*(yellow or red) 4. *P*(green or not blue)

You pick a marble, replace it, and pick again.

5. *P*(red, green) 6. *P*(green, green) 7. *P*(green , yellow)

You pick a marble, do NOT replace it, and pick again.

8. *P*(yellow, yellow) 9. *P*(green, green) 10. *P*(red, green)

11. Are the events in Exercise 5 independent or dependent events?

Lily sells cotton and nylon shirts in blue, white, and gray.

12. Draw a tree diagram to show the combinations of fabrics and colors.

13. Find the probability of randomly selecting a blue cotton shirt.

14. Jen stopped for yogurt. There were 4 flavors, 3 toppings, and 2 sizes. Find the number of possible choices for a yogurt with one topping.

15. Andy is taking his two sisters to a garden show. He knows that admittance is $4.25, programs are $1.00, and plants are $5.95 each. Should he use an exact or estimated amount to decide how much money to take to the show? Explain your answer.

16. Shari had 14 hits in 35 times at bat in June. Predict the number of hits Shari can expect if she bats 45 times in July.

17. A kitten in a litter is equally likely to be brown or black. Find the probability that both kittens in a litter are brown.

Cathy has a red, a white, a pink, and a yellow rose.

18. How many two-rose arrangements can she make?

19. How many arrangements can she make if order does **NOT** matter?

20. Use the simulation table and the information on page 440. Find *P*(Team B wins only 1 game).

Multiple-Choice Chapter 11 Test

Choose the correct letter for each answer.

Use the table for Questions 1–5.

After-School Activities		
Arts	Sports	Performing Arts
Pottery	Soccer	Band
Painting	Lacrosse	Orchestra
Sketching	Basketball	Chorus
	Softball	Drama
		Ballet

1. Misty cannot decide which after-school activity she wants. She randomly picks one. What is the probability she picks a sport?

   A $\frac{1}{6}$ C $\frac{1}{3}$

   B $\frac{1}{4}$ D $\frac{1}{2}$

2. What is the probability Misty picks a performing art when she randomly picks an after-school activity?

   F 20%

   G 25%

   H About 33%

   J About 42%

3. Find the number of possible choices if Misty chooses one art and one sport.

   A 7 choices

   B 12 choices

   C 15 choices

   D 20 choices

4. Ashley randomly selects a performing art and Brock randomly selects a sport. Which of the following is most reasonable?

   F Ashley is more likely to get chorus than Brock is to get soccer.

   G Brock is more likely to get soccer than Ashley is to get chorus.

   H Ashley is more likely to get soccer than Brock is to get chorus.

   J Brock is more likely to get soccer than softball.

5. Melissa wants to play two sports. How many different choices does she have?

   A 5 choices

   B 6 choices

   C 10 choices

   D 12 choices

6. The probability that Marcus will be in Mr. Bolt's math class is $\frac{1}{8}$. What is the probability he will *not* be in Mr. Bolt's math class?

   F 0

   G $\frac{1}{8}$

   H $\frac{7}{8}$

   J 1

7. The probability of picking a red marble from a bag with 5 marbles is $\frac{3}{5}$. You add a green marble to the bag. Now what is the probability of picking a red marble?

A $\frac{2}{5}$

B $\frac{1}{2}$

C $\frac{2}{3}$

D $\frac{4}{5}$

Use the following information for Questions 8 and 9.

A carnival game has 10 plastic fish in a pond. Without looking, you use a fishing pole to catch a fish two times. You must get a red fish each time to win. The pond has 2 red fish, 4 yellow fish, 3 blue fish, and 1 green fish.

8. The student running the game puts your first fish back before you catch your second fish. What is the probability you will win?

F   25%   **H**   8%

G   16%   **J**   4%

9. Another student takes over the game. She says you should keep your first fish until you catch the second one. Now what is the probability you will win?

A   About 2%   **C**   About 6%

B   About 4%   **D**   About 8%

10. In how many ways can 4 books be arranged on a shelf?

F   1 way   **H**   12 ways

G   4 ways   **J**   24 ways

11. A fruit stand serves orange juice and apple juice in three sizes: large, medium, and small. If you randomly make a selection, what is the probability you will get a medium orange juice?

A $\frac{2}{3}$ **C** $\frac{1}{6}$

B $\frac{1}{3}$ **D** $\frac{1}{12}$

12. Sarah's dad is taking her and her two friends to the movies. Tickets are \$4.50 for children and \$6.50 for adults. They will buy some popcorn while they are there. Which of the following is exact information?

F   Sarah's dad expects to spend about \$30.

G   Sarah's dad expects to spend \$20 on tickets.

H   Sarah's dad expects to spend about \$10 on popcorn.

J   Sarah's dad expects to spend about \$22 on the tickets.

13. Thomas has scored 40 points in the first 8 games of the basketball season. The season has 12 games in all. How many points could Thomas expect to score during the season?

A   About 5 points

B   About 45 points

C   About 60 points

D   About 80 points

Reteaching

Set A *(pages 418–419)*

You place the letters of the word ALGEBRA in a bag and draw one letter from the bag without looking. Find P(consonant).

4 favorable outcomes: L, G, B, R
7 possible outcomes: A, L, G, E, B, R, A

$P(consonant) = \dfrac{4}{7}$ ← favorable outcomes
← possible outcomes

Remember that the **probability** of an event is this ratio:

$$P = \dfrac{\text{number of favorable outcomes}}{\text{number of possible outcomes}}$$

Find each probability for the situation in the example at the left.

1. $P(A)$ **2.** $P(\text{not A})$

3. $P(\text{vowel})$ **4.** $P(\text{A or B})$

5. $P(K)$ **6.** $P(\text{A or not A})$

Set B *(pages 420–421)*

You place the letters of the word PERCENTS in a bag and draw one letter from the bag without looking. Write P(C or T) as a fraction, a decimal, and a percent.

$P(\text{C or T}) = \dfrac{\text{number of favorable outcomes}}{\text{number of possible outcomes}}$

$= \dfrac{2}{8} = \dfrac{1}{4}$

$1 \div 4 = 0.25 = 25\%$

So, $P(\text{C or T}) = \dfrac{1}{4} = 0.25 = 25\%$

Remember that you can represent a probability as a fraction, a decimal, or a percent.

Use the situation in the example. Find each probability as a fraction, a decimal, and a percent.

1. $P(E)$ **2.** $P(\text{consonant})$

3. $P(\text{not T})$ **4.** $P(A)$

5. $P(\text{E or R})$ **6.** $P(\text{N or not P})$

Set C *(pages 422–423)*

You have a number cube labeled 1 through 6. Tell whether "tossing a 4" and "tossing an odd number" are mutually exclusive events. Then find P(4 or odd).

"Tossing a 4" and "tossing an odd number" cannot happen at the same time. So they are mutually exclusive events.

$P(\text{4 or odd}) = P(4) + P(\text{odd})$

$$= \dfrac{1}{6} + \dfrac{3}{6} = \dfrac{4}{6} = \dfrac{2}{3}$$

Remember you add probabilities only when the events are **mutually exclusive.**

You toss a number cube labeled 1 through 6. Decide whether the events in each exercise are mutually exclusive. Then find each probability.

1. $P(\text{2 or multiple of 5})$

2. $P(\text{2 or even})$

Set D (pages 426–428)

How many outcomes are possible for choosing a bread and a meat?

Bread	Meat
rye	turkey
wheat	ham
	beef

Draw a tree diagram.

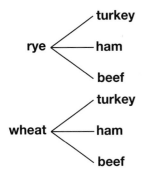

There are 6 possible outcomes.

Remember that you can use a tree diagram, a grid, or the counting principle to find all possible outcomes.

Find the number of possible outcomes in each exercise.

1. 3 breads, 3 meats

2. 3 breads, 4 meats

3. 2 breads, 3 meats, and 4 toppings

4. 3 breads, 4 meats, and 4 toppings

5. 5 colors of car exterior, 4 colors of car interior

6. 4 types of dress, 3 types of cloth, 9 colors of cloth

Set E (pages 430–431)

How many 2-digit numbers can be made from the digits 1, 2, 3, and 4? Do not repeat digits.

List the possible numbers.

12	21	31	41
13	23	32	42
14	24	34	43

Twelve 2-digit numbers can be made from the digits 1, 2, 3, and 4.

Remember when the order of the items in an arrangement is important, each possible arrangement is a **permutation**.

If order is **not** important, each arrangement is a **combination**.

Decide whether or not order matters in each situation. Write Yes or No. Then find the number of possible arrangements.

1. How many different pairs can you make with the numbers 1, 2, 3, and 4? Do not repeat digits.

2. Abby, Ellie, and Lori are running for president and secretary of their club. How many different ways can the positions be filled?

Reteaching (continued)

Set F (pages 432–433)

You place the letters of the word EQUATION in Bag 1 and the letters of the word EXPRESSION in Bag 2. You then draw one letter from each bag, in order, without looking. Find $P(N, S)$.

$P(N, S) = P(\text{N from Bag 1}) \times P(\text{S from Bag 2})$

$$= \frac{1}{8} \times \frac{2}{10}$$

$$= \frac{2}{80} = \frac{1}{40}$$

Remember that you can multiply probabilities to find the probability that the events will happen together.

Find the probability of picking the first letter from Bag 1 and the second letter from Bag 2.

1. $P(N, N)$ 2. $P(\text{vowel, vowel})$

3. $P(\text{not A, S})$ 4. $P(Q, \text{vowel})$

5. $P(\text{consonant, E})$ 6. $P(T, T)$

7. $P(E, Q)$ 8. $P(\text{letter, letter})$

Set G (pages 436–437)

Lisa has 5 containers of fruit yogurt in the refrigerator. Three are cherry and 2 are strawberry. She grabs one without looking and gives it to her friend. Then she grabs one for herself without looking. Find $P(2 \text{ cherry})$.

$P(\text{cherry 1st}) = \dfrac{3}{5}$

The events are dependent. After Lisa grabs a container of cherry yogurt, there are only 4 containers left and 2 that are cherry.

$P(\text{cherry 2nd}) = \dfrac{2}{4}$

$P(2 \text{ cherry})$

$P(\text{cherry 1st}) \times P(\text{cherry 2nd})$

$\dfrac{3}{5} \qquad \times \quad \dfrac{2}{4} = \dfrac{3}{10}$

$\dfrac{3}{10} \qquad = \quad 30\%$

Remember that in some compound events, the outcome of the first event affects the outcome of the second event. The second event *depends* on the first one. These are called **dependent events**.

Find each probability for the situation in the example.

1. $P(2 \text{ strawberry})$

2. $P(\text{strawberry, cherry})$

Use the following situation. Find each probability. Round to the nearest whole percent.

Students have 9 colors of cloth to use to make a banner. Four are shades of blue, 3 are shades of green, 1 is red, and 1 is white. They randomly choose 2 different colors.

3. $P(\text{blue, blue})$ 4. $P(\text{blue, red})$

5. $P(\text{green, not blue})$ 6. $P(\text{green, green})$

7. $P(\text{red, white})$ 8. $P(\text{white, not white})$

More Practice

Set A (pages 418–419)

Find each probability. Use the spinner at the right.

1. $P(X)$
2. $P(Z)$
3. $P(y \text{ or not } y)$

4. $P(\text{not } Z)$
5. $P(y \text{ or } Z)$
6. $P(\text{not } X)$

7. Katrina's probability of being selected class president is $\frac{1}{5}$. What is the probability she will not be selected?

Set B (pages 420–421)

The letters of the word BLINDFOLD are put in a hat. You choose a letter without looking. Find each probability as a fraction, a decimal rounded to the nearest hundredth, and a percent rounded to the nearest whole percent.

1. $P(B)$
2. $P(\text{not } F)$
3. $P(D)$
4. $P(B \text{ or } D)$

5. $P(\text{not a vowel})$
6. $P(D \text{ or } L)$
7. $P(S)$
8. $P(F, D, \text{ or } L)$

9. Are you more likely to get the letter L from a hat with the word BLINDFOLD or from a hat with the word BLUFF? Explain your answer.

Set C (pages 422–423)

You toss a number cube labeled 1 through 6. Find each probability. Express your answer as a fraction and a percent. Round to the nearest whole percent.

1. $P(\text{odd or number less than 4})$
2. $P(4 \text{ or prime number})$

3. $P(\text{even or 4})$
4. $P(\text{even or prime number})$

Tell whether the events are mutually exclusive. Explain your answer.

5. You run fewer than 5 miles this Friday. You run more than 2 miles this Friday.

6. A number is an even prime number. A number is greater than 2.

More Practice (continued)

Set D (pages 426–428)

Use the counting principle to find the number of possible outcomes taking one from each category.

1. 5 vegetables, 7 fruits

2. 12 colors, 4 cards

3. 4 colors, 3 sizes

4. 10 meals, 4 desserts, 2 salads

5. 5 pastas, 4 sauces, 2 meats

Use the table at the right for Exercises 6–9.

6. Draw a tree diagram to show all the possible outcomes for choosing a cereal and a fruit. How many possible outcomes are there?

7. What is the number of possible outcomes for choosing a cereal, a milk, and a fruit?

Cereals	Milks	Fruits
corn flakes	skim	strawberries
rice puffs	1%	raisins
oat puffs	2%	blueberries
corn puffs	whole	
wheat flakes		

8. What is the number of possible outcomes for choosing a cereal and a milk?

9. What is the probability of choosing rice puffs and whole milk?

Set E (pages 430–431)

For Exercises 1–4, decide whether or not order matters in each situation. Write Yes or No.

1. Choosing class president, vice-president, secretary, and treasurer

2. Choosing a committee to organize a canned food drive

3. Choosing 10 people to play a game

4. Following the steps of a recipe

5. In how many ways can 4 people line up for a line dance?

6. In how many ways can an 8-member club select 3 officers?

7. In how many ways can a 2-person team be selected from 5 people?

Set F (pages 432–433)

You toss two cubes each labeled A–F. Find each probability.

1. *P*(A, B)

2. *P*(C, vowel)

3. *P*(A, not A)

4. *P*(not C, not D)

5. *P*(vowel, vowel)

6. *P*(A, not vowel)

7. *P*(G, A)

8. *P*(consonant, consonant)

9. *P*(not G, not H)

Use the bag at the right for Exercises 10 and 11.

10. You pick 2 letters, one at a time, replacing the letter each time. What is the probability of picking 2 vowels?

11. What is the probability of spelling OR?

12. You are taking a multiple-choice test. Each question has 4 possible answers. You need to guess on 2 questions. What is the probability that you will guess both correctly?

Set G (pages 436–437)

Use the information to find each probability.

The letters of the word STUDENTS are placed in a bag as shown above. You pick 2 letters, one at a time, but do not replace them.

1. *P*(D, T)

2. *P*(T, S)

Karen and Karl are twins. They go to a movie with their friends Lisa, Roberto, and Maria. After the movie, two of the five students are randomly selected to be interviewed.

3. *P*(twin, twin)

4. *P*(girl, girl)

5. *P*(boy, girl)

6. *P*(twin, not twin)

7. Your class has 21 students. 12 are girls and 9 are boys. Your teacher chooses two students at random to prepare a report. Find the probability that she chooses 2 boys.

Problem Solving: Preparing for Tests

Choose the correct letter for each answer.

1. The biology class did a project on the growth of plants. They recorded the growth of a bean seed over a 3-week period. The seed sprouted and grew $\frac{3}{16}$ inch during the first week, $1\frac{1}{16}$ inches during the second week, and $\frac{5}{16}$ inch during the third week. How much more must the bean plant grow to reach a height of 2 inches?

   A $\frac{5}{16}$ inch

   B $\frac{7}{16}$ inch

   C $1\frac{1}{16}$ inch

   D $1\frac{9}{16}$ inch

Tip

First find how much the bean plant grew over the 3-week period.

2. Luis left a 15% tip on his bill at the restaurant. If he left $3.00 for the tip, how much was his bill?

   F $10.00

   G $15.00

   H $20.00

   J $30.00

Tip

Write an Equation and then *Work Backwards* to find the total amount of the bill.

3. How many right angles are there at the intersection of Pine and Third?

   A   0

   B   1

   C   2

   D   3

Tip

Remember that a right angle has a measure of 90°.

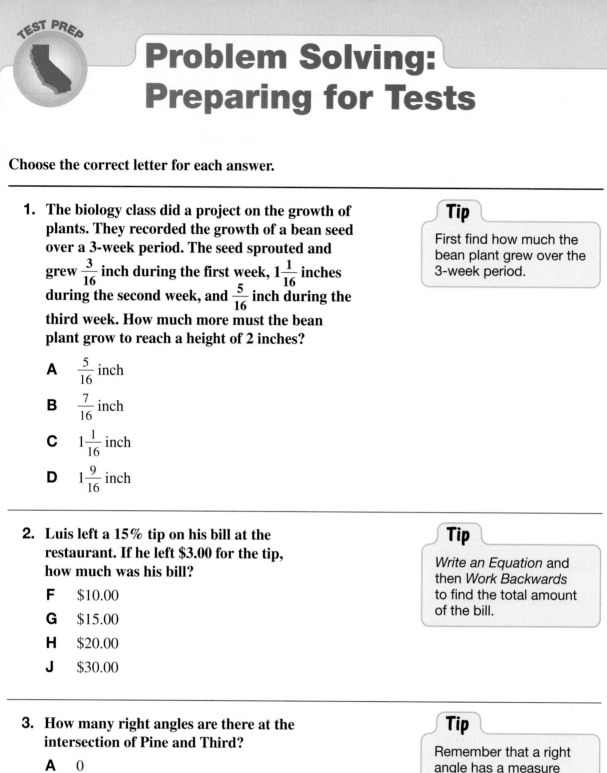

4. An airplane flight is scheduled to land at 3:30 P.M. Which information do you need to estimate the length of the flight?

   F The time the plane is scheduled to take off

   G How fast the plane will travel

   H The distance the plane will fly

   J The size and type of the plane

5. Sue and Beth are weaving identical rugs. After one week, Sue completed $\frac{1}{2}$ of the rug and Beth completed $\frac{1}{3}$ of the rug. How much more of the rug had Sue completed than Beth?

   A $\frac{2}{3}$ of the rug

   B $\frac{1}{2}$ of the rug

   C $\frac{1}{4}$ of the rug

   D $\frac{1}{6}$ of the rug

6. Square boxes 3 inches on each side are packed in a larger box 24 inches on each side. How many small boxes can be packed on the bottom layer of the box?

   F 20 boxes   **H** 72 boxes

   G 64 boxes   **J** 100 boxes

7. Forty-eight schools decided to plant trees for Earth Day. If a total of 240 trees were planted and each school planted the same number, how many trees did each school plant?

   A 5 trees   **C** 24 trees

   B 10 trees   **D** 48 trees

8. It takes $\frac{3}{8}$ pound of dough to make a small doll. How many small dolls can you make from 2 pounds of dough?

   F 3 dolls   **H** 5 dolls

   G 4 dolls   **J** 6 dolls

9. Louise wants to buy a pair of jeans on sale. About how much less will she pay than the regular price of $49.96 if the jeans are on sale for 25% off?

   A $5.00   **C** $8.00

   B $6.15   **D** $12.50

10. Mr. Hunt started to hike up a mountain trail at 10:15 A.M. He reached the observatory at 1:00 P.M. How long did it take Mr. Hunt to reach the observatory?

    F 2 hours

    G 2 hours 15 minutes

    H 2 hours 30 minutes

    J 2 hours 45 minutes

11.

Favorite Rides of 160 people	
Ferris Wheel	25%
Roller Coaster	30%
Water Ride	45%

How many people chose the roller coaster as their favorite ride?

   A 40   **C** 48

   B 46   **D** 50

Multiple-Choice Cumulative Review

Choose the correct letter for each answer.

Number Sense

1. Chicago's O'Hare International Airport is one of the busiest airports in the world. Suppose 352 airplanes take off in 8 hours. How many airplanes take off each hour on average?

   A   16 airplanes

   B   44 airplanes

   C   347 airplanes

   D   2816 airplanes

2. Donald, Liz, and Jake each ordered new computer modems. If each modem weighed 2.2 pounds, what was the total weight of the modems?

   F   6.6 pounds

   G   8.8 pounds

   H   10 pounds

   J   22 pounds

3. Marcy, Kayla, Dominic, and Trisha split the cost of a $10 taxi ride equally. How much did each person pay?

   A $1.25   C $2.25

   B $2.00   D $2.50

4. Which operation should you do first to find $18 - 6 \div 2 + 1 \times 3$?

   F   Division

   G   Subtraction

   H   Multiplication

   J   Addition

5. Twelve students weeded their garden. Each student weeded $\frac{2}{3}$ of a row of vegetables. How many rows got weeded?

   A $2\frac{2}{3}$ rows   C   12 rows

   B   8 rows   D   24 rows

6. Rick sold peanuts at the snack stand. Each bag of peanuts weighed $\frac{1}{4}$ pound. How many bags could he fill from a 12-pound sack of peanuts?

   F   3 bags   H   24 bags

   G   12 bags   J   48 bags

7. Complete.
   3 canisters for $51.00
   1 canister for ■

   A $14.00   C $16.75

   B $15.25   D $17.00

8. Trail A is $5\frac{1}{8}$ miles. Trails B and C are each $2\frac{1}{3}$ miles. Trail D is $2\frac{1}{2}$ miles longer than Trail A. Estimate the total length of the trails.

   F   About 10 miles

   G   About 12 miles

   J   About 17 miles

   H   About 25 miles

Measurement and Geometry

9. Two angles of an isosceles right triangle are the same measure. What is the measure?

   A $12\frac{1}{2}°$

   B 24°

   C 33°

   D 45°

10. Jerry measured the length of his room to be 300 inches long. How long is his room in feet?

    F 10 feet

    G 20 feet

    H 25 feet

    J 250 feet

11. How many lines of symmetry does the figure below have?

    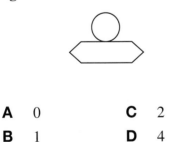

    A 0   C 2

    B 1   D 4

12. One cup of water is equal to 8 ___?___ of water.

    F ounces

    G pints

    H liters

    J gallons

Statistics, Data Analysis, and Probability

13. There are 16 marbles in a box. The marbles are red, white, or blue. If $P(red) = \frac{1}{2}$ and $P(blue) = \frac{1}{4}$, how many marbles are white?

    A 2   C 4

    B 3   D 6

Use the description below for Questions 14–16.

A cube is labeled with the numbers 1–6. Player A wins when a 4 is tossed. Player B wins when an odd number is tossed.

14. What are the possible outcomes for Player B to win?

    F 2, 4, 6

    G 0

    H 1, 3, 5

    J 3

15. What is the probability of Player A not winning?

    A $\frac{5}{6}$ C $\frac{1}{2}$

    B $\frac{2}{3}$ D $\frac{1}{3}$

16. What is the probability of tossing an even number?

    F $\frac{5}{6}$ H $\frac{1}{2}$

    G $\frac{2}{3}$ J $\frac{1}{3}$

CHAPTER

12

Perimeter, Area and Volume

Diagnosing Readiness

In Chapter 12, you will use these skills:

Ⓐ Adding and Subtracting Whole Numbers and Decimals

(pages 14–19)

1. $120 + 35 + 35 + 75$

2. $2.26 + 0.83 + 9.9 + 0.21$

3. $180.3267 - 127.365$

4. $92.375 - 20.125$

5. The length of Mr. Gillano's fence is 31.7 meters long. Mr. Nykamp has a horse fence that extends from Mr. Gillano's fence. The horse fence is 97.6 meters long. What is the total length of both fences combined?

Ⓑ Evaluating Expressions

(pages 26–27)

Evaluate each expression.

6. $262 - 3x + 12.6x$ for $x = 6$

7. $3a + 4b - c$ for $a = 5, b = 1$ and $c = 10$

8. When David is x years old, his brother is $x + 5$ years old. If David is 12, how old is his brother?

C Multiplying Decimals and Fractions

(pages 52–54, 192–193)

9. $6 \times 0.967 \times 11.2$

10. $85 \times \frac{3}{10} \times \frac{6}{12}$

11. $0.5 \times 90.9 \times 3.24$

12. 319×2.9

13. $\frac{2}{3} \times 24$

14. Laura made duplicates of 78 photographs and then gave the original photos and the duplicates away. She gave $\frac{1}{3}$ of them to her mom, $\frac{1}{4}$ of them to her brother, and let her little sister have the rest. How many photos did each person receive?

D Finding Percents

(pages 350–351, 354–355, 358–359)

Solve. Round to the nearest tenth.

15. 23 is what percent of 108?

16. 45 is what percent of 27?

17. What is 120% of 86.57?

18. 75 is what percent of 218?

19. What is 57% of 35?

E Using Order of Operations

(pages 24–25)

Use the order of operations to evaluate each of the following.

20. $33 + 15 \times 7 + 8$

21. $\frac{1}{4} + 1.8 \times 2.1 - 0.25$

22. $2{,}100 \times 2.8 - 1{,}300 + 21.09$

23. $25 \times \frac{15}{5} + 22 - (22 + 27)$

24. Hank divided 265 baseball cards into stacks of 5. From each stack he removed 10. He traded the cards he removed and added 7 new cards to each stack. Now, how many cards are in each stack?

F Converting Measurements

(pages 260–262)

25. 165 in. = ■ ft

26. 68 yd = ■ ft

27. 3 mile = ■ yd

28. The top of an oak tree in Jarrod's backyard measures 52 feet from the ground. His house is 11 yards high. How much taller, in feet, is the oak tree?

To the Family and Student

Looking Back	Chapter 12	Looking Ahead
In Grade 5 students learned how to construct geometric figures.	**Perimeter, Area, and Volume** In this chapter, students will learn how to determine the perimeter, area, and volume of geometric figures.	In Grade 7 students will extend their work with three-dimensional geometric figures.

Math and Everyday Living

Opportunities to apply the concepts of Chapter 12 abound in everyday situations. During the chapter, think about how perimeter, area, and volume can be used to solve a variety of real-world problems. The following examples suggest just several of the many situations that could launch a discussion about perimeter, area, and volume.

Math in the Budget
Your family has plans to recarpet your bedroom this year. They budgeted $680 for the improvement. Your bedroom measures 12 feet by $13\frac{1}{4}$ feet. What is the most your family can pay per square yard of carpet and stay within the budget?

Math in the Neighborhood
Your family is hosting a neighborhood barbecue this Saturday. You are in charge of decorating each side of the deck, except for the steps, with red, white, and blue crepe paper. The design of the deck is shown below. How much crepe paper of each color do you need?

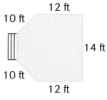

Math in Design Your family is working on a design for a banner for a celebration. The preliminary design is shown below.

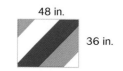

Your job is to add streamers to each corner as well as every 6 inches around the perimeter of the banner. Determine how many streamers you will need.

Math and Recreation
You and your family are considering purchasing a dart board for your game room. A dart board designed for adults has a 24 in. diameter while the dart board for children has a diameter of 18 in. What is the difference in area between the two dart boards?

Math and Fitness Your bike tire has a circumference of about 50 inches. If you pedal fast enough for the tire to complete 200 full revolutions each minute, about how many feet does the bike travel in one minute?

Math in the Yard Over the summer you and your friend run a lawn-cutting business. You charge $10.00 for a lawn under 350 ft², $20.00 for a lawn between 350 ft² and 700 ft², and $40.00 for a yard larger than 700 ft². Use the diagrams below to determine the pricing for Mrs. Roshek's yard and for Mr. McGrove's yard.

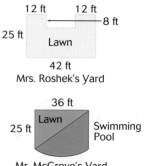

California Content Standards in Chapter 12 Lessons*

Algebra and Functions	Teach and Practice	Practice
1.1 (🗝) Write and solve one-step linear equations in one variable.		12-8
3.1 Use variables in expressions describing geometric quantities (e.g., $P = 2w + 2\ell$, $a = 1/2\ bh$, $C = \pi d$ the formulas for the perimeter of a rectangle, area of a triangle, and the circumference of a circle, respectively).	12-1, 12-3	12-2, 12-4, 12-5, 12-6, 12-9, 12-10
3.2 Express in symbolic form simple relationships arising from geometry.	12-2	12-1, 12-3, 12-4, 12-5, 12-6, 12-9, 12-10

Measurement and Geometry	Teach and Practice	Practice
1.1 (🗝) Understand the concept of a constant such as π; know the formulas for the circumference and area of a circle.	12-5, 12-6	
1.2 Know common estimates of π (3.14, 22/7) and use these values to estimate and calculate the circumference and the area of circles; compare with actual measurements.	12-5, 12-6	12-8, 12-10
1.3 Know and use the formulas for the volume of triangular prisms and cylinders (area of base × height); compare these formulas and explain the similarity between them and the formula for the volume of a rectangular solid.	12-9, 12-10	

Mathematical Reasoning	Teach and Practice	Practice
1.1 Analyze problems by identifying relationships, distinguishing relevant from irrelevant information, identifying missing information, sequencing and prioritizing information and observing patterns.		12-2, 12-3, 12-5
1.2 Formulate and justify mathematical conjectures based on a general description of the mathematical question or problem posed.		12-2
1.3 Determine when and how to break a problem into simpler parts.	12-4	12-2, 12-3, 12-8, 12-9, 12-10
2.2 Apply strategies and results from simpler problems to more complex problems.		12-6, 12-7, 12-8, 12-9, 12-10
2.4 Use a variety of methods, such as words, numbers, symbols, charts, graphs, tables, diagrams, and models, to explain mathematical reasoning.	12-7, 12-8	
2.5 Express the solution clearly and logically by using the appropriate mathematical notation and terms and clear language; support solutions with evidence in both verbal and symbolic work.		12-3, 12-4, 12-8
3.2 Note the method of deriving the solution and demonstrate a conceptual understanding of the derivation by solving similar problems.		12-3, 12-7
3.3 Develop generalizations of the results obtained and the strategies used and apply them in new problem situations.		12-6, 12-7

* The symbol (🗝) indicates a key standard as designated in the Mathematics Framework for California Public Schools. Full statements of the California Content Standards are found at the beginning of this book following the Table of Contents.

Area of Quadrilaterals

California Content Standard *Algebra and Functions 3.2: Express in symbolic form simple relationships arising from geometry.*

Warm-Up Review

Evaluate each expression.

1. s^2 when $s = 2.4$

2. xy when $x = 6\frac{1}{2}$ and $y = 1\frac{1}{3}$.

3. Find the perimeter of the baseball infield below. It is a square.

Math Link You know how to find the perimeter of a polygon. Now you will learn how to find the area of a quadrilateral.

The number of square units needed to cover a region is the **area** *(A)* of the region.

Word Bank

area

Area Formulas

Square $A = s^2$

Rectangle $A = lw$

Example 1

The infield of a baseball diamond is a square that is 90 feet on each side. Find the area of the infield.

$A = s^2$

$A = 90^2$ Substitute $s = 90$.

$A = 8,100$ $90^2 = 90 \times 90$

The infield has an area of 8,100 square feet.

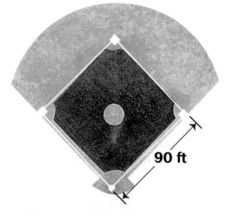

90 ft

The area of any figure is expressed in square units, such as square feet, or ft^2.

Example 2

Find the area of the rectangle below.

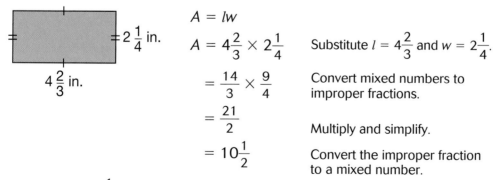

$2\frac{1}{4}$ in.

$4\frac{2}{3}$ in.

$A = lw$

$A = 4\frac{2}{3} \times 2\frac{1}{4}$ Substitute $l = 4\frac{2}{3}$ and $w = 2\frac{1}{4}$.

$= \dfrac{14}{3} \times \dfrac{9}{4}$ Convert mixed numbers to improper fractions.

$= \dfrac{21}{2}$ Multiply and simplify.

$= 10\frac{1}{2}$ Convert the improper fraction to a mixed number.

The area is $10\frac{1}{2}$ square inches.

Additional Standards: Algebra and Functions 3.1; Mathematical Reasoning 1.1, 1.2, 1.3 (See p. 457.)

You can use what you know about the area of a rectangle to find the area of a parallelogram. Look at the parallelogram at the right. If the triangle is cut out and moved to the opposite side, a rectangle is formed. The parallelogram and the rectangle have the same area.

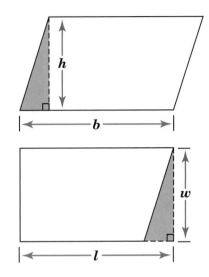

$A = lw$ The length of the rectangle is the base (b) of the parallelogram. The width of the rectangle is the height (h) of the parallelogram.

$A = bh$

Formula for the Area of a Parallelogram

$A = bh$

Example 3

Find the area of a parallelogram with base of 2.8 centimeters and height of 0.9 centimeters.

$A = bh$
$A = 2.8 \times 0.9$ Substitute $b = 2.8$ and $h = 0.9$.
$A = 2.52$ cm^2 Multiply.

Example 4

A 7 meter by 7 meter square has an area of 49 square meters. What happens to the area if the length of each side is doubled?

Step 1 Find the area of a 14 meter by 14 meter square.

$A = s^2$
$A = (14)^2 = 196$

Step 2 Find the ratio of the new area to the original area.

$$\frac{\text{new area}}{\text{original area}} = \frac{196}{49} = 4$$

When the length of a side of a square is doubled, the new area is 4 times the original area.

Guided Practice *For another example, see Set B on p. 488.*

Find the area of each quadrilateral.

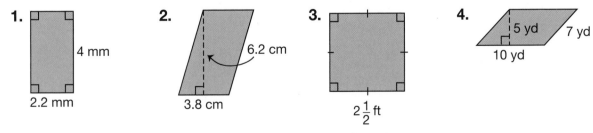

1. 4 mm 2.2 mm

2. 6.2 cm 3.8 cm

3. $2\frac{1}{2}$ ft

4. 5 yd 7 yd 10 yd

5. Find the area of a parallelogram with a height of 1.5 in. and a base of 15 in.

Algebra Find the area of each quadrilateral.

6. 2 mm
8 mm

7. 10 ft
30 ft

8. 12 yd
24 yd

9. $1\frac{1}{2}$ in.
6 in.

10. A 6 foot by 9 foot rectangle has an area of 54 square feet. What happens to the area if the length of each side is multiplied by 3? Explain.

Use the diagram at the right for Exercises 11–13.

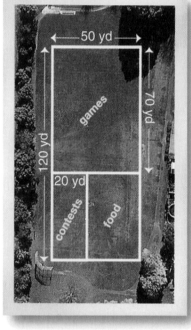

11. A section of the field will be used for games. What is the area of this section?

12. What is the area of the section roped off for food?

13. In the diagram, how much rope is needed to rope off the perimeter of the field and each section?

Mixed Review

Use the information to find each probability.

A carnival fish tank has 25 plastic fish, with 6 red, 3 blue, 7 yellow, 5 orange, and 4 green fish. You select one fish without looking, do **not** replace it, and select another fish.

14. *P*(blue, blue)

15. *P*(red, red)

16. *P*(orange, orange)

Test Prep   Choose the correct letter for each answer.

Use the following information for Questions 17 and 18.

Max wants to buy a $560 refrigerator that is on sale for 25% off. Tax is 6%. He can afford to spend $450.

17. To see if he can afford the refrigerator, what must Max calculate?
(1-3)

   A The exact cost with the discount and tax

   B An approximate cost with discount and tax

   C The exact change he would get from $450

   D The approximate tax

18. How much does the refrigerator cost with the discount and tax?
(9-9)

   F $420   **G** $445.20   **H** $526.40   **J** $593.60

Multiple-Choice Cumulative Review

Choose the correct letter for each answer.

1. Which of the following is the number of sides in a pentagon?

   A 5   **C** 8

   B 6   **D** 10

2. There are 12 marbles in a box. If P (red) $= \frac{3}{6}$, P(blue) $= \frac{1}{6}$, and P(white) $= \frac{2}{6}$, how many red marbles are in the box?

   F 2   **H** 4

   G 3   **J** 6

3. You get a $6.95 discount on a gift you buy for a friend. You pay $27.80 for the gift. If there is no sales tax, what was the original price?

   A $20.85   **C** $34.75

   B $32.15   **D** $35.67

4. A square has a perimeter of 48 centimeters. What is the length of one side?

   F 8 cm   **H** 36 cm

   G 12 cm   **J** 48 cm

5. A miner was 40 feet below the surface. he then descended another 30 feet through a shaft. How many feet below the surface was he then?

   A 10 ft   **C** 50 ft

   B 30 ft   **D** 70 ft

6. Scott is a writer. He has completed $\frac{2}{5}$ of his latest book and sent it to his editor. What percent of the book does he still have left to complete?

   F 20%   **H** 40%

   G 30%   **J** 60%

7. What is the area in square yards of a platform that measures 3 yards by 10 yards? (1 yd = 3 ft)

   A 300 yd^2 **C** 30 yd^2

   B 90 yd^2 **D** 19 yd^2

8. A number cube is labeled 1, 1, 2, 3, 3, 4. What is the probability of NOT tossing a 2?

   F 0   **H** $\frac{1}{2}$

   G $\frac{1}{6}$ **J** $\frac{5}{6}$

9. An airplane flies at an average speed of 330 miles per hour. The distance between Boston, MA, and Houston, TX, is approximately 1,600 miles. If the plane flies a direct route nonstop, about how long does it take to get from Boston to Houston?

   A $3\frac{1}{2}$ hours

   B 4 hours

   C 5 hours

   D 7 hours

LESSON

12-3

Area of Triangles

 Algebra

California Content Standard *Algebra and Functions 3.1: Use variables in expressions describing geometric quantities (e.g., A = $\frac{1}{2}bh$, . . . —the formula for . . . the area of a triangle . . .).*

Math Link You know how to evaluate variable expressions using the order of operations. Now you will learn how to evaluate formulas to find areas.

Warm-Up Review

Find the area of a parallelogram with each base (*b*) and height (*h*).

1. $b = 12.4$ km, $h = 9.5$ km

2. $b = 6\frac{1}{4}$ ft, $h = 3\frac{1}{5}$ ft

3. A rectangle is 1.5 feet by 42 inches. Find the area of the rectangle in square feet.

Example 1

The grassy area shown at the right is covered with plywood for a dance. Compare the area of the grassy area to the entire area. The entire area is a parallelogram. The diagram below shows the parallelogram can be divided into two congruent triangles. The area of each triangle is half the area of the parallelogram.

The grassy area is half the entire area.

You can use this relationship to write the formula for the area of a triangle.

Parallelogram	Triangle
$A = bh$	$A = \frac{1}{2}bh$

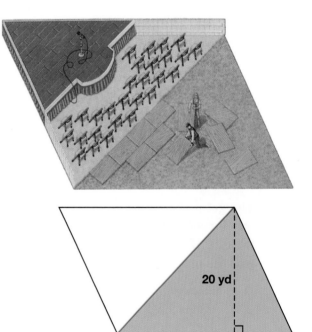

20 yd

30 yd

Example 2

Use the formula for the area of a triangle to find the area of the triangular section to be covered with plywood.

$A = \frac{1}{2}bh$

$= \frac{1}{2}(30 \times 20)$ Substitute 30 for *b* and 20 for *h*.

$= \frac{1}{2} \times 600$ Multiply.

$= 300$ square yards

The area of the section to be covered is 300 square yards.

464

Additional Standards: Algebra and Functions 3.2; Mathematical Reasoning 1.1, 1.3, 2.5, 3.2 (See p. 457.)

Guided Practice *For another example, See Set C on p. 488.*

Find the area of each triangle.

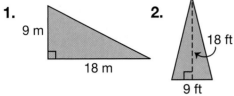

1. 9 m, 18 m

2. 18 ft, 9 ft

3. 6 in., 24 in.

4. 10 cm, 20 cm

5. Math Reasoning A triangle has a base of 1.5 meters and a height of 850 centimeters. Find the area of the triangle in square meters.

Independent Practice *For more practice, see Set C on p. 491.*

Find the area of each triangle.

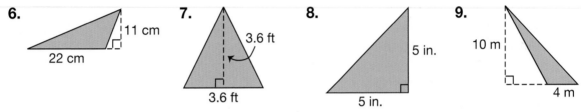

6. 11 cm, 22 cm

7. 3.6 ft, 3.6 ft

8. 5 in., 5 in.

9. 10 m, 4 m

10. Find the area of the triangle at the right. Each square of the grid is equal to 1 square unit.

11. Mental Math A square piece of green paper is cut along the diagonal to make two triangular place mats. If the area of each triangular place mat is 200 in.², how long is each side of the green square?

Mixed Review

12. The base paths of a baseball diamond form a square with 90 feet on a side. Suppose there are runners on first base and third base. If the batter hits a home run, how far do the three players run altogether?

13. Find the area of a rectangle with a width of 8 meters and a length of 4.6 meters.

Test Prep   Choose the correct letter for each answer.

14. $8\frac{1}{4} \div 5\frac{1}{2} =$
(5-8)

A $\frac{2}{3}$ **B** $1\frac{1}{2}$ **C** $2\frac{3}{4}$ **D** $13\frac{3}{4}$ **E** NH

15. Carly paid $36 for 24 tennis balls. Find the unit price to the nearest cent.
(8-6)

F $0.67   **G** $1.25   **H** $1.50   **J** $12

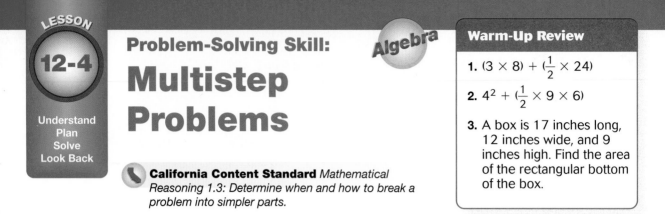

LESSON
12-4

Understand
Plan
Solve
Look Back

Problem-Solving Skill:

Multistep Problems

Algebra

California Content Standard *Mathematical Reasoning 1.3: Determine when and how to break a problem into simpler parts.*

Warm-Up Review

1. $(3 \times 8) + (\frac{1}{2} \times 24)$

2. $4^2 + (\frac{1}{2} \times 9 \times 6)$

3. A box is 17 inches long, 12 inches wide, and 9 inches high. Find the area of the rectangular bottom of the box.

Read For Understanding

You have decided to have a miniature golf contest at your school picnic. Your contest will take place on a miniature golf course hole like the one shown at the right in the diagram.

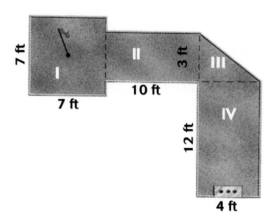

1 What are the dimensions of the rectangular area around the tee?

2 What are two of the dimensions of the triangle where the course hole turns?

THINK AND DISCUSS

MATH FOCUS

Multistep Problems

To solve some problems, you may need more than one step. Each step gives you some of the information you need.

Reread the paragraph at the top of the page.

Think about what steps are needed to find the area of green carpet used to cover the playing surface.

3 What is the area of Figure II? Figure III?

4 Write an expression that can be used to find the area of the green carpet.

5 What is the area of green carpet used to cover the playing surface?

6 What steps were needed to find the area of green carpet?

 Additional Standards: Algebra and Functions 3.1, 3.2; Mathematical Reasoning 2.5 (See p. 457.)

Guided Practice

Selena needs to mow the grass in the yard shown in the diagram at the right. How much area does she need to mow?

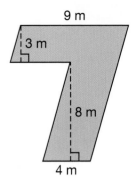

1. What do you need to do first to solve this problem?

   a. Divide the area into two rectangles.

   b. Divide the area into a parallelogram and a triangle.

   c. Divide the area into two parallelograms.

2. Which expression could you use to solve the problem?

   a. $(9 \times 3) + (4 \times 8)$

   b. 9×11

   c. $(4 \times 11) + (9 \times 3)$

Independent Practice

At a picnic, food will be placed on one long table. The long table will be created by placing two smaller tables end-to-end as shown in the diagram below. A paper skirt will be wrapped around the long table and held in place by thumbtacks. If the thumbtacks are placed every 6 inches, how many thumbtacks are needed?

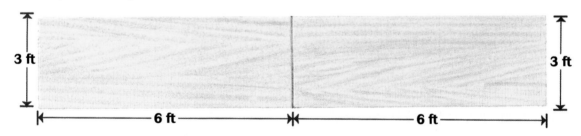

3. What do you need to do first to solve this problem?

   a. Find the perimeter of the long table.

   b. Find the area of the long table.

   c. Find the height of the long table.

4. Which expression could you use to solve the problem?

   a. $(2l + 2w) \div 6$

   b. $((2l + 2w) \times 12) \div 6$

   c. $(l \times w) \times 2$

5. **Math Reasoning** If three inches of paper on each side are folded under, how many square feet of paper are needed to cover the long table? Explain your answer.

12-5

Circumference

Algebra

California Content Standard *Measurement and Geometry 1.1(   ): Understand the concept of a constant such as π, know the formulas for the circumference . . . of a circle. Also, Measurement and Geometry 1.2*

Math Link You know how to find the perimeter and area of polygons. Now you will learn how to find the circumference of a circle.

Circumference is the distance around a circle.

Example 1

Rachel and Sheldon measured three circular objects. They found the circumference and diameter of each and recorded them in a table. Find the ratio of the circumference, *C*, to the diameter, *d*, of each object.

Object	Circumference	Diameter	$\frac{C}{d}$
Pan lid	71.4 cm	22.7 cm	$71.4 \div 22.7 \approx 3.145$
Juice glass	11 in.	$3\frac{1}{2}$ in.	$11 \div 3.5 \approx 3.143$
Swimming pool	47 ft	15 ft	$47 \div 15 \approx 3.133$

Each ratio is close to 3.14.

The ratio of the circumference to the diameter of every circle is the same. The Greek letter π (read **pi**) is used to represent this ratio.

$\pi = \frac{C}{d}$, so $C = \pi d$.

Since the diameter of a circle is twice the radius, $C = \pi d$ is the same as $C = \pi 2r$, or $C = 2\pi r$.

Word Bank

circumference

pi

Formula for Circumference of a Circle
$C = \pi d$ or $C = 2\pi r$

Differences in the ratios for $\frac{C}{d}$ appear in the table because it is impossible to measure exactly. Approximate values for π that are commonly used are 3.14 and $\frac{22}{7}$.

Additional Standards: Algebra and Functions 3.1, 3.2; Mathematical Reasoning 1.1 (See p. 457.)

Example 2

How much plastic tubing is needed to make the hoop in the photograph at the right? Use $\frac{22}{7}$ for π.

$C = \pi d$

$C \approx \frac{22}{7} \times 28$

$C \approx 88$

You need about 88 inches of plastic tubing.

28 in.

Example 3

Find the circumference of a circle with radius $r = 8$ m.

You can use 3.14 for π.

$C = 2\pi r$

$C \approx 2 \times 3.14 \times 8$

$C \approx 50.24$

The circumference is about 50.24 meters.

With a calculator:

Press: $\boxed{2}$ $\boxed{\times}$ $\boxed{\pi}$ $\boxed{\times}$ $\boxed{8}$ $\boxed{=}$

Display: $\boxed{50.265482}$

The answers differ slightly because the π key uses 3.1415927 as an approximation for π.

Guided Practice *For another example, see Set D on p. 490.*

Find the circumference of each circle to the nearest whole number. Use 3.14 or $\frac{22}{7}$ for π.

1. 5 m

2. 3 in.

3. 4.5 cm

4. 7 ft

5. A tire has a radius of 11 inches. What is its circumference?

Independent Practice *For more practice, see Set D on p. 492.*

Find the circumference of each circle to the nearest whole number. Use 3.14 or $\frac{22}{7}$ for π.

6. $3\frac{1}{2}$ ft

7. 2.1 m

8. 11 in.

9. 4.9 cm

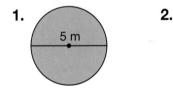

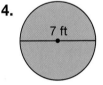
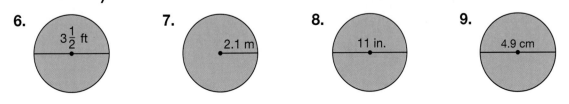

10. **Math Reasoning** Write a formula for the distance, D, around the figure at the right. The figures on the ends are semicircles.

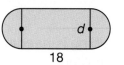
d

18

Use the photograph of a playground merry-go-round at the right for Exercises 11–13. Use 3.14 for π. Round to the nearest whole number.

11. Brittany's head is 48 inches from the middle of the merry-go-round. How far does her head travel each time it goes all the way around?

12. Branden's feet are 16 inches from the middle of the merry-go-round. How far do they travel each time they go around?

13. The diameter of the merry-go-round is 100 inches. If the children stand on the edge of the merry-go-round, how far will they travel in 10 revolutions of the merry-go-round?

Mixed Review

14. Use translation, rotation, or reflection to describe the motion used to move the children from one position to another on a merry-go-round.

Find the area of each figure.

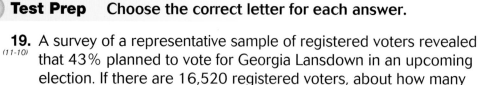

15.
9 mm
16 mm
7 mm

16.
7 in.
$2\frac{4}{5}$ in.

17.
2 in.
4 in.
4 in.

18.
3 km
4.5 km

🔺 **Test Prep** Choose the correct letter for each answer.

19. A survey of a representative sample of registered voters revealed
(11-10) that 43% planned to vote for Georgia Lansdown in an upcoming election. If there are 16,520 registered voters, about how many votes is Georgia Lansdown likely to get?

   A 70,000   **B** 9,000   **C** 7,000   **D** 710

20. Which term best describes the relationship between
(7-6) $\angle MON$ and $\angle POQ$ in the figure at the right?

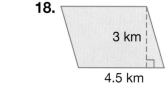

   F vertical   **H** complementary

   G supplementary   **J** adjacent

Diagnostic Checkpoint

Match the formula in Column A with the best description in Column B.

Column A

1. $P = 4s$
(12-1)

2. $P = 2l + 2w$
(12-1)

3. $C = 2\pi r$
(12-5)

4. $A = s^2$
(12-2)

5. $A = lw$
(12-2)

6. $A = \frac{1}{2}bh$
(12-3)

Column B

a. Area of a square

b. Area of a triangle

c. Perimeter of a square

d. Area of a rectangle

e. Circumference of a circle

f. Perimeter of a rectangle

Find the perimeter of each polygon.

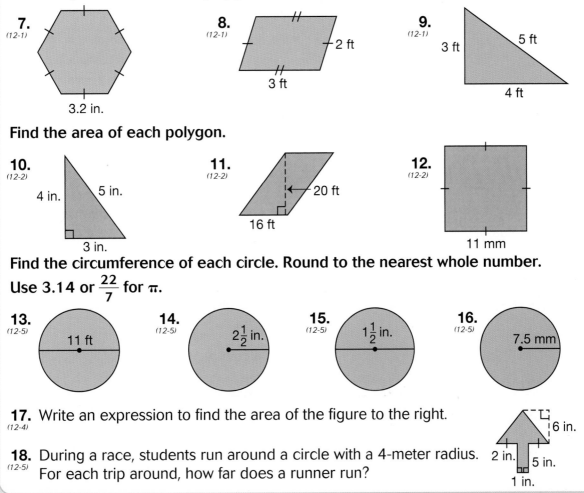

7. 3.2 in.
(12-1)

8. 2 ft, 3 ft
(12-1)

9. 3 ft, 5 ft, 4 ft
(12-1)

Find the area of each polygon.

10. 4 in., 5 in., 3 in.
(12-2)

11. 20 ft, 16 ft
(12-2)

12. 11 mm
(12-2)

Find the circumference of each circle. Round to the nearest whole number. Use 3.14 or $\frac{22}{7}$ for π.

13. 11 ft
(12-5)

14. $2\frac{1}{2}$ in.
(12-5)

15. $1\frac{1}{2}$ in.
(12-5)

16. 7.5 mm
(12-5)

17. Write an expression to find the area of the figure to the right.
(12-4)

6 in., 2 in., 5 in., 1 in.

18. During a race, students run around a circle with a 4-meter radius. For each trip around, how far does a runner run?
(12-5)

Area of a Circle

12-6

 Algebra

Warm-Up Review

Find the circumference of each circle.

1. $d = 8$ cm

2. $r = 11$ ft.

3. Find the circumference of the shaded region.

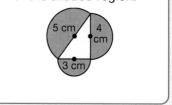

Math Link You know how to use π to find the circumference of a circle. Now you will learn how to use π to find the area of a circle.

Example 1

Divide a circle into sections as shown at the right. Rearrange the sections to approximate a parallelogram. Use the formula for the area of a parallelogram to write the formula for the area of a circle.

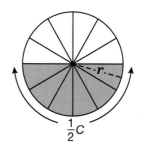

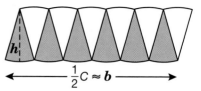

$A = b \times h$ Area of a parallelogram

$= \frac{1}{2}C \times h$ The base, b, is $\frac{1}{2}$ the circumference.

$= \frac{1}{2}(2\pi r) \times r$ The height, h, is the radius r.

$= \pi r \times r$ $r \times r = r^2$

$A = \pi r^2$ Area of a circle

> **Formula for Area of a Circle**
>
> $A = \pi r^2$

More Examples

A. Find the area of a circle with a radius of 7 ft.

$A = \pi r^2$
$A = \pi \times 7^2$
$A \approx \frac{22}{7} \times \frac{49}{1} = \frac{154}{1} = 154$

The area of the circle is about 154 square feet.

With a calculator:

Press: $\boxed{\pi}$ $\boxed{\times}$ $\boxed{7}$ $\boxed{x^2}$ $\boxed{=}$

Display: $\boxed{153.93804}$

B. Find the area of a circle with a diameter of 12 cm. Remember, if $d = 12, r = 6$.

$A = \pi r^2$
$A = \pi \times 6^2$
$A \approx 3.14 \times 36$
$A \approx 113.04$

With a calculator:

Press: $\boxed{\pi}$ $\boxed{\times}$ $\boxed{6}$ $\boxed{x^2}$ $\boxed{=}$

Display: $\boxed{113.09734}$

The area of the circle, to the nearest whole number, is 113 square centimeters.

Guided Practice *For another example, see Set E on p. 489.*

Find the area of each circle to the nearest whole number. Use 3.14 or $\frac{22}{7}$ for π.

1. 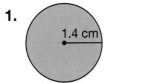 1.4 cm

2. 2 cm

3. 6 yd

4. 1.9 ft

5. Math Reasoning Find the area of the shaded region at the right.

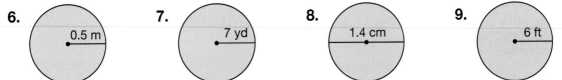
7
7
5
7
7

Independent Practice *For more practice, see Set E on p. 492.*

Find the area of each circle to the nearest whole number. Use 3.14 or $\frac{22}{7}$ for π.

6. 0.5 m

7. 7 yd

8. 1.4 cm

9. 6 ft

Use the archery target at the right for Exercises 10–12.

10. What is the area of the yellow bullseye?

11. What is the area of the whole target?

12. What percent of the target is the yellow bullseye?

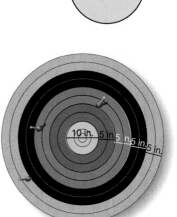
10 in. 5 in. 5 in. 5 in. 5 in.

Mixed Review

13. What is the circumference of a circle with a radius of 10 inches?

Find the circumference of each circle to the nearest whole number. Use 3.14 or $\frac{22}{7}$ for π.

14. $d = 84$ in.　　**15.** $d = 3.5$ yd　　**16.** $r = 2.5$ m

17. Find the area of the shaded triangle at the right. Each square of the grid is equal to 1 square unit.

Test Prep　Choose the correct letter for each answer.

18. Find m∠a in the figure at the right.
(7-6)
　A 35°　　　**B** 55°　　　**C** 70°　　　**D** 160°

19. Find m∠b in the figure at the right.
(7-7)
　F 35°　　　**G** 55°　　　**H** 70°　　　**J** 160°

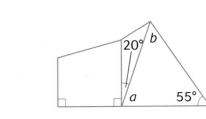
20° b
a 55°

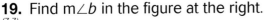

Problem-Solving Strategy:
Draw a Diagram

California Content Standard *Mathematical Reasoning 2.4: Use a variety of methods such as words, numbers, symbols, charts, graphs, tables, diagrams and models, to explain mathematical reasoning.*

Warm-Up Review

1. Find the perimeter of the parallelogram.

4 in.   2 in.   3 in.

2. Lois wants to divide a long piece of chain into 5 pieces. How many cuts does she need to make?

Barry's kite for the kite-flying contest is made up of two triangles that share the same base. Two sides of one triangle are each 24 inches long. Two sides of the other triangle are each 30 inches long. Barry wants to attach two colored streamers to each corner of the kite and single streamers 6 inches apart around the rest of the kite. How many colored streamers does he need?

Understand

What do you need to know?

You need to know how many corners the kite has and at how many points streamers will be placed along the sides of the kite.

Plan

How can you solve the problem?

You can draw a diagram of the kite to solve the problem. On the diagram, label the length of each side. Then, starting at one corner, mark 6-inch intervals around the kite.

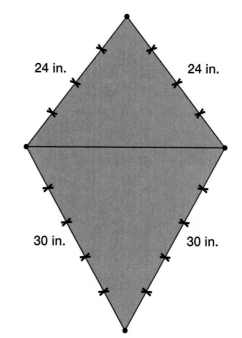

24 in.   24 in.   30 in.   30 in.

Solve

Find the number of streamers for the corners. (4 × 2 = 8). Count the number of streamers for the sides (14). Barry will need 22 streamers.

Look Back

How did using the diagram help you understand and solve the problem?

Additional Standards: Mathematical Reasoning 2.2, 3.2, 3.3; (See p. 457.)

Guided Practice

1. Kim is designing a poster made up of six congruent equilateral triangles having 22-inch sides. Each triangle shares two of its sides with other triangles. What is the shape of Kim's poster? How many feet of tape will she need to trim the poster's edges?

Independent Practice

2. Mia's rectangular art case is 22 inches long and 17 inches wide. She wants to decorate the surface of her case with square stickers 3 inches on a side. If she places the stickers 2 inches apart and 2 inches away from each edge of the case, how many stickers will she need?

3. The design for Emily's square kite has two congruent right isosceles triangles. The congruent sides of each isosceles triangle measure 3 feet. Will 8 square feet of fabric be enough to make the kite? Explain.

4. Barry is designing a second kite. This kite is made up of two congruent equilateral triangles, each having 36-inch sides and sharing the same base. If he places streamers as he did on his first kite, how many streamers does he need?

Mixed Review

Try these or other strategies to solve each problem. Tell which strategy you used.

> ## Problem-Solving Strategies
> - *Make a List*
> - *Make a Table*
> - *Make a Graph*
> - *Work Backward*

5. Barry's scores in the kite-flying contest were 8 for design, 6 for construction, and 5 for performance. In the same categories, Kim scored 9, 4, and 7: Emily scored 6, 8, and 3; and Mia scored 8, 4, and 7. Who came first in each category? Who had the highest overall score?

6. Emily spent a total of $5.85 on materials for her kite. She spent $2.40 for fabric, $0.95 for string, and $0.69 for tape. The rest was spent on balsa wood for the frame. How much did the wood cost?

LESSON
12-8

Understand
Plan
Solve
Look Back

Problem-Solving Application:

Using Circle Graphs

Algebra

Warm-Up Review

1. What percent of 85 is 17?

2. What is 45% of $28?

3. A $48 pair of jeans is marked 25% off. What is the sale price?

California Content Standard *Mathematical Reasoning 2.4: Use a variety of methods, such as . . . graphs, . . . to explain mathematical reasoning.*

Example 1

The total cost for 25 students to go to Fun World Amusement Park and participate in everything is $1,050. The circle graph shows how each separate cost relates to the total cost. How much will Linda pay if she does not go to the show?

Understand

What do you need to know?

You need to know what it costs per person to go on the trip and to go to the show.

Plan

How can you solve the problem?

Use the information in the circle graph to write equations.

Comparing Costs

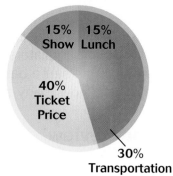

15% Show
15% Lunch
40% Ticket Price
30% Transportation

Solve

Step 1 Find the cost per student.	**Step 2** Find the cost of the show.	**Step 3** Subtract to find the cost without the show.
Number of students × Cost per student = Total cost ↓ ↓ ↓ 25 × C = $1,050 C = $42	15% of Cost per student = Cost of show ↓ ↓ ↓ ↓ 0.15 × 42 = $6.30	Cost per student − Cost of show = Cost without show ↓ ↓ ↓ $42.00 − $6.30 = $35.70
The cost per student is $42.	The show costs $6.30.	Linda will pay $35.70.

Look Back

Check by multiplying $42 × 85%.

Additional Standards: Algebra and Functions 1.1 (🔑); Mathematical Reasoning 1.3, 2.2, 2.5 (See p. 457.)

Example 2

Use the circle graph on page 476. What is the cost of transportation for one student?

Let t = cost of transportation.

30%	of	cost per student		cost of transportation
0.30	$\times$	$42	=	t
		$12.60	=	t

Each student must pay $12.60 for transportation.

Guided Practice

Use the circle graph on page 476 for Exercises 1 and 2.

1. If you did not want to pay for lunch or the show, how much would the trip cost?

2. What is the cost of one admission ticket?

Independent Practice

The total amount of money raised at the school fair was $3,500. Use the circle graph at the right for Exercises 3–5.

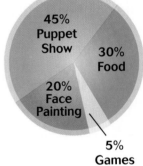

Money Raised At Each Booth

45% Puppet Show
30% Food
20% Face Painting
5% Games

3. Which booths together raised one-fourth of the total?

4. If the fair lasted 8 hours, how much money did the face-painting booth average per hour?

5. If the fair lasted 8 hours, which booth made about $22.00 per hour? Explain how you know.

Mixed Review

6. Next year the people organizing the school fair expect to make $4,000. Use the circle graph above to determine how much they can expect to earn on food.

7. In 1997, 12 boys and 4 girls competed in a swimming contest. In 1998 there were 7 girls and 10 boys. In 1999 there were 8 girls and 9 boys and in 2000 there were 7 boys and 10 girls. Describe the trend in the participation of boys and girls in the contest from 1997 through 2000.

Volume of Rectangular Prisms

Algebra

Warm-Up Review

Find the area of each rectangle.

1. ℓ = 5 in., w = $3\frac{1}{2}$ in.

2. ℓ = 11.7 cm, w = 4.8 cm

3. Find the area of the figure.

4 in.

3 in.

5 in.

4 in.

California Content Standard *Measurement and Geometry 1.3: Know and use . . . the formula for the volume of a rectangular solid.*

Math Link You know how to use formulas to find area and perimeter. Now you will learn how to use formulas to find the volume of rectangular prisms.

Example 1

How much sand was used to fill the long-jump pit at the right?

To find out, you need to find the volume of the pit. The volume, *V*, is the number of cubic units needed to fill a space figure.

Look at the model showing the cubes. Find the number of cubes in one layer.

$12 \times 7 = 84$

Next, multiply the number of cubes in one layer by the number of layers in the model.

$2 \times 84 = 168$

There are 168 cubic units in the model.

The pit was filled with 168 cubic feet of sand, or 168 ft³.

You can find the **volume** of any prism by multiplying the area of the base by the height

12 ft

7 ft

2 ft

number of cubes in one layer × number of layers = total number of cubes
↓   ↓   ↓

     area of the base   ×   height   =   volume
           ↓   ↓   ↓

            B   ×   *h*   =   *V*

$V = Bh$

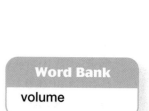

Word Bank

volume

The volume of any figure is expressed in cubic units, such as cubic feet, ft³, or cubic meters, m³.

Additional Standards: Algebra and Functions 3.1, 3.2; Mathematical Reasoning 1.3, 2.2 (See p. 457.)

Example 2

Write a formula for the volume of a rectangular prism with length *l*, width *w*, and height *h*.
Since the base is a rectangle, it has area *l* × *w*.
For a rectangular prism, $B = l \times w$.

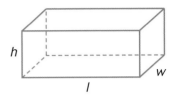

$V = B \times h$ Substitute *lw* for *B*.
$V = l \times w \times h$ or $V = lwh$

Formulas for the Volume of a Prism
Any prism: $V = Bh$
Rectangular prism: $V = lwh$

Example 3

Find the volume of a rectangular prism with a length of $5\frac{3}{4}$ inches, a width of $2\frac{1}{4}$ inches, and a height of $1\frac{1}{3}$ inches.

$V = l \times w \times h$

$V = 5\frac{3}{4} \times 2\frac{1}{4} \times 1\frac{1}{3}$ Substitute $l = 5\frac{3}{4}$, $w = 2\frac{1}{4}$, and $h = 1\frac{1}{3}$.

$V = \frac{23}{4} \times \frac{9}{4} \times \frac{4}{3} = \frac{69}{4}$ Convert mixed numbers to improper fractions.

$V = \frac{69}{4}$ Multiply.

$V = 17\frac{1}{4}$ Simplify.

The volume of the prism is $17\frac{1}{4}$ cubic inches.

Guided Practice *For another example, see Set F on p. 490.*

Find the volume of each space figure.

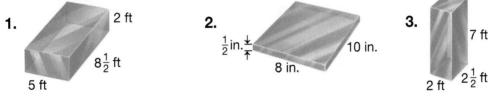

1. 2 ft, $8\frac{1}{2}$ ft, 5 ft

2. $\frac{1}{2}$ in., 10 in., 8 in.

3. 7 ft, $2\frac{1}{2}$ ft, 2 ft

4. Bags of sand measure 2 feet long, $1\frac{1}{2}$ feet wide, and 6 inches high. What is the volume of a stack of 8 bags?

5. **Math Reasoning** A cube is a special type of rectangular prism with all sides the same length. Write a formula for the volume of a cube with sides of length *s*.

Independent Practice *For more practice, see Set F on p. 493.*

Find the volume of each rectangular prism.

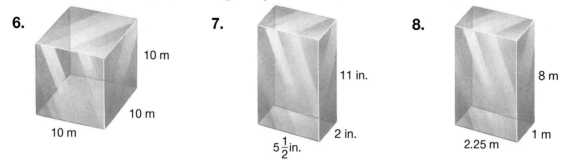

6. 10 m, 10 m, 10 m

7. 11 in., 2 in., $5\frac{1}{2}$ in.

8. 8 m, 1 m, 2.25 m

9. **Mental Math** How many cubic feet are in one cubic yard? Explain your answer.

Math Reasoning The surface area of a rectangular prism is the sum of the areas of all faces of the figure. Find the surface area of the rectangular prism shown in

10. Exercise 6. 11. Exercise 7. 12. Exercise 8.

Mixed Review

13. Use the information in the table at the right. How many possible one-topping pizzas could you order?

Toppings	Size
Mushroom	Small
Pineapple	Medium
Pepperoni	Large
Green Peppers	
Broccoli	

Find the circumference of each circle to the nearest whole number. Use 3.14 or $\frac{22}{7}$ for π.

14. $r = 2.4$ yd 15. $d = 2.1$ km 16. $r = 56$ in.

Find the area of each circle to the nearest whole number. Use 3.14 or $\frac{22}{7}$ for π.

17. $r = 4.2$ in. 18. $d = 7.8$ m 19. $d = 18$ cm

20. The base of a parallelogram is 10 ft, and the height is half the base. What is the area of the parallelogram?

Test Prep   Choose the correct letter for each answer.

21. There is a 68% probability of rain. What is the probability
(11-1) it does not rain?

   A 32%   **B** 42%   **C** 68%   **D** 100%

22. Evaluate $4x + 3y$ when $x = 7$ and $y = 2$.
(1-10)

   F 63   **G** 62   **H** 52   **J** 34

Volume of Triangular Prisms and Cylinders

Algebra

California Content Standard *Measurement and Geometry 1.3: Know and use the formulas for the volume of triangular prisms and cylinders (area of base × height); compare these formulas and explain the similarity between them and the formula for the volume of a rectangular solid.*

Math Link You know the formulas to find the volume of a rectangular prism, the area of a triangle, and the area of a circle. Now you will learn how to use these formulas to find the volume of triangular prisms and cylinders.

The formula for a rectangular prism, $V = Bh$, can be used to find the volume of a triangular prism or a cylinder. Remember that volume is measured in cubic units.

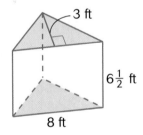

Example 1

Find the volume of the triangular prism at the right.

Step 1 Find B, the area of the base.	**Step 2** Use the volume formula.
$B = \dfrac{1}{2}b \times h$	$V = B \times h$
$B = \dfrac{1}{2} \times 8 \times 3$	$V = 12 \times 6\dfrac{1}{2}$
$B = 12$	$V = 12 \times \dfrac{13}{2}$
	$V = 78$

The volume of the triangular prism is 78 ft³.

Example 2

Find the volume of the cylinder at the right.

Step 1 Find B, the area of the base.	**Step 2** Use the volume formula.
$B = \pi r^2 = \pi \times 2^2$	$V = B \times h$
$B \approx 3.14 \times 4$	$V \approx 12.56 \times 8.5$
$B \approx 12.56$	$V \approx 106.76$

The volume of the cylinder is about 106.76 cm³.

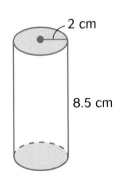

Additional Standards: Measurement and Geometry 1.2; Algebra and Functions 3.1, 3.2; Mathematical Reasoning 1.3, 2.2 (See p. 457.)

Sometimes, when the dimensions of a cylinder include fractions, it is easier to use $\frac{22}{7}$ for π rather than 3.14.

Example 3

Find the volume of the cylinder at the right.

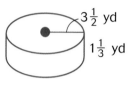

3½ yd

1⅓ yd

Step 1 Find B, the area of the base. Use $\frac{22}{7}$ for π.

$B = \pi r^2 = \pi \times \left(\frac{7}{2}\right)^2$

$B \approx \overset{11}{\underset{1}{\cancel{\frac{22}{7}}}} \times \overset{7}{\underset{2}{\cancel{\frac{49}{4}}}} = \frac{77}{2}$

Step 2 Use the volume formula.

$V = Bh$

$V \approx \frac{77}{2} \times 1\frac{1}{3} = \overset{}{\underset{1}{\cancel{\frac{77}{2}}}} \times \overset{2}{\cancel{\frac{4}{3}}}$

$V \approx \frac{154}{3} = 51\frac{1}{3}$

The volume of the cylinder is about $51\frac{1}{3}$ cubic yards.

Guided Practice   For another example, see Set G on p. 490.

Find the volume of each space figure. Use either 3.14 or $\frac{22}{7}$ for π.

1.

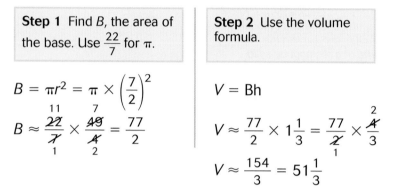

7 m   4 m

5.5 m

2.

5 mm

4 mm

3.

1¾ ft

4 ft

4. Math Reasoning How are the formulas for finding the volumes of rectangular prisms, triangular prisms, and cylinders similar? How are they different?

5.6 in.   5 in.

5. What is the volume of the crystal vase at the right?

11 in.

Independent Practice   For more practice, see Set G on p. 493.

Find the volume of each space figure. Use either 3.14 or $\frac{22}{7}$ for π.

6.

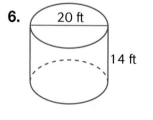

20 ft

14 ft

7.

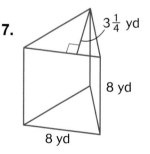

3¼ yd

8 yd

8 yd

8.

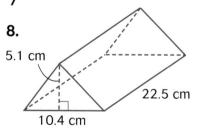

5.1 cm

10.4 cm

22.5 cm

A children's wading pool is 10 feet in diameter and 18 inches high.
Use 3.14 for π. Round to the nearest whole number.

9. What is the volume of the wading pool in cubic feet?

10. What is the volume of the wading pool in cubic inches?

11. The volume of a gallon of water is about 231 cubic inches. How many gallons of water does the wading pool hold?

12. One block of cheese is 8 inches in diameter and 2 inches high. A second block of cheese is 4 inches in diameter and 6 inches high. Which has the greater volume? Explain your answer, giving the volume of each block of cheese.

13. **Math Reasoning** Use the formulas $A = \pi r^2$ and $V = Bh$ to write a formula for the volume of a cylinder.

Mixed Review

14. A local park expects a group of four visitors to spend $120.00. If 25% of the money is spent on food, and the rest of the money is spent on tickets, what is the price per ticket?

15. Marc has 10 red marbles and 15 blue in a bag. He reaches into the bag, chooses one without looking, and sets it aside. He draws another. What is the probability that he draws 2 blue marbles?

Find the volume of each rectangular prism.

16. $l = 10$ cm
$w = 4$ cm
$h = 15$ cm

17. $l = 15$ m
$w = 4$ m
$h = 3$ m

18. $l = 10$ ft
$w = 7$ ft
$h = 11\frac{1}{2}$ ft

19. $l = 19$ mm
$w = 13$ mm
$h = 4.3$ mm

Find the area of each circle to the nearest whole number. Use 3.14 or $\frac{22}{7}$ for π.

20. $d = 6$ cm

21. $r = 15$ in.

22. $d = 8$ yd

23. $d = 1.2$ m

Test Prep Choose the correct letter for each answer.

24. $\frac{2}{3}(12 - 9) + 4 =$
(5-7)

A 3   **B** $3\frac{2}{3}$ **C** 6   **D** 10   **E** NH

25. Which of the following is true?
(6-1)

F $-\frac{7}{8} < -\frac{3}{4}$ **G** $-0.5 > \frac{1}{4}$ **H** $0 < -4\frac{1}{5}$ **J** $-2\frac{1}{8} < -3\frac{3}{4}$

Diagnostic Checkpoint

For Exercises 1–4 choose words from the word bank.

1. The distance around any polygon is called the ___?___.
<small>(12-1)</small>

2. The ___?___ is the distance around a circle.
<small>(12-5)</small>

3. The number of cubic units needed to fill a space figure is called the ___?___.
<small>(12-9)</small>

4. The ___?___ is the number of square units needed to cover a region.
<small>(12-2)</small>

Find the area of each circle to the nearest whole number. Use 3.14 or $\frac{22}{7}$ for π.

5. <small>(12-6)</small> 3.2 cm

6. <small>(12-6)</small> 1 m

7. <small>(12-6)</small> 2 mi

8. <small>(12-6)</small> 9 ft

9. <small>(12-6)</small> 3 km

Find the volume of each space figure to the nearest tenth. Use 3.14 for π.

10. <small>(12-9)</small> 5.2 cm, 2.1 cm, 1.1 cm

11. <small>(12-9)</small> $3\frac{1}{2}$ ft, $3\frac{1}{2}$ ft, $3\frac{1}{2}$ ft

12. <small>(12-9)</small> 4 ft, 4 ft, 4 ft

13. <small>(12-10)</small> 13 ft, 2 ft

Solve.

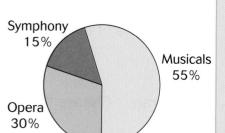

Symphony 15%

Musicals 55%

Opera 30%

14. Jack made the circle graph at the right to display the results of his survey. If 280 students were surveyed, how many students prefer musicals?
<small>(12-4)</small>

15. Tina plans to decorate the lid of a keepsake trunk with 6-inch square photos. The lid measures 36 in. long and 24 in. wide. How many photos can she use to cover the lid of her trunk?
<small>(12-7)</small>

16. Mrs. Bentz's rectangular swimming pool is 12 feet by 9 feet by 8 feet deep. How many cubic feet of water can it hold?
<small>(12-9)</small>

Chapter 12 Test

Write each formula.

1. Perimeter of a rectangle

2. Area of a circle

3. Area of a triangle

4. Circumference of a circle

Find the area of each figure to the nearest whole number. Use 3.14 or $\frac{22}{7}$ for π.

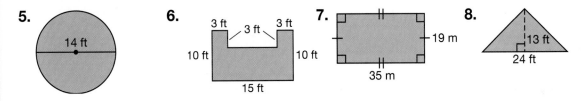

5. 14 ft

6. 3 ft   3 ft   3 ft   10 ft   10 ft   15 ft

7. 19 m   35 m

8. 13 ft   24 ft

Find the area and circumference of each circle. Round to the nearest tenth, if necessary. Use 3.14 or $\frac{22}{7}$ for π.

9. $d = 28$ ft

10. $r = 2.5$ m

11. $r = 5$ m

12. $d = 21$ in.

Find the volume of each space figure. Round to the nearest tenth, if necessary. Use 3.14 or $\frac{22}{7}$ for π.

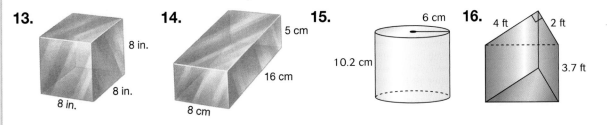

13. 8 in.   8 in.   8 in.

14. 5 cm   16 cm   8 cm

15. 6 cm   10.2 cm

16. 4 ft   2 ft   3.7 ft

17. Which has the larger area, a square 11 inches on a side or a circle with a 12-inch diameter? How much larger?

Use the graph on the right for Exercises 18–19.

18. How often do most people visit the park each year?

19. How many people visit the park more than twice a year?

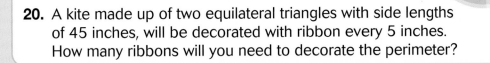

AMUSEMENT PARK SURVEY
OF 1,000 PEOPLE
VISITS PER YEAR

54% 1 visit
2% 5 or more visits
22% 2 visits
8% 4 visits
14% 3 visits

20. A kite made up of two equilateral triangles with side lengths of 45 inches, will be decorated with ribbon every 5 inches. How many ribbons will you need to decorate the perimeter?

Multiple-Choice
Chapter 12 Test

Choose the correct letter for each answer.

1. Given the following dimensions, which statement is true?

Triangle	Parallelogram
$b = 11$ in.	$b = 16$ yd
$h = 12$ in.	$h = 4$ yd

  A The parallelogram has a larger area than the triangle.

  B The triangle has a larger area than the parallelogram.

  C The triangle has a larger perimeter than the parallelogram.

  D The parallelogram has a perimeter of 32 yards.

2. What is the approximate area of a circular tabletop with a 70-inch diameter?

  F 110 in.^{2} H 3,850 in.^{2}

  G 220 in.^{2} J 15,400 in.^{2}

3. Which expression best represents how to calculate the perimeter of the following polygon?

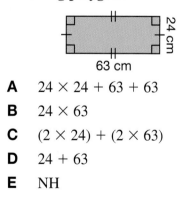
63 cm
24 cm

  A $24 \times 24 + 63 + 63$

  B 24×63

  C $(2 \times 24) + (2 \times 63)$

  D $24 + 63$

  E NH

Use the diagram for Question 4.

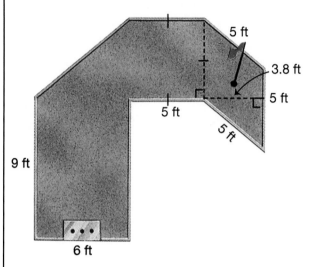
5 ft
3.8 ft
5 ft
5 ft
5 ft
9 ft
6 ft

4. What is the total area of the figure?

  F 94 ft^2 H 103.5 ft^2

  G 96.2 ft^2 J 113 ft^2

5. A triangular prism is filled with water. The prism is 12 cm high. Its base is a triangle with height 8 cm and base 16 cm. What is the volume of this prism?

  A 64 cm^2 C 192 cm^3

  B 96 cm^3 D 768 cm^3

6. A square has an area of 100 m^2, what is its perimeter?

  F 128 m

  G 40 m

  H 32 m

  J 16 m

  K NH

7. What is the circumference of a circle with a diameter of 63 cm? Use $\pi = \frac{22}{7}$.

   A   198 cm

   B   298 cm

   C   396 cm

   D   1386 cm

---

8. Monique plans to decorate a rectangular flag with 4-inch square patches. The flag is 5 feet long and 4 feet wide. How many patches does Monique need?

   F   12 patches

   G   15 patches

   H   30 patches

   J   180 patches

---

9. Find the area of the parallelogram.

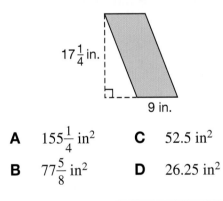

   A $155\frac{1}{4}$ in^2 **C**   52.5 in^2

   B $77\frac{5}{8}$ in^2 **D**   26.25 in^2

---

10. Find the area of the triangle.

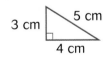

   F   6 cm^2

   G   7.5 cm^2

   H   10 cm^2

   J   12 cm^2

The graph shows the percent of types of shoes sold by Shoe City.

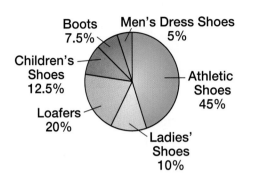

11. If Shoe City sold $200,000 worth of shoes last year, how much was from the sale of loafers?

   A $40,000   **C** $10,000

   B $20,000   **D** $5,000

---

12. Calculate the volume of the prism.

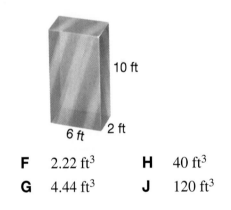

   F   2.22 ft^3 **H**   40 ft^3

   G   4.44 ft^3 **J**   120 ft^3

---

13. A 90-foot long section of an oil pipeline is in need of replacement. The radius of the pipe is about 8 ft. When the pipeline is full, what volume of oil does this particular section hold?

   A   About 25,800 ft^3

   B   About 18,500 ft^3

   C   About 4,600 ft^3

   D   About 1,000 ft^3

Reteaching

Set A *(pages 458–459)*

Find the perimeter of the polygon.

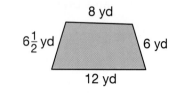

8 yd

$6\frac{1}{2}$ yd   6 yd

12 yd

P = sum of the sides

$P = 6\frac{1}{2} + 8 + 6 + 12$

$P = 32\frac{1}{2}$ yd

Remember you can find the perimeter of a polygon by adding the lengths of its sides.

Find the perimeter of each polygon.

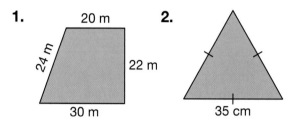

1. 20 m   **2.**

24 m   22 m

30 m   35 cm

Set B *(pages 460–462)*

Find the area of the quadrilateral.

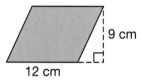

9 cm

12 cm

$A = bh$

$A = 12 \times 9$ Substitute $b = 9$ and $h = 3$.

$A = 108$ cm^2 Multiply.

Remember You can use a formula to find the area of a square, rectangle, and parallelogram.

$$\text{Square: } A = s^2$$
$$\text{Rectangle: } A = lw$$
$$\text{Parallelogram: } A = bh$$

Find the area of each quadrilateral.

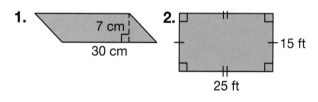

1. 7 cm   **2.**

30 cm   15 ft

25 ft

Set C *(pages 464–465)*

Find the area of the triangle.

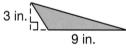

3 in.

9 in.

$A = \frac{1}{2}bh$

$A = \frac{1}{2} \times 9 \times 3$ Substitute $b = 9$ and $h = 3$.

$A = \frac{1}{2} \times 27$ Multiply.

$A = \frac{27}{2}$

$A = 13\frac{1}{2}$ in.^{2} Convert to mixed number.

Remember area is always measured in square units.

Find the area of each triangle.

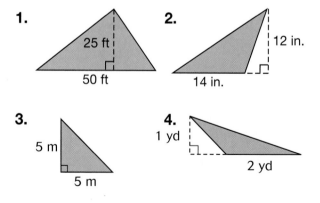

1.   **2.**

25 ft   12 in.

50 ft   14 in.

3.   **4.**

5 m   1 yd

5 m   2 yd

Set D *(pages 468–470)*

Find the circumference of the circle to the nearest whole number.

12 m

$C = \pi d$

$C \approx 3.14 \times 12$ Substitute $\pi \approx 3.14$ and $d = 12$.

$C \approx 37.68$

The circumference is about 38 meters.

Remember the formula for circumference of a circle is $C = \pi d$ or $C = 2\pi r$.

Find the circumference of each circle to the nearest whole number. Use 3.14 or $\frac{22}{7}$ for π.

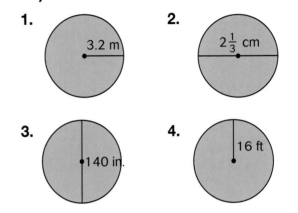

1. 3.2 m

2. $2\frac{1}{3}$ cm

3. 140 in.

4. 16 ft

Set E *(pages 472–473)*

Find the area of the circle to the nearest whole number.

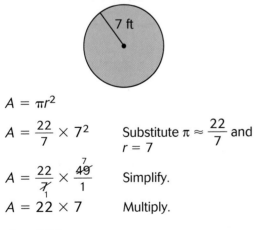

7 ft

$A = \pi r^2$

$A = \frac{22}{7} \times 7^2$ Substitute $\pi \approx \frac{22}{7}$ and $r = 7$.

$A = \frac{22}{\cancel{7}_1} \times \frac{\cancel{49}^{7}}{1}$ Simplify.

$A = 22 \times 7$ Multiply.

$A = 154$

The area is about 154 square feet.

Remember the formula for the area of a circle is $A = \pi r^2$.

Find the area of each circle to the nearest whole number. Use 3.14 or $\frac{22}{7}$ for π.

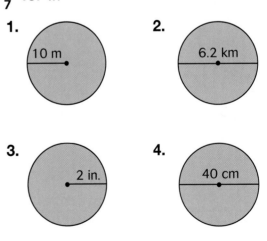

1. 10 m

2. 6.2 km

3. 2 in.

4. 40 cm

Reteaching (continued)

Set F (pages 478–480)

Find the volume of the space figure.

9.5 ft

7 ft

8.5 ft

$V = \ell wh$

$V = 8.5 \times 7 \times 9.5$

$V = 565.25 \text{ ft}^3$

Remember the formulas for volume.

Any prism: $V = Bh$

Rectangular prism: $V = lwh$

Find the volume of each space figure.

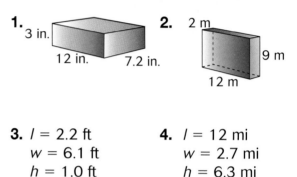

1. 3 in.

12 in. 7.2 in.

2. 2 m

12 m 9 m

3. $l = 2.2$ ft
   $w = 6.1$ ft
   $h = 1.0$ ft

4. $l = 12$ mi
   $w = 2.7$ mi
   $h = 6.3$ mi

Set G (pages 481–483)

Find the volume of the space figure.

14 in.

6 in.

Find B, the area of the base.

$B = \pi r^2$

$B \approx 3.14(6)^2$ Substitute $\pi \approx 3.14$ and

                  $r = 6$.

$B \approx 3.14(36)$

$B \approx 113.04$

$V = Bh$

$V \approx 113 \times 14$ Substitute $B \approx 113$ and

                  $h = 14$.

$V \approx 1582 \text{ in.}^3$

Remember when finding the volume of triangular prisms and cylinders, first find the area of the base. Then multiply it by the height.

Find the volume of each space figure. Use 3.14 or $\frac{22}{7}$ for π.

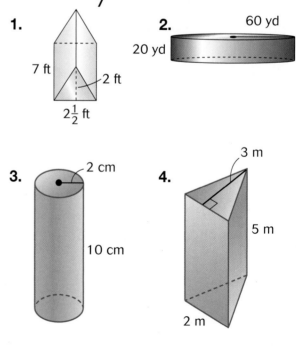

1.

7 ft

2 ft

$2\frac{1}{2}$ ft

2. 60 yd

20 yd

3. 2 cm

10 cm

4. 3 m

5 m

2 m

More Practice

Set A (pages 458–459)

Find the perimeter of each polygon.

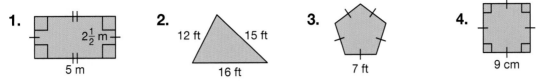

1. $2\frac{1}{2}$ m, 5 m
2. 12 ft, 15 ft, 16 ft
3. 7 ft
4. 9 cm

5. Ron's yard is 4 times longer than it is wide. If his yard is 30 feet wide, what is the perimeter of Ron's yard?

6. Jessie's yard is 25 feet wide and 140 feet long. Casey's yard has a perimeter of 325 feet. Whose yard has a greater perimeter, Casey's or Jessie's?

Set B (pages 460–462)

Find the area of each polygon.

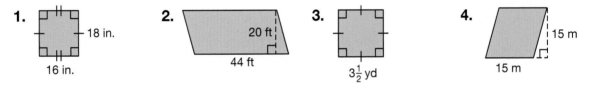

1. 18 in., 16 in.
2. 20 ft, 44 ft
3. $3\frac{1}{2}$ yd
4. 15 m, 15 m

5. The length of a rectangle is five times the width. What is the area of the rectangle if the width is 3.5 m?

Set C (pages 464–465)

Find the area of each triangle.

1.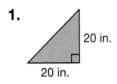
   20 in., 20 in.

2.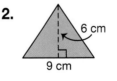
   6 cm, 9 cm

Use the grid to find the area of each triangle. Each square is equal to 1 square unit.

3.

4.

5. A piece of cloth is 39 inches long and 39 inches wide. If it is folded in half to form a triangle, what is the area of the triangle?

More Practice (continued)

Set D (pages 468–470)

Find the circumference of each circle to the nearest whole number.
Use 3.14 or $\frac{22}{7}$ for π.

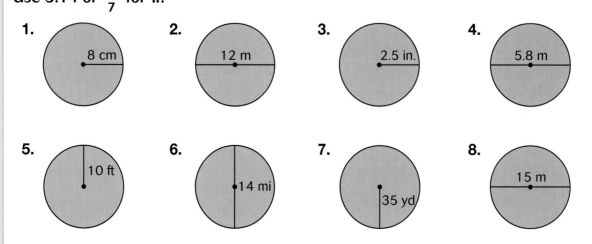

1. 8 cm

2. 12 m

3. 2.5 in.

4. 5.8 m

5. 10 ft

6. 14 mi

7. 35 yd

8. 15 m

9. A tire has a diameter of 18 in. What is its circumference to the nearest whole number?

10. Look at Question 9. Imagine the tire is rolling down a hill. About how many times does the tire go around if it travels 100 ft before stopping?

Set E (pages 472–473)

Find the area of each circle to the nearest whole number.
Use 3.14 or $\frac{22}{7}$ for π.

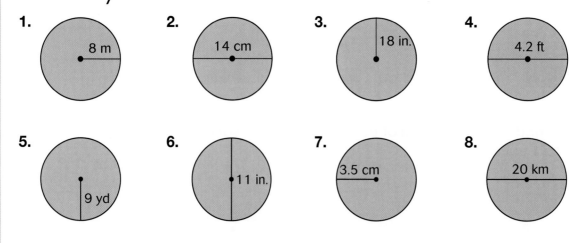

1. 8 m

2. 14 cm

3. 18 in.

4. 4.2 ft

5. 9 yd

6. 11 in.

7. 3.5 cm

8. 20 km

9. A round table has a radius of 45 inches. Spence purchased a 48 ft² circular tablecloth. Will the tablecloth cover the table?

Set F *(pages 478–480)*

Find the volume of each space figure.

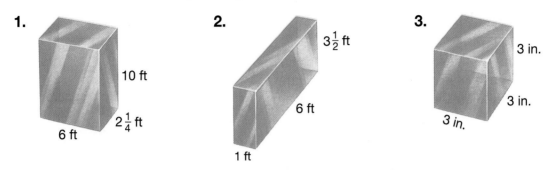

1.

10 ft

$2\frac{1}{4}$ ft

6 ft

2.

$3\frac{1}{2}$ ft

6 ft

1 ft

3.

3 in.

3 in.

3 in.

4. A cereal box is 3 inches wide, 10 inches long, and 18 inches high. What volume of cereal does it hold?

Set G *(pages 481–483)*

Find the volume of each figure. Use 3.14 or $\frac{22}{7}$ for π.

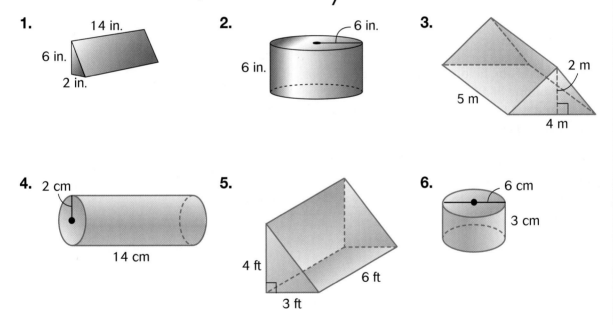

1.

14 in.

6 in.

2 in.

2.

6 in.

6 in.

3.

2 m

5 m

4 m

4. 2 cm

14 cm

5.

4 ft

3 ft

6 ft

6.

6 cm

3 cm

4. What is the volume of a cylindrical tunnel with a length of 45 feet and a radius of 5 feet?

Problem Solving: Preparing for Tests

Choose the correct letter for each answer.

1. The pictograph below shows the results of a survey of a local neighborhood. Which is the best estimate for the percent of people shown in this survey who live on Elm Street?

Tip

Start by making sure you understand the key for the pictograph.

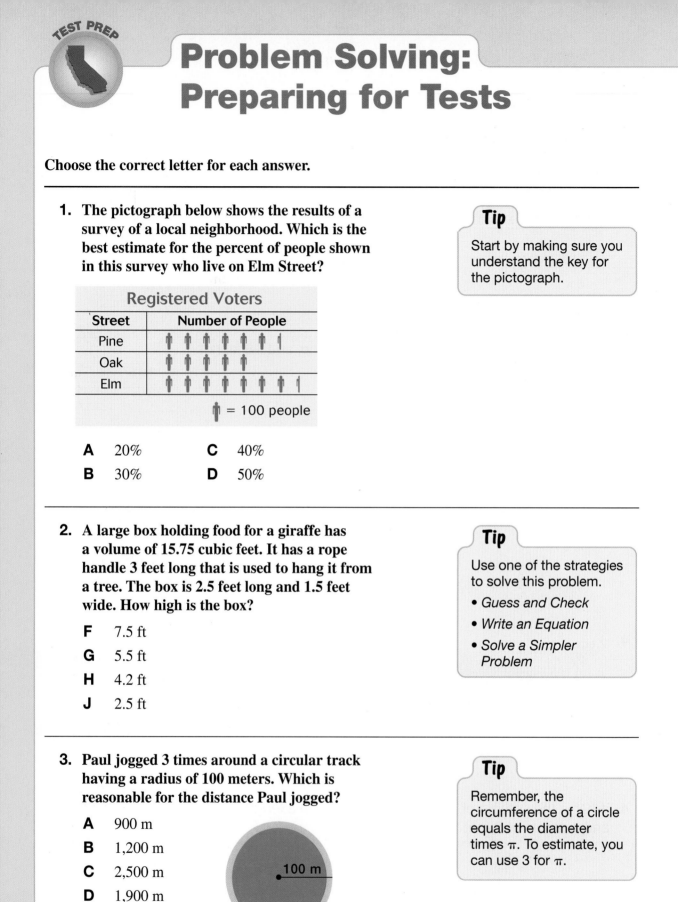

Registered Voters

Street	Number of People
Pine	👤 👤 👤 👤 👤 👤 ⃒
Oak	👤 👤 👤 👤 👤
Elm	👤 👤 👤 👤 👤 👤 👤 ⃒

👤 = 100 people

A 20% **C** 40%

B 30% **D** 50%

2. A large box holding food for a giraffe has a volume of 15.75 cubic feet. It has a rope handle 3 feet long that is used to hang it from a tree. The box is 2.5 feet long and 1.5 feet wide. How high is the box?

F 7.5 ft

G 5.5 ft

H 4.2 ft

J 2.5 ft

Tip

Use one of the strategies to solve this problem.
- *Guess and Check*
- *Write an Equation*
- *Solve a Simpler Problem*

3. Paul jogged 3 times around a circular track having a radius of 100 meters. Which is reasonable for the distance Paul jogged?

A 900 m

B 1,200 m

C 2,500 m

D 1,900 m

100 m

Tip

Remember, the circumference of a circle equals the diameter times π. To estimate, you can use 3 for π.

4. Sally bought 6 CDs that ranged in cost from $6.45 to $24.37. Which is reasonable for the total amount Sally spent?

 F Less than $100

 G Between $35 and $55

 H Between $55 and $130

 J Between $100 and $150

5. This figure is part of a scale drawing. What is the length of one curved side if each square represents 10 feet by 10 feet? (Use $\pi \approx 3.14$)

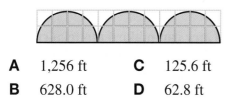

 A 1,256 ft C 125.6 ft

 B 628.0 ft D 62.8 ft

6. Bert used a computer program to create a series of figures with areas that decreased in this pattern.

Figure	1	2	3	4	5
Area	122	101	82	65	50

What will be the area of Figure 8 in square units?

 F 10 sq units H 17 sq units

 G 16 sq units J 25 sq units

7. Vanna cut a circle 40 in. in diameter from some fabric measuring 45 in. by 54 in. Which equation could you use to find ▧, the approximate amount of fabric left over?

 A $(3.14 \times 400) - (54 \times 45) =$ ▧

 B $(3.14 \times 1{,}600) - (54 \times 45) =$ ▧

 C $(45 \times 54) - (3.14 \times 400) =$ ▧

 D $(54 \times 45) - (3.14 \times 1{,}600) =$ ▧

8. This figure shows a design for a quilt. What is the area of the shaded part of the design?

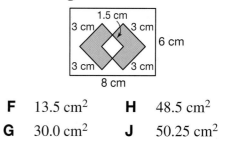

 F 13.5 cm² H 48.5 cm²

 G 30.0 cm² J 50.25 cm²

9. Five friends stood in line for tickets to a movie. Toni was between Jana and Fay. Jana was behind Toni and ahead of Cal. Fay was right behind Yuri. Which is a reasonable conclusion?

 A Yuri was first in line.

 B Jana was last in line.

 C Cal was ahead of Toni.

 D Yuri was between Jana and Cal.

10. The graph shows the amount of money raised for a hospital.

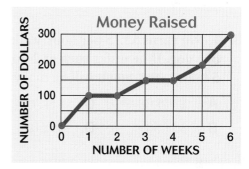

Which accurately compares the amount of money raised in the first 3 weeks to the amount raised in the last 3 weeks?

 F $50 more in the first 3 weeks

 G $20 less in the first 3 weeks

 H $50 less in the first 3 weeks

 J The amounts were the same.

Multiple-Choice Cumulative Review

Choose the correct letter for each answer.

Number Sense

1. It takes John about half as long to get home as it takes Kate. John left school at 4:30 P.M. If John got home today in 20 minutes, about how many minutes did it probably take Kate to get home?

    A 5 min   **C** 30 min

    B 10 min   **D** 40 min

2. What is the sum of 2.532, 1.2367, and 2.75?

    F 4.233

    G 6.5187

    H 6.523

    J 6.82103

    K NH

3. Kevin earns $3.75 per hour walking one dog. If he walks each of 2 dogs for 5 hours, how much will he make?

    A $375.00   **C** $17.75

    B $37.50   **D** $7.50

4. What is the quotient of $375.00 divided by 12?

    F $37.50

    G $31.25

    H $31.00

    J $25.00

    K NH

Algebra and Functions

5. Which number is missing from this pattern?

    ..., ■, 37, 31, 25, 19

    A 39   **D** 45

    B 40   **E** NH

    C 43

6. Gary can make 4 model airplanes in 6 hours. He needs to make 10 model airplanes for a project. Which proportion can be used to find out how long this will take?

    F $\frac{4}{?} = \frac{6}{10}$ **H** $\frac{4}{6} = \frac{?}{10}$

    G $\frac{4}{4} = \frac{10}{?}$ **J** $\frac{4}{6} = \frac{10}{?}$

7. A pool is 50 meters long. A lap is one length of the pool. If a swimmer can swim about 10 laps in 8 minutes, about how many laps would she be able to swim in 20 minutes?

    A 16   **C** 45

    B 25   **D** 140

8. Which equation can be used to solve for ■?

x	3	15	37	x
y	8	20	42	■

    F $x + 5 = ■$ **H** $x + ■ = 5$

    G $5 + ■ = x$ **J** $x - 5 = ■$

Measurement and Geometry

9. A playing field is 3 times as long as it is wide. If the length of the field is 150 yards, what is its perimeter?

    A   1,200 yd

    B   600 yd

    C   400 yd

    D   300 yd

10. What is the area of the right triangle shown? (1 yd = 3 ft)

    F   162 yd^2

    G   81 yd^2

    H   27 yd^2

    J   13.5 yd^2

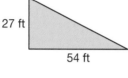

11. What are the dimensions of a rectangle that has a perimeter of 40 feet and the greatest area possible?

    A   10 ft × 10 ft

    B   12 ft × 8 ft

    C   15 ft × 5 ft

    D   16 ft × 2 ft

12. The picture shows a design for a playground. What is the area of the playground?

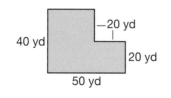

    F   400 yd^2

    G   1,200 yd^2

    H   1,600 yd^2

    J   2,400 yd^2

Statistics, Data Analysis, and Probability

13. Dana received these grades:

89%, 90%, 83%, 94%, 100%, 91%

What was her mean (average) grade, rounded to the nearest whole percent?

    A   90%   **C**   92%

    B   91%   **D**   93%

Use the graph below to answer Questions 14–16.

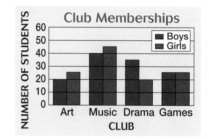

14. Which club was more popular with boys than with girls?

    F   Art   **H**   Drama

    G   Music   **J**   Games

15. Which club was most popular with girls?

    A   Art   **C**   Drama

    B   Music   **D**   Games

16. Which is a reasonable conclusion that can be drawn from the graph?

    F   The Games Club was the most popular club overall.

    G   The Art Club was more popular than the Drama Club.

    H   The Music Club was the least popular club overall.

    J   The Games Club was equally popular with boys and girls.

Credits

Photographs

Front Cover and Back Inset: Thomas Winz/Panoramic Images; Front and Back Cover Background: Jeffry Myers/Panoramic Images

14: John McGrail/Panoramic Images

70(TC): Alon Reininger/The Stock Market

70(B): Scott Gog/The Stock Market

138: Larry E. Neibergall/Stone

194: Gail Dickel/Christ the King Catholic School

270: Bonnie Kamin/PhotoEdit

304: Daemmrich Photography

458: Alex S. MacLean/Landslides

459: Alex S. MacLean/Landslides

460: Alex s. MacLean/Landslides

470: Don Mason/The Stock Market

Illustrations

19: Tom McKee

48: George Hamblin

326: George Hamblin

Additional Resources

Tables

Measures—*Customary*

Length
1 foot (ft) = 12 inches (in.)
1 yard (yd) = 36 inches
1 yard = 3 feet
1 mile (mi.) = 5,280 feet
1 mile = 1,760 yards

Weight
1 pound (lb) = 16 ounces (oz)
1 ton (T) = 2,000 pounds

Capacity
1 cup (c) = 8 fluid ounces (fl oz)
1 pint (pt) = 2 cups
1 quart (qt) = 2 pints
1 gallon (gal) = 4 quarts

Area
1 square foot (ft^2) = 144 square inches (in.^{2})
1 square yard (yd^2) = 9 square feet
1 acre = 43,560 square feet
1 square mile (mi^2) = 640 acres

Measures—*Metric*

Length
1 millimeter (mm) = 0.001 meter (m)
1 centimeter (cm) = 0.01 meter
1 kilometer (km) = 1,000 meters

Mass/Weight
1 milligram (mg) = 0.001 gram (g)
1 centigram (cg) = 0.01 gram
1 kilogram (kg) = 1,000 grams
1 metric ton (t) = 1,000 kilograms

Capacity
1 milliliter (mL) = 0.001 liter (L)
1 centiliter (cL) = 0.01 liter
1 kiloliter (kL) = 1,000 liters

Area
1 square centimeter (cm^2) = 100 square millimeters (mm^2)
1 square meter (m^2) = 10,000 square centimeters
1 hectare (ha) = 10,000 square meters
1 square kilometer (km^2) = 1,000,000 square meters

Measures—*Customary and Metric Unit Equivalents*

Length
1 in. = 2.54 cm
1 m ≈ 39.37 in.
1 m ≈ 1.09 yd
1 mi ≈ 1.61 km

Weight and Mass
1 oz ≈ 28.35 g
1 kg ≈ 2.2 lb
1 metric ton (t) ≈ 1.102 tons (T)

Capacity
1 L ≈ 1.06 qt
1 gal ≈ 3.79 L

Symbols

=	is equal to	π pi (approximately 3.14)	2:5 ratio of 2 to 5
≠	is not equal to	° degree	10^2 ten to the second
>	is greater than	°C degree Celsius	power
<	is less than	°F degree Fahrenheit	$^+4$ positive 4
≥	is greater than or equal to	$\overleftrightarrow{AB}$ line AB	$^-4$ negative 4
≤	is less than or equal to	$\overline{AB}$ line segment AB	(3, 4) ordered pair 3, 4
≈	is approximately equal to	$\overrightarrow{AB}$ ray AB	P(E) probability of event E
≅	is congruent to	∠ABC angle ABC	⊥ is perpendicular to
∼	is similar to	△ABC triangle ABC	
%	percent	‖ is parallel to	

Formulas

$P = 2\ell + 2w$	Perimeter of a rectangle	$C = \pi \times d$	Circumference of a circle
$A = \ell \times w$	Area of a rectangle	$A = \pi \times r^2$	Area of a circle
$A = b \times h$	Area of a parallelogram	$V = \ell \times w \times h$	Volume of a rectangular prism
$A = \frac{1}{2} \times b \times h$	Area of a triangle	$I = p \times r \times t$	Simple interest

Test-Taking Tips

Follow Instructions
- Listen carefully as your teacher explains the test.

Budget Your Time
- Do the questions in order if you can.
- If a question seems very hard, skip it and go back to it later.

Read Carefully
- Watch for extra information in a problem.
- Watch for words like *not*.
- Be sure to answer the question asked.

Make Smart Choices
- **Estimate** when you can so that you have a better idea what the answer might be.
- **Eliminate** answer choices that are not reasonable or are clearly wrong.
- **Check** an answer that you *think* is correct by working backward.

Mark Answers Correctly
- If you are using a "bubble" answer sheet or a gridded response form, be careful to match each question number with the correct number of the answer row.
- If you skip a question, be sure to leave that question's answer space blank.

Glossary

A

absolute value The absolute value of a number is its distance from zero on the number line. (p. 219)

acute angle An angle with a measure less than 90°. (p. 271)

acute triangle A triangle with three acute angles. (p. 276)

adjacent angles Two angles that have a common vertex and a common side but do not overlap. (p. 274)

angle Two rays with a common endpoint called the vertex. (p. 270)
Example:

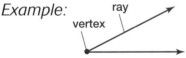

area The number of square units needed to cover a region. (p. 460)

associative (grouping) property of addition The way that addends are grouped does not change the sum. (p. 10) *Example:*
(2 + 3) + 4 = 2 + (3 + 4)

associative (grouping) property of multiplication The way that factors are grouped does not change the product. (p. 50) *Example:*
(2 × 3) × 4 = 2 × (3 × 4)

B

bar graph A graph that uses vertical or horizontal bars to represent numerical data. (p. 96)

base (in geometry) A particular side of a figure. See *height*. (p. 461)
Example:

base (in numeration) The number that is multiplied by itself when raised to a power. (p. 132) *Example:* In 5^3, 5 is the base.

biased A sample which does not mirror the population. (p. 104)

C

capacity The amount a container can hold. (p. 260)

centimeter (cm) A unit of length in the metric system equal to 0.01 meter. (p. 263)

certain event An event that is sure to happen. A certain event has a probability of one. (p. 418)

circle A closed plane figure with all of its points the same distance from a point called the center. (p. 468)

circle graph A graph that represents a total divided into parts. (p. 96)

circumference The distance around a circle. (p. 468)

combination Each possible arrangement of the outcomes of an event where order is not important. (p. 430)

commutative (order) property of addition The order of the addends does not change the sum. (p. 10) *Example:* 9 + 7 = 7 + 9

commutative (order) property of multiplication The order of the factors does not change the product. (p. 50)

compatible numbers Numbers that are easy to compute mentally. (p. 10) *Example:* 5 + 15 = 20

compensation strategy A mental math method in which numbers are adjusted up or down to make addition and subtraction easier. (p. 10)

complementary angles Two angles whose sum of their measures equals 90°. (p. 274)

composite number A whole number greater than one that has more than two factors. (p. 136)

compound event A combination of two or more simple events. (p. 432)

congruent figures Figures that have the same size and shape. (p. 271)

convenience sampling A sampling method where any convenient method is used to choose the sample. (p. 104)

coordinate grid A plane with a horizontal number line, called the *x*-axis, and a vertical number line, called the *y*-axis, intersecting at a point called the origin. Each point of the grid corresponds to an ordered pair of numbers. (p. 390)

corresponding angles Matching angles of congruent and similar figures. (p. 322)

corresponding sides Matching sides of congruent and similar figures. (p. 322)

counting principle If one choice can be made in m ways and a second choice can be made in n ways, then the two choices can be made together in $m \times n$ ways. (p. 427)

cross products In a proportion, the product of a numerator of one ratio with the denominator of the other ratio. (p. 310)

cup (c) A unit of capacity in the customary system equal to 8 ounces (2 cups equals 1 pint). (p. 260)

customary system of measurement A system of weights and measure that measures length in inches, feet, yards, and miles; capacity in fluid ounces, cups, pints, quarts, and gallons; weight in ounces, pounds, and tons; and temperature in degrees Fahrenheit. p. 260)

Glossary

cylinder A space figure with two parallel and congruent bases that are circles. (p. 481)

D

data Information that is gathered. (p. 8)

decimal A number with one or more digits to the right of a decimal point. (p. 4) *Examples:* 0.7, 1.8, 2.06, 0.175

decimal point The dot used to separate dollars from cents and ones from tenths. (p. 6)

decimeter (dm) A unit of length in the metric system equal to 0.1 meter. (p. 263)

degree (°) A unit for measuring angles. (p. 270)

dekameter (dam) A unit of length in the metric system equal to 10 meters. (p. 263)

denominator The number below the fraction bar in a fraction. (p. 148) *Example:* $\frac{2}{5}$. The denominator is 5.

dependent events Two events in which the outcome of the second is affected by the outcome of the first. (p. 436)

diagonal A segment that joins two vertices of a polygon but is not a side. (p. 280)
Example:

diameter A line segment that passes through the center of a circle and has both endpoints on the circle. (p. 468)

digit Any of the symbols used to write numbers: 0, 1, 2, 3, 4, 5, 6, 7, 8, and 9. (p. 4)

distributive property Multiplying a sum by a number produces the same results as multiplying each addend by the number and adding the products. (p. 50) *Example:*
$2 \times (3 + 4) = (2 \times 3) + (2 \times 4)$

divisible A number is divisible by another number if the remainder is zero after dividing. (p. 135)

double bar graph A graph that uses pairs of bars to compare information. (p. 96)
Example:

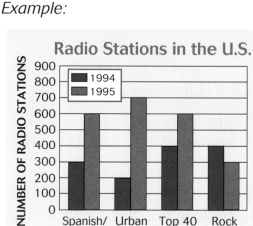

E

equation A number sentence stating that two expressions are equal. (p. 30)

equilateral triangle A triangle with all three sides congruent. (p. 276)
Example:

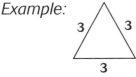

equivalent fractions Fractions that name the same number. (p. 148)

equivalent ratios Ratios that represent the same rate or make the same comparison. (p. 306)

event One or more outcomes of an experiment. (p. 418)

expanded form A number written as the sum of the values of its digits. (p. 4) *Example:* $500 + 50 + 5$ is the expanded form for 555.

exponent A number that tells how many times the base is used as a factor. (p. 132) *Example:*
$10^3 = 10 \times 10 \times 10$
The exponent is 3 and the base is 10.

expression A mathematical phrase made up of a combination of variables and/or numbers and operations. Expressions with variables are also called algebraic expressions. (p. 28)
Examples: $5n$, $4x - 7$, $(5 \times 2) - \frac{6}{3}$

F

factor The numbers that are multiplied to give a product. (p. 140) *Example:* $3 \times 5 = 15$. The factors are 3 and 5.

factor tree A diagram used to show the prime factors of a number. (p. 136)
Example:

fluid ounce (fl oz) A unit of capacity in the customary system equal to 2 tablespoons. (p. 260)

foot (ft) A unit of length in the customary system equal to 12 inches. (*pl. feet*). (p. 260)

formula An equation that expresses a rule. (p. 398)

fraction A number that names part of a whole or part of a set. (p. 148)
Examples: $\frac{1}{2}, \frac{2}{3}, \frac{6}{6}$

G

gallon (gal) A unit of capacity in the customary system equal to 4 quarts. (p. 260)

gram (g) The basic unit of mass in the metric system. (p. 264)

graph A drawing used to show information. (p. 32)

Glossary

greatest common factor (GCF) The greatest number that is a factor of each of two or more numbers. (p. 140)

H

hectometer (hm) A unit of length in the metric system equal to 100 meters. (p. 263)

height The length of a segment drawn from a vertex of a figure perpendicular to the base. See *base*. (p. 461)
Example:

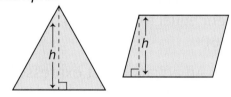

hundredth One of one hundred equal parts of a whole. (p. 4)
Examples: 0.01, $\frac{1}{100}$

I

identity property of addition The sum of any number and zero is that number. (p. 10)

identity property of multiplication The product of any number and one is that number. (p. 50)

impossible event An event that cannot happen. An impossible event has a probability of zero. (p. 418)

improper fraction A fraction in which the numerator is greater than or equal to the denominator. (p. 152)
Examples: $\frac{4}{3}, \frac{6}{6}$

inch (in.) A basic unit of length in the customary system. (p. 260)

independent events Events where the outcome of the first event does not affect the outcome of the second event. (p. 432)

inequality Comparison of two expressions using one of the symbols <, or >. (p. 6)

integers The set of numbers, . . . $-3, -2, -1, 0, +1, +2, +3, \ldots$ (p. 219)

interest The amount of money paid for the use of money. (p. 366)

intersecting lines Lines that have exactly one point in common. (p. 274)
Example:

inverse operations Two operations with an opposite effect. Addition and subtraction are inverse operations. Multiplication and division are inverse operations. (pp. 30, 68)

isosceles triangle A triangle with two congruent sides. (p. 276)

K

kilogram (kg) A unit of mass in the metric system equal to 1,000 grams. (p. 264)

kiloliter (kL) A unit of capacity in the metric system equal to 1,000 liters. (p. 264)

kilometer (km) A unit of length in the metric system equal to 1,000 meters. (p. 263)

L

least common denominator (LCD) The least common multiple of the denominators of two or more fractions. (p. 149) *Example:* 12 is the least common denominator of $\frac{1}{4}$ and $\frac{1}{6}$

least common multiple (LCM) The least number, other than zero, that is a multiple of each of two or more numbers. (p. 144) *Example:* 12 is the least common multiple of 4 and 6.

length The distance from one end of an object to the other. (p. 260)

line An endless collection of points along a straight path. A line has no endpoints. (p. 270)
Example:
E   F

line graph A graph used to show changes over a period of time. (p. 96)

line of symmetry A line that divides a figure in half into two congruent parts when folded. (p. 284)
Example:

line segment A part of a line having two endpoints. (p. 270)
Example:
A   D

liter (L) The basic unit of capacity in the metric system. (p. 264)

M

map Representation of part of the earth's surface on a plane often showing physical features, cities, etc. (p. 328)

mass The amount of matter an object contains that causes it to have weight. (p. 264)

mean The average of the numbers in a set of data. (p. 88)

measures of central tendency The mean, median, and mode are measures of central tendency. (p. 88)

median The middle number or average of the two middle numbers in a collection of data when the data are arranged in order from least to greatest. (p. 88)

Glossary

mental math Performing a computation without the use of paper and pencil or a calculator. (p. 10)

meter (m) The basic unit of length in the metric system. (p. 263)

metric system of measurement A measurement system that measures length in millimeters, centimeters, meters, and kilometers; capacity in liters and milliliters; mass in grams and kilograms; and temperature in degrees Celsius. (p. 263–264)

metric ton (t) A unit of mass equal to 1,000 kilograms. (p. 264)

mile (mi) A unit of length in the customary system equal to 5,280 feet, or 1,760 yards. (p. 260)

milligram (mg) A unit of mass in the metric system equal to 0.001 gram. (p. 264)

milliliter (mL) A unit of capacity in the metric system equal to 0.001 liter. (p. 264)

millimeter (mm) A unit of length in the metric system equal to 0.001 meter. (p. 263)

mixed numbers A number written as a whole number and a fraction. (p. 152)
Example: $2\frac{5}{6}$

mode The number(s) that occur most often in a set of data. (p. 88)

multiples The product of a given number and another whole number. (p. 144)
Example: 2, 4, 6 are multiples of 2.

mutually exclusive events Two events that cannot happen at the same time. (p. 422)

N

negative integers An integer whose value is less than zero. (p. 218)
Examples: -5, -10, -456

numerator The number above the fraction bar in a fraction. (p. 148)
Example: $\frac{3}{4}$. The numerator is 3.

O

obtuse angle An angle that measures more than 90° and less than 180°. (p. 271)

obtuse triangle A triangle with an obtuse angle. (p. 276)
Example:

opposites Pairs of numbers that are the same distance from 0 on a number line. (219)

order of operations The order in which operations are done in calculations. Work inside parentheses is done first. Then multiplication and division from left to right, and finally addition and subtraction from left to right. (p. 24)

ordered pair A pair of numbers used to locate a point on a coordinate grid. (p. 390)

origin The point of intersection of the *x*- and *y*-axes on a coordinate grid. (p. 390)

ounce (oz) The basic unit of weight in the customary system. (p. 260)

outcome A result in a probability experiment. (p. 418)

outlier A number in a data set that is very different from the rest of the numbers. (p. 92)

P

parallelogram A quadrilateral with each pair of opposite sides parallel and congruent. (p. 279)
Example:

percent A special ratio that compares a number with one hundred. (p. 346)

perimeter The distance around a polygon. (p. 458)

period In a large number, a group of three digits of a number, set off by commas. (p. 4) *Example:* In 23,456,789; 456 is in the thousands period.

permutation Each possible arrangement of the outcomes of an event where order is important. (p. 430)

pi (π) The ratio of the circumference of a circle to its diameter. π is approximately 3.14 or $\frac{22}{7}$. (p. 468)

pictograph A graph that represents numerical data using pictures. (p. 70)

pint (pt) A unit of capacity in the customary system equal to 2 cups. (p. 260)

place value The value determined by the position of a digit in a number. (p. 4)

plane A flat surface extending endlessly in all directions. (p. 270)

point An exact location in space. (p. 270)

population The entire group of people or things being considered in a statistical study. (p. 100)

positive integers An integer greater than zero. (p. 218)

pound (lb) A unit of weight in the customary system equal to 16 ounces. (p. 260)

power The number of times a number is multiplied by itself, 4^2 is read 4 to the second power. Since 4^2 equals 16, the second power of 4 is 16. See *exponent*. (p.132)

predict To declare in advance based on observation, experience, or reasoning. (p. 438)

prime factorization Writing a number as the product of its prime factors. (p. 136) *Example:* 24 = 2 × 2 × 2 × 3

Glossary

prime number A whole number greater than one with only two factors—itself and one. (p. 136)

principal An amount of money borrowed or loaned. (p. 366)

prism A space figure with two parallel and congruent bases that are polygons. (p. 479)

probability The ratio of the number of favorable outcomes to all possible outcomes. (p. 418)

product The answer in multiplication. (p. 28)

proper fraction A fraction in which the numerator is less than the denomintor. (p. 152) *Examples:* $\frac{3}{4}, \frac{5}{8}$

property of zero The product of any number and zero is zero. (p. 50)

proportion An equation stating that two ratios are equivalent. (p. 308)

protractor An instrument used to measure or draw angles. (p. 270) *Example:*

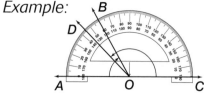

quadrilateral A polygon with four sides. (p. 279)

quart (qt) A unit of capacity in the customary system equal to 4 cups. (p. 260)

R

radius A line segment with one endpoint on the circle and the other endpoint at the center. The radius is one-half the diameter. (p. 468)

random sampling A sampling method in which each person or thing has an equal chance of being chosen. (p.104)

range The difference between the greatest and least numbers in a set of data. (p. 89)

rate A ratio that compares different kinds of units. (p. 314)

rate of interest A percent of the principal that determines how much interest is paid or owed. (p. 366)

ratio A comparison of two quantities. (p. 306)

ray A part of a line that has one endpoint and goes on and on in one direction. (p. 270)

reciprocals Two fractions whose product is 1. (p. 194) *Example:* $\frac{3}{4} \times \frac{4}{3} = 1$

rectangle A parallelogram with four right angles. (p. 279)

rectangular prism A prism whose bases are rectangles. (p. 479)
Example:

reflection The mirror image of a figure about a line of symmetry. (p. 284)
Example:

representative A random sample which is a good match for the population. (p. 104)

responses to a survey A form of sampling that is usually biased. (p. 104)

rhombus A parallelogram with all sides congruent. (p. 279)

right angle An angle that measures 90°. (p. 271)

right triangle A triangle with a right angle. (p. 276)

rotation A transformation obtained by rotating a figure through a given angle about a point. (p. 284)

S

sample A set of data that can be used to predict the results of a particular situation. A part of the population. (p. 100)

scale The ratio of the measurements in a drawing to the measurements of the actual objects. (p. 112, 324)

scale drawing A drawing made so that actual measurements can be determined from the drawing by using the scale. (p. 324)

scalene triangle A triangle with no sides congruent. (p. 276)

short word form A number written using both numerals and words. (p. 4)
Example: 2 thousand, 1 hundred, 36

similar figures Figures that have the same shape but not necessarily the same size. (p. 322)

simplest form A fraction is in simplest form when the greatest common factor of the numerator and denominator is one. (p. 149)

simulation Representing the conditions of a problem using models, drawings, or a computer rather than actual objects or events. (p. 434)

space figure A geometric figure with points that are in more than one plane. (p. 478)

square A rectangle with all sides congruent. (p. 279)

standard form A number written with commas separating adjacent groups of three digits. (p. 4)

statistics Collecting, organizing, and analyzing data. (p. 88)

Glossary

stem-and-leaf plot A display that shows data in order of place value. The leaves are the last digits of the numbers. The stems are the digits to the left of the leaves. (p. 94)

straight angle An angle with measure 180°. (p. 271)
Example:

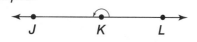

supplementary angles Two angles whose sum of their measures equals 180°. (p. 274)

survey To collect data to study some characteristic of a group. (p. 104)

symmetry A figure has symmetry if it can be folded along a line so that the two resulting parts match exactly. (p. 284)

T

tenth One of ten equal parts of a whole. (p. 4) *Example:* $0.1, \frac{1}{10}$

thousandth One of one thousand equal parts of a whole. (p. 4) *Example:* $0.001, \frac{1}{1,000}$

time zone A geographical region within which the same standard time is used. (p. 286)

ton (T) A unit of weight in the customary system equal to 2,000 pounds. (p. 260)

transformation The turning, sliding, or flipping of a plane figure. (p. 284)

translation A change in position resulting from a slide without any turn or flip. (p. 284)
Example:

trapezoid A quadrilateral with only one pair of opposite sides parallel. (p. 279)
Example:

tree diagram A diagram used to organize outcomes of an experiment to make them easier to count. (p. 426)

triangle A polygon with three sides. (p. 276)

triangular prism A space figure with two parallel and congruent bases that are triangles. (p. 481)

U

unit price The rate of price per unit of measure. (p. 318)

unit rate A ratio that compares a quantity to a unit of one. (p. 314)

V

variable A letter used to stand for a number in an expression or equation. (p. 26)

vertex The common endpoint of the two rays that form the sides of an angle. The point of intersection of two sides of a polygon. The point of intersection of three edges of a space figure. (p. 270, 277, 479)

vertical angles Two angles formed by intersecting lines and having no sides in common. (p. 274)

volume The number of cubic units that fit inside a space figure. (p. 479)

W

whole numbers The numbers in the set {0, 1, 2, 3, . . .}. (p. 4)

X

x- **and** *y-***axes** The horizontal and vertical number lines that intersect to form a coordinate plane. (p. 390)
Example:

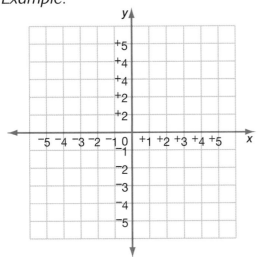

Y

yard (yd) A unit of length in the customary system equal to 36 inches, or 3 feet. (p. 260)

Z

zero property of multiplication See *property of zero*.

Index

Index

Index

Index

Index

Index

Index

Index

Index

Index

Index